메가스터디 N제

영어영역 고난도·3점

241제

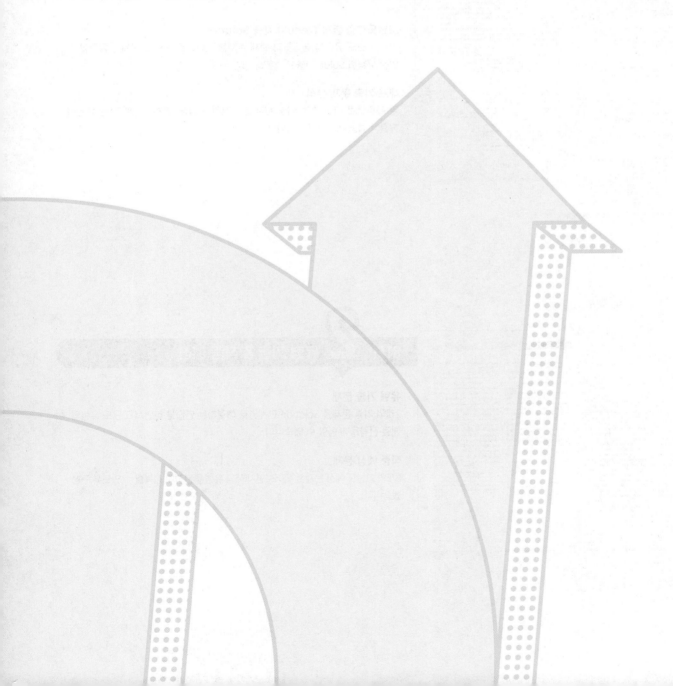

구성과 특징 STRUCTURE

✓ 수능에서 주로 3점으로 출제되는 유형과 등급을 결정짓는 고난도 유형으로만 구성되어 있어 영어 1등급을 목표로 하는 수험생이 효율적으로 학습할 수 있습니다.

✓ 특히 최근 수능에서 최고난도로 출제되는 유형의 정답 및 오답을 철저히 분석하여 고난도 유형의 최근 경향에 맞는 실질적인 해결 전략을 제공하고 있습니다.

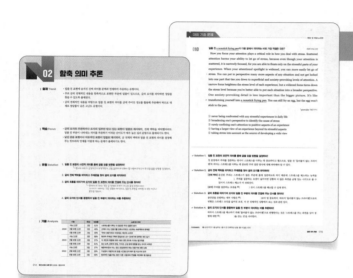

STEP 1 출제 Trend & 대표 기출 문제

고난도·3점 출제 Trend와 학습 Solution
최근 고난도 유형의 정답률과 출제 주제를 바탕으로 고난도 문제를 공략할 수 있는 유형별 Solution을 소개했습니다.

대표 기출 문제 분석
각 유형별로 최신 수능 기출 문제를 철저히 분석해 보면서 그에 따른 유형별 해결 비법을 제시하고 있습니다.

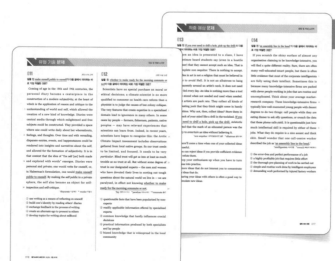

STEP 2 유형 기출 & 적중 예상

유형 기출 문제
2개의 기출 문제를 Solution 단계별로 해결하는 연습을 하면서 고난도 유형의 해결 전략을 체험할 수 있습니다.

적중 예상 문제
6개의 고난도 예상 문제를 풀어보면서 해당 유형을 완전히 정복할 수 있도록 구성했습니다.

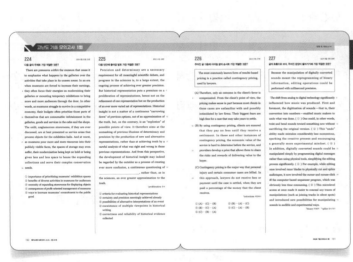

STEP 3   3점 공략 모의고사

- 주로 3점으로 출제되는 유형을 모두 포함하는 8문항으로 구성된 모의고사 16회분을 풀어보면서 실력을 다질 수 있도록 구성했습니다.

- 특히 3점으로 가장 많은 문항이 출제되는 빈칸 추론 유형의 비중을 높여 실질적인 고난도 연습이 될 수 있도록 구성했습니다.

STEP 4   고난도 기출 모의고사

최근 수능 및 평가원 모의고사에서 등급을 가른 진짜 고난도 문제를 뽑아 6문항씩 3회분으로 수록하여 최종적으로 자신의 실력을 확인하고 고난도 문항의 최근 경향에 대비할 수 있도록 구성했습니다.

친절하고 자세한 해설

모든 문제에 지문요약, 전문해석, 정답풀이, 구문풀이와 어휘풀이까지 친절하고 자세한 해설을 제공합니다.

➕ 미니 단어장

들고 다니면서 외울 수 있도록
전체 문항의 중요 어휘들만 모아
별책의 미니 단어장으로 구성하였습니다.

고난도·3점 유형 9개를 어떻게 선정했을까?

Q1. 수능에서는 어떤 문제가 3점으로 출제되었나요?

Q2. 3점으로 출제된 문제들은 모두 고난도 문제였나요?

이런 질문에 답하기 위한 분석을 함으로써 실제 어떤 문제가 3점으로 출제되고, 배점 3점인 문제가 모두 다 고난도 문제였는지 알 수 있습니다.

이러한 분석을 통해 실제로 3점으로 출제되는 유형, 3점 유형의 체감 난이도를 알 수 있습니다.

◆ 3점 기출 문제, 이렇게 출제되었다! ▶▶▶ 독해 28문항 중 7문항이 3점

3점 출제 횟수	2024 수능		2023 수능		2022 수능		2021 수능		2020 수능	
	3점 유형	정답률	3점 유형	정답률	3점 유형	정답률	3점 유형	정답률	3점 유형	정답률
5회	빈칸 추론	18%	빈칸 추론	48%	빈칸 추론	51%	빈칸 추론	55%	빈칸 추론	48%
	빈칸 추론	25%	빈칸 추론	23%	빈칸 추론	32%	빈칸 추론	43%	빈칸 추론	45%
	글의 순서	37%	글의 순서	35%	글의 순서	67%	글의 순서	49%	글의 순서	52%
	문장 삽입	53%	문장 삽입	56%	문장 삽입	48%	문장 삽입	69%	문장 삽입	40%
4회	함의 추론	61%	함의 추론	68%	함의 추론	37%			함의 추론	72%
3회			글의 주제	69%	글의 주제	77%	글의 주제	62%		
	밑줄 어휘	66%	밑줄 어휘	59%					밑줄(어휘)	55%
2회					밑줄 어법	56%	밑줄 어법	61%		
							장문(어휘)	73%	장문(어휘)	53%
1회	글의 제목	70%								

1. 3점 출제 유형은?
- 빈칸 추론(2문항), 글의 순서 파악(1문항), 문장 삽입(1문항)은 5번의 수능에서 5번 모두 3점으로 출제되었다.
- 함의 추론 유형은 5번의 수능에서 4번 3점으로 출제되었다.
- 글의 주제, 밑줄 어휘 유형은 5번의 수능에서 3번 3점으로 출제되었다.
- 밑줄 어법, 장문(어휘) 유형은 5번의 수능에서 2번 3점으로 출제되었다.
- 글의 제목 유형이 1번 2024 수능에서 3점으로 출제되었다.

2. 3점 유형의 정답률은?
- 빈칸 추론, 글의 순서 파악, 문장 삽입 유형은 정답률 낮은 진짜 고난도이다.
- 함의 추론은 정답률로 보면 최고난도는 아니므로 자신감을 가지고 풀어야 할 유형이다.
- 밑줄 어휘, 밑줄 어법, 장문(어휘) 유형은 노력하면 정복할 수 있는 난이도의 유형이다.
- 글의 주제, 글의 제목 유형은 정답률은 높고 배점은 3점이므로 반드시 맞혀야 할 유형이다.

◆ 오답률 Top 7 문항과 배점, 이렇게 출제되었다!

※ 메가스터디교육 제공

오답 순위	2024 수능		2023 수능		2022 수능		2021 수능		2020 수능	
1	33. 빈칸 추론	3점	34. 빈칸 추론	3점	34. 빈칸 추론	3점	34. 빈칸 추론	3점	39. 문장 삽입	3점
2	34. 빈칸 추론	3점	37. 글의 순서	3점	38. 문장 삽입	2점	37. 글의 순서	3점	31. 빈칸 추론	2점
3	37. 글의 순서	3점	29. 밑줄 어법	2점	21. 함축 의미	3점	24. 글의 제목	2점	34. 빈칸 추론	3점
4	36. 글의 순서	2점	31. 빈칸 추론	2점	39. 문장 삽입	3점	31. 빈칸 추론	2점	33. 빈칸 추론	3점
5	32. 빈칸 추론	2점	33. 빈칸 추론	3점	32. 빈칸 추론	2점	38. 문장 삽입	2점	37. 글의 순서	3점
6	38. 문장 삽입	2점	38. 문장 삽입	2점	24. 글의 제목	2점	33. 빈칸 추론	3점	41. 장문(제목)	2점
7	39. 문장 삽입	3점	39. 문장 삽입	3점	29. 밑줄 어법 30. 밑줄 어휘	3점 2점	40. 요약문 완성	2점	42. 장문(어휘)	3점

1. 3점 문항의 비중은?
- · 2020 수능의 경우, 오답률 Top 7에 5문항이 3점 문항으로 가장 많았다.
- · 2021 수능에서는 오답률 Top 7에 3문항이 3점으로 가장 적었다.
- · 2022 ~ 2024 수능에서는 오답률 Top 7에 4문항이 3점, 3문항이 2점이었다.

2. 2점 문항의 비중은?
- · 오답률 Top 7에 2점 문항도 평균 3문항 정도 포함되었다.
- · 빈칸 추론, 어법, 글의 순서 파악, 문장 삽입 유형은 2점짜리 문제도 정답률이 낮았다.
- · 글의 주제 유형은 3점으로 출제되지만 한 번도 오답률 Top 7에 포함되지 않았다.
- · 요약문 완성, 글의 제목, 장문(제목) 유형의 경우 배점은 2점이지만 오답률 Top 7에 포함되기도 하였다.

🏅 고난도·3점 유형
- · **최고난도 3점 유형** : 빈칸 추론, 글의 순서, 문장 삽입
- · **고난도 3점 유형** : 함의 추론, 밑줄 어휘, 밑줄 어법, 장문(어휘)
- · **비((非)고난도 3점 유형** : 글의 주제, 글의 제목
- · **고난도 2점 유형** : 빈칸 추론, 글의 순서, 문장 삽입, 요약문 완성

차례 CONTENTS

I 고난도·3점 유형

II 3점 공략 모의고사

III 고난도 기출 모의고사

N I 고난도·3점 유형

01 글의 주제

출제 Trend

- 글의 주제를 묻는 문제는 매년 수능에서 1문항씩 빠지지 않고 출제된다.
- 선택지가 영어이므로 한글로 제시되는 요지 유형보다는 정답률이 낮다. 하지만 선택지가 영어로 제시되는 글의 제목 유형보다는 전반적으로 정답률이 높은 편이다.
- 정답률로 보면 글의 주제는 최고난도 유형은 아니지만, 항상 3점으로 출제되기 때문에 절대 틀려서는 안 되는 유형이다.

학습 Focus

- 글에서 필자가 말하고자 하는 중심 내용을 요지라고 할 때, 요지를 압축적으로 나타낸 것이 주제다.
- 주제문은 대개 글의 처음이나 끝에 제시되지만, 주제문이 명시적으로 드러나지 않은 경우라면 반복적으로 제시되는 어구를 통해 주제를 추론해야 한다.
- 글의 내용에 비해 범위가 너무 좁거나, 글의 내용보다 범위가 너무 넓은 것은 주제로 부적합하다.

유형 Solution

1. 주제문을 찾기 위해 단락의 구성 방식을 이해한다.

지문 구성 방식	지문 구조 설명(주제문의 위치)
두괄식 구성	주제문+보충 설명문(근거 제시, 구체적 예시 등)
중괄식 구성	정보[객관적 사실]+주제문+보충 설명문
미괄식 구성	정보[객관적 사실]+주제문[결론, 결과]
함축식 구성	주제문이 명시적으로 드러나지 않고 글 내용 중에 암시

2. 글의 소재와 반복적으로 제시되는 핵심 개념을 파악한다.

3. 핵심 개념과 관련하여 필자가 제시하는 중심 내용을 파악한다.

4. 주제를 가장 잘 표현한 선택지를 고른다.
↳ 역으로 선택지의 주제로 글을 쓴다면 본문과 같은 글을 구성할 수 있을지 생각해 본다.

기출 Analysis

	시험	배점	정답률	소재 및 주제
2024	수능 23번	2점	55%	천연자원[숲]의 비시장 가치
	9월 모평 23번	3점	62%	음악 라디오 업계의 대규모 청취자를 끌어들이기 위한 시도의 결과
	6월 모평 23번	3점	56%	박물관의 이윤 지향적 운영의 결말
2023	수능 23번	3점	69%	자유로운 선택을 보장하기 위해 정보를 공개하는 것의 이점
	9월 모평 23번	3점	73%	농업에서 경험적 관찰을 사용하는 것의 한계
	6월 모평 23번	3점	65%	문화적으로 구성되는 감정 표현
2022	수능 23번	3점	77%	과학 연구에 있어 패러다임의 기능적 측면
	9월 모평 23번	3점	70%	제약받지 않은 것으로부터 얻는 미학적 쾌감
	6월 모평 23번	3점	67%	아동기 이후 변화된 놀이 형태에 대한 지속적 참여

● 정답 및 해설 p.003

001

다음 글의 주제로 가장 적절한 것은?

2024 수능 23번

Managers of natural resources typically face market incentives that provide financial rewards for exploitation. For example, owners of forest lands have a market incentive to cut down trees rather than manage the forest for carbon capture, wildlife habitat, flood protection, and other ecosystem services. These services provide the owner with no
5 financial benefits, and thus are unlikely to influence management decisions. But the economic benefits provided by these services, based on their non-market values, may exceed the economic value of the timber. For example, a United Nations initiative has estimated that the economic benefits of ecosystem services provided by tropical forests, including climate regulation, water purification, and erosion prevention, are over three
10 times greater per hectare than the market benefits. Thus cutting down the trees is economically inefficient, and markets are not sending the correct "signal" to favor ecosystem services over extractive uses.

*exploitation 이용 **timber 목재

① necessity of calculating the market values of ecosystem services
② significance of weighing forest resources' non-market values
③ impact of using forest resources to maximize financial benefits
④ merits of balancing forests' market and non-market values
⑤ ways of increasing the efficiency of managing natural resources

....

✓ **Solution 1.** **주제문을 찾기 위해 단락의 구성 방식을 이해하라!**

글의 중반부 But 문장에 글의 주제가 드러나는 중괄식 구조의 지문이다.

✓ **Solution 2.** **글의 소재와 반복적으로 제시되는 핵심 개념을 파악하라!**

But 이전 도입부에서 천연자원[숲]의 ❶(   ) 가치와 비시장 가치에 관한 글임을 파악할 수 있다.

✓ **Solution 3.** **핵심 개념과 관련하여 필자가 제시하는 중심 내용을 파악하라!**

But 이후에서 숲의 비시장 가치에 근거한 이익이 경제적 가치를 ❷(   ) 수 있음을 설명하고, 마지막 문장에서 벌목은 경제적으로 ❸(   )이고, 시장은 올바른 신호를 보내고 있지 않다고 정리하고 있다.

✓ **Solution 4.** **주제를 가장 잘 표현한 선택지를 골라라!**

숲[산림]이 제공하는 ❹(   ) 가치의 중요성을 언급하는 것을 주제로 선택한다.

Answers ❶ 경제적 ❷ 초과할 ❸ 비효율적 ❹ 비시장적

002

다음 글의 주제로 가장 적절한 것은?

An important advantage of disclosure, as opposed to more aggressive forms of regulation, is its flexibility and respect for the operation of free markets. Regulatory mandates are blunt swords; they tend to neglect diversity and may have serious unintended adverse effects. For example, energy efficiency requirements for appliances may produce goods that work less well or that have characteristics that consumers do not want. Information provision, by contrast, respects freedom of choice. If automobile manufacturers are required to measure and publicize the safety characteristics of cars, potential car purchasers can trade safety concerns against other attributes, such as price and styling. If restaurant customers are informed of the calories in their meals, those who want to lose weight can make use of the information, leaving those who are unconcerned about calories unaffected. Disclosure does not interfere with, and should even promote, the autonomy (and quality) of individual decision-making.

*mandate 명령   **adverse 거스르는   ***autonomy 자율성

① steps to make public information accessible to customers
② benefits of publicizing information to ensure free choices
③ strategies for companies to increase profits in a free market
④ necessities of identifying and analyzing current industry trends
⑤ effects of diversified markets on reasonable customer choices

003

다음 글의 주제로 가장 적절한 것은?

Scientists *use* paradigms rather than believing them. The use of a paradigm in research typically addresses related problems by employing shared concepts, symbolic expressions, experimental and mathematical tools and procedures, and even some of the same theoretical statements. Scientists need only understand *how* to use these various elements in ways that others would accept. These elements of shared practice thus need not presuppose any comparable unity in scientists' beliefs about what they are doing when they use them. Indeed, one role of a paradigm is to enable scientists to work successfully without having to provide a detailed account of what they are doing or what they believe about it. Thomas Kuhn noted that scientists "can agree in their *identification* of a paradigm without agreeing on, or even attempting to produce, a full *interpretation* or *rationalization* of it. Lack of a standard interpretation or of an agreed reduction to rules will not prevent a paradigm from guiding research."

① difficulty in drawing novel theories from existing paradigms
② significant influence of personal beliefs in scientific fields
③ key factors that promote the rise of innovative paradigms
④ roles of a paradigm in grouping like-minded researchers
⑤ functional aspects of a paradigm in scientific research

004

다음 글의 주제로 가장 적절한 것은?

  Matt Kluger, a physiologist at the Lovelace Institute, believes that "there is overwhelming evidence in favor of fever being an adaptive host response to infection that has persisted throughout the animal kingdom for hundreds of millions of years." He believes that using drugs to suppress fever may sometimes make people sicker—and even kill them. Some of the best evidence comes from his laboratory. In one experiment, he showed that even cold-blooded lizards benefit from a fever. When infected, they seek out a place warm enough to raise their body temperature about two degrees Celsius. If they cannot move to a warm place, they are more likely to die. Baby rabbits also cannot generate a fever, so when they are sick they too seek out a warm place to raise their body temperature. Adult rabbits do get a fever when infected, but if the fever is blocked with a fever-lowering drug, they are more likely to die.

① the necessity of reducing fevers in children
② the importance of fever in fighting infections
③ advantages of using medications to treat a fever
④ effective methods to maintain body temperature
⑤ why fever is dangerous for cold-blooded animals

005

다음 글의 주제로 가장 적절한 것은?

  Democracy depends on the formation of the collective will. Today, that means the formation of public opinion. Because of the close relationship between public opinion and government legitimacy, a democracy is necessarily concerned with regulation of the public space within which public opinion forms. Authoritarian regimes tend to try to shut down this space. Democratic regimes are skeptical of regulation, but no longer do they have the luxury of relying upon a "free market of ideas." Such a market is as subject to monopolization and distortion as an economic market; neither is self-correcting. In addition, the digital space has transformed the public sphere: Easier access to information has undermined traditional authoritative sources of knowledge; information bubbles have multiplied and fed polarized politics; misinformation has expanded and become more insidious and dangerous. The pandemic as an information emergency has amplified these trends, making more pressing the problem of regulation.

*insidious 은밀히 퍼지는

① the role of the digital space in forming public opinion
② the contribution of financial markets to democratic politics
③ necessity of public space regulation to avoid distortions
④ public opinion as a means of securing government legitimacy
⑤ differences between democratic states and authoritarian states

006

다음 글의 주제로 가장 적절한 것은?

People are equipped with powerful psychological defenses that operate offstage, rationalizing, reinterpreting, and distorting negative information in ways that make its impact better. When someone tells us that our hair looks like a poorly trimmed hedge, we assume they are joking and can't be serious. When someone turns us down for a date, we convince ourselves that he or she was not right for us after all. When a journal editor rejects one of our articles for publication, we decide that the editor must have extremely poor judgment. These events hurt when they first occur, but very quickly we find ways of warding off the pain by reinterpreting or rationalizing them. Just as we have a physiological immune system that identifies dangerous foreign bodies and minimizes their impact, so do we have a psychological immune system that identifies threats to our self-esteem and finds ways of neutralizing these threats. In short, the psychological immune system is an extra weapon people use to fight negative emotions. The psychological immune system selects, interprets, and evaluates incoming information in ways that maintain our self-esteem.

*ward off (공격 등을) 막다, 피하다

① various tactics to fight negative emotions
② examples of physiological defense mechanisms
③ self-defense strategies to reveal basic human emotion
④ protecting self-esteem through psychological resistance
⑤ reasons we prevent psychological defense systems from working

007

다음 글의 주제로 가장 적절한 것은?

Private acts are important not just in themselves but also for what they tell us about society. Feminist researchers have demonstrated how the private sphere is a site where social inequalities are produced and displayed. Interviews can shed light on the dynamics that take place within households, including the relationships between paid domestic workers and their employers as well as the relationships among family members. In her interviews with domestic workers, for example, Pierrette Hondagneu-Sotelo discovered how employers of domestic workers failed to acknowledge their status as "real" employees, justifying decisions to keep wages low and withhold benefits. Interviews like these help us investigate how gender, race, and class structure unequal relationships in private settings, which may go unnoticed but have profound consequences. In this way, interview findings have provided much of what we know about the experiences of both marginalized and privileged groups.

*marginalize 사회에서 소외하다

① factors that make it difficult to identify household problems
② how to root out the practice of treating domestic workers unfairly
③ researchers' difficulties when interviewing about private problems
④ interview surveys effective in revealing private unequal relationships
⑤ reasons why unequal relationships are not acknowledged in the private sector

008

다음 글의 주제로 가장 적절한 것은?

Scientists first developed the concept of mimicry to describe the patterns on butterflies' wings. For instance, the viceroy butterfly looks almost exactly like the monarch butterfly, which birds do not attack because they want to avoid the toxins the monarch caterpillar gets from eating milkweed leaves. The viceroy has no such toxins, but birds mistake it for its bitter lookalike and likewise shun it. Examples are now also known in many other animal groups. Any edible species that by chance resembles a toxic species will have an advantage, and natural selection will make this mimic species look increasingly like the toxic model. This is bad for the model because predators that eat the edible mimic learn to go after the model as well. This sets up an arms race between the mimic, which evolves an ever closer resemblance to the model, and the model, which evolves to be as different as possible from its edible neighbors. Some environmental circumstances favor the mimic to such an extent that really detailed resemblances between unrelated species may evolve.

*milkweed 유액을 분비하는 식물 **shun 피하다

① the rapid coevolution of predators and their prey
② environmental factors for mimicry to be successful
③ evolutionary war between the mimic and mimicked
④ positive effects of mimicry on the mimicked species
⑤ impossibility of resemblances among unrelated species

009

다음 글의 주제로 가장 적절한 것은?

In a world of social media, the published "version of record" of scientific research is no longer the primary means for alerting the community to the latest developments in their area of interest. Instead, there is a proliferation of preprints and data exchanges among and between colleagues, peers and even competitors. The attractiveness of early online disclosure of findings and discussions with colleagues is an important facet of the new research process. It requires appropriate carriers to convey research outputs, new carriers which marginalise the published article in terms of speed, impact and relevance. In this context, informal exchange becomes a useful adjunct to support of the formal research process. It is uncertain the extent to which such informal systems could even eventually eliminate the established primary journal article as a forum for information exchange and particularly for inter-peer communication, but erosion of the primacy of the scientific journal article for information exchange remains an issue to be addressed in the future.

*proliferation 확산   **marginalise 하찮은 존재로 만들다
***adjunct 부속물, 부가물

① potential value of peer reviews in scientific research
② efforts to popularize traditional scientific knowledge
③ ways to preserve the accuracy of scientific journal articles
④ dual aspects of social media's role in scientific communication
⑤ negative consequences of exchanging scientific findings online

02 함축 의미 추론

| 출제 Trend

- 밑줄 친 표현에 숨겨진 진짜 의미를 문맥과 연계하여 추론하는 유형이다.
- 주로 글의 전체적인 내용을 함축적으로 표현한 부분에 밑줄이 있으므로, 글의 요지를 파악하면 정답을 찾을 수 있도록 출제된다.
- 글의 전체적인 내용을 바탕으로 밑줄 친 표현의 의미를 글에 주어진 정보를 활용해 추론해야 하므로 대체로 정답률이 낮은 고난도 유형이다.

| 학습 Focus

- 글의 요지와 무관하거나 요지의 일부만 담고 있는 표현이 밑줄로 제시되어, 전체 맥락을 파악했더라도 밑줄 친 부분이 나타내는 의미를 추론하기 어려운 난이도가 매우 높은 킬러 문항으로 출제되기도 한다.
- 낯선 관용 표현이나 비유적인 표현이 밑줄로 제시되어, 글 전체의 맥락과 밑줄 친 표현의 의미를 결정해 주는 힌트와의 연계를 어렵게 하는 문제가 출제되기도 한다.

| 유형 Solution

1. 밑줄 친 표현의 사전적 의미를 통해 글을 읽을 방향을 설정하라!
> → 필자의 태도가 긍정적인지 부정적인지, 글을 읽으며 파악해야 할 내용이 무엇인지 등 글을 읽을 방향을 설정한다.

2. 글의 전체 맥락을 파악하고 주제문을 찾아 글의 요지를 파악하라!

3. 글의 흐름을 따라가며 요지와 밑줄 친 표현의 의미를 연결해 주는 단서를 찾아라!
> → 문제가 요구하는 것은 글 전체의 주제가 아니라 특정 표현의 의미!
> 지시어가 가리키는 것을 정확히 파악하고, 밑줄 친 표현을 대체할 수 있는 어구나 문장을 찾는다.

4. 글의 요지와 단서를 종합하여 밑줄 친 부분이 의미하는 바를 추론하라!

| 기출 Analysis

	시험	배점	정답률	소재 및 주제
2024	수능 21번	3점	61%	스트레스를 다루는 데 중요한 주의 집중의 방식
	9월 모평 21번	3점	40%	고객이 아닌 전문가를 만족시키려고 시도하는 프로젝트의 문제점
	6월 모평 21번	3점	59%	'막대 다발'이라고 비유되는 재산의 소유권
2023	수능 21번	3점	68%	현대적 주체성 구축의 중심으로 18~19세기에 정착된 개인 일기
	9월 모평 21번	3점	57%	각 개인의 취향에 따라 서로 다른 곳으로 이끄는 알고리즘
	6월 모평 21번	3점	61%	정신 능력, 문화적 관점, 가치관, 신념 등에 영향을 받는 우리의 세계관
2022	수능 23번	3점	37%	제한적이면서 어느 정도 보장되어야 하는 전문가에 대한 신뢰
	9월 모평 21번	3점	39%	구성원이 개별적으로 일할 시간을 갖게 해야 할 지도자의 임무
	6월 모평 21번	3점	59%	창의적인 일을 하는 동안 다른 사람과의 연결을 차단해야 할 필요성

010

밑줄 친 a nonstick frying pan이 다음 글에서 의미하는 바로 가장 적절한 것은?

2024 수능 21번

How you focus your attention plays a critical role in how you deal with stress. Scattered attention harms your ability to let go of stress, because even though your attention is scattered, it is narrowly focused, for you are able to fixate only on the stressful parts of your experience. When your attentional spotlight is widened, you can more easily let go of
⁵ stress. You can put in perspective many more aspects of any situation and not get locked into one part that ties you down to superficial and anxiety-provoking levels of attention. A narrow focus heightens the stress level of each experience, but a widened focus turns down the stress level because you're better able to put each situation into a broader perspective. One anxiety-provoking detail is less important than the bigger picture. It's like
¹⁰ transforming yourself into a nonstick frying pan. You can still fry an egg, but the egg won't stick to the pan.

*provoke 유발시키다

① never being confronted with any stressful experiences in daily life
② broadening one's perspective to identify the cause of stress
③ rarely confining one's attention to positive aspects of an experience
④ having a larger view of an experience beyond its stressful aspects
⑤ taking stress into account as the source of developing a wide view

....

✓ **Solution 1.** **밑줄 친 표현의 표면적 의미를 통해 글을 읽을 방향을 설정하라!**

첫 문장에서 주의를 집중하는 방식이 스트레스를 다루는 데 중요하다고 했으므로, 밑줄 친 '들러붙지 않는 프라이팬'의 의미는 스트레스를 다루는 데 중요한 주의 집중 방식에 대해 파악해야 알 수 있다.

✓ **Solution 2.** **글의 전체 맥락을 파악하고 주제문을 찾아 글의 요지를 파악하라!**

[전체 맥락] 분산된 주의는 스트레스가 많은 부분에 좁게 집중하도록 하기 때문에 스트레스를 해소하는 능력을 ❶(   ). 주의를 집중하는 초점이 넓어지면 상황의 더 많은 측면을 균형 있는 시각으로 볼 수 있어서 스트레스 해소가 더 쉬워진다.

[요지] 주의를 집중하는 초점을 ❷(   ) 것이 스트레스를 해소할 수 있게 한다.

✓ **Solution 3.** **글의 흐름을 따라가며 요지와 밑줄 친 부분의 의미를 연결해 주는 단서를 찾아라!**

불안감을 유발하는 세부 사항은 ❸(   )보다 덜 중요하다. 따라서 '들러붙지 않는 프라이팬'으로의 변형은 스트레스 요인을 넓어진 초점, 더 큰 전체적인 상황에서 보는 것과 관련 있다.

✓ **Solution 4.** **글의 요지와 단서를 종합하여 밑줄 친 부분이 의미하는 바를 추론하라!**

따라서 스트레스를 해소하기 위해 '들러붙지 않는 프라이팬'으로 변형한다는 것은 '스트레스를 주는 측면을 넘어 경험에 대한 ❹(   )을 갖는 것'을 의미한다.

Answers ❶ 손상시킨다 ❷ 넓히는 ❸ 더 큰 전체적인 상황 ❹ 더 넓은 시각

011
2023 수능 21번

밑줄 친 make oneself public to oneself가 다음 글에서 의미하는 바로 가장 적절한 것은?

Coming of age in the 18th and 19th centuries, the personal diary became a centerpiece in the construction of a modern subjectivity, at the heart of which is the application of reason and critique to the understanding of world and self, which allowed the creation of a new kind of knowledge. Diaries were central media through which enlightened and free subjects could be constructed. They provided a space where one could write daily about her whereabouts, feelings, and thoughts. Over time and with rereading, disparate entries, events, and happenstances could be rendered into insights and narratives about the self, and allowed for the formation of subjectivity. It is in that context that the idea of "the self [as] both made and explored with words" emerges. Diaries were personal and private; one would write for oneself, or, in Habermas's formulation, one would make oneself public to oneself. By making the self public in a private sphere, the self also became an object for self-inspection and self-critique.

*disparate 이질적인 ** render 만들다

① use writing as a means of reflecting on oneself
② build one's identity by reading others' diaries
③ exchange feedback in the process of writing
④ create an alternate ego to present to others
⑤ develop topics for writing about selfhood

012
2022 수능 21번

밑줄 친 whether to make ready for the morning commute or not이 다음 글에서 의미하는 바로 가장 적절한 것은?

Scientists have no special purchase on moral or ethical decisions; a climate scientist is no more qualified to comment on health care reform than a physicist is to judge the causes of bee colony collapse. The very features that create expertise in a specialized domain lead to ignorance in many others. In some cases lay people — farmers, fishermen, patients, native peoples — may have relevant experiences that scientists can learn from. Indeed, in recent years, scientists have begun to recognize this: the Arctic Climate Impact Assessment includes observations gathered from local native groups. So our trust needs to be limited, and focused. It needs to be very *particular.* Blind trust will get us into at least as much trouble as no trust at all. But without some degree of trust in our designated experts — the men and women who have devoted their lives to sorting out tough questions about the natural world we live in — we are paralyzed, in effect not knowing whether to make ready for the morning commute or not.

*lay 전문가가 아닌 **paralyze 마비시키다 ***commute 통근

① questionable facts that have been popularized by non-experts
② readily applicable information offered by specialized experts
③ common knowledge that hardly influences crucial decisions
④ practical information produced by both specialists and lay people
⑤ biased knowledge that is widespread in the local community

013

밑줄 친 If you ever need to drill a hole, pick up the drill.이 다음 글에서 의미하는 바로 가장 적절한 것은?

When an idea is presented to a class, I have sometimes heard students say (even in a hostile manner) that they cannot accept such an idea. That is a complete non sequitur. There is nothing to accept.
5 An idea in art is not a religion that must be believed in order to avoid Hell. It is not an albatross to hang permanently around an artist's neck. It does not need to be fed every day. An idea is nothing more than a tool to be stored when not needed and used when needed.
10 Most artists are pack rats. They collect all kinds of interesting junk that they think might come in handy sometime. Why not, then, collect ideas? Store them in the back of your mind like a drill in the toolshed. If you ever need to drill a hole, pick up the drill. Aristotle
15 insisted that the mark of an educated person was the ability to *entertain* an idea without believing it.

*non sequitur 그릇된[불합리한] 결론 **albatross 골칫거리

① There'll come a time when one of your collected ideas is useful.
② You can reject ideas if you provide sufficient evidence to refute them.
③ Keep your enthusiasm up when you have to turn ideas into practice.
④ Ignore ideas that do not interest you to concentrate on ideas that do.
⑤ Sharing your ideas with others is often a good way to stimulate new ideas.

014

밑줄 친 'an assembly line in the head'가 다음 글에서 의미하는 바로 가장 적절한 것은?

If you scratch the shiny surface of almost any organisation claiming to be knowledge-intensive, you will find a quite different reality. Sure, there are often many well-educated smart people, but there is often little evidence that most of the corporate intelligentsia 5 are fully using their intellect. Sometimes this is because many knowledge-intensive firms are packed with clever people working in jobs that are routine and uncomplicated. Think about your average market-research company. These knowledge-intensive firms 10 typically hire well-mannered young people with decent degrees to do two things: call people while they are eating dinner to ask silly questions, or crunch the data that these phone calls yield. It is questionable just how much intellectual skill is required by either of these 15 jobs. What they do require is a nice accent and thick skin. Small wonder that one call-centre worker described the job as 'an assembly line in the head.'

*intelligentsia 지식인들 **crunch 빠르게 처리하다

① the error-free and perfect performance of a job
② a highly profitable job that requires little effort
③ the thorough pre-planning of work to be carried out
④ simple and routine work done by intelligent employees
⑤ demanding work performed by injured factory workers

015

밑줄 친 want more than Oreos and milk가 다음 글에서 의미하는 바로 가장 적절한 것은?

Recent research in social psychology has shown that happy people are not people who have more; rather, they are people who are happy with what they already have. Happy people engage in satisficing all of the time, even if they don't know it. Warren Buffett can be seen as embracing satisficing to an extreme — one of the richest men in the world, he lives in Omaha, a block from a highway, in the same modest home he has lived in for fifty years. He once told a radio interviewer that for breakfasts during his weeklong visit to New York City, he'd bought himself a gallon of milk and a box of Oreo cookies. But Buffett does not satisfice with his investment strategies; satisficing is a tool for not wasting time on things that are not your highest priority. For your high-priority endeavors, the old-fashioned pursuit of excellence remains the right strategy. Do you want your surgeon or your airplane mechanic or the director of a $100 million feature film to do just good enough or do the best they possibly can? Sometimes you <u>want more than Oreos and milk</u>.

① invest a small amount of time and get great results
② place a high priority on becoming the best in your field
③ value meeting basic needs over pursuing mental satisfaction
④ feel great satisfaction in the small things you do on a daily basis
⑤ seek high quality solely in areas of greatest important to you

016

밑줄 친 You can't tell someone to turn on a creativity switch.가 다음 글에서 의미하는 바로 가장 적절한 것은?

College degrees are academic knowledge, but not necessarily applied knowledge. Not all applied knowledge is learned through books or in the classroom. Applied knowledge requires creativity, experience, and implementation skills. As a manager, I noticed that early on in their careers, the employees in my organization with the most applied knowledge were more successful than the employees with all the academic achievements. Creativity is not taught in school or, for that matter, anywhere in the known practical world. Applied knowledge is basically showing what you can do. Academic knowledge is basically all that you know. As a manager, I'll take the person in the room that can get things done rather than choose the smartest person in the room. I'm a big fan of implementation. <u>You can't tell someone to turn on a creativity switch.</u> I have observed my employees for a long time and what I have learned is that people who are creative really do two things their co-workers do not do. They look at things from a different perspective and connect ideas to form new ones.

① You cannot teach creativity, but you can kill it.
② People's creativity comes from their education.
③ The creative switch is always on and ideas flow effortlessly.
④ Creativity is not a matter of talent but of carrying out tasks.
⑤ People who are not born with creativity struggle to acquire it.

017

밑줄 친 history is a "special kind" of science가 다음 글에서 의미하는 바로 가장 적절한 것은?

According to Carl Becker, what we refer to as historical facts are not really facts at all in any ordinary sense. Instead of being observable or measurable, historical facts are merely symbolic representations of vanished past events. History neither unfolds in nor is written in a laboratory. Because the conclusion of an historical inquiry cannot be confirmed or falsified by comparing it with the conclusions of any other kind of inquiry, and it cannot be tested against independent criteria of credibility, history is not subject to the same rigorous standards of exactness as the physical sciences. In the words of novelist Cormac McCarthy, "In history there are no control groups." Historians generally have no way in which they may objectively test their hypotheses. Not only are there no control groups in history, but historians are usually not even firsthand observers of their subjects. Because of these limitations, R. G. Collingwood admitted that history is a "special kind" of science. If history can in any sense be considered scientific, observed Frederic W. Maitland, "it is only in the sense in which the method of a Sherlock Holmes would be scientific."

*disparate 이질적인, 별개의

① history has very strict standards of exactness
② past historical events cannot predict future events
③ scientific investigation is invalid in historical inquiry
④ scientific methods are of great help to historical investigation
⑤ historians stand in no less need of imagination than novelists

018

밑줄 친 a return to reality가 다음 글에서 의미하는 바로 가장 적절한 것은?

People argue endlessly about what constitutes reality, but let us start our definition with a simple, undeniable fact; some 4 billion years ago, life began on this planet in the shape of simple cells. These cells were the common ancestors to all life forms that followed. From these cells various branches of life emerged. In the remarkably complex chain of circumstances, we can identify, at certain turning points, a single ancestor from whom we humans have evolved. Let's call this interrelatedness of life the ultimate reality. And perhaps today we are witnessing the early signs of a return to reality. In the sciences, the first seeds of this began with Faraday, Maxwell, and Einstein, who focused on the relationships between phenomena, fields of force instead of individual particles. In addition, many scientists are now seeking to relate their various specializations to others. We can see this in the growing interest in complex theories applied to such disparate fields as economics, biology, and computers. We can also see it in health and medicine, in the way many are considering the body as a whole. This trend is the future, because the purpose of consciousness itself has always been to link us to reality.

① concentrating on practical alternatives rather than theoretical knowledge
② focusing on the essential whole to connect various branches of knowledge
③ making the finest distinctions between closely related or overlapping disciplines
④ finding a solution to the problem at hand by studying the origin of life on Earth
⑤ seeking one reality, manifesting itself in various forms and having various attributes

N 03 어법

| 출제 Trend
- 네모 안에서 어법에 맞는 표현을 고르는 유형과 밑줄 친 부분 중 어법상 틀린 표현을 고르는 유형이 출제되었는데, 최근 수능에는 밑줄 어법 유형만 출제되고 있다.
- 세부적인 어법 지식을 묻기보다는 수 일치, 관계사, 준동사, 접속사, 대명사, 대동사 등 내용 이해와 연관된 기본적인 어법 사항을 묻는 경우가 많다.
- 중요한 어법 사항은 반복적으로 출제되므로 기출 문제의 경우, 정답뿐만 아니라 오답으로 출제된 어법 사항들도 함께 확인해야 한다.

| 학습 Focus
- 단순 암기에 기초한 문법 지식보다는 글 전체의 흐름을 이해해야 풀 수 있게 출제한다.
- 문장과 절을 구성하는 원리를 묻는 문제가 자주 출제되는데, 특히 하나의 문장에 여러 개의 절이 있는 경우 각 절의 역할을 파악해야 하는 문제가 고난도로 출제되기도 한다.
- 동사와 준동사(부정사, 동명사, 분사)의 역할에 집중하여 문장의 구조를 파악해야 풀 수 있는 문제도 고난도로 출제되기도 한다.

| 유형 Solution

1. 밑줄 친 부분을 보고 묻고 있는 어법 개념이 무엇인지 파악하여 확인해야 한다.

밑줄 친 부분	확인할 어법 개념
동사, 준동사	수 일치, 동사의 태, 본동사와 준동사 구분, 병렬구조 확인
do동사, be동사	대동사로서의 do동사와 be동사 구분
분사	현재분사와 과거분사 구분
대명사	수 일치, 목적격 대명사와 재귀대명사 구분, 대명사와 관계대명사 구분
형용사, 부사	형용사 자리(명사 수식, 보어 역할)인지 부사 자리(동사, 형용사, 부사 수식)인지 구분
관계사, 접속사	선행사의 유무와 이어지는 절의 구조가 완전한지의 여부 확인

2. 문맥과 어법을 동시에 고려하여 밑줄 친 부분의 어법성을 판단해야 한다.

3. 기출 문제의 어법 사항을 한 번에 볼 수 있도록 정리해 두어야 한다.
└→ 기출 어법 사항을 정리하면 자주 출제되는 개념을 알 수 있다.

| 기출 Analysis

시험		배점	정답률	출제 어법 개념
2024	수능 29번	2점	57%	① 분사구문의 태 ② 관계대명사 which ③ 동사의 강조 ④ 대명사 those ⑤ to부정사(목적격보어)
	9월 모평 29번	2점	62%	① help의 목적격보어 ② 대명사 it ③ 문장 구조 파악(명령문) ④ 접속사 that ⑤ to부정사(진주어)
	6월 모평 29번	2점	41%	① 대명사 them ② to부정사(명사 수식) ③ 문장 구조 파악(본동사) ④ 전치사+관계대명사 ⑤ 과거분사(명사 수식)
2023	수능 29번	2점	42%	① 접속사 that ② 재귀대명사 themselves ③ 분사의 태 ④ 부사 ⑤ 분사구문
	9월 모평 29번	2점	58%	① 동사의 태 ② 문장 구조 파악(동명사 주어) ③ 병렬구조 ④ 관계대명사 that ⑤ whether+to부정사
	6월 모평 29번	3점	56%	① 대명사 those ② 현재분사 ③ 관계대명사 whose ④ 분사구문 ⑤ enable의 목적격보어(to부정사)
2022	수능 29번	3점	56%	① 분사구문의 태 ② 생략 ③ 병렬구조 ④ 관계대명사 what(→ 접속사 that) ⑤ being 생략된 분사구문
	9월 모평 29번	2점	63%	① 주어와 동사의 수 일치 ② 대명사 ③ 관계대명사 which(→ 접속사 that) ④ 형용사(보어) ⑤ 분사의 태
	6월 모평 29번	2점	60%	① 대명사 ② 주어와 동사의 수 일치 ③ 관계부사 where ④ 동사의 태 ⑤ 병렬구조

정답 및 해설 p.013

019

다음 글의 밑줄 친 부분 중, 어법상 틀린 것은?

2024 수능 29번

A number of studies provide substantial evidence of an innate human disposition to respond differentially to social stimuli. From birth, infants will orient preferentially towards the human face and voice, ①seeming to know that such stimuli are particularly meaningful for them. Moreover, they register this connection actively, imitating a variety of facial gestures that are presented to them — tongue protrusions, lip tightenings, mouth openings. They will even try to match gestures ②which they have some difficulty, experimenting with their own faces until they succeed. When they ③do succeed, they show pleasure by a brightening of their eyes; when they fail, they show distress. In other words, they not only have an innate capacity for matching their own kinaesthetically experienced bodily movements with ④those of others that are visually perceived; they have an innate drive to do so. That is, they seem to have an innate drive to imitate others whom they judge ⑤to be 'like me'.

*innate 타고난 **disposition 성향 ***kinaesthetically 운동감각적으로

....

✓ **Solution 1.** 밑줄 친 부분을 살펴보고, 묻고 있는 어법 개념이 무엇인지 파악하라!

밑줄 친 부분	확인할 어법 개념	어법성 판단 Solution
① seeming	분사구문의 태	의미상 주어와의 관계가 능동이면 현재분사를, 수동이면 과거분사를 써야 한다.
② which	관계대명사의 쓰임	앞에 수식하는 명사가 있는지, 뒤에 불완전한 구조의 절이 이어지는지 확인한다.
③ do	동사의 강조	일반동사를 강조하는 조동사 do를 인칭의 수나 시제에 맞게 사용하고 있는지 확인한다.
④ those	대명사의 수 일치	대명사가 대신하고 있는 명사(구)의 수와 일치하는지 확인한다.
⑤ to be	문장에서의 역할	문장 구조와 문맥을 고려하여 to부정사가 문장에서 어떤 역할을 하는지 파악한다.

✓ **Solution 2.** 문맥과 어법을 동시에 고려하여 밑줄 친 부분의 어법성을 판단하라!

① 주절에 대해 부가적 설명을 하는 분사구문으로, 의미상의 주어인 infants는 '알고 있는 것 같은' 주체로 seem to know와 ❶(   )의 관계를 이룬다.

② 관계대명사 which 뒤에 ❷(   ) 구조의 절이 이어져야 하는데, 여기서는 주어, 동사, 목적어를 갖춘 ❸(   ) 구조의 문장이 이어지고 있다.

③ 주어가 3인칭 복수이고 현재시제이므로 일반동사 succeed를 강조하는 조동사도 이에 수와 시제를 ❹(   ) 시킨다.

④ 지시대명사 those가 대신하고 있는 것은 bodily movements로 ❺(   ) 형태이다.

⑤ 동사 judge의 목적어 역할을 하는 것은 앞에 위치한 whom이고 to be 이하는 judge의 ❻(   )이다.

Answers ❶능동 ❷불완전한 ❸완전한 ❹일치 ❺복수 ❻목적격보어

020

2023 수능 29번

다음 글의 밑줄 친 부분 중, 어법상 **틀린** 것은?

Trends constantly suggest new opportunities for individuals to restage themselves, representing occasions for change. To understand how trends can ultimately give individuals power and freedom, one must first discuss fashion's importance as a basis for change. The most common explanation offered by my informants as to why fashion is so appealing is ① that it constitutes a kind of theatrical costumery. Clothes are part of how people present ② them to the world, and fashion locates them in the present, relative to what is happening in society and to fashion's own history. As a form of expression, fashion contains a host of ambiguities, enabling individuals to recreate the meanings ③ associated with specific pieces of clothing. Fashion is among the simplest and cheapest methods of self-expression: clothes can be ④ inexpensively purchased while making it easy to convey notions of wealth, intellectual stature, relaxation or environmental consciousness, even if none of these is true. Fashion can also strengthen agency in various ways, ⑤ opening up space for action.

*stature 능력

021

2022 수능 29번

다음 글의 밑줄 친 부분 중, 어법상 **틀린** 것은?

Like whole individuals, cells have a life span. During their life cycle (cell cycle), cell size, shape, and metabolic activities can change dramatically. A cell is "born" as a twin when its mother cell divides, ① producing two daughter cells. Each daughter cell is smaller than the mother cell, and except for unusual cases, each grows until it becomes as large as the mother cell ② was. During this time, the cell absorbs water, sugars, amino acids, and other nutrients and assembles them into new, living protoplasm. After the cell has grown to the proper size, its metabolism shifts as it either prepares to divide or matures and ③ differentiates into a specialized cell. Both growth and development require a complex and dynamic set of interactions involving all cell parts. ④ What cell metabolism and structure should be complex would not be surprising, but actually, they are rather simple and logical. Even the most complex cell has only a small number of parts, each ⑤ responsible for a distinct, well-defined aspect of cell life.

*metabolic 물질대사의 **protoplasm 원형질

022

다음 글의 밑줄 친 부분 중, 어법상 틀린 것은?

No one knows your product's features or its benefits for the consumer better than you ①do. That's why it is important for you to personally train any and every person who will be selling your product. And of equal importance is the fact ②that you must also train this sales force to push your products, instead of the competition's or, better yet, train them to love and want to push only your products to their customers. If your products sell through vendor distribution channels then make sure to develop a training program ③which you visit all vendors who sell your products and train their staff about the benefits of your products. ④Create incentives for these salespeople so that they want to sell your products over your competitors' products. The incentive could be money, but it is better to make your products easier to sell than the competition because they are better to begin with and the people selling them have been trained to understand all the benefits and ⑤what the product will do for the customer.

023

다음 글의 밑줄 친 부분 중, 어법상 틀린 것은?

The physical situation surrounding a communication event includes the location, the environmental conditions (temperature, lighting, noise level), and the physical proximity of participants to each other. The physical situation can influence ①how we interpret the messages we send and receive. We are likely to be most successful when we are present with ②those with whom we are interacting, either literally, as in face-to-face situations, or virtually. The term we use for creating a sense of "being there" with another person virtually is social presence. One technology-enhanced communication channel that does not lend itself to conveying social presence ③is e-mail. As a result, e-mail messages can often be misinterpreted, cause hurt feelings, or damage relationships. Joy, for instance, gasped when she read the e-mail from her professor that seemed to be accusing ④herself of cheating. She began to fire off a reply but stopped and made an appointment to speak in person so as to avoid the misinterpretation that can come from the lack of social presence ⑤provided via e-mail.

*proximity 근접(성)

024

다음 글의 밑줄 친 부분 중, 어법상 틀린 것은?

Before early naturalists could begin to understand the many forms of organic life, they had to list and describe ①them. And as research progressed, scholars were increasingly impressed with the amount of biological diversity they saw. It wasn't until the seventeenth century that John Ray, a minister ②educated at Cambridge University, developed the concept of species, as we think of it today. He was the one who first recognized that groups of plants and animals could be distinguished from other groups by their ability to mate with one another and produce offspring. He placed such groups of reproductively isolated organisms into a single category, ③which he called the species. Thus, by the late 1600s, the biological criterion of reproduction was used to define species, much as it ④does today. Ray also recognized that species frequently shared similarities with other species, and he grouped these together in a second level of classification he called the *genus*. He was the first ⑤to use the labels *genus* and *species* in this way, and they're the terms we still use today.

*genus (생물 분류의) 속(屬)

025

다음 글의 밑줄 친 부분 중, 어법상 틀린 것은?

A domain in which humans often reflect on and compensate for their future-thinking limitations ①is prospective memory, which involves remembering to perform an action at some particular future occasion. Because we recognize the chance that we will forget to perform the action, many of us use calendars, alarms, lists, and other external reminders as aids. Indeed, many human institutions would collapse entirely if it were not for future-oriented record-keeping procedures ②that preclude the need for perfect memories (e.g., consider legal and financial systems). There have been some claims for prospective memory in great apes, with experiments ③showing that they remember to request or exchange a token for food after completing an irrelevant task. Nevertheless, it remains possible that no future-thinking ④involved in these studies but, instead, that the apes were simply cued into action after completing the irrelevant task. There is nothing to indicate that great apes or other animals ⑤spontaneously set their own reminders in order to improve their likelihood of remembering to perform future actions.

*preclude 배제하다, 차단하다

026

다음 글의 밑줄 친 부분 중, 어법상 틀린 것은?

The earliest written records of Hispaniola's birds date from Christopher Columbus's expeditions to the island between 1492 and 1504. These and subsequent explorations of Hispaniola ① during the following two centuries, however, provided little more than general narrative accounts and incidental natural history observations. France's occupation of Haiti in the early 1700s spawned advances in bird study and led to a number of published works, many of them ② based on specimen collections which were subsequently lost or destroyed. The first ornithological explorations of eastern Hispaniola ③ were conducted by a French biologist, Auguste Salle, who published in 1857 a thorough account of his collections, which included 61 species. Systematic documentation of Hispaniola's avifauna began with collecting expeditions by the U.S. ornithologist Charles Cory, who visited both Haiti and the Dominican Republic from 1881 to 1883 and ④ publishing an important reference work, *The Birds of Haiti and San Domingo*, in 1885. Several follow-up collecting trips through 1896, under Cory's direction, gathered several thousand bird specimens, most of ⑤ which are housed in U.S. museums.

*specimen 표본 **ornithological 조류학의
***avifauna 조류상(한 지방[시대]의 조류의 분포 상태)

027

다음 글의 밑줄 친 부분 중, 어법상 틀린 것은?

Like the Mayans, the Aztec were deeply interested in calendars, which were linked to concepts of creation. The Aztec Calendar Stone is large—over eleven feet in diameter and over twenty-five tons. Also ① called the Sun Stone, the carved stone emphasizes the Aztec concept of cyclical time and reflects the Aztec's cosmology and mythology. At the center of the stone is an image of the creature Ollin, its tongue in the shape of a knife. Also depicted on the stone ② are the first four suns, and the bodies of two fire gods, according to Aztec tradition. The monumental carving is not exactly a marker of time, though there are markings that indicate the twenty-day Aztec calendar, and the date of the birth of the current (fifth) sun. The stone was excavated in the center of Mexico City, ③ in which now lies at the heart of the former Aztec empire: the city of Teotihuacán. Teotihuacán ④ was considered the birthplace of the fifth and current sun, and was the political center of the empire. Although the meaning of the Aztec Calendar Stone remains mysterious, ⑤ its image continues to influence modern Mexican art and culture.

*excavate 발굴하다

| 출제 Trend
- 하나의 주제로 전개되는 글의 내용을 고려하여 주어진 두 단어 중 알맞은 것을 선택하는 네모 어휘 유형과, 밑줄을 친 단어가 글의 흐름에 적절한지를 판단하는 밑줄 어휘 유형이 있다.
- 2018수능부터는 밑줄 어휘 유형만 출제되었는데, 2024 6월 평가원 모의고사에서 네모 어휘 유형이 출제되었다.
- 2019수능부터 장문(1지문 2문항)에도 밑줄 어휘 유형이 출제되고 있어서 어휘 유형의 중요성이 더 커졌다고 볼 수 있다.

| 학습 Focus
- 내용 자체가 어려운 지문에서 복잡한 문맥을 고려해 두 개의 반의어 가운데 하나를 선택해야 할 때, 또는 밑줄 친 단어가 반의어의 가능성이 열려 있을 때 상당히 어려울 수 있다.
- 특히 부정어가 사용된 문장의 경우, 잘못된 정답을 선택하지 않도록 주의해야 한다.
- 단어의 의미를 알고 문맥까지 정확히 파악해야 풀 수 있는 유형이므로 체감 난이도가 높다. 실수하지 않으려면 기계적인 단어 암기보다는 문맥의 흐름에 적절한 어휘가 사용되었는지를 판단할 수 있는 독해력이 필요하다.

| 유형 Solution

1. 글의 도입부에서 무엇에 관한 글인지를 파악하라!
└→ 필자의 어조가 주제에 대해 긍정적인지 비판적인지 판단하며 글을 읽는다!

2. 전체 맥락을 고려하여 각 선택지 어휘의 적절성 여부를 판단하라!
└→ 밑줄 친 어휘를 포함한 문장이 글의 주제에 부합해야 한다!

3. 밑줄 친 어휘를 훑어보고 각 어휘의 반의어를 떠올려 봐라!
└→ 특정한 반의어가 없는 어휘들은 정답일 가능성이 낮다.

| 기출 Analysis

	시험	배점	정답률	출제 어휘
2024	수능 30번	3점	65%	① restrictions ② assess ③ necessity ④ low(→ high) ⑤ similar
	9월 모평 30번	3점	57%	① particular ② increased ③ added ④ countered(→ resulted in) ⑤ reconnect
	6월 모평 30번	3점	46%	(A) compensate / prepare (B) purposefully / randomly (C) independent / protective
2023	수능 30번	3점	59%	① remote ② absorption ③ affected ④ adapt ⑤ maintain(→ delay)
	9월 모평 30번	2점	61%	① qualifications ② preventing ③ differentiate ④ challenged ⑤ diminished(→ amplified)
	6월 모평 30번	2점	56%	① limit ② persuading ③ alternative ④ accommodating(→ managing) ⑤ reinforce
2022	수능 30번	2점	55%	① reduce ② essential ③ benefits(→ constraints) ④ fewer ⑤ contribution
	9월 모평 30번	3점	49%	① demand ② stored ③ later ④ seized(→ missed) ⑤ unforeseen
	6월 모평 30번	2점	64%	① identifying ② passionate ③ failure ④ increase(→ ignore) ⑤ defeated

028

다음 글의 밑줄 친 부분 중, 문맥상 낱말의 쓰임이 적절하지 <u>않은</u> 것은?

2024 수능 30번

Bazaar economies feature an apparently flexible price-setting mechanism that sits atop more enduring ties of shared culture. Both the buyer and seller are aware of each other's ① <u>restrictions</u>. In Delhi's bazaars, buyers and sellers can ② <u>assess</u> to a large extent the financial constraints that other actors have in their everyday life. Each actor belonging to a
5 specific economic class understands what the other sees as a necessity and a luxury. In the case of electronic products like video games, they are not a ③ <u>necessity</u> at the same level as other household purchases such as food items. So, the seller in Delhi's bazaars is careful not to directly ask for very ④ <u>low</u> prices for video games because at no point will the buyer see possession of them as an absolute necessity. Access to this type of knowledge
10 establishes a price consensus by relating to each other's preferences and limitations of belonging to a ⑤ <u>similar</u> cultural and economic universe.

*constraint 압박 **consensus 일치

✓ **Solution 1.** 글의 도입부에서 무엇에 관한 글인지 파악하라!

문화 공유라는 유대 속에 상점가 경제의 유연한 가격 설정 메커니즘에 관한 글이다.

✓ **Solution 2.** 전후 맥락을 고려하여 각 선택지의 적절성 여부를 판단하라!

① restrictions: 다음 문장에 델리의 상점에서 구매자와 판매자는 서로의 재정적 압박을 평가할 수 있다는 내용이 기술되고 있다. 따라서 구매자와 판매자 둘 다 서로의 ❶(　　　)을 알고 있다고 할 수 있다.

② assess: 다음 문장에 특정 경제 계층에 속하는 행위자의 필수품과 사치품을 이해한다는 내용이 기술되고 있다. 따라서 구매자와 판매자는 대체로 다른 행위자들이 그들의 일상생활에서 가지는 재정적인 압박을 ❷(　　　) 수 있다고 할 수 있다.

③ necessity: 판매 제품으로 비디오 게임과 식품의 경우, 전자는 식품과 같은 가정에서의 구매 ❸(　　　)이 아니다.

④ low: 앞 문장에서 비디오 게임은 식품과 같은 필수품은 아니라고 했다. 따라서 절대적 필수 소유 품목이 아닌 비디오 게임에 대해 판매자는 곧바로 ❹(　　　) 가격을 요구하지 않도록 주의할 것이다.

⑤ similar: 상점가의 판매자와 구매자가 특정 경제 계층에 속하는 경우, 둘 다 서로의 ❺(　　　) 문화적, 경제적 세계를 고려하여 선호와 한계를 토대로 가격 합의에 도달할 것이라고 할 수 있다.

Answers ❶ 제약 ❷ 평가할 ❸ 필수품 ❹ 높은 ❺ 비슷한

029

다음 글의 밑줄 친 부분 중, 문맥상 낱말의 쓰임이 적절하지 <u>않은</u> 것은?

Everywhere we turn we hear about almighty "cyberspace"! The hype promises that we will leave our boring lives, put on goggles and body suits, and enter some metallic, three-dimensional, multimedia otherworld. When the Industrial Revolution arrived with its great innovation, the motor, we didn't leave our world to go to some ① remote motorspace! On the contrary, we brought the motors into our lives, as automobiles, refrigerators, drill presses, and pencil sharpeners. This ② absorption has been so complete that we refer to all these tools with names that declare their usage, not their "motorness." These innovations led to a major socioeconomic movement precisely because they entered and ③ affected profoundly our everyday lives. People have not changed fundamentally in thousands of years. Technology changes constantly. It's the one that must ④ adapt to us. That's exactly what will happen with information technology and its devices under human-centric computing. The longer we continue to believe that computers will take us to a magical new world, the longer we will ⑤ maintain their natural fusion with our lives, the hallmark of every major movement that aspires to be called a socioeconomic revolution.

*hype 과대광고 **hallmark 특징

030

(A), (B), (C)의 각 네모 안에서 문맥에 맞는 낱말로 가장 적절한 것은?

To the extent that an agent relies on the prior knowledge of its designer rather than on its own percepts, we say that the agent lacks autonomy. A rational agent should be autonomous — it should learn what it can to (A) compensate / prepare for partial or incorrect prior knowledge. For example, a vacuum-cleaning agent that learns to foresee where and when additional dirt will appear will do better than one that does not. As a practical matter, one seldom requires complete autonomy from the start: when the agent has had little or no experience, it would have to act (B) purposefully / randomly unless the designer gave some assistance. So, just as evolution provides animals with enough built-in reflexes to survive long enough to learn for themselves, it would be reasonable to provide an artificial intelligent agent with some initial knowledge as well as an ability to learn. After sufficient experience of its environment, the behavior of a rational agent can become effectively (C) independent / protective of its prior knowledge. Hence, the incorporation of learning allows one to design a single rational agent that will succeed in a vast variety of environments.

	(A)	(B)	(C)
①	compensate	randomly	protective
②	compensate	purposefully	protective
③	prepare	randomly	protective
④	compensate	randomly	independent
⑤	prepare	purposefully	independent

031

다음 글의 밑줄 친 부분 중, 문맥상 낱말의 쓰임이 적절하지 <u>않은</u> 것은?

In multicultural societies, some cultural identity groups come closer to providing a comprehensive context of choice for their members than others. Since minority cultural groups must compete with the dominant culture to provide a context of choice for their members, they find themselves at a ① <u>disadvantage</u>. The context of choice for their members is not the one favored by governmental institutions and practices. Government ② <u>protects</u> the dominant culture, whether intentionally or not, through the language it uses, the education it accredits, the history it honors, and the holidays that it keeps. The state and the dominant public culture that it supports, both indirectly and directly, cannot be culturally ③ <u>biased</u> in this sense. Government conducts its business, public schools teach, and the mass media broadcast in the dominant language. Family law ④ <u>conforms</u> to the dominant culture. The civic associations with the highest social status favor people who identify with the dominant culture. Distance from the dominant culture also carries with it economic and educational drawbacks through no fault of the individuals whose cultural upbringing ⑤ <u>differs</u> from the dominant one.

*accredit 인가하다

032

다음 글의 밑줄 친 부분 중, 문맥상 낱말의 쓰임이 적절하지 <u>않은</u> 것은?

In international relations, conflict regularly occurs when actors interact and disputes over incompatible interests arise. In and of itself, conflict is not necessarily threatening because war and conflict are ① <u>different</u>. Conflict may be seen as inevitable and occurs whenever two parties perceive differences between themselves and seek to resolve those differences to their own ② <u>satisfaction</u>. Some conflict results whenever people interact and may be generated by religious, ideological, ethnic, economic, political, or territorial issues; therefore, it should not be regarded as ③ <u>abnormal</u>. Nor should we regard conflict as necessarily destructive. Conflict can ④ <u>undermine</u> social solidarity, creative thinking, learning, and communication — all factors critical to the resolution of disputes and the durability of cooperation. However, the costs of conflict do become ⑤ <u>threatening</u> when the parties take up arms to settle perceived irreconcilable differences or to settle old scores. When that happens, violence occurs, and we enter the sphere of warfare.

*irreconcilable 화해할 수 없는

033

다음 글의 밑줄 친 부분 중, 문맥상 낱말의 쓰임이 적절하지 <u>않은</u> 것은?

Rituals involve any behavior that is done repeatedly in order to produce a desired outcome. Generally, rituals express a person's anxiety ① <u>symbolically</u>. This means the behavior is an attempt to lead to a result through an unrelated action. Those who believe in the power of rituals often feel that ② <u>breaking</u> the ritual will produce negative consequences, perhaps even supernatural punishment. Psychologically, ritualistic behavior can ③ <u>reduce</u> a sense of control over often uncontrollable situations. For instance, Wayne Gretzky, a Hall-of-Fame hockey player, tucked in his jersey in the exact same manner before each game. The outcome of a hockey game obviously cannot be ④ <u>controlled</u> solely by a single hockey player. However, a ritual may give a player the feeling that he has control over the team's success, even if it is through the ⑤ <u>superstitious</u> habit of putting on jersey in a certain way.

034

(A), (B), (C)의 각 네모 안에서 문맥에 맞는 낱말로 가장 적절한 것은?

In ancient nonalphabet societies, the world was conceived of as a whole, composed of meaningful interrelations, fluid interactions, and cycles, as opposed to discrete, abstract, and hierarchical ideas and pieces of information — the artifacts of literacy. Face-to-face communication and the immediate social and natural environment are of (A) minor / primary importance in an oral culture. In such a specific social organization, a sense of well-being would no doubt be linked more to the cohesiveness of the social collective than to separate individuals. Privacy would not be understood as a(n) (B) collective / individual value, if it would exist at all. The sense of oneself as an individual did not resonate with primarily oral people. Personal autonomy in a psychological sense did not exist. Notions of privacy and individuality did not become important until after about AD 1500. In an oral society well-being would be determined by the social body in terms of complete interconnectedness. A(n) (C) integration / separation between the social and the individual begins with the inventions of alphabets and writing.

*resonate with ~에 반향을 일으키다

	(A)	(B)	(C)
①	minor	collective	integration
②	minor	collective	separation
③	primary	individual	integration
④	primary	collective	integration
⑤	primary	individual	separation

035

다음 글의 밑줄 친 부분 중, 문맥상 낱말의 쓰임이 적절하지 <u>않은</u> 것은?

Entertainment is a luxury, not a necessity. Movies won't give you a ① <u>dependable</u> ride to work, and a downloaded song won't feed your family for a week. People will only consume entertainment when they have the time, money, and desire to do so. That desire comes about through any number of variables, but once it's there, you'd better ② <u>deliver</u> — *now*. Entertainment must be available to the public when the public wants it, not a minute sooner or a second later. It is this perishability that poses the biggest ③ <u>challenge</u> to the industry. Trends in automobiles or home furnishings — large investments — may ebb and flow over several years. Those industries can follow a ④ <u>linear</u> path in the life of a product, taking more time to create the new version, model, or style. Entertainment? Today's hot thing can be a cold thing tomorrow. The consuming public is fickle, so if you want to take advantage of their interest, you need to ⑤ <u>withhold</u> *all* your forces immediately.

*perishability 사멸성 **fickle 변덕스러운

036

다음 글의 밑줄 친 부분 중, 문맥상 낱말의 쓰임이 적절하지 <u>않은</u> 것은?

Defensive pessimists are characterized by anticipatory coping strategies, that is, those used *before* entering a performance setting. A hallmark of defensive pessimism is setting ① <u>low</u> performance expectations, which serves the self-protective goal. By thinking about how the worst might happen, they may ② <u>cushion</u> themselves preemptively against potential bad outcomes. If something bad does happen, defensive pessimists are able to think, "I expected it all along," making the outcome seem less damaging. Convincing themselves that they will do poorly also serves a motivational goal by impelling them to redouble their efforts and preparation to ③ <u>ensure</u> that they actually will do well. This helps to harness the anxiety or negative effect over possible failure. Defensive pessimists' use of anticipatory strategies may appear ④ <u>ironic</u>. First, they are very high performers, and in fact they did perform well in the past. Second, convincing themselves that poor performances will happen does not actually make them happen. Low performance expectations are not ⑤ <u>self-contradicting</u>.

*anticipatory 예방적인, 예상한 **preemptively 선제적으로, 예방을 위해

05 빈칸 추론(1)

출제 Trend

- 글의 흐름을 파악하여 빈칸에 들어갈 낱말이나 어구, 절을 추론하는 유형이다.
- 빈칸은 주제문, 요지를 나타내는 문장, 또는 요지를 뒷받침하는 논거가 제시되는 문장에 위치할 수 있다.
- 빈칸 추론은 최근 4문항씩 출제되고 있으며, 그중 2문항이 3점이므로 수능에서 출제 비중이 가장 높은 유형이라고 할 수 있다.
- 배점에 상관없이 빈칸 추론 문제는 대체로 낮은 정답률을 보이는 고난도 유형이다.

학습 Focus

- 빈칸 문장이 글의 구조상 주제, 결론, 예시, 대조, 첨가 중 어떤 역할을 하는지 판단한 후, 그에 부합하는 어구를 골라야 한다.
- 글의 주제가 명확하게 드러나 있지 않은데 빈칸에 적절한 말을 넣어 결론이나 주제문을 완성해야 하는 경우, 글에 주어진 정보를 종합해서 필자가 말하고자 하는 바를 유추해야 한다.
- 자신의 상식이 아닌 지문에 제시된 정보에 근거하여 정답을 찾는 연습을 해야 한다.
- 정답을 고르기 어려운 경우에는 절대 정답이 아닌 것부터 소거하는 방식으로 접근하는 것도 방법이다.

유형 Solution

1. 빈칸의 위치를 확인하고 단서의 위치를 파악하라!

빈칸의 위치	단서의 위치
글의 첫 부분	보통 빈칸 문장이 주제문으로, 글의 마지막 부분에 재진술되는 주제나 결론에 빈칸의 단서가 있을 가능성이 높다.
글의 중반부	빈칸 문장의 앞부분은 도입부이고 뒷부분에 근거가 제시되는 경우가 많으므로 뒷부분에 단서가 있을 가능성이 높다.
글의 마지막 부분	보통 빈칸 문장이 글의 결론에 해당하며 전반부의 또 다른 주제문에 단서가 있을 가능성이 높다.
구체적 사례 바로 앞	빈칸 문장이 주제문일 가능성이 높으므로, 이어지는 사례를 일반화하여 빈칸 내용을 추론한다.
반전이 있는 부분	빈칸 문장부터 글의 내용이 반전되므로 뒷부분에 단서가 있을 가능성이 높다.

2. 글의 전반부에서 핵심 소재를 파악하고 글의 전개를 예측하라!
↳ 전반부에 반복적으로 드러내는 표현이 글의 핵심 소재!

3. 반복되는 유사한 개념의 표현에서 빈칸의 단서를 찾아라!
↳ 같은 표현을 반복하기보다 개념적으로 연결되는 표현을 사용한다.

4. 파악한 단서와 글의 주제를 바탕으로 빈칸에 들어갈 말을 추론하라!

기출 Analysis

시험		배점	정답률	소재 및 주제
2024	수능 31번	2점	76%	그림, 사진 등 다양한 형태로 확대된 읽기 텍스트의 범주
	수능 32번	2점	45%	친숙한 음악으로 관객의 영화 이해를 돕는 영화 음악
	수능 33번	3점	18%	상황이나 맥락까지 알아야 이해할 수 있는 얼굴의 감정 표현
	수능 34번	3점	25%	도로에 관한 교통정책 토론에서 자기중심적 주장을 하는 이유
2023	수능 31번	2점	48%	많이 읽히면서 존경받지 못하는 스포츠 저널리즘의 전문적 지위에 대한 역설적 측면
	수능 32번	2점	68%	빈번한 접촉을 제공하여 예술, 음악, 패션, 언어 등 모든 사회적 변화의 발전기 역할을 하는 도시
	수능 33번	3점	48%	꿀벌 군집이 그들의 노동력을 조절하도록 정보를 교환하는 상호작용 방법
	수능 34번	3점	23%	기후 변화에 대한 우리의 책임을 부인하도록 오도하는 과거, 현재, 미래로 시간 나누기

037

다음 빈칸에 들어갈 말로 가장 적절한 것은?

Over the last decade the attention given to how children learn to read has foregrounded the nature of *textuality*, and of the different, interrelated ways in which readers of all ages make texts mean. 'Reading' now applies to a greater number of representational forms than at any time in the past: pictures, maps, screens, design graphics and photographs are all regarded as text. In addition to the innovations made possible in picture books by new printing processes, design features also predominate in other kinds, such as books of poetry and information texts. Thus, reading becomes a more complicated kind of interpretation than it was when children's attention was focused on the printed text, with sketches or pictures as an adjunct. Children now learn from a picture book that words and illustrations complement and enhance each other. Reading is not simply _____. Even in the easiest texts, what a sentence 'says' is often not what it means.

*adjunct 부속물

① knowledge acquisition
② word recognition
③ imaginative play
④ subjective interpretation
⑤ image mapping

....

✔ **Solution 1. 빈칸의 위치를 확인하고 단서의 위치를 파악하라!**

후반부에 위치한 빈칸 문장이 Reading으로 시작하므로 글의 전반부에서 Reading에 대한 단서를 찾아야 한다.

✔ **Solution 2. 글의 전반부에서 핵심 소재를 파악하고 글의 전개를 예측하라!**

글의 전반부에서 텍스트가 단지 글을 의미했던 예전과 달리, 이제는 그림, 지도, 화면, 디자인 그래픽, 사진도 텍스트로 여겨지므로 Reading도 이러한 ❶(   ) 표현 형태에 적용된다고 했으므로 후반부에도 Reading 범주의 형태 변화에 대한 설명이 이어질 것이다.

✔ **Solution 3. 반복적으로 제시되는 단서를 찾아라!**

읽기(Reading)가 다양한 표현 형태에 적용되면서 글에만 집중되던 때보다 더 ❷(   ) 종류의 해석이 되고, 글과 다른 표현 형태가 서로를 ❸(   )하고 향상시킨다고 하므로, 결국 이 글은 '읽기(Reading) 형태의 확대'에 관한 내용이라고 할 수 있다.

✔ **Solution 4. 파악한 단서를 바탕으로 빈칸에 들어갈 말을 추론하라!**

빈칸에 들어갈 말은 읽기 형태의 확대와 관련이 있는데, 읽기는 단지 ❹(   )의 인식에만 집중하는 것이 아니라 그림, 사진, 디자인 등의 다른 표현 형태를 함께 봐야 한다고 추론할 수 있다.

Answers   ❶ 다양한 ❷ 복잡한 ❸ 보완 ❹ 글자[문자]

038

다음 빈칸에 들어갈 말로 가장 적절한 것은?

There is something deeply paradoxical about the professional status of sports journalism, especially in the medium of print. In discharging their usual responsibilities of description and commentary,
5　reporters' accounts of sports events are eagerly consulted by sports fans, while in their broader journalistic role of covering sport in its many forms, sports journalists are among the most visible of all contemporary writers. The ruminations of the elite
10　class of 'celebrity' sports journalists are much sought after by the major newspapers, their lucrative contracts being the envy of colleagues in other 'disciplines' of journalism. Yet sports journalists do not have a standing in their profession that corresponds to the
15　size of their readerships or of their pay packets, with the old saying (now reaching the status of cliché) that sport is the 'toy department of the news media' still readily to hand as a dismissal of the worth of what sports journalists do. This reluctance to take sports
20　journalism seriously produces the paradoxical outcome that sports newspaper writers are much read but little _____.

*discharge 이행하다 **rumination 생각 ***lucrative 돈을 많이 버는

① paid
② admired
③ censored
④ challenged
⑤ discussed

039

다음 빈칸에 들어갈 말로 가장 적절한 것은?

Humour involves not just practical disengagement but cognitive disengagement. As long as something is funny, we are for the moment not concerned with whether it is real or fictional, true or false. This is why
5　we give considerable leeway to people telling funny stories. If they are getting extra laughs by exaggerating the silliness of a situation or even by making up a few details, we are happy to grant them comic licence, a kind of poetic licence. Indeed, someone listening to a
10　funny story who tries to correct the teller — 'No, he didn't spill the spaghetti on the keyboard and the monitor, just on the keyboard' — will probably be told by the other listeners to stop interrupting. The creator of humour is putting ideas into people's heads for the
15　pleasure those ideas will bring, not to provide _____ information.

*cognitive 인식의 **leeway 여지

① accurate
② detailed
③ useful
④ additional
⑤ alternative

040

다음 빈칸에 들어갈 말로 가장 적절한 것은?

George Herbert Mead, American philosopher and social theorist, gave an example of a very simple act of communication between two dogs to explain the point about the social constitution of meaning. One dog
5 makes the gesture of a snarl and this may call forth a counter-snarl, which means 'fight'; or the gesture could call forth flight, which means victory and defeat; or the response to the gesture could be crouching, which means submission and domination. Meaning,
10 therefore, does not lie in the gesture alone but in the social act as a whole. In other words, meaning arises in the responsive interplay between actors; gesture and response can never be separated but must be understood as moments in one act. Meaning does not
15 arise first in each individual, to be subsequently expressed in action, nor is it transmitted from one individual to another. Meaning is not attached to an object, formed as a representation, or stored but is created in the _____.

*snarl (이빨을 드러내고) 으르렁거림

① hierarchy   ② agreement
③ convention   ④ interaction
⑤ utterance

041

다음 빈칸에 들어갈 말로 가장 적절한 것은?

It is becoming increasingly evident that not only are nonhuman animals capable of intentional and instrumental communication, but their vocabulary can be impressively broad. For instance, prairie dogs,
5 extensively studied by Con Slobodchikoff from Northern Arizona University, have a sophisticated language, which includes, among other things, social chatter and vocalisations for distinguishing triangular from circular shapes. Hens have specific vocalisations
10 to distinguish aerial predators from threats on the ground. Dolphins call one another by name. Nightingales have elaborated songs in which each note is sung in one-tenth of a second, making it difficult for humans to appreciate the nuances unless the song is
15 recorded and slowed down for replay. What to us might sound like a chirp could in fact be conveying a full balladic stanza to the informed listener; that is, another nightingale. These and other known or not-yet-discovered communication skills leave little doubt
20 that the nonhuman animal world is also filled with vibrant _____.

*chirp 짹짹거리는 소리 **stanza (시의) 연(聯), 시

① collective rituals
② social structures
③ instrument usage
④ defense strategies
⑤ information exchanges

042

다음 빈칸에 들어갈 말로 가장 적절한 것은?

To model _____ of our judgments, Jonathan Haidt uses the analogy of a person riding an elephant and believing that he or she has full control of the elephant's movements. However, the elephant is much stronger than the rider, who (unless he engages in careful and prolonged reflection) has minimal effect on this irrational, instinctive, and powerful animal force. As the rider goes through various routines, he clings to the delusion that he is in charge. In the realm of ordinary judgments, Haidt argues, people believe they derive their judgments from reason, when the beliefs are actually shaped by unreflecting and often biased intuition. When we think that our judgments are grounded in reason, we are as deluded as the rider who thinks he or she is in charge of the elephant. After all, research shows that two people, looking at the same evidence, will assess it differently according to whether it supports their intuition-based judgments. However strong the evidence, it is weaker than our feelings.

① the final and binding effect
② the diverse and discrete aspects
③ the biased yet empathetic quality
④ the intuitive and emotional nature
⑤ the descriptive and evaluative roles

043

다음 빈칸에 들어갈 말로 가장 적절한 것은?

Ethics codes for criminalists frequently include a requirement that the work of the criminalist is _____. This is also generally a legal requirement. This requirement originates from the concept of the scientific method, which essentially requires the scientific investigator to provide experimental verification of their hypotheses. The scientist does not simply assert that something is true; he or she provides the process and information by which another observer can independently verify the truth of the proposition. This scientific requirement, reflected in the law and in codes of ethics, means that the data, the methods, and the materials are preserved for review by other interested investigators—the data upon which conclusions were based, the methods by which the data were obtained, and the material that was used for the analysis. Unlike most other fields of science, where the material that is subjected to analysis is generally in plentiful supply, the material available to the forensic scientist is often in very short supply; and the possibility of getting more is usually nonexistent.

① negotiable   ② consistent
③ reviewable   ④ legitimate
⑤ replaceable

044

다음 빈칸에 들어갈 말로 가장 적절한 것은?

There are several ways to actively encourage new knowledge to come forward. But even more importantly, there are things you need to do to keep the ideas flowing. One is _____. There's an interesting phenomenon in the high-tech sector. Developing the information age on the ground has meant a series of experiments and failures, with companies starting up and failing with great consistency over and over until the industry gets the new idea right. Christopher Meyer at Stanford University believes that the high-tech sector succeeds partially because "failure here is understood to be an integral aspect of the growth process." In fact, venture capitalists effectively reward failure by preferring to invest in companies whose executives are "seasoned"—i.e., have been involved in one or more start-ups that didn't fly.

① not punishing failure
② offering a big reward
③ relying on group wisdom
④ not repeating the same error
⑤ appreciating the gravity of failure

045

다음 빈칸에 들어갈 말로 가장 적절한 것은?

Our thoughts, and the language we use to express them, can remind us of the consequences of bad habits, guide us to other actions, and heighten the reinforcement value of success. We can introduce ideas that countermand others. Instead of "That pint of chocolate ice cream looks really good to me; I'll have just a few bites," we can say to ourselves, "I know that I can't have one bite, because it will lead to twenty." We can remind ourselves of our goals: "If I don't eat that now, I'll feel better about myself tomorrow." Or we can repeat statements of self-efficacy: "I don't have to respond that way; I can respond this way," or "I can do this; I can control this." Instead of responding habitually to the promise of immediate reward, we can make ourselves conscious of the long-term impact of eating highly palatable food. This shift of attention is a tool for _____ that "involves changing the way you think about the meaning of the stimulus," according to Kevin Ochsner, who studies the psychological and neural processes involved in emotion, self-regulation, and perception at Columbia University.

*countermand 취소하다, 중지시키다 **palatable 입맛에 맞는

① gaining cognitive control
② evoking specific emotions
③ shutting off external stimuli
④ expressing unconscious desire
⑤ reducing the influence of others

대표 기출 문제

정답 및 해설 p.027

046

다음 빈칸에 들어갈 말로 가장 적절한 것은?

2024 수능 34번

Everyone who drives, walks, or swipes a transit card in a city views herself as a transportation expert from the moment she walks out the front door. And how she views the street _____. That's why we find so many well-intentioned and civic-minded citizens arguing past one another. At neighborhood meetings in school auditoriums, and in back rooms at libraries and churches, local residents across the nation gather for often-contentious discussions about transportation proposals that would change a city's streets. And like all politics, all transportation is local and intensely personal. A transit project that could speed travel for tens of thousands of people can be stopped by objections to the loss of a few parking spaces or by the simple fear that the project won't work. It's not a challenge of the data or the traffic engineering or the planning. Public debates about streets are typically rooted in emotional assumptions about how a change will affect a person's commute, ability to park, belief about what is safe and what isn't, or the bottom line of a local business.

*swipe 판독기에 통과시키다 **contentious 논쟁적인 ***commute 통근

① relies heavily on how others see her city's streets
② updates itself with each new public transit policy
③ arises independently of the streets she travels on
④ tracks pretty closely with how she gets around
⑤ ties firmly in with how her city operates

....

✔ **Solution 1.** 빈칸의 위치를 확인하고 단서의 위치를 파악하라!

전반부에 빈칸이 있고 빈칸 다음에 그 내용의 ❶(   )가 이어지고 있음을 염두에 둔다.

✔ **Solution 2.** 글의 전반부에서 핵심 소재를 파악하고 글의 전개를 예측하라!

도시의 도로를 바꿀 교통 제안을 논의할 때 각자 자기주장만 하는 결과를 초래하는 ❷(   )에 관해 파악해야 함을 알고 글의 전개를 따라간다.

✔ **Solution 3.** 반복적으로 제시되는 단서를 찾아라!

수만 명의 이동 속도를 높이는 교통 프로젝트도 주차 공간의 상실이나 단순한 두려움 같은 자기중심적 이유로 중단될 수 있는데, 도로 정책에 대한 일반 대중의 주장은 자신의 통근, 주차 능력, 안전한 것에 대한 믿음 등 개인의 ❸(   ) 추정에 뿌리를 둔다고 한다. 따라서 일반 대중이 도로를 바라보는 방식은 '각 개인의 도로 이용 방식과 관련이 있다'고 할 수 있다.

✔ **Solution 4.** 파악한 단서를 바탕으로 빈칸에 들어갈 말을 추론하라!

빈칸에 들어갈 말은 도로 정책에 대한 개인의 감정적 추정과 관련이 있으므로, 도시의 도로를 바꿀 프로젝트에 대한 논쟁에서 각자는 그 변화가 ❹(   )에게 미칠 영향에 근거하여 주장한다고 추론할 수 있다.

Answers ❶ 결과 ❷ 이유 ❸ 감정적 ❹ 자신

047

다음 빈칸에 들어갈 말로 가장 적절한 것은?

The entrance to a honeybee colony, often referred to as the dancefloor, is a market place for information about the state of the colony and the environment outside the hive. Studying interactions on the dancefloor provides us with a number of illustrative examples of how individuals changing their own behavior in response to local information _____ _____. For example, upon returning to their hive honeybees that have collected water search out a receiver bee to unload their water to within the hive. If this search time is short then the returning bee is more likely to perform a waggle dance to recruit others to the water source. Conversely, if this search time is long then the bee is more likely to give up collecting water. Since receiver bees will only accept water if they require it, either for themselves or to pass on to other bees and brood, this unloading time is correlated with the colony's overall need of water. Thus the individual water forager's response to unloading time (up or down) regulates water collection in response to the colony's need.

*brood 애벌레 **forager 조달자

① allow the colony to regulate its workforce
② search for water sources by measuring distance
③ decrease the colony's workload when necessary
④ divide tasks according to their respective talents
⑤ train workers to acquire basic communication patterns

048

다음 빈칸에 들어갈 말로 가장 적절한 것은?

We understand that the segregation of our consciousness into present, past, and future is both a fiction and an oddly self-referential framework; your present was part of your mother's future, and your children's past will be in part your present. Nothing is generally wrong with structuring our consciousness of time in this conventional manner, and it often works well enough. In the case of climate change, however, the sharp division of time into past, present, and future has been desperately misleading and has, most importantly, hidden from view the extent of the responsibility of those of us alive now. The narrowing of our consciousness of time smooths the way to divorcing ourselves from responsibility for developments in the past and the future with which our lives are in fact deeply intertwined. In the climate case, it is not that _____. It is that the realities are obscured from view by the partitioning of time, and so questions of responsibility toward the past and future do not arise naturally.

*segregation 분리 **intertwine 뒤얽히게 하다 ***obscure 흐릿하게 하다

① all our efforts prove to be effective and are thus encouraged
② sufficient scientific evidence has been provided to us
③ future concerns are more urgent than present needs
④ our ancestors maintained a different frame of time
⑤ we face the facts but then deny our responsibility

049

다음 빈칸에 들어갈 말로 가장 적절한 것은?

Sustainability threats are embedded in cultural and social structures as well as in physical infrastructures that can only be changed in the long run. Sustainability is therefore a value-laden concept, entailing assumptions of what is worth sustaining, and at what costs. This is already indicated by the difficulties in integrating the 'three pillars' of sustainability — environmental, economic and sociocultural — which are not mutually compatible, as a gain in one dimension is easily a loss in another. There is a tension between sustainability and economic development, between environmental requirements and socio-cultural desires, between needs of the present generation and those of future generations, and so on. Even deeper tensions can be found between sustaining what is, and developing the capacity to bounce back after a collapse and to adapt to change. Thus, sustainability issues _____.

① are best tackled through voluntary initiative
② involve a profound lack of agreement on values
③ can be easily incorporated into our daily practices
④ have both immediate and generational implications
⑤ cannot be addressed without any ethical considerations

050

다음 빈칸에 들어갈 말로 가장 적절한 것은?

An important contribution of Descartes was that he improved the negative image emotions had had since antiquity. Rather than viewing them as experiences that compromise rational thought and that therefore should be avoided, he assigned them a functional significance. With a surprisingly Darwinian spirit, he postulated that emotions "dispose the soul to will the things nature tells us are useful and to persist in that volition." If we feel fear, it is likely because flight is a beneficial action in that circumstance. If we feel anger, it is likely because confrontation or fighting is a beneficial action in that circumstance. Thus, emotions _____. Despite their having an obvious function, however, Descartes warned that excessive emotions may be bad for a person and suggested ways in which such excess may be prevented.

*postulate 가정하다   **volition 자유의지

① help us remember what is important
② arise from desires for certain pleasures
③ bias us to behave in a self-serving manner
④ are regarded as conditional, temporary, mental states
⑤ are reflected in the characteristics of one's face and voice

051

다음 빈칸에 들어갈 말로 가장 적절한 것은?

Most of our brain's activity is spent on primitive processes—like walking—that we can't even perceive consciously. Instead, we are aware of only a thin, newly evolved layer of cognition that sits on and depends upon the reliable workings of older processes. You can't do calculus unless you do counting. Likewise, you can't do cell phones unless you do wires. You can't do digital infrastructure unless you do industrial. For example, a recent high-profile effort to computerize every hospital in Ethiopia was abandoned because the hospitals did not have reliable electricity. According to a study by the World Bank, a fancy technology introduced in developing countries typically reaches only 5 percent penetration before it stops. It doesn't spread further until _____. Big-budget infrastructure—roads, waterworks, airports, machine factories, electrical systems, power plants—are needed to make the high-tech stuff work. Thus, countries that failed to adopt old technologies are at a disadvantage when it comes to new ones."

*calculus 미적분 **high-profile 세간의 이목을 끄는

***penetration (현지) 진출, 보급

① cultural diversity is highly respected
② older foundational technologies catch up
③ people learn how to operate the technology
④ they get more support from foreign countries
⑤ companies invest more in talent development

052

다음 빈칸에 들어갈 말로 가장 적절한 것은?

What are scientific revolutions, and what role do they play in scientific development? Scientific revolutions occur when _____. However, there is one further question that needs to be asked. Why should a change of paradigm be called a revolution? When comparing the large number of differences between political and scientific development, how can we justify using a metaphor that finds revolutions in both? One aspect of the similarity should be quite obvious. Political revolutions are begun by a growing sense, often by a small part of the political community, that existing institutions are unable to correct the problems posed by an environment that they have helped create. In much the same way, scientific revolutions are begun by a growing sense, again often by a small number of the scientific community, that an existing paradigm does not do enough in the exploration of an area it has previously led the way in. In both political and scientific development, the sense of malfunction that can lead to crisis is needed for a revolution to occur.

① a scientific community considers them to be necessary
② too many unexpected results creep into a field of study
③ geniuses switch their ideas from one paradigm to another
④ general similarities are found between political and scientific development
⑤ new paradigms cannot exist alongside the old paradigm either completely or in part

053

다음 빈칸에 들어갈 말로 가장 적절한 것은?

It seems that _____ is a universal condition of life. Even such seemingly infallible predators as the African lion fail in their attacks on gazelles and zebras two-thirds of the time. The basic problem facing both attacker and victim is that success depends on each doing a host of tasks well. Ideally, a predator should be able to detect, catch those it has detected, and overcome the resistance defenses of the prey. A potential prey should remain undetected or, failing that, flee or, failing that, thwart the predator's attempts to kill it. Success in each of these endeavors calls for abilities that often clash. For example, the agility needed for effective capture or for successful escape is usually incompatible with heavy armor. Excelling at one task entails diminished performance in others, unless the animal's energy budget enlarges so that both functions can increase without interfering with each other or with other functions. Within the budget's constraints, the resulting compromise means no task is done as well as it could be were it the only task to be accomplished.

*thwart 좌절시키다 **agility 민첩함

① the stable coexistence of predator and prey populations
② cooperation between different animal species for survival
③ imperfection as a necessary accompaniment to adaptation
④ the expression of the instinctive desire for self-preservation
⑤ reliance on social learning for the acquisition of survival skills

054

다음 빈칸에 들어갈 말로 가장 적절한 것은?

Enormous amounts of money are expended on new product development projects, with workers making tremendous efforts _____ to increase their success rates. Thus, food companies outsource huge sensory evaluation projects to expert research firms. The sensory experts try to minimize test errors, in other words, minimize the influence of various factors that might affect the results. For example, since the perceived flavor changes according to the order of the test samples, they control the comparison group, centralization tendency error, time dependency, and location influence through various experimental designs and statistical analysis methods. Psychological deviation in particular is also treated as a significant factor. In addition, they carefully control for expectation error (if the goal is cost reduction), stimulation error (if it is held in a luxurious container), logic error (if the color is different), and halo effect (if it tastes good, the rest of the examining factors are also evaluated as good). Therefore, all sensory evaluations are conducted individually in independent booths.

*halo effect 후광 효과

① to innovate their production process and to reduce defects
② to produce quality goods and to attract potential consumers
③ to analyze buyers' needs and to take the initiative in the market
④ to arouse consumers' emotional stimuli and to promote products
⑤ to decrease individual deviations and to produce unbiased results

| 출제 Trend

- 흐름이 자연스러운 글이 되도록 단락을 알맞게 배열하는 유형으로, 단락 간의 논리 관계를 이해하고 있는지를 측정한다.
- 2015수능부터 2문항씩 출제되고 있으며, 변별력 확보를 위해 두 문항 중 한 문항은 고난도 3점으로 출제되고 있다.
- 최근에는 글이 길어지고 2~3개의 문장을 한 단락으로 묶어 제시하고 있어 깊은 사고력을 요하는 고난도 문항으로 출제되고 있다.

| 학습 Focus

- 일반적으로 문단의 요지와 이를 뒷받침하는 주요 세부 사항들을 활용하여 문제를 출제하며 문장 간의 유기적 연결성이 비교적 명확한 지문을 이용한다. 따라서 지시어와 연결어, (정)관사 등이 중요한 단서가 된다.
- 문장 간의 논리적인 순서를 추론할 수 있는 직접적인 연결고리가 없을 경우에는 주어진 글에 담겨있는 글의 소재나 주제를 정확히 파악하여, 이를 바탕으로 글의 전개 방향을 논리적으로 추론해야 한다.

| 유형 Solution

1. 주어진 글을 통해 글의 소재, 주제, 이어질 내용 등을 예측하라!

2. 연결어와 지시어, 반복되는 어구 등을 단서로 (A), (B), (C) 사이의 순서를 예측하라!
   └→ 지시어, 대명사, such, 「the+명사」 등이 있는 문장 앞에는 이것들이 가리키는 것이 있어야 한다.

3. 글 (A), (B), (C)의 내용을 토대로 자연스러운 글의 순서를 구성하라!
   └→ 가장 확실한 순서를 먼저 정하고, 그 순서를 기준으로 나머지 순서를 결정하라.

4. 결정한 순서대로 글을 읽어보고, 흐름이 논리적인지 확인하라!

| 기출 Analysis

	시험	배점	정답률	소재 및 주제
	수능 36번	2점	38%	공통의 이익 달성과 갈등의 영역을 밝히려는 목적의 협상
	수능 37번	3점	37%	집단에서 순응의 결과로 생겨나는 규범
2024	9월 모평 36번	2점	54%	분류하고 일반화하는 직관적인 능력의 유용한 면과 부정적인 면
	9월 모평 37번	3점	42%	식물의 영양분이 제한적일 때 식물들이 보이는 반응
	6월 모평 36번	2점	58%	컴퓨터 소프트웨어의 복잡성 증가가 불러온 전세계 보안과 안전의 문제
	6월 모평 37번	3점	58%	사회적 목적에 긍정적으로 부합하는 당황했을 때 얼굴이 붉어지는 인간의 특징
	수능 36번	2점	61%	종의 환경 적응과 생식에 이바지하는 물벼룩이라는 종의 적응 가소성
	수능 37번	3점	35%	변호사가 사용하는 '승소 시 보수 약정'이라는 제도로 알아본 결과 기반 가격 책정
2023	9월 모평 36번	2점	69%	서로 다른 수위에 있는 물길을 연결하기 위해 로크라는 물웅덩이를 만드는 운하
	9월 모평 37번	3점	57%	의식적인 방식뿐만 아니라 의식하지 못한 방식으로도 사용되는 문화적 관념
	6월 모평 36번	2점	56%	진화의 이야기를 제공하고 진화론의 예측에 대한 근거를 보여주는 화석 기록
	6월 모평 37번	3점	48%	투자하여 소유권을 가지게 된 것을 지나치게 중시하는 인간의 경향

055 주어진 글 다음에 이어질 글의 순서로 가장 적절한 것은?

2024 수능 37번

> Norms emerge in groups as a result of people conforming to the behavior of others. Thus, the start of a norm occurs when one person acts in a particular manner in a particular situation because she thinks she ought to.

(A) Thus, she may prescribe the behavior to them by uttering the norm statement in a prescriptive manner. Alternately, she may communicate that conformity is desired in other ways, such as by gesturing. In addition, she may threaten to sanction them for not behaving as she wishes. This will cause some to conform to her wishes and act as she acts.

(B) But some others will not need to have the behavior prescribed to them. They will observe the regularity of behavior and decide on their own that they ought to conform. They may do so for either rational or moral reasons.

(C) Others may then conform to this behavior for a number of reasons. The person who performed the initial action may think that others ought to behave as she behaves in situations of this sort.

*sanction 제재를 가하다

① (A) – (C) – (B) ② (B) – (A) – (C) ③ (B) – (C) – (A)
④ (C) – (A) – (B) ⑤ (C) – (B) – (A)

....

✓ **Solution 1.** **주어진 글을 통해 글의 소재, 주제, 전개 방향 등을 예측하라!**

집단에서 다른 사람의 행동에 ❶( )한 결과로 ❷( )이 발생한다는 것을 설명하는 글임을 예측할 수 있다.

✓ **Solution 2.** **연결어와 지시어, 반복되는 어구 등을 단서로 하여 주어진 글 다음에 올 글을 예측하라!**

(A): 주어진 글에 Thus가 있으므로, 다시 Thus로 연결하는 것은 자연스럽지 않다.

(B): 순응 행동을 지시받지 않고 스스로 관찰하여 순응할지의 여부를 결정하는 사람들도 있다는 내용으로 주어진 글과 논리적으로 연결되지 않는다.

(C): this behavior는 주어진 글의 한 사람이 특정 상황에서 특정 방식으로 행동하는 것을 가리키며, 다른 사람들도 그 행동에 순응한다는 내용으로 주어진 글과 자연스럽게 연결된다.

✓ **Solution 3.** **글 (A), (B), (C)의 내용을 간략하게 요약하면서 자연스러운 글의 순서를 구성하라!**

(C): this behavior는 주어진 글에서 말한 특정 상황에서의 특정 행동을 가리키며, 이 행동을 다른 사람들도 여러 이유로 순응하게 된다고 함으로써 규범의 시작을 설명한다.

(A): 규범 진술을 말로 함으로써 순응하는 행동을 ❸( ) she는 (C)에 나온 최초의 행동을 하는 사람을 가리키는 것이 적절하고, 다른 방식으로 순응이 요망된다고 전달하거나 순응하도록 협박해서 순응하게 할 수도 있다고 설명한다.

(B): (A)에서 말한 것과 같은 지시가 아니라 다른 사람의 행동을 관찰함으로써 스스로 순응할지의 여부를 결정하는 사람들도 있다고 추가적인 설명을 하고 있다.

Answers ❶ 순응 ❷ 규범 ❸ 지시하는

056

주어진 글 다음에 이어질 글의 순서로 가장 적절한 것은?

A fascinating species of water flea exhibits a kind of flexibility that evolutionary biologists call *adaptive plasticity.*

(A) That's a clever trick, because producing spines and a helmet is costly, in terms of energy, and conserving energy is essential for an organism's ability to survive and reproduce. The water flea only expends the energy needed to produce spines and a helmet when it needs to.

(B) If the baby water flea is developing into an adult in water that includes the chemical signatures of creatures that prey on water fleas, it develops a helmet and spines to defend itself against predators. If the water around it doesn't include the chemical signatures of predators, the water flea doesn't develop these protective devices.

(C) So it may well be that this plasticity is an adaptation: a trait that came to exist in a species because it contributed to reproductive fitness. There are many cases, across many species, of adaptive plasticity. Plasticity is conducive to fitness if there is sufficient variation in the environment.

*spine 가시 돌기 **conducive 도움되는

① (A) − (C) − (B)
② (B) − (A) − (C)
③ (B) − (C) − (A)
④ (C) − (A) − (B)
⑤ (C) − (B) − (A)

057

주어진 글 다음에 이어질 글의 순서로 가장 적절한 것은?

In spite of the likeness between the fictional and real world, the fictional world deviates from the real one in one important respect.

(A) The author has selected the content according to his own worldview and his own conception of relevance, in an attempt to be neutral and objective or convey a subjective view on the world. Whatever the motives, the author's subjective conception of the world stands between the reader and the original, untouched world on which the story is based.

(B) Because of the inner qualities with which the individual is endowed through heritage and environment, the mind functions as a filter; every outside impression that passes through it is filtered and interpreted. However, the world the reader encounters in literature is already processed and filtered by another consciousness.

(C) The existing world faced by the individual is in principle an infinite chaos of events and details before it is organized by a human mind. This chaos only gets processed and modified when perceived by a human mind.

*deviate 벗어나다 **endow 부여하다 *** heritage 유산

① (A) − (C) − (B)
② (B) − (A) − (C)
③ (B) − (C) − (A)
④ (C) − (A) − (B)
⑤ (C) − (B) − (A)

058

주어진 글 다음에 이어질 글의 순서로 가장 적절한 것은?

> Human superiority over other beings is not by any means absolute or all-inclusive. The only superiority we have is our thinking and reasoning ability and our strong sense of morality.

(A) Yet even this is subject to question, as the lifestyles of animals often seem to be more rational than ours. For instance, one can learn a great deal from observing how bees, termites, and ants live harmoniously in densely populated nests, an order the likes of which humans would never be able to achieve.

(B) So my response to those offended by comparing humans to lower beings is that perhaps we have an inflated image of our own species and are neither as intelligent nor as civilized as we would like to think. The time has come for us to pause and take an objective inventory of what our species is made of.

(C) In the last century alone, it is estimated that about 182 million humans were killed by organized violence for no good reason at all. Despite the fact that the lower forms of beings are devoid of our intelligence, they never unnecessarily engage one another or try to eradicate one another.

*eradicate 근절하다, 절멸시키다

① (A) − (C) − (B)
② (B) − (A) − (C)
③ (B) − (C) − (A)
④ (C) − (A) − (B)
⑤ (C) − (B) − (A)

059

주어진 글 다음에 이어질 글의 순서로 가장 적절한 것은?

> Since prehistoric times, we have all been genetically programmed to maintain our bodies in a state best suited for our individual and collective survival. Our DNA directs where every protein, every lipid, in every cell, is to be placed.

(A) However, it is very unrealistic to believe that the many months or years of eating that led up to being overweight can be rapidly overcome by decreasing the amount one eats for several days or weeks. As noted, the body is programmed to want the fat and does not care about an individual's health goals or wish to work on their physical appearance.

(B) Since fat is a better source of energy than is muscle, the body is pre-programmed to prefer a higher amount of body fat and less muscle mass. The supposed rationale for this is that during times of famine the body is able to feed off its fat stores for the energy needed to survive.

(C) While this may serve a practical biological purpose, it tends to serve as a source of great frustration for those wishing to lose weight through dieting. For dieting runs counter to the body's programmed desire to maintain high fat stores. People will sometimes starve themselves in an attempt to attain long-term weight reduction.

*lipid 지방질

① (A) − (C) − (B)
② (B) − (A) − (C)
③ (B) − (C) − (A)
④ (C) − (A) − (B)
⑤ (C) − (B) − (A)

060

주어진 글 다음에 이어질 글의 순서로 가장 적절한 것은?

Much of what people do in a culture is linked to other people and linked to the culture generally. Even a seemingly private activity such as brushing your teeth is a form of cultural participation.

(A) Moreover, brushing teeth is not instilled in our genes via some evolutionary process that weeded out non-tooth brushers and left us all with an innate urge to brush. On the contrary, you probably brush because you were taught to do so by your parents.

(B) You probably also accept on faith the cultural teaching that doing so will increase your dental health. If you fail to do it, your teeth will go bad, and either you or someone else will have to pay for treatment, such as filling cavities; the services of dentists are likewise provided as part of economy.

(C) The brand of toothpaste you choose reflects what the market has produced to offer you, and if there are several brands your choice is probably shaped by cultural messages such as advertising slogans. In turn, your choices combine with those of many other toothpaste purchasers to determine which brands remain on the market and which ones fail and disappear.

*instill 주입하다

① (A) − (C) − (B)　　② (B) − (A) − (C)
③ (B) − (C) − (A)　　④ (C) − (A) − (B)
⑤ (C) − (B) − (A)

061

주어진 글 다음에 이어질 글의 순서로 가장 적절한 것은?

In many cases, the nonverbal channel trumps the impact of the verbal channel. That is, when there is a discrepancy between the verbal message and the nonverbal message, the latter typically weighs more in forming a judgment.

(A) That is, the nonverbal message is deliberate, but designed to let the partner know one's candid reaction indirectly. It is then the partner's responsibility to interpret the nonverbal message and make some adjustment in the plan.

(B) In such a case, the purpose of the positive comment might be to avoid a disagreement and support the friend, but the lack of a positive expression unintentionally leaks a more candid, negative reaction to the plan. Of course, the muted expressive display might also be strategic and intentional.

(C) For example, a friend might react to a plan for dinner with a comment like "that's good," but with little vocal enthusiasm and a muted facial expression. In spite of the verbal comment, the lack of expressive enthusiasm suggests that the plan isn't viewed very positively.

*discrepancy 차이, 불일치

① (A) − (C) − (B)　　② (B) − (A) − (C)
③ (B) − (C) − (A)　　④ (C) − (A) − (B)
⑤ (C) − (B) − (A)

062

주어진 글 다음에 이어질 글의 순서로 가장 적절한 것은?

Green turtles that hatch on the shores of Ascension Island in the South Atlantic swim across thousands of miles of ocean before returning, every three years, to breed on the exact same eggshell-littered beach from which they emerged.

(A) Moreover, Darwin's obsession with the geographical distribution of animal species and the mystery of why isolated island species of mockingbirds tend to be so specialized led him to propose his theory of evolution.

(B) Similarly, many species of birds, whales, spiny lobsters, frogs, and even bees are all capable of undertaking journeys that would challenge the greatest human explorers. How animals manage to find their way around the globe has been a mystery for centuries.

(C) However, mysteries are fascinating because there's always the possibility that their solution may lead to fundamental shift in our understanding of the world. Copernicus's thoughts in the sixteenth century on a problem concerning the geometry of the Ptolemaic Earth-centered model of the solar system, for instance, led him to shift the center of gravity of the entire universe away from humankind.

① (A) − (C) − (B)
② (B) − (A) − (C)
③ (B) − (C) − (A)
④ (C) − (A) − (B)
⑤ (C) − (B) − (A)

063

주어진 글 다음에 이어질 글의 순서로 가장 적절한 것은?

Even before a very young child can read, that child is hearing "lessons about life" transmitted through proverbs. Whether called maxims, truisms, clichés, idioms, expressions, or sayings, proverbs are small packages of truth about a people's values and beliefs.

(A) They are, in a sense, regarded as storehouses of a culture's wisdom. Proverbs are so important to every culture that there are even proverbs about proverbs. A German proverb states, "A country can be judged by the quality of its proverbs," and the Yoruba of Africa teach, "A wise man who knows proverbs overcomes difficulties."

(B) The idea that you can learn about a people through their proverbs is emphasized in these proverbs. Communicated in colorful, vivid language and with very few words, proverbs reflect the insights, wisdom, biases, and even superstitions of a culture.

(C) David Olajide, a famous sociolinguist, notes the significance of proverbs to a culture when he writes, "Proverbs are an aspect of culture cherished all over the world and preserved in language which is the medium for expressing them. Also, proverbs have psychological, cosmological and sociocultural roots."

① (A) − (C) − (B)
② (B) − (A) − (C)
③ (B) − (C) − (A)
④ (C) − (A) − (B)
⑤ (C) − (B) − (A)

문장 삽입

| 출제 Trend
- 글이 논리적으로 완성되도록 주어진 한 문장을 지문 속 적절한 위치에 삽입하는 유형이다.
- 2015수능부터 2문항씩 출제되고 있으며 두 문항 중 한 문항은 배점 3점으로 출제된다.
- 개별 문장 간의 연결성과 글 전체의 흐름을 동시에 파악해야 하기 때문에 배점에 관계없이 대부분의 수험생이 어려워하는 대표적인 고난도 유형이다.

| 학습 Focus
- 최근에는 지시적 표현이나 연결어에 의해서 풀기보다는 문장 간 의미의 논리성을 파악하도록 출제되는 추세이다. 따라서 정확한 문제 해결을 위해서는 형식적인 연결고리를 감지하는 능력뿐 아니라, 전체적인 흐름을 파악하여 문장 간의 논리적 상관관계를 추론해 내는 능력도 길러야 한다.
- 문장 간의 논리적인 관계를 추론할 수 있는 직접적인 연결고리가 없을 경우에는 주어진 문장이 글 전체에서 담당하는 역할(원인, 결과, 예시, 반박, 구체화 등)을 정확하게 파악하여 논리적 공백이 있는 곳을 찾아낸다.

| 유형 Solution

1. 주어진 문장에서 필요한 정보를 최대한 확인하라!
  └▸ 연결어, 지시어, 소재, 주어진 문장의 역할 등을 파악한다.

2. 글의 전반부에서 글의 소재와 주제를 파악하라!
  └▸ 첫 한두 문장에서 무엇에 관한 글인지를 파악한다.

3. 글을 읽으며 논리적 공백이 있는지를 살펴라!
  └▸ 주어진 문장이 들어가야 할 곳 전후에는 반드시 논리적 단절이 발생한다!

4. 주어진 문장을 선택한 곳에 넣어 보고 앞뒤 문맥이 자연스럽게 연결되는지 확인하라!

| 기출 Analysis

시험		배점	정답률	소재 및 주제
2024	수능 38번	2점	45%	때로 승자 독식으로 묘사되는 과학 대회에 대한 부정확한 설명
	수능 39번	3점	53%	문서의 오타와 유기체에서 발생하는 돌연변이의 유사점과 차이
	9월 모평 38번	2점	24%	아날로그에서 디지털 기술로의 변화가 음악 제작 방식에 미친 영향
	9월 모평 39번	3점	43%	예술 작품의 제작 과정을 이해하는 데 필요한 것
	6월 모평 38번	2점	55%	공식적 교육으로 전문화가 가능한 기관과 공식적 교육이 어려운 기관
	6월 모평 39번	3점	40%	숲에서 함께 자랄 때 영양분과 물을 최적으로 분배하는 나무들
2023	수능 38번	2점	55%	도시의 다른 사물과는 구분되도록 자연을 담으려는 공원 설계
	수능 39번	3점	56%	큰 문제를 작은 조각으로 나누는 협상가들이 사용하는 '살라미 전술'
	9월 모평 38번	2점	41%	일반인이 생각하는 것과 다른 사회심리학자의 집단에 대한 정의
	9월 모평 39번	3점	41%	보안과 사용자 편의성 향상을 시도하지만 서로 속도가 맞지 않을 수 있는 새로운 기술
	6월 모평 38번	2점	53%	수확량 유지를 위해 해충 저항력이 있는 품종의 지속적 개발 필요성
	6월 모평 39번	3점	42%	개별 개체가 아닌 여러 개체의 이탈을 포식자 공격의 증거로 인식하는 역학

064

글의 흐름으로 보아, 주어진 문장이 들어가기에 가장 적절한 곳은?

2024 수능 39번

At the next step in the argument, however, the analogy breaks down.

Misprints in a book or in any written message usually have a negative impact on the content, sometimes (literally) fatally. (①) The displacement of a comma, for instance, may be a matter of life and death. (②) Similarly most mutations have harmful consequences
5 for the organism in which they occur, meaning that they reduce its reproductive fitness. (③) Occasionally, however, a mutation may occur that increases the fitness of the organism, just as an accidental failure to reproduce the text of the first edition might provide more accurate or updated information. (④) A favorable mutation is going to be more heavily represented in the next generation, since the organism in which it occurred
10 will have more offspring and mutations are transmitted to the offspring. (⑤) By contrast, there is no mechanism by which a book that accidentally corrects the mistakes of the first edition will tend to sell better.

*analogy 유사 **mutation 돌연변이

···

✓ **Solution 1.** 주어진 문장에서 필요한 정보를 확인하라!

하지만(however), 논거의 다음 단계에서 그 ❶(　　　　)이 깨진다고 했으므로, 주어진 문장의 앞에는 어떤 두 대상의 유사점이 제시될 것이고, 그 뒤에는 두 대상의 유사점이 깨진 내용이 나올 것임을 예상할 수 있다.

✓ **Solution 2.** 글을 읽으며 논리적 공백이 있는지를 살펴라!

문서의 오타는 부정적[치명적] 영향을 끼침 (①) 예시: 잘못 찍힌 쉼표의 치명성 (②) Similarly(마찬가지로), 생식 적합성을 감소시키는 해로운 돌연변이 (③) However(그러나), 적합성을 높이는 유리한 돌연변이가 있음 = 초판 텍스트의 실수(= 돌연변이)가 더 정확한 정보 제공의 기회일 수 있음 (④) 유리한 돌연변이는 더 많은 자손을 낳게 함 (⑤) By contrast(대조적으로), 초판의 오류를 바로잡은 책이 더 잘 팔리는 메커니즘은 없음

▶ ❷(　　　)번 앞 문장에서는 텍스트에 있는 오타를 유기체의 ❸(　　　　)에 비유해서 서로 유사점을 설명하고 있는 반면에, 마지막 두 문장에서는 유리한 돌연변이는 ❹(　　　) 결과를 만들지만, 책의 오타를 수정한 판이 판매량 증가라는 유리한 결과로 이어지는 것만은 아니라고 함으로써, 오타 수정과 돌연변이 간의 유사점이 깨진 상황을 설명한다.

✓ **Solution 3.** 주어진 문장을 선택한 곳에 넣어 보고 앞뒤 문맥이 자연스럽게 연결되는지 확인하라!

주어진 문장을 ❺(　　)에 넣으면, 책의 오류와 돌연변이 간의 유사성이 나오는 앞 부분과 그 유사성이 깨진 것에 대해 설명하는 뒤 부분이 논리적 비약 없이 자연스럽게 연결된다.

Answers ❶ 유사점 ❷ ④ ❸ 돌연변이 ❹ 유리한 ❺ ④

065

글의 흐름으로 보아, 주어진 문장이 들어가기에 가장 적절한 곳은?

> There's a reason for that: traditionally, park designers attempted to create such a feeling by planting tall trees at park boundaries, building stone walls, and constructing other means of partition.

Parks take the shape demanded by the cultural concerns of their time. Once parks are in place, they are no inert stage—their purposes and meanings are made and remade by planners and by park users. Moments of park creation are particularly telling, however, for they reveal and actualize ideas about nature and its relationship to urban society. (①) Indeed, what distinguishes a park from the broader category of public space is the representation of nature that parks are meant to embody. (②) Public spaces include parks, concrete plazas, sidewalks, even indoor atriums. (③) Parks typically have trees, grass, and other plants as their central features. (④) When entering a city park, people often imagine a sharp separation from streets, cars, and buildings. (⑤) What's behind this idea is not only landscape architects' desire to design aesthetically suggestive park spaces, but a much longer history of Western thought that envisions cities and nature as antithetical spaces and oppositional forces.

*aesthetically 미적으로 **antithetical 대조적인

066

글의 흐름으로 보아, 주어진 문장이 들어가기에 가장 적절한 곳은?

> It may be easier to reach an agreement when settlement terms don't have to be implemented until months in the future.

Negotiators should try to find ways to slice a large issue into smaller pieces, known as using *salami tactics*. (①) Issues that can be expressed in quantitative, measurable units are easy to slice. (②) For example, compensation demands can be divided into cents-per-hour increments or lease rates can be quoted as dollars per square foot. (③) When working to fractionate issues of principle or precedent, parties may use the time horizon (when the principle goes into effect or how long it will last) as a way to fractionate the issue. (④) Another approach is to vary the number of ways that the principle may be applied. (⑤) For example, a company may devise a family emergency leave plan that allows employees the opportunity to be away from the company for a period of no longer than three hours, and no more than once a month, for illness in the employee's immediate family.

*increment 증가 **fractionate 세분하다

067

글의 흐름으로 보아, 주어진 문장이 들어가기에 가장 적절한 곳은?

There will be a point at which the clip will be bent out of shape and will not return to the flat pattern that it had when fresh out of the box.

The paper clip works because its loops can be spread apart just enough to get it around some papers and, when released, can spring back to grab the papers and hold them. (①) This springing action, more than its shape per se, is what makes the paper clip work. (②) Springiness, and its limits, are also critical for paper clips to be made in the first place. (③) To appreciate this, open a paper clip a bit wider than needed to get the loops around some papers. (④) When this happens, the clip's elastic limit is said to have been exceeded (or the wire is said to have been plastically deformed), and it is extremely difficult to restore the clip to the shape it had in the box. (⑤) Needless to say, the clip is also no longer as effective in holding papers or in lying flat upon them.

068

글의 흐름으로 보아, 주어진 문장이 들어가기에 가장 적절한 곳은?

Their life experiences had tagged their genes in ways that meant these identical twins were, in terms of their genetic function, no longer identical.

In 2005, scientists in Spain found that, in a sense, our genes can learn. They prepared chromosomes from two sets of identical twins, one set aged three and the other aged fifty. (①) Using fluorescent green and red molecules that bind, respectively, to epigenetically modified and unmodified segments of DNA, they examined the two sets of genes. (②) The children's genes looked very similar, indicating that, as one would expect, twins start life with essentially identical genetic tags. (③) In contrast, the fifty-year-old chromosomes lit up green and red like two Christmas trees with different decorations. (④) This means the tagging is not just due to aging but also a direct result of how we live our lives. (⑤) In photographing the different patterns of red and green on the two fifty-year-old chromosomes, scientists were capturing the two different "personalities" the twins' genes had developed.

*epigenetically 후성적으로

069

글의 흐름으로 보아, 주어진 문장이 들어가기에 가장 적절한 곳은?

> Sometimes determining the safety of a food additive can be quite challenging because they undergo transformations within our foods and bodies.

Government agencies routinely reevaluate food additives to ensure they are safe, especially if any new toxicology data arises. Each government has a detailed list of additives that are acceptable for use, as well as the maximum levels that can be employed and the types of foods they can be used in. (①) Sometimes these lists vary between countries so that an additive is assumed to be safe in one country but not in another, which causes problems for food companies trying to sell their products in a global market. (②) These differences arise due to different interpretations of the toxicological data by scientists — establishing safety is not always clear-cut. (③) For instance, they may chemically degrade during cooking, after being exposed to light, or after reacting with other food ingredients, thereby changing their toxicity. (④) Consequently, it is essential to understand how additives actually behave in real foods. (⑤) It is likely that some of the additives currently accepted for use in foods will be banned in the future, but, that does not mean that all additives are bad.

*toxicology 독물학

070

글의 흐름으로 보아, 주어진 문장이 들어가기에 가장 적절한 곳은?

> In contrast, in integrative situations the negotiators should employ win-win strategies and tactics.

The structure of the interdependence shapes the strategies and tactics that negotiators employ. In distributive situations, negotiators are motivated to win the competition and beat the other party or to gain the largest piece of the fixed resource that they can. (①) To achieve these objectives, negotiators usually employ win-lose strategies and tactics. (②) This approach to negotiation — called *distributive bargaining* — accepts the fact that there can only be one winner given the situation and pursues a course of action to be that winner. (③) The purpose of the negotiation is to claim value — that is, to do whatever is necessary to claim the reward, gain the lion's share of the prize, or gain the largest piece possible. (④) This approach to negotiation attempts to find solutions so both parties can do well and achieve their goals. (⑤) The purpose of the negotiation is to create value — that is, to find a way for all parties to meet their objectives, either by identifying more resources or finding unique ways to share and coordinate the use of existing resources.

071

글의 흐름으로 보아, 주어진 문장이 들어가기에 가장 적절한 곳은?

> If the same type of food is searched for by humans and their predators, conflicts are likely to occur.

It is logical to postulate that organisms, such as human beings, who grew up under different conditions have developed different survival strategies, and different optimal levels of risk taking. Prehistoric humans living in environments rich in vegetation and with little dangers from predators were hardly encouraged or forced to expose themselves to any of the dangers around. (①) They could afford to wait until the threat was removed before continuing to look for food. (②) This type of environment would have encouraged patient and risk-avoiding temperaments. (③) On the other hand, an environment with scarce resources, and more predators would have forced inhabitants into a fierce competition for food. (④) To provide themselves and their offspring with essential resources, like food, these humans had to take considerably higher risks, both to outwit other predators, as well as to acquire the necessary resources, because their prey would also be more cautious and harder to overcome. (⑤) This type of environment would have encouraged more risky behavior, as a patient, risk-avoiding person would have been less likely to gain access to the necessary resources.

*postulate 가정하다 **outwit (~보다) 한 수 앞서다

072

글의 흐름으로 보아, 주어진 문장이 들어가기에 가장 적절한 곳은?

> In 2009, some experts identified the relative anonymity of Internet users as a key issue that enables cybercrime and proposed Internet 'passports' to help combat the problem.

In most cases, the police know who the criminal is and their main problem is how to gather enough evidence to prove guilt. But Internet-based crime is different: the police simply do not know who the criminals are! (①) With online crime there are so many ways to hide one's identity. (②) There are numerous services that will mask a user's IP address by routing traffic through various servers, making it difficult to track down the criminal. (③) However, attempts to better track online identity raise serious issues for privacy advocates and result in a political backlash. (④) And end to anonymity on the Internet could have serious consequences in countries where the government punishes dissenters. (⑤) So even if the technological challenge of identifying every online user could be overcome, many lawmakers would be hesitant to mandate it.

09 요약문 완성

| 출제 Trend

- 글의 요지를 한 문장으로 요약한 문장에서 (A), (B) 두 개의 빈칸에 들어갈 알맞은 어휘를 추론하는 유형이다.
- 요약문 완성 문제는 2점으로 출제되는 경우가 많지만 정답률을 보면 체감 난이도가 높은 고난도 유형이라고 할 수 있다.
- 심리학 등의 연구나 실험을 제시하고 도출된 결론의 빈칸을 채우는 문제들이 많이 출제되었으나 최근 수능에서는 제시되는 글의 범위가 다양해져서 일반적인 내용의 글에서 요지를 찾는 방향으로 출제되기도 한다.

| 학습 Focus

- 지문의 길이가 상대적으로 길고 지문과 요약문을 비교하여 빈칸에 들어갈 표현을 찾아야 하므로 문제를 푸는 데 시간이 더 걸릴 수 있다. 따라서 요약문의 빈칸에 들어갈 표현의 단서를 찾기 위한 지문 읽기 연습을 해야 한다.
- 선택지에 있는 표현을 빈칸에 넣어 보고 말이 되는 것을 고르는 식으로 접근하면 지문의 내용과 어긋나는 답을 고르는 실수를 할 수 있다. 따라서 지문의 내용을 정확하게 파악하고 반드시 지문 속에서 정답의 단서를 찾아야 한다.

| 유형 Solution

1. 요약문을 먼저 읽고 글의 내용을 예측하라!
  └→ 요약문은 글의 중심 내용을 표현한 것이고, 빈칸에 들어갈 말은 글의 핵심어에 해당한다.

2. 요약문의 빈칸에 들어갈 내용을 찾기 위한 목적 의식을 가지고 지문을 읽어라!

3. 지문에서 요약문의 내용과 대응되는 부분을 찾으면 그 부분을 근거로 빈칸에 들어갈 말을 추론하라!
  └→ 지문에 쓰인 것과 다른 표현을 써서 같은 뜻을 전달하는 선택지를 찾아야 한다.

| 기출 Analysis

	시험	배점	정답률	소재 및 주제
	수능 40번	2점	58%	기간 차이를 두고 연구함으로써 가능한 다양한 과학 분야에서 성과 내기
2024	9월 모평 40번	2점	55%	역사적 사건에 살을 붙인 설명을 제공함으로써 대중의 이해를 돕는 역사 소설
	6월 모평 40번	2점	53%	진화의 과정에서 미래의 진화에 제약이 될 수도 있는 생존 특성 발달
	수능 40번	2점	75%	장인정신의 온전한 발전을 방해하는 현대사회의 사회적, 경제적 요인
2023	9월 모평 40번	2점	71%	팀원들과 큰 규모의 프로젝트를 진행할 때 중요한 디자이너의 관리 능력
	6월 모평 40번	2점	63%	기술과 정보 사회에서 인간의 이동성에 관련하여 나타난 사회적 불평등의 문제
	수능 40번	2점	53%	과학적 설명에 대한 두 가지 철학적 관점
2022	9월 모평 40번	2점	49%	탈맥락적 방식의 정보처리에 유능하지만 종합적 판단을 방해하는 컴퓨터
	6월 모평 40번	2점	59%	땅에 대한 소유권과 국가에 대한 충성심을 보여주는 영국 귀족의 나무 심기

정답 및 해설 p.041

073

다음 글의 내용을 한 문장으로 요약하고자 한다. 빈칸 (A), (B)에 들어갈 말로 가장 적절한 것은?   2024 수능 40번

Even those with average talent can produce notable work in the various sciences, so long as they do not try to embrace all of them at once. Instead, they should concentrate attention on one subject after another (that is, in different periods of time), although later work will weaken earlier attainments in the other spheres. This amounts to saying that the brain adapts to universal science in *time* but not in *space*. In fact, even those with great abilities proceed in this way. Thus, when we are astonished by someone with publications in different scientific fields, realize that each topic was explored during a specific period of time. Knowledge gained earlier certainly will not have disappeared from the mind of the author, but it will have become simplified by condensing into formulas or greatly abbreviated symbols. Thus, sufficient space remains for the perception and learning of new images on the cerebral blackboard.

*condense 응축하다 **cerebral 대뇌의

↓

Exploring one scientific subject after another _____(A)_____ remarkable work across the sciences, as the previously gained knowledge is retained in simplified forms within the brain, which _____(B)_____ room for new learning.

	(A)		(B)			(A)		(B)
①	enables	………	leaves		②	challenges	………	spares
③	delays	………	creates		④	requires	………	removes
⑤	invites	………	diminishes					

✓ **Solution 1.** 요약문을 먼저 읽고 글의 내용을 예측하라!

과학 주제를 하나씩 순차적으로 탐구하는 것이 가져오는 결과를 설명하는 글로, (A)에는 순차적 탐구와 주목할 만한 연구의 관계를 나타내는 표현이, (B)에는 이전 연구 지식이 단순화되어 유지되는 것이 새로운 학습에 미치는 영향을 나타내는 표현이 들어가야 한다.

✓ **Solution 2.** 글을 읽으며 글의 주제 및 요지를 파악하라!

과학 주제를 차례로 탐구하게 되면 이전에 얻은 지식이 단순화되어 보유되면서 다음의 새로운 학습을 위한 공간이 남아 있게 되어 다양한 과학 분야에서 주목할 만한 과학적 성과를 이룰 수 있다.

✓ **Solution 3.** 글에서 요약문의 내용과 대응되는 부분을 찾아 그 부분을 근거로 요약문의 빈칸에 들어갈 말을 추론하라!

(A) 처음 두 문장과 다섯 번째 문장에서 과학 주제를 하나씩 차례로 탐구하면 다양한 과학 분야에서 주목할 만한 성과를 ❶(   )는 것을 알 수 있다.

(B) 마지막 두 문장에서 이전에 얻은 지식은 ❷(   )되며, 그 결과 뇌에 새로운 학습이 이루어질 수 있는 공간이 ❸(   )다는 것을 알 수 있다.

Answers ❶ 가능하게 한다 ❷ 단순화 ❸ 남아 있는

074

다음 글의 내용을 한 문장으로 요약하고자 한다. 빈칸 (A), (B)에 들어갈 말로 가장 적절한 것은?

"Craftsmanship" may suggest a way of life that declined with the arrival of industrial society—but this is misleading. Craftsmanship names an enduring, basic human impulse, the desire to do a job well for its own sake. Craftsmanship cuts a far wider swath than skilled manual labor; it serves the computer programmer, the doctor, and the artist; parenting improves when it is practiced as a skilled craft, as does citizenship. In all these domains, craftsmanship focuses on objective standards, on the thing in itself. Social and economic conditions, however, often stand in the way of the craftsman's discipline and commitment: schools may fail to provide the tools to do good work, and workplaces may not truly value the aspiration for quality. And though craftsmanship can reward an individual with a sense of pride in work, this reward is not simple. The craftsman often faces conflicting objective standards of excellence; the desire to do something well for its own sake can be weakened by competitive pressure, by frustration, or by obsession.

*swath 구획

↓

> Craftsmanship, a human desire that has _____(A)_____ over time in diverse contexts, often encounters factors that _____(B)_____ its full development.

	(A)		(B)
①	persisted	………	limit
②	persisted	………	cultivate
③	evolved	………	accelerate
④	diminished	………	shape
⑤	diminished	………	restrict

075

다음 글의 내용을 한 문장으로 요약하고자 한다. 빈칸 (A), (B)에 들어갈 말로 가장 적절한 것은?

Philip Kitcher and Wesley Salmon have suggested that there are two possible alternatives among philosophical theories of explanation. One is the view that scientific explanation consists in the *unification* of broad bodies of phenomena under a minimal number of generalizations. According to this view, the (or perhaps, a) goal of science is to construct an economical framework of laws or generalizations that are capable of subsuming all observable phenomena. Scientific explanations organize and systematize our knowledge of the empirical world; the more economical the systematization, the deeper our understanding of what is explained. The other view is the *causal/mechanical* approach. According to it, a scientific explanation of a phenomenon consists of uncovering the mechanisms that produced the phenomenon of interest. This view sees the explanation of individual events as primary, with the explanation of generalizations flowing from them. That is, the explanation of scientific generalizations comes from the causal mechanisms that produce the regularities.

*subsume 포섭(포함)하다 **empirical 경험적인

↓

> Scientific explanations can be made either by seeking the _____(A)_____ number of principles covering all observations or by finding general _____(B)_____ drawn from individual phenomena.

	(A)		(B)
①	least	………	patterns
②	fixed	………	features
③	limited	………	functions
④	fixed	………	rules
⑤	least	………	assumptions

076

다음 글의 내용을 한 문장으로 요약하고자 한다. 빈칸 (A), (B)에 들어갈 말로 가장 적절한 것은?

Have you ever wondered why you commit yourself so often to something in the future that seems like a good idea at the time but becomes more and more awful as the day approaches? "Why did I ever agree to this?" we lament. "How did I think I could get into med school with a C in biology?" "Why did I think I had room in my house for a dozen more people?" And now the panic sets in — because when you decided your goal was to become a doctor, when you decided to fill your house with your husband's family, you didn't really spend all that much time thinking about whether or not you could make it work. You were thinking why, not what, and if it's any consolation, it's a situation most of us fall into again and again. Because we are biased to think about future events more in terms of why we want to do them and less in terms of how we'll actually get it done, we adopt goals and plans with potentially rich rewards that are also logistical nightmares.

*logistical nightmare 실제 실행상의 어려움

↓

We readily agree to goals and plans beyond our _____(A)_____ because we pay more attention to their _____(B)_____ than to whether or not they will work out.

	(A)		(B)
①	focus	·········	origins
②	focus	·········	potential
③	capacity	·········	causes
④	capacity	·········	alternatives
⑤	comprehension	·········	applications

077

다음 글의 내용을 한 문장으로 요약하고자 한다. 빈칸 (A), (B)에 들어갈 말로 가장 적절한 것은?

Imagine that you have just moved to a desert town and are trying to determine if the local weather forecaster can accurately predict whether it will be sunny or rainy. The forecaster often predicts sunshine and rarely predicts rain. One day, you observe that the forecaster predicts sunshine and is correct. On another day, she predicts rain and is correct. Which of these correct predictions would leave you more convinced that the forecaster can accurately predict the weather? According to information-theoretic accounts, the more informative of the two observations is the correct prediction of rain. This is because a correct prediction of sunshine is not surprising in the desert, where it is sunny almost every day. That is, even if the forecaster knew only that the desert is sunny, you would expect her to make lots of correct predictions of sunshine just by chance. Because rainy days are rare in the desert, a correct prediction of rain is less likely to occur by chance and therefore provides stronger evidence that the forecaster can distinguish between future sunny and rainy days.

↓

Whether or not the _____(A)_____ of prediction for an event is considered significant depends on the _____(B)_____ of the event.

	(A)		(B)
①	precision	·········	objective
②	precision	·········	rarity
③	rapidity	·········	uniqueness
④	frequency	·········	popularity
⑤	frequency	·········	location

078

다음 글의 내용을 한 문장으로 요약하고자 한다. 빈칸 (A), (B)에 들어갈 말로 가장 적절한 것은?

The terms *narrow* and *weak* AI are used to contrast with *strong, human-level, general* or *full-blown* AI (sometimes called AGI, or artificial general intelligence)—that is, the AI that we see in movies,
5 that can do most everything we humans can do, and possibly much more. General AI might have been the original goal of the field, but achieving it has turned out to be much harder than expected. Over time, efforts in AI have become focused on particular well-
10 defined tasks—speech recognition, chess playing, autonomous driving, and so on. Creating machines that perform such functions is useful and often lucrative, and it could be argued that each of these tasks individually requires "intelligence." But no AI
15 program has been created yet that could be called intelligent in any general sense. A recent appraisal of the field stated this well: "A pile of narrow intelligences will never add up to a general intelligence. General intelligence isn't about the number of abilities, but
20 about the integration between those abilities."

*lucrative 수익성이 있는

↓

At present, AI has the ability to perform ___(A)___ functions or tasks, but its abilities cannot be ___(B)___ to reach the level of general intelligence.

	(A)		(B)
①	specific	....	combined
②	multiple	....	subdivided
③	integrated	....	extended
④	specific	....	recognized
⑤	integrated	....	aroused

079

다음 글의 내용을 한 문장으로 요약하고자 한다. 빈칸 (A), (B)에 들어갈 말로 가장 적절한 것은?

One study compared how people make car-buying decisions under two conditions. In one condition, they were offered the car loaded with options, and their task was to eliminate the options they didn't want. In the second condition, they were offered the car devoid of 5 options, and their task was to add the ones they wanted. People in the first condition ended up with many more options than people in the second. This is because when options are already attached to the car being considered, they become part of the endowment and passing them 10 up triggers a feeling of loss. When the options are not already attached, they are not part of the endowment and choosing them is perceived as a gain. But because losses hurt more than gains satisfy, people judging, say, a $400 stereo upgrade that is part of the car's 15 endowment may decide that giving it up will hurt worse than its $400 price. In contrast, when the upgrade is not part of the car's endowment, they may decide that choosing it won't produce $400 worth of good feeling. So the endowment effect is operating even before people 20 actually close the deal on their new car.

*devoid of ~이 없는

↓

The study suggests that losses have more ___(A)___ impact than equivalent gains do because once something is seemingly ___(B)___ by someone, it is worth more to the person than its mere cash value.

	(A)		(B)
①	social	....	used
②	monetary	....	chosen
③	psychological	....	possessed
④	monetary	....	abandoned
⑤	psychological	....	evaluated

080

다음 글의 내용을 한 문장으로 요약하고자 한다. 빈칸 (A), (B)에 들어갈 말로 가장 적절한 것은?

Social Darwinism refers to a loose group of theories that arose in the late-nineteenth and early-twentieth centuries, following publication of Charles Darwin's theory of evolution. This was a time of European 5 imperialism, intense immigration to the United States, and growing masses of urbanized poor due to the industrial revolution. Thus, social prejudices spread among the European and American elite who convinced themselves that the conquered and the 10 impoverished were somehow deserving of their status. Likewise, the idea of survival of the fittest was used to justify this viewpoint. Darwin did not intend evolution to be racist or a justification of social inequity. His theory was an explanation of how animals adapted to 15 their environments. It was not a moral prescription for society. But his work was misinterpreted to mean that only the strongest and most worthy survive and that social disadvantage is a reflection of genetic inferiority.

↓

Social Darwinism is considered to be an ___(A)___ of Darwinism because it attempted to ___(B)___ social inequality for the ruling group.

	(A)		(B)
①	opposition	········	justify
②	opposition	········	intensify
③	improvement	········	minimize
④	exploitation	········	contradict
⑤	exploitation	········	rationalize

081

다음 글의 내용을 한 문장으로 요약하고자 한다. 빈칸 (A), (B)에 들어갈 말로 가장 적절한 것은?

One of the greatest values of cross-cultural comparisons is that they can tell us whether a developmental phenomenon is or is not universal. For example, are masculine and feminine roles universal? Could biological differences between the sexes lead 5 inevitably to sex differences in behavior? Many years ago, anthropologist Margaret Mead compared the gender roles adopted by people in three tribal societies on the island of New Guinea, and her observations are certainly thought-provoking. In the Arapesh tribe, 10 both men and women were taught to play what we would regard as a feminine role: they were cooperative, non-aggressive, and sensitive to the needs of others. Both men and women of the Mundugumor tribe were brought up to be aggressive and emotionally 15 unresponsive to other people—a masculine pattern of behavior by Western standards. Finally, the Tchambuli displayed a pattern of gender-role development that was the direct opposite of the Western pattern: males were passive, emotionally dependent, and socially 20 sensitive, whereas females were dominant, independent, and assertive. Mead's research shows that whatever holds true in our society doesn't hold true everywhere.

↓

Mead's cross-cultural comparison suggests that ___(A)___ learning may have far more to do with the characteristic behavior patterns of men and women than ___(B)___ differences do.

	(A)		(B)
①	individual	········	emotional
②	cultural	········	biological
③	collective	········	developmental
④	universal	········	social
⑤	comparative	········	psychological

장문(1지문 2문항)

출제 Trend

- 두 단락 길이 정도의 긴 지문을 주고, 41번과 42번 두 문항을 출제하는 유형이다.
- 두 문항 중 첫 번째는 글의 전체 내용을 포괄하는 제목을 묻는 문제이고, 두 번째 문제로는 2019수능 이전까지는 빈칸 추론이 출제되었는데, 2019수능부터 밑줄 어휘의 적절성을 판단하는 어휘 추론 유형이 출제되고 있다.
- 두 번째 어휘 문항이 3점으로 출제된 적이 있기는 하지만 대체로 2점으로 출제되고 있으며, 전반적으로 정답률은 높지 않은 편이다.

학습 Focus

- 지문의 내용에 따라 상당히 어렵게 출제될 수 있으며, 글 전체의 내용을 파악하는 동시에 세부적인 내용의 흐름을 정확하게 파악하는 연습을 해야 한다.
- 제목 추론은 글 전체를 아우르는 내용을 가장 잘 표현한 선택지를 골라야 한다. 따라서 각 단락의 중심 내용 및 전체적인 글의 주제를 파악하고, 글의 전체 내용을 포괄하는 하나의 핵심어(구)를 떠올려 본다.
- 어휘 추론은 글의 흐름에 대한 정확한 이해를 요구한다. 따라서 밑줄 친 어휘가 전체적인 글의 흐름을 해치지 않는지, 밑줄 친 어휘 대신 반의어가 오는 게 맞지 않을지 의심하면서 글을 읽는다.

유형 Solution

1. 제목 추론 문항의 선택지를 먼저 읽고 글의 내용을 예측하라!
→ 선택지에 제시된 제목으로 글을 쓴다면 어떤 내용을 담아야 할지 생각해 본다.

2. 글을 읽으며 글의 주제 및 요지를 파악하라!

3. 글의 주제 및 요지를 잘 압축한 제목을 골라라!
→ 너무 포괄적이나 지엽적이어서는 안 되며 전체 내용을 함축적이고 상징적으로 표현해야 한다.

4. 글의 요지와 선택지의 전후 맥락을 고려하여 밑줄 친 어휘의 적절성 여부를 판단하라!
→ 선택지 어휘의 반의어를 떠올려 보는 것도 한 방법이다.

기출 Analysis

	시험	배점	정답률	소재 및 주제
2024	수능 41번	2점	58%	매우 개인적으로 결정되는 과학자들의 언론과의 접촉 여부
	수능 42번	2점	58%	
	9월 모평 41번	2점	52%	내용에 대한 기억과는 다른 절차로 다루어지는 맥락 정보
	9월 모평 42번	2점	50%	
	6월 모평 41번	2점	57%	협상은 고정된 파이라는 잘못된 통념에서 벗어나야 할 필요성
	6월 모평 42번	2점	37%	
2023	수능 41번	2점	58%	의사 결정에서 인간 전문가의 판단 능력을 능가하기도 하는 단순 공식
	수능 42번	2점	62%	
	9월 모평 41번	2점	63%	근원적으로 상상력의 위기로 인해 초래된 기후 변화의 위기
	9월 모평 42번	2점	61%	
	6월 모평 41번	2점	68%	상황을 판단하는 데 있어 중요한 근거가 되는 다른 사람들의 반응
	6월 모평 42번	2점	57%	

082~083 다음 글을 읽고, 물음에 답하시오.

2024 수능 41~42번

One way to avoid contributing to overhyping a story would be to say nothing. However, that is not a realistic option for scientists who feel a strong sense of responsibility to inform the public and policymakers and/or to offer suggestions. Speaking with members of the media has (a)advantages in getting a message out and perhaps receiving favorable recognition, but it runs the risk of misinterpretations, the need for repeated clarifications, and entanglement in never-ending controversy. Hence, the decision of whether to speak with the media tends to be highly individualized. Decades ago, it was (b)unusual for Earth scientists to have results that were of interest to the media, and consequently few media contacts were expected or encouraged. In the 1970s, the few scientists who spoke frequently with the media were often (c)criticized by their fellow scientists for having done so. The situation now is quite different, as many scientists feel a responsibility to speak out because of the importance of global warming and related issues, and many reporters share these feelings. In addition, many scientists are finding that they (d)enjoy the media attention and the public recognition that comes with it. At the same time, other scientists continue to resist speaking with reporters, thereby preserving more time for their science and (e)running the risk of being misquoted and the other unpleasantries associated with media coverage.

*overhype 과대광고하다   **entanglement 얽힘

082

윗글의 제목으로 가장 적절한 것은?

① The Troubling Relationship Between Scientists and the Media
② A Scientist's Choice: To Be Exposed to the Media or Not?
③ Scientists! Be Cautious When Talking to the Media
④ The Dilemma over Scientific Truth and Media Attention
⑤ Who Are Responsible for Climate Issues, Scientists or the Media?

083

밑줄 친 (a)~(e) 중에서 문맥상 낱말의 쓰임이 적절하지 <u>않은</u> 것은?

① (a)   ② (b)   ③ (c)   ④ (d)   ⑤ (e)

Solution 1. 제목 추론 문항의 선택지를 먼저 읽고 글의 중심 소재와 내용을 예측하라!

① 과학자와 언론 간의 골치 아픈 관계

② 과학자의 선택: 언론과 접할 것인가, 말 것인가?

③ 과학자여! 언론에 말할 때 조심하시오

④ 과학적 진실과 언론의 주목에 대한 딜레마

⑤ 누가 기후 문제에 책임이 있나, 과학자인가, 언론인가?

→ '과학자'와 '언론'이 중심 소재이고, 이 둘의 관계에서 파생되는 문제를 다루고 있는 글임을 추론할 수 있다.

Solution 2. 글을 빠르게 읽으면서 글의 주제 및 요지를 파악하라!

과학자가 언론과 접촉해 대화할지의 여부는 개인적으로 결정되는 경향이 있다.

Solution 3. 글의 주제 및 요지를 잘 압축한 제목을 골라라!

과학자가 ❶(   )과 접촉할 것인가 말 것인가는 과학자 스스로가 선택할 문제라는 내용을 담고 있는 선택지를 고른다.

Solution 4. 글의 요지와 각 선택지의 전후 맥락을 고려하여 밑줄 친 어휘의 적절성 여부를 판단하라!

① advantages: 언론과의 대화를 통해 메시지를 알리고 호의적인 인정을 받을 수 있다는 것은 언론과의 접촉이 가진 ❷(   )이라고 할 수 있다.

② unusual: 수십 년 전에 지구과학자가 언론과 접촉하는 것이 예상되거나 권장되는 일이 거의 없었던 것은 그들이 언론의 흥미를 끄는 연구 결과를 가지는 일이 ❸(   ) 때문이라고 볼 수 있다.

③ criticized: 지금은 과학자나 기후 문제에 대해 공개적으로 의견을 발표하는 것이 필요하다고 생각하지만, 과거에는 언론과 대화하는 과학자들이 동료들로부터 ❹(   )을 받았을 것임을 추론할 수 있다.

④ enjoy: 과학자가 언론과 접촉해도 된다고 생각하는 현재의 상황과 관련된 추가 진술이므로, 과학자들이 언론의 주목과 대중의 인정을 ❺(   ) 있다는 문맥이 되어야 한다.

⑤ running: 현재 상황에서 일부 과학자들은 아직도 기자들과의 대화를 거부함으로써 자신들의 연구가 잘못 인용되는 위험과 언론 보도로 인한 불쾌한 상황을 ❻(   ) 있다는 문맥이다.

Answers   ❶ 언론 ❷ 장점들 ❸ 드물었기 ❹ 비판 ❺ 즐기고 ❻ 피하고

084~085 다음 글을 읽고, 물음에 답하시오. `2023 수능 41~42번`

There is evidence that even very simple algorithms can outperform expert judgement on simple prediction problems. For example, algorithms have proved more (a) accurate than humans in predicting whether a
5 prisoner released on parole will go on to commit another crime, or in predicting whether a potential candidate will perform well in a job in future. In over 100 studies across many different domains, half of all cases show simple formulas make (b) better significant
10 predictions than human experts, and the remainder (except a very small handful), show a tie between the two. When there are a lot of different factors involved and a situation is very uncertain, simple formulas can win out by focusing on the most important factors and
15 being consistent, while human judgement is too easily influenced by particularly salient and perhaps (c) irrelevant considerations. A similar idea is supported by further evidence that 'checklists' can improve the quality of expert decisions in a range of
20 domains by ensuring that important steps or considerations aren't missed when people are feeling (d) relaxed. For example, treating patients in intensive care can require hundreds of small actions per day, and one small error could cost a life. Using checklists
25 to ensure that no crucial steps are missed has proved to be remarkably (e) effective in a range of medical contexts, from preventing live infections to reducing pneumonia.

*parole 가석방 **salient 두드러진 ***pneumonia 폐렴

084

윗글의 제목으로 가장 적절한 것은?

① The Power of Simple Formulas in Decision Making
② Always Prioritise: Tips for Managing Big Data
③ Algorithms' Mistakes: The Myth of Simplicity
④ Be Prepared! Make a Checklist Just in Case
⑤ How Human Judgement Beats Algorithms

085

밑줄 친 (a)~(e) 중에서 문맥상 낱말의 쓰임이 적절하지 <u>않은</u> 것은?

① (a)　　　② (b)　　　③ (c)
④ (d)　　　⑤ (e)

086~087 다음 글을 읽고, 물음에 답하시오.   2022 수능 41~42번

Classifying things together into groups is something we do all the time, and it isn't hard to see why. Imagine trying to shop in a supermarket where the food was arranged in random order on the shelves: tomato soup
5 next to the white bread in one aisle, chicken soup in the back next to the 60-watt light bulbs, one brand of cream cheese in front and another in aisle 8 near the cookies. The task of finding what you want would be (a) time-consuming and extremely difficult, if not
10 impossible.

In the case of a supermarket, someone had to (b) design the system of classification. But there is also a ready-made system of classification embodied in our language. The word "dog," for example, groups
15 together a certain class of animals and distinguishes them from other animals. Such a grouping may seem too (c) abstract to be called a classification, but this is only because you have already mastered the word. As a child learning to speak, you had to work hard to
20 (d) learn the system of classification your parents were trying to teach you. Before you got the hang of it, you probably made mistakes, like calling the cat a dog. If you hadn't learned to speak, the whole world would seem like the (e) unorganized supermarket; you would
25 be in the position of an infant, for whom every object is new and unfamiliar. In learning the principles of classification, therefore, we'll be learning about the structure that lies at the core of our language.

086

윗글의 제목으로 가장 적절한 것은?

① Similarities of Strategies in Sales and Language Learning
② Classification: An Inherent Characteristic of Language
③ Exploring Linguistic Issues Through Categorization
④ Is a Ready-Made Classification System Truly Better?
⑤ Dilemmas of Using Classification in Language Education

087

밑줄 친 (a)~(e) 중에서 문맥상 낱말의 쓰임이 적절하지 <u>않은</u> 것은?

① (a)   ② (b)   ③ (c)
④ (d)   ⑤ (e)

088~089 다음 글을 읽고, 물음에 답하시오.

It can be helpful to realize that in our life, there are many more thoughts, feelings, memories, fantasies and desires than it seems. We are only familiar with one part of our inner world, while another part lies in the dark. When we are plagued by experiences that we do not understand, the decisive step might be to search for their origins in the (a)less conscious areas of our emotional life. It is important to uncover the sub-streams of emotion, desire and imagination that determine our life without us knowing it. If we succeed, unconscious emotional events turn into conscious experience. Part of this process is a growing (b)alertness towards the inner world, a verbal articulation of it and a biographical understanding that allows the hidden logic and dynamic of repressed and covered-up motives to come to light. At the end of this process, I can (c)gain a better knowledge of my inner world. And it does not stop with just knowledge. Growing self-knowledge can lead to liberating changes and to greater inner autonomy. The compulsive desires and the incomprehensible, uncontrollable emotions are, after I have explained them to myself, easier to (d)control and might perhaps even dissolve entirely. They become superfluous. Many experiences that earlier appeared like foreign bodies lose their strangeness through growing understanding and can be recognized as a part of the person — they can be appropriated and made into an explicit part of one's emotional identity. This appropriation means that they no longer (e)enhance one's inner autonomy.

*appropriate ~을 자신의 것으로 만들다 **superfluous 불필요한

088

윗글의 제목으로 가장 적절한 것은?

① Inner Autonomy: Crucial But Hard to Achieve
② You Must Seek Counsel to Resolve Inner Conflict
③ Don't Let Emotional Reactions Dictate Your Attitude
④ Unconscious Desires: The Hidden Obstacles of Daily Life
⑤ The Necessity of Inwardly Expanding Self-Understanding

089

밑줄 친 (a)~(e) 중에서 문맥상 낱말의 쓰임이 적절하지 않은 것은?

① (a) 　 ② (b) 　 ③ (c)
④ (d) 　 ⑤ (e)

If we forbid humans to drive not only taxis but vehicles altogether, and give computer algorithms a (a) monopoly over traffic, we can then connect all vehicles to a single network, thereby rendering car accidents far less likely. In August 2015 one of Google's experimental self-driving cars had an accident. As it approached a crossing and detected pedestrians wishing to cross, it applied its brakes. A moment later it was hit from behind by a sedan whose careless human driver was perhaps contemplating the mysteries of the universe instead of watching the road. This could not have happened if *both* vehicles had been guided by (b) interlinked computers. The controlling algorithm would have known the position and intentions of every vehicle on the road, and would not have allowed two of its marionettes to collide. Such a system would save lots of time, money and human lives — but would also (c) generate the human experience of driving a car and tens of millions of human jobs.

Some economists predict that sooner or later unenhanced humans will be completely (d) useless. Robots and 3D printers are already replacing workers in manual jobs such as manufacturing shirts, and highly intelligent algorithms will do the same to white-collar occupations. Bank clerks and travel agents, who a short time ago seemed completely secure from (e) automation, have become endangered species. How many travel agents do we need when we can use our smartphones to buy plane tickets from an algorithm? Stock-exchange traders are also in danger. Most financial trading today is already being managed by computer algorithms that can process in a second more data than a human can in a year, and can react to the data much faster than a human can blink.

090

윗글의 제목으로 가장 적절한 것은?

① AI Will Create More Jobs Than It Eliminates
② Computers Are on a Pathway to Replace Mankind
③ AI Should Amplify Human Intelligence, Not Replace It
④ Advantages and Disadvantages of Computer Algorithms
⑤ We Wouldn't Be Able to Control Super Intelligent Machines

091

밑줄 친 (a)~(e) 중에서 문맥상 낱말의 쓰임이 적절하지 <u>않은</u> 것은?

① (a)   ② (b)   ③ (c)
④ (d)   ⑤ (e)

092~093 다음 글을 읽고, 물음에 답하시오.

A mature patient who has an anxious personality, whose mind is constantly filled with doubts and suspicions, whose every effort is directed towards isolating himself from society, had (a)identical character traits and psychological activity in his third and fourth year of life. The only difference is that such traits are more transparent and easier to see in small children, who have not yet learned to (b)hide their real feelings. We made it a rule, therefore, to focus the greater part of our investigation on the childhood of our patients. In this way we were often able to infer the characteristics of a mature person whose childhood we were familiar with before we were told about them. The traits we observe in the adult are in fact the direct projection of childhood experiences. When we listen to the most vivid recollections of patients' childhoods, and know how to interpret these recollections correctly, we can accurately (c)construct the pattern of their present character. In doing this we bear in mind the fact that it is extremely difficult for individuals to deviate from the patterns of behaviour they developed in their early life. Very few individuals have ever been able to (d)maintain their childhood behaviour patterns, even though in adult life they may have found themselves in entirely different situations. Even a change of attitude in adult life need not necessarily lead to a change of behaviour pattern. The psyche does not change its foundation; individuals retain the same tendencies in childhood and in maturity, leading us to deduce that much of their personality is also (e)unaltered.

*deviate 벗어나다

092

윗글의 제목으로 가장 적절한 것은?

① Nature vs. Nurture: Which Is More Influential?
② Factors Affecting the Development of Personality
③ Why Are Certain Behavior Patterns So Changeable?
④ How to Overcome Childhood Psychological Problems
⑤ Childhood Experiences: The Basis of the Human Psyche

093

밑줄 친 (a)~(e) 중에서 문맥상 낱말의 쓰임이 적절하지 않은 것은?

① (a)　　② (b)　　③ (c)
④ (d)　　⑤ (e)

094~095 다음 글을 읽고, 물음에 답하시오.

With every passing year the Internet becomes further integrated into our lives. Trust on the Internet becomes increasingly important. This is especially true in the case of Internet voting, which may play a very

5 important role in the future of democracy. Internet voting has already been used widely by corporations for the purpose of share-holder voting. However, it must be recognized that the use of Internet voting for democratic elections would bring certain problems

10 with it. The Internet opens up whole new possibilities of fraud, verification problems, and exclusivity, which could have potentially (a)devastating effects on an election. One hurdle that Internet voting would have to overcome is the current "digital divide." That is, while

15 in theory Internet balloting would make voting more accessible for the masses, it would really only serve to further (b)widen the gap between the rich and the poor voters, as the rich are far more likely to have Internet access. Beyond this problem are the various

20 new (c)security issues that would crop up. A recurring theme in the discussion of Internet trust is the problem of verification, which would be especially problematic in the context of Internet voting. Since the voting would be taking place away from a polling station,

25 there would also be greater opportunity for voter bribery or coercion, as a third party could be present while a voter is casting his vote. Lastly, there is the ever-present danger of hackers (d)manipulating voter data or otherwise disrupting the system. Even if these

30 problems can be dealt with, as long as there is the public perception that Internet voting is less trustworthy than the current voting forms, Internet voting should be refined to (e)fuel the public's doubts. If trust cannot be established in Internet voting to the

extent that it is already established in current voting 35 procedures, then it should not be adopted.

*bribery 뇌물 수수, 매수(買收) **coercion 강압

094

윗글의 제목으로 가장 적절한 것은?

① Voting: A Right or a Duty of Citizens?
② Various Ways to Protect the Right to Vote
③ Internet Voting: An Opportunity for Democracy
④ Confidence Issues in Adopting a New Voting System
⑤ Increasing Voter Turnout: It's Tougher Than You Thin

095

밑줄 친 (a)~(e) 중에서 문맥상 낱말의 쓰임이 적절하지 <u>않은</u> 것은?

① (a)　　　　② (b)　　　　③ (c)
④ (d)　　　　⑤ (e)

01 글의 주제

01	distort	v	
02	disclosure	n	
03	undermine	v	
04	erosion	n	
05	attribute	n	
06	회의적인	a	
07	withhold	v	
08	eliminate	v	
09	유연성, 융통성	n	
10	amplify	v	
11	edible	a	
12	legitimacy	n	
13	neglect	v	
14	규제, 규정	n	
15	sphere	n	
16	multiply	v	
17	regime	n	
18	privilege	v	
19	suppress	v	
20	interfere with		

02 함축 의미 추론

01	hostile	a	
02	embrace	v	
03	rigorous	a	
04	stimulate	v	
05	refute	v	
06	hypothesis	n	
07	(학문의) 분야	n	
08	vanish	v	
09	criterion	n	
10	마비시키다	v	
11	corporate	a	
12	우선(권), 우선순위	n	
13	collapse	n	
14	constitute	v	
15	enthusiasm	n	
16	particle	n	
17	alternate	a	
18	falsify	v	
19	invalid	a	
20	reflect on		

03 어법

01	ambiguity	n	
02	distinguish	v	
03	spontaneously	ad	
04	expedition	n	
05	carve	v	
06	incidental	a	
07	새끼, 자손	n	
08	progress	v	
09	흡수하다	v	
10	gasp	v	
11	isolated	a	
12	생식, 번식	n	
13	subsequent	a	
14	diameter	n	
15	distinct	a	
16	mythology	n	
17	procedure	n	
18	depict	v	
19	institution	n	
20	compensate for		

04 어휘

01	aspire	v	
02	incompatible	a	
03	inevitable	a	
04	ritual	n	
05	hierarchical	a	
06	인공의	a	
07	variable	n	
08	discrete	a	
09	harness	v	
10	추상적인	a	
11	impel	v	
12	소수 민족, 소수 집단	n	
13	resolve	v	
14	incorporation	n	
15	dominant	a	
16	dispute	n	
17	declare	v	
18	association	n	
19	cohesiveness	n	
20	comprehensive	a	

05 빈칸 추론(1)

01	transmit	v
02	reluctance	n
03	evoke	v
04	consistent	a
05	integral	a
06	realm	n
07	delusion	n
08	과장하다	v
09	analogy	n
10	assert	v
11	편향된	a
12	sophisticated	a
13	직관(력)	n
14	verify	v
15	executive	n
16	empathetic	a
17	proposition	n
18	paradoxical	a
19	submission	n
20	correspond to	

06 빈칸 추론(2)

01	integrate	v
02	metaphor	n
03	defect	n
04	detect	v
05	tremendous	a
06	persist	v
07	상호 간에, 서로	ad
08	constraint	n
09	entail	v
10	지속 가능성	n
11	divorce	v
12	군집, 서식지	n
13	flee	v
14	assign	v
15	primitive	a
16	victim	n
17	coexistence	n
18	compromise	n
19	diminish	v
20	confrontation	n

07 글의 순서 파악

01	conserve	v
02	rationale	n
03	innate	a
04	inventory	n
05	vivid	a
06	obsession	n
07	알을 깨고 나오다	v
08	deliberate	a
09	seemingly	ad
10	offend	v
11	중립적인	a
12	modify	v
13	포식자	n
14	collective	a
15	cherish	v
16	variation	n
17	idiom	n
18	undertake	v
19	superstition	n
20	devoid of	

08 문장 삽입

01	inert	a
02	implement	v
03	identical	a
04	ingredient	n
05	tactic	n
06	embody	v
07	precedent	n
08	옹호, 옹호자	n
09	scarce	a
10	최적의	a
11	coordinate	v
12	segment	n
13	settlement	n
14	초과하다	v
15	ban	v
16	inhabitant	n
17	mandate	v
18	compensation	n
19	temperament	n
20	anonymity	n

09 요약문 완성

01	impulse	*n*
02	significant	*a*
03	consolation	*n*
04	commitment	*n*
05	trigger	*v*
06	autonomous	*a*
07	이주, 이민	*n*
08	prescription	*n*
09	금전적인, 통화의	*a*
10	misinterpret	*v*
11	appraisal	*n*
12	버리다, 포기하다	*v*
13	alternative	*n*
14	causal	*a*
15	enduring	*a*
16	frustration	*n*
17	lament	*v*
18	equivalent	*a*
19	manual	*a*
20	intensify	*v*

10 장문(1지문 2문항)

01	monopoly	*n*
02	collide	*v*
03	remainder	*n*
04	inherent	*a*
05	deduce	*v*
06	의심, 의혹	*n*
07	maturity	*n*
08	contemplate	*v*
09	감염	*n*
10	decisive	*a*
11	명시적인	*a*
12	projection	*n*
13	occupation	*n*
14	recollection	*n*
15	transparent	*a*
16	forbid	*v*
17	trait	*n*
18	irrelevant	*a*
19	fraud	*n*
20	compulsive	*a*

N II 3점 공략 모의고사

학습 회차	학습일		맞은 문항 수
3점 공략 모의고사 **1회**	월	일	/ 8문항
3점 공략 모의고사 **2회**	월	일	/ 8문항
3점 공략 모의고사 **3회**	월	일	/ 8문항
3점 공략 모의고사 **4회**	월	일	/ 8문항
3점 공략 모의고사 **5회**	월	일	/ 8문항
3점 공략 모의고사 **6회**	월	일	/ 8문항
3점 공략 모의고사 **7회**	월	일	/ 8문항
3점 공략 모의고사 **8회**	월	일	/ 8문항
3점 공략 모의고사 **9회**	월	일	/ 8문항
3점 공략 모의고사 **10회**	월	일	/ 8문항
3점 공략 모의고사 **11회**	월	일	/ 8문항
3점 공략 모의고사 **12회**	월	일	/ 8문항
3점 공략 모의고사 **13회**	월	일	/ 8문항
3점 공략 모의고사 **14회**	월	일	/ 8문항
3점 공략 모의고사 **15회**	월	일	/ 8문항
3점 공략 모의고사 **16회**	월	일	/ 8문항

096

밑줄 친 *moral jazz*가 다음 글에서 의미하는 바로 가장 적절한 것은?

Jazz saxophonist Stan Getz said that jazz is "like a language. You learn the alphabet, which is the scales. You learn sentences, which are the chords. And then you talk with the horn without a rehearsal." Good improvisation is not making something out of nothing, but making something out of previous experience, practice, and knowledge. Likewise, we make ourselves wise with practice like jazz musicians. The more we learn how to perceive the relevant details of our situations and the more we build our skills at improvisation, the easier it becomes to improvise — to combine old skills and knowledge in new ways to deal with the unexpected. Thus, practical wisdom is a kind of *moral jazz*. It sometimes depends on rules and principles — like the notes on the page and the basic melodies in jazz. But rules by themselves can't do the job. Moral improvisation is the interpretative tune we play around these notes and melodies, in order to do the right thing.

① the right decision made by the agreement of participants

② the harmony of group members for the progress of a society

③ the spontaneous display of emotion when we listen to good music

④ the enhanced efficiency generated by following fundamental principles

⑤ the application of correct behavior in unforeseen, changeable situations

097

다음 글의 밑줄 친 부분 중, 어법상 틀린 것은?

Writing brings about fundamental changes in society. It makes permanent and accessible ①what once would have disappeared instantly. For example, the words of Socrates would be unknown to us ②were Plato not set them down in a permanent manner, but we can still read the transcriptions almost 2500 years later. This particular act of writing from the distant past has been tremendously influential on the very ways in which we conceptualize the world. Writing also makes it possible ③to organize societies in a systematic and repeatable way: books of rules and regulations allow bureaucrats to apply general principles to particular cases rather than having to work everything out from the details of each particular case. Written laws reduce the possibility of arbitrary decisions by creating guidelines for use beyond the immediate moment, and ④provide a basis on which to mount an argument about decisions. Writing can come to divide a society into those who write, those who read, those who do both and those who do neither. If writing is restricted to particular groups, then it is likely that it is the interests of these groups ⑤that will be promoted.

*bureaucrat 관료

098

다음 글의 밑줄 친 부분 중, 문맥상 낱말의 쓰임이 적절하지 <u>않은</u> 것은?

Credit cards capitalize on our desire to avoid the pain of paying. And that has given them the power to shift the way we perceive value. With easier, less salient payment and the shifting of time between payment and consumption, credit cards ① <u>minimize</u> the pain of paying we feel at the moment we buy something. They create a detachment that makes us more ② <u>willing</u> to spend. As Elizabeth Dunn and Mike Norton noted, this detachment is not just about how we feel in the moment; it also changes how we remember the purchasing experience in a way that "makes it ③ <u>harder</u> to remember how much we've spent." For example, if we go to the store and buy socks, pyjamas and an ugly sweater, the moment we get home, we're less likely to remember the amount of money we spent if we used a credit card than if we used cash. Credit cards are like memory ④ <u>erasers</u> from a science fiction movie, but they live in our wallets. Studies have found not only that people are more inclined to pay when they use credit cards, but also that they make larger purchases, leave larger tips, are more likely to ⑤ <u>overestimate</u> how much they spent and make spending decisions more quickly.

*salient 두드러진, 눈에 띄는

099

다음 빈칸에 들어갈 말로 가장 적절한 것은?

Doing conceptual work is a lot like solving a jigsaw puzzle. One of the reasons that I believe many people get bored in their work, and fail to engage with their full curiosity, is that they are overwhelmed by the uncertainty and options. They haven't truly defined the parameters of the problem. Consequently, their approach to their work is a little like dumping an entire jigsaw puzzle on the table and setting to work with little or no understanding of what they're trying to assemble. Overwhelmed, they may give up and settle in, happy to find that a piece or two fall together by chance. However, with a little intentional effort at the beginning of the process to define the "edges" of the problem you're solving, it's possible to get up to speed more quickly, explore more potentially relevant solutions, and leverage your full creative problem-solving skill. When you have _____ to work within, you can feel more comfortable asking extremely divergent questions and exploring initially irrelevant-seeming possibilities.

*parameter 한도, 한계 **leverage 끌어내다
***divergent (의견 등이) 다른, 분산되는

① various options
② a logical system
③ clear boundaries
④ an undefined space
⑤ the full responsibility

100

다음 빈칸에 들어갈 말로 가장 적절한 것은?

Wolfgang Köhler (1887−1967) was a German psychologist who contributed to the creation of Gestalt psychology. He conducted a famous series of studies on chimpanzees' methods of problem solving. He placed a bunch of bananas just out of the animals' reach and then watched how they figured out how to get to the bananas. At first frustrated, the chimps eventually reached an insight about how to use available objects as tools. This insight often came suddenly in a sort of A-Ha! moment. In one case, a chimpanzee put two sticks together to create a tool long enough to reach the bananas. Another chimp stacked three boxes on top of each other to reach the fruit hanging from the ceiling. Besides showing us the remarkable ingenuity of these animals, this work supported the Gestalt notion that the mind actively creates complete solutions to problems, often arriving at them all at once. This is in contrast to the behaviorist assumption that problem solving _____.

① is an ability that only humans possess
② can only proceed gradually by trial and error
③ is reinforced by using rewards and punishments
④ can only be made as a result of a sudden insight
⑤ is used in new situations only after being learned

101

주어진 글 다음에 이어질 글의 순서로 가장 적절한 것은?

There are two old adages about the people we tend to choose as friends or romantic partners. One is "Birds of a feather flock together," and the other is "Opposites attract." Then do we want someone who is similar to us, or are we looking for someone who is different to complement our personality?

(A) One possible explanation for the influence of similarity on attraction is balance theory, which is related to cognitive dissonance theory. It states that when we like someone who does not like the things we like, we experience an imbalance that causes dissonance. This dissonance motivates change that restores consonance.

(B) Furthermore, similarity seems to predict attraction across a variety of cultures, including Mexico, India, and Japan. Similarity also seems to be a factor in the friends we choose.

(C) Research on this issue indicates that, indeed, "Birds of a feather flock together." When choosing a romantic partner, we tend to gravitate to people who are of similar age, socioeconomic status, education, intelligence, race, religion, attitudes, power, and physical attractiveness to ourselves.

*cognitive dissonance 인지부조화

① (A) − (C) − (B) ② (B) − (A) − (C)
③ (B) − (C) − (A) ④ (C) − (A) − (B)
⑤ (C) − (B) − (A)

102

글의 흐름으로 보아, 주어진 문장이 들어가기에 가장 적절한 곳은?

> A hazardous, polluting, and energy-intensive process of extraction and purification follows, within which lurks the majority of our material world's ecological and social destruction.

A cheap radio-controlled child's tank contains a thumbnail-sized microchip within which you will find over two-thirds of the elements of the periodic table. Let us not forget, these elements do not come out of the ground in clear glass test tubes, labeled and ready for use. (①) On the contrary, these rare compounds are mined and clawed from the earth, encased in thousands of tons of rock and mud. (②) An industry in itself occupies this level of resource conversion, behind the scenes, transforming the earth's rare resources into miraculous modern materials. (③) The plethora of electronic products that surround us are infused with a rich cocktail of complex minerals, precious metals, and noxious compounds. (④) To most of us, these are completely unseen, lurking just beneath the surface of our material experience. (⑤) Despite their genius, these wonders of industrial alchemy become waste surprisingly quickly, and they certainly are not designed to last.

*lurk 숨다 **plethora 차고 넘침, 과다 ***alchemy 연금술

103

다음 글의 내용을 한 문장으로 요약하고자 한다. 빈칸 (A), (B)에 들어갈 말로 가장 적절한 것은?

Most scientists agree on a description of quantum mechanics known as the Copenhagen interpretation, which says that at a very fundamental level, atoms act randomly. Quantum mechanics can be used to predict the chances that an atom might be in this place or that one, at this speed or that speed, at this energy level or that one, but it can't predict any of these qualities exactly. Einstein was an important pioneer in the development of quantum mechanics and he knew that it predicted these chances with incredible accuracy, but other scientists believed the accuracy of quantum mechanics meant reality itself was random. Einstein, on the other hand, believed reality operated with definite laws of cause and effect, actions that could be predicted—if you had all the information possible—precisely and perfectly. To his death, Einstein insisted that we simply didn't understand nature well enough, there must be additional factors, some hidden variables at work that we didn't yet understand.

*quantum mechanics 양자 역학

↓

> Einstein objected to the fundamentally ___(A)___ nature of quantum mechanics, proposing that reality is actually governed by some ___(B)___ hidden variables that we hadn't yet identified.

	(A)		(B)
①	probabilistic	········	predictable
②	definite	········	causal
③	universal	········	specific
④	definite	········	random
⑤	probabilistic	········	deterministic

104

다음 글의 주제로 가장 적절한 것은?

Dissent in organizations is rarely so dramatic. It is defined as the expression of disagreement or contradictory opinions regarding contextual phenomena — a form of feedback about employee discontent with organizational actions and decisions. Feedback loops are central to how individuals, groups, and organizations learn and improve their practices. Dissent thus ought to be welcomed, given that learning and improvement is crucial for people to fulfill given purposes, missions, and tasks. Theorists and researchers have shown that when individuals explicitly assume the role of dissenter in groups, they help prevent conformity of thought and action. Social conflicts that are constructive — offered and waged in the spirit of making enterprises more effective — are functional rather than dysfunctional across the spectrum of social systems. Without dissent, people risk acting reflexively rather than reflectively, unquestioningly moving along paths that lead to places they ought not to go. To interrupt the easy flow of agreement and create moments of pause that press others to reflect on their own possible biases is therefore essential to any organization's success.

*wage (전쟁, 투쟁 등을) 행하다, 벌이다

① ways of voicing dissent in organizations
② beneficial effects of questioning the majority
③ the importance of constructive feedback in enterprises
④ acknowledging dissenters' voices to avoid social conflict
⑤ structural means of conveying dissatisfaction in organizations

105

다음 글의 밑줄 친 부분 중, 어법상 틀린 것은?

A justification is a type of explanation; however, a justification includes an attempt to persuade the listener that the actions taken ①were correct or at least understandable. Explanations don't include any overt attempt to convince the listener to believe what is being said, while justifications ②do. There are, of course, good justifications and bad justifications. A bad justification is one ③which, rather than providing a rational and compelling explanation, the person offering it is simply making excuses for herself or for someone else. Another word for the kind of self-serving and inappropriate attempt at justification is rationalization. Rationalizations, despite the fact that they sound like they must be logical, because the word contains the idea of reason, are weak explanations which attempt to excuse behaviour that the person offering the rationalization knows ④was wrong. The professor who falsifies data in a study and then tries to justify it by saying that there was a lot of pressure from the pharmaceutical company ⑤paying for the research is offering a rationalization.

106

다음 글의 빈칸에 들어갈 말로 가장 적절한 것은?

The world and all that is in it are the sphere of interest not only of scientists but also of theologians, philosophers, poets, and politicians. How can one make a demarcation between their concerns and those of scientists? Scientists assume that this world is not chaotic but is structured in some way, and that most, if not all, aspects of this structure will yield to the tools of scientific investigation. A primary tool used in all scientific activity is testing. Every new fact and every new explanation must be tested again and again, preferably by different investigators using different methods. Every confirmation strengthens the probability of the "truth" of a fact or explanation, and every falsification or refutation strengthens the probability that an opposing theory is correct. One of the most characteristic features of science is this _____. The willingness to abandon a currently accepted belief when a new, better one is proposed is an important demarcation between science and religious dogma.

*demarcation 구분, 경계 **falsification 반증

① openness to challenge
② contribution to society
③ conformity to authority
④ resistance to innovation
⑤ objection to modification

107

다음 빈칸에 들어갈 말로 가장 적절한 것은?

In a hunter-gatherer society, it was highly adaptive to be seen by one's group as someone who really belonged. How should people be best equipped to convince others they belong to their group? By having evolved nonconscious mental processes, including self-deception and compromised critical thinking. Such bases for knowledge resistance would reduce tensions with the main knowledge beliefs and values of the group. When we wish to be a member of a group — such as a religious, political, or even a scientific community — it isn't just for conscious, tactical reasons that we often don't challenge their fundamental knowledge beliefs. We are equipped with the capacity to believe the dominant knowledge claims of the group in question. Why? Because our body language and nonconscious signals communicate far more to others than our clever and well-measured words do. Therefore, a crucial part of human adaptation in hunter-gatherer society must have included the ability to _____.

*compromise 굽히다, 타협하다

① express our feelings both clearly and respectfully
② challenge our old beliefs and accept new convictions
③ allow ourselves to be fooled by others in some matters
④ devote ourselves to the welfare and happiness of others
⑤ lead a group of people towards the group's common goal

108

주어진 글 다음에 이어질 글의 순서로 가장 적절한 것은?

When Westerners draw on their own cultural knowledge to interpret practices such as veiling in the Muslim world, they may misinterpret the meaning of the veil to the women who wear it.

(A) In fact, neither of these conclusions is necessarily accurate; for instance, some Muslim women voluntarily choose to cover—sometimes against the wishes of male family members—as a statement of modern religious and political identity.

(B) For example, Westerners may assume that veiling is a practice imposed by men on unwilling women or that Muslim women who veil do so to hide their beauty.

(C) By the same token, some women think of the veil as a way to accentuate, not conceal, beauty. Yet if Westerners interpret these practices through the lens of their own prior cultural knowledge and assumptions, they may emerge with a distorted understanding that can impede further learning.

*accentuate 강조하다

① (A) − (C) − (B)
② (B) − (A) − (C)
③ (B) − (C) − (A)
④ (C) − (A) − (B)
⑤ (C) − (B) − (A)

109

글의 흐름으로 보아, 주어진 문장이 들어가기에 가장 적절한 곳은?

Understanding such patterns is necessary if we are to alter or change the characteristics of plants in an informed way.

The development of genetically modified (GM) plant technology raises two kinds of issues: the scientific and the ethical. (①) Science is concerned with understanding the world in which we live and in particular the causal relationships that shape that world: for example, the association between genes as a molecular sequence and the characteristics, such as resistance to frost, that the genes express. (②) Ethics, by contrast, is concerned with what we ought or ought not to do. (③) Ethical principles provide standards for the evaluation of policies or practices, for example, indicating that it would be wrong to carry out a certain genetic modification because to do so would threaten human health or harm the environment. (④) Although it may be scientifically possible to undertake a certain experiment or introduce a new type of crop for commercial planting, it does not follow that it would be ethically right to do so. (⑤) Working out what it is right or permissible to do involves, therefore, bringing together our scientific understanding with our ethical principles to decide what we should do given the capacities for genetic modification that have been developed.

110~111 다음 글을 읽고, 물음에 답하시오.

The cow is a valuable source of food, but no one worries that the cow will soon be extinct. Indeed, the great demand for beef seems to ensure that the species will continue to thrive. Why does the commercial value
5 of ivory threaten the elephant, while the commercial value of beef protects the cow? The reason is that elephants are a common resource, whereas cows are a private good. Elephants roam freely without any owners. Each poacher has a strong incentive to kill as
10 many elephants as he can find. Because poachers are numerous, each poacher has (a)little incentive to preserve the elephant population. By contrast, cattle live on ranches that are privately owned. Each rancher makes a great effort to maintain the cattle population
15 on his ranch because he reaps the (b)benefit.

Governments have tried to solve the elephant's problem in two ways. For example, Kenya and Tanzania have made it illegal to kill elephants and sell their ivory. Yet these laws have been hard to enforce,
20 and the battle between the authorities and the poachers has become increasingly violent. Meanwhile, elephant populations have continued to (c)increase. By contrast, other countries, such as Namibia and Zimbabwe, have made elephants a private good by
25 (d)allowing people to kill elephants, but only those on their own property. Landowners now have an incentive to preserve the species on their own land, and as a result, elephant populations have started to rise. With private ownership and the profit motive now on its
30 side, the African elephant might someday be as (e)safe from extinction as the cow.

110

윗글의 제목으로 가장 적절한 것은?

① The Changing Concept of Animals as Property
② The Economic Value of Some Endangered Animals
③ To Protect Endangered Species, Let Them Be Owned
④ On the Sustainability of Common Property Resources
⑤ Common Property as a Concept in Natural Resources Policy

111

밑줄 친 (a)~(e) 중에서 문맥상 낱말의 쓰임이 적절하지 <u>않은</u> 것은?

① (a)   ② (b)   ③ (c)
④ (d)   ⑤ (e)

112

밑줄 친 the whole really does add up to more than the sum of its parts가 다음 글에서 의미하는 바로 가장 적절한 것은?

When Indigenous Mesoamerican people first domesticated corn, some five thousand years ago, they knew better than to grow it alone. By itself, this highly productive grain would rapidly use up the nutrients in the soil, particularly nitrogen, and large stands of it would be attractive to pests, which might decimate the crop. So alongside corn, people planted beans, which could gather nitrogen from the atmosphere and provide their own fertility. They also planted squash, which covered the ground with its broad leaves, protecting against erosion and smothering weeds. The squash even contained special weed-suppressing chemicals in its leaves, which leached out during rainstorms. Together, the corn, beans, and squash made the most of the sunlight, each catching the sun's rays at a different angle. The complex three-dimensional structure of the intercrop provided habitat for beneficial insects, while confusing pests. As farmers have long known and researchers have confirmed in recent decades, the whole really does add up to more than the sum of its parts.

*decimate (특정 지역의 동식물을) 대량으로 죽이다 **smother 성장을 저지하다

① dynamic ecological balance supports diverse crop growth
② each component of an ecosystem has its role to play in it
③ harmony between humans and nature brings a larger yield
④ immeasurable benefits result from cultivating various crops
⑤ integrating diverse farming methods improves farming outcomes

113

다음 글의 밑줄 친 부분 중, 어법상 **틀린** 것은?

I always advise my clients, family, and friends to not only trust the advice that someone gives them but to also do a substantial amount of research on any conditions ①that they are challenged by to make informed decisions about what actions to pursue. This is particularly relevant when they have been ②pressured to do something that they don't understand or feel comfortable with by a doctor or an intuitive healer. For instance, I have met people who have spent a substantial amount of time doing certain breathing techniques without properly understanding ③them, literally becoming incapacitated and bedridden as they shattered different circuits in their body and nervous system. I have also known people who have spent tens of thousands of dollars on their healing, always searching for the next miracle, only ④to end up sicker than ever. Make sure that you research ⑤whenever system of healing you work with, ask a lot of questions, and have a profound understanding of what you are doing.

114

다음 글의 밑줄 친 부분 중, 문맥상 낱말의 쓰임이 적절하지 <u>않은</u> 것은?

We generally assume that the world is as we see it, and that others see it the same way—that our senses reflect an ① objective and shared reality. We assume that our senses represent the world in which we live as
5 ② accurately as a mirror reflects the face that looks into it. Of course, if our senses did not provide us with somewhat accurate information, we could not rely on them as we do, but nevertheless psychologists have found that these assumptions about perception are
10 ③ flawless. Picking up information about our worlds is not a passive, reflective process, but a complex, active one in which the mind and senses work together, helping us to ④ construct a *perception* of reality. We do not just see patterns of light, dark, and color—we
15 organize these patterns of stimulation so that we see objects that are ⑤ meaningful to us. We can name or recognize them, and identify them as entirely new or similar to other objects.

115

다음 빈칸에 들어갈 말로 가장 적절한 것은?

It can be argued that monkeys tend to _____ much more than humans are. In a 1950 experiment, a monkey had to choose between an object identical to one previously shown and a different object. In the experiment, the monkey saw an object. Then the 5 monkey saw another object which was either identical to the baited object or different from it. Two conditions were compared: when choosing the identical (familiar) object was reinforced and when choosing the different (new) object was reinforced. On the whole, the 10 monkeys responded to new stimuli faster than to familiar ones. In comparable experiments, humans have acted in a very different manner. The preferences exhibited by human subjects on the Cognitive Bias Task (when humans are asked to look at a target and 15 then two choices and afterwards to choose the one they "like the best") are very different from those of monkeys. Humans almost invariably choose items most similar to the target rather than ones that show greater differences. 20

① be attracted to novelty
② be unaware of differences
③ be influenced by their peers
④ be inconsistent in their preferences
⑤ be afraid to choose unfamiliar things

116

다음 빈칸에 들어갈 말로 가장 적절한 것은?

In one study, Ziva Kunda, a psychologist who devoted her career to motivated cognition, gave students an article about the risks caffeine consumption posed for the development of fibrocystic disease in women. Kunda told them it was from the *New York Times* Science section but had really taken it from a medical journal. She then asked them to rate their own risk for developing the disease within fifteen years and to evaluate how convincing they found the article itself. A curious pattern soon emerged. Women who were heavy or moderate caffeine drinkers themselves acknowledged that they might be at higher risk, but were also far more skeptical of the article. They wanted, they said, to see some additional evidence; to them, the study seemed shaky at best. Everyone else, however — men and women who drank little or no caffeine — found the work convincing. So what does this suggest? Simply put, when it comes to ourselves — our traits, our lives, our decisions — _____.

*fibrocystic disease 섬유낭종성 질환

① our tendency is to attribute bad things to external events
② we only want to hear what we have been trained to hear
③ our personal attachments overpower our objective understanding
④ we suspect that health-related news articles are frequently biased
⑤ we systematically misevaluate evidence based on general reputation

117

주어진 글 다음에 이어질 글의 순서로 가장 적절한 것은?

The members of society which the free-rider exploits are forced to behave altruistically: they contribute to the fitness of the free-rider at the expense of their own fitness.

(A) At that point, the implicit agreements that bind the society together will fall apart. Suspicion and a reluctance to engage in reciprocal deals, will increase, making the natural flow of interactions and relationships less fluid. Willingness to co-operate on trust will decrease and gradually the virtual bonds that hold the social system together will dissolve.

(B) Free-riding will eventually be held in check by our personal experience of an individual free-rider's behaviour: once bitten, we will be reluctant to trust that particular person again. But once we reach that point, the element of trust that helps to hold society together has been lost.

(C) These costs may be small in the short term, especially if they are shared between all the other members of the society. But they necessarily add up in the long term. And if the pressures are great enough, the effect of many individuals behaving as free-riders will be such as to impose a very significant burden on the rest of the community.

① (A) − (C) − (B)
② (B) − (A) − (C)
③ (B) − (C) − (A)
④ (C) − (A) − (B)
⑤ (C) − (B) − (A)

118

글의 흐름으로 보아, 주어진 문장이 들어가기에 가장 적절한 곳은?

> However, as the related terminology—degradable, biodegradable, and compostable—entered more general use, consumer awareness of the terms grew, though consumers still lacked a complete understanding.

Biodegradable goods generally refer to the products that can be broken down by natural processes and biological organisms, including fungi and bacteria. (①) Until recently, consumer appreciation of the issues behind biodegradability was limited for a number of reasons. (②) The proliferation of terminology and the complexity of the different processes involved prevented the general public from engaging with this feature of sustainable practice. (③) As a result of this lack of understanding, the purchase decision-making process had not been duly influenced by considerations of the life cycle of products or packaging, and the possibilities of reuse or recycling. (④) This has been stimulated by government campaigns encouraging more household recycling, coupled with local government recycling plans and curbside collections. (⑤) Retailer and consumer lobbying actions, particularly those concerning packaging and the reduction of single-use plastic bags, together with increasing media attention have also contributed to greater consumer engagement.

119

다음 글의 내용을 한 문장으로 요약하고자 한다. 빈칸 (A), (B)에 들어갈 말로 가장 적절한 것은?

The first source of technological uncertainty derives from the fortunate fact that there always exist a variety of solutions to perform a particular task. It is always uncertain which might be the "best," taking into account technical criteria, economic criteria, and social criteria. Uncertainty prevails at all stages of technological evolution, from initial design choices, to success or failure in the marketplace, to eventual environmental impacts and spin-off effects. The technological and management literature labels such uncertainty a "snake pit" problem. It is like trying to pick a particular snake out of a pit of hundreds that all look alike. Others use the biblical quote "many are called, but few are chosen." Technological uncertainty continues to be a notorious embarrassment in efforts to "forecast" technological change. But there is also nothing to be gained by a strategy of "waiting until the sky clears." It will not clear, uncertainty will go on, and the correct strategy is experimentation with technological variety.

*spin-off effect 파급 효과　**biblical 성경의

↓

> Since technical uncertainty is ___(A)___ in all the stages of technical development, it would be unreasonable to ___(B)___ an experiment because of concerns over the uncertainty of the results.

	(A)		(B)
①	unlikely	………	re-evaluate
②	persistent	………	suspend
③	expectable	………	undertake
④	constant	………	repeat
⑤	absent	………	postpone

120

다음 글의 밑줄 친 부분 중, 어법상 틀린 것은?

Herodotus was called *The Father of History* by the Roman writer Cicero, but has also been rejected as *The Father of Lies* by critics, ancient and modern, ① who claim his work is little more than tall tales. While it is true that Herodotus sometimes relays inaccurate information or ② exaggerates for effect, his accounts have consistently been found to be more or less reliable. Some early criticism of his work has been refuted by later archaeological evidence which proves ③ that his most-often criticized claims were, in fact, accurate, and were based on accepted information of the time. While it is clear that he makes a number of claims now ④ recognizing as wrong, there is still much in his work that he has gotten right. His Histories often points the way to ⑤ understanding a given event or cultural paradigm even when the details he provides are wrong or exaggerated. In the present day, Herodotus continues to be recognized as 'The Father of History' and a reliable source of information on the ancient world by the majority of historians.

121

다음 빈칸에 들어갈 말로 가장 적절한 것은?

Certain information seems to be stored around general concepts that help us understand more subordinate concepts. So for example, if someone asks whether a flounder has gills, you can easily answer without ever having considered the question before, and, more important, without actually having that information in your memory at all. All you need to know is that a flounder is a fish and that fish have gills. Similarly, you know that a Buick has wheels because it is a car and that a female horse has teats because it is a mammal. The idea behind semantic memory is simply that this kind of information is shared _____. We store the information that female mammals have teats and infer that therefore horses have teats because they are mammals. Clearly, people must have information organized at least to some extent in this way because they know a great deal more than they have ever actually experienced.

*flounder 가자미 **teat (동물 암컷의) 젖꼭지

① differently   ② collectively
③ horizontally   ④ hierarchically
⑤ subconsciously

122

다음 빈칸에 들어갈 말로 가장 적절한 것은?

Citizens of the new millennium need what is referred to as cognitive complexity, which is made up of the twin abilities of differentiating and integrating. Differentiation involves being able to see how a single entity is composed of a number of different parts; integration, on the other hand, involves the capacity to identify how the various parts are interconnected. The cognitively complex person is able to engage in both types of thinking and can move comfortably between the two. One must be able to focus on the unique needs of the local situation while at the same time understanding how it fits into the operations of the total organization. The study of cultural anthropology encourages one to examine another culture as well as one's own, compare the two, and understand the relationship of both cultures to the generalized concept of culture. Thus the student of anthropology gets practice at becoming cognitively complex by _____ _____.

① gaining much knowledge from real-life experiences
② analyzing various patterns of cross-cultural communication
③ moving from the specific parts to the whole and back again
④ examining concrete examples of the effects of external events
⑤ concentrating on a certain aspect to give a competitive advantage

123

주어진 글 다음에 이어질 글의 순서로 가장 적절한 것은?

What kinds of materials and tools are involved in different artistic media? Some materials and tools are physical in nature — for example, paint and canvas, or film stock and film cameras.

(A) Of course storytelling is also possible in paint but, this function is achieved in a markedly different way than in filmmaking — for example, with a sequence of still images or image parts that are understood, according to convention, to represent a sequence of events. It is interesting to note that films are sometimes ascribed a painterly quality when the image sequence gives the impression of a series of still compositions.

(B) Conversely, paintings are sometimes ascribed a cinematic quality when they vividly convey a sense of unfolding events. Digital films, moreover, can become painterly when they are largely or entirely composited.

(C) Different physical materials and tools allow for the realization of different creative goals. There are things that you can do with paint that you can't do with stone — for example, create a two-dimensional, abstract expressionist composition — and there are artistically significant functions such as storytelling that moving image sequences are particularly and distinctively well suited to accomplish.

*ascribe 부여하다 **composited 조합된

① (A) − (C) − (B)　　　② (B) − (A) − (C)
③ (B) − (C) − (A)　　　④ (C) − (A) − (B)
⑤ (C) − (B) − (A)

124

글의 흐름으로 보아, 주어진 문장이 들어가기에 가장 적절한 곳은?

> In exchange for efficiency, however, the grid format makes it more difficult for the retailer to influence the flow of shopper traffic.

Retailers have a number of generic store layouts on which to base their interiors. The most common approach is the grid, in which aisles are organized parallel to each other with shelves on both sides. (①) This layout is popular because it is efficient. (②) Customers are familiar with this type of store, are comfortable moving around in it, and can quickly find the products they want to buy. (③) It is also cost-efficient for the retailer, because the interior fixtures can be standardized and a great deal of merchandise can be displayed per square foot. (④) Larger grocery and warehouse stores, with tens of thousands of products, emphasize efficiency and, as a result, favor the grid layout. (⑤) To address this limitation, stores have become very creative with their signage and product displays.

*generic 총괄적인

125

다음 글의 내용을 한 문장으로 요약하고자 한다. 빈칸 (A), (B)에 들어갈 말로 가장 적절한 것은?

In the first half of the twentieth century there were more than six million farms in the United States. Today only a third of them, or two million farms, remain. Half of the remaining farms are tiny, part-time operations with annual sales below $5,000. The only group of farms that has consistently grown is farms over two thousand acres. The globalized food commodity system rewards economies of scale, and the U.S. program of agricultural subsidies reinforces this by providing cash incentives—corporate welfare—for large-scale, industrial-type production. The largest farms are receiving more subsidies than ever. The largest 2 percent of farms are receiving nearly 30 percent of U.S. agricultural subsidies, while the largest 30 percent are receiving more than 80 percent of total subsidies. According to the *Des Moines Register*, "The countryside is being divvied up into Wal-Mart-like mega-farms, which profit most from federal farm payments, and thousands of small farms, comprising niche, part-time or hobby farmers who almost always require off-farm income to stay afloat."

*divvy 분배하다, 나누다

↓

> Large-scale farms have been increasingly ____(A)____ in the U.S. due to the ____(B)____ distribution of federal subsidies in the globalized food commodity system.

	(A)	(B)
①	dwindling	equivalent
②	thriving	inequitable
③	dwindling	inconsistent
④	integrated	limited
⑤	thriving	unlimited

126~127 다음 글을 읽고, 물음에 답하시오.

Our instinct or what we sometimes call intuition isn't some magical or mysterious thing. It is an innate universal animalistic behaviour. Our instincts help us navigate the world. Socrates wrote, 'I decided that it
5 was not wisdom that enabled poets to write their poetry, but a kind of Instinct.' For artists, instinct is considered an (a) asset. But when it comes to making important decisions about people or situations, we cannot always rely on instinct. Darwin defined instinct
10 as independent of experience, but more recent research in psychology and neuroscience has shown that it is continually being honed; it is (b) fluid. When new memories are formed in our brains, the millions of neurons in our cerebral cortex fuse. But this fusion
15 is not permanent and depends to a great extent on subsequent use and reinforcement. So our instinct is not based on some sort of innate behavioural patterns, but on our past experiences, interactions, our situations and our contexts. Our instinct is a result of
20 an (c) accumulated knowledge and so its value cannot be discounted, especially when making quick decisions. But it is also shaped by our biases and prejudices, and so cannot be (d) inferior to acting with complete rationality in accordance with evidence. The key is to
25 not fall back on it for decision-making but rather to use it as a trigger for sparking analytical and logical thought. It is vital to filter possibilities quickly at a subconscious level and (e) direct our decision-making to a point where our rational, conscious mind can take
30 over, one where we can acknowledge and evaluate our biases openly.

*hone 연마하다 **cerebral cortex 대뇌 피질

126
윗글의 제목으로 가장 적절한 것은?

① Supposed Function of Instinct in Artistic Creation
② Instinctive Intuition: A Barrier to Overcoming Biases
③ Role of Instinct: Providing a Cue for Rational Reasoning
④ How Hard Instinctive Animalistic Behavior Is to Change
⑤ Rationality Is Activated Only When instinct Is Suppressed

127
밑줄 친 (a)~(e) 중에서 문맥상 낱말의 쓰임이 적절하지 않은 것은?

① (a)   ② (b)   ③ (c)
④ (d)   ⑤ (e)

128

다음 글의 주제로 가장 적절한 것은?

Being an effective teacher clearly requires much more than expert-level musical knowledge and performance skill. This fact challenges the traditional idea (among some) that teaching makes a good "fallback job" for people who leave a performance career. In fact, exceptional performing musicians may be at a distinct disadvantage when it comes to reaching music students as a teacher. Although elite musicians surely learn a lot through the experience of their own advanced skill development, there is usually reason to doubt whether they can effectively guide the musical growth of other musicians who are different from them. With reference to the broad stages of skill acquisition, among exceptional musicians, many of their performance skills have become highly automatized, such that they may not remember when those skills required more conscious attention or effortful learning strategies. They may not be able to draw upon their own experiences in guiding others at the early stages of skill development.

① importance of students learning from experts
② challenges of skilled musicians in teaching music
③ similarities between performing music and teaching music
④ necessity to participate in competitions for skill development
⑤ effects of teaching experience on musical skill development

129

다음 글의 밑줄 친 부분 중, 어법상 틀린 것은?

Studying is like most things in life: It is not how long it takes to do something but what you accomplish during that time. So it's not how long you sit at your desk that is important but what you learn while ①sitting there. Fifteen minutes of intensive study are better than a whole hour of careless study. Now I'm not advocating that you only work for fifteen minutes; I'm saying that by studying ②effectively you can gain more from your hours at the desk. I often hear from students after they fail an exam ③which they "studied really hard for this exam." But what do they mean when they say they studied really hard? Did they spend a lot of hours using their body heat ④to warm their lecture notes or did they truly study? While both are possible, the probability is that they had their notes ⑤open in front of them for a long time but they were not studying.

130

다음 글의 밑줄 친 부분 중, 문맥상 낱말의 쓰임이 적절하지 <u>않은</u> 것은?

For centuries, American medicine has regarded the question of whether our emotions can affect our health as ①unimportant. Our two-hundred-year span of medical miracles has led us to ②disrespect the technological and scientific approach while giving little thought to the impact that emotions might have on our health. In large part that's because, until very recently, we have ③lacked scientific proof that our feelings can influence our physical well-being. In the last two decades, however, researchers have developed ④technology to see — in real time — how our emotions influence our bodies' cells by changing the chemical and electrical activity in our brains. Slowly, the divide that has long separated mind and body is beginning to disappear as the two spheres of study increasingly ⑤overlap, and researchers are focusing on how our emotions, stress levels, and thought patterns might influence our basic immune cells.

131

다음 빈칸에 들어갈 말로 가장 적절한 것은?

One feature of virtues, according to Philippa Foot, is that they are _____. Aristotle recognizes that people have natural tendencies toward pleasure and cautions us to ward against them becoming too dominant in our lives. And Foot adds that "there is, for instance, a virtue of industriousness only because idleness is a temptation; and of humility only because men tend to think too well of themselves. Hope is a virtue because despair too is a temptation; it might have been that no one cried that all was lost except where he could really see it to be so, and in this case there would have been no virtue of hope." Virtues, then, help us overcome obstacles to living a consistently good life and guard against the tendency to get too caught up in a self-centered world-view with its attendant motives and inclinations. In other words, they motivate us where we are deficient or bolster us where we are inclined to fall short of goodness.

*bolster 북돋우다, 기운 나게 하다

① subjective
② corrective
③ self-confirming
④ ambiguous
⑤ self-contradictory

132

다음 빈칸에 들어갈 말로 가장 적절한 것은?

You may have heard this argument: "I think all these claims about smoking being bad for you are overblown. My grandfather smoked all his life and died in his nineties." This is an argument that needs little critical thinking. You don't need to know the horrifying statistics on smoking-related mortality to show what's wrong with that reasoning. The claim that "smoking being a bad idea is overblown" is both vague and contrary to well-established evidence of the dangers of smoking. Because the claim conflicts with existing scientific evidence we would want some really good evidence before being persuaded. The grandfather's impressive lifespan just isn't enough. This quote is a classic example of the fallacy of anecdotal evidence: _____. That's why we have research and statistics. That's also why we need critical thinking.

① numbers or statistics are emphasized more than necessary
② there is critical evidence for your case that needs to be analyzed
③ one good example or story can't support a broad generalization
④ a strong argument can have true premises and a false conclusion
⑤ the existing evidence is more important than potential evidence

133

주어진 글 다음에 이어질 글의 순서로 가장 적절한 것은?

The !Kung Bushmen of the Kalahari typically spend twelve to nineteen hours a week collecting food, and the Hazda nomads of Tanzania spend less than fourteen hours. That leaves a lot time free for leisure activities, socializing, and so on.

(A) It used to be thought that the switch to farming gave people more time to devote to artistic pursuits, the development of new crafts and technologies, and so on. Farming, in this view, was a liberation from the anxious hand-to-mouth existence of the hunter-gatherer. But in fact the opposite turns out to be true.

(B) When asked by an anthropologist why his people had not adopted farming, one Bushman replied, "Why should we plant, when there are so many fruits and nuts in the world?" In effect, hunter-gatherers work two days a week and have five-day weekends. The hunter-gatherer lifestyle in preagricultural times would probably have been even more pleasant.

(C) Farming is more productive in the sense that it produces more food per unit of land: a group of twenty-five people can subsist by farming on a mere twenty-five acre, a much smaller area than the tens of thousands of acres they would need to subsist by hunting and gathering. But farming is less productive when measured by the amount of food produced per hour of labor.

*subsist 근근이 생계를 유지하다

① (A) − (C) − (B)　　② (B) − (A) − (C)
③ (B) − (C) − (A)　　④ (C) − (A) − (B)
⑤ (C) − (B) − (A)

134

글의 흐름으로 보아, 주어진 문장이 들어가기에 가장 적절한 곳은?

> The meaning of this metaphorical exercise is clear: 'If you try to communicate too much information, you risk communicating nothing.'

There may be many features and benefits that could be used to help sell a brand, but the agency needs to decide which of those benefits is the single most important one; the one that is most likely to interest the target audience. (①) One senior creative used to demonstrate this to advertising students by throwing a tennis ball into groups that would attend his talks and lectures. (②) One student in the audience would invariably catch the ball and hurl it back. (③) The creative would then instruct the student to try catching the ball again. (④) However, this time the creative would throw several balls at the student, who would predictably catch none. (⑤) The truth of the matter is that in a society where the average person is exposed to thousands of advertisements a day, the advertising message has to cut through a great deal of virtual 'noise.'

*hurl 던지다

135

다음 글의 내용을 한 문장으로 요약하고자 한다. 빈칸 (A), (B)에 들어갈 말로 가장 적절한 것은?

Knowledge and knowhow are crucial for the accumulation of information. Simply put, knowledge involves relationships between entities. These relationships are often used to predict the outcomes of events without having to act them out. For instance, we know that tobacco use increases the likelihood of lung cancer, and we can use that connection to anticipate the consequences of tobacco use without the need to use tobacco ourselves. Knowhow is different from knowledge because it involves the capacity to perform actions, which is tacit. For example, most of us know how to walk, even though we do not know how we walk. Most of us know how to identify and label objects in an image, even though we do not know how we accomplish those perceptual and verbal tasks. Most of us know how to recognize objects from different angles, identify faces, and recognize emotions, even though we cannot explain how we do it. We can do these tasks, however, because we have knowhow. Knowhow is the tactic computational capacity that enables us to perform actions, and it is accumulated at both the individual and collective levels.

*tacit 암묵적인

↓

> Knowledge is different from knowhow in that the former enables us to predict the results of actions through ___(A)___ the linkages between them without actually performing them, while the latter allows us to go through certain actions ___(B)___ of what we are doing.

	(A)		(B)
①	reasoning	········	convinced
②	inferring	········	unaware
③	accumulating	········	uninformed
④	preventing	········	unsure
⑤	generating	········	mindful

136

밑줄 친 giving a peck and getting a bushel이 다음 글에서 의미하는 바로 가장 적절한 것은?

Ever pick dandelions out of your yard? Good luck. You may start with 20 in your basket, increase to 60, commit to "pick them all," only to find that you have picked 80 after several hours and that 85 more (that you had not seen before) are now in your side yard—and so forth. In the evolutionary story of a modern yard, dandelions show an extraordinary failure rate (they get picked and mowed a lot), only to be outdone by an even more extraordinary success rate (they find good environments and grow a lot). Dandelion, and so many other natural forms of life, have the greatest possible lessons for us, "giving a peck and getting a bushel." And here it is: Dandelions cannot help but fail at times. They don't seem to have evolved mechanisms designed to reduce failure at all! They don't bite; they are actually pleasant to eat (with few if any toxins): they are helpless! Rather, their strategy toward proliferation seems more like this: grow a lot, grow quickly, grow wherever, and turn to seed as soon as possible. Ever see a field full of dandelions? I bet you have. And that is because this particular evolved strategy—resilience—works.

*proliferation 증식, 확산

① learning from others' failures and successes
② replacing failed attempts with successful ones
③ moving forward through failure for more success
④ developing strategies not to repeat the same failure
⑤ cooperating with other plants for successful survival

137

다음 글의 밑줄 친 부분 중, 어법상 틀린 것은?

When you establish a loyal customer relationship with a business, you are in essence building a mutually beneficial partnership with that business. Building a partnership is ①what allows you, the consumer, to use your loyalty as a valuable investment. This investment pays huge dividends and greatly ②enhances the way these companies treat you. Remember, your repeat business has value to even the biggest companies, no matter ③how much (or little) you spend. After all, the long-term promise of even the modest amount of income your business ④bringing to a company is worth a great deal, especially when multiplied by the hundreds of thousands of other loyal customers who are just like you. Think about it: If you were the CEO of a major airline, wouldn't you feel secure ⑤knowing that hundreds of thousands of people will continue to spend even a few hundred dollars flying your airline every year?

*pay dividends 보상이 돌아오다

138

다음 빈칸에 들어갈 말로 가장 적절한 것은?

The trend toward leisurely, in-depth holidays, like so many others, stems from the baby boomers. They've worked hard—their white-collar toil has largely driven the past few years of global productivity growth—and now they have the money and the time to enjoy themselves. Travelers since they were teens, they've already seen the great museums of Europe, and probably the key monuments of Asia and the plains of Africa. Rather than zip through 20 countries in 20 days, they are more interested in hanging out in a remote corner of one, interacting with locals and sampling new customs. _____ than crossing hot spots off a checklist. This is reflected in the travel industry's new marketing campaigns, notes Alex Kyriakidis, managing partner of Deloitte's global tourism practice. "Greece invites people to 'Explore your senses'," he says. "Intercontinental Hotels asks, 'Are you living an Intercontinental life?'" Holidaymakers are getting plenty of time and space to tailor their days and delve deep into a topic rather than skim the surface.

*delve into ~을 파고들다, ~을 파헤치다

① Luxury high-end travel is more sought after
② Quality and depth of experience matter far more
③ A free-wheeling improvisational trip is more rewarding
④ Adding educational activities for kids is a higher priority
⑤ Visiting as many places as possible is more cost-effective

139

다음 빈칸에 들어갈 말로 가장 적절한 것은?

We can understand why it's not possible for fierce super-dragons to evolve on Earth. This is because the energy supply will not stretch to the support of super-dragons. Great white sharks or killer whales in the sea, and lions and tigers on the land, are apparently the most formidable animals that can survive in the current world. Even these are very thinly spread. One may swim many lifetimes in the world's oceans without encountering a great white shark; and an ancient Chinese proverb asserts that a hill shelters only one tiger. Evolutionary principle tells us that the existence of these animals creates a theoretical possibility for other animals to evolve to eat them, but the food calories to be won from a career or niches of hunting great white sharks and tigers are too few to support a minimum population of animals as large and horribly ferocious as these would have to be. Such animals, therefore, have never evolved. Great white sharks and tigers represent the largest predators that _____.

*niche 활동 범위 **ferocious 사나운, 잔인한

① ecological systems depend on to maintain their balance
② evolutionary theory has no explanation for the origin of
③ geographical limitations force to remain in specific habitats
④ destructive human activities have relatively small impact on
⑤ the laws of physics allow the contemporary Earth to support

140

주어진 글 다음에 이어질 글의 순서로 가장 적절한 것은?

Thousands of years ago, we humans lived a nomadic life, wandering across deserts and plains, hunting and gathering. Then we shifted into living in settlements and cultivating our food.

(A) Over the centuries this reaction has become more psychological: the feeling that we have options in a situation translates into something like the feeling of open space. Our minds thrive on the sense that there is a possibility to break free.

(B) Conversely, the sense of psychological enclosure is deeply disturbing to us, often making us overreact. When someone or something encircles us, we lose control of our emotions and make the kinds of mistakes that render the situation more hopeless.

(C) The change brought us comfort and control, but in a part of our spirit we remain nomads: we cannot help but associate the room to roam and wander with a feeling of freedom. To a cat, tight, enclosed spaces may mean comfort, but to us they conjure suffocation.

*conjure 상기시키다

① (A) − (C) − (B)
② (B) − (A) − (C)
③ (B) − (C) − (A)
④ (C) − (A) − (B)
⑤ (C) − (B) − (A)

141

글의 흐름으로 보아, 주어진 문장이 들어가기에 가장 적절한 곳은?

For these complicated tasks, the business needed to employ people with marketing knowledge.

When businesses started to develop, they were at first small and located within the community. It was easy to keep customers satisfied by producing goods they wanted to buy. Because businesses were located in the community, marketing practices could be based on the owners' personal knowledge of their customers' needs and desires. (①) However, the mass production of products resulted in larger businesses that needed to sell to customers over a larger geographic area. (②) Because business owners could no longer communicate personally with their customers, they had to seriously consider how to market their products. (③) They also had to communicate the benefits of the product to potential consumers who now had many products from which to choose. (④) As a result, during the early twentieth century the demand from businesses for trained marketing professionals began to increase. (⑤) To supply these professionals, marketing became a field of academic study at colleges and universities.

142~143 다음 글을 읽고, 물음에 답하시오.

In one study, undergraduates read a report ostensibly written by a graduate of the math department at their college. The report described a positive experience in the department and presented the report author as
5 academically (a)<u>successful</u>. All participants were thus exposed to a positive role model in math. Researchers manipulated a single datum in the report — the author's birthday, embedded in a small box along with the author's name and hometown. In the same-
10 birthday condition, the author's birthday (b)<u>matched</u> the participant's birthday. In the different-birthday condition, the two birthdays differed by several months. As past research indicates, a shared birthday creates a "unit relationship" between individuals,
15 inducing greater cooperation and liking. If people adopt the goals and interests of others to whom they feel socially (c)<u>disconnected</u>, they should be more motivated to achieve in math in the same-birthday condition than in the different-birthday condition.
20 They were. The primary measure of motivation was how long participants persisted on an insoluble math puzzle task. The task was completed in private, minimizing social desirability pressure, and thus provides a relatively clear index of (d)<u>intrinsic</u>
25 motivation for math. Participants in the same-birthday condition persisted 65% longer on the puzzle than did participants in the different-birthday condition. They also displayed (e)<u>greater</u> motivation for math along several self-reporting instruments (e.g., reporting that
30 it was "more important" for them to be good at math).

*ostensibly 수박 겉핥기식으로

142

윗글의 제목으로 가장 적절한 것은?

① Sameness Increases Motivation for Achievement
② Persistence: An Integral Part of Academic Success
③ Importance of Having a Good Role Model at College
④ Social Desirability Motivates People Not to Cooperate
⑤ Differences: Sometimes More Attractive than Similarities

143

밑줄 친 (a)~(e) 중에서 문맥상 낱말의 쓰임이 적절하지 <u>않은</u> 것은?

① (a)   ② (b)   ③ (c)
④ (d)   ⑤ (e)

144

다음 글의 주제로 가장 적절한 것은?

One of the great challenges in understanding the health consequences of climate variability and change is the lack of temporally and spatially compatible data to underpin evidence based on scientifically sound knowledge and action. Robust results require data from many different disciplines, including from health, medical, social, and behavioral sciences to environmental, oceanographic, and climate sciences. And within that are further challenges to accessibility and availability — ranging from privacy concerns and private sector ownership surrounding some health data, making it altogether unavailable, or available but without the granularity needed for robust analysis, to accessing massive climate data sets in a usable way. And though it may sound like an oxymoron, while we may not have a robust temporally and spatially matched dataset for a given problem, as more and more data are gathered across disciplines, the challenge becomes how to integrate and use all this big data.

*granularity 세분화 **oxymoron 모순어법

① global climate changes and their influence on public health
② innovative healthcare systems for climate change adaptation
③ growing need for community engagement in climate data awareness
④ obstacles in obtaining and utilizing data for climate-health analysis
⑤ protection of privacy in the research on climate-related health issues

145

다음 글의 밑줄 친 부분 중, 어법상 틀린 것은?

Disease is a disvalue, one that may wipe out whole groups of organisms or cause them much suffering and pain. It is notable that disease usually can be attributed to microorganisms seeking to maintain their lives in the world, so disease is yet another way in which the flourishing of some creatures is at cross-purposes with ①that of others, at least in the short run. Loss of mates and progeny and the deterioration of habitats are still other kinds of disvalues, as ②is the overpopulation of one or more species at the expense of others. Nature is a dynamic, volatile system, as we have seen. Its various aspects are radically dependent on one another, and all are therefore made highly ③vulnerable to change. The future is not always dependable for nature's creatures and can bring ④themselves severe frustrations, setbacks, and losses. ⑤Whatever interferes with a creature's *telos* or characteristic mode of developing and flourishing is a disvalue in nature, and there is much such interference in the natural world, quite apart from any role that human beings might play in it.

*progeny 자손 **telos (궁극의) 목적

146

다음 글의 밑줄 친 부분 중, 문맥상 낱말의 쓰임이 적절하지 <u>않은</u> 것은?

The urgency instinct makes us want to take ① <u>immediate</u> action in the face of a perceived imminent danger. It must have served us humans well in the distant past. If we thought there might be a lion in the grass, it wasn't ② <u>sensible</u> to do too much analysis. Those who stopped and carefully analyzed the probabilities are not our ancestors. We are the offspring of those who decided and acted quickly with ③ <u>sufficient</u> information. Today, we still need the urgency instinct—for example, when a car comes out of nowhere and we need to take evasive action. But now that we have ④ <u>eliminated</u> most immediate dangers and are left with more complex and often more abstract problems, the urgency instinct can also lead us astray when it comes to our understanding the world around us. It makes us stressed, amplifies our other instincts and makes them harder to control, blocks us from thinking analytically, tempts us to make up our minds too fast, and ⑤ <u>encourages</u> us to take drastic actions that we haven't thought through.

147

다음 빈칸에 들어갈 말로 가장 적절한 것은?

One problem that results from our personal selections and interpretations in our daily life is that we are all set on self-fulfilling missions. That is, we formulate our model for coping with the world, and it is then only in terms of that model's framework that we experience the world. We accept or receive information that confirms and consolidates our model, while conversely rejecting anything that might serve to challenge or change it. We are in a sense 'imprisoned' within our own interpretations. So, for example, in personal relationships we tend to notice and record evidence that _____ which we have made of people; or we interpret people's actions in such a way that, on the whole, we can continue to speak of them acting 'characteristically' (i.e. in a way that we would, on the basis of past experience, expect of them); and we find prolonged 'uncharacteristic' behavior so disturbing, that we would probably attribute it to another person's temporary drunkenness or emotional disorder, rather than to our own previous fundamental misjudgment.

① helps us to let go of stereotypes
② contradicts favorable impressions
③ only enhances emotional connections
④ serves to confirm previous evaluations
⑤ enables us to recognize misconceptions

148

다음 빈칸에 들어갈 말로 가장 적절한 것은?

Coffee is a product that stands at the heart of contemporary debates about globalization, international trade, human rights and environmental destruction. As coffee has grown in popularity, it has become 'branded' and politicized: the decisions that consumers make about what kind of coffee to drink and where to purchase it have become lifestyle choices. Individuals may choose to drink only organic coffee, decaffeinated coffee or coffee that has been 'fairly traded' (through schemes that pay full market prices to small coffee producers in developing countries). They may opt to patronize 'independent' coffee houses, rather than 'corporate' coffee chains. Coffee drinkers might decide to boycott coffee from certain countries with poor human rights and environmental records. As shown in the trade and consumption of coffee, globalization heightens people's awareness of issues occurring in distant corners of the planet and _____.

*patronize (상점 등을) 애용하다

① enables the developing countries to share its benefits
② raises expectations of what companies should deliver
③ prompts them to act on new knowledge in their own lives
④ urges companies to comply with stricter environmental guidelines
⑤ helps the have-nots to access resources otherwise off-limits

149

주어진 글 다음에 이어질 글의 순서로 가장 적절한 것은?

> Computer users who wish to share files and make use of them in common must be utilizing compatible software programs. As the number of users with compatible software increases, the advantages of the ability to share files expand.

(A) This will be true not only because of file compatibility across users, but also because more users will be familiar with a particular program, reducing training costs for businesses and increasing the availability of informal sources of assistance for learning how to use a program for both business and home users.

(B) All the users of MS Word constitute a network, and the bigger the network the greater the advantage of using MS Word. The computer program that is able to attract the most users will exercise a clear marketplace advantage.

(C) If MS Word is used by more computer users than any other word processing program, then it pays for someone who wants to exchange files with others to purchase MS Word as opposed to competing programs such as WordPerfect.

① (A) − (C) − (B)
② (B) − (A) − (C)
③ (B) − (C) − (A)
④ (C) − (A) − (B)
⑤ (C) − (B) − (A)

150

글의 흐름으로 보아, 주어진 문장이 들어가기에 가장 적절한 것은?

> For Berridge, this discovery offers a fruitful way for thinking about some of the "disorders of desire" that bedevil humans.

The foods we eat the most are not always the ones we like the most. In 1996, the psychologist Kent Berridge changed the way many neuroscientists thought about eating when he introduced a distinction between "wanting" (the motivation to eat something) and "liking" (the pleasure the food actually gives). (①) Berridge found that "wanting" or craving was neurally as well as psychologically distinct from "liking." (②) Specifically, whereas the zone of the brain that controls our motivation to eat stretches across the entire *nucleus accumbens*, the sections of the brain that give us pleasure when we eat occupy smaller "hotspots" within this same area. (③) For example, binge eating may be associated with "excessive wanting without corresponding 'liking.'" (④) You may feel a potent drive to purchase an extra-large portion of cheesy nachos, even though the pleasure they deliver when you actually consume them is much less potent than you expected. (⑤) Indeed, binge eaters often report that the foods they crave do not even taste good when they are eating them: the desire is greater than the enjoyment.

*nucleus accumbens 측좌핵(동기 및 보상과 관련된 정보를 처리하는 뇌의 보상체계)

**binge eating 폭식

151

다음 글의 내용을 한 문장으로 요약하고자 한다. 빈칸 (A), (B)에 들어갈 말로 가장 적절한 것은?

In numerous designs, crucial parts are carefully hidden away. Handles on cabinets distract from some design aesthetics, and so they are deliberately made invisible or left out. The cracks that signify the existence of a door can also distract from the pure lines of the design, so these significant cues are also minimized or eliminated. The result can be a smooth expanse of gleaming material, with no sign of doors or drawers, let alone of how those doors and drawers might be opened. This same aesthetic principle is usually applied to electrical devices, so many electrical devices have the on/off switches hidden somewhere. For example, many printers and photocopiers have the on/off switch in the rear or the side making it difficult to find and awkward to use. Furthermore, the switches that control kitchen garbage disposal units are often hidden away and are sometimes nearly impossible to find. Many systems can be vastly improved by the act of making visible what is invisible now.

↓

> The principle of ____(A)____, which makes it much easier to use devices, is ____(B)____ in the design of many everyday items.

	(A)		(B)
①	visibility	………	applied
②	visibility	………	violated
③	simplicity	………	emphasized
④	multi-function	………	ignored
⑤	multi-function	………	integrated

152

밑줄 친 "simply human"이 다음 글에서 의미하는 바로 가장 적절한 것은?

Given two categories, we overestimate the differences between them. We underestimate the variation among members of each group. We also tend to see our own group as beautifully diverse and people outside it as homogeneous. The technical term for this is "outgroup homogeneity," and it helps explain, for example, the different ways the American media cover violence. When White, Christian people commit hate crimes, they are largely portrayed in mainstream media as disturbed individuals whose actions issue from their own particular psychological state. Crime committed by a Muslim person is likely to be ascribed not to individual pathology but to group identity: violent acts by people from marginalized groups are seen as a reflection of that group to which they belong. The term "Black on Black crime" exists, while the term "White on White crime" does not, even though more than 80 percent of White murder victims in the United States are killed by other White people. In the cultural imagination, the White perpetrator and the White victim are not seen as part of a meaningful group. White people are, as philosopher George Yancy puts it, "simply human."

*homogeneous 동질적인 **pathology 병리, 병적 측면

***perpetrator 가해자

① regarded as always generous to those in need
② recognized as individuals free from group stereotypes
③ often perceived as a distinct social group in their societies
④ respecting all humans regardless of religious differences
⑤ taking a stand against hate crimes and race-related violence

153

다음 글의 밑줄 친 부분 중, 어법상 틀린 것은?

Baby Boomers, born between 1946 and 1964, grew up in the midst of economic prosperity, in contrast with their parents who came of age during times of economic depression. Still, like their parents, they believe in working hard and putting in long hours, but unlike members of the generation before them, they expect to be acknowledged publicly for their work and ① rewarded for their efforts. Baby Boomers associate ② them closely with their professions and many work considerably long hours. On the other hand, generation X or Xers, born between 1965 and 1980, have a different view of work than their predecessors. Having witnessed their parents ③ laid off despite years of dedication and loyal service, they don't see the necessity of putting in excessively long hours or working extra hard to impress employers they perceive as not likely to be concerned with their well-being. Instead, they believe in "working smarter," ④ which often translates into developing transferable skills and devoting less time on the job. They further value being able to work independently, ⑤ focusing more on outcomes than tasks.

154

다음 빈칸에 들어갈 말로 가장 적절한 것은?

Pluralist democracy makes a virtue of the struggle between competing interests. It argues for government that accommodates the struggle and channels the result into government action. According to pluralist democracy, the public is best served if the government structure provides access for different groups to press their claims in competition with one another. Note that pluralist democracy does not insist that all groups have equal influence on government decisions. In the political struggle, wealthy, well-organized groups have an inherent advantage over poorer, inadequately organized groups. In fact, unorganized segments of the population may not even get their concerns placed on the agenda for government consideration. Indeed, studies of the congressional agenda demonstrate that it is characterized by little in the way of legislation concerned with poor or low-income Americans, while business-related bills are plentiful. Pluralist democracy appears to _____ in levels of political organization and resources among different segments of society.

① justify great disparities
② resolve social inequality
③ value diversity of opinion
④ intensify political struggle
⑤ support the legislative activities

155

다음 빈칸에 들어갈 말로 가장 적절한 것은?

Adding to the obstacles that confront anthropologists when doing research abroad is their own cultural baggage. It probably can be claimed that anthropologists have a greater capacity than most people to hold their cultural backgrounds at bay; that is a central part of their training. Yet the very fact that they have been socialized at birth into a particular culture (or more precisely a location within a culture) encompasses specific values and institutions and occupies a particular moral and political niche in their world order. This inevitably suggests, without even considering the individual anthropologist's personality, that _____. Sometimes anthropologists joke, at least in private, that our ethnographies consist partly of cultural projection and personal confession, reflecting our own vision of the world, rather than the vision of people who are studied. However, it would be difficult to point to any other discipline engaged in cross-cultural studies that has done the job better.

*encompass 포함하다 **ethnography 민족지(民族誌)

① many other disciplines are related to anthropology
② some amount of ethnocentrism must always creep in
③ there are common grounds between different cultures
④ different ethnic groups are becoming better integrated
⑤ cultural backgrounds do not affect cross-cultural studies

156

주어진 글 다음에 이어질 글의 순서로 가장 적절한 것은?

Studying the development of modern ecosystems and the plants and animals in them would be simpler if we could assume that past ecosystems in any given area had the same climate, soil, and geography which now characterize that area.

(A) For example, during the Miocene epoch, the plains near what is now the Salmon River in east central Idaho were covered with a dense forest dominated by dawn redwood but also containing many other species of trees.

(B) Frequently, however, fossil records reveal ecosystems so different from those of today in the same sites that we know there has been a considerable change in the climate and/or the natural environment.

(C) Today, that forest is covered with 15 million years' accumulation of volcanic ash. On top of the layers of ash lies semi-desert rangeland, on which sagebrush and grass are growing. The rise of the Cascade Mountains about a million years ago turned much of Idaho into a rain shadow desert.

*Miocene epoch 중신세
**dawn redwood 메타세쿼이아(중국에서 자생종이 발견된 낙엽 교목)
***sagebrush 산쑥(미국 서부 건조지의 대표적 식물)

① (A) − (C) − (B) ② (B) − (A) − (C)
③ (B) − (C) − (A) ④ (C) − (A) − (B)
⑤ (C) − (B) − (A)

157

글의 흐름으로 보아, 주어진 문장이 들어가기에 가장 적절한 곳은?

A low score might simply indicate that someone was feeling ill during the examination.

Data are typically numbers: the results of measurements, counts, or other processes. We can think of such data as providing a simplified representation of whatever we are studying. (①) If we are concerned with school children, and in particular their academic ability and suitability for different kinds of careers, we might choose to study the numbers giving their results in various tests and examinations. (②) These numbers would provide an indication of their abilities and inclinations, but the representation would not be perfect. (③) A missing value, in the same vein, does not tell us much about their ability, but merely that they did not sit the examination. (④) Data quality matters because of the general principle (which applies throughout life, not merely in statistics) that if we have poor material to work with then the results will be poor. (⑤) Statisticians can perform amazing feats in extracting understanding from numbers, but they cannot perform miracles.

*missing value 결측값(실험에서 얻어지지 않은 값)

158~159 다음 글을 읽고, 물음에 답하시오.

In order to appreciate how the producer-audience relationship is changing, we should first remind ourselves how the arts and entertainment industry traditionally operates. Despite the recent social inclusion of the arts including arts education and audience development agendas, whose communal aim is partly to (a)reveal the creative process, and despite the increasing popularity of the academic discipline of arts and entertainment management, the creative process itself often remains a mystery. There are various reasons for this. First, many artists, producers and audiences would contend that the secret behind the process is precisely what gives arts and entertainment experiences their overriding (b)appeal. The powerful image and symbolism of a curtain slowly revealing a stage hints at a closed, mysterious and escapist world, which can briefly transport its audience from one side of the curtain to the other. Second, the creative process itself is inherently (c)complex, requiring a diverse body of creative agents coming together to stage a new experience. This involves many (d)intangibles such as human and artistic chemistry, which are forced into a crucible to produce an unknown new element for the audience. Finally, like many other professional activities, writing, composing, choreography, filming, rehearsals and other related creative activities generally take place behind closed doors so that writers, directors and artists can experiment, focus and work in a spirit of artistic freedom and (e)transparency.

*crucible 도가니   **choreography (무용) 안무

158

윗글의 제목으로 가장 적절한 것은?

① Concealing the Artistic Process is Natural
② Art Reflects the Artists' Desire for Secrecy
③ The Arts Reflect Social and Cultural Trends
④ The Great Difficulty to Appreciate Artworks
⑤ The Interdependence of Artistic Disciplines

159

밑줄 친 (a)~(e) 중에서 문맥상 낱말의 쓰임이 적절하지 <u>않은</u> 것은?

① (a)   ② (b)   ③ (c)
④ (d)   ⑤ (e)

3점 공략 모의고사 1회

01 detachment   *n* _____

02 arbitrary   *a* _____

03 initially   *ad* _____

04 complement   *v* _____

05 noxious   *a* _____

06 개척자, 선구자   *n* _____

07 hazardous   *a* _____

08 inclined   *a* _____

09 화합물   *n* _____

10 restore   *v* _____

11 definite   *a* _____

12 conversion   *n* _____

13 통찰력   *n* _____

14 reinforce   *v* _____

15 adage   *n* _____

16 proceed   *v* _____

17 influential   *a* _____

18 ingenuity   *n* _____

19 pollute   *v* _____

20 extraction   *n* _____

3점 공략 모의고사 2회

01 contradictory   *a* _____

02 roam   *v* _____

03 overt   *a* _____

04 alter   *v* _____

05 dissent   *n* _____

06 sequence   *n* _____

07 impose   *v* _____

08 informed   *a* _____

09 저항, 내성   *n* _____

10 fulfill   *v* _____

11 compelling   *a* _____

12 멸종한   *a* _____

13 impede   *v* _____

14 thrive   *v* _____

15 conformity   *n* _____

16 dominant   *a* _____

17 정체성   *n* _____

18 modification   *n* _____

19 reap   *v* _____

20 refutation   *n* _____

3점 공략 모의고사 3회

01	notorious	*a*	
02	attribute	*v*	
03	substantial	*a*	
04	cognition	*n*	
05	moderate	*a*	
06	평판, 명성	*n*	
07	skeptical	*a*	
08	retailer	*n*	
09	implicit	*a*	
10	domesticate	*v*	
11	말 그대로	*ad*	
12	fertility	*n*	
13	서식지	*n*	
14	fungus	*n*	
15	altruistically	*ad*	
16	terminology	*n*	
17	indigenous	*a*	
18	identical	*a*	
19	novelty	*n*	
20	reciprocal	*a*	

3점 공략 모의고사 4회

01	evaluate	*v*	
02	equivalent	*a*	
03	suppress	*v*	
04	integration	*n*	
05	conversely	*ad*	
06	barrier	*n*	
07	잠재의식의	*a*	
08	subordinate	*a*	
09	포유동물	*n*	
10	consistently	*ad*	
11	differentiate	*v*	
12	merchandise	*n*	
13	평행의	*a*	
14	exaggerate	*v*	
15	abstract	*a*	
16	subsidy	*n*	
17	comprise	*v*	
18	prejudice	*n*	
19	infer	*v*	
20	dwindle	*v*	

3점 공략 모의고사 5회

01	nomad	*n*	
02	tactic	*a*	
03	obstacle	*n*	
04	anticipate	*v*	
05	invariably	*ad*	
06	미덕	*n*	
07	deficient	*a*	
08	겸손함	*n*	
09	dominant	*a*	
10	advocate	*v*	
11	면역의	*a*	
12	exceptional	*a*	
13	span	*n*	
14	liberation	*n*	
15	fallacy	*n*	
16	metaphorical	*a*	
17	accumulation	*n*	
18	perceptual	*a*	
19	inclination	*n*	
20	attendant	*a*	

3점 공략 모의고사 6회

01	wander	*v*	
02	resilience	*n*	
03	loyal	*a*	
04	manipulate	*v*	
05	외딴, 외진	*a*	
06	기념물, 기념비	*n*	
07	apparently	*ad*	
08	integral	*a*	
09	induce	*v*	
10	assert	*v*	
11	cultivate	*v*	
12	현대의, 동시대의	*a*	
13	enhance	*v*	
14	embed	*v*	
15	insoluble	*a*	
16	persist	*v*	
17	secure	*a*	
18	settlement	*n*	
19	multiply	*v*	
20	formidable	*a*	

3점 공략 모의고사 7회

01 vulnerable   *a* _____

02 consolidate   *v* _____

03 potent   *a* _____

04 setback   *n* _____

05 urgency   *n* _____

06 compatible   *a* _____

07 고정관념   *n* _____

08 imminent   *a* _____

09 spatially   *ad* _____

10 formulate   *v* _____

11 즉각적인   *a* _____

12 contradict   *v* _____

13 미학   *n* _____

14 drastic   *a* _____

15 imprison   *v* _____

16 misconception   *n* _____

17 offspring   *n* _____

18 prompt   *v* _____

19 evasive   *a* _____

20 comply to _____

3점 공략 모의고사 8회

01 prosperity   *n* _____

02 accommodate   *v* _____

03 inherent   *a* _____

04 고백   *n* _____

05 agenda   *n* _____

06 contend   *v* _____

07 통계학, 통계 수치   *n* _____

08 dedication   *n* _____

09 민족의   *a* _____

10 communal   *a* _____

11 extract   *v* _____

12 feat   *n* _____

13 segment   *n* _____

14 integrate   *v* _____

15 confront   *v* _____

16 legislation   *n* _____

17 transport   *v* _____

18 inevitably   *ad* _____

19 predecessor   *n* _____

20 portray   *v* _____

160

밑줄 친 the class of particulars so defined가 다음 글에서 의미하는 바로 가장 적절한 것은?

The sociologist must define as well as observe social facts, and there are rules for arriving at each definition. It is unnecessary to observe all the facts that one can include under a given definition, for that would defeat
5 the economy of effort, which is one of science's purposes. It is not necessary to observe every single instance of murder in order to define it. Neither is it necessary to observe every single aspect of a phenomenon that fits under a definition, for the
10 infinity of attributes makes this impossible. Instead, the sociologist should arrive at those characteristics essential to his purpose, use these as his definition, and by observation determine which particular instances share the defining characteristics. These, and
15 only these, fall into the class of particulars so defined. Durkheim pointed to crime as an illustration. All actions that evoke punishment by society fall under this class of behaviour. Hence, punishment is the definition of crime, all crimes sharing this attribute. All
20 actions that fail to elicit this collective reaction do not belong to the class and therefore do not fit the definition.

① the strategy that is based on making an economy of effort

② the kind of actions that are not judged by a moral standard

③ the general rule that can be applied to all social phenomena

④ the particular phenomenon that every action has its own result

⑤ the categorized social facts that have defining attributes in common

161

다음 글의 밑줄 친 부분 중, 어법상 틀린 것은?

The power of sport can be used to address myriad social objectives. As a powerful and emotive socioeconomic institution, sport offers a way for individuals, groups, and cultures ① to build relationships and engage with one another. On a local level, sport 5 provides an arena for individual engagement and exchange; at the same time, its structural power and function as a social institution mean ② that it can also be used to influence societies on a large scale. Because sport is enormously popular and, indeed, pervades the 10 social fabric of many countries, its ability to reach across social, political, and economic areas ③ makes sport one of the few institutions that can serve as a catalyst for change. The power of the social institution of sport generates huge economic investment, ④ which 15 creates opportunity for extensive social impact. Whether or not that opportunity is realized ⑤ depending on the conduct of sport, and that conduct is ultimately determined by current practitioners and by aspiring sport managers embarking on careers in the industry. 20

*myriad 무수히 많은 **catalyst 촉매(제)

162

다음 글의 밑줄 친 부분 중, 문맥상 낱말의 쓰임이 적절하지 <u>않은</u> 것은?

Uncertainty is an important part of our experience of life. The making of decisions is one of the many things associated with this feeling of uncertainty. Yet although it is a feeling that we are all familiar with, it is still something that we are anxious to ① avoid. Uncertainty is a condition that people experience aversively. In other words, people are highly motivated to ② eliminate this condition from their lives—at least, as far as possible. The feeling that we can exercise control over what we do and the results that we achieve is a more ③ comforting one. This means that we have a strong belief in the idea that we must try to control the uncontrollable. This is clearly not possible—but it doesn't stop us from trying. We are eager to experience the ④ illusion of control. This attempt to achieve a 'false' feeling of control is therefore, in reality, irrational behaviour. And an aspect of this behaviour, which we often use in our attempt to trick ourselves in this manner, is the ⑤ implementing of decisions.

163

다음 빈칸에 들어갈 말로 가장 적절한 것은?

Scientists' theoretical commitments, beliefs, previous knowledge, training, experiences, and expectations actually influence their work. All these background factors form a mind-set that affects the problems scientists investigate and how they conduct their investigations, what they observe (and do not observe), and how they make sense of, or interpret their observations. It is this (sometimes collective) mind-set that accounts for _____ in the production of scientific knowledge. It is noteworthy that, contrary to common belief, science rarely starts with neutral observations. Observations (and investigations) are motivated and guided by, and acquire meaning in reference to questions or problems, which, in turn, are derived from within certain theoretical perspectives. Often, hypothesis or model testing serves as a guide to scientific investigations. For example, a researcher operating from a Darwinian framework might focus his/her efforts on the location of transitional species. By contrast, from a punctuated equilibrist perspective, transitional species would not be expected, nor would what a Darwinian considered a transitional species be considered as such.

*punctuated equilibrist (진화가 일정한 정체기 후 한순간 폭발적으로 일어난다는) 단속평형설을 믿는 사람

① the value of evidence
② the role of subjectivity
③ the power of collaboration
④ the presence of uncertainty
⑤ the importance of objectivity

164

다음 빈칸에 들어갈 말로 가장 적절한 것은?

European Americans moved further west in the 1800s into the lands of the Native Americans. The majority of the period's writings either presented the extermination of the American Indians as justified or needed in the name of progress. Even when the "noble savage" image was emphasized, underlying self-serving purposes often existed. For example, in 1887, a bill, the Dawes Act, designed to support the breakup of tribal lands into parcels to allow individual Indians to farm or ranch their own land was passed. Created to encourage Indians to assimilate into the European American culture, the "noble savage" image was used to summon support for the act. The Dawes Act actually had a long-lasting negative impact. It paved the way for ill-intentioned European Americans to grab precious land that had belonged to Indian tribes, and often left many American Indians landless and in poverty. In the American west in the 1800s, _____.

*extermination 말살, 근절

① conflict and cooperation coexisted
② sentiments of sympathy became a rarity
③ new economic activities were not to be seen
④ the "noble savage" image was undermined by law
⑤ the colonists' culture was projected onto tribal cultures

165

주어진 글 다음에 이어질 글의 순서로 가장 적절한 것은?

Perhaps the commonest circumstances under which societies fail to perceive a problem is when it takes the form of a slow trend concealed by wide up-and-down fluctuations. The prime example in modern times is global warming.

(A) With such large and unpredictable fluctuations, it has taken a long time to discern the average upwards trend of 0.01 degree per year within that noisy signal. That's why it was only a few years ago that most professional climatologists previously skeptical of the reality of global warming became convinced.

(B) Instead, as we all know, climate fluctuates up and down erratically from year to year: three degrees warmer in one summer than in the previous one, then two degrees warmer the next summer, down four degrees the following summer, down another degree the next one, then up five degrees, etc.

(C) We now realize that temperatures around the world have been slowly rising in recent decades, due in large part to atmospheric changes caused by humans. However, it is not the case that the climate each year has been exactly 0.01 degree warmer than in the previous year.

*erratically 불규칙하게, 변덕스럽게

① (A) − (C) − (B)
② (B) − (A) − (C)
③ (B) − (C) − (A)
④ (C) − (A) − (B)
⑤ (C) − (B) − (A)

166

글의 흐름으로 보아, 주어진 문장이 들어가기에 가장 적절한 곳은?

> Yet there is some specialized genre such as academic discourse which tends to rely heavily on writing as opposed to speaking.

Most scholars would now agree with anthropologist Ruth Finnegan's observation that "no firm line can be drawn between the oral and the written." (①) Neither linguistic structure nor social functions split nicely down the line between the oral and the written. (②) Almost everything that can or could be written could be said and vice versa and there is no grammar or vocabulary that is unique to one but unavailable to the other. (③) Even speech acts such as asserting and promising, although varying somewhat from one society to another, are more or less universal with no speech act uniquely associated with the written tradition. (④) As we all know, if you want to take part in any specialized discipline, such as psychology, you have to learn how to read and write psychological articles and texts. (⑤) All disciplines possess, as we say, a *literature*, and to participate one must know the literature.

167

다음 글의 내용을 한 문장으로 요약하고자 한다. 빈칸 (A), (B)에 들어갈 말로 가장 적절한 것은?

Recent empirical work has examined the interesting fact that our sense of how long ago events occurred does not always map onto their actual distance in time. Friends at college reunions will relive their undergraduate antics, remarking "it seems like yesterday," whereas graduating seniors looking back on awkward moments from freshman year feel as if those events occurred ages ago. It turns out that beliefs about the self contribute to feelings of temporal distance and feelings of temporal distance can impact beliefs about the self. Another recent area of interest involves the mental images people experience as they recall past events. An interesting fact about these images is that they are not always pictured from the "first-person" visual perspective that was experienced as the event unfolded. Sometimes people picture past events from the "third-person" perspective of an outside observer, so that they see their past selves in the image.

*antics 익살스러운 짓

↓

> When we look back on the past, the temporal distance is ____(A)____ measured, and sometimes we view past events that happened to us from a(n) ____(B)____ point of view.

	(A)		(B)
①	obejctively	········	multiple
②	obejctively	········	impartial
③	selectively	········	biased
④	subjectively	········	neutral
⑤	subjectively	········	unclear

168

밑줄 친 'frozen images'가 다음 글에서 의미하는 바로 가장 적절한 것은?

Often, indigenous people wear traditional costumes to be more exotic and to live up to the expectations of the tourists. All this adds to keeping the picture of a traditional culture alive. In the late 1990s, some scholars claimed that cultural markers tended to be unchanged in a tourism context and they called them 'frozen images.' It might have changed in many places, but there are still such expectations which, when fulfilled, add to tendencies such as stereotyping, othering and related phenomena. Nonetheless, as has been noted by some scholars, indigenous people are not automatically passive victims of such a process. Instead, they sometimes actively participate in this process in order to gain economic benefits. What is permitted and what is forbidden in indigenous tourism is tested and negotiated in various ways among indigenous and non-indigenous stakeholders, and is furthermore dependent on current ethnopolitical discourses.

① static and rigid representations of indigenous people
② conceptions of indigenous people as passive victims of tourism
③ negative portrayals of indigenous tourism as a necessary evil
④ neglected traditional values versus economic gain in indigenous tourism
⑤ cultural expressions transferred to goods and services for indigenous tourism

169

다음 글의 밑줄 친 부분 중, 어법상 틀린 것은?

We read fiction partly because it is entertaining or enjoyable, but some fiction is read also because it provides examples of interpersonal relating. Reading allows us to ①be exposed to experiments in interpersonal living without having to suffer the negative consequences of making mistakes. Instead of ruining our own lives, we can watch Tolstoy's Anna Karenina ②ruin hers. While it is not tailored to our specific circumstances, good literature is applicable to a large audience. In this respect, literature functions as myths ③do in some cultures. Some Apaches, for example, use stories associated with specific places in the surrounding landscape ④to guide people through life's tangles. Religious and cultural myths are often cited by seniors as navigational guides for younger members of the society. Freud used one specific myth — that of Oedipus — as a guide to the psychology of most boys, and Gilligan used the myth of Cupid and Psyche as a guide to romantic love. These myths, like literature, presumably have been retained and reshaped to fit situations ⑤where members of the culture may face from time to time.

170

다음 빈칸에 들어갈 말로 가장 적절한 것은?

If a film camera is placed in a particular spot, it sees the objects one behind the other exactly as does the human eye (when the observer is standing still), one object obstructing the view of another. And this limitation helps to achieve quite special effects. In Eisenstein's film *The General Line* a poor peasant woman comes to the farm of a rich, fat man to borrow a horse. The man is lying on a couch. The woman stands before him and addresses him humbly. He sits up. The camera is then placed behind him. His broad back is seen looming large and heavy in the foreground, finally blotting out entirely the woman who is standing in the background. The whole picture is suddenly filled and dominated by his huge back. Here his authority over her is expressed by means of a clever choice of position. Through being close to the camera, his back appears particularly large, fat, and space-devouring. The peasant woman in the background is very small by contrast. The image highlights the fact that there is little she can do. Therefore, the idea that _____ is suggested, and the woman disappears from the picture altogether.

① the film is just an illusion
② power overshadows helplessness
③ gender stereotyping pervades films
④ close-up shots add emotion to scenes
⑤ camera angles make all the difference

171

다음 빈칸에 들어갈 말로 가장 적절한 것은?

My travels and encounters with diverse cultures have taught me an important thing about miracles. I have learned that the less people know about basic science, the more they talk about miracles. In places where there is little awareness of astronomy and medical science, for example, one hears much talk of miracle eclipses and healings. In societies with higher levels of science literacy, one hears claims of miracles, but they are less frequent and almost always limited to unusual events, such as people surviving a plane crash or the rescue of some lost hiker. The correlation is clear: _____ means less reliance on miracles to explain events. This can be seen in history as well. Centuries ago, things we now understand were thought to be unexplainable and therefore supernatural. It is likely that this trend will hold true in the future. Today's miraculous occurrence will probably be tomorrow's routine occurrence, thanks to future generations' greater understanding of how the universe works.

*eclipse (해와 달의) 식(蝕)

① more diversity in scientific literature
② a higher position in the social hierarchy
③ more understanding of the natural world
④ a less close association with religious beliefs
⑤ a less frequent occurrence of supernatural events

172

주어진 글 다음에 이어질 글의 순서로 가장 적절한 것은?

> In some circumstances, scientists can control conditions deliberately and precisely to obtain their evidence.

(A) Often, however, control of conditions may be impractical (as in studying stars), or unethical (as in studying people), or likely to distort the natural phenomena (as in studying wild animals in captivity).

(B) In such cases, observations have to be made over a sufficiently wide range of naturally occurring conditions to infer what the influence of various factors might be. Because of this reliance on evidence, great value is placed on the development of better instruments and techniques of observation, and findings of any one investigator or group are usually checked by others.

(C) They may, for example, control the temperature, change the concentration of chemicals, or choose which organisms mate with others. By varying just one condition at a time, they can hope to identify its exclusive effects on what happens, uncomplicated by changes in other conditions.

① (A) − (C) − (B)
② (B) − (A) − (C)
③ (B) − (C) − (A)
④ (C) − (A) − (B)
⑤ (C) − (B) − (A)

173

글의 흐름으로 보아, 주어진 문장이 들어가기에 가장 적절한 곳은?

> However, the rate of change and progress created by these innovations is not the same in every country.

Individuals in every society derive certain meaning or value from their lives. (①) That meaning is individualized and varies from one person to another, and it constitutes that particular individual's quality of life. (②) As societies advance and become more sophisticated, inventive minds imagine and create new things, which we call innovations, to make consumers' lives better, easier, and, it is hoped, more enjoyable. (③) From the wheel to penicillin and to the computer, and many others, each and every major development has changed and continues changing how people live and work in societies. (④) It is hypothesized that "productivity growth rates tend to vary inversely with productivity levels", implying that economically less developed countries have a greater opportunity to catch up and forge ahead than do industrialized countries. (⑤) During the past several decades, newly industrialized countries such as Asia's four tigers (Hong Kong, Singapore, Taiwan, and South Korea) have shown that this supposition is correct.

*forge ahead 빠른 진전을 보이다

174~175 다음 글을 읽고, 물음에 답하시오.

The idea of categorizing humans into groups is an old one: who are the members of our family, extended family, village, tribe, religion, region, nation, and a number of other social categories? It's (a) natural to create groups based on perceived differences and we do so based on a huge number of social categories. But race has a specific biological meaning, where it is identical to the term 'sub-species' for groups of organisms within a species that are genetically distinct from one another. In fact, we show a relative low level of genetic diversity when compared to chimps and gorillas. So what can we say about the different human 'races'? On the genetic level, there is next to no (b) variation between a person from Africa, Europe, or Asia—pick any two people at random from anywhere on the planet and they will be very closely related when you look at their DNA, much more so than is normal for such a widely dispersed animal species.

The simple fact is that modern biology (c) confirms the way we have traditionally created different human races using skin color as well as made western civilization the global 'standard.' Both ideas are deeply (d) flawed. Skin color is controlled by a simple genetic switch that controls the production of melanocytes, the cells that produce melanin, which pigments the skin, but this difference is very slight. Also, the use of western culture as an absolute measure of sophistication simply does not reflect the range and diversity of human society. In short, the idea that there are (e) separate 'human races' simply cannot be sustained in light of twenty-first century biology.

*pigment 색소를 제공하다

174

윗글의 제목으로 가장 적절한 것은?

① Race Is an Illusion, Not a Biological Reality
② Racial Discrimination: Its Roots and Causes
③ Differences Between Human and Animal Biology
④ The Reason Biology Pays Attention to Skin Colors
⑤ Genetics Reveals the Biological Concept of Race is Valid

175

밑줄 친 (a)~(e) 중에서 문맥상 낱말의 쓰임이 적절하지 <u>않은</u> 것은?

① (a)   ② (b)   ③ (c)
④ (d)   ⑤ (e)

176

다음 글의 주제로 가장 적절한 것은?

Postindustrial society has a socially liberating effect. The service-based economy tends to reverse the disciplined, standardized ways in which industrial society organizes people's daily activities. In the industrial age, the mass-production system subjected the labor force to rigid centralized control, and workers were embedded in closely knit groups with strong conformity pressures. By contrast, post-industrialization destandardizes economic activities and social life. The flexible organization of the service-based economy and the autonomy it gives workers radiate into all domains of life: human interaction is increasingly freed from the bonding ties of closely knit groups, enabling people to make and break social ties readily. The welfare state supports this individualization trend. Formerly, children's survival largely depended on whether their parents provided for them, and children took care of their parents when they reached old age. Although the role of the family is still important, the life-or-death nature of this relationship has been eroded by the welfare state.

① necessity to maintain social ties despite societal changes
② benefits and limitations of the welfare state for individuals
③ reasons for economic instability in a post-industrial society
④ various solutions to the problems of the mass-production system
⑤ impact of post-industrial society on economic and social structures

177

다음 글의 밑줄 친 부분 중, 어법상 틀린 것은?

When a high-pressure fine weather spell subsides and a low-pressure weather system sits threateningly on the doorstep, the air humidity level gradually rises. And many plants don't like this because the coming rain plays havoc with their offspring. Many species send their seeds off on their way, ① bearing on small fluffy hairs, which are carried away by even the gentlest breeze. But when they're wet, these little hairs are effectively grounded. The opportunity to conquer new territories ② is lost. The same applies to the pollen in fresh flowers: if ③ knocked to the ground by rain, it can't be carried away by bees and used for fertilization. When the air gets more humid, suggesting rain is on the way, certain flowers react with a precautionary measure, closing their petals protectively over their interior. One example is the silver thistle, ④ whose large flowers are particularly decorative and the way it folds up is no less striking. It's not for nothing ⑤ that their common name in German is "weather thistles."

*havoc 큰 피해 **thistle 엉겅퀴

178

다음 글의 밑줄 친 부분 중, 문맥상 낱말의 쓰임이 적절하지 <u>않은</u> 것은?

The chemistry of individual plants, fungi and insects in the garden cannot be considered in isolation. The chemistry of a plant is the summation of its intrinsic properties and the consequences of its ①interaction with its environment. A plant will produce a number of natural products in response to environmental challenges. A plant is essentially ②stationary. When attacked it cannot flee but it must fight. The formation of some natural products is elicited as a response to microbial or herbivore attack. These natural products can have a defensive role and may be ③toxic to the predator. The production of insect anti-feedants in leaves can be seasonal. Their presence in leaves prior to flowering can ④protect the plant against predators early in the season. After flowering and later in the year, the anti-feedants may not be present and the leaves are damaged prior to leaf fall and their decay. The damaged tissue ⑤blocks a route of entry for micro-organisms involved in autumnal decay.

*anti-feedant 섭식 저해 물질(해충이 식물의 잎·줄기를 먹는 것을 방해하는 물질)

179

다음 빈칸에 들어갈 말로 가장 적절한 것은?

Suppose that you work for an organization that sells many varieties of one product. Although it may seem against your intuition at first, it may be worth _____ provided by your business in order to drum up maximum interest in your offerings. There are a number of major manufacturers of a variety of consumer products that in recent years have been reviewing their product lines and cutting out redundant items, sometimes in response to a modest rebellion by clients against the excessive choices they were offered. Clients who are uncertain about what they want are being driven to competitors by excessive choices. Simply put, fewer choices can increase sales. Of course, there could be additional benefits of offering less, such as more storage space, reduced spending on raw materials, and a reduction in the marketing and point-of-sale materials needed to support a smaller portfolio. A worthwhile exercise would be to review the extent of your product range and ask yourself the question: Where we have customers who may not be clear about their requirements, might the number of choices we offer be causing them to seek alternatives elsewhere?

*point-of-sale 매장의

① expanding the product line
② streamlining the range of options
③ specifying information about each option
④ reducing the number of marketing routes
⑤ canceling the strategy of product sampling

180

다음 빈칸에 들어갈 말로 가장 적절한 것은?

In 1999, two psychologists, Dan Kindlon and Michael Thompson, coauthored a book entitled *Raising Cain*. The authors argue that America, as a society, has so mishandled the emotional lives of boys that it has produced many distant and troubled men. They suggest that fathers and mothers, male and female teachers alike, all unconsciously _____. As Kindlon and Thompson put it, we want our boys to be "tough" and "strong" based on images of manliness we absorb from our culture. So when a child is hurting, when he's sad, angry, frustrated, disappointed, or frightened, we don't allow him to learn about what he's feeling. We push him back inside himself with comments like "Just tough it out" or "You need to be strong." The authors contend that we don't teach boys "emotional literacy," the ability to recognize, interpret, and comprehend emotional experiences. As a result, boys not only lack the ability to express their own feelings, they also fail to recognize emotions in others.

① urge boys to challenge gender stereotypes and roles
② conspire to limit the emotional development of boys
③ try to control the aggression of boys by emotional intervention
④ place more emphasis on intellectual rather than emotional development
⑤ press boys to express their emotions through actions rather than words

181

주어진 글 다음에 이어질 글의 순서로 가장 적절한 것은?

The idea of sacrificing present joy for the sake of greater joy in the future would be foreign, difficult, even incomprehensible to most animals. A dramatic demonstration of this point emerged from a study with chimpanzees.

(A) Yet, despite repeated trials, they never learned to store food for later. Even the short span of 24 hours was apparently beyond their cognitive capacity for adjusting their behavior. In contrast, humans routinely acquire and store food for days, or even weeks and months.

(B) A sensible response would have been to keep some of the available food for later, especially for the hungry hours the next morning, but the animals never learned to do this. They would rejoice over the food when it came. They would eat their fill, and then they would ignore the rest, sometimes even engaging in food fights in which they would throw the unwanted leftover food at each other.

(C) They were fed only once a day, always at the same time, and they were allowed to have all the food they wanted. Like humans and many other animals, chimps prefer to eat multiple times during the day, so they were always very hungry in the last couple hours before their next scheduled feeding.

① (A) − (C) − (B)
② (B) − (A) − (C)
③ (B) − (C) − (A)
④ (C) − (A) − (B)
⑤ (C) − (B) − (A)

182

글의 흐름으로 보아, 주어진 문장이 들어가기에 가장 적절한 곳은?

> Efforts, however, are now being made to develop alternative energy sources to replace fossil fuels, as they pollute the environment and are nonrenewable.

Humans utilize supplemental energy, which is derived from biological materials such as firewood, oil, and gas.(①) For most of human history, the energy derived from plants and animals has been used by people to accomplish various tasks. (②) In the United States in the 1850s, about 91 percent of the energy used came from burning wood and other biological materials. (③) At the beginning of the 21st century, about 81 percent of the supplemental energy used to power the machinery Americans needed came from fossil fuels such as gas, coal, and oil. (④) This demand for fossil fuel energy has also been aided in certain sectors by the federal government giving out fuel subsidies for such items as the gasoline farmers need for farm equipment. (⑤) Some are very pessimistic about our ability to find an appropriate alternative and predict the demise of industrialized culture as a result, but others believe the current progress in solar and wind power makes this fate avoidable.

*demise 종말

183

다음 글의 내용을 한 문장으로 요약하고자 한다. 빈칸 (A), (B)에 들어갈 말로 가장 적절한 것은?

An example of how the context in which a question is asked can affect survey results is provided by research on Americans' "interest in public affairs." When survey respondents were asked about "how much you follow what's going on in government and public affairs," 18% more said they followed it "most of the time" when this question was asked as the first question in the survey than when it was asked after questions on whether the person remembered anything special that their U.S. representative had done for their district and how their congressman/congresswoman had voted on any legislative bills. Because most people did not remember anything that their representatives had done for their district or how they had voted, they said "don't know" to these items. When they were then asked how often they followed government and public affairs, they were less likely to say "most of the time." The "hard knowledge" questions had provided a different context for what the interviewer meant by "following government and public affairs."

↓

> The ___(A)___ of questions in a survey can have a significant effect on its results as ___(B)___ questions may influence how the subject responds to any other questions.

	(A)		(B)
①	order	………	subsequent
②	number	………	open-ended
③	validity	………	pointed
④	order	………	preceding
⑤	number	………	exploratory

184

다음 글의 밑줄 친 부분 중, 어법상 틀린 것은?

Most classic theories and research on human development are based on Western samples, and developmental researchers once believed that the processes of human development ①were universal. More recent observations suggest that development varies dramatically with context. For example, ②consider milestones, such as the average age that infants begin to walk. In Uganda, infants begin to walk at about 10 months of age, in France at about 15 months, and in the United States at about 12 months. These differences are influenced by parenting practices that vary by culture. African parents tend to handle infants in ways ③that stimulate walking, by playing games that allow infants to practice jumping and walking skills. The cultural context in which individuals live influences the timing and expression of many aspects of development, even physical developments long ④thought to be influenced only by biological maturation. Some scientists argue that applying principles of development derived from Western samples to children of other cultures ⑤to be unscientific and even unethical because it may yield misleading conclusions about children's capacities.

185

다음 빈칸에 들어갈 말로 가장 적절한 것은?

For people who are engaged in negotiations, concessions are often the focus of reciprocation. After receiving a concession, most people feel obligated to make a concession in return. A compliance tactic designed to engage this felt obligation is called the reciprocal concessions or door-in-the-face technique. Rather than starting with a small request and then advancing to the desired favor, someone using the door-in-the-face procedure goes in the opposite direction. Here, the requester begins with a large request that, if rejected, temporarily places him or her in the unique position of being significantly more likely to hear "yes" on making a subsequent, but smaller request. The reciprocal concessions tactic is a unique influence strategy because it actually _____. By retreating from a large first request to a smaller second one, the requester makes a concession to the target, who (through the rule for reciprocity) feels obligated to provide a return.

① causes a deadlock in negotiations
② clouds the other party's judgment
③ goes beyond the concept of reciprocity
④ empowers the requester through rejection
⑤ forces the requester to compromise on his goal

186

다음 빈칸에 들어갈 말로 가장 적절한 것은?

Animals cannot live without knowing what is of immediate use to them and what is needed for their survival: where to find food, how to avoid predators, where to find mates, etc. However, the human species differs from other animals because we _____ _____. We look around us and we wonder. We wonder aimlessly and passively about our surroundings and about what we observe both near and far, but we want to understand it all. Indeed, we fear the unknown. This sense of wonder and the urgent desire for understanding not only makes us human, but is also one of the foundation stones of civilization. The satisfaction of our curiosity becomes easier and more proficient when the search for answers and their retention in a generally accessible memory is pursued in an organized fashion, helping to transform primitive groups into the grand historical confederations we call civilizations, such as the Chinese, the Babylonian, the Egyptian, the Mayan, the Indian, the ancient Greek, the contemporary Western civilization, and perhaps others that have left no record.

*confederation 연합, 연맹

① pursue collective security that is beneficial to evolution
② symbolize almost anything that is easily stored in our memory
③ thirst for knowledge that reaches far beyond our personal needs
④ avoid unnecessary risks that may put the whole species in danger
⑤ are subject to competition that results in the survival of the fittest

187

주어진 글 다음에 이어질 글의 순서로 가장 적절한 것은?

Easterners tend to have a *holistic* perspective on the world. They see objects (including people) in their contexts, they're inclined to attribute behavior to situational factors, and they attend closely to relationships between people and between objects.

(A) But the holistic perspective saves Easterners from some serious errors in understanding why other people behave as they do. Moreover, the reluctance to make dispositional attributions contributes to Eastern belief in the capacity of people to change.

(B) Westerners have a more analytic perspective. They attend to the object, notice its attributes, categorize the object on the basis of those attributes, and think about the object in terms of the rules that they assume apply to objects of that particular category.

(C) Both perspectives have their place. I have no doubt that the analytic perspective has played a role in Western dominance in science. And in fact, the Greeks invented science at a time when Chinese civilization, though making great progress in mathematics and many other fields, had no real tradition of science in the modern sense.

*holistic 전체적인 **dispositional 성향의, 기질의

① (A) − (C) − (B)
② (B) − (A) − (C)
③ (B) − (C) − (A)
④ (C) − (A) − (B)
⑤ (C) − (B) − (A)

188

글의 흐름으로 보아, 주어진 문장이 들어가기에 가장 적절한 곳은?

> With such help a particular organic plot can match non-organic yields, but only by using extra land elsewhere to grow those plants and feed the cattle, effectively doubling the area under the plough.

Organic farming is low-yield, whether you like it or not. The reason for this is simple chemistry. (①) Since organic farming eschews all synthetic fertilizer, it exhausts the mineral nutrients in the soil—especially phosphorus and potassium, but eventually also sulphur, calcium and manganese. (②) It gets round this problem by adding crushed rock and squashed fish to the soil, which have to be mined or netted. (③) Its main problem, though, is nitrogen deficiency, which it can reverse by growing legumes (clover, alfalfa or beans), which fix nitrogen from the air, and either ploughing them into the soil or feeding them to cattle whose manure is then ploughed into the soil. (④) Conventional farming, by contrast, gets its nitrogen from factories, which fix it from the air. (⑤) Given this, should the world decide to go organic—that is, should farming get its nitrogen from plants and fish rather than direct from the air using factories and fossil fuels—and leave many of the nine billions starved and all rainforests cut down?

*eschew 피하다   **legume 콩과의 식물

189

다음 글의 내용을 한 문장으로 요약하고자 한다. 빈칸 (A), (B)에 들어갈 말로 가장 적절한 것은?

If meanings are attached to pieces of music, they are usually of a highly individual nature, perhaps relating to memories of past times when the same music was heard—the 'they're playing our tune, darling' syndrome. As Ian Cross has recently stated, 'one and the same piece of music can bear quite different meanings for the performer and listener, or for two different listeners; it may even bear multiple disparate meanings for a single listener or participant at a particular time.' This is most evidently the case with religious music; I am an atheist, so when I listen to the great eighteenth-century choral works that were written to glorify God, such as Handel's *Messiah* or Bach's *St Matthew Passion*, they 'mean' something quite different to me than they would to someone of religious faith. As John Blacking has explained, the music of Handel and Bach cannot be fully understood without reference to the eighteenth-century view of the world—just as northern Indian music cannot be fully understood outside the context of Hindu culture.

*atheist 무신론자

↓

> The meaning of a piece of music can be ____(A)____ to listeners because the listener's ____(B)____ plays a crucial role in the appreciation of the music.

	(A)		(B)
①	distinctive	········	background
②	distinctive	········	personality
③	intricate	········	intent
④	universal	········	culture
⑤	universal	········	education

190~191 다음 글을 읽고, 물음에 답하시오.

Entertainment has almost always been described as an activity where there is rather little challenge, or only as much challenge as the media user can still handle (a)successfully. This, of course, would be the optimal challenge, the level that allows people to feel the greatest sense of competence. The feeling of competence is therefore almost ensured, and it can be created without much effort. Where else can somebody feel competent so often, so easily, and so profoundly? Video games, which are among the most appealing facilitators of entertainment these days, particularly among younger males, provide an excellent example of this. The level of complexity, difficulty, and challenge of a given game varies and is (b)dependent on the settings that are either chosen by the player or automatically set by the game. The game itself may choose an optimal difficulty level based on the amount of skill or expertise a player has demonstrated previously. In other words, a video game (c)forbids the player to be challenged at a level he or she can master without becoming bored or overwhelmed. The importance of competition and challenge for a video game player's entertainment experience is often mentioned, which seems to (d)support the notion that individuals often seek to experience competence in entertainment. As in many examples of players' entertainment experiences, we can consider how carefully they prepare for a situation in which they will be able to avoid boredom and find some challenge while making sure that this situation will not overwhelm them or give them a sense of being (e)incompetent.

190

윗글의 제목으로 가장 적절한 것은?

① Entertainment as a Self-Regulatory Resource
② The Value of Entertainment: A Stress Reliever
③ Entertainment Brings Out Feeling of Competence
④ Gamer Psychology: What Makes Games Engaging
⑤ Too Much Competition in Games: A Blow to Confidence

191

밑줄 친 (a)~(e) 중에서 문맥상 낱말의 쓰임이 적절하지 <u>않은</u> 것은?

① (a)　　② (b)　　③ (c)
④ (d)　　⑤ (e)

192

다음 글의 주제로 가장 적절한 것은?

We all have implicit frames of reference—with luck, less extreme—that produce habitual thinking and behavior. Our experiences and actions always *seem* to be rooted in conscious thought, and we can find it difficult to accept that there are hidden forces at work behind the scenes. But though those forces may be invisible, they still exert a powerful pull. In the past there was a lot of speculation about the unconscious mind, but the brain was like a black box, its workings inaccessible to our understanding. The current revolution in thinking about the unconscious came about because, with modern instruments, we can watch as different structures and substructures in the brain generate feelings and emotions. We can measure the electrical output of individual neurons and map the neural activity that forms a person's thoughts. Today scientists can go beyond talking to us and guessing how our experiences affected us; today they can actually pinpoint the brain alterations that result from traumatic early experiences and understand how such experiences cause physical changes in stress-sensitive brain regions.

① the insights into the unconscious mind with modern technology
② the impact of traumatic early experiences on changes in the brain
③ the intricate operation of brain generating feelings and emotions
④ the frame of reference that influences our thinking and behavior
⑤ the difficulty of distinguishing consciousness from unconsciousness

193

다음 글의 밑줄 친 부분 중, 어법상 틀린 것은?

It was not until the nineteenth century that hand washing became standard practice in medical settings. Hungarian physician Ignaz Semmelweis realized while working on the maternity ward of Vienna Hospital ①that women whose babies were delivered by doctors had a significantly higher likelihood of dying of "childbed fever" than did women whose babies had been delivered by midwives. Semmelweis instituted an aggressive policy of hand washing on his maternity ward with the hypothesis ②which the poor outcomes of the women attended by doctors were somehow related to the autopsies that doctors performed alongside their obstetric work. This dramatically reduced rates of maternal death from "childbed fever." Despite this, his forceful campaign ③to convert others to his new techniques bore little fruit. ④Pained by what he saw as needless deaths of thousands of women, he became increasingly disturbed and eventually died in a mental hospital. Semmelweis' theories were not widely accepted until after his death, when Louis Pasteur's work with microorganisms ⑤provided an understandable mechanism through which Semmelweis' tactics could have operated.

*midwife 조산사, 산파 **autopsy 검시
***obstetric work 분만을 돕는 (의사의) 일

194

다음 글의 밑줄 친 부분 중, 문맥상 낱말의 쓰임이 적절하지 <u>않은</u> 것은?

Anthony Giddens refers to the paradox of democracy which is that democracy is spreading throughout the world, yet at the same time people in mature democracies are becoming increasingly ① <u>disillusioned</u> with democratic processes. This in turn has meant that fewer people are turning out to vote, and trust in politicians is low. Giddens suggests that the ② <u>lack</u> of interest in democracy is due, in part, to the impact of globalization. Democracy at the level of the nation-state has a ③ <u>limited</u> impact on global changes such as increased ecological risks, globalization of the economy, and technological change. Individuals therefore feel that little difference can be made by participating in national politics. In contrast, public distrust in traditional democratic processes has led to an ④ <u>increase</u> in groups involved in "single-issue" politics. Moreover, the globalization process is affecting nation-states in such a way that they are increasingly unable to make unilateral decisions, which in turn ⑤ <u>challenges</u> the view that individuals have little control over decisions made by national governments.

*unilateral 일방적인

195

다음 빈칸에 들어갈 말로 가장 적절한 것은?

Southwest Airlines, a company renowned for its customer focus, does not, as a matter of policy, believe the customer is always right. Southwest will not tolerate customers who abuse their staff. They would rather those customers fly on a different airline. It's a subtle irony that one of the best customer service companies in the country _____. The trust between the management and the employees, not dogma, is what produces the great customer service. It is a prerequisite, then, for someone to trust the culture in which they work to share the values and beliefs of that culture. Without it, that employee, for example, is simply a bad fit and likely to work only for self-gain without consideration for the greater good. But if those inside the organization are a good fit, the opportunity to "go the extra mile," to explore, to invest, to innovate, to advance and, more importantly, to do so again and again and again, increases dramatically. Only with mutual trust can an organization become great.

*dogma 신조

① does not care about its customers
② values customer trust more than its profits
③ focuses on its employees before its customers
④ relies solely on its employees for customer service
⑤ prioritizes organizational values over personal values

196

다음 빈칸에 들어갈 말로 가장 적절한 것은?

If I'm a stock clerk and you want me to use my knowledge for the good of the company, you need to help me understand exactly what that means. For example, unless I know we're having trouble financially, I may not bother redesigning the inventory controls so that they're cheaper and simpler. Of course, I know, based on the exhortations of all the higher-ups, that I'm always supposed to improve my job, but let's face it, I've got a life outside stock clerking. I'm only going to do it if there is a compelling reason to pay attention. Knowledge and innovation cannot be ordered but only invited. The challenge for all managers is to make the invitation so irresistible that all will respond. Some part of that compelling invitation is ensuring that workers know _____. This often entails releasing information that has hitherto been largely management's province (e.g., financial and other confidential information) and helping people to understand how it relates to their jobs.

*exhortation (간곡한) 권고

① what is happening in the company
② what areas of expertise are required of them
③ what the financial rewards to be obtained are
④ what is an acceptable risk in project management
⑤ how important critical thinking is to the company's future

197

주어진 글 다음에 이어질 글의 순서로 가장 적절한 것은?

Try to keep the pace of your meals slow and relaxed. It takes about twenty minutes for your stomach to communicate the "I'm full" message to your brain for processing.

(A) Because they require more chewing, they take longer to eat than low-fiber foods. When your kids slow down the pace, they'll be able to focus more fully on the foods that they're eating. This higher level of awareness will help them eat less at each meal.

(B) Before their brains get the signal that their stomachs are full, they'll probably be reaching for seconds. If your kids need help slowing down while they're eating, serve plenty of fiber-rich foods.

(C) It takes another moment or two for your brain to send a message to your hand that you've had enough to eat, and it's time to put the fork down. If you have a family of fast eaters who like to eat the entire meal in five minutes flat, they'll probably end up eating more than their bodies need.

① (A) – (C) – (B)
② (B) – (A) – (C)
③ (B) – (C) – (A)
④ (C) – (A) – (B)
⑤ (C) – (B) – (A)

198

글의 흐름으로 보아, 주어진 문장이 들어가기에 가장 적절한 곳은?

> Scientists work to remove the narrative, to boil it away, leaving behind only the raw facts.

The people who came before you invented science because your natural way of understanding and explaining what you experience is terrible. When you have zero evidence, every assumption is basically equal. (①) You prefer to see causes rather than effects, signals in the noise, patterns in the randomness. (②) You prefer easy-to-understand stories, and thus turn everything in life into a narrative so that complicated problems become easy. (③) Those data sit there naked and exposed so they can be reflected upon and rearranged by each new visitor. (④) Scientists and laypeople will conjure up new stories using the data, and they will argue, but the data will not budge. (⑤) They may not even make sense for a hundred years or more, but thanks to the scientific method, the stories, full of biases and fallacies, will crash against the facts and recede into history.

*budge 조금 움직이다

199

다음 글의 내용을 한 문장으로 요약하고자 한다. 빈칸 (A), (B)에 들어갈 말로 가장 적절한 것은?

Excavations during 2003 at the Liang Bang rock-shelter on Flores Island in Indonesia produced the remains of seven individuals who had been no more than one metre high, even though they were fully grown adults. These were designated as a new species, *Homo floresiensis*. One interpretation of these finds is that a small population of *Homo erectus* made a short water-crossing to Flores Island, around 800,000 years ago in light of the date of stone artefacts found on the island. That population became isolated and evolved into a dwarf form of *Homo*. This is a process known to happen to any large terrestrial mammal when isolated on small islands, especially if predators are absent. Hence remains of dwarf elephants, hippos, deer, and mammoths have been found on islands around the world. If correct, then this is the only discovery of dwarf humans, and shows us just how physiologically diverse our genus can be. Perhaps just as remarkable as their size is the young geological age of the remains. The fossils range in age from 74,000 to 18,000 years, the latter of which falls well within the range of modern humans elsewhere in the Old and quite possibly New World.

*rock-shelter 선사 시대 주거지 **artefact 문화 유물

↓

> It is speculated that *Homo floresiensis*, which demonstrates a new range of biological diversity in the genus *Homo*, may have evolved its tiny physique as a result of long-term geographical ___(A)___, and this species ___(B)___ with modern humans.

	(A)		(B)
①	isolation	....	resembled
②	transformation	....	conflicted
③	expansion	....	interacted
④	isolation	....	coexisted
⑤	transformation	....	associated

200

밑줄 친 had brains in his legs가 다음 글에서 의미하는 바로 가장 적절한 것은?

When asked to explain the idea that led to 'total football,' a strategy that revolutionized soccer, Dutch coach Rinus Michels claimed that: 'In starting, you have no exact idea about the aims after which you are going to strive.' In a sense, he went on to explain, you simply start by trying a few things, and if you are observant and are open to good influences and can connect ideas to one another as things unfold, then a good strategy starts to become clear. There has never been a better articulation of this idea than Alfred Polgar's description of the famous Austrian footballer Matthias Sindelar: 'In a way he had brains in his legs ... and many remarkable and unexpected things occurred to them while they were running.' While we may lack this level of artistry, many of the best strategic ideas we have been a part of have occurred only as a group's emergent thoughts were whiteboarding.

① played the game according to the coach's instructions
② had the physical conditioning to run throughout the game
③ found an appropriate strategy while carrying out some trials
④ exercised his brain as well as his body by learning something new
⑤ was in control of his body and mind from the very start of the game

201

다음 글의 밑줄 친 부분 중, 어법상 틀린 것은?

Superstars and Supermen don't chase money. Money is the way score is kept in capitalism and ①that makes it a result of doing well, not a goal that should be pursued. Trying too hard to get money will prove counterproductive to getting it. What happens is you focus on the goal rather than the fundamentals that are critical to obtaining the goal. In both arenas the chase is far more tempting than the catch. Sounds weird but true! Focusing on the target ②leading to all kinds of bad decisions and self-serving moves. People become too enamored with goals and begin chasing instant gratification and the quick win. Really big wins take time and nurturing ③whether they are finding a soulmate or a successful profession. Those into quick hits and instant success are the ones always ④attributing super success to luck. The trek to fame and fortune ⑤is long and arduous — about twenty years in most cases. Get-rich-quick schemes are destined for failure so beware getting caught up in that trap.

*gratification 만족 **arduous 고된, 힘든

202

다음 빈칸에 들어갈 말로 가장 적절한 것은?

Indeed, people usually like the kind of paintings they have grown up with. For example, students from Cornell University preferred those Impressionist paintings that were most frequently depicted in books in the Cornell University Library. Frequency with which depictions of paintings appeared was taken as a substitute for the frequency with which students had seen the painting in their lifetime. The same preference for more frequent paintings was found in older adults, but not in children, who obviously have not seen as many paintings as students or older adults. In a similar vein, people like the kind of music they grew up with. Sociologist Pierre Bourdieu observed that different social classes differ in their musical tastes because they grow up with different kinds of music in their homes. What people like and find beautiful depends on _____.

① what helps them to grow mentally
② what they have encountered before
③ what they have been educated about
④ what left a strong impression on them
⑤ what is considered to be artistically worthwhile

203

다음 빈칸에 들어갈 말로 가장 적절한 것은?

Will a global language eliminate the motivation for adults to learn other languages? Clear signs of linguistic complacency, common observation suggests, are already present in the typical British or American tourist who travels the world assuming that everyone speaks English, and that it is somehow the fault of the local people if they do not. But these days, there are signs of growing awareness, within English-speaking communities, of the need to break away from the traditional monolingual bias. In economically hard times, success in boosting exports and attracting foreign investment can depend on subtle factors, and sensitivity to the language spoken by a country's potential foreign partners is known to be particularly influential. At least at the levels of business and industry, many firms have begun to make fresh efforts in this direction. But at ordinary tourists' level, too, there are signs of a growing respect for other cultures, and a greater readiness to engage in language learning. Language attitudes are changing all the time, and more and more are discovering, to their great delight, that they are not at all bad at _____.

*complacency 안주, 자기만족

① picking up a foreign language
② eliminating a bias against bilingual minorities
③ enhancing the presence of English as a global language
④ traveling with the aid of a device that has translation software
⑤ attracting foreign investors and fostering economic growth

204

주어진 글 다음에 이어질 글의 순서로 가장 적절한 것은?

All of the media messages we view, whether we like them or not, are constitutive of our reality. They help us to see and feel the world around us. Sociologists have long recognised that the news media not only reflects social opinion but can construct it too.

(A) However, there is never a direct correlation between authorial or editorial intention and reception. Emotional responses are individual, but, simultaneously, individual responses are shaped by shared cultural and social contexts.

(B) As a result, messages can sometimes tap into a shared concern, promoting a shared sense of feeling and, thanks to social media, such messages can be in turn 'shared,' becoming viral.

(C) The same goes for emotions: media can indicate to audiences what should be important to them as an emotional community, and can also suggest how they should respond emotionally to situations or stimuli. From instilling fear to inspiring hope, the media produces emotional responses.

① (A) − (C) − (B) ② (B) − (A) − (C)
③ (B) − (C) − (A) ④ (C) − (A) − (B)
⑤ (C) − (B) − (A)

205

글의 흐름으로 보아, 주어진 문장이 들어가기에 가장 적절한 곳은?

This is accomplished through the thoroughness of testing, the credibility of the organization, compliance with industry standards, and the case histories of other users, etc.

To succeed in the long run, a brand must offer added values over and above the basic product characteristics. (①) In the services sector, when all other factors are equal, this could be as simple as being addressed by name when getting foreign exchange at a bank. (②) In the business-to-business market, it could be conveyed by the astute sales engineer presenting the brand as a no-risk purchase. (③) It is most important to realise that the added values must be relevant to the customer and not just to the manufacturer or distributor. (④) Car manufacturers who announced that their brands had the added value of electronic circuits emitting 'computer speak' when seat belts were not worn didn't take long to discover that this so-called benefit was intensely disliked by customers. (⑤) A hotel promoting a quality service will win loyal customers by offering a special late night food menu rather than simply placing promotional literature around guest rooms.

*astute 빈틈없는

206~207 다음 글을 읽고, 물음에 답하시오.

Studies of birds provide a clear answer to the nature/nurture issue concerning verbal and nonverbal behavior. The European male robin attacks strange robins that enter his territory during the breeding
5 season. Research using stuffed models has shown that a red breast alone triggers this attack mechanism. The female robin who shares the nest, however, also has a red breast and is not attacked. Thus, this aggressive behavior, which is believed to be innate, is (a) modified
10 by certain conditions or situations in the environment. As another example, some birds (b) instinctively sing a song common to their own species without ever having heard another bird sing the song. These birds may, on hearing the songs of their particular group, develop a
15 variation on the melody that reflects a local dialect. It has also been noted that without exposure to mature songs, the young bird's song remains (c) perfect. And even when a bird is born with its basic song, it may have to learn to whom the call should be addressed,
20 and under what circumstances, and how to recognize signals from other birds. Many of the innate components of human behavior can be altered (d) similarly. It is like our human predisposition for, or capacity to learn, verbal language. Although we are born with the
25 capacity to learn language, it is not learned without (e) cultural training. Children isolated from human contact do not develop linguistic competence. Some nonverbal signals probably depend primarily on inherited neurological programs; others probably
30 depend primarily on environmental learning; and, of course, many behaviors are influenced by both.

*predisposition 성향, 경향

206

윗글의 제목으로 가장 적절한 것은?

① Human Language Evolved from Birdsong
② Understanding the Biological Roots of Behavior
③ Biology and Environment Jointly Shape Behavior
④ Is Communication Only a Human Characteristic?
⑤ Vocal Learning Differences Between Birds and Humans

207

밑줄 친 (a)~(e) 중에서 문맥상 낱말의 쓰임이 적절하지 <u>않은</u> 것은?

① (a) ② (b) ③ (c)
④ (d) ⑤ (e)

208

다음 글의 주제로 가장 적절한 것은?

Some countries have the phrase in their constitutions that once elected to the parliament only the member's own conscience should guide his or her voting. This is probably fair but removes the representative function.
5 The members of parliament no longer need to promote the matters their constituency elected them for. The situation is worse if the parliament is based on political parties, as most parties require their delegates to vote as the party leader or prime minister dictates,
10 independent of any private 'conscience'. In fact, this is connected with the introduction of cabinet responsibility, meaning that a government should always be backed by a majority in parliament. This requirement was added to the constitution of several countries, after
15 several cases of so-called democratic governments ruling by 'provisional laws' which were not supported by parliament. In any case, all these issues point in the direction of criticizing representative democracy for having weakened or eliminated the influence of citizens
20 on government.

*constituency 유권자 **delegate 대리자 ***provisional 임시의, 잠정적인

① the need for representatives to act on their conscience
② the significant role of election in representative democracy
③ reasons why a government should be supported by parliament
④ problems created by not allowing members to vote on their conscience
⑤ factors causing representative democracy to lose its representativeness

209

다음 글의 밑줄 친 부분 중, 어법상 틀린 것은?

Human beings exist in and depend on a world of living organisms. The oxygen in the air we breathe is produced by photosynthesis ①conducted by countless billions of individual organisms. The food that fuels our bodies comes from the tissues of other living 5 organism. The fuels ②that drive our cars and power our electric plants are, for the most part, various forms of carbon molecules produced by living organisms — mostly millions of years ago. Inside and out, our bodies are covered in complex communities of living unicellular 10 organisms, most of ③them help us maintain our health. There are also harmful species that invade our bodies and can cause mild to serious diseases, or even death. These interactions with other species ④are not limited to humans. Ecosystem function depends on 15 thousands of complex interactions among the millions of species that inhabit Earth. In other words, ⑤understanding biological principles is essential to our lives and for maintaining the functioning of Earth as we know it and depend on it. 20

210

다음 글의 밑줄 친 부분 중, 문맥상 낱말의 쓰임이 적절하지 <u>않은</u> 것은?

Capitalism is commonly defined as a market-based social and economic system in which individuals are free to own private property and the means of production in order to ① <u>maximize</u> profit by employing the labor of others. Resource allocation is determined via the price system. In other words, all commodities, including labor, find their natural price through the ② <u>relative</u> strength of supply and demand in the market. Scarce resources, which at any particular time could be skilled labor, gold, or, indeed, any commodity, command high prices. Moreover, such high prices ③ <u>discourage</u> investment in this area and a resulting greater supply of this particular good to meet the demand. Thus capitalism is ④ <u>expansive</u> and constantly produces greater amounts and improved quality of goods. For this reason, capitalism has brought greater ⑤ <u>wealth</u> to human society than was ever imaginable in precapitalist society.

211

다음 빈칸에 들어갈 말로 가장 적절한 것은?

We descend from a long line of group-living primates with a high degree of interdependence. _____ became clear when primatologists counted long-tailed macaques on different islands in the Indonesian archipelago. Some islands have cats (such as tigers and clouded leopards), whereas others don't. The same monkeys were found traveling in large groups on islands with cats, but in small groups on islands without. Predation thus forces individuals together. Generally, the more vulnerable a species is, the larger its aggregations. Ground-dwelling monkeys, like baboons, travel in larger groups than tree dwellers, which enjoy better escape opportunities. And chimpanzees, which because of their size have little to fear in the daytime, typically forage alone or in small groups.

*primatologist 영장류 동물학자

① How group size influences collective action
② How the need for security shapes social life
③ Why the survival of the fittest is a scientific truth
④ That a complex hierarchy is related to intelligence
⑤ How hunting methods affect the safety of the pack

212

다음 빈칸에 들어갈 말로 가장 적절한 것은?

If you want a creative organization, inaction is the worst kind of failure—and the only kind that deserves to be punished. From multiple studies, Researcher Dean Keith Simonton provides strong evidence of what leads to creativity. Renowned geniuses like Picasso, da Vinci, and physicist Richard Feynman didn't succeed at a higher rate than their peers. They simply produced more, which meant that they had far more successes and failures than their unheralded colleagues. In every occupation Simonton studied, from composers, artists, and poets to inventors and scientists, the story is the same: Creativity _____. These findings mean that measuring whether people are doing something—or nothing—is one of the ways to assess the performance of people who do creative work. Companies should demote, transfer, and even fire those who spend day after day talking about and planning what they are going to do but never do anything.

*unheralded 알려지지 않은 **demote 강등시키다

① is inspired by the art of doing nothing
② is a variable that is difficult to measure
③ grows out of a social and cultural matrix
④ results from active unconscious processes
⑤ is a function of the quantity of work produced

213

주어진 글 다음에 이어질 글의 순서로 가장 적절한 것은?

Suppose that you're driving to work one day and see an accident victim sitting on the side of the road, clearly in shock and needing medical assistance. Because you know first aid and are in no great hurry to get to your destination, you could easily stop and assist the person.

(A) Moral theorists would agree, however, that if you sped away without rendering aid or even calling for help, your action might be perfectly legal but would be morally suspect. Regardless of the law, such conduct would almost certainly be wrong.

(B) Legally speaking, though, you are not obligated to stop and render aid. Under common law, the prudent thing would be to drive on, because by stopping you would bind yourself to use reasonable care and thus incur legal liability if you fail to do so and the victim thereby suffers injury.

(C) Many states have enacted so-called Good Samaritan laws to provide immunity from damages to those rendering aid (except for gross negligence or serious misconduct). But in most states the law does not oblige people to give such aid or even to call an ambulance.

*gross negligence 중과실

① (A) – (C) – (B)   ② (B) – (A) – (C)
③ (B) – (C) – (A)   ④ (C) – (A) – (B)
⑤ (C) – (B) – (A)

214

글의 흐름으로 보아, 주어진 문장이 들어가기에 가장 적절한 곳은?

> This is because making mistakes is very "normal" and not "abnormal" in activities that involve a vast majority of persons from a given population.

Most efforts to reduce traffic injuries are termed "accident prevention" campaigns. (①) We should be clear that *accident prevention* is just one aspect—and not always the most rewarding one—of a much larger range of countermeasures used in effective road traffic injury control programmes. (②) It is important that all programmes also include measures of reducing injury severity if a crash does occur, and well-designed systems for emergency care, treatment and rehabilitation after the crash. (③) It is normal for professional drivers to be distracted during some periods of their long driving hours; it is normal for executives driving to work to be day-dreaming at some point in the journey; and it is normal for a teenager to take more risks than an elderly person while driving a motorcycle. (④) In short, we will never eliminate carelessness, absentmindedness, and even neglect in day-to-day activity. (⑤) However, by designing our products and environment to be more tolerant of these normal variations in human performance, we can minimize the number of resulting accidents and injuries.

*rehabilitation 재활

215

다음 글의 내용을 한 문장으로 요약하고자 한다. 빈칸 (A), (B)에 들어갈 말로 가장 적절한 것은?

A fascinating study asked the question: Do chimpanzees, orangutans, and two-year-old human children differ in how influential peers are to solving a problem? To test this, the researchers first gave all three groups a task to solve. The task was to drop a ball into a set of boxes that had three different holes. Dropping the ball into only one of the holes would release a reward—peanuts for the great apes and chocolate chips for the human children. Once the three groups figured out which hole released the food by dropping the ball themselves, they then watched similar peers drop the ball into a different hole that also released food. The three groups were then given the chance to go back to the set of boxes and to drop balls in again. The results clearly showed that only human children were likely to switch by dropping the ball into the hole their peers did. The great apes stuck with their original solution. Moreover, human children were even more likely to copy the behavior of others if the peer was present in the same room. For the great apes, the presence of a peer did not influence their behavior.

↓

> The study revealed that human children were more likely to ___(A)___ to their peers' behavior compared to great apes, which was ___(B)___ by the presence of their peers in the room.

	(A)		(B)
①	object	········	influenced
②	object	········	triggered
③	respomd	········	recognized
④	conform	········	unaffected
⑤	conform	········	reinforced

216

밑줄 친 science itself has so sadly misled us가 다음 글에서 의미하는 바로 가장 적절한 것은?

Because we are ourselves alive we are much more conscious of the processes of growth than we are of the processes involved in death and decay. This is perfectly natural and justifiable. Indeed, it is a very powerful instinct in us and a healthy one. Yet, if we are fully grown human beings, our education should have developed in our minds so much knowledge and reflection as to enable us to grasp intelligently the vast role played in the universe by the processes making up the other or more hidden side of the Wheel of Life. In this respect, however, our general education in the past has been gravely defective partly because science itself has so sadly misled us. Those branches of knowledge dealing with the vegetable and animal kingdoms — botany and zoology — have confined themselves almost entirely to the study of *living* things and have given little or no attention to what happens to these units of the universe when they die and to the way in which their waste products and remains affect the general environment on which both the plant and animal world depend.

① scientific studies have only focused on living things
② all the disciplines have been developed interdependently
③ the balance of ecosystems has been neglected until recently
④ science has been used not for conservation but for development
⑤ science has failed to find the link between humans and other living things

217

다음 글의 밑줄 친 부분 중, 어법상 틀린 것은?

Women today have a huge influence in buying decisions, can often ①be found at the helm of giant corporations and, thanks to their shrewd investments, have controlling interests in major operations throughout the world. Despite this, most businesses are still tending to treat target audiences as though they ②were all male. In a UK survey conducted a couple of years ago it was found that 91 percent of women felt that advertisers didn't understand ③them, despite the fact that a fifth of all media advertising was aimed at women rather than men. Marketing to women is a hot topic today, and businesses that assume that adding a few pink shades to their marketing materials or logo will suffice to reach their female targets ④ending up in the loser's seat quickly. In order to include women successfully in brand strategies, we need to understand the ways ⑤in which they think differently from men.

*helm 지도적 위치 **shrewd 빈틈없는

218

다음 글의 밑줄 친 부분 중, 문맥상 낱말의 쓰임이 적절하지 <u>않은</u> 것은?

Regardless of the reason, many different sociological, psychological, and biological theories acknowledge a process called *maximizing the difference* through which people attempt to ①distinguish their group from others, whether or not there is personal gain. People strongly identify with their own group and ②exaggerate positive traits, especially at the expense of the lesser-regarded others. Groups and societies create myths and rationales that justify the dominance of some groups over others. Such stories and myths ③undermine beliefs that differences are fundamental, natural, and beyond human invention or social convention. Race, ethnicity, and gender are particularly good examples of socially constructed differences, greatly ④magnified and encrusted with mythology and custom. However, whatever differences in genetic and biological endowments that exist among these groups are exceedingly ⑤small and by no means support the vast differences in social roles and treatment.

*encrust (외피로) 덮다

219

다음 빈칸에 들어갈 말로 가장 적절한 것은?

Sometimes it's not material possessions that make us envious, but other people's kids. This is most likely to happen if we regard our children as extensions of ourselves, and believe that their achievements reflect upon us. There will always be children who are better, faster, smarter, or more attractive than our children, giving us unlimited opportunities to be envious. But here again, we can choose how to look at the situation. Instead of seeing our children's inabilities, it's far better to focus on their strengths. Then when comparisons inevitably arise, we will be able to appreciate what is special about each child. In addition, we must recognize that our children's successes and failures are their own, not ours. We love our kids, and it's only natural that we rejoice when they succeed and feel pain when they don't. But we must make sure that our hopes and expectations for our kids are tailored to their personalities and strengths, not to _____.

① our ability to support their growth
② our own unfulfilled wishes for ourselves
③ their endeavors to progress step by step
④ their inability to set a goal for themselves
⑤ the continuous challenges that they will face

220

주어진 글 다음에 이어질 글의 순서로 가장 적절한 것은?

Life is beautiful and harmonious and most people share this perception. What is the cause of such beauty and order? Charles Darwin answered this hard and probably one of the most central scientific and philosophical questions.

(A) Now 150 years after this incredible revelation and countless attempts to test and even to disprove the Darwinian view, this is the most convincing and factually supported theory of evolution.

(B) Certainly those efforts were not in vain. The progress in understanding of intricate life processes was amazing and this is very much relevant to both random hereditary variation and natural selection.

(C) He came to the conclusion that there are two forces of paramount importance. One of them is random hereditary variation, which is a wild and blind force of nature. Another force is natural selection, capable of transforming this randomness into adaptations and harmony.

*revelation 시현, 나타내 보임 **hereditary 유전적인

① (A) − (C) − (B)　　② (B) − (A) − (C)
③ (B) − (C) − (A)　　④ (C) − (A) − (B)
⑤ (C) − (B) − (A)

221

글의 흐름으로 보아, 주어진 문장이 들어가기에 가장 적절한 곳은?

It is impossible to decide between these two conflicting judgments of value in a rational scientific way.

According to a certain ethical conviction, human life, the life of every human being, is the highest value. (①) Consequently it is, according to this ethical conviction, absolutely forbidden to kill a human being, even in war and even as capital punishment. (②) This is, for instance, the opinion of so-called conscientious objectors who refuse to perform military service; and of those who repudiate in principle, and in any case, the death penalty. (③) However, there is another ethical conviction, according to which the highest value is the interest and honor of the nation. (④) Consequently, everybody is, according to this opinion, morally obliged to sacrifice his own life and to kill other human beings as enemies of the nation in war if the interest or the honor of the nation requires such action, and it is justified to kill human beings as criminals in inflicting capital punishment. (⑤) It is, in the last instance, our feeling, our will, and not our reason; the emotional, and not the rational element of our consciousness which decides this conflict.

*conscientious objector 양심적 병역 거부자 **repudiate 거부하다

222~223 다음 글을 읽고, 물음에 답하시오.

When we are in a situation in which we lack trust, we use tools and methods to impose constraints on the interactions. We do not meet strangers in a dark alley, we use third parties to (a) assure major financial transactions, we go with a friend to a club, and so on. The same is true online. When we communicate with someone we do not fully trust, we invoke mechanisms to constrain the communication. We want checking, validation, witnesses (trusted third parties), and so on. We want viruses removed from incoming email, we want spam stripped out, and so on. But such constraints on behavior are not a basis for trust. Constraint is in some sense the (b) opposite of trust. Because one person trusts another, the trustee is expected to "do the right thing," even though he/she is not externally constrained to. A police state may greatly constrain what its citizens do, and this may provide a certain sort of predictability and assurance of behavior, but it does not induce trust. For real trust to develop, there must be freedom for that trust to be tested; there must be the potential for that trust to be (c) maintained. It is this risk, and the freedom that accompanies it, that is the essence of human trust. Society gives us the tools to constrain interaction as well as the means to (d) bypass them. The nature of the original Internet, which has been called "open" or "transparent," is the constraint-free context in which trusting parties interact. And it is among trusting parties, where the overhead of interaction is (e) lowest, that we most easily find innovation, novelty, and originality.

*invoke 발동[실시]하다 **overhead 간접비

222

윗글의 제목으로 가장 적절한 것은?

① Why It's Hard to Secure Real Trust Online
② Various Ways to Compensate for a Lack of Trust
③ Freedom: An Essential Element of Trust Confirmation
④ The Internet: A Space of Interaction through Real Trust
⑤ Increasingly Sophisticated and Complex Online Regulations

223

밑줄 친 (a)~(e) 중에서 문맥상 낱말의 쓰임이 적절하지 <u>않은</u> 것은?

① (a)　　② (b)　　③ (c)
④ (d)　　⑤ (e)

3점 공략 모의고사 9회

01	pervade	v	
02	implement	v	
03	commitment	n	
04	savage	n	
05	empirical	a	
06	impartial	a	
07	환상	n	
08	mind-set	n	
09	시간의	a	
10	discern	v	
11	investigate	v	
12	부족의	a	
13	discourse	n	
14	neutral	a	
15	assimilate	v	
16	fluctuation	n	
17	undermine	v	
18	awkward	a	
19	ultimately	ad	
20	embark on		

3점 공략 모의고사 10회

01	authority	v	
02	obstruct	v	
03	discrimination	n	
04	sophisticated	a	
05	sustain	v	
06	고의로, 일부러	ad	
07	correlation	n	
08	exclusive	a	
09	static	a	
10	왜곡하다	v	
11	exotic	a	
12	풍경, 경치	n	
13	ruin	v	
14	peasant	n	
15	derive	v	
16	hierarchy	n	
17	dominate	v	
18	tailor	v	
19	rigid	a	
20	retain	v	

3점 공략 모의고사 11회

01	reverse	v
02	erode	v
03	humidity	n
04	intervention	n
05	intrinsic	a
06	pollen	n
07	rebellion	n
08	부패, 부식	n
09	supplemental	a
10	희생하다	v
11	utilize	v
12	validity	n
13	비관적인	a
14	preceding	a
15	subside	v
16	petal	n
17	flexible	a
18	stationary	a
19	modest	a
20	incomprehensible	a

3점 공략 모의고사 12회

01	proficient	a
02	compliance	n
03	exhaust	v
04	disparate	a
05	retreat	v
06	competent	a
07	deficiency	n
08	intricate	a
09	분석적인	a
10	overwhelm	v
11	낳다, 산출하다	v
12	deadlock	n
13	오도하는	a
14	concession	n
15	attribution	n
16	boredom	n
17	squash	v
18	empower	v
19	subsequent	n
20	compromise on	

3점 공략 모의고사 13회

01	disillusion	v	
02	subtle	a	
03	excavation	n	
04	speculate	v	
05	confidential	a	
06	designate	v	
07	abuse	v	
08	alternation	n	
09	성숙한	a	
10	entail	v	
11	참다, 용인하다	v	
12	terrestrial	a	
13	substructure	n	
14	분만시키다	v	
15	isolate	v	
16	recede	v	
17	hitherto	ad	
18	prerequisite	n	
19	prioritize	v	
20	conjure up		

3점 공략 모의고사 14회

01	substitute	n	
02	foster	v	
03	minority	n	
04	emergent	a	
05	boost	v	
06	bilingual	a	
07	nurture	n	
08	방언	n	
09	inherited	a	
10	emit	v	
11	simultaneously	ad	
12	영토, 영역	n	
13	instill	v	
14	credibility	n	
15	unfold	v	
16	stimulus	n	
17	depict	v	
18	arena	n	
19	역효과를 낳는	a	
20	articulation	n	

3점 공략 모의고사 15회

01 dwell   *v* _____

02 eliminate   *v* _____

03 primate   *n* _____

04 conscience   *n* _____

05 fascinating   *a* _____

06 prudent   *a* _____

07 헌법   *n* _____

08 renowned   *a* _____

09 distracted   *a* _____

10 침입하다   *v* _____

11 enact   *v* _____

12 forage   *v* _____

13 parliament   *n* _____

14 영감을 주다   *v* _____

15 dictate   *v* _____

16 photosynthesis   *n* _____

17 allocation   *n* _____

18 scarce   *a* _____

19 executive   *n* _____

20 be obligated to *do* _____

3점 공략 모의고사 16회

01 validation   *n* _____

02 confine   *v* _____

03 remains   *n* _____

04 defective   *a* _____

05 magnify   *v* _____

06 bypass   *v* _____

07 constraint   *n* _____

08 동반하다   *v* _____

09 forbid   *v* _____

10 suffice   *v* _____

11 envious   *a* _____

12 conservation   *n* _____

13 반영하다, 반사하다   *v* _____

14 endowment   *n* _____

15 inflict   *v* _____

16 신념, 확신   *n* _____

17 rationale   *n* _____

18 disprove   *v* _____

19 paramount   *a* _____

20 transaction   *n* _____

너 절대로 포기하지 마.

"이 길의 끝에 넌
세상에서 가장 환하게 웃게 될 거야.
그러니 너, 절대로 포기하지 마."

– 〈이토록 공부가 재미있어지는 순간〉 중에서

N Ⅲ 고난도 기출 모의고사

224

다음 글의 주제로 가장 적절한 것은?

There are pressures *within* the museum that cause it to emphasise what happens in the galleries over the activities that take place in its unseen zones. In an era when museums are forced to increase their earnings, they often focus their energies on modernising their galleries or mounting temporary exhibitions to bring more and more audiences through the door. In other words, as museums struggle to survive in a competitive economy, their budgets often prioritise those parts of themselves that are consumable: infotainment in the galleries, goods and services in the cafes and the shops. The unlit, unglamorous storerooms, if they are ever discussed, are at best presented as service areas that process objects for the exhibition halls. And at worst, as museums pour more and more resources into their publicly visible faces, the spaces of storage may even suffer, their modernisation being kept on hold or being given less and less space to house the expanding collections and serve their complex conservation needs.

① importance of prioritising museums' exhibition spaces
② benefits of diverse activities in museums for audiences
③ necessity of expanding storerooms for displaying objects
④ consequences of profit-oriented management of museums
⑤ ways to increase museums' commitment to the public good

225

다음 빈칸에 들어갈 말로 가장 적절한 것은?

Precision and determinacy are a necessary requirement for all meaningful scientific debate, and progress in the sciences is, to a large extent, the ongoing process of achieving ever greater precision. But historical representation puts a premium on a proliferation of representations, hence not on the refinement of one representation but on the production of an ever more varied set of representations. Historical insight is not a matter of a continuous "narrowing down" of previous options, not of an approximation of the truth, but, on the contrary, is an "explosion" of possible points of view. It therefore aims at the unmasking of previous illusions of determinacy and precision by the production of new and alternative representations, rather than at achieving truth by a careful analysis of what was right and wrong in those previous representations. And from this perspective, the development of historical insight may indeed be regarded by the outsider as a process of creating ever more confusion, a continuous questioning of _____, rather than, as in the sciences, an ever greater approximation to the truth.

*proliferation 증식

① criteria for evaluating historical representations
② certainty and precision seemingly achieved already
③ possibilities of alternative interpretations of an event
④ coexistence of multiple viewpoints in historical writing
⑤ correctness and reliability of historical evidence collected

226

주어진 글 다음에 이어질 글의 순서로 가장 적절한 것은?

> The most commonly known form of results-based pricing is a practice called contingency pricing, used by lawyers.

(A) Therefore, only an outcome in the client's favor is compensated. From the client's point of view, the pricing makes sense in part because most clients in these cases are unfamiliar with and possibly intimidated by law firms. Their biggest fears are high fees for a case that may take years to settle.

(B) By using contingency pricing, clients are ensured that they pay no fees until they receive a settlement. In these and other instances of contingency pricing, the economic value of the service is hard to determine before the service, and providers develop a price that allows them to share the risks and rewards of delivering value to the buyer.

(C) Contingency pricing is the major way that personal injury and certain consumer cases are billed. In this approach, lawyers do not receive fees or payment until the case is settled, when they are paid a percentage of the money that the client receives.

*intimidate 위협하다

① (A) − (C) − (B)
② (B) − (A) − (C)
③ (B) − (C) − (A)
④ (C) − (A) − (B)
⑤ (C) − (B) − (A)

227

글의 흐름으로 보아, 주어진 문장이 들어가기에 가장 적절한 곳은?

> Because the manipulation of digitally converted sounds meant the reprogramming of binary information, editing operations could be performed with millisecond precision.

The shift from analog to digital technology significantly influenced how music was produced. First and foremost, the digitization of sounds — that is, their conversion into numbers — enabled music makers to undo what was done. (①) One could, in other words, twist and bend sounds toward something new without sacrificing the original version. (②) This "undo" ability made mistakes considerably less momentous, sparking the creative process and encouraging a generally more experimental mindset. (③) In addition, digitally converted sounds could be manipulated simply by programming digital messages rather than using physical tools, simplifying the editing process significantly. (④) For example, while editing once involved razor blades to physically cut and splice audiotapes, it now involved the cursor and mouse-click of the computer-based sequencer program, which was obviously less time consuming. (⑤) This microlevel access at once made it easier to conceal any traces of manipulations (such as joining tracks in silent spots) and introduced new possibilities for manipulating sounds in audible and experimental ways.

*binary 2진법의   **splice 합쳐 잇다

228~229 다음 글을 읽고, 물음에 답하시오. 2024 6월 모평 41~42번

Many negotiators assume that all negotiations involve a fixed pie. Negotiators often approach integrative negotiation opportunities as zero-sum situations or win-lose exchanges. Those who believe in the mythical fixed pie assume that parties' interests stand in opposition, with no possibility for integrative settlements and mutually beneficial trade-offs, so they (a) suppress efforts to search for them. In a hiring negotiation, a job applicant who assumes that salary is the only issue may insist on $75,000 when the employer is offering $70,000. Only when the two parties discuss the possibilities further do they discover that moving expenses and starting date can also be negotiated, which may (b) block resolution of the salary issue.

The tendency to see negotiation in fixed-pie terms (c) varies depending on how people view the nature of a given conflict situation. This was shown in a clever experiment by Harinck, de Dreu, and Van Vianen involving a simulated negotiation between prosecutors and defense lawyers over jail sentences. Some participants were told to view their goals in terms of personal gain (e.g., arranging a particular jail sentence will help your career), others were told to view their goals in terms of effectiveness (a particular sentence is most likely to prevent recidivism), and still others were told to focus on values (a particular jail sentence is fair and just). Negotiators focusing on personal gain were most likely to come under the influence of fixed-pie beliefs and approach the situation (d) competitively. Negotiators focusing on values were least likely to see the problem in fixed-pie terms and more inclined to approach the situation cooperatively. Stressful conditions such as time constraints contribute to this common misperception, which in turn may lead to (e) less integrative agreements.

*prosecutor 검사 **recidivism 상습적 범행

228

윗글의 제목으로 가장 적절한 것은?

① Fixed Pie: A Key to Success in a Zero-sum Game
② Fixed Pie Tells You How to Get the Biggest Salary
③ Negotiators, Wake Up from the Myth of the Fixed Pie!
④ Want a Fairer Jail Sentence? Stick to the Fixed Pie
⑤ What Alternatives Maximize Fixed-pie Effects?

229

밑줄 친 (a)~(e) 중에서 문맥상 낱말의 쓰임이 적절하지 <u>않은</u> 것은?

① (a) ② (b) ③ (c)
④ (d) ⑤ (e)

230

2024 9월 모평 21번

밑줄 친 "The best is the enemy of the good."이 다음 글에서 의미하는 바로 가장 적절한 것은?

Gold plating in the project means needlessly enhancing the expected results, namely, adding characteristics that are costly, not required, and that have low added value with respect to the targets—in other words, giving more with no real justification other than to demonstrate one's own talent. Gold plating is especially interesting for project team members, as it is typical of projects with a marked professional component—in other words, projects that involve specialists with proven experience and extensive professional autonomy. In these environments specialists often see the project as an opportunity to test and enrich their skill sets. There is therefore a strong temptation, in all good faith, to engage in gold plating, namely, to achieve more or higher-quality work that gratifies the professional but does not add value to the client's requests, and at the same time removes valuable resources from the project. As the saying goes, "The best is the enemy of the good."

*autonomy 자율성   **gratify 만족시키다

① Pursuing perfection at work causes conflicts among team members.
② Raising work quality only to prove oneself is not desirable.
③ Inviting overqualified specialists to a project leads to bad ends.
④ Responding to the changing needs of clients is unnecessary.
⑤ Acquiring a range of skills for a project does not ensure success.

231

2022 수능 30번

다음 글의 밑줄 친 부분 중, 문맥상 낱말의 쓰임이 적절하지 <u>않은</u> 것은?

It has been suggested that "organic" methods, defined as those in which only natural products can be used as inputs, would be less damaging to the biosphere. Large-scale adoption of "organic" farming methods, however, would ①<u>reduce</u> yields and increase production costs for many major crops. Inorganic nitrogen supplies are ②<u>essential</u> for maintaining moderate to high levels of productivity for many of the non-leguminous crop species, because organic supplies of nitrogenous materials often are either limited or more expensive than inorganic nitrogen fertilizers. In addition, there are ③<u>benefits</u> to the extensive use of either manure or legumes as "green manure" crops. In many cases, weed control can be very difficult or require much hand labor if chemicals cannot be used, and ④<u>fewer</u> people are willing to do this work as societies become wealthier. Some methods used in "organic" farming, however, such as the sensible use of crop rotations and specific combinations of cropping and livestock enterprises, can make important ⑤<u>contributions</u> to the sustainability of rural ecosystems.

*nitrogen fertilizer 질소 비료   **manure 거름   ***legume 콩과(科) 식물

232

다음 빈칸에 들어갈 말로 가장 적절한 것은?

An invention or discovery that is too far ahead of its time is worthless; no one can follow. Ideally, an innovation opens up only the next step from what is known and invites the culture to move forward one hop. An overly futuristic, unconventional, or visionary invention can fail initially (it may lack essential not-yet-invented materials or a critical market or proper understanding) yet succeed later, when the ecology of supporting ideas catches up. Gregor Mendel's 1865 theories of genetic heredity were correct but ignored for 35 years. His sharp insights were not accepted because they did not explain the problems biologists had at the time, nor did his explanation operate by known mechanisms, so his discoveries were out of reach even for the early adopters. Decades later science faced the urgent questions that Mendel's discoveries could answer. Now his insights _____. Within a few years of one another, three different scientists each independently rediscovered Mendel's forgotten work, which of course had been there all along.

*ecology 생태 환경 **heredity 유전

① caught up to modern problems
② raised even more questions
③ addressed past and current topics alike
④ were only one step away
⑤ regained acceptance of the public

233

다음 빈칸에 들어갈 말로 가장 적절한 것은?

Development can get very complicated and fanciful. A fugue by Johann Sebastian Bach illustrates how far this process could go, when a single melodic line, sometimes just a handful of notes, was all that the composer needed to create a brilliant work containing lots of intricate development within a coherent structure. Ludwig van Beethoven's famous Fifth Symphony provides an exceptional example of how much mileage a classical composer can get out of a few notes and a simple rhythmic tapping. The opening da-da-da-DUM that everyone has heard somewhere or another _____ throughout not only the opening movement, but the remaining three movements, like a kind of motto or a connective thread. Just as we don't always see the intricate brushwork that goes into the creation of a painting, we may not always notice how Beethoven keeps finding fresh uses for his motto or how he develops his material into a large, cohesive statement. But a lot of the enjoyment we get from that mighty symphony stems from the inventiveness behind it, the impressive development of musical ideas.

*intricate 복잡한 **coherent 통일성 있는

① makes the composer's musical ideas contradictory
② appears in an incredible variety of ways
③ provides extensive musical knowledge creatively
④ remains fairly calm within the structure
⑤ becomes deeply associated with one's own enjoyment

234

주어진 글 다음에 이어질 글의 순서로 가장 적절한 것은?

> Plants show finely tuned adaptive responses when nutrients are limiting. Gardeners may recognize yellow leaves as a sign of poor nutrition and the need for fertilizer.

(A) In contrast, plants with a history of nutrient abundance are risk averse and save energy. At all developmental stages, plants respond to environmental changes or unevenness so as to be able to use their energy for growth, survival, and reproduction, while limiting damage and nonproductive uses of their valuable energy.

(B) Research in this area has shown that plants are constantly aware of their position in the environment, in terms of both space and time. Plants that have experienced variable nutrient availability in the past tend to exhibit risk-taking behaviors, such as spending energy on root lengthening instead of leaf production.

(C) But if a plant does not have a caretaker to provide supplemental minerals, it can proliferate or lengthen its roots and develop root hairs to allow foraging in more distant soil patches. Plants can also use their memory to respond to histories of temporal or spatial variation in nutrient or resource availability.

*nutrient 영양소 **fertilizer 비료 ***forage 구하러 다니다

① (A) − (C) − (B)   ② (B) − (A) − (C)
③ (B) − (C) − (A)   ④ (C) − (A) − (B)
⑤ (C) − (B) − (A)

235

글의 흐름으로 보아, 주어진 문장이 들어가기에 가장 적절한 곳은?

> As a result, they are fit and grow better, but they aren't particularly long-lived.

When trees grow together, nutrients and water can be optimally divided among them all so that each tree can grow into the best tree it can be. If you "help" individual trees by getting rid of their supposed competition, the remaining trees are bereft. They send messages out to their neighbors unsuccessfully, because nothing remains but stumps. Every tree now grows on its own, giving rise to great differences in productivity. (①) Some individuals photosynthesize like mad until sugar positively bubbles along their trunk. (②) This is because a tree can be only as strong as the forest that surrounds it. (③) And there are now a lot of losers in the forest. (④) Weaker members, who would once have been supported by the stronger ones, suddenly fall behind. (⑤) Whether the reason for their decline is their location and lack of nutrients, a passing sickness, or genetic makeup, they now fall prey to insects and fungi.

*bereft 잃은 **stump 그루터기 ***photosynthesize 광합성하다

236

밑줄 친 Flicking the collaboration light switch가 다음 글에서 의미하는 바로 가장 적절한 것은?

Flicking the collaboration light switch is something that leaders are uniquely positioned to do, because several obstacles stand in the way of people voluntarily working alone. For one thing, the fear of being left out of the loop can keep them glued to their enterprise social media. Individuals don't want to be—or appear to be—isolated. For another, knowing what their teammates are doing provides a sense of comfort and security, because people can adjust their own behavior to be in harmony with the group. It's risky to go off on their own to try something new that will probably not be successful right from the start. But even though it feels reassuring for individuals to be hyperconnected, it's better for the organization if they periodically go off and think for themselves and generate diverse—if not quite mature—ideas. Thus, it becomes the leader's job to create conditions that are good for the whole by enforcing intermittent interaction even when people wouldn't choose it for themselves, without making it seem like a punishment.

*intermittent 간헐적인

① breaking physical barriers and group norms that prohibit cooperation
② having people stop working together and start working individually
③ encouraging people to devote more time to online collaboration
④ shaping environments where higher productivity is required
⑤ requiring workers to focus their attention on group projects

237

다음 글의 밑줄 친 부분 중, 어법상 틀린 것은?

Consider *The Wizard of Oz* as a psychological study of motivation. Dorothy and her three friends work hard to get to the Emerald City, overcoming barriers, persisting against all adversaries. They do so because they expect the Wizard to give ①them what they are missing. Instead, the wonderful (and wise) Wizard makes them aware that they, not he, always had the power ②to fulfill their wishes. For Dorothy, *home* is not a place but a feeling of security, of comfort with people she loves; it is wherever her heart is. The courage the Lion wants, the intelligence the Scarecrow longs for, and the emotions the Tin Man dreams of ③being attributes they already possess. They need to think about these attributes not as internal conditions but as positive ways ④in which they are already relating to others. After all, didn't they demonstrate those qualities on the journey to Oz, a journey ⑤motivated by little more than an *expectation*, an idea about the future likelihood of getting something they wanted?

*adversary 적(상대)

238

2023 6월 모평 33번

다음 빈칸에 들어갈 말로 가장 적절한 것은?

Manufacturers design their innovation processes around the way they think the process works. The vast majority of manufacturers still think that product development and service development are always done by manufacturers, and that their job is always to find a need and fill it rather than to sometimes find and commercialize an innovation that _____. Accordingly, manufacturers have set up market-research departments to explore the needs of users in the target market, product-development groups to think up suitable products to address those needs, and so forth. The needs and prototype solutions of lead users—if encountered at all—are typically rejected as outliers of no interest. Indeed, when lead users' innovations do enter a firm's product line—and they have been shown to be the actual source of many major innovations for many firms—they typically arrive with a lag and by an unusual and unsystematic route.

*lag 지연

① lead users tended to overlook
② lead users have already developed
③ lead users encountered in the market
④ other firms frequently put into use
⑤ both users and firms have valued

239

2024 9월 모평 34번

다음 빈칸에 들어갈 말로 가장 적절한 것은?

Prior to photography, _____. While painters have always lifted particular places out of their 'dwelling' and transported them elsewhere, paintings were time-consuming to produce, relatively difficult to transport and one-of-a-kind. The multiplication of photographs especially took place with the introduction of the half-tone plate in the 1880s that made possible the mechanical reproduction of photographs in newspapers, periodicals, books and advertisements. Photography became coupled to consumer capitalism and the globe was now offered 'in limitless quantities, figures, landscapes, events which had not previously been utilised either at all, or only as pictures for one customer'. With capitalism's arrangement of the world as a 'department store', 'the proliferation and circulation of representations ... achieved a spectacular and virtually inescapable global magnitude'. Gradually photographs became cheap massproduced objects that made the world visible, aesthetic and desirable. Experiences were 'democratised' by translating them into cheap images. Light, small and mass-produced photographs became dynamic vehicles for the spatiotemporal circulation of places.

*proliferation 확산 **magnitude (큰) 규모 ***aesthetic 미적인

① paintings alone connected with nature
② painting was the major form of art
③ art held up a mirror to the world
④ desire for travel was not strong
⑤ places did not travel well

240

주어진 글 다음에 이어질 글의 순서로 가장 적절한 것은?

Spatial reference points are larger than themselves. This isn't really a paradox: landmarks are themselves, but they also define neighborhoods around themselves.

(A) In a paradigm that has been repeated on many campuses, researchers first collect a list of campus landmarks from students. Then they ask another group of students to estimate the distances between pairs of locations, some to landmarks, some to ordinary buildings on campus.

(B) This asymmetry of distance estimates violates the most elementary principles of Euclidean distance, that the distance from A to B must be the same as the distance from B to A. Judgments of distance, then, are not necessarily coherent.

(C) The remarkable finding is that distances from an ordinary location to a landmark are judged shorter than distances from a landmark to an ordinary location. So, people would judge the distance from Pierre's house to the Eiffel Tower to be shorter than the distance from the Eiffel Tower to Pierre's house. Like black holes, landmarks seem to pull ordinary locations toward themselves, but ordinary places do not.

*asymmetry 비대칭

① (A) − (C) − (B)　　② (B) − (A) − (C)
③ (B) − (C) − (A)　　④ (C) − (A) − (B)
⑤ (C) − (B) − (A)

241

글의 흐름으로 보아, 주어진 문장이 들어가기에 가장 적절한 곳은?

Personal stories connect with larger narratives to generate new identities.

The growing complexity of the social dynamics determining food choices makes the job of marketers and advertisers increasingly more difficult. (①) In the past, mass production allowed for accessibility and affordability of products, as well as their wide distribution, and was accepted as a sign of progress. (②) Nowadays it is increasingly replaced by the fragmentation of consumers among smaller and smaller segments that are supposed to reflect personal preferences. (③) Everybody feels different and special and expects products serving his or her inclinations. (④) In reality, these supposedly individual preferences end up overlapping with emerging, temporary, always changing, almost tribal formations solidifying around cultural sensibilities, social identifications, political sensibilities, and dietary and health concerns. (⑤) These consumer communities go beyond national boundaries, feeding on global and widely shared repositories of ideas, images, and practices.

*fragmentation 파편화　**repository 저장소

정답 및 해설 p.123

고난도 기출 모의고사 1회

01	alternative	*a*
02	integrative	*a*
03	approximation	*n*
04	conversion	*n*
05	audible	*a*
06	constraint	*n*
07	mindset	*n*
08	simulated	*a*
09	convert	*v*
10	explosion	*n*
11	조작	*n*
12	suppress	*v*
13	trade-off	*n*
14	misperception	*n*
15	당사자	*n*
16	refinement	*n*
17	undo	*v*
18	mount	*v*
19	representation	*n*
20	합의, 합의금	*n*

고난도 기출 모의고사 2회

01	cohesive	*a*
02	mighty	*a*
03	자율성	*n*
04	overqualified	*a*
05	patch	*n*
06	finely	*ad*
07	gratify	*v*
08	inventiveness	*n*
09	justification	*n*
10	supplemental	*a*
11	proliferate	*v*
12	reproduction	*n*
13	spatial	*n*
14	contradictory	*a*
15	sustainability	*n*
16	temporal	*a*
17	unconventional	*a*
18	수확량, 산출량	*n*
19	unevenness	*n*
20	visionary	*a*

고난도 기출 모의고사 3회

01	address	v	11	democratise	v
02	multiplication	n	12	reference point	n
03	정기간행물	n	13	barrier	n
04	persist	v	14	security	n
05	distribution	n	15	coherent	a
06	dwelling	n	16	segment	n
07	emerging	a	17	solidify	v
08	enforce	v	18	vehicle	n
09	inclination	n	19	위반하다	v
10	commercialize	v	20	attribute	n

메가스터디 N제

메가스터디 N제

메가스터디 N제

영어영역 고난도 · 3점

수능 완벽 대비 예상 문제집

정답 및 해설

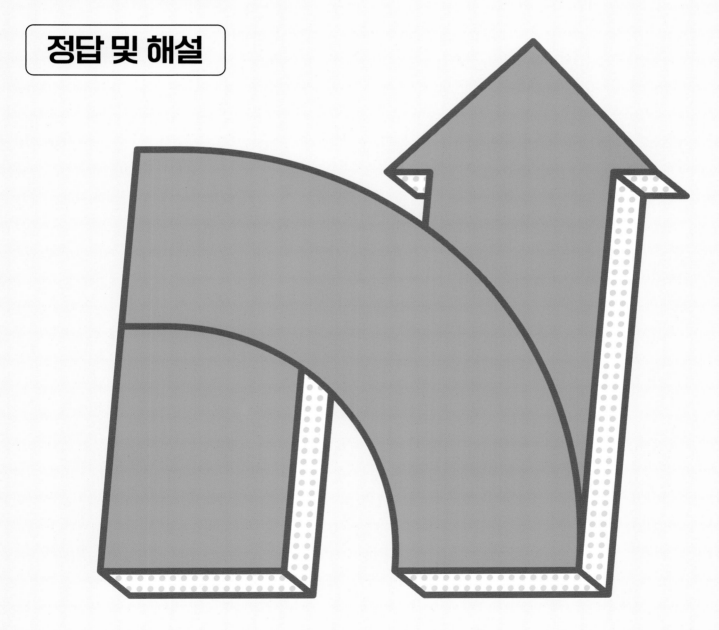

241제

메가스터디BOOKS

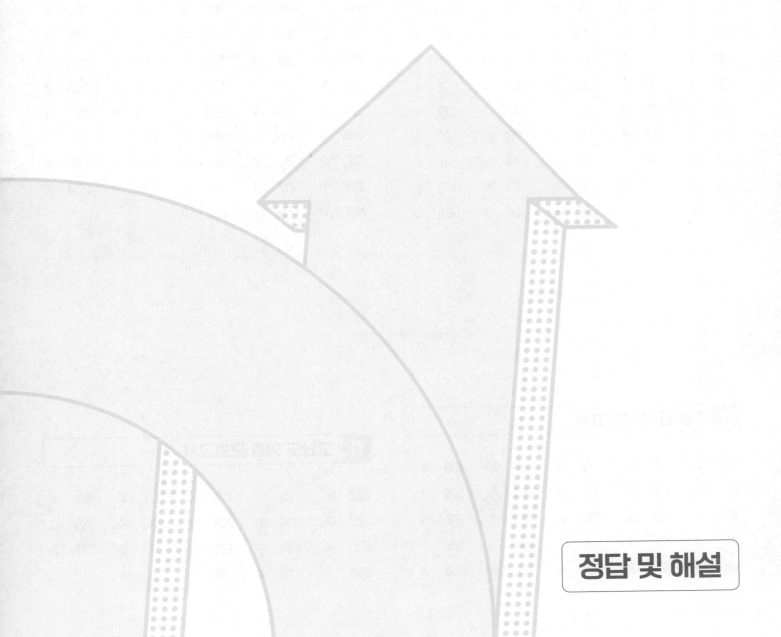

메가스터디 N제

영어영역 고난도·3점

241제

정답 및 해설

I 고난도 · 3점 유형

001 ②	002 ②	003 ⑤	004 ②	005 ③
006 ④	007 ④	008 ③	009 ④	010 ④
011 ①	012 ②	013 ①	014 ④	015 ⑤
016 ④	017 ③	018 ②	019 ②	020 ②
021 ④	022 ③	023 ④	024 ④	025 ④
026 ④	027 ③	028 ④	029 ⑤	030 ④
031 ③	032 ④	033 ③	034 ⑤	035 ⑤
036 ⑤	037 ②	038 ②	039 ①	040 ④
041 ⑤	042 ④	043 ③	044 ①	045 ①
046 ④	047 ①	048 ②	049 ②	050 ③
051 ②	052 ⑤	053 ④	054 ⑤	055 ④
056 ②	057 ⑤	058 ①	059 ③	060 ④
061 ⑤	062 ③	063 ④	064 ④	065 ⑤
066 ④	067 ④	068 ④	069 ③	070 ④
071 ④	072 ③	073 ①	074 ①	075 ①
076 ③	077 ②	078 ①	079 ③	080 ⑤
081 ②	082 ②	083 ⑤	084 ①	085 ④
086 ②	087 ③	088 ⑤	089 ⑤	090 ②
091 ③	092 ⑤	093 ④	094 ④	095 ⑤

121 ④	122 ③	123 ④	124 ⑤	125 ②
126 ③	127 ④	128 ②	129 ③	130 ②
131 ④	132 ③	133 ④	134 ⑤	135 ②
136 ③	137 ④	138 ②	139 ⑤	140 ④
141 ④	142 ①	143 ③	144 ④	145 ④
146 ④	147 ④	148 ③	149 ⑤	150 ③
151 ②	152 ②	153 ②	154 ①	155 ②
156 ②	157 ③	158 ①	159 ⑤	160 ⑤
161 ⑤	162 ⑤	163 ②	164 ②	165 ⑤
166 ④	167 ④	168 ①	169 ⑤	170 ②
171 ③	172 ④	173 ④	174 ①	175 ③
176 ⑤	177 ①	178 ⑤	179 ②	180 ②
181 ⑤	182 ⑤	183 ④	184 ⑤	185 ④
186 ③	187 ③	188 ④	189 ①	190 ④
191 ③	192 ①	193 ②	194 ⑤	195 ③
196 ①	197 ⑤	198 ③	199 ④	200 ③
201 ②	202 ②	203 ①	204 ④	205 ③
206 ③	207 ③	208 ⑤	209 ③	210 ③
211 ②	212 ⑤	213 ③	214 ④	215 ⑤
216 ①	217 ④	218 ③	219 ②	220 ④
221 ⑤	222 ④	223 ③		

II 3점 공략 모의고사

096 ⑤	097 ②	098 ⑤	099 ③	100 ②
101 ⑤	102 ②	103 ⑤	104 ②	105 ③
106 ①	107 ③	108 ②	109 ②	110 ③
111 ③	112 ④	113 ⑤	114 ③	115 ①
116 ③	117 ④	118 ④	119 ②	120 ④

III 고난도 기출 모의고사

224 ④	225 ②	226 ④	227 ⑤	228 ③
229 ②	230 ②	231 ③	232 ④	233 ②
234 ⑤	235 ②	236 ②	237 ③	238 ②
239 ⑤	240 ①	241 ⑤		

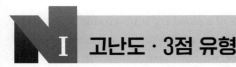

I 고난도 · 3점 유형

01 글의 주제
본문 p.009

001 답 ②

📖 산림[숲]의 경제적 가치를 훨씬 넘어서는 비시장 가치

전문해석

천연자원의 관리자는 일반적으로 이용에 대한 재정적 보상을 제공하는 시장 인센티브에 직면한다. 예를 들어, 산림 지대의 소유자는 탄소 포집, 야생동물 서식지, 홍수 방어, 그리고 다른 생태계 서비스를 위해 산림을 관리하기보다는 벌목을 위한 시장 인센티브를 가지고 있다. 이러한 (생태계) 서비스는 소유자에게 어떠한 재정적 이익도 제공하지 않으며, 따라서 관리 결정에 영향을 미칠 것 같지는 않다. 그러나 이러한 서비스가 제공하는 경제적 이익은, 그것의 비시장적 가치에 근거하여, 목재의 경제적 가치를 초과할 수도 있다. 예를 들어, 유엔의 한 계획은 기후 조절, 수질 정화 및 침식 방지를 포함하여 열대 우림이 제공하는 생태계 서비스의 경제적 이익이 시장 이익보다 헥타르당 3배 이상이라고 추정했다. 따라서 벌목은 경제적으로 비효율적이며, 시장은 채취하는 사용보다 생태계 서비스를 선호하게 하는 올바른 '신호'를 보내지 않고 있다.

정답풀이

산림[숲]의 소유자가 생태계 서비스를 위해 산림을 보호하기보다는 벌목을 하게 되면 시장 인센티브라는 경제적 가치를 가지겠지만, 산림이 주는 생태계 서비스의 비시장적 가치는 목재의 경제적 가치를 훨씬 초과할 수도 있다는 점에 주목해야 한다는 요지의 글이다. 따라서 글의 주제로 가장 적절한 것은 ② '산림 자원의 비시장적 가치를 따져 보는 것의 의의'이다.

오답풀이

① 생태계 서비스의 시장 가치 산정의 필요성
 └ 숲이 주는 생태계 서비스의 시장 가치가 아니라 비시장 가치의 중요성을 말하고 있는 글이므로 적절하지 않다.

③ 재정적 이익을 극대화하기 위한 산림 자원 이용의 영향
④ 산림의 시장 가치와 비시장 가치의 균형을 맞추는 장점
 └ 지문의 어휘를 사용해서 혼동을 주고 있지만 산림의 비시장 가치가 시장 가치보다 크기에 벌목은 경제적으로 비효율적이라는 내용이므로 적절하지 않다.

⑤ 천연자원 관리의 효율성을 높이는 방법

구문풀이

5행 But the economic benefits [provided by these services], [based on their non-market values], **may exceed** the economic value of the timber.

: 첫 번째 [ ]는 문장의 핵심 주어인 the economic benefits를 수식하는 과거분사구이고, 동사는 may exceed이다. 두 번째 [ ]는 주어와 동사 사이에 삽입된 어구이다.

10행 Thus [cutting down the trees] is economically inefficient, / and markets are not sending the correct "signal" [to favor ecosystem services over extractive uses].

: 첫 번째 [ ]는 and 앞 절의 주어로 쓰인 동명사구이고, 두 번째 [ ]는 the correct "signal"을 수식하는 형용사적 용법의 to부정사구이다.

002 답 ②

📖 자유로운 선택을 보장하기 위해 정보를 공개하는 것의 이점

전문해석

공개의 중요한 이점은 더 공격적인 형태의 규제와는 대조적으로 자유 시장의 운용에 대한 유연성과 존중이다. 규제하는 명령은 무딘 칼인데, 그것은 다양성을 무시하는 경향이 있으며, 의도하지 않은 심각한 역효과를 가질 수도 있다. 예를 들어, 가전제품에 대한 에너지 효율 요건은 덜 잘 작동하거나 소비자가 원하지 않는 특성을 가진 제품을 만들어 낼 수도 있다. 반대로 정보 제공은 선택의 자유를 존중한다. 자동차 제조사들이 자동차의 안전 특성을 측정하고 공개해야 한다면, 잠재적인 자동차 구매자는 가격과 스타일 같은 다른 속성과 안전에 대한 우려를 맞바꿀 수 있다. 식당 손님들에게 음식에 들어 있는 칼로리를 알려주면, 살을 빼고 싶은 사람들은 그 정보를 이용할 수 있고, 칼로리에 신경 쓰지 않는 사람들은 영향을 받지 않은 채로 있게 된다. 공개는 개인 의사 결정의 자율성(그리고 질)을 방해하지 않으며 심지어 촉진할 것이다.

정답풀이

정보 공개는 규제와는 대조적으로 선택의 자유를 존중하며 의사 결정의 자율성과 질을 촉진한다는 내용의 글이다. 따라서 글의 주제로 가장 적절한 것은 ② '자유로운 선택을 보장하기 위해 정보를 공개하는 것의 이점'이다.

오답풀이

① 공공정보를 고객이 이용할 수 있게 하는 절차
③ 기업들이 자유 시장에서 이윤을 늘리는 전략들
④ 현재의 산업 동향을 파악하고 분석할 필요성
⑤ 다양화된 시장이 소비자의 합리적 선택에 미치는 영향
 └ 공개된 정보를 보고 소비자가 선택하도록 하는 자율성을 주는 것의 이점에 대한 내용으로 다양화된 시장의 영향에 대한 설명은 없다.

구문풀이

6행 For example, energy efficiency requirements for appliances may produce goods [that work less well] or [that have characteristics {that consumers do not want}].

: or로 연결된 두 개의 [ ]는 선행사 goods를 수식하는 주격 관계대명사절이고, 두 번째 [ ] 안의 { }는 characteristics를 수식하는 목적격 관계대명사절이다.

14행 [If restaurant customers are informed of the calories in their meals], those [who want to lose weight] can make use of the information, [**leaving** those {who are unconcerned about calories} **unaffected**].

: 첫 번째 [ ]는 조건을 나타내는 부사절이다. 두 번째 [ ]는 바로 앞의 those를 수식하는 주격 관계대명사절이다. 세 번째 [ ]는 부대상황을 나타내는 분사구문이고, those who are ~ calories는 leaving의 목적어, unaffected는 목적격보어이며, { }는 바로 앞의 those를 수식하는 주격 관계대명사절이다.

어휘풀이

- disclosure *n* 공개, 폭로, 드러냄
- aggressive *a* 공격적인
- flexibility *n* 유연성, 융통성
- blunt *a* 무딘
- diversity *n* 다양성
- efficiency *n* 효율성
- provision *n* 제공
- publicize *v* 공개하다, 알리다
- inform *A* of *B* A에게 B를 알리다
- interfere with ~을 방해하다
- as opposed to ~와는 대조적으로
- regulation *n* 규제, 규정
- regulatory *a* 규제하는
- neglect *v* 무시하다, 소홀히 하다
- unintended *a* 의도하지 않은
- appliance *n* 가전제품
- manufacturer *n* 제조업체
- attribute *n* 속성, 특성
- unaffected *a* 영향을 받지 않는

003 답 ⑤

📖 과학 연구에 있어 패러다임의 기능적 측면

전문해석

과학자들은 패러다임을 믿기보다 그것을 '사용한다.' 연구에서 패러다임의 사용은 일반적으로 공유된 개념, 상징적 표현, 실험적 및 수학적 도구와 절차, 그리고 심지어 동일한 이론적 진술의 일부를 사용함으로써 관련된 문제들을 다룬다. 과학자들은 다른 사람들이 받아들일 방식으로 이러한 다양한 요소들을 사용하는 '방법'을 이해하기만 하면 된다. 따라서 이러한 공유된 실행의 요소들은 과학자들이 그것들을 사용할 때 그들이 하고 있는 것에 관한 그들의 믿음에서 그 어떤 비슷한 통일성을 전제로 할 필요는 없다. 실제로, 패러다임의 한 가지 역할은 과학자들이 그들이 무엇을 하고 있는지 또는 그들이 그것에 관해 무엇을 믿고 있는지에 대한 상세한 설명을 제공할 필요 없이 성공적으로 일할 수 있게 하는 것이다. Thomas Kuhn이 언급하기를, 과학자들은 "패러다임에 대한 완전한 '해석'이나 '합리화'에 동의하거나, 심지어 그런 것을 만들어 내려고 시도조차 하지 않고도, 그것[패러다임]을 '확인'하는 데 있어서 의견의 합치를 보일 수 있다. 표준 해석이나 규칙에의 합의적 수렴이 없다 해도 패러다임이 연구를 안내하는 것을 막지는 못할 것이다."

정답풀이

패러다임은 과학자들이 연구에서 그것을 사용함으로써 성공적으로 일할 수 있게 해주며 연구를 안내한다는 내용의 글이다. 따라서 글의 주제로 가장 적절한 것은 ⑤ '과학 연구에서 패러다임의 기능적 측면'이다.

오답풀이

① 기존의 패러다임으로부터 새로운 이론을 도출하는 데 있어서의 어려움
② 과학 분야에서 개인 신념의 상당한 영향력
③ 혁신적 패러다임의 출현을 고취하는 핵심 요인
④ 생각이 비슷한 연구원들을 분류하는 데 있어서 패러다임의 역할
 └ 패러다임의 역할에서 연구원들을 분류하는 기능에 대한 언급이 없다.

구문풀이

2행 **The use of a paradigm in research** typically **addresses** related problems **by employing** [shared concepts, symbolic expressions, experimental and mathematical tools and procedures, and even some of the same theoretical statements].

: 문장의 주어는 The use of a paradigm in research(핵은 use)이고 동사는 addresses이다. 「by+-ing」는 '~함으로써'라는 의미를 나타내고, [ ]는 동명사 employing의 목적어 역할을 하는 명사구이다.

6행 Scientists need only understand [***how to use*** these various elements in ways {that others would accept}].

: [ ]는 「how+to부정사: ~하는 방법」 구문이 쓰인 명사구로 understand의 목적어 역할을 하며, 그 안의 { }는 ways를 수식하는 목적격 관계대명사절이다.

11행 Indeed, one role of a paradigm is [to **enable** scientists **to work** successfully without {having to provide a detailed account **of** (what they are doing) or (what they believe about it)}].

: [ ]는 주격보어로 쓰인 to부정사구이고, 「enable+목적어+to부정사(목적격보어)」는 '~가 …할 수 있게 하다'라는 의미를 나타낸다. { }는 전치사 without의 목적어 역할을 하는 동명사구이고, 그 안의 두 개의 ( )는 전치사 of의 목적어 역할을 하는 명사절이다.

어휘풀이

- typically *ad* 일반적으로
- employ *v* 사용하다
- theoretical *a* 이론적인
- comparable *a* 비슷한
- account *n* 설명
- interpretation *n* 해석
- rationalization *n* 합리화, 이론적 설명
- reduction *n* 정리, 단순화, 축약, 축소
- address *v* (문제 등을) 다루다
- procedure *n* 절차
- presuppose *v* 전제하다
- unity *n* 통일성
- identification *n* 식별, 확인

004 답 ②

📖 감염되었을 때 발열이 중요한 이유

전문해석

Lovelace Institute의 생리학자인 Matt Kluger는 '발열이 수억 년 동안 동물의 왕국 전체에 걸쳐 지속되어온 **감염에 대한 숙주의 적응적 반응**이라는 것을 지지하는 결정적인 증거가 있다'고 믿는다. **그는 발열을 억제하려고 약을 쓰는 것이 때로는 사람들을 더 아프게 하고 심지어 사람들을 죽인다고 믿는다.** 최고의 증거 중 일부는 그의 실험실에서 나온다. 한 실험에서 그는 냉혈 동물인 도마뱀조차도 발열로부터 혜택을 본다는 것을 보여주었다. 감염되면 그들은 자신의 체온을 섭씨 약 2도 올리기에 충분히 따뜻한 장소를 찾는다. 따뜻한 장소로 이동할 수 없으면 그들은 죽을 가능성이 더 크다. 새끼 토끼 또한 열을 낼 수 없어서 그들이 아플 때 자신의 체온을 높이기 위해 따뜻한 장소를 찾는다. 어른 토끼가 감염되면 정말 열이 나지만 열을 낮추는 약으로 발열이 차단되면 그들은 죽을 가능성이 더 크다.

정답풀이

발열은 감염에 대한 숙주의 적응적 반응이므로, 감염되었을 때 약을 써서 발열을 억제하는 것이 더 아프거나 위험하게 만들 수 있다는 내용이다. 이에 대한 증거로 냉혈 동물인 도마뱀과 토끼의 사례를 설명하고 있으므로, 글의 주제로는 ② '감염병과 싸울 때 발열의 중요성'이 가장 적절하다.

오답풀이

① 아이의 발열을 낮출 필요성
③ 발열을 치료하기 위해 약을 사용하는 것의 이점
 └ 열을 낮추기 위해 약을 먹는 것이 더 아프거나 위험하다고 했으므로 적절하지 않다.
④ 체온을 유지하는 효과적인 방법
 └ 효과적인 체온 유지 방법에 대한 설명은 전혀 없다.
⑤ 냉혈 동물에게 발열이 위험한 이유
 └ 발열은 냉혈 동물에게도 혜택일 수 있다고 설명했다.

구문풀이

1행 Matt Kluger, a physiologist at the Lovelace Institute, believes [that "there is overwhelming evidence in favor of {**fever being** an adaptive host response to infection (that has persisted throughout the animal kingdom for hundreds of millions of years)}]."

: [ ]는 believes의 목적어로 쓰인 명사절이고, 그 안의 { }는 전치사 of의 목적어 역할을 하는 동명사구로 fever가 being ~의 의미상 주어이다. ( )는 an adaptive host response to infection을 수식하는 주격 관계대명사절이다.

- physiologist *n* 생리학자
- in favor of ~을 지지[찬성]하여
- host *n* 숙주
- persist *v* 지속되다
- laboratory *n* 실험실
- body temperature 체온
- overwhelming *a* 결정적인
- adaptive *a* 적응적인
- infection *n* 감염
- suppress *v* 억제하다
- lizard *n* 도마뱀
- generate *v* 만들어 내다, 발생하다

- regulation *n* 규제, 규정
- regime *n* 정권
- luxury *n* 사치
- monopolization *n* 독점
- self-correcting *a* 자기 수정적인
- multiply *v* 증식하다, 갑자기 증가하다
- expand *v* 확대하다
- pressing *a* 긴급한
- authoritarian *a* 권위주의적인
- skeptical *a* 회의적인
- be subject to ~의 대상이다
- distortion *n* 왜곡
- undermine *v* 약화시키다
- polarized *a* 양극화된
- amplify *v* 증폭시키다

005 답 ③

📖 여론이 형성되는 공적 공간을 규제할 필요성의 증가

전문해석
민주주의는 집단적 의지의 형성에 달려 있다. 오늘날 그것은 여론의 형성을 의미한다. 여론과 정부의 정당성 사이의 밀접한 관계 때문에, 민주국가는 필연적으로 여론이 형성되는 공적 공간에 대한 규제에 관심이 있다. 권위주의적인 정권은 이 공간을 폐쇄하려고 노력하는 경향이 있다. 민주적인 정권은 규제에 회의적이지만, 더 이상 '사상의 자유 시장'에 의존하는 사치를 누리고 있지는 않다. 그러한 시장은 경제 시장만큼 독점과 왜곡의 대상이며, 또한 자기 수정적이지도 않다. 게다가 디지털 공간이 공적 영역을 변형시켰는데, 정보에 대한 보다 쉬운 접근은 전통적으로 권위 있는 지식의 원천을 약화시켰고, 정보 거품이 증식해 양극화된 정치를 공급했으며, 잘못된 정보는 확대되고 더 은밀히 퍼지고 위험해졌다. 정보 비상사태로서의 팬데믹은 이러한 추세를 증폭시켜 규제 문제를 더욱 시급하게 만들었다.

정답풀이
권위주의적인 정권은 원래부터 여론이 형성되는 공적 공간을 폐쇄하려고 했고, 이제는 민주적인 정권도 왜곡의 대상이면서 자기 수정적이지 않은 사상의 자유 시장에 의존하기 어려워졌다고 했다. 또한 쉽게 접근이 가능한 디지털 공간까지 정보 거품과 잘못된 정보로 여러 문제를 증폭시키기 때문에 여론을 형성하는 공적인 공간에 대한 규제의 필요성이 증가하고 있다는 내용이므로, 글의 주제로 가장 적절한 것은 ③ '왜곡을 피하기 위한 공적 공간 규제의 필요성'이다.

오답풀이
① 여론을 형성하는 데 있어서 디지털 공간의 역할
　↳ 왜곡된 정보로 여론을 형성하는 디지털 공간의 문제를 지적함으로써 규제의 필요성을 말하는 글이다.
② 민주적인 정치에 대한 금융 시장의 기여
④ 정부의 정당성을 확보하는 수단으로서의 여론
⑤ 민주적인 정부와 권위주의적인 정부의 차이점

구문풀이
3행 [Because of the close relationship between public opinion and government legitimacy], a democracy is necessarily concerned with regulation of the public space [within which public opinion forms].

: 첫 번째 [ ]는 「because of+명사구」로 이루어진 부사구이고, 두 번째 [ ]는 the public space를 수식하는 관계절이다.

8행 Democratic regimes are skeptical of regulation, but **no longer do they have** the luxury of relying upon a "free market of ideas."

: but 다음에서 부정어인 no longer가 절 앞에 위치해 「조동사(do)+주어(they)+본동사(have)」의 도치가 일어났다.

어휘풀이
- formation *n* 형성
- legitimacy *n* 정당성, 합법성
- collective *a* 집단적인
- be concerned with ~에 관심이 있다

006 답 ④

📖 심리적 면역 시스템으로서의 심리 방어 기제

전문해석
사람들은 무대 뒤에서 작동하는 강력한 심리 방어 기제를 갖고 있으며, 그 영향력을 더 좋게 하기 위한 방식으로 부정적인 정보를 합리화하고 재해석하고 왜곡한다. 누군가가 우리 머리가 형편없이 다듬어진 울타리처럼 보인다고 말하면, 우리는 그들이 농담을 하고 있으며, 진지한 것이 아니라고 생각한다. 누군가가 우리의 데이트 제안을 거절하면, 그(녀)가 우리에게 전혀 맞지 않았다고 자신을 납득시킨다. 학술지 편집자가 우리의 논문 중 하나를 출판하는 것을 거부하면, 우리는 그 편집자가 판단력이 매우 부족한 것이 틀림없다고 확신한다. 이러한 사건들은 처음에는 상처를 주지만, 우리는 그것들을 재해석하거나 합리화함으로써 그 고통을 막는 방법을 아주 빠르게 찾는다. 마치 우리가 위험한 외부 물질을 식별하고 그 영향을 최소화하는 생리학적 면역 시스템을 가지고 있는 것처럼, 우리는 우리의 자존감에 대한 위협을 식별하고 그러한 위협을 중화시키는 방법을 찾는 심리적 면역 시스템을 가지고 있다. 요약하면, 심리적 면역 시스템은 사람들이 부정적인 감정과 싸우기 위해 사용하는 추가적인 무기이다. **심리적 면역 시스템은 우리의 자존감을 유지하는 방식으로 들어오는 정보를 선택하고 해석하며 평가한다.**

정답풀이
우리는 자신의 자존감에 상처를 주는 정보를 접하게 되면 그것을 자신에게 상처를 주지 않는 방식으로 재해석하거나 합리화하는 심리적 방어 기제를 작동시킨다는 내용의 글이다. 따라서 글의 주제로 가장 적절한 것은 ④ '심리적 저항을 통한 자존감 보호하기'이다.

오답풀이
① 부정적인 감정과 싸우기 위한 다양한 전술들
② 생리학적 방어 기제의 예들
③ 기본적인 인간 감정을 드러내는 자기방어 전략
⑤ 우리가 심리적 방어 시스템의 작동을 막는 이유
　↳ 심리적 방어 시스템의 작동을 막는 이유가 아니라 작동시키는 이유를 설명하는 내용이다.

구문풀이
1행 People are equipped with powerful psychological defenses [that operate offstage], [**rationalizing**, **reinterpreting**, and **distorting** negative information in ways {that make its impact better}].

: 첫 번째 [ ]는 powerful psychological defenses를 수식하는 주격 관계대명사절이다. 두 번째 [ ]는 분사구문으로 rationalizing, reinterpreting, distorting이 병렬구조로 연결되어 있으며, 그 안의 { }는 ways를 수식하는 주격 관계대명사절이다.

4행 [When someone tells us {that our hair looks like a poorly trimmed hedge}], we assume [they are joking and can't be serious].

: 첫 번째 [ ]는 때를 나타내는 부사절이고, 그 안의 { }는 tells의 직접목적어 역할을 하는 명사절이다. 두 번째 [ ]는 주절의 동사 assume의 목적어 역할을 하는 목적절로 앞에 접속사 that이 생략되었다.

14행 [**Just as** we have a physiological immune system {that identifies dangerous foreign bodies and minimizes their impact}], **so do we have** a psychological immune system [that identifies threats to our self-esteem and finds ways of neutralizing these threats].

: 첫 번째 [ ]는 Just as(마치 ~처럼)가 이끄는 부사절이고, 그 안의 { }는 a physiological immune system을 수식하는 주격 관계대명사절이다. 주절에는 「so+조동사(do)+주어(we)+본동사(have) ~」의 도치구문이 쓰여 '~도 또한 …하다'라는 의미를 나타내고 있다. 두 번째 [ ]는 a psychological immune system을 수식하는 주격 관계대명사절이다.

어휘풀이

- be equipped with ~을 갖추다
- rationalize *v* 합리화하다
- distort *v* 왜곡하다
- assume *v* 가정하다
- convince *v* 설득하다
- article *n* 논문, 기사
- physiological *a* 생리적인
- identify *v* 식별하다
- self-esteem *n* 자존감
- evaluate *v* 평가하다
- tactic *n* 전술, 전략

- offstage *ad* 무대 뒤에서
- reinterpret *v* 재해석하다
- trim *v* 다듬다
- hedge *n* 울타리
- reject *v* 거절하다
- publication *n* 출판
- immune system 면역 체계
- minimize *v* 최소화하다
- neutralize *v* (효과 등을) 무효화시키다
- maintain *v* 유지하다

007 답 ④

📖 **사적 영역의 불평등한 관계를 밝혀내는 데 유용한 면접 방법**

전문해석

사적 행위는 그 자체로뿐만 아니라 그것이 사회에 대해 우리에게 말하는 것을 위해서도 중요하다. 페미니스트 연구원은 사적 영역이 어떻게 사회적 불평등이 생산되고 드러나는 장소인지를 보여주었다. 인터뷰는 가족 구성원 간의 관계뿐만 아니라 유급 가사 노동자와 고용주 사이의 관계를 포함해 가정 내에서 일어나는 역학관계를 밝힐 수 있다. 예를 들어, 가사 노동자들과의 인터뷰에서 Pierrette Hondagneu-Sotelo는 가사 노동자의 고용주들이 임금을 낮게 유지하고 수당을 주지 않는 결정을 정당화하면서 '진짜' 직원으로서의 그들의 지위를 어떻게 인정하지 않았는지를 발견했다. 이와 같은 인터뷰는 사적 환경에서 성, 인종 및 계층이 어떻게 불평등한 관계를 구조화하는지를 우리가 연구하는 데 도움을 주는데, 그것은[그러한 구조화는] 눈에 띄지 않고 넘어갈 수 있지만 중대한 결과를 가져올 수 있다. 이러한 방식으로, 인터뷰 결과는 우리가 소외 집단과 특권 집단의 경험에 대해 우리가 알고 있는 많은 것을 제공했다.

정답풀이

인터뷰를 통해 가사 노동자들이 어떻게 차별을 받고 있는지가 밝혀진 예를 들면서, 우리 사회의 사적인 영역에서 발생하는 성, 인종, 계층별 불평등 관계를 밝히는 데 인터뷰가 효과적이라고 말하고 있다. 따라서 글의 주제로 가장 적절한 것은 ④ '사적인 불평등한 관계를 밝히는 데 효과적인 인터뷰 조사'이다.

오답풀이

① 가정 문제를 밝히는 것을 어렵게 만드는 요인들
② 가사 노동자를 부당하게 대우하는 관행을 근절하는 법
③ 사적인 문제에 대해 인터뷰할 때의 연구원들의 어려움들
⑤ 사적인 영역에서 불평등한 관계가 인정되지 않는 이유
    ↳ 사적인 영역에서 구조화된 불평등한 관계가 있음을 인터뷰를 통해 알 수 있다는 내용이다.

구문풀이

2행 Feminist researchers have demonstrated [how the private sphere is a site {where social inequalities are produced and displayed}].

: [ ]는 have demonstrated의 목적어로 쓰인 명사절이고, 그 안의 { }는 a site를 수식하는 관계부사절이다.

5행 Interviews can shed light on the dynamics [that take place within households, including {the relationships between paid domestic workers and their employers} **as well as** {the relationships among family members}].

: [ ]는 the dynamics를 수식하는 주격 관계대명사절이며, 「*A* as well as *B*: B뿐만 아니라 A도」 구문에 의해 두 개의 { }가 연결되고 있다.

9행 In her interviews with domestic workers, for example, Pierrette Hondagneu-Sotelo discovered [how employers of domestic workers failed to acknowledge their status as "real" employees, {justifying decisions (**to keep** wages low and **withhold** benefits)}].

: [ ]는 discovered의 목적어로 쓰인 명사절이고, 그 안의 { }는 동시상황을 나타내는 분사구문이며, ( )는 decisions를 수식하는 형용사적 용법의 to부정사구로 keep과 withhold가 병렬구조로 연결되어 있다.

13행 Interviews like these **help** us **investigate** [how gender, race, and class structure unequal relationships in private settings], [which may go unnoticed but have profound consequences].

: 동사 help는 목적격보어로 동사원형(investigate)이나 to부정사가 올 수 있다. 첫 번째 [ ]는 investigate의 목적어로 쓰인 명사절이고, 두 번째 [ ]는 앞의 명사절을 부연 설명하는 계속적 용법의 주격 관계대명사절이다.

어휘풀이

- demonstrate *v* 보여주다, 증명[입증]하다
- sphere *n* 영역
- display *v* 드러내다, 보이다
- dynamics *n* 역학(관계)
- acknowledge *v* 인정하다
- justify *v* 정당화하다
- benefit *n* 수당
- structure *v* 구조화하다
- unnoticed *a* 눈에 띄지 않는, 간과되는
- profound *a* 중대한
- privilege *v* 특권을 주다

- inequality *n* 불평등
- shed light on ~을 밝히다
- domestic worker 가사 노동자
- status *n* 지위
- withhold *v* ~을 주지 않다, 보류하다
- investigate *v* 연구하다
- setting *n* 환경
- consequence *n* 결과

008 답 ③

📖 **모방 종과 모방 대상 종 사이의 진화 전쟁**

전문해석

과학자들은 처음에 나비 날개의 무늬를 묘사하기 위해 모방이라는 개념을 개발했다. 예를 들어 바이스로이나비는 제주왕나비와 거의 정확히 똑같아 보이는데, 새는 제주왕나비 유충이 유액을 분비하는 식물의 잎을 먹음으로써 갖게 되는 독소를 피하려고 하므로 그것을 공격하지 않는다. 바이스로이나비는 그런 독소가 없지만, 새는 그것을 그것의 씁쓸레한 닮은꼴로 착각하여 마찬가지로 그것을 피한다. 사례는 이제 많은 다른 동물 집단에서도 알려져 있다. 우연히 독성이 있는 종을 닮은 먹을 수 있는 어떤 종도 이점이 있을 것이며, 자연 선택은 이 모방 종을 점점 더 독성이 있는 본보기(모방 대상 종)처럼 보이게 만들 것이다. 이것은 그 본보기에는 나쁜데, 먹을 수 있

는 모방자를 먹는 포식자들이 그 본보기를 쫓는 것 또한 배우기 때문이다. **이것은 본보기에 점점 더 가깝게 닮아가도록 진화하는 모방자와 자기의 먹을 수 있는 이웃과 가능한 한 다르도록 진화하는 본보기 사이의 군비 확대 경쟁을 설정한다.** 어떤 환경적 상황은 관계없는 종 사이에 진정 정밀한 유사함이 진화할 수 있을 정도로 모방자에게 유리하다.

정답풀이

독성이 있는 종을 모방하는 종은 포식자를 피하는 이점을 얻지만, 모방의 대상이 되는 종은 포식자에게 쫓기는 신세가 된다. 따라서 모방하는 종은 최대한 독성이 있는 종과 흡사하도록 진화하고 모방의 대상이 되는 종은 모방하는 종과 최대한 달라 보이도록 진화하게 된다. 결국 이 둘 사이에는 쫓고 달아나는 진화 전쟁이 일어나게 된다는 내용이므로, 글의 주제로 가장 적절한 것은 ③ '모방자와 모방 대상자 사이의 진화 전쟁'이다.

오답풀이

① 포식자와 그 먹잇감의 신속한 공진화
② 모방이 성공적이기 위한 환경 요인
④ 모방이 모방의 대상이 되는 종에 미치는 긍정적 영향
  └ 모방의 대상이 되는 종에게 모방은 부정적 영향이 있다는 내용이다.
⑤ 관계없는 종들 사이에 유사성의 불가능함

구문풀이

2행 For instance, the viceroy butterfly looks almost exactly like the monarch butterfly, [which birds do not attack {because they want to avoid the toxins (the monarch caterpillar gets from eating milkweed leaves)}].

: [ ]는 선행사 the monarch butterfly를 부연 설명하는 계속적 용법의 목적격 관계대명사절이고, 그 안의 { }는 이유를 나타내는 부사절이며, ( )는 the toxins를 수식하는 관계절로 앞에 목적격 관계대명사 which[that]가 생략되었다.

15행 This sets up an arms race **between** the mimic, [which evolves an ever closer resemblance to the model], **and** the model, [which evolves to be **as** different **as possible** from its edible neighbors].

: 「between A and B」에 의해 the mimic과 the model이 연결되어 있고, 두 개의 [ ]는 각각 선행사 the mimic과 the model을 부연 설명하는 계속적 용법의 주격 관계대명사절이다. 「as+원급+as possible」은 '가능한 한 ~한'이라는 의미를 나타낸다.

어휘풀이

- mimicry *n* 모방, 흉내
- monarch butterfly 제주왕나비
- caterpillar *n* 유충
- edible *a* 먹을 수 있는, 식용의
- predator *n* 포식자, 육식 동물
- resemblance *n* 닮음, 유사함
- circumstance *n* 상황, 주위의 사정
- viceroy butterfly 바이스로이나비
- toxin *n* 독소
- lookalike *n* 닮은꼴, 닮은 것
- by chance 우연히
- arms race 군비 확대 경쟁
- evolve *v* 진화하다
- extent *n* 정도, 범위

009 답 ④

📖 소셜 미디어를 통한 비공식적 연구 결과 교환의 의미

전문해석

소셜 미디어의 세계에서, 과학 연구의 출판된 '기록 버전'은 더 이상 공동체에게 그들의 관심 영역에서의 최신 발전에 대한 주의를 환기시키는 주요한 수단이 아니다. 대신에 동료들과 심지어 경쟁자들 사이에 예비 프린트물 및 자료의 교환이 확산되고 있다. 연구 결과와 동료들과의 토론을 온라인으로 먼저 공개하는 것의 매력은 새로운 연구 과정의 중요한 측면이다. 그것은 연구 산출물을 전달하기 위한 적절한 운반자, 즉 속도, 영향 및 적합성 측면에서 출판된 기사를 하찮은 존재로 만드는 새로운

운반자가 필요하다. **이런 맥락에서 비공식적인 교환은 공식적인 연구 과정을 지원하는 유용한 부속물이 된다.** 그러한 비공식 체제가 정보 교환 및 특히 동료 간 의사소통을 위한 공개 토론의 장으로 자리를 잡고 있는 주요 학술지의 기사를 결국 어느 정도까지 제거할 수 있는지는 불확실하지만, **정보 교환에 있어서 과학 학술지 기사의 우선권에 대한 침해는 앞으로 다루어야 할 문제로 남아 있다.**

정답풀이

소셜 미디어 세계에서, 학술지 기사와 같은 출판된 기록물보다는 온라인을 통한 예비 프린트물 및 자료의 교환 활동이 확산되면서 이것이 공식적인 연구 과정을 지원하고 있는데, 과학계의 의사소통에서 과학 학술지 기사의 우선권에 대한 소셜 미디어의 침해는 다루어져야 할 문제로 남아 있다는 내용이다. 따라서 글의 주제로 가장 적절한 것은 ④ '과학적 의사소통에 있어서 소셜 미디어의 역할의 이중적 측면'이다.

오답풀이

① 과학 연구에 있어서 동료 검토의 잠재적인 가치
② 전통적인 과학 지식을 대중화하려는 노력
③ 과학 학술지 기사의 정확성을 지키는 법
⑤ 온라인으로 과학적 연구물을 교환하는 것의 부정적 결과
  └ 온라인으로 연구 결과를 교환하는 것이 공식적 연구 과정을 지원하는 측면이 있지만, 앞으로 그로 인한 문제도 다루어져야 한다는 내용이다.

구문풀이

9행 It requires [appropriate carriers {to convey research outputs}], [new carriers {which marginalise the published article in terms of speed, impact and relevance}].

: 두 개의 [ ]는 동격 관계이며, 첫 번째 { }는 appropriate carriers를 수식하는 형용사적 용법의 to부정사구이고, 두 번째 { }는 new carriers를 수식하는 주격 관계대명사절이다.

14행 It is uncertain the extent [to which such informal systems could even eventually eliminate the established primary journal article as a forum {for information exchange and particularly for inter-peer communication}], / but [erosion of the primacy of the scientific journal article for information exchange] **remains** an issue [to be addressed in the future].

: 첫 번째 [ ]는 the extent를 수식하는 관계절이고, 그 안의 { }는 a forum을 수식하는 전치사구이며, 여기서 as는 '~로서'라는 의미로 쓰였다. 두 번째 [ ]는 but 다음 절에서 주어(핵심은 erosion) 역할을 하고 이에 이어지는 동사는 remains이다. 세 번째 [ ]는 an issue를 수식하는 형용사적 용법의 to부정사구이다.

어휘풀이

- primary *a* 주요한
- alert A to B B에 대해 A에게 주의를 환기시키다
- preprint 예비 프린트, 견본 인쇄본
- peer *n* 동료, 또래
- disclosure *n* 공개, 드러냄
- facet *n* 측면
- carrier *n* 운반자
- article *n* 기사, 논문
- extent *n* 정도
- forum *n* 토론의 장
- primacy *n* 우수성
- preserve *v* 유지하다
- colleague *n* 동료
- competitor *n* 경쟁자
- finding *n* 연구 결과
- appropriate *a* 적절한
- output *n* 출력, 산출물
- relevance *n* 적절성
- eliminate *v* 제거하다
- erosion *n* 침해, 침식
- address *v* (문제 등을) 처리하다

- transform _v_ 변형시키다, 바꾸다
- be confronted with ~에 직면하다
- take ~ into account ~을 고려하다
- nonstick _a_ 들러붙지 않는
- confine _v_ 한정하다

---

010 답 ④

📖 스트레스 해소를 위해 넓은 시각의 관점 갖기

전문해석

여러분이 주의를 집중하는 방식은 여러분이 스트레스를 다루는 방식에 매우 중요한 역할을 한다. 분산된 주의는 여러분이 스트레스를 해소하는 능력을 손상시키는데, 왜냐하면 여러분의 주의가 분산되더라도, 여러분은 경험한 것 중에서 스트레스가 많은 부분에만 집착할 수 있으므로, 그것이 좁게 집중되기 때문이다. **여러분이 주의를 기울이는 초점이 넓어지면, 여러분은 스트레스를 더 쉽게 해소할 수 있다.** 여러분은 어떤 상황의 더 많은 측면을 균형 있는 시각으로 볼 수 있으며, 피상적이고 불안을 유발하는 주의 수준으로 여러분을 얽어매는 한 부분에 갇히지 않을 수 있다. 좁은 초점은 각 경험의 스트레스 수준을 높이지만, **넓어진 초점은 스트레스 수준을 낮추는데,** 왜냐하면 여러분은 각 상황을 더 넓은 시각으로 더 잘 볼 수 있기 때문이다. 불안감을 유발하는 하나의 세부 사항은 더 큰 전체적인 상황보다 덜 중요하다. 그것은 여러분 자신을 들러붙지 않는 프라이팬으로 변형시키는 것과 같다. 여러분은 여전히 달걀을 부칠 수 있지만, 그 달걀은 팬에 들러붙지 않을 것이다.

정답풀이

분산된 주의로 인해 초점이 좁아지면 불안감을 유발하는 측면에 얽매이게 되고 스트레스를 해소하는 능력이 손상되는 반면, 초점을 넓히면 상황의 더 많은 측면을 균형 있는 시각으로 볼 수 있어 스트레스 수준을 낮추므로 전체적인 상황을 볼 수 있도록 주의의 초점을 넓혀야 한다는 것이 글의 핵심이다. 따라서 밑줄 친 부분이 글에서 의미하는 바로 가장 적절한 것은 ④ '스트레스를 주는 측면을 넘어 경험에 대한 더 넓은 시각을 갖는 것'이다.

오답풀이

① 일상생활에서 스트레스가 많은 어떤 경험에도 결코 직면하지 않는 것
② 스트레스의 원인을 파악하기 위해 자신의 시각을 넓히는 것
  ↳ 스트레스를 유발하는 원인에 얽매이는 것에서 벗어나 상황을 더 넓은 시각에서 보는 내용이므로 적절하지 않다.
③ 경험의 긍정적인 측면에 자신의 주의를 거의 한정하지 않는 것
⑤ 넓은 시각을 개발하는 원천으로 스트레스를 고려하는 것

구문풀이

[5행] You **can put** in perspective [many more aspects of any situation] and not **get** locked into one part [that ties you down to superficial and anxiety-provoking levels of attention].

: 조동사 can에 이어지는 동사원형 put과 get이 병렬구조로 연결되었다. 첫 번째 [ ]는 put의 목적어로 쓰인 명사구이고, 두 번째 [ ]는 one part를 수식하는 주격 관계대명사절이다.

어휘풀이

- critical _a_ 중대한, 결정적인
- harm _v_ 손상시키다, 해롭게 하다
- let go of ~을 해소하다, ~을 놓아주다[풀어주다]
- fixate on ~에 집착하다
- put ~ in perspective ~을 균형 있는 시각으로 보다
- tie ~ down to … ~을 …에 옭아[얽어]매다
- superficial _a_ 피상적인
- anxiety-provoking _a_ 불안을 유발하는
- scatter _v_ 분산시키다, 흩뜨리다
- spotlight _n_ 초점, 주시, 관심

---

011 답 ①

📖 근대의 주체성 구축의 중심적 매체 역할을 한 개인 일기

전문해석

18세기와 19세기에 완전히 발달한 상태가 된, 개인 일기는 근대적 주체성을 구성하는 데 중심물이 되었는데, 그것의 중심에 있는 것은 이성과 비평을 세계와 자아의 이해에 적용하는 것이고, 이는 새로운 종류의 지식을 창조할 수 있게 해주었다. **일기는 그것을 통해 깨우치고 자유로운 주체가 구성될 수 있는 중심 매체였다.** 그것은 개인이 자신의 행방, 감정, 생각에 대해 매일 쓸 수 있는 공간을 제공했다. 시간이 지남에 따라 그리고 다시 읽어짐으로써, 이질적인 기입 내용, 사건 및 우연이 자아에 관한 통찰력과 이야기로 만들어질 수 있었으며, 주체성 형성을 가능하게 해주었다. '말로 만들어지기도 하고 탐구되기도 하는 (대로의) 자아'라는 개념이 나타나는 것은 바로 그러한 상황이다. 일기는 개인적이고 사적인 것이었는데, 사람들이 자신을 위해 쓰곤 했거나, Habermas의 명확한 표현에 따르면, 사람들이 자기 자신을 스스로에게 공개되게 하곤 했다. **자아를 사적 영역에서 공개함으로써, 자아는 또한 자기 점검과 자기비판의 대상이 되었다.**

정답풀이

일기는 그것을 통해 계몽되고 자유로운 주체를 구성할 수 있는 중심 매체로서 자신의 행방, 감정, 생각에 대해 매일 쓸 수 있도록 해주었으며, 일기에 기입한 내용이 자아에 관한 통찰력과 이야기로 만들어질 수 있었고, 주체성 형성을 가능하게 해주었다. 또한 마지막 문장에서 일기를 통해 자아는 또한 자기 점검과 자기비판의 대상이 되었다고 했으므로, 밑줄 친 부분이 의미하는 바로는 ① '글을 자신을 되돌아보는 수단으로 사용하다'가 가장 적절하다.

오답풀이

② 타인의 일기를 읽음으로써 자신의 정체성을 확립하다
  ↳ 타인의 일기가 아니라 자신이 쓴 일기를 다시 읽음으로써 주체성 형성이 가능하다는 내용이다.
③ 글 쓰는 과정에서 피드백을 교환하다
④ 다른 사람에게 보이기 위한 대체 자아를 만들어 내다
  ↳ 일기는 사적인 것으로 다른 사람이 아니라 스스로에게 자기 자신을 보여주는 수단이다.
⑤ 자아에 관한 글쓰기 주제를 개발하다

구문풀이

[1행] [Coming of age in the 18th and 19th centuries], the personal diary became a centerpiece in the construction of a modern subjectivity, [**at the heart of which** is {the application of reason and critique to the understanding of world and self}], [which allowed the creation of a new kind of knowledge].

: 첫 번째 [ ]는 문장의 주어(the personal diary)에 대한 부가적인 설명을 하는 분사구문이다. 두 번째 [ ]는 the construction of a modern subjectivity를 부연 설명하는 관계절인데, 부사구 at the heart of which가 절 앞으로 나와서 관계절의 주어인 { }와 동사 is가 도치되었다. 세 번째 [ ]는 the application of reason ~ world and self를 부연 설명하는 주격 관계대명사절이다.

어휘풀이

- come of age (어떤 것이) 발달한 상태가 되다, 성년이 되다
- centerpiece _n_ 중심물, 중심적 존재
- subjectivity _n_ 주체성, 주관성
- reason _n_ 이성
- enlightened _a_ 깨우친, 계몽된
- construction _n_ 구성, 건설
- application _n_ 적용
- critique _n_ 비평, 비판
- whereabouts _n_ 행방, 소재

- entry *n* 기입 사항
- insight *n* 통찰력
- formulation *n* 명확한 표현
- public *a* 공개의
- self-inspection *n* 자기 점검
- alternate *a* 대체의, 대안의
- happenstance *n* 우연, 뜻밖의 일
- narrative *n* 이야기
- emerge *v* 나타나다, 등장하다
- sphere *n* 영역, 분야
- reflect on ~을 되돌아보다[반성하다]

012 답 ②

📖 때로는 한정적이어야 하지만 어느 정도 보장되어야 하는 전문가에 대한 신뢰

전문해석
과학자들이 도덕적 혹은 윤리적 결정에 대해 특별히 유리한 입장에 있는 것은 아닌데, 기후 과학자가 의료 개혁에 대해 의견을 말할 자격이 없는 것은 물리학자가 꿀벌 군집의 붕괴 원인을 판단할 자격이 없는 것과 같다. 특화된 영역에서 전문 지식을 만들어 내는 바로 그 특징이 많은 다른 특화된 영역에서는 무지로 이어진다. 어떤 경우에는, 비전문가들, 즉 농부, 어부, 환자, 원주민들이, 과학자들에게 배움의 원천이 될 수 있는 관련된 경험을 가지고 있을지도 모른다. 실제로, 최근에 과학자들은 이 점을 인식하기 시작했는데, 북극 기후 영향 평가는 지역 토착 집단에게서 수집된 관찰을 포함한다. 그러므로 우리의 신뢰는 제한되고 집중적일 필요가 있다. 신뢰는 매우 '까다로워' 한다. 맹목적 신뢰는 적어도 신뢰가 전혀 없는 것만큼이나 우리를 곤란에 빠뜨릴 것이다. 하지만 우리가 특별히 전문가라고 부르는 사람들, 즉 우리가 사는 자연 세계에 관한 어려운 질문들을 해결하는 데 자신의 삶을 바친 남녀들에 대한 어느 정도의 신뢰가 없으면, 우리는 마비되고, 사실상 아침 통근 준비를 해야 할지 하지 말아야 할지를 알지 못하게 될 것이다.

정답풀이
과학자와 같은 전문가들도 때로는 일반인들로부터 배워야 할 경우가 있으므로 전문가의 전문 지식에 대한 신뢰는 한정되고 특화된 영역으로 초점이 맞춰져야 하지만, 그렇다 해도 평생을 연구에 바친 전문가들의 전문성에 대해 어느 정도의 신뢰가 없다면 '아침에 통근을 준비해야 할지'와 같은 일상의 문제도 알 수 없을 정도로 세상이 마비될 것이라는 내용이다. But으로 시작하는 부분부터 전문가에 대한 신뢰가 필요함을 말하고 있으므로, 밑줄 친 부분이 의미하는 바로 가장 적절한 것은 ② '전문화된 전문가들에 의해 제공된 쉽게 적용할 수 있는 정보'이다.

오답풀이
① 비전문가에 의해 보급된 의심스러운 사실
③ 중차대한 결정에 거의 영향을 주지 않는 일반 지식
④ 전문가와 전문가가 아닌 사람들 모두에 의해 생산된 실용적인 지식
　↳ 전문가가 자신의 특화된 영역에서 만들어 내는 지식에 대한 신뢰는 필요하다는 문맥이다.
⑤ 지역 공동체에 널리 퍼져 있는 편향된 지식

구문풀이
1행 Scientists have no special purchase on moral or ethical decisions; a climate scientist **is no more** qualified to comment on health care reform **than** a physicist is to judge the causes of bee colony collapse.

: 세미콜론(;) 다음에는 「*A* is no more *B* than *C* is *D*」 구문이 쓰여 'A가 B가 아닌 것은 C가 D가 아닌 것과 같다'라는 의미를 나타내고 있다. to judge 앞에는 qualified가 생략된 것으로 볼 수 있다.

15행 But [without some degree of trust in **our designated experts** – the men and women {who have devoted their lives to <sorting out tough questions about the natural world (we live in)>}

—] we are paralyzed, [in effect **not knowing** {whether to make ready for the morning commute or not}].

: 첫 번째 [ ]는 전치사 without이 이끄는 부사구이고, 대시(–)로 표시된 부분은 our designated experts를 구체적으로 설명하는 동격 어구이다. 첫 번째 [ ] 안의 { }는 the men and women을 수식하는 주격 관계대명사절이고, 〈 〉는 전치사 to의 목적어 역할을 하는 동명사구이며, ( )는 the natural world를 수식하는 관계절로 앞에 목적격 관계대명사가 생략되었다. 두 번째 [ ]는 부대상황을 나타내는 분사구문이고, 그 안의 { }는 knowing의 목적어로 쓰인 명사구이다.

어휘풀이
- purchase *n* 유리한 입장, 강점
- qualified *a* 자격이 있는
- colony *n* (개미, 벌 등의) 군집, 군체
- feature *n* 특징
- domain *n* 영역
- Arctic *a* 북극의
- particular *a* 까다로운
- designated *a* 특별히 (~이라고) 불리는
- devote *v* 바치다, 헌신하다
- in effect 사실상
- popularize *v* 보급하다, 널리 알리다
- biased *a* 편향된
- ethical *a* 윤리적인
- physicist *n* 물리학자
- collapse *n* 붕괴, 와해
- expertise *n* 전문 지식
- relevant *a* 관련이 있는
- assessment *n* 평가
- sort out (문제 등을) 해결하다
- paralyze *v* 마비시키다
- applicable *a* 적용[응용]할 수 있는

013 답 ①

📖 아이디어를 보관해야 할 필요성

전문해석
어떤 아이디어가 학급에 제시될 때, 나는 이따금 학생들이 그런 아이디어를 받아들일 수 없다고 (심지어 적대적인 태도로) 말하는 것을 들었다. 그것은 완전히 그릇된 결론이다. 받아들일 것은 아무것도 없다. 예술에서 아이디어는 지옥을 피하기 위해 믿어야 하는 종교가 아니다. 그것은 영원히 예술가의 목을 죄는 골칫거리가 아니다. 그것에게 매일 먹을 것을 줄 필요가 없다. 아이디어는 필요 없을 때 보관되고 필요할 때 사용되는 도구에 지나지 않는다. 대부분의 예술가는 잡동사니 수집가이다. 그들은 언젠가 유용하게 쓰일 것이라고 생각하는 온갖 종류의 흥미로운 잡동사니를 수집한다. 그렇다면 아이디어를 수집하는 것은 어떤가? 그것을 공구 창고에 있는 드릴처럼 자신의 마음속 깊이 보관하라. 구멍을 뚫어야 할 일이 있으면 그 드릴을 집어 들라. 아리스토텔레스는 교육받은 사람의 특징은 어떤 아이디어를 믿지 않고 그것을 '즐길 수 있는' 능력이라고 주장했다.

정답풀이
예술에서 아이디어는 받아들여야 하고 종교처럼 믿어야 하는 것이거나 예술가의 마음을 억누르는 골칫거리가 아니라 보관해 두었다가 필요할 때 꺼내 쓰는 도구에 지나지 않는다고 하면서 어떤 아이디어든 거부하지 말고 일단 마음속에 보관해 두라는 요지의 글이다. 구멍을 뚫어야 할 일이 있으면 공구 창고에 있는 드릴을 집어 들라는 것은 아이디어를 마음속에 보관해 두면 언제든 필요할 때 쓸 수 있다는 의미이다. 따라서 밑줄 친 부분이 글에서 의미하는 바로는 ① '모아 둔 아이디어 중 하나가 쓸모 있을 때가 올 것이다.'가 가장 적절하다.

오답풀이
② 아이디어를 반박할 충분한 증거를 제시한다면 그것을 거부할 수 있다.
③ 아이디어를 실행에 옮겨야 할 때 열정을 유지하라.
④ 흥미를 끄는 아이디어에 집중하기 위해서 그렇지 않은 아이디어를 무시하라.
⑤ 다른 사람들과 자신의 아이디어를 공유하는 것은 흔히 새로운 아이디어를 자극하는 좋은 방법이다.

10행 They collect all kinds of interesting junk [that {they think} might come in handy sometime].

: [ ]는 all kinds of interesting junk를 수식하는 주격 관계대명사절이고, 그 안의 { }는 삽입절이다.

어휘풀이
- hostile *a* 적대적인
- religion *n* 종교
- permanently *ad* 영원히, 영구적으로
- nothing more than ~에 지나지 않는
- store *v* 저장[보관]하다
- pack rat 잡동사니 수집가
- junk *n* 잡동사니, 고물
- come in handy 도움이 되다, 유용하게 쓰이다
- toolshed *n* 공구 창고
- insist *v* 주장하다
- mark *n* 특색, 특징
- refute *v* 반박하다
- keep up ~을 유지하다
- enthusiasm *n* 열정, 열의
- concentrate on ~에 집중하다
- stimulate *v* 자극하다, 촉진시키다

014 답 ④

📖 지식 집약적인 회사의 직원들이 수행하는 단순하고 기계적인 일

전문해석
지식 집약적이라고 주장하는 거의 모든 조직의 빛나는 표면을 긁어내면, 꽤 다른 현실을 발견할 것이다. 물론, 교육을 잘 받은 똑똑한 사람들이 흔히 많이 있지만, 기업의 지식인들 대부분이 그들의 지력을 충분히 사용하고 있다는 증거가 거의 없는 경우가 흔하다. **때때로 이것은 많은 지식 집약적인 회사들이 일상적이고 복잡하지 않은 일자리에서 일하는 머리 좋은 사람들로 꽉 차 있기 때문이다.** 보통의 시장 조사 회사에 대해 생각해 보라. 이러한 지식 집약적인 회사들은 일반적으로 두 가지 일을 하기 위해 번듯한 학위를 가진 예절 바른 젊은이들을 고용하는데, 저녁 식사를 하고 있는 사람들에게 전화를 해서 멍청한 질문을 하거나 이러한 전화 통화에서 얻는 자료를 고속으로 처리하는 일이다. **이러한 일 중 어느 하나가 얼마나 많은 지적 기술을 필요로 하는지는 의심스럽다.** 그것들이 정말 필요로 하는 것은 멋진 억양과 낯두꺼움이다. 한 콜센터 직원이 그 일을 '머릿속의 조립 라인'이라고 묘사한 것은 놀랄 일이 아니다.

정답풀이
지식 집약적인 회사의 머리 좋은 직원들이 수행하는 단순하고 일상적인 업무에 대한 내용이다. 시장 조사 회사의 머리 좋은 지식인들을 예로 들고 있는데, 그들이 하는, 사람들에게 전화해 멍청한 질문을 하거나 그 질문에서 얻은 자료를 빠르게 처리하는 일은 많은 지식적 기술을 필요로 하지 않는다고 했다. 따라서 그러한 일을 머릿속에 있는 조립 라인에서 처리되는 단순하고 반복적인 일로 비유하고 있으므로 밑줄 친 부분이 의미하는 바로는 ④ '지적인 직원들에 의해 행해지는 단순하고 판에 박힌 일'이다.

오답풀이
① 실수가 전혀 없는 완벽한 업무 수행
└▸ 머리 좋은 직원들이 수행하는 단순하고 일상적인 업무를 비유적으로 나타낸 말이지, 정해진 틀에 맞춰져 실수 없이 수행되는 일을 말하고 있는 게 아니다.
② 노력을 거의 요구하지 않는 아주 수익성이 높은 일
③ 수행되는 일에 대한 철저한 사전 계획
⑤ 상해를 입은 공장 노동자들에 의해 수행되는 힘든 일

구문풀이

6행 Sometimes this is because many knowledge-intensive firms are packed with clever people [working in jobs {that are routine and uncomplicated}].

: [ ]는 clever people을 수식하는 현재분사구이고, 그 안의 { }는 jobs를 수식하는 주격 관계대명사절이다.

어휘풀이
- scratch *v* 긁다
- organisation *n* 조직체
- knowledge-intensive *a* 지식 집약적인
- corporate *a* 기업의
- intellect *n* 지력, 지성
- be packed with ~로 꽉 차다
- routine *a* 반복적인
- uncomplicated *a* 복잡하지 않은
- typically *ad* 보통
- hire *v* 고용하다
- well-mannered *a* 예의 바른
- decent *a* 번듯한, 남 부끄럽지 않은
- degree *n* 학위
- yield *v* (결과, 대답 등을) 가져오다
- questionable *a* 의심스러운
- thick skin 낯두꺼움
- demanding *a* 힘든

015 답 ⑤

📖 최우선 순위의 일과 그렇지 않은 일에서의 만족감

전문해석
사회 심리학에서 최근의 연구는 행복한 사람들은 더 많은 것을 가진 사람들이 아니라, 오히려 자신이 이미 가지고 있는 것에 만족해하는 사람들이라는 것을 보여 주었다. **행복한 사람들은 비록 그들이 그것을 알지는 못하더라도 '항상' 최소한의 필요조건을 충족시키는 데 몰두한다.** Warren Buffett은 최소한의 필요조건을 충족시키는 것을 극단적으로 수용하는 것으로 보일 수 있는데, 세계에서 가장 부유한 사람 중 한 사람인 그는 고속도로에서 한 블록 떨어진 Omaha에 있는 50년 동안 살아온 똑같은, 아담한 집에 살고 있다. 그는 이전에 한 라디오 인터뷰 진행자에게 일주일간의 뉴욕시 방문 동안 아침식사로 우유 1갤런과 오레오 쿠키 한 상자를 직접 구입했다고 말했다. 그러나 Buffet은 그의 투자 전략에 있어서는 최소한의 필요조건을 충족시키지 않는데, **최소한의 필요조건을 충족시키는 것은 자신의 최우선 순위가 아닌 것들에 시간을 낭비하지 않기 위한 도구이다. 최우선 순위의 시도에 있어서는 탁월함에 대한 구식의 추구가 여전히 올바른 전략이다.** 여러분은 자신의 외과의사나 비행기 정비사 또는 1억 달러짜리 장편 영화의 감독이 그저 충분히 잘하기를 원하는가 아니면 그들이 할 수 있는 최선을 다하기를 원하는가? 때때로 여러분은 오레오와 우유 이상을 원한다.

정답풀이
최우선 순위가 아닌 일들에서 최소한의 필요조건만 충족시키는 것은 그러한 일들에 시간을 낭비하지 않기 위해서이며, 최우선 순위의 일에서는 탁월함을 추구하는 것이 여전히 올바른 전략임을 Warren Buffett의 사례를 들어 이야기하고 있다. Warren Buffett이 일화에서 아침식사로 오레오 쿠키와 우유를 구입한 것은 최우선 순위가 아닌 일들에서 최소한의 필요조건을 충족시키는 것을 뜻하므로 '오레오와 우유 이상을 원한다'는 것은 최소한의 필요조건이 아닌 탁월함을 추구하기를 원한다는 것임을 추론할 수 있다. 따라서 밑줄 친 부분이 글에서 의미하는 바로는 ⑤ '자신에게 가장 중요한 분야에서만 탁월함을 추구한다'가 가장 적절하다.

오답풀이
① 적은 시간을 투자해서 큰 결과를 얻는다
② 자신의 분야에서 최고가 되는 것에 최우선 순위를 둔다
③ 정신적인 만족을 추구하는 것보다 기본적인 욕구를 충족시키는 것을 가치 있게 여긴다
④ 매일 하는 작은 일들에서 큰 만족을 느낀다

구문풀이

17행 Do you **want** [your surgeon or your airplane mechanic or the director of a $100 million feature film] [**to do** just good enough or

---

do the best {they possibly **can**}]?

: 첫 번째 [ ]는 want의 목적어이고, 두 번째 [ ]가 목적격보어 역할을 하는 to부정사구이며, 두 개의 do가 병렬구조를 이룬다. { }는 the best를 수식하는 목적격 관계대명사절로 can은 can do를 대신한다.

어휘풀이
- psychology *n* 심리학
- engage in ~에 몰두하다, ~에 참여하다
- satisfice *v* 최소한의 필요조건을 충족시키다, 작은 성과에 만족하다
- embrace *v* 수용하다, 받아들이다
- modest *a* 아담한
- strategy *n* 전략
- endeavor *n* 시도, 노력
- excellence *n* 탁월함
- mechanic *n* 정비사
- to an extreme 극도로, 극단적으로
- investment *n* 투자
- priority *n* 우선(권), 우선순위
- pursuit *n* 추구
- surgeon *n* 외과의사
- feature film 장편 영화

016 답 ④

📖 배움이 아니라 실행을 통해서 드러나는 창의력

전문해석
대학교 학위는 학업 지식이지 그것이 꼭 응용 지식인 것은 아니다. 모든 응용 지식이 책을 통해서 또는 교실에서 학습되는 것은 아니다. 응용 지식은 창의성, 경험 그리고 실행력을 필요로 한다. 매니저로서 나는 나의 조직에서 가장 많은 응용 지식을 가진 직원들이 경력 초기부터 그 모든 학업적 성취를 이룬 직원들보다 더 성공한다는 것을 알아차렸다. 창의력은 학교에서뿐 아니라 알려진 실제 세상 어디에서도 가르쳐주지 않는다. 응용 지식은 기본적으로 당신이 할 수 있는 것을 보여준다. 학업 지식은 기본적으로 당신이 알고 있는 전부이다. 매니저로서 나는 방에서 가장 현명한 사람을 고르기보다는 일을 완수할 수 있는 사람을 고를 것이다. 나는 실행의 열렬한 팬이다. 당신은 누군가에게 창의력 스위치를 켜라고 말할 수 없다. 나는 나의 직원들을 오랜 시간 동안 관찰해 왔고 내가 알게 된 것은 창의적인 사람들은 그들의 동료들이 하지 않는 두 가지를 실제로 한다는 것이다. 그들은 다른 관점에서 사물들을 보며 새로운 아이디어를 만들기 위해서 아이디어들을 연결한다.

정답풀이
창의력은 배울 수 있는 것이 아니라 다른 관점에서 사물들을 보고 기존의 아이디어를 결합하는 실천을 통해서 나오는 것이라는 내용의 글이다. 창의력 스위치를 켜라고 할 수 없다는 것은 창의력이 내재해 있어서 전등처럼 마음대로 켜거나 끌 수 있는 것이 아니라는 의미이다. 따라서 밑줄 친 부분이 의미하는 바로는 ④ '창의력은 재능의 문제가 아니라 과업 실행의 문제이다.'가 가장 적절하다.

오답풀이
① 창의력을 가르칠 수는 없지만 그것을 없앨 수는 있다.
② 사람들의 창의력은 그들의 교육에서 나온다.
③ 창의력 스위치는 언제나 켜져 있고 아이디어는 술술 나온다.
   └ '창의력 스위치를 켜다'라는 표현이 내재된 창의력의 발현과 관련이 있다고 생각할 수 있으나, 이는 창의력에 있어 실행의 중요성을 담고 있는 이 글의 주제와 연관 지어 생각해 보면 적절하지 않다.
⑤ 창의력을 가지고 태어나지 않은 사람들은 그것을 얻기 위해 고군분투한다.

구문풀이
17행 I have observed my employees for a long time / and [what I have learned] is [that <u>people</u> {who are creative} really do <u>two things</u> {their co-workers do not do}].

: and로 두 개의 절이 연결된 구조이다. 첫 번째 [ ]는 관계대명사 what이 이끄는 명사절로 and 다음 절에서 주어 역할을 한다. 두 번째 [ ]는 is의 보어로 쓰인 명사절이며,

---

그 안의 첫 번째 { }는 people을 수식하는 주격 관계대명사절이고, 두 번째 { }는 two things를 수식하는 목적격 관계대명사절이다.

어휘풀이
- degree *n* 학위
- creativity *n* 창의력, 창조력
- achievement *n* 성취
- for that matter 그 점에 있어서는 (마찬가지로)
- practical *a* 실제적인
- perspective *n* 관점
- effortlessly *ad* 쉽게, 힘들이지 않고
- academic *a* 학업의, 학문의
- implementation *n* 실행, 이행
- observe *v* 관찰하다
- form *v* 만들어 내다
- carry out ~을 수행하다

017 답 ③

📖 과학적 조사 방법이 유효하지 않은 역사

전문해석
Carl Becker에 따르면, 우리가 역사적 사실이라고 말하는 것은 진정 어떤 통상적인 의미에서도 전혀 사실이 아니다. 관찰하거나 측정할 수 있는 대신, 역사적 사실은 그저 사라진 과거 사건들을 상징적으로 나타낸 것일 뿐이다. 역사는 실험실에서 밝혀지지도 기록되지도 않는다. 역사적 탐구의 결론은 그것을 어떤 다른 종류의 탐구의 결론과 비교함으로써 확증되거나 반증될 수 없고, 그것(역사적 탐구의 결론)이 진실성이라는 독자적인 기준과 대조하여 검증될 수 없기 때문에, 역사는 물리 과학과 동일한 정확성의 엄격한 기준에 얽매이지 않는다. 소설가 Cormac McCarthy의 말로 '역사에는 대조군이 없다'. 역사가는 일반적으로 자신의 가설을 객관적으로 검증할 어떠한 방법도 갖고 있지 않다. 역사에는 대조군이 없을 뿐만 아니라, 역사가는 보통 그들의 대상에 대한 직접적인 관찰자도 아니다. 이러한 한계 때문에 R. G. Collingwood는 역사가 '특별한 종류'의 과학이라는 것을 시인했다. Frederic W. Maitland는 만약 역사가 어떤 의미에서든 과학적으로 여겨질 수 있다면, '명탐정의 방법이 과학적일 수도 있다는 의미에서일 뿐'이라고 말했다.

정답풀이
역사적 사실은 사라진 과거의 사건들을 상징적으로 나타낸 것이므로 물리 과학의 연구에서처럼 객관적으로 검증할 수 있는 어떤 과학적 방법의 대상도 될 수 없다는 내용의 글이다. 따라서 밑줄 친 부분이 의미하는 바로는 ③ '과학적 연구는 역사 탐구에 유효하지 않다'가 가장 적절하다.

오답풀이
① 역사는 매우 엄격한 정확성의 기준을 가지고 있다
② 과거의 역사적 사건은 미래의 사건을 예측할 수 없다
④ 과학적 방법은 역사 연구에 큰 도움이 된다
   └ 글의 요지와는 상반된 내용을 담고 있어서 오답!
⑤ 역사가들은 소설가 못지않은 상상력을 필요로 한다

구문풀이
15행 **Not only** [<u>are</u> there no control groups in history], **but** [historians are usually not even firsthand observers of their subjects].

: 두 개의 [ ]로 표시된 절이 「not only ~, but (also) ...(~일 뿐만 아니라 …도)」의 상관접속사로 연결되었다. 부정어구인 Not only가 절 맨 앞으로 나오면서 there와 are가 도치되었다.

어휘풀이
- refer to as ~라고 말하다[일컫다]
- vanish *v* 사라지게 하다
- inquiry *v* 탐구
- falsify *v* 반증하다
- representation *n* 표현, 나타낸 것
- unfold *v* 펼쳐지다, 밝혀지다
- confirm *v* 확증하다
- criterion *n* 기준 (*pl.* criteria)

- credibility *n* 진실성, 신뢰성
- be subject to ~에 얽매이다, ~ 하에 놓이다
- rigorous *a* 엄격한　　　・exactness *n* 정확성
- hypothesis *n* 가설 (*pl.* hypotheses)
- firsthand *a* 직접의　　　・investigation *n* 연구, 조사
- invalid *a* 유효하지 않은, 근거 없는　　・be of help 도움이 되다
- stand in need of ~을 필요로 하다　・no less *A* than *B* B 못지않게 A한

018 답 ②

BB 전문적인 지식 분야들을 연결시켜 본질을 이루는 전체를 찾으려는 노력

전문해석

사람들은 무엇이 본질을 구성하는가에 대해 끝없이 논쟁하지만, 우리의 정의를 단순하고 부인할 수 없는 사실로부터 시작하자. 즉, 약 40억 년 전에 이 행성에서 생명체가 단순한 세포의 형태로 시작되었다. 이 세포들은 뒤따르는 모든 생명체의 공통 조상이었다. 이 세포들로부터 다양한 생명체의 자손이 생겨났다. 놀랍도록 복잡한 일련의 상황 속에서, 우리는 특정한 전환점에서 우리 인간이 진화해 온 하나의 조상을 확인할 수 있다. 이러한 생명체의 상호 연관성을 궁극적인 본질이라고 하자. 그리고 아마도 오늘날 우리는 본질로의 복귀에 대한 초기 징후를 목격하고 있을 수 있다. 과학에서 이것의 첫 씨앗은 Faraday, Maxwell 그리고 Einstein에서 시작되었는데, 그들은 개별적인 입자 대신에 현상들, 즉 힘의 장들 사이의 관계에 초점을 맞추었다. 게다가, 많은 과학자들은 현재 그들의 다양한 전문 분야들을 다른 것들과 연결시키기 위해 노력하고 있다. 우리는 경제학, 생물학 그리고 컴퓨터와 같이 너무나 이질적인 분야들에 적용되는 복잡한 이론들에 대한 관심이 증가하는 것에서도 이것을 볼 수 있다. 우리는 또한 그것을 건강과 의학의, 많은 사람들이 신체를 하나의 완전체로 여기고 있는 방식에서 볼 수 있다. 이러한 경향이 미래인데, 왜냐하면 의식 그 자체의 목적은 항상 우리를 본질과 연결시키는 것이었기 때문이다.

정답풀이

태초에 단순한 형태의 세포에서 생명체가 시작되었고, 어느 시점에서 인간이 진화해 온 하나의 조상을 확인할 수 있다고 하면서 이러한 생명체의 상호 연관성을 궁극적인 본질이라고 정의하고 있다. 또 많은 과학자들이 다양한 전문 분야들을 다른 것들과 연결시키기 위해 노력하고 있고, 경제학이나 생물학, 컴퓨터와 같은 이질적인 분야들에 적용되는 복잡한 이론에 대한 관심이 증가하고 있으며, 건강과 의학에서 신체를 하나의 완전체로 여기고 있다는 것에서 오늘날 나타난 '본질로의 복귀'란 ② '다양한 지식 분야를 연결하기 위해 본질적인 전체에 집중하는 것'임을 추론할 수 있다.

오답풀이

① 이론적인 지식보다는 실용적인 대안에 집중하는 것
③ 밀접하게 관련되거나 중복되는 분야들 사이의 아주 미묘한 차이를 구별하는 것
④ 지구 생명체의 기원을 연구하여 당면한 문제에 대한 해결책을 찾는 것
⑤ 다양한 형태로 나타나며 다양한 속성을 가진 하나의 본질을 찾는 것
└→ 본질을 찾는다는 것에서 정답이라고 생각할 수 있지만, 다양한 지식 분야를 연결하는 본질적인 전체를 추구한다는 요지를 담고 있지 않아서 오답!

구문풀이

17행 We can see this in the growing interest in complex theories [applied to such disparate fields **as** economics, biology, and computers].

: [ ]는 과거분사구로 complex theories를 수식하며, as는 전치사로 '~와 같은, ~처럼'의 의미로 쓰였다.

어휘풀이
- constitute *v* 구성하다
- ancestor *n* 조상
- remarkably *ad* 놀라울 정도로
- turning point 전환점
- ultimate *ad* 궁극적인
- witness *v* 목격하다
- phenomenon *n* 현상 (*pl.* phenomena)
- field of force 힘의 장(전기장이나 자기장 같은 힘이 작용하는 공간)
- particle *n* 입자　　　・specialization *n* 전문 분야
- disparate *a* 서로 이질적인, 서로 관련 없는
- consciousness *n* 의식, 자각　　・alternative *n* 대안
- theoretical *a* 이론적인　　・overlap *v* 겹치다
- discipline *n* (학문의) 분야　　・manifest oneself 나타나다
- attribute *n* 속성
- undeniable *a* 부인할 수 없는, 확실한
- emerge *v* 나타나다, 나오다
- identify *v* 확인하다
- interrelatedness *n* 상호 관련성
- reality *n* 본질, 실재, 현실

- orient towards ~쪽으로 향하다
- register *v* 마음속에 새기다, 명심하다
- protrusion *n* 내밀기
- experiment *v* 실험하다
- capacity *n* 능력
- drive *n* 욕구, 추진력
- preferentially *ad* 우선적으로
- imitate *v* 모방하다
- tighten *v* (입을) 다물다
- distress *n* 괴로움, 고통
- perceive *v* 지각하다, 인식하다

019 답 ②

📖 사회적 자극에 차별적으로 반응하는 타고난 인간의 성향

전문해석

많은 연구가 사회적 자극에 차별적으로 반응하는 타고난 인간 성향에 대한 상당한 증거를 제시한다. 태어날 때부터, 아기들은 사람의 얼굴과 목소리 쪽으로 우선하여 향하게 될 것인데, 이러한 자극이 자신들에게 특별하게 의미가 있다는 것을 알고 있는 것 같다. 게다가, 그들은 혀 내밀기, 입술 다물기, 입 벌리기와 같이 자신들에게 보여지는 다양한 얼굴 제스처를 모방하면서 이러한 연결을 적극적으로 마음속에 새긴다. 심지어 그들은 자신들이 다소 어려워하는 제스처에 맞추려고 노력하고, 성공할 때까지 자기 자신의 얼굴로 실험한다. 그들은 정말 성공하면 눈을 반짝이면서 즐거움을 보여주고, 실패하면 괴로움을 나타낸다. 다시 말해, 그들은 운동감각적으로 경험한 그들 자신의 신체적 움직임과 시각적으로 지각되는 다른 사람의 그것들을 일치시키는 타고난 능력을 가지고 있을 뿐만 아니라, 그렇게 하려는 타고난 욕구도 가지고 있다. 즉, 그들은 자신들이 '나와 비슷하다'라고 판단하는 타인을 모방하려는 타고난 욕구를 가지고 있는 것 같다.

정답풀이

② **관계대명사 which:** 뒤에 주어, 동사, 목적어를 갖춘 완전한 절이 왔으므로 관계대명사 which를 단독으로 쓸 수 없다. 앞의 선행사 gestures가 which 뒤의 절과 연결되려면 부사적인 역할을 해야 하는데, '그들이 (타인들의) 제스처에 어려움을 가진다'라는 문맥이므로 which를 with which와 같은 '전치사+관계대명사' 표현으로 바꿔 써야 한다.

오답풀이

① **분사구문의 태:** 주어인 infants의 상태를 부가적으로 설명하는 분사구문으로, 아기들이 '알고 있는 것 같다'는 능동의 의미이므로 현재분사 seeming은 어법상 적절하다.

③ **동사의 강조:** 주어가 3인칭 복수이고 현재시제이므로 일반동사 succeed를 강조하는 조동사 do는 어법상 적절하다.

④ **대명사:** bodily movements를 대신하므로 복수형 대명사인 those는 어법상 적절하다.

⑤ **to부정사:** 동사 judge의 목적어는 앞에 위치한 whom이고, to be 'like me'는 목적어를 보충하는 목적격보어 역할을 하고 있으므로 to be는 어법상 적절하다.

└ 「judge+목적어+(to be) 목적격보어: ~을 …라고 판단하다」의 구문으로, 목적어 역할을 하는 whom이 앞으로 나가면서 동사 다음에 to be가 바로 연결되었다.

구문풀이

[4행] Moreover, they register this connection actively, [imitating a variety of facial gestures {that are presented to them} – tongue protrusions, lip tightenings, mouth openings].

: [ ]는 주절에 이어지는 부수적 상황을 나타내는 분사구문으로 의미상의 주어는 주절의 주어와 동일한 they이다. { }는 a variety of facial gestures를 수식하는 주격 관계대명사절이고, 대시(—) 다음에 a variety of facial gestures that are presented to them의 구체적인 예시를 열거하고 있다.

어휘풀이

- substantial *a* 상당한
- stimulus *n* 자극 (*pl.* stimuli)
- differentially *ad* 차별적으로
- infant *n* 아기, 유아

020 답 ②

📖 자기표현의 가장 단순하고 값싼 방법 중 하나인 패션

전문해석

유행은 사람들이 자신을 재조정할 새로운 기회를 끊임없이 제시하고, 변화의 때를 나타낸다. 유행이 궁극적으로 어떻게 개인에게 힘과 자유를 줄 수 있는지를 이해하기 위해서는 먼저 변화를 위한 기반으로서의 패션의 중요성에 대해 논의해야 한다. 왜 패션이 그렇게 매력적인지에 대해 나의 정보 제공자들이 한 가장 흔한 설명은 그것이 일종의 연극적인 의상을 구성한다는 것이다. 옷은 사람들이 자신을 세상에 보여주는 방식의 일부이고, 패션은 사회에서 일어나고 있는 일, 그리고 패션 자체의 역사와 관련하여 그들을 현재에 위치시킨다. 표현 형태로서 패션은 다수의 모호함을 담고 있어 개인이 특정한 옷과 연관된 의미를 재창조할 수 있게 한다. 패션은 자기표현의 가장 단순하고 값싼 방법 중 하나로, 옷은 저렴하게 구매할 수 있으며, 부, 지적 능력, 휴식 또는 환경 의식에 대한 개념을, 비록 이것 중 어느 것도 사실이 아니라 해도, 쉽게 전달할 수 있다. 패션은 또한 행동을 위한 공간을 열어주며 다양한 방법으로 행동력을 강화할 수 있다.

정답풀이

② **대명사:** 주어인 people이 자신들을 세상에 보여준다는 문맥으로 주어와 목적어가 동일한 대상을 가리키므로 them을 재귀대명사인 themselves로 고쳐야 한다.

오답풀이

① **접속사 that:** 문장의 주격보어 역할을 하는 명사절을 이끌어야 하며, 뒤에 주어, 동사, 목적어를 갖춘 완전한 구조의 절이 이어지고 있으므로 접속사 that은 어법상 적절하다.

③ **분사의 태:** 앞의 the meanings를 수식하는 어구를 이끌고, the meanings는 associate(~을 연관시키다)의 대상이므로 과거분사 associated는 어법상 적절하다.

└ enabling 이하는 결과를 나타내는 분사구문인데, enabling individuals to recreate the meanings를 동명사구 주어로 착각하면 동사가 와야 하는 자리로 생각할 수 있는 함정 오답!

④ **부사:** 동사의 과거분사형인 purchased를 수식하므로 부사 inexpensively는 어법상 적절하다.

⑤ **분사구문:** Fashion을 의미상의 주어로 하며 부대상황을 나타내는 분사구문을 이끄는 opening은 어법상 적절하다.

구문풀이

[6행] The most common explanation [offered by my informants **as to** {why fashion is so appealing}] is [that **it** constitutes a kind of theatrical costumery].

: 첫 번째 [ ]는 문장의 주어인 The most common explanation을 수식하는 과거분사구이고, 그 안의 { }는 전치사구 as to(~에 관하여)의 목적어 역할을 하는 명사절이다. 두 번째 [ ]는 주격보어로 쓰인 명사절이고, 대명사 it은 fashion을 가리킨다.

[8행] Clothes are part of [how people present themselves to the world], and fashion locates **them** in the present, **relative** [to {what is happening in society}] and [**to** fashion's own history].

: 첫 번째 [ ]는 전치사 of의 목적어 역할을 하는 명사절이고, them은 people을 가리킨다. 두 번째와 세 번째 [ ]는 relative에 이어지는 어구로 relative to는 '~에 관하여'라는 의미를 나타내고, 두 번째 [ ] 안의 { }는 선행사를 포함하는 관계대명사 what이 이끄는 명사절로 전치사 to의 목적어로 쓰였다.

어휘풀이

- constantly *ad* 끊임없이, 계속
- occasion *n* 때, 경우
- basis *n* 기반
- appealing *a* 매력적인
- theatrical *a* 연극적인
- a host of 다수의
- consciousness *n* 의식

- restage *v* 재공연하다
- ultimately *ad* 궁극적으로
- informant *n* 정보 제공자
- constitute *v* 구성하다
- costumery *n* 의상, 복장
- ambiguity *n* 모호함
- strengthen *v* 강화하다

021 답 ④

📖 생명 주기 동안에 크기, 모양, 물질대사 활동이 극적으로 변화하는 세포

전문해석

온전한 개체와 마찬가지로, 세포도 수명이 있다. 그것의 생명 주기(세포 주기) 동안에, 세포의 크기, 모양, 물질대사 활동은 극적으로 변할 수 있다. 세포는 모세포가 분열하여 두 개의 딸세포를 생성할 때 쌍둥이로 '탄생'한다. 각각의 딸세포는 모세포보다 더 작으며, 특이한 경우를 제외하고는 각각 모세포의 크기만큼 커질 때까지 자란다. 이 기간에, 세포는 물, 당, 아미노산, 그리고 그 밖의 다른 영양소들을 흡수하고 그것들을 조합하여 새로운 살아 있는 원형질로 만든다. 세포가 적절한 크기로 성장한 후, 그것은 분열할 준비를 하거나 혹은 성숙하여 특화된 세포로 분화하면서 그것의 물질대사가 변화한다. 성장과 발달 모두 모든 세포 부분을 포함하는 복잡하고 역동적인 일련의 상호 작용을 필요로 한다. 세포의 물질대사와 구조가 복잡하리라는 것은 놀라운 일이 아닐 테지만, 실제로 그것들은 꽤 단순하고 논리적이다. 가장 복잡한 세포조차도 그저 몇몇 부분만을 가지고 있는데, 각각은 세포 생명의 뚜렷이 다른, 명확한 한 측면을 담당한다.

정답풀이

④ 관계대명사 **what**: but 앞에서 What cell metabolism and structure should be complex가 주어이고 동사는 would not be이다. What 다음에 주어(cell metabolism and structure), 동사(should be), 보어(complex)를 갖춘 완전한 구조의 절이 이어지므로 What은 어법상 적절하지 않다. 따라서 관계대명사 What을 명사절을 이끄는 접속사 That으로 고쳐야 한다.

오답풀이

① 분사구문의 태: producing 이하는 its mother cell을 의미상 주어로 하는 분사구문으로, its mother cell이 produce의 주체이고 뒤에 목적어 two daughter cells를 취하고 있으므로 능동의 현재분사 producing은 어법상 적절하다.

② 생략: 원래 as the mother cell was large에서 보어인 large가 생략된 것이므로 어법상 적절하다.

③ 병렬구조: as절의 동사가 「either A or B」 구문에 의해 연결된 형태로 prepares와 병렬구조를 이루는 matures and differentiates는 어법상 적절하다.

┗ to divide의 divide와 병렬구조를 이룬다고 생각할 수도 있지만, 문맥상 '분열될 준비를 하거나 다 자라서 분화한다'는 의미가 자연스럽고 앞의 matures의 형태를 보아서도 differentiates가 맞는 표현이다.

⑤ 분사구문: each를 의미상의 주어로 하는 분사구문 each being responsible ~에서 being이 생략된 형태이므로 responsible의 쓰임은 어법상 적절하다.

구문풀이

8행 During this time, **the cell** [absorbs water, sugars, amino acids, and other nutrients] and [assembles **them** into new, living protoplasm].

: 두 개의 [ ]는 주어 the cell에 이어지는 술어부로 and로 연결되어 있고, them은 water, sugars, amino acids, and other nutrients를 가리킨다.

어휘풀이

- life span 수명
- absorb *v* 흡수하다
- amino acid 아미노산(단백질의 기본 구성단위)
- nutrient *n* 영양소, 영양분
- assemble A into B A를 조합하여 B를 만들다
- mature *v* 다 자라다
- logical *a* 논리적인
- distinct *a* 뚜렷이 구별되는[다른]
- well-defined *a* (정의가) 명확한, (윤곽이) 뚜렷한

- dramatically *ad* 극적으로, 급격하게

- differentiate *v* 분화하다
- responsible for ~을 담당하고 있는

022 답 ③

📖 제품을 판매하는 인력들을 훈련시켜야 할 필요성

전문해석

그 누구도 당신 제품의 특징이나 그것이 소비자에게 주는 이점을 당신이 아는 것보다 더 잘 알지는 못한다. 그것이 바로 당신이 당신의 제품을 팔게 될 모든 사람을 개인적으로 훈련시키는 것이 중요한 이유이다. 그리고 똑같이 중요한 것은 당신이 또한 이 판매 인력으로 하여금 경쟁사의 것이 아닌 당신의 제품을 판촉하도록 훈련시켜야 한다는 즉 더 바람직하게는 그들로 하여금 그들의 고객들에게 당신의 제품만을 판촉하는 것을 좋아하고 원하도록 훈련시켜야 한다는 사실이다. 당신의 제품이 판매사의 유통망을 통해 판매된다면, 당신의 제품을 판매하는 모든 판매사들을 방문해서 당신 제품의 이점에 대해 그들의 직원들을 훈련시키는 훈련 프로그램을 반드시 개발하도록 하라. 이 판매원들이 당신 경쟁사들의 제품보다 당신의 제품을 팔고 싶어 하도록 그들을 위한 장려책을 마련하라. 그 장려책은 돈이 될 수도 있겠으나, 당신의 제품을 경쟁 제품보다 판매하기 더 수월하게 만드는 것이 더 나은데, 왜냐하면 그런 제품들은 시작하기에 더 좋고 그것들을 판매하는 사람들은 모든 이점과 그 제품이 소비자를 위해 무엇을 할 수 있는지를 이해하도록 훈련되어 있기 때문이다.

정답풀이

③ 관계대명사 **which**: 뒤에 주어, 동사, 목적어를 모두 갖춘 완전한 구조의 절이 이어지므로 관계대명사 which는 어법상 적절하지 않다. a training program을 선행사로 하며 관계사절에서 in the training program의 의미를 대신하도록 which를 in which로 고쳐야 한다.

오답풀이

① 대동사: do는 반복되는 동사구 know ~ the consumer를 대신하는 대동사로 어법상 적절하다.

② 접속사 that: 뒤에 주어, 동사, 목적어, 목적격보어를 모두 갖춘 절이 이어지고, 이 절은 문맥상 the fact와 동격의 관계를 이루므로 명사절을 이끄는 접속사 that은 어법상 적절하다.

③ 문장의 구조 파악: so that 이하의 부사절을 제외하면 Create ~ salespeople은 명령문의 주절로 동사원형 Create는 어법상 적절하다.

⑤ 관계대명사 **what**: understand의 목적어 역할을 하는 명사절을 이끌면서 이어지는 절의 동사 will do의 목적어 역할을 하는 관계대명사 what은 어법상 적절하다. all the benefits와 what 이하는 병렬구조를 이룬다.

구문풀이

4행 And **of equal importance** is **the fact** [that you must also train this sales force to push your products, instead of the competition's or, better yet, train them to love and want to push only your products to their customers].

: 원래는 The fact that ~ is of equal importance.의 문장인데, 보어가 문장 앞으로 나가면서 「보어+동사(is)+주어」의 어순으로 도치되었다. 보어인 of equal importance는 equally important의 뜻을 나타내는 형용사구이다. [ ]는 the fact의 구체적인 내용을 설명하는 동격의 명사절이다.

어휘풀이

- feature *n* 특징
- sales force 판매 인력
- push *v* ~의 판매를 촉진하다, 홍보하다
- competition *n* 경쟁 상대
- distribution channel 유통망
- competitor *n* 경쟁자, 경쟁 상대
- any and every 온갖, 모든
- vendor *n* 판매사, 판매자
- staff *n* (전체) 직원
- incentive *n* 장려책, 유인책

구문풀이

6행 We are likely to be most successful when we are present with those [**with whom** we are interacting], **either** literally, [as in face-to-face situations], **or** virtually.

: 첫 번째 [ ]는 those를 수식하는 관계사절이다. 「either ~ or ....」의 상관접속사가 동사를 수식하는 두 개의 부사를 연결하고 있으며, 두 번째 [ ]는 literally와 관련하여 '~에서와 같이'의 뜻을 나타내는 부사구이다.

어휘풀이

- interpret *v* 해석하다
- face-to-face 얼굴을 마주하는
- virtually *ad* 가상적으로, 온라인상으로
- enhance *v* 향상시키다
- misinterpret *v* 잘못 이해하다
- accuse A of *doing* ~한 것으로 A를 나무라다
- cheating *n* (시험) 부정행위
- via *prep* ~에 의해, ~을 통해
- literally *ad* 문자 그대로
- lend oneself to ~에 적합하다
- gasp *v* (놀라서) 숨을 헐떡이다
- fire off 급히 ~을 하다

023 답 ④

📖 의사소통에서 사회적 실재감의 부재로 인한 오해의 가능성

전문해석

하나의 의사소통 활동을 둘러싼 물리적 상황은 장소, 환경 조건(기온, 조명, 소음 수준) 그리고 참여자들의 서로에 대한 물리적 근접성을 포함한다. 물리적 상황은 우리가 보내고 받는 메시지를 해석하는 방식에 영향을 줄 수 있다. 우리는 우리가 소통하고 있는 사람들과 얼굴을 마주하고 있는 상황에서와 같이 문자 그대로든 아니면 가상적으로든 함께 있을 때 (의사소통에) 가장 성공적일 것이다. 우리가 다른 사람과 가상적으로 '그곳에(소통의 공간에 함께) 있다'는 느낌을 만들어 내기 위해 사용하는 용어는 사회적 실재감이다. 사회적 실재감을 전하는 데 적합하지 않은, 기술에 의해 향상된 의사소통 수단의 하나는 이메일이다. 그 결과, 이메일 메시지는 흔히 잘못 해석되거나 불쾌한 기분을 초래하거나 관계를 손상시킨다. 예를 들면, Joy는 부정행위를 한 것으로 자신을 나무라고 있는 듯 보이는 교수의 이메일을 읽었을 때 놀라서 숨이 막혔다. 그녀는 급히 답장을 쓰기 시작하지만 멈추고 이메일에 의해 주어지는 사회적 실재감의 부재로부터 생겨날 수 있는 오해를 피하려고 직접 이야기를 나누기 위한 약속을 잡았다.

정답풀이

④ **재귀대명사**: accusing의 주체는 주격 관계대명사 that의 선행사인 the e-mail from her professor로, 그 목적어인 herself(= Joy)와 동일하지 않다. 따라서 재귀대명사 herself를 목적격 대명사 her로 고쳐야 한다.

오답풀이

① **관계부사 how**: 동사 influence의 목적어로 쓰인 절은 주어, 동사, 목적어를 모두 갖춘 완전한 구조를 이루며 문맥상 '~하는 방법'이라는 의미를 나타내므로 관계부사 how는 어법상 적절하다.

② **대명사 those**: with whom 이하의 관계사절의 수식을 받으면서 문맥상 '~인 사람들'의 뜻을 나타내는 대명사 those는 어법상 적절하다.

③ **주어와 동사의 수 일치**: One ~ social presence가 문장의 주어부이고 that ~ social presence는 핵심 주어인 One ~ channel을 수식하는 주격 관계대명사절이다. 따라서 단수 주어에 수를 맞춘 단수형 동사 is는 어법상 적절하다.

   └ 문장의 주어부가 길어서 문장의 구조를 파악하기가 쉽지 않은 형태이다. 수식어구를 모두 걸어 낸 후 핵심 주어와 동사를 파악하도록 한다.

⑤ **분사의 태**: 수식을 받는 the lack of social presence는 '제공되는' 대상이므로 과거분사 provided를 쓴 것은 어법상 적절하다.

024 답 ④

📖 '종(種)'과 '속(屬)'의 개념을 만든 John Ray

전문해석

초기 동식물 연구가들은 유기체의 다양한 형태를 이해하기 시작하기 전에 그것들의 목록을 만들고 자세히 설명해야 했다. 그리고 연구가 진행됨에 따라, 학자들은 그들이 발견한 생물학적 다양성의 양에 점점 더 깊은 인상을 받았다. 17세기가 되어서야 Cambridge 대학에서 교육받은 목사인 John Ray가 오늘날 우리가 생각하는 종(種)의 개념을 발전시켰다. 그는 식물 및 동물의 무리가 서로 짝짓기하고 새끼를 낳는 능력에 의해 다른 집단과 구별될 수 있다는 것을 처음으로 인지한 사람이었다. 그는 그러한 생식적으로 분리되는 유기체들을 단일한 범주에 넣었고, 그는 그것을 '종(種)'이라고 불렀다. 따라서 1600년대 후반 무렵에 생식이라는 생물학적 기준은 오늘날과 마찬가지로 종을 정의하는 데 사용되었다. Ray는 또한 종들이 다른 종들과 자주 유사점을 공유한다는 것을 인지했고, 그는 이것을 자신이 '속(屬)'이라고 불렀던 두 번째 차원의 범주로 분류했다. 그는 이런 식으로 '속(屬)'과 '종(種)'이라는 분류 표시를 사용한 최초의 사람이었고, 그것들은 우리가 오늘날에도 여전히 사용하는 용어이다.

정답풀이

④ **대동사**: as절의 주어인 it은 주절의 주어인 the biological criterion of reproduction을 가리키며, 동사로는 반복되는 동사구 is used to define species를 대신하는 대동사가 와야 한다. 따라서 대동사 does를 is로 고쳐야 어법상 적절하다.

오답풀이

① **대명사**: they(= early naturalists)가 목록을 만들고 자세히 설명해야 하는 것은 the many forms of organic life이므로 복수형 대명사 them은 어법상 적절하다.

② **분사의 태**: 「It is[was] ~ that ....」 강조구문으로 부사구 not until the seventeenth century를 강조하고 있다. 주어는 John Ray이고 동사는 developed이며 a minister ~ University는 John Ray와 동격을 이루는 명사구이다. a minister는 '교육을 받은' 대상이므로 수동의 의미로 이를 수식하는 과거분사 educated는 어법상 적절하다.

③ **관계대명사 which**: a single category를 부연 설명하는 관계사절을 이끄는 목적격 관계대명사 which는 어법상 적절하다. 관계사절에서 the species는 called의 목적어가 아니라 목적격보어임에 유의한다.

⑤ **to부정사**: the first를 수식하는 형용사적 용법의 to부정사구를 이끄는 to use는 어법상 적절하다.

구문풀이

8행 He was the one [who first recognized {that groups of plants and animals could be distinguished from other groups by their ability (**to mate** with one another and **produce** offspring)}].

: [ ]는 the one을 수식하는 주격 관계대명사절이고, 그 안의 { }는 recognized의 목적어 역할을 하는 명사절이다. ( )는 their ability를 수식하는 형용사적 용법의 to부정사구이며 mate와 produce가 병렬구조를 이룬다.

어휘풀이
- naturalist *n* 동식물 연구가, 박물학자
- biological diversity 생물의 다양성
- distinguish *v* 구별하다
- offspring *n* 새끼, 자손
- isolated *a* 분리된, 고립된
- reproduction *n* 생식, 번식
- progress *v* 진행되다
- minister *n* 목사
- mate with ~와 짝짓기를 하다
- reproductively *ad* 생식적으로
- criterion *n* 기준
- classification *n* 범주, 분류

025 답 ④

📖 동물의 미래 지향적 사고의 유무

전문해석
인간이 미래를 생각하는 한계를 종종 되돌아보고 보상하는 영역은 장래에 대한 기억인데, 그것은 미래에 어떤 특정한 때에 행동을 수행할 것을 기억하는 것을 포함한다. 우리는 행동을 수행하는 것을 잊어버릴 가능성을 인식하기 때문에, 우리 중 많은 사람들은 달력, 알람, 목록 및 기타 외부의 상기시켜주는 것을 보조 도구로 사용한다. 실제로, 완벽한 기억에 대한 필요를 배제하는 미래 지향적인 기록 보관 방법이 없다면 많은 인간의 기관들은 완전히 붕괴될 것이다(예로 법적 그리고 재정적 시스템을 고려해 보라). 유인원이 어떤 관련 없는 일을 완료한 후 음식을 얻기 위해 토큰을 요청하거나 교환하는 것을 기억한다는 것을 보여주는 실험과 함께, 유인원의 미래 기억에 대한 일부 주장이 있었다. 그럼에도 불구하고 이러한 연구에 미래에 대한 사고가 전혀 관여되지 않았으며, 그 대신 유인원이 관련 없는 일을 완료한 후 단순히 행동을 하라는 신호를 받았을 가능성이 남아 있다. 유인원이나 다른 동물들이 미래의 행동을 수행하는 것을 기억할 자신들의 가능성을 높이기 위해 자발적으로 그들 자신의 상기시키는 것을 설정한다는 것을 나타내는 것은 아무것도 없다.

정답풀이
④ **문장의 구조 파악**: it remains possible that ~, but that ~의 구조로 이루어진 문장으로 it은 가주어이고, 문장의 진주어는 but으로 연결된 두 개의 that절이다. 첫 번째 that절에서 주어 no future-thinking에 대한 술어동사가 필요한데, 주어가 '관여되는' 대상이므로 involved를 was involved로 바꿔 써야 한다.

오답풀이
① **주어와 동사의 수 일치**: 주어의 핵은 A domain이고 in which ~ limitations는 A domain을 수식하는 관계절이므로 단수 동사 is는 어법상 적절하다.
② **관계대명사 that**: future-oriented record-keeping procedures를 수식하는 절을 이끌면서, 뒤에 이어지는 절에서 preclude의 주어 역할을 하는 주격 관계대명사 that은 어법상 적절하다.
③ **분사의 태**: 「with+명사+분사」 구문은 '~가 …하면서'라는 의미로 주어의 부수적인 상황을 표현한다. experiments가 show의 주체에 해당하므로 현재분사 showing은 어법상 적절하다.
⑤ **부사**: that절의 주어 great apes or other animals에 이어지는 동사 set

을 수식하는 부사 spontaneously는 어법상 적절하다.

구문풀이

1행 A domain [**in which** humans often reflect on and compensate for their future-thinking limitations] is prospective memory, [which involves remembering to perform an action at some particular future occasion].

: 첫 번째 [ ]는 문장의 핵심 주어인 A domain을 수식하는 관계절로 in which는 관계부사 where로 바꿔 쓸 수 있다. 두 번째 [ ]는 prospective memory를 부연 설명하는 계속적 용법의 주격 관계대명사절이다.

7행 Indeed, many human institutions **would collapse** entirely **if it were not for** future-oriented record-keeping procedures [that preclude the need for perfect memories] (e.g., consider legal and financial systems).

: 「주어+조동사의 과거형(would)+동사원형 ~ if it were not for …」 형태의 가정법 과거 구문이 사용된 문장으로 '만약 …이 없다면, ~할 것이다'라는 의미를 나타내며, if it were not for는 without으로 바꿔 쓸 수 있다. [ ]는 future-oriented record-keeping procedures를 수식하는 주격 관계대명사절이다.

18행 There is nothing [to indicate {that great apes or other animals spontaneously set their own reminders <**in order to improve** their likelihood of (remembering to perform future actions)>}].

: [ ]는 nothing을 수식하는 형용사적 용법의 to부정사구이고, 그 안의 { }는 indicate의 목적어 역할을 하는 명사절이다. < >는 「in order+to부정사: ~하기 위해서」 구문이 쓰인 어구이고, ( )는 their likelihood와 동격 관계의 동명사구로 전치사 of의 목적어 역할을 한다.

어휘풀이
- domain *n* 영역
- compensate for ~을 보상하다
- prospective *a* 장래의, 가망이 있는
- reminder *n* 상기시키는 것
- collapse *v* 붕괴하다, 무너지다
- claim *n* 주장, 권리
- token *n* 토큰, 상징(물)
- cue ~ into … ~에게 …하라는 신호를 주다
- indicate *v* 나타내다, 가리키다
- likelihood *n* 가능성
- reflect on ~을 되돌아보다[반성하다]
- limitation *n* 한계
- occasion *n* 때, 경우
- institution *n* 기관, 제도
- procedure *n* 방법, 절차
- great ape 유인원
- irrelevant *a* 관련 없는
- spontaneously *ad* 자발적으로

026 답 ④

📖 Hispaniola 섬에 사는 조류에 관한 기록

전문해석
Hispaniola 섬에 사는 조류에 관한 최초의 문서 기록은 1492년과 1504년 사이에 Christopher Columbus가 그 섬을 탐험한 것으로 거슬러 올라간다. 하지만 Hispaniola 섬에 대한 이 탐험과 그 후 2세기 동안의 후속 탐험은 그저 일반적인 설명과 부차적인 자연사 관찰 기록만을 제공할 뿐이었다. 1700년대 초반 프랑스의 아이티 점령은 조류 연구의 발전을 가져왔으며 많은 출판물로 이어졌는데, 그중 많은 것들은 그 후에 사라지거나 파괴된 표본 수집물에 기반을 두었다. 동부 Hispaniola에 대한 최초의 조류학 탐험은 프랑스 생물학자 Auguste Salle에 의해서 이루어졌는데, 그는 1857년에 자신의 수집물에 대한 상세한 설명을 출판했고, 이것은 61종을 포함했다. Hispaniola 섬의 조류상(鳥類相)에 관한 체계적인 기록은 미국 조류학자 Charles Cory의 수집 탐험과 함께 시작되었는데, 그는 1881년부터 1883년까지 아이티섬과 도미니카 공화국을 둘 다 방문했으며, 1885년에 중

요한 참고 서적인 〈The Birds of Haiti and San Domingo〉를 출판했다. Cory 의 지휘 하에 1896년까지 여러 차례의 후속 수집 여행을 통해 수천 개의 새 표본을 수집했는데, 그 대부분은 미국의 박물관에 소장되어 있다.

정답풀이

④ **병렬구조**: 문맥상 who가 이끄는 관계사절의 동사 visited와 and에 의해 병렬로 연결된 구조이므로 준동사 publishing을 본동사 published로 고쳐야 한다.

오답풀이

① **전치사**: 뒤에 명사구 the following two centuries가 이어지고 있으므로 전치사 during은 어법상 적절하다.
  ⌐ 문장의 동사인 provided를 the following two centuries에 이어지는 동사로 착각하면 접속사 while이 와야 한다고 생각할 수 있는 함정 오답!

② **분사구문**: 원래 and many of them were based on ~이 분사구문이 되면서 의미상의 주어 many of them은 생략되지 않고 남아 있고 being은 생략되어 many of them based on ~의 형태가 된 것으로 과거분사 based는 어법상 적절하다.

③ **주어와 동사의 수 일치**: 주어인 The first ornithological explorations of eastern Hispaniola에 이어지는 동사 자리로, 주어의 핵은 explorations이므로 복수형 동사 were는 어법상 적절하다.

⑤ **관계대명사 which**: several thousand bird specimens를 선행사로 하며 관계사절에서 of의 목적어 역할을 하는 관계대명사 which는 어법상 적절하다.

구문풀이

`7행` France's occupation of Haiti in the early 1700s **spawned** advances in bird study and **led** to a number of published works, [many of them **based** on specimen collections {which were subsequently lost or destroyed}].

: 문장의 동사는 and로 연결된 spawned와 led이다. [ ]는 분사구문으로 의미상의 주어는 many of them이고, 그 안의 { }는 specimen collections를 수식하는 주격 관계대명사절이다.

`11행` The first ornithological explorations of eastern Hispaniola were conducted by a French biologist, Auguste Salle, [who published in 1857 a thorough account of his collections, {which included 61 species}].

: [ ]와 { }는 각각 Auguste Salle와 a thorough account of his collections를 부연 설명하는 주격 관계대명사절이다.

어휘풀이

- date from ~부터 존재해 오다
- subsequent *a* 뒤의, 차후의
- little more than 겨우 ~밖에
- account *n* 설명, 기술
- occupation *n* 점령
- conduct *v* 실시하다, 수행하다
- documentation *n* 참고 문서
- follow-up *a* 후속의, 뒤따르는
- expedition *n* 탐험, 원정
- exploration *n* 탐험, 탐사
- narrative *a* 서술의, 서술적인
- incidental *a* 부차적인, 우연의
- spawn *v* 낳다, 생겨나게 하다
- thorough *a* 빈틈없는, 철저한
- reference *n* 참고, 참조
- house *v* 소장하다, 보관하다

027 답 ③

📖 **아즈텍 달력 석판**

전문해석

마야인처럼 아즈텍인도 달력에 깊은 관심이 있었는데, 그것은 창조의 개념과 연결되

었다. Aztec Calendar Stone은 거대하며, 지름이 11피트가 넘고 무게는 25톤이 넘는다. Sun Stone이라고도 불리는 이 조각된 돌은 순환하는 시간이라는 아즈텍의 개념을 강조하고 아즈텍의 우주론과 신화를 반영한다. 그 돌의 중심에는 상상의 동물인 Ollin의 모습이 있는데, 그것의 혀는 칼 모양이다. 또한 아즈텍 전통에 따라 돌에는 최초의 네 개의 태양과 불의 두 신들의 몸이 묘사되어 있다. 20일짜리 아즈텍 달력과 현재 (다섯 번째) 태양의 탄생일을 나타내는 표시가 있지만, 이 기념비적인 조각은 시간을 표시하는 것이라고 할 수는 없다. 이 돌은 멕시코시티의 중심에서 발굴되었는데, 그것은 현재 이전 아즈텍 제국의 중심부인 Teotihuacán 시에 있다. Teotihuacán은 다섯 번째이자 현재 태양의 탄생지로 여겨졌고, 제국의 정치적 중심지였다. Aztec Calendar Stone의 의미는 여전히 불가사의하지만, 그것의 이미지는 현대 멕시코 예술과 문화에 계속해서 영향을 미치고 있다.

정답풀이

③ **전치사+관계대명사**: 뒤에 동사 lies의 주어가 없는 불완전한 구조의 절이 이어지므로 관계사절에서 부사구 역할을 하는 「전치사+관계대명사」 형태의 in which는 적절하지 않다. The stone을 선행사로 하는 계속적 용법의 주격 관계대명사 which로 고쳐야 한다.

오답풀이

① **분사구문의 태**: called의 의미상의 주어는 the carved stone이고, 이는 Sun Stone이라 불리는 대상이므로 과거분사 called를 쓴 것은 어법상 적절하다.

② **주어와 동사의 수 일치**: depicted on the stone은 강조되어 문장 앞으로 나간 보어이고, 주어는 the first four suns, and ~ gods이므로 복수형 동사 are를 쓴 것은 어법상 적절하다.

④ **동사의 태**: 주어인 Teotihuacán은 탄생지로 여겨지는 대상이므로 수동태 was considered를 쓴 것은 어법상 적절하다. 이어지는 the birthplace of ~ sun은 목적어가 아니라 5형식 능동태 문장에서 considered의 목적격보어였던 명사구이다.

⑤ **대명사**: 양보 부사절에 이어지는 주절에서 the Aztec Calendar Stone을 대신하는 소유격 대명사 its는 어법상 적절하다.

구문풀이

`7행` [At the center of the stone] is [an image of the creature Ollin], [**its tongue** in the shape of a knife].

: 첫 번째 [ ]로 표시된 위치[장소] 부사구가 문두로 나가 두 번째 [ ]로 표시된 주어와 동사 is가 도치되었다. 세 번째 [ ]는 분사구문으로 의미상의 주어인 its tongue 다음에 being이 생략된 형태이다.

어휘풀이

- diameter *n* 지름, 직경
- emphasize *v* 강조하다
- reflect *v* 반영하다
- mythology *n* 신화
- monumental *a* 기념비적인
- empire *n* 제국
- mysterious *a* 불가사의한
- carve *v* 조각하다
- cyclical *a* 순환하는, 주기적인
- cosmology *n* 우주론
- depict *v* 그리다, 묘사하다
- indicate *v* 나타내다
- birthplace *n* 탄생지

028 답 ④

📖 상점가 경제의 유연한 가격 설정 메커니즘

전문해석

상점가 경제는 공유되는 문화라는 보다 지속적인 유대 위에 자리 잡은, 겉보기에 유연한 가격 설정 메커니즘을 특징으로 한다. 구매자와 판매자 둘 다 서로의 제약을 알고 있다. 델리의 상점가에서, 구매자와 판매자는 대체로 다른 행위자들이 그들의 일상생활에서 가지는 재정적인 압박을 평가할 수 있다. 특정 경제 계층에 속하는 각 행위자는 상대방이 무엇을 필수품으로 여기고 무엇을 사치품으로 여기는지를 이해한다. 비디오 게임 같은 전자 제품의 경우, 그것들은 식품과 같은 다른 가정 구매품과 같은 수준의 필수품이 아니다. 따라서 델리의 상점가에서 판매자는 비디오 게임에 대해 곧바로 매우 낮은(→ 높은) 가격을 요구하지 않도록 주의하는데, 구매자가 비디오 게임 소유를 절대적 필수 사항으로 볼 이유가 전혀 없기 때문이다. 이러한 유형의 지식에 대한 접근은 비슷한 문화적, 경제적 세상에 속한 것에서 비롯한 서로의 선호와 한계를 관련지어 가격 합의를 정립한다.

정답풀이

④ 델리의 상점가에서 특정 경제 계층의 구매자와 판매자는 서로 문화를 공유하고 있으므로 서로가 가진 제약을 알고 있다고 했다. 따라서 판매자는 필수품으로 여겨지지 않는 비디오 게임에 대해 너무 높은 가격을 제시하면 구매자가 구매를 포기할 수도 있으니 가격을 너무 높게 제시하지 않도록 주의한다는 내용이 문맥상 적절하다. 따라서 low(낮은)를 반대 개념인 high(높은)로 바꿔야 한다.

오답풀이

① 구매자와 판매자의 재정적 압박에 관한 내용이 이어지고 있으므로, 구매자와 판매자 둘 다 서로의 '제약(restrictions)'을 알고 있다는 문맥은 적절하다.
② 서로 특정 경제 계층에 속하는 행위자의 필수품과 사치품을 이해한다는 내용이 이어지고 있으므로 구매자와 판매자는 대체로 다른 행위자들이 그들의 일상생활에서 가지는 재정적인 압박을 '평가할(assess)' 수 있다는 문맥은 적절하다.
③ 비디오 게임과 식품의 경우, 비디오 게임은 식품과 같은 가정에서의 구매 '필수품(necessity)'이 아니라고 하는 것은 문맥상 적절하다.
⑤ 상점가의 판매자와 구매자가 특정 경제 계층에 속하므로 둘 다 서로의 '비슷한(similar)' 문화적, 경제적 세계를 고려하여 선호와 한계를 토대로 가격 합의에 도달할 것이라는 문맥은 적절하다.

구문풀이

3행 In Delhi's bazaars, buyers and sellers can **assess** to a large extent [the financial constraints {that other actors have in their everyday life}].

: [ ]는 동사 assess의 목적어로 쓰인 명사구이고, { }는 the financial constraints를 수식하는 목적격 관계대명사절이다.

4행 Each actor [belonging to a specific economic class] understands [what the other sees as a necessity and a luxury].

: 첫 번째 [ ]는 문장의 핵심 주어인 Each actor를 수식하는 현재분사구이고, 두 번째 [ ]는 동사 understand의 목적어 역할을 하는 명사절이다.

7행 So, **the seller** in Delhi's bazaars **is** careful not to directly ask for very high prices for video games / because **at no point** will the buyer see possession of **them** as an absolute necessity.

: 주절의 핵심 주어는 the seller이고 동사는 is이다. because가 이끄는 이유의 부사절에서 부정의 부사구 at no point가 부사절 맨 앞으로 나와서 '조동사(will)+주어(the buyer)+동사원형(see)'으로 도치가 이루어졌다. 대명사 them은 video games를 대신한다.

어휘풀이

- bazaar *n* 상점가, 시장 거리
- apparently *ad* 겉보기에, 외관상
- mechanism *n* 메커니즘(사물의 작용 원리)
- atop *ad* 위에, 맨 꼭대기에
- restriction *n* 제약
- to a large extent 대체로, 대부분은
- necessity *n* 필수품, 필수 사항
- possession *n* 소유
- access *n* 접근
- relate to ~을 관련짓다
- feature *v* 특징으로 하다
- flexible *a* 유연한, 융통성 있는
- enduring *a* 지속적인
- assess *v* 평가하다
- financial *a* 재정적인
- luxury *n* 사치품
- absolute *a* 절대적인
- establish *v* 정립하다, 확립하다
- limitation *n* 한계

029 답 ⑤

📖 컴퓨터와 우리 삶의 자연스러운 융합을 위한 사고방식

전문해석

우리가 어디로 몸을 돌리든 우리는 전능한 '사이버공간'에 대해 듣게 된다! 과대광고는 우리가 따분한 생활을 벗어나 고글과 바디 수트를 착용하고, 어떤 금속성의, 3차원의, 멀티미디어로 이루어진 다른 세계로 들어갈 것으로 약속한다. 산업 혁명이 그것의 위대한 혁신품인 모터와 더불어 도래했을 때, 우리는 우리의 세상을 떠나 어떤 멀리 떨어진 모터의 공간으로 가지 않았다! 반대로, 우리는 모터를 자동차, 냉장고, 드릴 프레스, 연필깎이와 같은 것들로서 우리 삶에 가져왔다. 이러한 흡수는 너무 완전해서 우리는 그것들의 '모터성'이 아니라 그것들의 용처를 분명히 밝히는 이름으로 이 모든 도구를 일컫는다. 이러한 혁신품들은 정확히 우리의 일상생활에 들어와 지대한 영향을 미쳤기 때문에 주요 사회경제적 움직임으로 이어졌다. 사람들은 근본적으로 수천 년간 변하지 않았다. 기술은 끊임없이 변화한다. **우리에게 적응해야 하는 것은 바로 기술이다. 그것이 바로 인간 중심의 컴퓨터 활용 하에서 정보 기술과 그 장치들에 일어날 일이다.** 컴퓨터가 우리를 마법의 신세계로 데려다줄 것이라고 우리가 계속 더 오래 믿을수록, 우리는 컴퓨터와 우리 삶의 자연스러운 융합을 더 오래 유지할(→ 지연할) 것인데, 이는 사회경제적 혁명이라고 불리기를 열망하는 모든 주요 운동의 특징이기도 하다.

정답풀이

⑤ 과거의 기술 혁신이 인간을 신세계로 데려다준 것이 아니라 우리 삶으로 들어와 유용한 물건들의 형태로 존재했듯이, 현재의 정보 기술과 그것에서 나온 장치들 또한 그래야 한다는 취지를 담고 있는 글이다. 따라서 컴퓨터가 우리를 마법 같은 신세계로 데려다줄 것이라고 믿는 것은 결국 컴퓨터와 우리 삶의 자연스러운 융합에 지장을 줄 것이므로, maintain(유지하다)을 delay(지연하다) 정도의 어휘로 바꿔야 한다.

오답풀이

① 앞에 otherworld라는 표현을 썼고, 우리가 우리의 세상을 떠난다는 내용이 있으므로 '모터의 공간(다른 세상)'을 수식하는 remote(멀리 떨어진)는 문맥상 적절하다.
② 모터를 유용한 여러 가지 물건의 형태로 우리의 삶에 들여왔다고 했으므로 이러한 상황을 '흡수(absorption)'로 표현한 것은 문맥상 적절하다.
③ 혁신품들이 주요 사회경제적 움직임으로 이어졌다고 했으므로 그것들이

우리의 일상생활에 지대한 '영향을 미쳤다(affected)'고 한 것은 문맥상 적절하다.

④ 앞에서 사람은 오랜 기간 변하지 않고 기술은 끊임없이 변한다고 했으므로 기술이 사람에 '적응해야(adapt)' 한다는 흐름은 문맥상 적절하다.
    ⌐ 문맥상 us와 the one이 앞에서 비교되고 있는 '사람'과 '기술'이라는 것을 알 수 있다.

구문풀이

10행 This absorption has been **so** complete [**that** we refer to all these tools with names {that declare their usage, not their "motorness."}]

: [ ]는 「so+형용사[부사]+that절: 너무 ~해서 …하다」 구문의 that절로 결과의 부사절이고, 그 안의 { }는 names를 수식하는 주격 관계대명사절이다.

19행 **The longer** we continue to believe [that computers will take us to a magical new world], **the longer** we will delay their natural fusion with our lives, [the hallmark of every major movement {that aspires to be called a socioeconomic revolution}].

: 「the+비교급 ~, the+비교급 …」는 '~하면 할수록 더 …하다'라는 의미를 나타낸다. 첫 번째 [ ]는 believe의 목적어 역할을 하는 명사절이고, 두 번째 [ ]는 앞의 내용을 부연 설명하는 어구이며, 그 안의 { }는 every major movement를 수식하는 주격 관계대명사절이다.

어휘풀이

- almighty *a* 전능한
- three-dimensional *a* 3차원의
- refer to ~을 일컫다
- usage *n* 용처, 용법
- profoundly *ad* 지대하게
- constantly *ad* 끊임없이
- fusion *n* 융합
- metallic *a* 금속성의
- absorption *n* 흡수
- declare *v* 분명하게 밝히다
- precisely *ad* 정확히
- fundamentally *ad* 근본적으로
- human-centric *a* 인간 중심의
- aspire *v* 열망하다

030 답 ④

📖 인공 지능 에이전트의 학습 능력의 필요성

전문해석

에이전트가 자신의 인식 결과가 아니라 설계자의 사전 지식에 의존하는 만큼, 우리는 그 에이전트가 자율성이 부족하다고 말한다. **합리적 에이전트는 자율적이어야 하는데, 즉 불완전하거나 부정확한 사전 지식을 보완할 수 있도록 학습할 수 있는 것은 학습해야 한다.** 예를 들어, 추가적인 먼지가 언제, 어디에서 나타날지 예측하는 법을 학습하는 진공 청소 에이전트는 그렇게 하지 않는 것보다 더 잘할 것이다. 실질적으로는 처음부터 완전한 자율성은 거의 필요하지 않은데, 에이전트가 경험이 거의 또는 전혀 없을 때는 설계자가 얼마간의 지원을 제공하지 않는다면, 그것은 **무작위**로 작동해야 할 것이다. 그러므로 진화가 동물에게 스스로 학습할 수 있을 만큼 충분히 오래 생존할 수 있도록 필요한 만큼의 타고난 반사 신경을 제공하는 것처럼, 인공 지능 에이전트에게 학습 능력뿐만 아니라 약간의 초기 지식을 제공하는 것이 합리적일 것이다. 환경에 대한 충분한 경험 후에, 합리적인 에이전트의 행동은 사전 지식으로부터 실질적으로 독립할 수 있다. 그리하여 **학습의 통합은 아주 다양한 환경에서 성공할 하나의 단일한 합리적 에이전트를 설계할 수 있게 한다.**

정답풀이

(A) 합리적 에이전트는 불완전하고 부정확한 사전 지식에 의존하기보다는 이를 보완하기 위해서 스스로 학습하고 자율적이어야 한다는 흐름이므로 '보완하다'라는 뜻의 compensate가 적절하다. (prepare: 준비하다)

(B) 앞에서 에이전트가 처음부터 완전한 자율성이 필요한 것은 아니라고 했고, 에이전트가 경험이 거의 없는 상황을 전제했다. 이러한 상황에서 설계자의

지원이 제공되지 않는다면 에이전트는 특정한 목적 없이 되는대로 작동할 것이므로 '무작위로, 임의로'라는 뜻의 randomly가 적절하다. (purposefully: 목적을 갖고, 의도적으로)

(C) 처음에는 자율성이 부족했던 에이전트가 약간의 초기 지식과 충분한 환경 경험을 통해 학습을 하게 되면 사전 지식의 영향으로부터 벗어나 자율성을 갖게 될 것이다. 따라서 자율성과 맥을 같이 하는 independent(독립적인)가 적절하다. (protective: 보호하는)

구문풀이

6행 For example, a vacuum-cleaning agent [that learns to foresee {where and when additional dirt will appear}] will do better than one [that **does not**].

: 첫 번째 [ ]는 문장의 핵심 주어인 a vacuum-cleaning agent를 수식하는 주격 관계대명사절이고, 그 안의 { }는 foresee의 목적어 역할을 하는 명사절이다. 두 번째 [ ]는 one(= a vacuum-cleaning agent)을 수식하는 주격 관계대명사절이고, does not 다음에는 learn to foresee where and when additional dirt will appear가 생략되었다.

13행 So, [**just as** evolution **provides** animals **with** enough built-in reflexes {to survive long enough (to learn for themselves)}], **it** would be reasonable [to **provide** an artificial intelligent agent **with** some initial knowledge **as well as** an ability to learn].

: 첫 번째 [ ] just as(마치 ~처럼)가 이끄는 부사절이고, 그 안의 { }는 enough built-in reflexes를 수식하는 형용사적 용법의 to부정사구이며, ( )는 long enough를 수식하는 부사적 용법의 to부정사구이다. 주절에서 it은 형식상의 주어이고, 두 번째 [ ]의 to부정사구가 내용상의 주어이다. 「provide A with B」는 'A에게 B를 제공하다'라는 의미이고, 「A as well as B」는 'B뿐만 아니라 A도'라는 의미이다.

어휘풀이

- to the extent that ~ ~인 만큼
- autonomy *n* 자율성
- compensate *v* 보완하다, 보상하다
- prior *a* 사전의
- assistance *n* 지원, 도움
- reflex *n* 반사 능력
- initial *a* 초기의, 처음의
- effectively *ad* 실질적으로, 사실상
- percept *n* 인식 결과
- rational *a* 합리적인
- partial *a* 불완전한, 부분적인
- foresee *v* 예측하다
- built-in *a* 타고난, 내재한
- artificial *a* 인공의
- sufficient *a* 충분한
- incorporation *n* 통합

031 답 ③

📖 다문화 사회에서 소수 문화 집단이 겪는 불이익

전문해석

다문화 사회에서 일부 문화 정체성 집단은 다른 집단들보다 그 구성원들에게 포괄적인 선택 상황을 제공하는 데 더 근접한다. **소수 문화 집단은 구성원들에게 선택 상황을 제공하기 위해 지배 문화와 경쟁해야만 하므로, 자신들이 불리한 상황에 있음을 알게 된다.** 그 구성원들을 위한 선택 상황은 정부 기관이나 관행이 호의를 보이는 것이 아니다. 정부는 그것이 사용하는 언어, 그것이 인가하는 교육, 그것이 경의를 표하는 역사 그리고 그것이 지키는 기념일을 통해 의도적이든 아니든 지배 문화를 보호한다. 국가와 그것이 지지하는 지배적인 대중문화는 이런 의미에서 간접적으로나 직접적으로나 문화적으로 편향될(→ 중립적일) 수 없다. 정부는 그것의 업무를 지배 언어로 수행하고, 공립학교는 지배 언어로 가르치며, 대중 매체는 지배 언어로 방송한다. 가족법은 지배 문화를 따른다. 최고의 사회적 지위를 가진 시민 단체는 지배 문화와 일체감을 느끼는 사람들에게 호의를 보인다. **지배 문화로부터의 거리는 또한 문화적 양육이 지배 문화의 것과는 다른 개인들의 잘못이 아닌데도 경제적 그리고 교육적 불이익을 수반한다.**

③ 언어, 교육, 역사, 기념일과 관련된 사항이 지배 문화를 중심으로 돌아간다는 내용이 앞에 언급되었고, 정부의 사업, 공립학교의 교육, 대중 매체의 방송이 지배 언어로 이루어진다는 내용이 뒤에 이어지고 있다. 따라서 지배 문화와 경쟁하는 소수 문화 집단의 입장에서 볼 때 국가와 그것이 지지하는 지배적인 대중문화가 문화적으로 편향적이지 않다는 흐름은 적절하지 않다. 부정어 cannot을 고려할 때 biased(편향된)를 neutral(중립적인) 정도의 어휘로 바꿔야 한다.

오답풀이

① 지배 문화와 경쟁해야 한다는 것과, 정부 기관이나 관행이 소수 문화 집단의 선택 상황에 호의를 보이지 않는다는 것에서 소수 문화 집단이 '불리한(disadvantage)' 상황에 있다는 흐름은 적절하다.

② 정부 기관이나 관행이 소수 문화 집단의 선택 상황에 호의를 보이지 않는다는 것과 대조적으로 지배 문화에 대해서는 우호적이라는 문맥이 적절하므로 정부가 지배 문화를 '보호한다(protects)'는 흐름은 적절하다.

④ 정부 업무, 공교육, 방송 등에서 지배 언어가 사용된다는 흐름에서 가족법 또한 지배 문화를 '따른다(conforms)'는 문맥은 적절하다.

⑤ '지배 문화로부터의 거리'라는 개념은 소수 문화 집단 구성원을 전제로 한 것이므로, 그들의 문화적 양육이 지배 문화의 것과 '다르다(differs)'는 문맥은 적절하다.

구문풀이

`9행` Government protects the dominant culture, [whether intentionally or not], **through** [the language {it uses}], [the education {it accredits}], [the history {it honors}], and [the holidays {that it keeps}].

: 첫 번째 [ ]는 양보의 부사절 whether it does so intentionally or not에서 it does so를 생략한 형태로 볼 수 있다. 이어지는 네 개의 [ ]는 모두 전치사 through의 목적어이며, 네 개의 { }는 각각 the language, the education, the history, the holidays를 수식하는 목적격 관계대명사절이다.

어휘풀이

- identity *n* 정체성
- minority *n* 소수 민족, 소수 집단
- favor *v* ~에 호의를 보이다
- intentionally *ad* 의도적으로, 고의로
- conform to ~을 따르다, ~에 순응하다
- association *n* 단체, 연합
- identify with ~와 일체감을 느끼다
- through no fault of ~의 잘못이 아닌데도
- upbringing *n* 양육
- comprehensive *a* 포괄적인
- dominant *a* 지배적인, 우세한
- institution *n* 제도, 기관
- broadcast *v* 방송하다
- civic *a* 시민의
- status *n* 지위
- drawback *n* 불이익, 결점

032 답 ④

📖 갈등의 필연성과 긍정적 기능

전문해석

국제 관계에서 갈등은 당사자들이 상호작용하며 양립할 수 없는 이해관계에 대한 논쟁이 일어날 때 빈번히 발생한다. 그것 자체로 갈등은 반드시 위협적인 것은 아닌데, 전쟁과 갈등은 다르기 때문이다. **갈등은 필연적인 것으로 여겨질 수 있을 것이며, 양자가 자신들 사이에서 차이를 인식하고 자신이 만족하도록 그 차이를 해결하려고 노력할 때마다 발생한다.** 어떤 갈등은 사람들이 상호작용할 때마다 일어나며, 종교적이거나 이념적이거나 민족적이거나 경제적이거나 정치적이거나 또는 영토적인 사안들에 의해 발생될 수 있으며, 따라서 비정상적인 것으로 여겨져서는 안 된다. **또한 우리는 갈등을 반드시 파괴적인 것으로 간주해서도 안 된다.** 갈등은 사회적 결속, 창

의적 사고, 학습 그리고 의사소통을 약화시킬(→ 촉진시킬) 수 있는데, 이것들 모두 논쟁의 해결과 협력의 지속에 매우 중요한 요소들이다. 하지만 갈등의 대가는 양자가 화해할 수 없는 인식된 차이를 해결하거나 묵은 원한을 풀기 위해 무기를 들 때에는 진정 위협적이 될 수 있다. 그런 일이 일어날 때는 폭력이 발생하며, 우리는 전쟁의 영향권으로 들어가게 된다.

정답풀이

④ 갈등은 이해관계가 대립되는 상황에서 필연적으로 발생하는데, 그것이 비정상적이거나 반드시 파괴적인 것만은 아니라는 내용이다. However로 시작하는 문장 앞에서는 갈등의 필연성과 순기능을, 뒤에서는 갈등이 위협적이 되는 경우를 설명하고 있다. 따라서 갈등의 순기능을 설명하는 문맥에 맞도록 undermine(약화시키다)을 promote(촉진하다) 정도의 어휘로 바꿔야 한다.

오답풀이

① 진정한 위협이 되는 전쟁과 달리 갈등은 반드시 위협적인 것은 아니라고 했으므로 different(다른)의 쓰임은 문맥상 적절하다.

② 갈등은 양자가 이해관계를 논할 때 발생하는 것이므로 자신이 '만족(satisfaction)'하도록 노력할 때 발생한다는 흐름은 자연스럽다.

③ 갈등은 다양한 사안들에 의해 상시적으로 일어나기 때문에 자연스런 현상으로 받아들여야 한다는 흐름이므로 not과 함께 쓰인 abnormal(비정상적인)은 문맥상 적절하다.

└ '갈등'은 일반적으로 부정적인 것으로 인식되는데다 앞에 있는 not을 간과한다면 쉽게 고를 수 있는 함정 오답!

⑤ 갈등의 순기능을 설명한 앞의 문맥과 반대로 화해할 수 없는 차이를 해결하기 위해 무기를 들 때는 갈등이 '위협적(threatening)'이 된다는 흐름은 자연스럽다.

구문풀이

`12행` **Nor should we regard** conflict as necessarily destructive.

: Nor는 앞에 나온 부정문에 이어서 '~ 또한 …가 아니다'의 의미를 나타내는 문장을 이끄는 접속사로서 「Nor+조동사(should)+주어(we)+본동사(regard)」와 같이 반드시 어순이 도치된다.

어휘풀이

- dispute *n* 논쟁
- in and of itself 그것 자체로
- resolve *v* 해결하다
- generate *v* 일으키다
- ethnic *a* 인종의, 민족의
- regard *A* as *B* A를 B로 여기다
- solidarity *n* 결속
- durability *n* 지속(성), 내구성
- take up ~을 집어 올리다
- settle *v* (논쟁 등)을 해결하다
- sphere *n* 영향권
- incompatible *a* 양립할 수 없는
- inevitable *a* 필연적인, 불가피한
- result *v* 생기다, 일어나다
- ideological *a* 이념적인
- territorial *a* 영토의
- undermine *v* 약화시키다
- resolution *n* 해결
- cooperation *n* 협력, 협동
- arms *n* 무기
- old scores 묵은 원한, 구원(舊怨)
- warfare *n* 전쟁

033 답 ③

📖 의식적인 행동의 특성

전문해석

의식은 바람직한 결과를 만들어 내기 위해 반복적으로 행해지는 어떠한 행동도 포함한다. 일반적으로, 의식은 개인의 불안을 상징적으로 표현한다. 이것은 이 행동이 관련 없는 행동을 통하여 어떤 결과를 가져오게 하려는 시도라는 것을 의미한다. 의식의 힘을 믿는 사람들은 종종 의식을 깨는 것이 부정적인 결과, 아마도 심지어는 초자연적인 벌을 가져올 것이라고 믿는다. 심리학적으로, 의식적인 행동은 종종 제어할 수 없는 상황에 대한 통제감을 줄일(→ 제공할) 수 있다. 예를 들어, 명예의 전당에

오른 하키 선수 Wayne Gretzky는 매 경기 전에 정확히 똑같은 방식으로 그의 운동복 셔츠를 안에 넣어 입었다. 하키 경기의 결과는 분명히 전적으로 단 한 명의 하키 선수에 의해서 제어될 수 없다. 그러나 의식은 특정한 방식으로 운동복 셔츠를 입는 미신적인 습관에 의한 것이라고 할지라도, 한 선수에게 그가 팀의 성공을 제어하고 있다는 느낌을 줄 수도 있다.

정답풀이

③ 글의 후반부에 나오는 내용(하키 선수의 예)으로 보아, 의식적으로 하는 행동은 제어할 수 없는 상황에 대한 통제감을 '제공한다'는 것을 알 수 있으므로 reduce(줄이다)를 provide(제공하다) 또는 increase(늘리다) 같은 어휘로 바꿔야 한다.

오답풀이

① 의식은 관련 없는 행동을 통하여 바람직한 결과를 가져오게 하려는 것이라고 했으므로, 의식은 '상징적으로(symbolically)' 한 개인의 불안감을 표현하는 것이라는 문맥은 적절하다.
② 의식의 힘을 믿는 사람들은 의식을 '깨뜨리는' 것이 부정적인 결과를 가져온다고 생각한다는 문맥이므로 breaking의 쓰임은 적절하다.
④ 하키 경기가 한 개인의 행동으로 '제어될' 수 있는 것은 아니라는 문맥이므로 cannot과 함께 쓰인 controlled는 적절하다.
⑤ 한 선수가 팀의 성공을 제어하기 위해 운동복 셔츠를 특정한 방식으로 입는 것은 '미신적인' 습관이라고 할 수 있으므로 superstitious의 쓰임은 적절하다.

구문풀이

[5행] Those [who believe in the power of rituals] often **feel** [that breaking the ritual will produce negative consequences, perhaps even supernatural punishment].

: 핵심 주어는 첫 번째 [ ]로 표시된 주격 관계대명사절의 수식을 받는 Those이고, 동사는 feel이다. 두 번째 [ ]는 feel의 목적어로 쓰인 명사절이다.

[14행] However, a ritual may give a player **the feeling** [that he has control over the team's success], / **even if** it is through the superstitious habit of putting on jersey in a certain way.

: [ ]는 the feeling과 동격을 이루는 명사절이며, even if는 양보의 부사절을 이끈다.

어휘풀이

- ritual *n* 의식, 의례
- desired *a* 바람직한
- symbolically *ad* 상징적으로
- supernatural *a* 초자연적인
- psychologically *ad* 심리[정신]적으로
- ritualistic *a* 의례적인, 의식적인
- tuck *v* 집어넣다
- manner *n* 방법, 방식
- superstitious *a* 미신적인
- repeatedly *ad* 반복적으로
- anxiety *n* 불안감
- consequence *n* 결과
- punishment *n* 벌, 처벌
- Hall-of-Fame 명예의 전당
- jersey *n* (운동 경기용) 셔츠
- solely *ad* 단지, 오로지

034 답 ⑤

📖 문자의 등장과 프라이버시 개념의 형성

전문해석

글자가 없는 고대 사회에서는 세상이 별개이고, 추상적이며, 위계적인 아이디어와 문자 활용의 인공물인 정보 조각이 아니라, 뜻깊은 상호 관계, 유동적인 상호 작용, 그리고 순환으로 구성된 전체로 생각되었다. 대면 의사소통과 직접적인 사회적, 자연적 환경은 구전 문화에서 최우선으로 중요하다. 그런 특정한 사회 구성에서, 안녕

감은 의심의 여지없이 개별적인 개인에게보다는 사회 집단의 결속에 더 많이 연결되곤 했다. 프라이버시는 혹시 존재하기라도 했다면, 개인적 가치로 이해되지 않곤 했다. **개인으로서의 자기 정체성은 구전 위주의 민족에게 반향을 일으키지 못했다.** 심리적 의미에서 개인적 자율은 존재하지 않았다. 프라이버시와 개인성 개념은 기원후 1500년이 되어서야 중요해졌다. 구전 사회에서 안녕은 완전한 상호 연결성이라는 견지에서 사회체에 의해 결정되곤 했다. **사회와 개인 사이의 분리는 글자와 글의 발명과 더불어 시작된다.**

정답풀이

(A) 앞에서 글자가 없는 고대 사회는 상호 관계와 상호 작용, 순환으로 구성된 전체라고 제시되었으므로, 대면 의사소통은 그러한 구전 문화에서 매우 중요하다고 하는 것이 논리적이다. 따라서 '제1의, 최우선적인'이라는 뜻의 primary가 적절하다. (minor: (중요성이) 작은)
(B) 앞에서 안녕감이 사회 집단의 결속에 더 많이 연결된다고 했고, 뒤에서 개인으로서의 자기 정체성이 사회에 유의미한 영향을 주지 않았다고 했으므로, 프라이버시가 개인적 가치로 이해되지 않았다고 하는 것이 논리적이다. 따라서 '개인의'라는 뜻의 individual이 적절하다. (collective: 집단적인)
(C) 글자와 글이 없는 구전 사회에서 사회로부터 독립된 개인의 가치는 중요하지 않았으며, 프라이버시와 개인성의 개념은 글자의 발명 이후에 중요해졌다고 했으므로, 동사 begins를 고려하면 '분리'라는 뜻의 separation이 적절하다. (integration: 통합)

구문풀이

[1행] In ancient nonalphabet societies, **the world was conceived of as** a whole, [composed of meaningful interrelations, fluid interactions, and cycles], **as opposed to** [discrete, abstract, and hierarchical ideas and pieces of information — the artifacts of literacy].

: 「conceive of A as B: A를 B로 생각하다」에서 A에 해당하는 the world가 주어로 쓰인 수동태 문장이다. 첫 번째 [ ]는 a whole을 부가적으로 설명하는 과거분사구이고, 두 번째 [ ]는 as opposed to(~이 아니라)에 이어지는 명사구이며, pieces of information과 the artifacts of literacy는 동격 관계이다.

[6행] [{Face-to-face communication} and {the immediate social and natural environment}] are **of primary importance** in an oral culture.

: [ ]는 문장의 주어로 쓰인 명사구로 두 개의 { }가 and로 연결되어 있는 구조이다. of primary importance는 「of+형용사+명사」로 구성된 형용사구로 '최우선으로 중요한'이라는 의미를 나타내며 are의 보어 역할을 한다.

어휘풀이

- conceive of *A* as *B* A를 B로 생각하다
- composed of ~로 구성된
- discrete *a* 개별적인
- hierarchical *a* 위계의, 서열의
- literacy *n* 문자 활용 (능력)
- oral culture 구전 문화
- collective *n* 집단 *a* 집단적인
- autonomy *n* 자율
- fluid *a* 유동적인
- abstract *a* 추상적인
- artifact *n* 인공물
- immediate *a* 직접적인
- cohesiveness *n* 결속, 단결
- separate *a* 개별적인
- individuality *n* 개인성

035 답 ⑤

📖 대중의 욕구가 있을 때 바로 전달해야 하는 오락

전문해석

오락은 필수품이 아니라 사치품이다. 영화는 여러분에게 직장까지 신뢰할 수 있는

탑승을 제공해 주지 않을 것이며, 내려받은 음악이 한 주간 여러분의 가족에게 먹을 것을 주지도 않을 것이다. 사람들은 시간, 돈 그리고 그렇게 하고자 하는 욕구가 있을 때에 단지 오락을 소비할 것이다. **그런 욕구는 많은 변수를 통해 생겨나지만, 일단 그것(욕구)이 있게 되면, 여러분은 '즉시' 제공하는 것이 낫다. 오락은 대중이 그것을 원할 때, 잠시도 이르거나 늦지 않게 대중이 이용할 수 있어야 한다.** (오락)산업에 가장 큰 난제를 제기하는 것이 바로 이 (오락의) 사멸성이다. 큰 투자인 자동차 또는 가정의 가구는 유행이 몇 년에 걸쳐 성쇠를 되풀이한다. 그런 산업은 새로운 버전, 모델 또는 스타일을 만들어 내는 데 더 많은 시간이 필요하기 때문에 제품의 수명에서 단선적인 경로를 따라갈 수 있다. 오락은 어떤가? 오늘 인기 있는 것이 내일은 인기 없는 것이 될 수 있다. **소비하는 대중은 변덕스러우므로, 여러분이 그들의 관심을 이용하고자 한다면, 여러분의 '모든' 힘을 즉시 보류할(→ 동원할) 필요가 있다.**

정답풀이

⑤ 오락을 소비하는 대중은 변덕스럽기 때문에 그들의 관심을 이용하고자 한다면 모든 힘을 즉시 '동원해야' 한다는 문맥이 자연스럽다. 따라서 withhold (보류하다)를 mobilize(동원하다) 정도의 어휘로 바꿔야 한다.

오답풀이

① 영화는 오락의 일종으로 사치품에 해당하기 때문에 직장까지 '신뢰할 수 있는' 탑승을 제공하지 않는다는 문맥이므로 not과 함께 쓰인 dependable 은 적절하다.
② 이어지는 문장에서 오락은 대중이 원할 때 바로 이용할 수 있어야 한다고 했으므로 대중의 욕구가 있을 때 즉시 '제공하는(deliver)' 것이 낫다는 문맥은 적절하다.
③ 뒤에서 예로 든 자동차나 가구와 달리 오락은 시간의 제약을 받는데, 이러한 오락의 사멸성이 오락 산업에 가장 큰 '어려움'을 준다는 것을 추론할 수 있으므로 challenge는 적절하다.
④ 오락의 인기가 오늘과 내일을 예측하기 어려운 것과는 달리, 큰 투자에 해당하는 자동차나 가구의 유행은 수년에 걸쳐 성쇠를 되풀이하여 제품의 수명에서 '단선적인' 경로를 따른다는 문맥이므로 linear는 적절하다.

구문풀이

10행 **It is** this perishability **that** poses the biggest challenge to the industry.

: This perishability poses the biggest challenge to the industry.라는 문장에서 주어인 This perishability를 「It is ~ that ....」 강조구문을 써서 강조한 문장이다.

13행 Those industries can follow a linear path in the life of a product, [**taking** more time to create the new version, model, or style].

: [ ]는 분사구문으로 taking ~의 의미상 주어는 문장의 주어인 Those industries이다.

어휘풀이

- entertainment *n* 오락
- necessity *n* 필수품, 필요
- dependable *a* 신뢰할 수 있는, 믿을 수 있는
- come about 생기다, 일어나다
- deliver *v* 전달하다, 제공하다
- challenge *n* 난제, 도전
- investment *n* 투자
- ebb and flow (흥망)성쇠를 되풀이하다
- linear *a* 단선적인, 선형의
- withhold *v* 보류하다, 주지 않다
- luxury *n* 사치품
- variable *n* 변수
- pose *v* 제기하다
- furnishing *n* 가구, 비품
- take advantage of ~을 이용하다

---

036 답 ⑤

📖 방어적 비관주의의 특징

전문해석

방어적 비관주의자들은 예방적 대처 전략, 즉 수행 상황에 들어가기 '전에' 사용되는 전략에 의해서 특징지어진다. **방어적 비관주의의 특징은 낮은 성과 기대를 설정하는 것인데, 이는 자기 보호 목적에 기여한다.** 최악의 일이 발생할 수도 있다고 생각함으로써 그들은 잠재적인 나쁜 결과에 대해서 선제적으로 자신들의 충격을 완화시킬 수 있다. 만일 나쁜 일이 정말로 일어나면 방어적 비관주의자들은 "나는 이 모든 것을 예상했어."라고 생각할 수 있으며, 그 결과가 덜 해로워 보이게 만든다. 그들이 형편 없이 할 것이라고 자신을 설득시키는 것은 또한 그들에게 실제로 그들이 잘할 것이라는 것을 확실하게 하려는 노력과 준비를 배가하도록 강요함으로써 동기를 부여하는 목표에 도움이 된다. 이것은 가능한 실패에 대한 불안이나 부정적인 효과를 이용하도록 돕는다. 방어적 비관주의자들의 예방적 전략의 사용은 모순처럼 보일 수 있다. 먼저, 그들은 매우 높은 성과를 내는 사람들이며, 사실 그들은 과거에 좋은 성과를 냈다. 둘째, 형편없는 성과가 생길 것이라고 자신을 확신시키는 것은 실제로 그 성과가 일어나게 하지 않는다. 낮은 성과에 대한 기대는 자기 모순적이지(→ 자기 충족적이지) 않다.

정답풀이

⑤ 자신이 잘하지 못할 것이라고 미리 자신을 설득시키는 사람에게 실제로는 그런 일(형편없는 성과)이 일어나지 않는다고 했으므로 낮은 성과에 대한 기대는 자기 모순적이라고 할 수 있다. 따라서 앞에 있는 부정어 not을 고려할 때 self-contradicting(자기 모순적인)을 self-fulfilling(자기 충족적인, 예언대로 성취되는) 정도의 어휘로 바꿔야 한다.

오답풀이

① 방어적 비관주의는 최악의 일이 일어날 수도 있다고 선제적으로 마음을 다잡는 것이므로 '낮은(low)' 성과를 기대하는 것이다.
② 방어적 비관주의는 나쁜 결과가 생겼을 때 그 충격을 '완화시키기' 위한 전략이므로 cushion의 쓰임은 적절하다.
③ 더 많은 노력과 준비를 하는 것은 성공을 '확실하게 하기' 위함이므로 ensure의 쓰임은 적절하다.
④ 방어적 비관주의자들은 과거에 좋은 성과를 냈던 사람들이고 실제로 높은 성과를 내도록 한다는 점에서 방어 전략은 '모순적(ironic)'이라고 할 수 있다.

구문풀이

18행 Second, [**convincing** themselves that poor performances will happen] **does** not actually **make** them **happen**.

: [ ]는 동명사구 주어로 단수 취급하며, make는 사역동사로서 목적격보어로 원형부정사를 쓴다.

어휘풀이

- defensive *a* 방어적인
- characterize *v* 특징짓다
- hallmark 특징
- convince *v* 확신시키다, 납득시키다
- redouble one's efforts 노력을 배가하다
- preparation *n* 준비
- pessimist *n* 비관주의자
- cope *v* 대처하다
- cushion *v* ~의 충격을 완화하다
- impel *v* 강요하다
- harness *v* 이용하다

- interrelated *a* 상호 연관된
- representational *a* 표현의, 재현의
- predominate *v* 두드러지다, 지배적이다
- complicated *a* 복잡한
- illustration *n* 삽화
- enhance *v* 향상시키다
- apply to ~에 적용되다
- feature *n* 특징
- interpretation *n* 해석
- complement *v* 보완하다

037 답 ②

📖 읽기 텍스트 범주의 다양한 형태로의 확대

전문해석

지난 10년 동안 어린이가 읽기를 배우는 방법에 주어진 관심은 '텍스트성'의 본질과 모든 연령대의 독자가 텍스트를 의미하게 만드는 서로 다른, 상호 연관된 방식의 본질을 더 중요하게 만들었다. **이제 '읽기'는 과거 어느 때보다 더 많은 표현 형식에 적용되는데, 그림, 지도, 화면, 디자인 그래픽, 그리고 사진이 모두 텍스트로 여겨진다.** 새로운 인쇄 공정에 의해 그림책에서 가능해진 혁신에 더해, 시집과 정보 텍스트와 같은 다른 종류에서도 디자인적 특징이 두드러진다. **그래서 읽기는 어린이의 주의가 인쇄된 텍스트에 집중되고 스케치나 그림이 부속물이었을 때보다 더 복잡한 종류의 해석이 된다.** 이제 어린이는 그림책에서 글과 삽화가 서로를 보완하고 서로를 향상시킨다는 것을 알게 된다. 읽기는 결코 단어 인식이 아니다. 가장 쉬운 텍스트에서조차도 문장이 '말하는' 것은 흔히 그것이 의미하는 것이 아니다.

정답풀이

읽기(Reading)의 범주가 다양한 형태로 확대되어 이제는 글자[문자]뿐만 아니라 그림, 지도, 화면, 디자인 그래픽, 사진 역시 텍스트로 여겨진다는 내용으로, 어린이 그림책의 글과 삽화가 서로 읽기를 보완하고 향상시킨다고 했으므로, 빈칸에 들어갈 말로는 ② '단어 인식'이 가장 적절하다. 그래야 앞의 부정어(not)와 함께 '읽기는 단지 단어 인식만이 아니다'라는 흐름상 적절한 내용이 된다.

오답풀이

① 지식 습득
 ↳ 읽기는 이제 글 외의 다른 표현 형식도 함께 반영하여 보다 복잡한 해석을 할 수 있다는 의미이지, 읽기가 지식 습득과 관계없다는 말이 아니다.

③ 창의적인 놀이
④ 주관적인 해석
⑤ 이미지 맵핑

구문풀이

[1행] Over the last decade / the attention [given to {how children learn to read}] **has foregrounded** the nature [of *textuality*], and [of the different, interrelated ways {in which readers of all ages make texts mean}].

: 첫 번째 [ ]는 문장의 핵심 주어인 the attention을 수식하는 과거분사구이고, 그 안의 { }는 전치사 to의 목적어 역할을 하는 명사절이며, 문장의 동사는 has foregrounded이다. 두 번째와 세 번째 [ ]는 the nature에 이어지는 어구이고, 세 번째 [ ] 안의 { }는 the different, interrelated ways를 수식하는 관계절이다.

[5행] In addition to the innovations [made possible in picture books by new printing processes], / **design features** also **predominate** in other kinds, such as books of poetry and information texts.

: In addition to ~ processes는 부사구이고, [ ]는 the innovations를 수식하는 과거분사구이다. 문장의 주어는 design features이고, 술어 동사는 predominate이다.

어휘풀이

- foreground *v* 더 중요하게 만들다, 특히 중시하다
- nature *n* 본질
- textuality *n* 텍스트성

038 답 ②

📖 존중받지 못하는 스포츠 저널리즘의 전문적 지위

전문해석

스포츠 저널리즘의 전문적 지위에 관해서, 특히 인쇄 매체에서, 매우 역설적인 것이 있다. 기자들이 설명하고 논평하는 통상적으로 자신이 맡은 일을 이행할 때, 스포츠 팬들이 스포츠 경기에 관한 기자들의 설명을 열심히 찾아보는 한편, 여러 형식으로 스포츠를 취재하는 그들의 더 폭넓은 저널리스트의 역할에서 스포츠 저널리스트는 동시대의 모든 작가 중에서 가장 눈에 띄는 이들 가운데 있다. '유명인'급 스포츠 저널리스트 중 엘리트 계층의 생각은 주요 신문사들이 많이 원하고, 그들의 돈을 많이 버는 계약은 저널리즘의 다른 '부문'에 있는 동료들의 선망의 대상이 된다. **그러나 스포츠 저널리스트들이 하는 일의 가치를 묵살하는 말로 여전히 쉽게 건네는, 스포츠는 '뉴스 매체의 장난감 부서'라는 (이제는 상투적인 문구의 지위에 이르는) 옛말과 더불어, 그들의 독자 수나 급여 액수의 크기에 상응하는 그들 전문성에서의 지위를 스포츠 저널리스트는 누리지 못한다.** 이렇게 스포츠 저널리즘을 진지하게 여기기를 꺼리는 것은 스포츠 신문 작가들이 많이 읽히면서도 거의 존중받지 못하는 역설적인 결과를 낳는다.

정답풀이

스포츠 저널리스트는 그들의 기사를 찾아 읽는 독자층이 많고 저널리즘의 다른 부분에 있는 동료들보다 돈도 많이 벌지만, 스포츠는 '뉴스 매체의 장난감 부서'라는 말에서 알 수 있듯이 전문성을 인정받지는 못하고 있다고 했으므로, 스포츠 저널리스트들은 많이 읽히면서도 제대로 ② '존중받지(admired)'는 못한다고 해야 적절하다.

오답풀이

① 돈을 받지
 ↳ 유명 스포츠 저널리스트들은 돈을 많이 번다고 했으므로 오답! 앞에 있는 부정어 little을 고려해서 답을 골라야 한다.

③ 검열되지
④ 의문이 제기되지
⑤ 논의되지
 ↳ 스포츠 팬들이 많이 찾아본다는 것은 팬들 입방아에 많이 거론된다는 의미이므로 오답!

구문풀이

[9행] **The ruminations** of the elite class of 'celebrity' sports journalists **are** much **sought** after by the major newspapers, [their lucrative contracts **being** the envy of colleagues in other 'disciplines' of journalism].

: 주어의 핵은 The ruminations이고 동사는 are sought이다. [ ]는 분사구문으로, their lucrative contracts가 being ~의 의미상 주어이다.

[13행] Yet sports journalists do not have a standing in their profession [that corresponds to the size of their readerships or of their pay packets], with **the old saying** (now reaching the status of cliché) [that sport is the 'toy department of the news media'] [still readily **to hand** as a dismissal of the worth of {what sports journalists do}].

: 첫 번째 [ ]는 a standing in their profession을 수식하는 주격 관계대명사절이고, 두 번째 [ ]는 the old saying과 동격 관계의 명사절이다. 세 번째 [ ]는 the old saying을 수식하는 형용사적 용법의 to부정사구이고, 그 안의 { }는 선행사를 포함하는 관계대명사 what이 이끄는 명사절로 전치사 of의 목적어 역할을 한다.

어휘풀이

- paradoxical *a* 역설적인
- medium *n* 매체
- account *n* 설명
- consult *v* (서적, 기사 등을) 찾아보다, 조사[참고]하다
- cover *v* 취재하다
- celebrity *n* 유명인사
- envy *n* 선망의 대상
- discipline *n* 부문, 분야
- correspond to ~에 상응하다
- pay packet 급여 봉투, 급여 액수
- dismissal *n* 묵살

- status *n* 지위
- commentary *n* 논평
- eagerly *ad* 열심히, 열성적으로
- contemporary *a* 동시대의
- sought after 수요가 많은, 인기 있는
- colleague *n* 동료
- standing *n* 지위
- readership *n* 독자층[수]
- cliché *n* 상투적인 문구
- reluctance *n* 꺼림, 주저함

039 답 ①

📖 **유머에 담긴 정보의 부정확성**

전문해석

유머는 실제적인 이탈뿐만 아니라 인식의 이탈을 포함한다. **어떤 것이 재미있기만 하면, 우리는 잠깐 그것이 실제인지 허구인지, 진실인지 거짓인지에 관해 관심을 두지 않는다.** 이것이 우리가 재미있는 이야기를 하는 사람들에게 상당한 여지를 주는 이유이다. 만약 그들이 상황의 어리석음을 과장하여 또는 심지어 몇 가지 세부 사항을 꾸며서라도 추가 웃음을 얻고 있다면, 우리는 그들에게 기꺼이 희극적 허용, 일종의 시적 허용을 허락한다. 실제로, 재미있는 이야기를 듣고 있는 누군가가 '아니야, 그는 스파게티를 키보드와 모니터에 쏟은 것이 아니라 키보드에만 쏟았어.'라며 말하는 사람을 바로잡으려고 하면, 그 사람은 아마 듣고 있는 다른 사람들에게서 방해하지 말라는 말을 들을 것이다. 유머를 만드는 사람은 사람들의 머릿속에 생각을 집어넣고 있는데, 그 생각이 가져올 즐거움을 위해서이지 <u>정확한</u> 정보를 제공하기 위해서가 아니다.

정답풀이

유머는 재미있기만 하면 내용을 과장하거나 꾸며내는 것도 허용되며, 오히려 내용의 정확성을 바로잡으려고 하면 방해하지 말라는 말을 듣게 될 것이라고 했으므로, 유머는 사람들에게 즐거움을 주기 위한 것이지 ① '정확한(accurate)' 정보를 제공하기 위한 것이 아니라고 해야 적절하다.

오답풀이

② 상세한
↳ 유머에서 사람들이 관심을 두지 않는 것은 이야기의 진위 여부라고 했다.

③ 유용한   ④ 추가적인   ⑤ 대안적인

구문풀이

2행 [**As long as** something is funny], we are for the moment not concerned with [**whether** it is real **or** fictional, true **or** false].

: 첫 번째 [ ]는 as long as(~이기만 하면, ~인 한)이 이끄는 부사절이다. 두 번째 [ ]는 with의 목적어 역할을 하는 명사절로 「whether *A* or *B*」는 'A인지 아니면 B인지'라는 의미를 나타낸다.

9행 Indeed, <u>someone</u> [listening to a funny story] [who tries to correct the teller—'No, he didn't spill the spaghetti on the keyboard and the monitor, just on the keyboard'—] will probably **be told** by the other listeners [**to stop** interrupting].

: 첫 번째 [ ]는 someone을 수식하는 현재분사구이고, 두 번째 [ ]는 someone listening to a funny story를 수식하는 주격 관계대명사절이다. 「주어+tell+목적어+목적격보어(to부정사)」의 5형식이 수동태로 전환된 문장으로, 세 번째 [ ]는 능동태에서 목적격보어였던 to부정사구이다.

어휘풀이

- disengagement *n* 이탈, 해방
- considerable *a* 상당한
- silliness *n* 어리석음
- grant *v* 허가하다, 부여하다
- correct *v* 바로잡다, 정정하다
- interrupt *v* 방해하다, 끼어들다

- fictional *a* 허구의
- exaggerate *v* 과장하다
- make up ~을 꾸며내다[지어내다]
- licence *n* (창작상의) 파격, 허용
- spill *v* 쏟다, 흘리다

040 답 ④

📖 **의미의 사회적 구성**

전문해석

미국의 철학자이자 사회 이론가인 George Herbert Mead는 의미의 사회적 구성에 대한 요점을 설명하기 위해 두 마리 개 사이의 매우 단순한 의사소통 행위의 예를 제시했다. 개 한 마리가 으르렁거리는 몸짓을 하면, 이것은 '싸움'을 의미하는 대항의 으르렁거림을 불러일으킬 수 있거나 혹은 그 몸짓은 승리와 패배를 의미하는 도망을 불러일으킬 수 있거나 또는 그 몸짓에 대한 반응은 굴복과 지배를 의미하는 웅크리는 것이 될 수 있다. 그러므로 의미는 몸짓에만 있는 것이 아니라 사회적 행위 전체에 있다. 다시 말해서, **의미는 행위자들 사이의 반응하는 상호작용에서 생기는데, 몸짓과 반응은 결코 분리될 수 없으며 한 행동에서의 순간들로 이해되어야 한다**는 것이다. 의미는 각 개인에게서 먼저 발생하여 이후에 행동으로 표현되는 것이 아니고, 한 개인에서 다른 개인으로 전달되는 것도 아니다. **의미는 어떤 대상에 부여되거나, 표현으로 형성되거나, 저장되는 것이 아니라, 상호작용에서 만들어진다.**

정답풀이

의사소통에 있어서 의미의 사회적 구성에 대해 설명하는 글이다. 두 마리 개 사이의 의사소통에서 볼 수 있듯이 의미는 행위자들 사이의 반응하는 상호작용에서 생겨난다는 것이 글의 핵심이다. 빈칸이 있는 문장은 글의 결론에 해당하고, 따라서 빈칸에 들어갈 말로는 ④ '상호작용'이 가장 적절하다.

오답풀이

① 위계질서   ② 합의   ③ 관습   ⑤ 발화

구문풀이

14행 Meaning does not arise first in each individual, [**to be** subsequently expressed in action], [**nor is it** transmitted from one individual to another].

: 첫 번째 [ ]는 결과를 나타내는 부사적 용법의 to부정사구이고, 두 번째 [ ]는 '~도 또한 … 아니다'를 뜻하는 「nor+(조)동사+주어」의 도치구문이 쓰였다.

어휘풀이

- philosopher *n* 철학자
- call forth ~을 불러일으키다
- flight *n* 도망, 도피
- crouch *v* 웅크리다
- domination *n* 지배, 우세
- arise *v* 발생하다
- interplay *n* 상호작용
- transmit *v* 전달하다
- representation *n* 표현, 표상

- constitution *n* 구성, 구조, 조성
- counter- *a* 대항[대응]하는
- defeat *n* 패배
- submission *n* 굴복, 항복, 복종
- lie in ~에 있다
- responsive *a* 반응하는, 반응이 빠른
- subsequently *ad* 이후, 계속해서
- attach *v* 부여하다

041 답 ⑤

📖 동물들의 의사소통 능력

전문해석

인간이 아닌 동물들이 의도적이고 도구를 쓰는 의사소통을 할 수 있을 뿐만 아니라, 그들의 어휘도 인상적으로 폭이 넓을 수 있다는 것이 점점 더 분명해지고 있다. 예를 들어, Northern Arizona 대학의 Con Slobodchikoff에 의해 광범위하게 연구된 프레리도그는 정교한 언어를 가지고 있는데, 그것에는 무엇보다도 사회적인 꽥꽥 울기와 삼각형과 원형을 구별하기 위한 발성을 포함한다. 암탉들은 공중 포식자들과 지상의 위협을 구별하기 위한 특정한 발성을 가지고 있다. 돌고래들은 서로의 이름을 부른다. 나이팅게일(유럽산 지빠귓과의 작은 새)은 각각의 음이 10분의 1초 안에 불려지는 정교하게 만든 노래를 갖고 있는데, 이는 그 노래를 녹음하고 재생을 위해 속도를 늦추지 않는 한 인간이 그 뉘앙스들을 이해하기 어렵게 만든다. 우리에게 짹짹거리는 소리처럼 들릴지도 모르는 것은 잘 아는 청자, 즉 또 다른 나이팅게일에게는 발라드의 완전한 한 연을 전달하고 있는 것일 수도 있다. 이것들과 다른 알려지거나 아직 발견되지 않은 의사소통 기술들은 인간이 아닌 동물의 세계 또한 활기찬 <u>정보 교환</u>으로 가득 차 있다는 것에 의심의 여지가 거의 없다.

정답풀이

인간이 아닌 동물들의 의사소통을 설명하고 있는 글이다. 삼각형과 원형을 구분하는 프레리도그의 정교한 언어, 공중 포식자와 지상의 위협을 구별하는 암탉의 발성, 서로의 이름을 부르는 돌고래, 특히 완전한 발라드 한 연을 전달하는 것일 수도 있는 나이팅게일의 노래 등을 통해 동물도 그들만의 방식으로 의사소통한다는 것을 설명하고 있으므로, 빈칸에 들어갈 말로 가장 적절한 것은 ⑤ '정보 교환'이다.

오답풀이

① 집단적 의식   ② 사회적 구조   ③ 기구 사용
④ 방어 전략
   ↳ 예시에서 언급된 동물이 내는 특정 발성은 동물의 방어 전략이 아니라 의사소통 능력을 설명하기 위한 것이다.

구문풀이

[1행] **It** is becoming increasingly evident [that **not only** are nonhuman animals capable of intentional and instrumental communication, / **but** their vocabulary can be impressively broad].

: It은 형식상의 주어이고 [ ]의 명사절이 내용상의 진주어이다. 명사절은 「not only A but (also) B: A뿐만 아니라 B도」 구문에 의해 두 개의 절이 연결되어 있는데, A에 해당하는 절에서 부정어 not only가 절 앞으로 나와 주어(nonhuman animals)와 be동사(are)가 도치되었다.

[12행] Nightingales have elaborated songs [in which each note is sung in one-tenth of a second], [making **it** difficult {**for humans to appreciate** the nuances} {unless the song is recorded and slowed down for replay}].

: 첫 번째 [ ]는 elaborated songs를 수식하는 관계절이다. 두 번째 [ ]는 주절의 내용을 부가적으로 설명하는 분사구문이고, making의 목적어 자리에 있는 it은 형식상의 목적어이고, 첫 번째 { }의 to부정사구가 내용상의 진목적어이며 for humans는 to appreciate ~의 의미상 주어를 나타낸다. 두 번째 { }는 unless(~하지 않는다면)이 이끄는 조건의 부사절이다.

어휘풀이

- evident *a* 분명한, 명백한
- intentional *a* 의도적인
- instrumental *a* 도구를 사용하는
- impressively *ad* 인상적으로
- extensively *ad* 광범위하게
- sophisticated *a* 정교한
- chatter *n* 꽥꽥 울기, 수다
- vocalisation *n* 발성, 발화
- distinguish *A* from *B* A를 B와 구별하다

- triangular *a* 삼각형의
- circular *a* 원형의
- aerial *a* 공중의
- predator *n* 포식자
- threat *n* 위협
- elaborated *a* 정교하게 만든, 정성을 들인
- note *n* 음, 음조
- appreciate *v* 이해하다, 감상하다
- convey *v* 전달하다
- balladic *a* 발라드의
- informed *a* 잘 아는, 정보에 근거한
- leave little doubt 의심의 여지가 거의 없다
- vibrant *a* 활기찬, 생기 넘치는

042 답 ④

📖 우리 판단력의 직관적이고 비이성적인 본질

전문해석

우리 판단의 직관적이고 감정적인 본질을 모형으로 나타내기 위해, Jonathan Haidt는 코끼리를 타고 있으면서 자신이 그 코끼리의 움직임을 완전히 통제할 수 있다고 믿는 사람에 대한 비유를 이용한다. 하지만 코끼리는 타고 있는 사람보다 훨씬 더 강한데, 그 사람은 (세심하고 장기적인 숙고를 하지 않으면) 이 비이성적이고 본능적이며 강력한 동물의 힘에 아주 작은 영향을 미칠 뿐이다. 타고 있는 사람은 다양한 틀에 박힌 일을 경험하면서 자신이 주도권을 쥐고 있다는 착각을 고수한다. 일반적인 판단의 영역에서, 그 믿음은 실제로 분별없고 흔히 편향적인 직관에 의해 형성됨에도 불구하고 사람들은 자신들이 이성으로부터 판단을 이끌어 낸다고 믿는다고 Haidt는 주장한다. 우리의 판단이 이성에 근거하고 있다고 생각할 때, 우리는 코끼리를 타고 있으면서 자신이 코끼리를 통제하고 있다고 생각하는 사람만큼이나 착각하고 있는 것이다. 결국, 연구는 동일한 증거를 보고 있는 두 사람이 그것이 그들의 직관에 근거한 판단을 뒷받침하는지에 따라 그것을 다르게 평가할 것이라는 것을 보여준다. 아무리 강력한 증거라도 그것은 우리의 감정보다 약하다.

정답풀이

우리는 우리의 판단이 이성에 근거하고 있다고 생각하지만, 사실은 우리가 통제할 수 없는 분별없고 편향적인 직관에 의해 판단이 형성되고 아무리 강력한 증거가 있더라도 감정에 따라 그것을 다르게 판단하게 된다는 내용이다. 빈칸에는 우리 판단의 이러한 속성을 나타내는 말이 들어가야 하므로 ④ '직관적이고 감정적인 본질'이 가장 적절하다.

오답풀이

① 최종적이고 구속하는 효과
② 다양하고 개별적인 측면
③ 편파적이지만 공감하는 특성
   ↳ 우리 판단이 편향적인 직관에 의해 형성된다고는 했지만, 공감하는 특성을 보인다는 내용은 없으므로 오답!
⑤ 기술적이고 평가적인 역할들

구문풀이

[1행] To model the intuitive and emotional nature of our judgments, Jonathan Haidt uses the analogy of a person [**riding** an elephant and **believing** {that he or she has full control of the elephant's movements}].

: [ ]는 a person을 수식하는 현재분사구이며, 그 안에서 riding과 believing은 병렬 구조를 이룬다. { }는 believing의 목적어 역할을 하는 명사절이다.

어휘풀이

- analogy *n* 비유, 유추
- engage in ~을 하다
- prolonged *a* 장기간의, 연장된
- reflection *n* 숙고
- minimal *a* 아주 작은
- instinctive *a* 본능적인

- cling to ~을 고수하다, ~에 매달리다
- be in charge 주도권을 쥐다
- derive v 이끌어 내다
- biased a 편향된
- ground v ~에 근거를 두다
- discrete a 개별적인
- evaluative a 평가하는
- delusion n 착각, 망상 (v delude)
- realm n 영역
- unreflecting a 분별없는
- intuition n 직관(력)
- assess v 평가하다
- empathetic a 공감하는

043 답 ③

📖 재검토를 위해 자료나 방법을 보존해야 하는 범죄학자

전문해석
범죄학자를 위한 윤리 강령에는 범죄학자의 일이 **재검토될 수 있다는** 요건이 자주 포함된다. 이것은 또한 일반적으로 법적 요건이기도 하다. 이 요건은 과학적 방법의 개념에서 비롯되는데, 그것은 본질적으로 과학 수사관에게 자신의 가설에 대한 실험적인 검증을 제공할 것을 요구한다. **과학자는 단순히 무언가가 진실이라고 주장하는 것이 아니라, 또 다른 관찰자가 독립적으로 그 명제의 진실을 검증할 수 있는 과정과 정보를 제공한다.** 법과 윤리 강령에 반영되어 있는 이 과학적 요건은 데이터, 방법 그리고 자료, 즉 결론이 근거를 두고 있는 데이터, 그 데이터를 얻은 방법 그리고 분석을 위해 사용된 자료가 관심 있어 하는 다른 조사자들에 의한 검토를 위해 보존된다는 것을 의미한다. 분석 대상인 자료가 일반적으로 풍부하게 공급되는 대부분의 다른 과학 분야와 달리, 법의학자가 이용할 수 있는 자료는 종종 공급이 매우 부족하며, 더 많이 얻을 가능성이 대개 존재하지 않는다.

정답풀이
범죄학자의 일은 관심 있어 하는 다른 조사자에 의한 검토를 위해 자료나 방법이 보존되는데, 이는 자료가 매우 많은 다른 과학 분야와는 달리 법의학자가 이용할 수 있는 자료가 많지 않기 때문이라는 내용의 글이다. 따라서 빈칸에 들어갈 말로 가장 적절한 것은 ③ '재검토할 수 있는'이다.

오답풀이
① 협상 가능한
② 일관성이 있는
④ 합법적인
⑤ 대체할 수 있는

구문풀이
4행 This requirement originates from the concept of the scientific method, [which essentially **requires** the scientific investigator **to provide** experimental verification of their hypotheses].

: [ ]는 the concept of the scientific method를 부연 설명하는 주격 관계대명사절이며, 여기에는 「require+목적어+목적격보어(to부정사): (목적어)에게 ~할 것을 요구하다」 구문이 쓰였다.

어휘풀이
- ethics code 윤리 강령
- requirement n 요건, 필요조건
- originate from ~에서 비롯되다, ~에서 생기다
- essentially ad 본질적으로, 기본적으로
- verification n 검증
- assert v 주장하다
- proposition n 명제
- conclusion n 결론
- be subjected to ~의 대상이다, ~을 당하다
- plentiful a 풍부한
- nonexistent a 존재하지 않는
- legitimate a 합법적인, 타당한
- criminalist n 범죄학자
- legal a 법적인
- hypothesis n 가설
- verify v 검증하다, 확인하다
- preserve v 보존하다
- analysis n 분석
- forensic scientist 법의학자
- consistent a 일관성이 있는
- replaceable a 대체할 수 있는

044 답 ①

📖 실패를 경험으로 여기고 징벌하지 않기

전문해석
새로운 지식이 생기도록 적극적으로 권장하는 방법은 여러 가지이다. 그러나 **훨씬 더 중요한 것은 아이디어들이 계속 나오게 하기 위해서 해야 할 일이 있다는 것이다. 그중 하나는 실패를 징벌하지 않는 것이다.** 첨단 기술 분야에는 흥미로운 현상이 있다. (산업) 현장에서 정보화 시대를 발전시키는 것은 일련의 실험과 실패를 의미해 왔는데, 회사들이 아주 한결같이 반복적으로 창업하고 실패하다가 마침내 그 업계가 새로운 아이디어를 제대로 해내게 되는 것이다. Stanford 대학의 Christopher Meyer는, 첨단 기술 부문이 성공을 거두는 이유는 부분적으로 '이 분야에서의 실패가 성장 과정의 필수적인 측면으로 이해되기' 때문이라고 믿는다. 사실상 벤처 자본가들은, 그 경영진들이 '경험을 쌓은', 즉 성공하지 못한 하나 이상의 신규 업체에 관여한 적이 있는 회사에 투자하는 것을 선호함으로써 실패를 효과적으로 보상한다.

정답풀이
빈칸에는 새로운 지식이 계속해서 생겨나도록 권장하는 방법 중 하나가 들어가야 하는데, 빈칸이 있는 문장 다음에 실패를 성장 과정의 필수적인 측면으로 여기고 벤처 자본가들이 실패한 적이 있는 경영진을 오히려 선호한다는 내용이 이어지고 있다. 따라서 빈칸에 들어갈 말로 가장 적절한 것은 ① '실패를 징벌하지 않는 것'이다.

오답풀이
② 큰 보상을 제공하는 것
  └ 마지막 문장의 effectively reward를 확대 해석한 것으로, 글의 핵심인 실패에 대한 언급이 없으므로 오답!
③ 집단 지혜에 의존하는 것
④ 같은 실수를 되풀이하지 않는 것
⑤ 실패의 심각성을 인식하는 것

구문풀이
6행 [Developing the information age on the ground] **has meant** a series of experiments and failures, [**with** companies **starting** up and **failing** with great consistency over and over / until the industry gets the new idea right].

: 첫 번째 [ ]의 동명사구가 주어로 쓰여 단수형 동사 has meant가 쓰였다. 두 번째 [ ]는 「with+명사+현재분사」 구문이 쓰여 '~하면서, ~한 채로'라는 의미로 부수적인 상황을 나타내며, starting과 failing이 병렬구조를 이룬다.

어휘풀이
- phenomenon n 현상
- with consistency 한결같이
- partially ad 부분적으로
- invest v 투자하다
- seasoned a 경험을 쌓은
- fly v 성공하다
- gravity n 중대성, 심각성
- sector n 분야
- over and over 반복적으로
- integral a 필수의
- executive n 경영진
- start-up n 신규업체
- punish v 처벌하다, 벌주다

045 답 ①

📖 생각과 그것의 언어적 표현을 통해 행동 조절하기

전문해석
우리의 생각 그리고 그것을 표현하기 위해 우리가 사용하는 언어는 나쁜 습관의 결과를 우리에게 상기시키고, 우리를 다른 행동으로 인도하며, 성공의 강화 가치를 높일 수 있다. 우리는 다른 행동을 중지시키는 생각을 도입할 수 있다. "저 초콜릿 아

이스크림 파인트는 정말 맛있어 보이는데, 나는 몇 입만 먹을 것이다."라고 말하는 대신에, 우리는 스스로에게 이렇게 말할 수 있다. "나는 내가 한 입 먹을 수 없다는 것을 알고 있는데, 왜냐하면 그 한 입이 스무 입으로 이어질 것이기 때문이다." 우리는 우리 자신에게 목표를 상기시킬 수 있는데, 즉 "내가 지금 그것을 먹지 않는다면, 나는 내일 나 자신에 대해 더 낫다고 느낄 것이다." 또는 우리는 자기 효능감의 말을 반복할 수 있는데, 즉 "나는 그렇게 대응할 필요가 없고 이렇게 대응할 수 있다." 또는 "나는 이것을 할 수 있고 이것을 통제할 수 있다." 즉각적인 보상이라는 약속에 습관적으로 반응하는 대신, 우리는 아주 입맛에 맞는 음식을 먹는 것이 장기적으로 미치는 영향에 대해 우리 자신이 의식하도록 만들 수 있다. Columbia 대학교에서 감정, 자기 조절, 지각과 관련된 심리 및 신경 과정을 연구하는 Kevin Ochsner에 의하면 이러한 관심의 변화는 '자극의 의미에 관한 자신의 사고방식을 변화시키는 것을 수반하는' 인지적 제어를 얻기 위한 도구이다.

정답풀이
생각과 그것을 표현하는 언어를 통해 즉각적인 보상을 해주는 습관적인 행동을 그것의 장기적인 영향을 의식하면서 제어할 수 있다는 것이므로, 빈칸에 들어갈 말로 가장 적절한 것은 ① '인지적 제어를 얻기'이다.

오답풀이
② 특정한 감정을 불러일으키기
③ 외부의 자극을 차단하기
④ 무의식적인 욕망을 표현하기
⑤ 타인의 영향력을 감소시키기

구문풀이
1행 [Our thoughts, and the language {we use to express them}], **can remind** us of the consequences of bad habits, **guide** us to other actions, and **heighten** the reinforcement value of success.

: [ ]가 문장의 주어이고, and로 연결된 remind, guide, heighten이 조동사 can에 이어지는 술어 동사로 병렬구조를 이룬다. { }는 the language를 수식하는 목적격 관계대명사절이다.

어휘풀이
• remind A of B A에게 B를 상기시키다 • consequence *n* 결과
• heighten *v* 높이다
• reinforcement value 강화 가치(일종의 이득이나 쾌락이 지각되어 반복적으로 찾거나 갈구하는 어떤 대상이나 경험의 힘 또는 매력)
• pint *n* 파인트(액량·건량 단위) • statement *n* 말, 진술
• self-efficacy *n* 자기 효능감 • habitually *ad* 습관적으로
• shift *n* 변화, 이동 • involve *v* 수반하다, 포함하다
• stimulus *n* 자극 (*pl.* stimuli) • neural *a* 신경의
• self-regulation *n* 자기 조절 • perception *n* 지각, 인지
• evoke *v* 불러일으키다 • specific *a* 특정한, 구체적인

06 빈칸 추론(2) 본문 p.038

| **046** ④ | **047** ① | **048** ⑤ | **049** ② | **050** ③ |
| **051** ② | **052** ⑤ | **053** ③ | **054** ⑤ | |

046 답 ④

📖 도로를 만드는 교통 정책에 대한 자기중심적 시각

전문해석
도시에서 운전하거나 걷거나 교통 카드를 판독기에 통과시키는 모든 사람은 현관문을 나서는 순간부터 자신을 교통 전문가로 여긴다. 그리고 그 사람이 도로를 바라보는 방식은 그 사람이 돌아다니는 방식과 매우 밀접하게 일치한다. 그것이 우리가 매우 많은 선의의 시민 의식을 가진 시민이 서로 딴소리하며 자기주장만 하는 것을 발견하게 되는 이유이다. 학교 강당에서 열리는 주민 회의에서, 그리고 도서관과 교회의 뒷방에서, 전국의 지역 주민들이 도시의 도로를 바꿀 교통 제안에 대해 흔히 논쟁적인 토론을 위해 모인다. 그리고 모든 정치처럼, 모든 교통은 지역적이고 지극히 개인적이다. 수만 명의 이동 속도를 높일 수 있는 교통 프로젝트는 몇 개의 주차 공간 상실에 대한 반대나 프로젝트가 효과가 없을 것이라는 단순한 두려움 때문에 중단될 수 있다. 그것은 데이터나 교통 공학 또는 계획의 어려움이 아니다. 도로에 대한 대중 토론은 일반적으로 변화가 개인의 통근, 주차 능력, 무엇이 안전한지와 무엇이 안전하지 않은지에 대한 믿음, 또는 지역 사업체의 순익에 어떤 영향을 미칠 것인지에 대한 감정적인 추정에 뿌리를 두고 있다.

정답풀이
도시에서 도로를 이용하는 모든 사람은 도시의 도로를 바꿀 교통 제안에 대해 자신의 통근, 주차 능력, 안전한 것에 대한 믿음 등의 개인적인 관점에서 논쟁적인 토론을 한다는 내용의 글이다. 따라서 일반 대중이 도로를 바라보는 방식은 개인적인 관점, 즉 각 개인의 도로 이용 방식과 관련이 있다고 할 수 있으므로, 빈칸에 들어갈 말로 가장 적절한 것은 ④ '그 사람이 돌아다니는 방식과 매우 밀접하게 일치한다'이다.

오답풀이
① 다른 사람들이 그 사람의 도시 도로를 어떻게 보느냐에 크게 의존한다
② 각각의 새로운 대중교통 정책에 맞춰 자체를 업데이트한다
  └ 도로를 바라보는 방식을 업데이트한다는 언급 자체가 없다.
③ 그 사람이 이동하는 도로와 관계없이 발생한다
  └ 사람이 도로를 바라보는 방식은 그 사람이 도로에서 이동하는 방식과 매우 관련 있다는 내용이다.
⑤ 그 사람의 도시가 운영되는 방식과 견고하게 연계되어 있다

구문풀이
1행 Everyone [who drives, walks, or swipes a transit card in a city] **views** herself as a transportation expert from the moment [she walks out the front door].

: 첫 번째 [ ]는 문장의 핵심 주어인 Everyone을 수식하는 주격 관계대명사절이고, 문장의 동사는 views이다. 두 번째 [ ]는 the moment를 수식하는 관계절로 시간을 나타내는 관계부사 when이 생략되었다.

8행 A transit project [that could speed travel for tens of thousands of people] **can be stopped** [by objections to the loss of a few parking spaces] or [by **the simple fear** {that the project won't work}].

: 첫 번째 [ ]는 문장의 핵심 주어인 A transit project를 수식하는 주격 관계대명사절이고, 동사는 can be stopped이다. or로 연결된 두 번째와 세 번째 [ ]는 stopped에

이어지고, 세 번째 [ ] 안의 { }는 the simple fear를 구체적으로 설명하는 동격절이다.

어휘풀이

- transit card 교통 카드
- transportation *n* 교통, 운송, 수송
- expert *n* 전문가
- well-intentioned *a* 선의의
- civic-minded *a* 시민 의식을 가진
- argue past one another 서로 딴소리하며 자기 주장만 하다
- auditorium *n* 강당
- resident *n* 주민
- intensely *ad* 지극히
- objection *n* 반대
- challenge *n* 어려움, 난제
- engineering *n* 공학
- assumption *n* 추정, 가정
- bottom line 순익
- track with ~와 일치하다

047 답 ①

📖 꿀벌 군집의 정보 교환을 통한 노동력 조절 방법

전문해석

흔히 댄스 플로어라고 불리는 꿀벌 군집의 입구는 군집의 상태와 벌집 밖의 환경에 관한 정보를 교환하기 위한 시장이다. 댄스 플로어에서의 상호 작용을 연구하는 것은 우리에게 그 장소의 정보에 반응하여 자신의 행동을 바꾸는 개체들이 어떻게 군집이 그것의 노동력을 조절하게 할 수 있는지에 대한 많은 예증이 되는 예들을 제공한다. 예를 들어, 물을 모아온 꿀벌들은 자신들의 벌집으로 돌아오자마자 자신들의 물을 벌집 안으로 넘겨주기 위해 물을 받을 벌을 찾는다. 만약 이 (물을 받을 벌) 찾는 시간이 짧으면, 그 돌아오는 벌은 물이 있는 곳으로 데려갈 다른 벌들을 모집하기 위해 8자 춤을 출 가능성이 더 크다. 반대로, 이 찾는 시간이 길면 그 벌은 물을 가지러 가는 것을 포기할 가능성이 더 크다. 물을 받는 벌들은 자신들을 위해서든 다른 벌들과 애벌레들에게 전해주기 위해서든, 물이 필요할 때만 물을 받을 것이므로, 이러한 물을 넘겨주는 시간은 군집의 전반적인 물 수요와 상관관계가 있다. 따라서 (시간이 늘어나든 혹은 줄어들든 간에) 물을 넘겨주는 시간에 대한 개별적인 물 조달자의 반응은 군집의 수요에 맞춰서 물 수집(량)을 조절한다.

정답풀이

댄스 플로어에서 물을 가져온 꿀벌들의 행동이 물을 넘겨주는 데 걸리는 시간에 따라 달라지는데, 물을 받아줄 벌이 빨리 찾아지면 군집에 물이 많이 필요하다고 판단하여 물을 가지러 갈 다른 벌들을 더 모집하고, 물을 받는 벌을 찾는 데 시간이 길어지면 군집에 물이 많이 필요하지 않다고 판단하여 물을 가지러 가지 않을 것이라고 한다. 이는 댄스 플로어에서 획득한 정보에 반응하여 꿀벌이 행동을 바꿈으로써 군집의 노동력을 조절하는 한 예에 해당하므로, 빈칸에는 ① '군집이 그것의 노동력을 조절할 수 있게 하는지'가 가장 적절하다.

오답풀이

② 거리를 측정하여 물이 있는 곳을 찾는지

③ 필요할 때 군집의 작업 부담을 줄이는지
  └ 군집의 수요에 따라 물 수집량을 조절한다고 했는데, 작업 부담을 줄이는 경우만을 말하는 것이 아니므로 빈칸에 들어가기에는 지엽적이다.

④ 자신들 각자의 재능에 따라 일을 나누는지

⑤ 기본적인 의사소통 패턴을 습득하도록 일벌들을 훈련하는지

구문풀이

4행 [Studying interactions on the dancefloor] **provides** us **with** a number of illustrative examples of [how individuals {changing their own behavior in response to local information} **allow** the colony **to regulate** its workforce].

: 첫 번째 [ ]가 문장의 주어로 쓰인 동명사구이고, 문장의 동사는 provides이며 「provide A with B」는 'A에게 B를 제공하다'라는 의미이다. 두 번째 [ ]는 전치사 of

의 목적어 역할을 하는 명사절이고, 그 안의 { }는 명사절의 핵심 주어인 individuals 를 수식하는 현재분사구이다. 「allow+목적어+to부정사(목적격보어)」는 '~가 …하게 하다'라는 의미이다.

8행 For example, [**upon returning** to their hive] honeybees [that have collected water] **search out** a receiver bee [to unload their water to within the hive].

: 첫 번째 [ ]는 부사구이고 「upon+-ing」는 '~하자마자'라는 의미이다. 두 번째 [ ]는 문장의 핵심 주어인 honeybees를 수식하는 주격 관계대명사절이고, 문장의 동사는 search out이다. 세 번째 [ ]는 목적을 나타내는 부사적 용법의 to부정사구이다.

어휘풀이

- colony *n* (꿀벌 등의) 군집, 서식지
- hive *n* 벌집
- illustrative *a* 예증이 되는
- unload *v* (짐 등을) 넘겨주다
- waggle dance 8자 춤(꿀벌이 꽃, 물 등의 방향과 거리를 동료에게 알리는 동작)
- recruit *v* 모집하다
- conversely *ad* 반대로
- be correlated with ~와 관련이 있다
- overall *a* 전반적인
- regulate *v* 조절하다

048 답 ⑤

📖 과거, 현재, 미래로 나누는 시간 인식이 기후 변화 책임에 미치는 영향

전문해석

우리는 우리의 의식을 현재, 과거, 미래로 분리하는 것이 허구이며 또한 이상하게도 자기 지시적인 틀이라는 것을 이해하는데, 여러분의 현재는 여러분 어머니 미래의 일부였고 여러분 자녀의 과거는 부분적으로 여러분의 현재이다. 시간에 대한 우리의 의식을 이러한 전통적인 방식으로 구조화하는 것에는 일반적으로 잘못된 것이 전혀 없고 그것은 흔히 충분히 효과적이다. 그러나 기후 변화의 경우, 시간을 과거, 현재, 미래로 분명하게 구분하는 것은 심하게 잘못된 정보를 주었고 가장 중요하게는 지금 살아 있는 우리들의 책임 범위를 시야로부터 숨겨왔다. 시간에 대한 우리의 의식을 좁히는 것은 사실 우리의 삶이 깊이 뒤얽혀 있는 과거와 미래의 발전에 대한 책임으로부터 우리를 단절시키는 길을 닦는다. 기후의 경우, 우리가 사실을 직면하면서도 우리의 책임을 부인하는 것이 아니다. 시간을 나눔으로써 현실이 시야로부터 흐릿해지고 그래서 과거와 현재의 책임에 관한 질문이 자연스럽게 생겨나지 않는 것이다.

정답풀이

시간을 과거, 현재, 미래로 구분하여 인식하는 것은 기후 변화에 대한 우리의 책임 범위를 시야에서 안 보이게 하고, 과거와 현재의 책임에 대한 질문 자체가 생겨나지 않게 한다는 내용이다. 즉, 기후 변화에 대한 책임을 회피하는 것이 아니라 책임을 의식하지 못하게 된다는 맥락이므로, 빈칸에 들어갈 말로는 ⑤ '우리가 사실을 직면하면서도 우리의 책임을 부인하는'이 가장 적절하다.

오답풀이

① 우리의 모든 노력이 효과적으로 밝혀지고 따라서 장려되는
  └ 기후 변화에 대한 책임을 인식하지 못하는 이유를 설명하는 내용으로 책임을 지려는 노력에 대해서는 언급되지 않았다.

② 충분한 과학적인 증거가 우리에게 제공되어온

③ 미래의 우려가 현재의 필요보다 더 긴급한

④ 우리의 조상들이 다른 시간적 틀을 유지한

구문풀이

12행 [The narrowing of our consciousness of time] **smooths** the way to [divorcing ourselves from responsibility for developments in the past and the future {with which our lives are in fact deeply intertwined}].

: 첫 번째 [ ]가 문장의 주어이고, 동사는 smooths이다. 두 번째 [ ]는 전치사 to의 목적

어 역할을 하는 동명사구이고, 그 안의 { }는 developments in the past and the future를 수식하는 관계절이다.

어휘풀이
- consciousness *n* 의식
- oddly *ad* 이상하게
- framework *n* 틀
- conventional *a* 전통적인
- desperately *ad* 심하게, 극도로
- misleading *a* 오도하는, 잘못된 정보를 주는
- extent *n* 범위
- smooth the way to ~로 가는 길을 닦다[순탄하게 하다]
- divorce *v* 단절시키다, 분리하다
- arise *v* 생겨나다
- fiction *n* 허구
- self-referential *a* 자기 지시적인
- structure *v* 구조화[조직화]하다
- division *n* 구분
- partition *v* 나누다, 분할하다

어휘풀이
- sustainability *n* (환경 파괴 없는) 지속 가능성
- embed *v* 깊이 새겨두다
- in the long run 결국에는
- entail *v* 수반하다
- integrate *v* 통합하다
- mutually *ad* 상호 간에, 서로
- dimension *n* 일면, 측면
- requirement *n* 요구
- collapse *n* 붕괴
- tackle *v* ~에 대처하다, ~을 다루다
- profound *a* 심대한, 깊은, 심오한
- incorporate *v* 포함하다, 통합시키다
- implication *n* 영향
- infrastructure *n* 기간 시설
- value-laden *a* 가치 판단적인
- assumption *n* 추정, 가정
- pillar *n* 기둥
- compatible *a* 양립할 수 있는
- tension *n* 긴장
- bounce back 다시 회복하다
- adapt to ~에 적응하다
- initiative *n* 솔선, 자발성
- address *v* ~을 다루다, ~에 대응하다

049 답 ②

📖 지속 가능성 사안에 수반된 가치관적인 합의 결여

전문해석
(환경 파괴 없는) 지속 가능성에 대한 위협은 오직 장기적으로만 변화될 수 있는 물리적 기간 시설뿐만 아니라 문화적, 사회적 구조에도 내재되어 있다. 따라서 **지속 가능성은 가치 판단적인 개념으로서 무엇이 지속할 가치가 있는가와 어떤 대가를 치를 것인가에 대한 가정을 수반한다.** 이것은 이미 서로 양립할 수 없는 지속 가능성의 '3대 기둥', 즉 환경적, 경제적, 사회문화적인 것을 통합하는 데에서의 어려움에 의해 드러나고 있는데, 이는 한 면에서의 이득은 쉽게 다른 면에서의 손실이 되기 때문이다. 지속 가능성과 경제 발전 사이, 환경적 요구와 사회문화적 열망 사이, 현재 세대의 필요와 미래 세대의 필요 사이 등에 긴장이 있다. 훨씬 더 심한 긴장은 현재의 것을 지속하는 것과 붕괴 후에 다시 회복하고 변화에 적응하는 능력을 개발하는 것 사이에서 발견될 수 있다. 이처럼 **지속 가능성 관련 사안들은 가치관에 대한 심각한 합의 결여를 수반한다.**

정답풀이
문화적 그리고 사회적 구조에 내재되어 있는 지속 가능성에 대한 위협 요인은 서로 양립할 수 없는 환경, 경제, 사회문화 사이의 서로 다른 가치관으로 인해 일어나는 매우 다양한 측면에서의 긴장에 있다는 내용이다. 따라서 빈칸에는 지속 가능성과 관련된 사안들을 바라보는 각 부문의 가치관에 대한 시각 차이로 인해 일어나는 결과를 나타내는 ② '가치관에 대한 심각한 합의 결여를 수반한다'가 들어가는 것이 가장 적절하다.

오답풀이
① 자발성을 통해 가장 잘 해결된다
③ 우리의 일상생활에 쉽게 통합될 수 있다
④ 즉각적인 영향과 세대 간 영향 둘 다 가진다
  └ 서로 양립할 수 없는 가치관으로 인한 긴장의 하나로 언급된 현재와 미래 세대의 필요 사이의 긴장만을 담고 있어 오답!
⑤ 어떠한 윤리적 고려 없이는 해결될 수 없다

구문풀이
15행 Even deeper tensions can be found **between** [sustaining {what is}], **and** [developing the capacity {**to bounce** back after a collapse} and {**to adapt** to change}].

: 두 개의 [ ]는 각각 「between *A* and *B*」 구문의 *A*와 *B*에 해당한다. 첫 번째 [ ] 안의 { }는 sustaining의 목적어 역할을 하는 명사절로 '현재의 것'이라는 뜻이다. 두 번째 [ ]에서 두 개의 { }는 the capacity를 수식하는 형용사적 용법의 to부정사구로 and에 의해 병렬로 연결되었다.

050 답 ③

📖 감정의 기능에 관한 Descartes의 생각

전문해석
Descartes의 중요한 공헌은 감정이 옛날부터 가지고 있었던 부정적인 이미지를 개선했다는 것이다. 감정을 이성적인 사고를 위태롭게 하고 그래서 피해야 하는 경험으로 여기기보다는, 그는 감정에 기능적인 중요성을 부여했다. 놀랍게도 다윈주의적인 정신으로, 그는 감정이 '영혼으로 하여금 자연이 우리에게 유용하다고 말하는 것을 원하고 그 자유의지를 고집하고 싶은 마음이 들게 한다'고 가정했다. 우리가 공포를 느낀다면, 그것은 도망가는 것이 그 상황에서 유익한 행동이기 때문일 것이다. 우리가 분노를 느낀다면, 그것은 대립이나 싸움이 그 상황에서 유익한 행동이기 때문일 것이다. 따라서 **감정은 우리가 자신에게 도움이 되는 방식으로 행동하도록 치우치게 한다.** 그러나 Descartes는 감정이 분명한 기능을 가지고 있음에도 불구하고 지나친 감정은 사람에게 해로울 수 있다고 경고했으며, 그러한 과잉을 막을 수 있는 방법을 제시했다.

정답풀이
Descartes는 감정에 기능적인 중요성을 부여하여 특정한 상황에서 감정이 우리가 자신에게 유익하게 행동하고 싶은 마음이 들게 한다고 가정했는데, 예를 들면 도망가는 것이 유익할 때는 공포를 느끼고, 싸우는 것이 유익할 때는 분노를 느끼게 된다는 것이다. 따라서 빈칸에는 이런 내용을 요약한 ③ '우리가 자신에게 도움이 되는 방식으로 행동하도록 치우치게 한다'가 들어가는 것이 가장 적절하다.

오답풀이
① 무엇이 중요한지 우리가 기억하도록 돕는다
② 특정한 쾌락에 대한 욕망에서 발생한다
  └ 지나친 감정은 해로우니 그것을 막아야 한다는 마지막 문장의 내용을 확대 해석한 함정 오답!
④ 조건적이고 일시적인 정신 상태라고 여겨진다
⑤ 얼굴과 목소리 같은 특성에 반영된다

구문풀이
1행 An important contribution of Descartes was [that he improved the negative image {emotions had had since antiquity}].

: [ ]는 주격보어 역할을 하는 명사절이고, 그 안의 { }는 the negative image를 수식하는 목적격 관계대명사절이다.

6행 With a surprisingly Darwinian spirit, he postulated that emotions "dispose the soul [**to will** the things {(nature tells us) are useful}] and [**to persist** in that volition]."

: and로 연결된 두 개의 [ ]는 「dispose+목적어+목적격보어(to부정사): (목적어)로 하여금 ~하고 싶은 마음이 들게 하다」 구문을 이루는 to부정사구이다. { }는 the things를 수식하는 관계절로 주격 관계대명사가 생략되었다. ( )는 삽입절인데, 주격 관계대명사 바로 뒤에 삽입절이 이어질 때 주격 관계대명사는 생략이 가능하다.

어휘풀이

- contribution *n* 공헌
- compromise *v* 위태롭게 하다
- assign *v* 부여하다
- significance *n* 중요성
- dispose *v* ~하고 싶은 마음이 들게 하다
- will *v* 원하다
- flight *n* 도망
- confrontation *n* 대립
- self-serving *a* 자신의 이익을 도모하는
- antiquity *n* 아주 오래됨, 고대
- rational *a* 이성적인
- functional *a* 기능적인

- persist *v* 고집하다, 끈질기게 계속하다
- beneficial *a* 유익한
- excessive *a* 지나친, 과도한
- temporary *a* 일시적인

051 답 ②

📖 새로운 기술 도입에 앞서 갖춰져 있어야 하는 예전 기본 기술

전문해석

우리 두뇌 활동의 대부분은 우리가 의식적으로 지각하지도 못하는, 걷기와 같은, 원초적인 과정에 쓰인다. 그 대신 우리는 더 오래된 과정의 믿을 만한 작동에 기반을 두고 의지하는, 얇고 새롭게 진화된 인식의 층위만 의식한다. **계산을 하고나서야 미적분을 할 수 있다. 이와 마찬가지로 전선 작업을 수행하고서야 무선 전화를 사용할 수 있다. 산업화를 구현하고서야 디지털 기반 시설을 구현할 수 있다.** 예를 들어 에티오피아에서 모든 병원을 전산화하려는 최근 세간의 이목을 끄는 노력은 병원에 안정적인 전기가 없어서 취소되었다. 세계은행이 수행한 한 연구에 따르면, 개발도상국에 도입된 멋진 기술은 일반적으로 고작 5퍼센트 (현지) 진출한 후에 멈춘다. 그것(멋진 기술)은 <u>더 오래된 기본적인 기술들이 따라잡고</u> 나서야 더 확산된다. **첨단 기술을 사용하는 것이 작동하게 하려면 도로, 급수 시설, 공항, 기계 공장, 전기 시스템, 발전소와 같은 큰 예산이 드는 기반 시설이 필요하다.** 따라서 예전 기술을 채택하지 못한 나라들은 새로운 기술에 관한 한 불리한 처지에 있다.

정답풀이

병원을 전산화하려면 그에 앞서 전기 시설이 안정적으로 갖춰져 있어야 하듯이 첨단 기술의 도입과 확산이 이루어지려면 그 이전에 기반이 되는 기본적인 시설이 갖춰져 있어야 한다는 내용이므로, 빈칸에 들어갈 말로는 ② '더 오래된 기본적인 기술들이 따라잡고'가 가장 적절하다.

오답풀이

① 문화적 다양성이 매우 존중되고
③ 사람들이 그 기술을 작동하는 방법을 배우고
 ↳ 첨단 기술의 확산을 위해 사람들이 그 기술을 작동하는 방법을 배워야 한다는 설명은 없다.
④ 그들(개발도상국들)이 외국들로부터 더 많은 지원을 받고
 ↳ 첨단 기술의 확산을 위해 개발도상국에 대한 외국의 지원이 있어야 한다고 언급되지 않았다.
⑤ 기업들이 재능 개발에 더 많이 투자하고

구문풀이

11행 According to a study by the World Bank, / a fancy technology [introduced in developing countries] typically **reaches** only 5 percent penetration [before **it** stops].

: 첫 번째 [ ]는 주절의 주어인 a fancy technology를 수식하는 과거분사구이고, 주절의 동사는 reaches이다. 두 번째 [ ]는 시간의 부사절이고, it은 a fancy technology를 가리킨다.

19행 Thus, <u>countries</u> [that failed to adopt old technologies] **are** at a

disadvantage **when it comes to** new ones.

: [ ]는 문장의 주어인 countries를 수식하는 주격 관계대명사절이고, 동사는 are이다. when it comes to는 '~에 관한 한'이라는 의미이고, 부정대명사 ones는 technologies를 가리킨다.

어휘풀이

- primitive *a* 원초적인
- consciously *ad* 의식적으로
- reliable *a* 믿을 만한
- infrastructure *n* 기반 시설
- big-budget *a* 큰 예산이 드는
- at a disadvantage 불리한 입장에 있는
- perceive *v* 인식하다
- cognition *n* 인식
- process *n* 과정
- abandon *v* 취소하다, 포기하다
- adopt *v* 채택하다

052 답 ⑤

📖 과학 혁명과 패러다임의 전환

전문해석

과학 혁명이란 무엇이며, 그것은 과학 발전에서 어떤 역할을 하는가? **과학 혁명은 새로운 패러다임이 이전의 패러다임과 완전히 혹은 부분적으로라도 양립할 수 없을 때 일어난다.** 하지만 물어봐야 할 질문이 하나 더 있다. 왜 패러다임의 변화가 혁명으로 불려야 하는가? 정치 발전과 과학 발전 사이의 엄청난 차이를 비교해 볼 때, 양쪽 모두에서 혁명이라고 하는 은유를 사용하는 것은 어떻게 정당화할 수 있는가? 유사성의 한 측면은 상당히 명백하다. 정치 혁명은 흔히 정치 집단의 일부에 의해서 기존 제도가 그것이 도와 만들어 왔던 환경에 의해 제기되는 문제들을 바로잡을 수 없다는 의식이 커지면서 시작된다. 이와 마찬가지로, **과학 혁명 역시 흔히 일부 과학 집단에 의해서 기존의 패러다임이 그것이 이전에 주도해 왔던 어떤 분야를 탐구하는 데 있어 충분히 기능하지 못한다는 의식이 커지면서 시작된다.** 정치 발전과 과학 발전 모두에서, 혁명이 일어나기 위해서는 위기를 초래할 수 있는 기능적 결함에 대한 인식이 필요하다.

정답풀이

정치 혁명은 기존 제도가 제기되는 문제들을 바로잡을 수 없을 때, 과학 혁명은 기존의 패러다임이 더 이상 충분한 기능을 하지 못할 때 시작되며, 두 분야에서 혁명은 위기를 초래할 수 있는 기능적 결함에 대한 인식이 있어야 일어난다고 했다. 즉, 기존의 방식으로는 문제나 위기를 해결할 수 없을 때 혁명이 일어난다는 것을 알 수 있으므로, 빈칸에 들어갈 말로는 ⑤ '새로운 패러다임이 이전의 패러다임과 완전히 혹은 부분적으로라도 양립할 수 없을'이 가장 적절하다.

오답풀이

① 어떤 과학 집단에서 그것들이 필요하다고 생각할
② 너무나 많은 예상치 못한 결과들이 어떤 연구 분야에 발생할
③ 천재들이 하나의 패러다임에서 다른 패러다임으로 그들의 생각을 전환할
④ 정치 발전과 과학 발전 사이에 일반적인 유사점들이 발견될
 ↳ 지문에 제시된 단어들로 구성한 함정 오답! 이 글은 정치 발전과 과학 발전에서 혁명의 양상이 비슷하다는 내용이지, 정치 발전과 과학 발전 간의 유사성에 관한 내용이 아니다.

구문풀이

10행 Political revolutions are begun by **a growing sense**, often by a small part of the political community, [that existing institutions are unable to correct <u>the problems</u> {posed by <u>an environment</u> (that they have helped create)}].

: [ ]는 a growing sense와 동격 관계의 명사절이며, 그 안의 { }는 the problems를 수식하는 과거분사구이고, ( )는 an environment를 수식하는 목적격 관계대명사절이다.

어휘풀이

- revolution *n* 혁명
- justify *v* 정당화하다

- metaphor *n* 은유
- institution *n* 제도, 관습
- exploration *n* 탐험, 탐구
- lead the way 앞장서다, 선도하다
- creep into ~에 생기기 시작하다
- similarity *n* 유사점
- pose *v* (위협·문제 등을) 제기하다
- previously *ad* 이전에, 미리
- malfunction *n* 기능적 결함[불량]

어휘풀이
- seemingly *ad* 겉보기에는
- predator *n* 포식동물, 포식자
- victim *n* 희생자
- detect *v* 탐지하다
- flee *v* 달아나다
- clash *v* 상충하다, 충돌하다
- armor *n* 갑옷, 방호 기관
- diminish *v* 감소시키다
- enlarge *v* 커지다
- constraint *n* 제한, 제약
- coexistence *n* 공존
- instinctive *a* 본능적인
- infallible *a* 절대 확실한
- gazelle *n* 가젤
- a host of 다수의
- resistance *n* 저항
- endeavor *n* 노력, 정진
- incompatible *a* 양립할 수 없는
- entail *v* 수반하다
- budget *n* 경비, 예산
- interfere with ~을 방해하다
- compromise *n* 타협(안)
- accompaniment *n* 부속물
- acquisition *n* 습득

053 답 ③

📖 적응에 필수적으로 수반되는 불완전성

전문해석

적응의 필수적인 부속물로서의 불완전함은 생명체의 보편적인 조건인 듯하다. 아프리카의 사자 같은 겉보기에 완벽해 보이는 포식자조차 가젤과 얼룩말에 대한 공격 횟수 중 3분의 2를 실패한다. 공격자와 희생자 둘 다 직면하는 기본적인 문제는 성공이 각각 다수의 과업을 잘 행하는 것에 달려 있다는 것이다. 이상적으로 보면, 포식자는 탐지하고, 탐지한 것을 포획하며, 먹잇감의 저항 방어를 극복할 수 있어야 한다. 잠재적 먹잇감은 탐지되지 않은 상태로 남아 있거나, 그것이 실패하면 달아나거나, 그것도 실패하면 자신을 죽이려는 포식자의 시도를 좌절시켜야 한다. 이 각각의 노력에서의 성공은 흔히 상충하는 능력을 요구한다. 예를 들면, 효과적인 포획이나 성공적인 탈출을 위해 필요한 민첩함은 보통 무거운 갑옷(방호 기관)과 양립할 수 없다. 하나의 과업에 뛰어난 것은, 두 기능 모두 서로 또는 다른 기능을 방해하지 않고 강해질 수 있도록 그 동물의 에너지 수지가 커지지 않으면, 다른 과업에서의 수행력 감소를 수반한다. 에너지 수지의 제약 내에서 결과적인 타협안은 어느 과업도 오로지 그 과업만 성취되는 경우만큼 잘 이루어지지 않는다는 것을 의미한다.

정답풀이

포식자는 모든 사냥을 성공할 수 없고 먹잇감은 모든 사냥에서 무사히 빠져나올 수 없는데, 이는 포식자가 사냥을 위해 한편으로는 민첩함을 갖췄지만 다른 한편으로는 사냥에 필요한 무거운 신체 기관을 갖추도록 진화했기 때문이고, 먹잇감이 탈출을 위해 한편으로는 민첩함을 갖췄지만 다른 한편으로는 방어를 위해 무거운 신체 기관을 갖추도록 진화했기 때문이라는 내용의 글이다. 결국 사냥이 성공하기도 하고 실패하기도 하는 것은 포식자와 먹잇감 둘 다 진화를 통한 적응이 완벽하지 않기 때문이라고 추론할 수 있으므로, 빈칸에 들어갈 말로 가장 적절한 것은 ③ '적응의 필수적인 부속물로서의 불완전함'이다.

오답풀이

① 포식자와 먹잇감의 안정적인 공존
② 서로 다른 동물 종 사이의 생존을 위한 협력
④ 자기 보전에 대한 본능적인 욕구의 표현
⑤ 생존 기술 습득을 위한 사회적 학습에의 의존

구문풀이

7행 Ideally, a predator should be able to **detect, catch** those [it has detected], and **overcome** the resistance defenses of the prey.

: and로 연결된 detect, catch, overcome은 be able to에 이어지는 동사원형이다. [ ]는 those를 수식하는 목적격 관계대명사절이다.

19행 Within the budget's constraints, / the resulting compromise means [{no task is done} **as well as** {it could be / **were it** the only task to be accomplished}].

: [ ]는 means의 목적어로 쓰인 명사절이다. 이 절에는 「as+부사의 원급+as」의 원급 비교 구문이 쓰여 { }로 표시된 두 개의 절을 비교하고 있다. 두 번째 { }는 원래 it could be if it were the only task to be accomplished로 가정법 과거 구문이 쓰인 문장인데, 조건절의 if가 생략되어 주어 it과 be동사 were가 도치되었다.

054 답 ⑤

📖 신제품 개발을 위한 감각 평가의 오차 줄이기

전문해석

연구자들이 성공률을 높이기 위해서 개인별 편차를 줄이고 편향되지 않은 결과를 도출하기 위한 엄청난 노력을 하며, 막대한 액수의 돈이 신제품 개발 계획에 지출된다. 그래서 식품회사들은 거대한 감각 평가 계획을 전문 연구 기관에 위탁한다. 감각 전문가들은 시험 오차를 최소화하려고 하는데, 다시 말해서 결과에 영향을 미칠 수 있는 다양한 인자들의 영향을 최소화하려고 한다. 예를 들어, 인지된 맛은 시험 표본의 순서에 따라 변하므로, 그들은 다양한 실험 설계와 통계적 분석 방법을 통해 비교 집단, 중앙 집중화 경향 오류, 시간 의존성 및 장소의 영향을 통제한다. 특히 심리적 편차 또한 중요한 요인으로 취급된다. 게다가, 그들은 예상 오차(목표가 비용 절감인 경우), 자극 오차(고급 용기에 보관되는 경우), 논리 오차(색상이 다른 경우), 후광 효과(맛이 좋을 경우 나머지 검사 요인도 양호한 것으로 평가된다)를 세심하게 통제한다. 따라서 모든 감각 평가는 독립된 부스에서 개별적으로 실시된다.

정답풀이

식품회사들이 신제품을 개발하면서 감각 평가 계획을 실시할 때, 결과에 영향을 미칠 수 있는 시험 오차를 최소화하기 위해 하는 다양한 노력들을 열거하고 있다. 따라서 빈칸에는 ⑤ '개인별 편차를 줄이고 편향되지 않은 결과를 도출하기 위한'이 들어가는 것이 가장 적절하다.

오답풀이

① 자신들의 생산 과정을 혁신하고 결함을 줄이기 위한
② 양질의 제품을 생산하고 잠재 고객들을 유인하기 위한
 └ 이 글의 핵심인 신제품 개발 시 이루어지는 감각 평가 시험에서의 오차를 최소화하려는 연구원들의 노력을 확대 해석한 함정 오답!
③ 구매자의 요구를 분석하고 시장에서 주도권을 잡기 위한
④ 소비자들의 감정적 자극을 불러일으키고 제품을 홍보하기 위한

구문풀이

8행 For example, **since** the perceived flavor changes according to the order of the test samples, / they control [the comparison group, centralization tendency error, time dependency, and location influence] [**through** various experimental designs and statistical analysis methods].

: since가 이끄는 이유 부사절과 주절로 이루어진 문장이다. 첫 번째 [ ]는 주절의 동사 control의 목적어 역할을 하는 명사구이고, 두 번째 [ ]는 전치사 through가 이끄는 부사구로 방법을 나타낸다.

어휘풀이
- enormous *a* 막대한, 엄청난
- expend *v* 지출하다

- tremendous *a* 엄청난, 거대한
- sensory *a* 감각의
- centralization tendency error 집중화 경향 오류
- statistical analysis 통계 분석
- stimulation *n* 자극
- defect *n* 결함
- the initiative 주도권
- arouse *v* 불러일으키다, 자아내다
- unbiased *a* 편향적이지 않은
- outsource *v* 위탁하다
- evaluation *n* 평가
- deviation *n* 편차
- luxurious *a* 고급의, 사치스러운
- quality *a* 양질의, 고급의

07 글의 순서 파악

본문 p.044

055 ④	**056** ②	**057** ⑤	**058** ①	**059** ③
060 ④	**061** ⑤	**062** ③	**063** ④	

055 답 ④

📖 순응의 결과를 통해 발생하는 집단의 규범

전문해석

규범은 사람들이 다른 사람들의 행동에 순응하는 결과로 집단들 내에 생겨난다. 따라서 한 사람이 특정 상황에서 자신이 그래야만 한다고 생각하기 때문에 특정 방식으로 행동할 때 규범의 시작이 발생한다. (C) 그런 다음 다른 사람들은 여러 가지 이유로 이 행동에 순응할 수도 있다. 최초의 행동을 한 사람은 다른 사람들이 이러한 유형의 상황에서 자신이 행동하는 것처럼 행동해야 한다고 생각할 수도 있다. (A) 따라서 그 사람은 지시하는 방식으로 규범 진술을 함으로써 그들에게 행동을 지시할 수도 있다. 다른 방식으로는, 몸짓과 같은 다른 방식으로 순응이 요망된다는 것을 전달할 수도 있다. 더군다나 그 사람은 자신이 원하는 대로 행동하지 않으면 그들에게 제재를 가하겠다고 겁을 줄 수도 있다. 이것은 일부 사람들이 그 사람의 바람에 순응하고 그 사람이 행동하는 대로 행동하는 것을 초래할 것이다. (B) 그러나 다른 일부 사람들은 그 행동이 자신에게 지시되게 할 필요가 없을 것이다. 그들은 행동의 규칙성을 관찰하고 자신이 순응해야만 하는가를 스스로 결정할 것이다. 그들은 이성적이나 도덕적 이유로 그렇게 할 수도 있다.

정답풀이

집단에서 규범은 한 사람의 행동에서 시작되어 그것에 순응함으로써 발생한다고 언급한 주어진 글 다음에는, 다른 사람들도 최초의 그 사람의 행동에 순응하고, 최초의 행동을 한 사람은 자신처럼 행동해야 한다고 생각한다는 내용의 (C)가 이어져야 한다. 그다음에는 그러한 생각의 결과로 다른 사람에게 다양한 방법으로 순응에 대한 요망을 전달하는 내용의 (A)가 이어지고, 마지막으로 이성적 또는 도덕적 이유로 이러한 순응에 대한 지시를 따르지 않고 스스로 순응할지의 여부를 결정하는 사람들도 있다는 것을 말한 (B)가 오는 순서가 가장 적절하다.

구문풀이

12행 The person [who performed the initial action] **may think** [that others ought to behave {**as** she behaves in situations of this sort}].

: 첫 번째 [ ]는 문장의 핵심 주어인 The person을 수식하는 주격 관계대명사절이고, 동사는 may think이다. 두 번째 [ ]는 think의 목적어 역할을 하는 명사절이고, 그 안의 { }는 접속사 as(~처럼)가 이끄는 부사절이다.

어휘풀이

- norm *n* 규범
- conform to ~에 순응하다, ~을 따르다
- utter *v* 말하다, 소리를 내다
- prescriptive *a* 지시하는
- conformity *n* 순응, 따름
- observe *v* 관찰하다
- rational *a* 이성적인, 합리적인
- initial *a* 최초의, 초기의
- emerge *v* 생겨나다, 출현하다
- prescribe *v* 지시하다, 규정하다
- statement *n* 진술, 성명
- alternately *ad* 다른 방식으로
- threaten *v* 겁을 주다, 위협하다
- regularity *n* 규칙성
- moral *a* 도덕적인

056 답 ②

📖 종의 환경 적응과 생식에 이바지하는 물벼룩이라는 종의 적응 가소성

전문해석

물벼룩이라는 매력적인 종은 진화생물학자들이 '적응적 가소성'이라고 부르는 일종의 유연성을 보여준다. (B) 만일 물벼룩을 잡아먹고 사는 생물의 화학적인 특징을 포함하는 물에서 새끼 물벼룩이 성체로 발달하고 있으면, 그것은 자신을 포식자로부터 지키기 위해 머리 투구와 가시돌기를 발달시킨다. 만일 자신을 둘러싼 물이 포식자의 화학적인 특징을 포함하지 않으면, 그 물벼룩은 이러한 보호 장치를 발달시키지 않는다. (A) 그것은 영리한 수법인데, 에너지 면에서 가시돌기와 머리 투구를 만드는 것은 비용이 많이 들고 에너지를 보존하는 것은 살아남고 생식하는 유기체의 능력을 위해 필수적이기 때문이다. 물벼룩은 오직 필요할 때에만 가시돌기와 머리 투구를 만드는 데 필요한 에너지를 쓴다. (C) 그러므로 이러한 가소성은 아마 적응일 텐데, 즉 그것은 생식의 적합성에 기여하기 때문에 생물 종에 존재하게 된 특징이다. 많은 종에 걸쳐 적응적 가소성의 많은 사례가 있다. 가소성은 환경에 충분한 변화가 있을 때 적합성에 도움이 된다.

정답풀이

물벼룩이라는 종이 적응적 가소성이라는 유연성을 보여준다는 주어진 글 다음에, 그에 대한 구체적 내용으로 포식자의 화학적인 특징을 포함하는 물에서 성체로 발달하고 있는 새끼 물벼룩만 자신을 포식자로부터 지키기 위해 머리 투구와 가시돌기를 발달시킨다는 내용의 (B)가 와야 한다. 그다음으로 (B)의 내용을 That으로 받아 그것이 생존과 생식을 위해 에너지를 보존하는 영리한 수법이고 설명한 (A)가 이어지고, 이러한 가소성이 다른 종에서도 나타나는 보편적인 현상이며 환경 변화에 대한 적합성에 도움을 준다고 마무리하는 (C)가 마지막에 오는 것이 자연스럽다.

구문풀이

4행 That's a clever trick, [because {**producing** spines and a helmet} is costly, in terms of energy, / and {**conserving** energy} is essential for an organism's ability {to survive and reproduce}].

: [ ]는 이유를 나타내는 부사절로, and에 의해 두 개의 절이 연결되어 있는데 두 절 모두 { }로 표시된 명사구가 주어로 쓰였다. 세 번째 { }는 an organism's ability를 수식하는 형용사적 용법의 to부정사구이다.

10행 [If the baby water flea is developing into an adult in water {that includes the chemical signatures of creatures (that prey on water fleas)}], it develops a helmet and spines [to defend itself against predators].

: 첫 번째 [ ]는 조건을 나타내는 부사절이며, 그 안의 { }는 water를 수식하는 주격 관계대명사절이고, ( )는 creatures를 수식하는 주격 관계대명사절이다. 두 번째 [ ]는 목적을 나타내는 부사적 용법의 to부정사구이다.

어휘풀이

- fascinating a 매력적인
- exhibit v 보여주다, 나타내다
- adaptive plasticity 적응적 가소성
- organism n 유기체
- chemical a 화학적인
- prey on ~을 먹고 살다
- device n 장치, 기구
- trait n 특성, 특징
- fitness n 적합성
- variation n 변화, 차이
- water flea 물벼룩
- flexibility n 유연성, 융통성
- conserve v 보존하다
- reproduce v 생식하다, 번식하다
- signature n (고유한) 특징
- predator n 포식자
- may well 아마 ~일 것이다
- contribute to ~에 기여하다
- sufficient a 충분한

057 답 ⑤

📖 현실 세계에 작가가 개입함으로써 만들어지는 허구 세계

전문해석

허구의 세계와 현실 세계 사이의 유사성에도 불구하고, 허구의 세계는 한 가지 중요한 측면에서 현실 세계에서 벗어난다. (C) 개인이 직면하는 지금 존재하는 세계는 이론상으로 인간의 정신에 의해 조직되기 전에는 사건과 세부 사항의 무한한 혼돈 상태이다. 이 혼돈 상태는 인간 정신에 의해 인지될 때만 처리되고 수정된다. (B) 개인이 유산과 환경을 통해 부여받은 내적 특성 때문에 정신은 여과 장치로서 작용하며, 그것을 통과하는 모든 외부 인상은 걸러지고 해석된다. 그러나 문학에서 독자가 마주치는 세계는 이미 또 다른 의식에 의해 처리되고 여과되어 있다. (A) 작가는 중립적이고 객관적이고자 하거나, 또는 세계에 대한 어떤 주관적인 관점을 전달하고자 하는 시도로, 자기 자신의 세계관과 적절성에 대한 자신의 개념에 따라 내용을 선정해왔다. 동기가 무엇이든, 세계에 대한 작가의 주관적인 이해는 독자와 그 이야기의 기반이 되는 원래의 손대지 않은 세계 사이에 존재한다.

정답풀이

허구의 세계가 현실 세계와 한 가지 중요한 측면에서 다르다고 언급한 주어진 글 다음에, 현실 세계의 특징에 대해 말하는 (C)가 와야 한다. 그다음에 (C)의 마지막 문장에서 언급한 인간 정신의 역할을 부연하면서, 문학에서 독자가 접하는 세계의 특징에 대해 언급하는 (B)가 오고, 마지막으로 (B)에서 언급한 문학 세계를 여과시키는 또 다른 의식에 대해 구체적으로 설명하는 (A)가 오는 순서가 자연스럽다.

구문풀이

12행 [**Because of** the inner qualities {with which the individual is endowed through heritage and environment}], the mind functions as a filter; every outside impression [that passes through it] is filtered and interpreted.

: 첫 번째 [ ]는 「Because of+명사구」로 이루어진 부사구이고, 그 안의 { }는 the inner qualities를 수식하는 관계절이다. 두 번째 [ ]는 세미콜론(;) 다음에 이어진 절의 주어인 every outside impression을 수식하는 주격 관계대명사절이다.

19행 The existing world [faced by the individual] **is** in principle an infinite chaos of events and details [before it is organized by a human mind].

: 첫 번째 [ ]는 주절의 주어인 The existing world를 수식하는 과거분사구이고, 주절의 동사는 is이다. 두 번째 [ ]는 before가 이끄는 시간 부사절이다.

어휘풀이

- fictional a 허구의, 가상의
- conception n 개념, 이해
- neutral a 중립적인
- convey v 전달하다
- untouched a 손대지 않은, 본래 그대로의
- function v 작용하다, 기능하다
- encounter v 마주치다, 조우하다
- consciousness n 의식
- in principle 이론상으로
- chaos n 혼돈, 무질서
- perceive v 인지하다, 인식하다
- respect n 측면, 관점
- relevance n 적절성, 타당성
- objective a 객관적인
- subjective a 주관적인
- interpret v 해석하다
- literature n 문학
- existing a 현존하는, 기존의
- infinite a 무한한
- modify v 수정하다

058 답 ①

📖 동물보다 우월할 것이 없는 인간

전문해석

다른 존재에 대한 인간의 우월함은 결코 절대적이거나 포괄적이지 않다. 우리가 가진 유일한 우월함은 우리의 사고 및 추론 능력 그리고 우리의 강한 도덕성이다. (A) 하지만 동물의 생활방식이 종종 우리의 것보다 더 합리적으로 보이기 때문에 이것마

저도 의문시된다. 예를 들어, 우리는 개체 밀도가 높은 둥지에서 어떻게 벌, 흰개미 그리고 개미들이 조화롭게 사는지를 관찰함으로써 많은 것을 배울 수 있는데, 그와 같은 질서를 인간은 절대로 성취할 수 없을 것이다. (C) 지난 세기에서만 약 1억 8천 2백만 명의 인간들이 아무런 이유도 없이 조직화된 폭력으로 숨진 것으로 추정된다. 하등 동물들에게 우리의 지성이 없다는 사실에도 불구하고, 그것들은 불필요하게 서로 교전을 벌이거나 서로를 절멸시키려 하지 않는다. (B) 그래서 인간을 하등 동물들과 비교하는 것으로 인해 불쾌함을 느끼는 사람들에 대한 나의 대답은, 아마도 우리는 우리 종에 대한 부풀려진 이미지를 가지고 있으며 우리가 생각하고 싶어 하는 것만큼 지적이지도 문명화되지도 않다는 것이다. 우리가 잠시 멈춰서 우리 종이 무엇으로 구성되었는지에 대한 객관적인 목록을 만들 때가 왔다.

정답풀이
인간이 동물보다 유일하게 우월한 점은 사고 및 추론 능력과 강한 도덕성이라고 하는 주어진 글 다음에는, 하지만(Yet) 동물의 생활방식이 더 합리적으로 보이기도 한다는 점에서 이러한 우월성마저도 의문시된다고 하면서 조화롭게 사는 동물들을 예로 드는 (A)가 와야 한다. 동물들에게서 관찰되는 질서를 인간은 절대로 성취할 수 없다는 (A)의 마지막 문장에 이어서 인간들 사이에 일어나는 폭력과 전쟁을 언급하는 (C)가 오고, 그러므로(So) 인간을 객관적으로 다시 볼 필요가 있다는 내용의 (B)가 결론으로 이어지는 것이 가장 적절하다.

구문풀이
12행 So [**my response** to those {offended by comparing humans to lower beings}] **is** [that perhaps we **have** an inflated image of our own species and **are** neither **as** intelligent nor **as** civilized **as** we would like to think].

: 첫 번째 [ ]가 문장의 주어부로 주어의 핵은 my response이고 동사는 is이다. { }는 those를 수식하는 과거분사구이다. 두 번째 [ ]는 주격보어로 쓰인 명사절이고, 주어 we에 이어지는 동사는 have와 are이며, 「neither A nor B(A도 B도 아닌)」가 as ~ as 원급 비교 구문과 함께 쓰였다.

16행 The time has come [for us **to pause** and **take** an objective inventory of {what our species is made of}].

: [ ]는 문장의 주어인 The time을 수식하는 형용사적 용법의 to부정사구로 pause와 take가 병렬구조를 이루며, for us는 to부정사의 의미상 주어를 나타낸다. { }는 선행사를 포함하는 관계대명사 what이 이끄는 명사절로 전치사 of의 목적어로 쓰였다.

어휘풀이
- superiority *n* 우월(감)
- all-inclusive *a* 포괄적인
- be subject to ~이 될 수 있다
- termite *n* 흰개미
- densely populated 인구[개체] 밀도가 높은
- the likes of ~와 같은
- inflated *a* 부풀려진, 과장된
- inventory *n* 목록, 일람표
- devoid of ~이 없는
- not by any means 결코 ~ 않다
- morality *n* 도덕성
- rational *a* 이성적인
- offend *v* ~의 감정을 상하게 하다
- civilized *a* 문명화된
- estimate *v* 추정하다
- engage *v* 전투를 벌이다, 교전하다

059 답 ③

📖 음식 조절을 통해 체중을 감량하기가 어려운 이유

전문해석
선사 시대 이후로 우리 모두는 우리의 신체를 우리의 개인적인 그리고 집단적인 생존에 최적화된 상태로 유지하도록 유전적으로 프로그래밍되어 왔다. 우리의 DNA는 모든 세포의 모든 단백질, 모든 지방질이 어디에 배치되어야 하는가를 명령한다. (B) **지방은 근육보다 더 좋은 에너지원이므로 신체는 더 많은 양의 체지방과 더 적은 근육량을 선호하도록 사전에 프로그래밍되어 있다.** 이것에 대한 가정된 이론적 근거는

기근 기간 동안에 신체가 생존에 필요한 에너지를 위해 그것의 지방 축적물을 원료로 사용할 수 있다는 것이다. (C) 이것은 실용적인 생물학적 목적에 도움이 되기는 하지만, 음식 조절을 통해 체중 감량을 소망하는 이들에게는 커다란 좌절감의 원인이 되는 경향이 있다. 왜냐하면 음식 조절은 높은 지방 축적물을 유지하려는 신체의 프로그래밍된 열망에 역행하기 때문이다. 사람들은 때때로 장기적인 체중 감소를 이루려는 시도에서 굶을 것이다. (A) 하지만 과체중으로 이어진 여러 달 또는 여러 해의 섭식이 며칠 또는 몇 주 동안 먹는 양을 줄임으로써 신속하게 극복될 수 있다고 믿는 것은 매우 비현실적이다. 언급한 바와 같이, **신체는 지방을 원하도록 프로그래밍되어 있고 개인의 건강 목표나 신체적 외모를 가꾸려는 소망 따위에는 관심이 없다.**

정답풀이
우리의 신체가 생존에 최적화되도록 단백질과 지방질이 세포 내에 배치된다는 내용의 주어진 글 다음에는, 기근 기간 동안 신체가 생존에 필요한 에너지를 얻기 위해 지방이 단백질보다 체내에 더 많이 축적된다는 내용의 (B)가 오고, 이것(this)은 생물학적 목적에 도움이 되기는 하지만 체중 감량을 위해 노력하는 사람들에게는 좌절감을 준다는 내용의 (C)가 온 후, 그와 같은 사람들의 체중 감량 노력이 왜 실효를 거둘 수 없는지를 구체적으로 설명하는 내용의 (A)로 마무리되는 순서가 가장 적절하다.

구문풀이
1행 **Since** prehistoric times, we have all been genetically programmed to maintain our bodies in a state [best **suited** for our individual and collective survival].

: Since는 '~ 이후로'의 뜻을 나타내는 전치사로 쓰였으며, [ ]는 a state를 수식하는 과거분사구이다.

어휘풀이
- prehistoric *a* 선사 시대의
- collective *a* 집단적인
- lead up to ~에 가까이 가다, ~ 쪽으로 이끌다
- rationale *n* 이론적 근거
- feed off ~을 먹다, ~로부터 먹이를 얻다
- run counter to ~에 역행하다
- in an attempt to *do* ~하려는 시도로
- genetically *ad* 유전적으로
- famine *n* 기근, 기아
- frustration *n* 좌절감
- attain *v* ~을 이루다

060 답 ④

📖 문화적 참여의 한 형태로 여겨지는 사적인 행위

전문해석
한 문화 안에서 사람들이 하는 것의 많은 부분은 다른 사람들과 연결되어 있고 전반적으로 문화와 연결되어 있다. 여러분의 이를 닦는 것과 같이 외관상 사적인 행위조차도 문화적 참여의 한 형태이다. (C) 여러분이 선택하는 치약 브랜드는 시장이 여러분에게 제공하기 위해 생산한 것을 반영하고, 만약 몇몇 브랜드가 있다면 여러분의 선택은 아마도 광고의 선전 문구와 같은 문화적 메시지에 의해 형성될 것이다. 나아가, 여러분의 선택은 다른 많은 치약 구매자들의 그것들과 결합해 어떤 브랜드가 시장에 남아 있고 어떤 브랜드가 실패하고 사라지는지를 결정한다. (A) 또한, 이를 닦는 것은 양치질을 하지 않는 사람을 제거하고 칫솔질을 하려는 타고난 욕구를 가진 우리 모두만 남겨놓은 어떤 진화적인 과정을 통해 우리의 유전자에 주입되지 않는다. 반대로, 여러분은 아마도 부모님으로부터 그렇게 하라고 배웠기 때문에 양치질을 할 것이다. (B) 여러분은 또한 그렇게 하는 것이 치아 건강을 증진시킬 것이라는 문화적 가르침을 아마 의심하지 않고 받아들이고 있을 수도 있다. 여러분이 그것을 하지 않는다면, 여러분의 치아는 나빠질 것이고 여러분이나 혹은 다른 누군가가 충치를 메우는 것과 같은 치료에 비용을 지불해야 할 것인데, 치과의사들의 서비스는 마찬가지로 경제의 일부로서 제공된다.

우리가 하는 여러 활동이 문화적 참여의 한 형태라는 점을 설명하고 있는 글이다. 이를 닦는 것과 같이 사적인 행위처럼 보이는 것도 문화적 참여의 한 형태라고 언급한 주어진 글 다음에, 양치질에 연관된 문화적 측면으로 치약 브랜드의 선택에 대해 설명한 (C)가 오고, 여기에 Moreover로 추가해 양치질이 유전이 아니라 가정 교육에 의해 형성된 문화적 산물임을 설명한 (A)가 그 다음에 이어지며, 양치질에 관련된 문화적 가르침의 측면을 더 구체적으로 설명하고 있는 (B)가 마지막에 오는 순서가 가장 자연스럽다.

구문풀이

5행 Moreover, [brushing teeth] is not instilled in our genes via some evolutionary process [that {**weeded out** non-tooth brushers} and {**left** us all with an innate urge (to brush)}].

: 첫 번째 [ ]는 문장의 주어로 쓰인 동명사구이다. 두 번째 [ ]는 some evolutionary process를 수식하는 주격 관계대명사절로, { }로 표시된 두 개의 술어부가 and로 연결되어 있고, ( )는 an innate urge를 수식하는 형용사적 용법의 to부정사이다.

11행 You probably also **accept** on faith [**the cultural teaching** {that doing so will increase your dental health}].

: [ ]는 accept의 목적어로 쓰인 명사구이고, 그 안의 { }는 the cultural teaching의 구체적 내용을 설명하고 있는 동격절이다.

17행 The brand of toothpaste [you choose] **reflects** [what the market has produced {to offer you}], / and [if there are several brands] your choice is probably shaped by cultural messages such as advertising slogans.

: and 앞에서 첫 번째 [ ]는 주어인 The brand of toothpaste를 수식하는 목적격 관계대명사절이고, 동사는 reflects이다. 두 번째 [ ]는 reflects의 목적어로 쓰인 명사절(관계절)이고, 그 안의 { }는 목적을 나타내는 부사적 용법의 to부정사구이다. 세 번째 [ ]는 and 다음에서 조건을 나타내는 부사절이다.

어휘풀이

- seemingly *ad* 겉으로 보기에, 외관상
- via *prep* ~을 통하여
- innate *a* 타고난, 선천적인
- on faith 의심하지 않고
- reflect *v* 반영하다
- participation *n* 참여
- weed out ~을 제거하다
- urge *n* 욕구
- cavity *n* 충치(의 구멍)

061 답 ⑤

📖 언어적 메시지와 비언어적 메시지

전문해석

많은 경우에 비언어적 경로는 언어적 경로의 영향보다 중요하다. 다시 말해서, 언어적인 메시지와 비언어적인 메시지 사이에 차이가 있을 때, 판단을 형성하는 데 있어서 후자가 보통 더 큰 비중을 차지한다. (C) 예를 들어, 한 친구는 저녁 식사 계획에 대해 '괜찮은데'라고 말하지만 목소리에 열의가 거의 없고 활기 없는 얼굴 표정으로 응답할지도 모른다. 말로 답을 한 것에도 불구하고 표현상 열정의 부족은 그 계획을 아주 긍정적으로 보지는 않는다는 것을 암시한다. (B) 그러한 경우에, 긍정적인 말의 목적은 의견의 불일치를 피하고 친구를 지지하기 위한 것일 수도 있지만, 긍정적인 표정의 부족은 자신도 모르게 그 계획에 대한 보다 정직하고 부정적인 반응을 흘린다. 물론 활기 없는 표정의 드러냄은 또한 전략적이고 의도적일 수도 있다. (A) 다시 말해, 그 비언어적 메시지는 의도적이지만 상대방에게 자신의 솔직한 반응을 간접적으로 알리려고 고안된 것이다. 그러고 나면 비언어적인 메시지를 해석하고 계획에 약간의 조정을 하는 것은 상대방의 책임이다.

언어적 메시지와 비언어적 메시지 사이에 차이가 있을 때 비언어적 메시지가 더 중요하다는 내용의 주어진 글 다음에는, 한 친구의 저녁 식사 계획에 대한 반응을 예로 드는 (C)가 와야 한다. (C)에서 말한 상황에서(In such a case) 활기 없는 표정은 의도적인 것일 수 있다는 내용의 (B)가 그 다음에 오고, 그 의도적인 표정에 대한 해석은 상대방의 몫이라는 내용의 (A)가 마지막에 오는 순서가 가장 적절하다.

구문풀이

8행 **It** is then the partner's responsibility [**to interpret** the nonverbal message and **make** some adjustment in the plan].

: It은 형식상의 주어이고, [ ]로 표시된 to부정사구가 내용상의 주어이다. to interpret과 (to) make는 and에 의해 병렬구조로 연결되어 있다.

어휘풀이

- nonverbal *a* 비언어적인
- weigh *v* 중요시되다, 중요하다
- candid *a* 솔직한
- unintentionally *ad* 무심코, 자신도 모르게
- leak *v* 흘리다, 누출하다
- strategic *a* 전략적인
- trump *v* 앞지르다, 능가하다
- deliberate *a* 의도적인, 고의적인
- adjustment *n* 조정, 조절
- muted *a* (표정·표현에) 활기가 없는
- enthusiasm *n* 열정, 열의

062 답 ③

📖 미스터리 해결을 통한 세상에 대한 이해의 근본적 변화

전문해석

남대서양의 Ascension 섬의 해안에서 알을 깨고 나오는 푸른 거북은 그들이 출현했던, 알껍질이 흩어져 있는 정확히 같은 해변에서 알을 낳기 위해 3년마다 돌아오기 전에 수천 마일의 바다를 가로질러 헤엄친다. (B) 마찬가지로, 많은 종의 새, 고래, 닭새우, 개구리, 심지어 벌들까지 모두가 가장 위대한 인간의 탐험가들에게 도전할 여행에 착수할 수 있다. 어떻게 동물들이 전 세계에서 자신들이 갈 길을 찾아내는지는 수 세기 동안 미스터리였다. (C) 그러나 미스터리는 매혹적인데, 왜냐하면 그것의 해결이 세상에 대한 우리 이해에서의 근본적 변화로 이어질지도 모르는 가능성이 항상 있기 때문이다. 예를 들어, 16세기에 Copernicus가 Ptolemy의 지구 중심적 태양계 모형의 기하학과 관련한 문제에 관해 고찰한 것은 그가 우주 전체의 무게 중심을 인류로부터 멀리 옮겨가도록 이끌었다. (A) 게다가, 동물 종의 지리적 분포와 관련한, 그리고 고립된 섬에 사는 흉내지빠귀 종이 왜 그렇게 분화하는 경향이 있는지에 대한 미스터리와 관련한 Darwin의 집념은 그가 진화론을 제시하도록 이끌었다.

푸른 거북이 알을 낳기 위해 수천 마일의 바다를 가로질러 남대서양의 해안으로 돌아온다는 주어진 글 다음에는, 마찬가지로 먼 거리를 여행하는 다른 동물들을 열거하면서 동물들의 그런 행동이 수 세기 동안 미스터리였다는 내용의 (B)가 와야 한다. 그리고 (B)에서 언급한 미스터리가 매혹적인 것은 세상에 대한 이해의 근본적인 변화로 이어질 수 있기 때문이라고 하면서 Copernicus의 예를 드는 (C)가 오고, 미스터리를 해결하기 위한 Darwin의 집념과 진화론의 탄생을 덧붙이는 (A)가 오는 순서가 가장 적절하다.

구문풀이

6행 Moreover, [**Darwin's obsession** with {the geographical distribution of animal species} and {the mystery **of** (why isolated island species of mockingbirds tend to be so specialized)}] **led** him to propose his theory of evolution.

: [ ]가 문장의 주어부이고 주어의 핵은 Darwin's obsession이며, 문장의 동사는 led이다. 두 개의 { }는 전치사 with의 목적어인 명사구이고, ( )는 전치사 of의 목적어인

명사절(의문사절)이다.

어휘풀이
- hatch *v* 알에서 깨고 나오다
- breed *v* 새끼를 낳다
- eggshell-littered *a* 알껍질이 흩어져 있는
- obsession *n* 집념, 강박 관념
- geographical *a* 지리의, 지리적인
- distribution *n* 분포, 분배
- isolated *a* 고립된, 격리된
- mockingbird *n* 흉내지빠귀
- specialized *a* 분화한, 특수화한
- evolution *n* 진화
- spiny lobster 닭새우
- undertake *v* ~에 착수하다, ~을 떠맡다
- fascinating *a* 매혹적인
- fundamental *a* 근본적인
- shift *n* 변화
- geometry *n* 기하학
- gravity *n* 중력, 무게

063 답 ④

📖 속담의 전수와 학습을 통한 문화의 계승

전문해석
아주 어린 아이가 읽을 수 있기 전에도 그 아이는 속담을 통해서 전달되는 '인생에 관한 교훈'을 듣는다. 금언으로 불리든 또는 자명한 이치, 상투적 표현, 관용구, 격언, 속담으로 불리든, 속담은 한 민족의 가치관과 신념에 관한 작은 진실 꾸러미들이다. (C) 유명한 사회언어학자인 David Olajide는 "속담은 전 세계에서 소중히 여겨지고 그것들을 표현하는 매체인 언어에 보존되는 문화의 한 측면이다. 또한 속담은 심리적, 우주론적 그리고 사회문화적 뿌리를 가지고 있다."라고 쓰면서 한 문화에 대한 속담의 중요성을 언급한다. (A) 그것들(속담들)은 어떤 의미에서 한 문화가 가진 지혜의 저장 창고라고 여겨진다. 속담은 모든 문화에 매우 중요해서 심지어 속담과 관련한 속담도 있다. 한 독일 속담은 "한 나라는 그 속담의 질로 판단될 수 있다."라고 말하며, 아프리카의 요루바 부족은 "속담을 아는 현명한 사람은 어려운 일들을 극복한다."라고 가르친다. (B) 속담을 통해 한 민족에 대해 배울 수 있다는 생각은 이 속담들에서 강조된다. 화려하고 생생한 언어 그리고 몇 마디 안 되는 단어로 소통되는 속담들은 한 문화의 통찰력, 지혜, 편견 그리고 심지어 미신도 반영한다.

정답풀이
어떻게 불리든 속담은 한 민족의 가치관과 신념을 담고 있다는 내용의 주어진 글 다음에는, 문화에 있어 속담이 중요함을 언급한 (C)가 와야 한다. 그다음에 (C)의 proverbs를 They로 지칭하며 속담은 문화의 저장 창고라고 부연 설명하는 (A)가 이어지고, (B)의 these proverbs는 (A)에서 소개한 독일과 요루바 부족의 속담을 가리키므로 (A) 다음에 (B)가 오는 순서가 되어야 한다.

구문풀이
8행 Proverbs are **so** important to every culture **that** there are even proverbs about proverbs.

: 「so ~ that ....」은 '너무 ~해서 …하다'의 의미를 나타낸다.

어휘풀이
- transmit *v* 전달하다, 전승하다
- proverb *n* 속담
- maxim *n* 금언, 격언, 명언
- truism *n* 자명한 이치
- cliché *n* 상투적 표현, 진부한 표현
- idiom *n* 관용구, 숙어
- vivid *a* 생생한
- superstition *n* 미신
- significance *n* 중요성
- cherish *v* 소중히 여기다
- preserve *v* 보존하다
- cosmological *a* 우주학의, 우주론의

08 문장 삽입   본문 p.050

| **064** ④ | **065** ⑤ | **066** ④ | **067** ④ | **068** ④ |
| **069** ③ | **070** ④ | **071** ④ | **072** ③ | |

064 답 ④

📖 문서의 오타와 유기체에서 발생하는 돌연변이 간의 유사성과 차이

전문해석
책이나 어떤 문서로 된 메시지에서 오타가 발생하면 일반적으로 내용에 부정적인 영향을 미치며 때로는 (문자 그대로) 치명적이다. 예를 들어, 쉼표의 위치가 잘못 찍히는 것은 생사가 걸린 문제일 수 있다. 마찬가지로 대부분의 돌연변이는 그것이 발생하는 유기체에 해로운 결과를 가져오는데, 이는 그것들이 생식 적합성을 감소시킨다는 것을 의미한다. 그러나 때때로 우연히 초판의 텍스트를 복사하지 못한 것이 더 정확하거나 최신의 정보를 제공할 수도 있는 것처럼 유기체의 적합성을 높이는 돌연변이가 발생할 수 있다. 그러나 논거의 다음 단계에서는 그 유사성은 깨진다. 유리한 돌연변이가 발생한 유기체는 더 많은 자손을 낳을 것이고 돌연변이가 자손에게 전달되기 때문에, 유리한 돌연변이는 다음 세대에서 더 많이 발현될 것이다. 대조적으로, 우연히 초판의 오류를 바로잡은 책이 더 잘 팔리는 경향이 있을 메커니즘은 없다.

정답풀이
역접의 연결어 however를 사용하며, 논거의 다음 단계에서는 그 유사성이 깨진다는 내용의 주어진 문장은 문서의 오류와 돌연변이 간의 유사성을 언급하는 문장 다음, 그리고 그 유사성이 깨진 것에 대한 설명이 시작되는 문장 앞인 ④에 들어가는 것이 가장 적절하다.

구문풀이
4행 Similarly most mutations have harmful consequences for the organism [in which they occur], [meaning {that they reduce its reproductive fitness}].

: 첫 번째 [ ]는 the organism을 수식하는 관계절이고, 두 번째 [ ]는 주절의 내용을 부연 설명하는 분사구문이며, 그 안의 { }는 meaning의 목적어 역할을 하는 명사절이다.

10행 By contrast, there is no mechanism [by which a book {that accidentally corrects the mistakes of the first edition} will tend to sell better].

: [ ]는 mechanism을 수식하는 관계절이고, 그 안의 { }는 a book을 수식하는 주격 관계대명사절이다.

어휘풀이
- negative *a* 부정적인
- impact *n* 영향
- fatally *ad* 치명적으로
- literally *ad* 문자 그대로
- displacement *n* 잘못된 배치, (제자리에서 쫓겨난) 이동
- consequence *n* 결과
- organism *n* 유기체
- reproductive *a* 생식의, 번식의
- fitness *n* 적합성
- accidental *a* 우연한
- favorable *a* 유리한, 호의적인
- offspring *n* 자손, 새끼
- transmit *v* 전달하다

065 답 ⑤

📖 도시의 다른 공간과 구분되도록 자연을 표현한 공원 설계

전문해석
공원은 그것이 속한 시대의 문화적 관심사가 요구하는 형태를 취한다. 일단 공원이

마련되면, 그것은 비활성화된 단계가 아닌데 그것의 목적과 의미는 계획자와 공원 이용자에 의해 만들어지고 다시 만들어진다. 그러나 공원을 조성하는 순간들은 특히 의미가 있는데, 자연과 그것이 도시 사회와 갖는 관계에 대한 생각을 드러내고 실현하기 때문이다. **실제로 공원을 더 넓은 범주의 공공 공간과 구별되게 하는 것은 공원이 구현하려는 자연의 표현이다.** 공공 공간에는 공원, 콘크리트 광장, 보도, 심지어 실내 아트리움도 포함된다. 일반적으로 공원에는 그들의 중심적인 특색으로 나무, 풀, 그리고 다른 식물들이 있다. 도시의 공원에 들어갈 때, 사람들은 흔히 거리, 자동차, 그리고 건물과의 뚜렷한 분리를 상상한다. 거기에는 이유가 있는데, 전통적으로 공원 설계자들은 공원 경계에 키 큰 나무를 심고, 돌담을 쌓고, 다른 칸막이 수단을 세워 그런 느낌을 만들어 내려고 했다. 이 생각의 배후에는 미적인 암시가 있는 공원 공간을 설계하려는 조경가의 욕망뿐만 아니라 도시와 자연을 대조적인 공간과 반대 세력으로 상상하는 훨씬 더 오래된 서구 사상의 역사가 있다.

정답풀이

주어진 문장의 such a feeling은 ⑤ 앞 문장에서 언급된 도시의 다른 것들과는 뚜렷하게 분리되는 공원의 느낌을 가리키고, '공원 설계자들이 전통적으로 공원 경계에 나무를 심고 돌담 및 다른 칸막이 수단을 세웠다'는 주어진 문장의 내용은 ⑤ 앞 문장에서 사람들이 도시의 공원에서 갖게 되는 분리의 느낌에 대한 이유가 된다. 따라서 주어진 문장이 들어가기에 가장 적절한 곳은 ⑤이다.

구문풀이

13행 Indeed, [what distinguishes a park from the broader category of public space] **is** the representation of nature [that parks are meant to embody].

: 첫 번째 [ ]는 선행사를 포함하는 관계대명사 what이 이끄는 명사절로 문장의 주어로 쓰였고, 문자의 동사는 is이다. 두 번째 [ ]는 the representation of nature를 수식하는 목적격 관계대명사절이다.

어휘풀이

- boundary *n* 경계(선)
- construct *v* 건설하다
- partition *n* 칸막이
- inert *a* 비활성의
- telling *a* 효과적인, 유효한
- reveal *v* 드러내다
- actualize *v* 실현하다
- distinguish *A* from *B* A를 B와 구별하다
- representation *n* 표현, 묘사
- embody *v* 구현하다
- atrium *n* 아트리움, 중앙 홀, 안마당
- feature *n* 특징, 특색
- landscape architect 조경가
- suggestive *a* 암시[시사]하는, 연상시키는
- envision *v* 마음속에 그리다, 상상하다
- oppositional *a* 반대의

066 답 ④

📖 협상 시 이용하는 쟁점을 세분화하는 '살라미 전술'

전문해석

협상가들은 '살라미 전술'을 사용하는 것으로 알려진, 큰 문제를 더 작은 조각으로 나누는 방법을 찾으려고 노력해야 한다. 정량적이고 측정 가능한 단위로 표현될 수 있는 문제는 나누기 쉽다. 예를 들어, 보상 요구는 시간당 센트 증가로 나누거나 임대료는 평방 피트당 달러로 시세를 매길 수 있다. 원칙이나 관례의 쟁점을 세분화하는 작업을 할 때, 당사자들은 그 쟁점을 세분화하는 방법으로 시간 지평(원칙이 효력을 발휘하는 때나 지속되는 기간)을 사용할 수 있다. 합의 조건이 향후 몇 개월까지 이행될 필요가 없을 때 합의에 도달하는 것이 더 쉬울 수 있다. 또 다른 접근법은 원칙이 적용될 수 있는 방법의 수를 다양화하는 것이다. 예를 들어, 회사는 직원의 직계 가족의 질병에 대해 직원에게 3시간 이내, 한 달에 단지 한 번의 기간 동안 회사를 비울 기회를 제공하는 가족 비상 휴가 계획을 고안할 수 있다.

정답풀이

합의 조건의 이행 시기가 몇 개월 이후부터라면 합의에 도달하는 것이 더 쉬울 수 있다는 내용의 주어진 문장은 ④ 앞 문장에서 언급된 시간 지평(원칙이 효력을 발휘하는 때나 지속되는 기간)을 사용하는 하나의 사례에 해당되므로 주어진 문장이 들어가기에 가장 적절한 곳은 ④이다.

구문풀이

4행 Negotiators should try to find ways [to slice a large issue into smaller pieces], [known as {using *salami tactics*}].

: 첫 번째 [ ]는 ways를 수식하는 형용사적 용법의 to부정사구이고, 두 번째 [ ]는 ways to slice a large issue into smaller pieces를 부가적으로 설명하는 과거분사구이며, 그 안의 { }는 전치사 as(~로서)의 목적어 역할을 하는 동명사구이다.

15행 For example, a company may devise a family emergency leave plan [that **allows** employees the opportunity {to be away from the company for a period of no longer than three hours, and no more than once a month, for illness in the employee's immediate family}].

: [ ]는 a family emergency leave plan을 수식하는 주격 관계대명사절이고, 그 안의 { }는 the opportunity를 수식하는 형용사적 용법의 to부정사구이다. 여기서 allows는 뒤에 간접목적어(employees)와 직접목적어(the opportunity ~)를 갖는 4형식 동사로 쓰였다.

어휘풀이

- settlement *n* 합의, 해결
- terms *n* 조건
- implement *v* 이행하다
- negotiator *n* 협상가
- tactic *n* 전술, 전략
- quantitative *a* 양적인
- compensation *n* 보상
- lease rate 임대료
- quote *v* 시세를 매기다, (가격, 견적 비용 등을) 제시하다
- precedent *n* 선례, 전례
- time horizon 시간 지평
- devise *v* 고안하다
- emergency leave plan 비상 휴가 계획
- immediate family 직계 가족

067 답 ④

📖 종이 클립의 탄력성과 그것의 한계

전문해석

종이 클립은, 그것이 종이 둘레로 들어갈 만큼 충분히 그것의 고리를 서로 벌릴 수 있고 놓았을 때는 원래 상태로 다시 돌아가 종이를 붙잡아 그것을 유지할 수 있기 때문에 작용을 한다. **이 되돌아가는 작용은, 그것의 형태 그 자체 이상으로 종이 클립이 효과가 있게 만드는 것이다. 탄력성과 그것의 한계는 또한 애초에 종이 클립이 만들어지기 위해서도 매우 중요하다.** 이것을 이해하기 위해서, 고리가 종이 둘레로 들어가는 데 필요한 것보다 종이 클립을 조금 더 넓게 벌려 보라. 클립이 구부러져서 형태에서 벗어나고 그것이 처음 상자 밖으로 나올 때 그랬던 편평한 형태로 되돌아가지 못하는 어떤 시점이 있을 것이다. 이런 일이 생길 때, 클립의 탄력적인 한계는 초과되었다고들 하며(혹은 철사선이 가소성으로 인해 변형되었다고들 하며), 클립을 상자 안에 있었던 형태로 되돌리는 것은 아주 어렵다. 말할 필요도 없이, 클립은 종이를 붙잡거나 종이 위에 편평하게 놓여 있는 데 있어서 이제 더 이상 그만큼 효과적이지도 않다.

정답풀이

주어진 문장은 클립이 구부러져 본래의 편평한 형태를 회복하지 못한다는 내용이고, 이는 ④ 앞에서 언급한 필요한 것보다 종이 클립을 더 넓게 벌린 경우에 일어나는 일이다. 또한 ④ 다음 문장의 this는 종이 클립이 본래의 편평한

형태를 회복하지 못하는 경우를 가리키므로, 주어진 문장은 ④에 들어가는 것이 가장 적절하다.

구문풀이

`12행` When this happens, / the clip's elastic limit is said **to have been exceeded** (or the wire is said **to have been** plastically **deformed**), / and **it** is extremely difficult [**to restore** the clip to the shape {it had in the box}].

: 「to have+과거분사」 형태의 완료형 부정사가 사용되어, 문장의 시제보다 앞선 시제를 나타낸다. and 다음에서 it은 형식상의 주어이며 [ ]로 표시된 to부정사구가 내용상의 주어이다. { }는 the shape를 수식하는 목적격 관계대명사절이다.

어휘풀이

- out of shape 형태를 벗어난
- loop *n* 고리
- spring *v* 제자리로 돌아가다
- springiness *n* 탄력성, 제자리로 돌아감
- in the first place 우선, 애초에
- elastic *a* 탄력적인
- plastically *ad* 가소성으로 인해, 유연하게
- deform *v* 변형시키다
- fresh *a* 갓 나온, 새로운
- release *v* 놓아 주다, 풀어주다
- per se 그 자체로
- appreciate *v* 이해하다
- exceed *v* 초과하다
- restore *v* 돌아가게 하다, 회복시키다

068 답 ④

📖📖 일란성 쌍둥이의 염색체로 확인된 유전자의 학습 능력

전문해석

2005년에 스페인의 과학자들이 어떤 의미에서 보면 우리의 유전자가 학습할 수 있다는 것을 발견했다. 그들은 두 세트의 일란성 쌍둥이들의 염색체를 준비했는데, 한 세트는 3세의 것이고 다른 하나는 50세의 것이었다. 각각 DNA의 후성적으로 수정된 부분 및 수정되지 않은 부분과 결합하는 녹색과 붉은색의 형광성 분자를 이용하여 그들은 두 세트의 유전자를 검사했다. 아이들의 유전자는 매우 비슷해 보였는데, 예상하는 바대로 두 쌍둥이가 본질적으로 동일한 유전적 꼬리표를 가지고 생애를 시작한다는 것을 나타냈다. 대조적으로, 50세인 사람의 염색체는 다른 장식을 한 두 그루의 크리스마스트리처럼 녹색과 붉은색으로 빛났다. 그들 삶의 경험이 이 일란성 쌍둥이들이 유전적 기능 면에서 더 이상 동일하지 않다는 것을 뜻하는 방식으로 그들의 유전자에 꼬리표를 붙였던 것이다. 이것은 그 꼬리표 붙이기가 단지 노화 때문만이 아니라 또한 우리가 삶을 사는 방식의 직접적인 결과이기도 하다는 것을 의미한다. 두 명의 50세인 사람의 염색체상의 상이한 붉은색과 녹색 패턴을 촬영할 때 과학자들은 그 쌍둥이들의 유전자가 발달시킨 다른 두 '인격체'를 포착하고 있었다.

정답풀이

주어진 문장은 삶의 경험으로 인해 일란성 쌍둥이인 두 사람의 유전적 기능이 서로 달랐다는 내용이므로, 아이들의 유전자에 관한 언급이 끝나고 50세인 사람들의 유전자에 관한 언급이 시작된 다음인 ④에 들어가야 한다. 그래야 50세인 사람들의 유전자 꼬리표 붙이기에 대한 내용인 ④ 다음 문장과도 자연스럽게 연결된다.

오답풀이

⑤ 주어진 문장의 Their가 가리키는 대상이 ⑤ 앞의 문장에는 없으므로 ⑤에는 들어갈 수 없다.

구문풀이

`7행` [**Using** fluorescent green and red molecules {that bind, respectively, to epigenetically modified and unmodified segments of DNA}], they examined the two sets of genes.

: [ ]는 '~을 사용하여'의 뜻을 나타내는 분사구문이고, 그 안의 { }는 fluorescent green and red molecules를 수식하는 주격 관계대명사절이다.

어휘풀이

- tag *v* ~에 꼬리표를 붙이다
- in terms of ~의 면에서
- fluorescent *a* 형광성의
- respectively *ad* 각각
- segment *v* 부분, 조각
- identical *a* 일란성의, 동일한
- chromosome *n* 염색체
- molecule *n* 분자
- modified *a* 수정[변경]된
- capture *v* 포착하다

069 답 ③

📖📖 식품 첨가제의 안전성 판단의 어려움

전문해석

정부 기관은 식품 첨가제가 안전하다는 것을 확실히 하기 위해 그것을 정례적으로 재평가하는데, 특히 새로운 독물학 자료가 생기는 경우에 그렇다. 각 정부는 사용될 수 있는 최대 수치와 첨가제가 사용될 수 있는 식품의 유형은 물론 사용이 허용된 첨가제에 관한 상세한 목록을 가지고 있다. 때때로 이 목록은 나라마다 다양해서 한 나라에서 어떤 첨가제는 안전하다고 추정되지만 다른 나라에서는 그렇지 않은데, 이는 자사 제품을 세계 시장에서 판매하려고 하는 식품 회사들에게 문제를 초래한다. 이러한 차이는 과학자들에 의한 독물학 자료의 해석이 서로 달라서 생기는데, 안전성을 설정하는 것이 항상 분명하지는 않다. 때때로 식품 첨가제의 안전성을 결정하는 것은 매우 힘들 수 있는데, 첨가제가 우리의 식품이나 몸 안에서 변형을 거치기 때문이다. 예를 들어, 그것(첨가제)은 조리 동안에, 빛에 노출된 후에 또는 다른 식품 성분과 반응한 후에 화학적으로 분해될 수 있으며, 그로 인해 그것의 독성이 변화할 수 있다. 결과적으로, 첨가제가 실제 식품에서 실제로 어떻게 작용하는지를 이해하는 것이 필수적이다. 현재 식품에 사용이 허용되는 일부 첨가제는 금지될 가능성이 있지만, 그것이 모든 첨가제가 나쁘다는 것을 의미하는 것은 아니다.

정답풀이

식품 첨가제의 안전성을 설정하는 것이 매우 어려운 이유를 설명하는 글이다. 주어진 문장은 그 이유 중 하나로 첨가제의 변형 가능성에 관해 언급하고 있으므로, 식품 첨가제가 식품의 조리 과정이나 보관 과정에서 화학적으로 분해되어 그 독성이 변할 수 있다는 구체적 사례를 제시하는 문장 앞인 ③에 들어가는 것이 가장 적절하다.

구문풀이

`21행` Consequently, **it** is essential [**to understand** {how additives actually behave in real foods}].

: it은 형식상의 주어이고, [ ]로 표시된 to부정사구가 내용상의 주어이며, 그 안의 { }는 understand의 목적어로 쓰인 명사절(의문사절)이다.

`22행` **It** is likely [that some of the additives {currently accepted for use in foods} will be banned in the future], / but, **that** does not mean [that all additives are bad].

: It은 형식상의 주어이고, 첫 번째 [ ]로 표시된 명사절이 내용상의 주어이며, 그 안의 { }는 some of the additives를 수식하는 과거분사구이다. but 다음에 주어로 쓰인 that은 앞 절의 내용을 가리키고, 두 번째 [ ]는 mean의 목적어 역할을 하는 명사절이다.

어휘풀이

- additive *n* 첨가제
- transformation *n* 변형
- reevaluate *v* 재평가하다
- interpretation *n* 해석
- clear-cut *a* 확실한, 분명한
- ingredient *n* 성분, 재료
- undergo *v* ~을 거치다, ~을 겪다
- routinely *ad* 정례적으로, 일상적으로
- employ *v* 사용하다
- establish *v* 설정하다
- degrade *v* 분해되다
- toxicity *n* 독성

• ban *v* 금지하다

070 답 ④

📖 협상에 있어서 분배형과 통합형 접근방식의 차이점

전문해석
상호 의존의 구조는 협상가들이 사용하는 전략과 전술을 형성한다. **분배형 상황에서 협상가들은 경쟁에서 이기고 상대편을 이기거나 고정된 자원에서 그들이 얻을 수 있는 가장 큰 조각을 얻도록 동기 부여된다.** 이런 목적을 이루기 위해 협상가들은 보통 한쪽에만 유리한 (협상) 전략과 전술을 사용한다. 협상에 대한 이런 접근방식은 '분배형 협상'이라고 불리는데, 상황을 고려하면 오직 한 명의 승자만 있을 수 있다는 사실을 받아들이고 그 승자가 될 수 있는 행동 경로를 추구한다. 협상의 목적은 가치를 주장하는 것, 즉 보상을 주장하거나 상의 가장 큰 부분을 얻거나 가능한 한 가장 큰 조각을 얻는 데 필요한 것은 무엇이든 하는 것이다. **이와 대조적으로, 통합형 상황에서 협상가들은 양측에 유리한 (협상) 전략과 전술을 사용할 것이다.** 협상에 대한 이런 접근방식은 쌍방 모두 성공하고 자신의 목적을 이룰 수 있도록 해결책을 찾으려고 시도한다. 협상의 목적은 가치를 창조하는 것, 즉 더 많은 자원을 찾거나 기존의 자원 사용을 나누고 조정하는 독특한 방법을 찾음으로써 모든 당사자가 자신의 목적을 충족시키는 방법을 찾는 것이다.

정답풀이
④ 앞까지는 협상에서 한쪽에만 유리한 전략을 사용하는 접근방식인 분배형 협상에 해당하는 내용이고 ④ 다음 문장에서는 협상에서 쌍방 모두 만족하는 결과를 추구하는 접근방식에 대해 말하고 있다. 따라서 대조의 연결어 In contrast를 사용하며 통합형 상황에서 협상가들이 양측에 유리한 협상 전략을 사용한다는 내용의 주어진 문장은 ④에 들어가는 것이 가장 적절하다.

구문풀이
4행 In distributive situations, negotiators **are motivated** [**to win** the competition and **beat** the other party] or [**to gain** the largest piece of the fixed resource {that they **can**}].

: 두 개의 [ ]는 are motivated에 이어지는 to부정사구로 or에 의해 병렬구조를 이루고 있고, 첫 번째 [ ]에서 win과 beat가 and에 의해 병렬구조를 이룬다. 두 번째 [ ] 안의 { }는 the largest piece of the fixed resource를 수식하는 목적격 관계대명사절이고 can 뒤에는 gain이 생략되었다.

9행 This approach to negotiation—called *distributive bargaining*—**accepts** the fact [that there can only be one winner given the situation] and **pursues** a course of action [to be that winner].

: 문장의 주어 This approach to negotiation에 이어지는 동사 accepts와 pursues가 and로 연결되었다. 첫 번째 [ ]는 the fact와 동격 관계를 이루는 명사절이고, 두 번째 [ ]는 a course of action을 수식하는 형용사적 용법의 to부정사구이다.

13행 The purpose of the negotiation is to claim value—that is, to do [**whatever** is necessary **to** {**claim** the reward}, {**gain** the lion's share of the prize}, or {**gain** the largest piece possible}].

: [ ]는 do의 목적어 역할을 하는 명사절로 whatever는 anything that이라는 의미로 선행사를 포함하는 복합관계대명사이다. or로 연결된 세 개의 { }는 병렬구조로 to에 이어진다.

19행 The purpose of the negotiation is to create value—that is, to find a way [**for all parties** to meet their objectives], **either** by [identifying more resources] **or** [finding unique ways {to share and coordinate the use of existing resources}].

: 첫 번째 [ ]는 a way를 수식하는 형용사적 용법의 to부정사구이고, for all parties는 to meet ~의 의미상 주어를 나타낸다. 두 번째와 세 번째 [ ]는 전치사 by에 이어지는 동명사구로 「either *A* or *B*」에 의해 병렬구조로 연결되어 있고, 세 번째 [ ] 안의 { }는 unique ways를 수식하는 to부정사구이다.

어휘풀이
• integrative situation 통합형 상황
• negotiator *n* 협상가
• employ *v* 사용하다
• strategy *n* 전략
• tactic *n* 전술
• structure *n* 구조
• interdependence *n* 상호 의존
• distributive situation 분배형 상황
• beat *v* 이기다
• objective *n* 목적
• pursue *v* 추구하다
• the lion's share 가장 큰 조각
• identify *v* 찾다, 발견하다
• coordinate *v* 조정하다

071 답 ④

📖 자원의 이용 가능성과 위험 감수 수위

전문해석
상이한 조건 하에서 성장한 인간과 같은 유기체는 상이한 생존 전략을 개발해 왔고 위험 감수의 상이한 최적 수준을 발달시켜 왔다고 가정하는 것이 논리적이다. 식물이 풍부하고 포식자로부터의 위험이 거의 없는 환경에 살았던 선사 시대의 인간은 주위의 어떠한 위험에도 스스로를 노출시키도록 부추겨지거나 강요되는 경우가 거의 없었다. 그들은 위협이 제거될 때까지 기다렸다가 먹을 것을 찾는 것을 계속할 수 있는 여유가 있었다. **이런 유형의 환경은 참을성 있고 위험을 회피하는 기질을 촉진했을 것이다.** 반면에, 부족한 자원과 더 많은 포식자가 있는 환경은 거주자들을 먹을 것을 위한 격렬한 경쟁 속으로 몰아갔을 것이다. **같은 유형의 먹을 것이 인간과 그들의 포식자에 의해 탐색이 되면, 갈등이 일어날 것이다.** 자기 자신과 자식들에게 먹을 것과 같은 필수적인 자원을 공급하기 위해, 이 인간들은 다른 포식자들보다 한 수 앞서기 위해서 동시에 필요한 자원을 얻기 위해서 상당히 더 높은 위험들을 감수해야만 했는데, 그들의 먹잇감 역시 더 조심스럽고 제압하기에 더 힘들 것이기 때문이었다. **이런 유형의 환경은 더 위험스런 행동을 촉진했을 것인데,** 참을성 있고 위험을 회피하는 사람은 필요한 자원에 접근할 가능성이 더 적었을 것이기 때문이다.

정답풀이
위험이 없는 환경에서의 인간의 행동과 자원이 부족하고 포식자가 더 많은 환경에서의 인간의 행동을 대조적으로 설명하는 글이다. 인간과 인간의 포식자가 같은 유형의 먹을 것을 탐색하면 갈등이 일어날 가능성이 크다는 내용의 주어진 문장은 자원이 부족하고 포식자가 더 많은 환경에서 일어날 수 있는 갈등에 대한 설명이다. 따라서 주어진 문장은 On the other hand로 시작하는 ④ 앞 문장의 부연 설명에 해당하며, 또 주어진 문장의 humans를 ④ 다음 문장에서 these humans로 받으며 추가로 부연 설명하고 있으므로 주어진 문장이 들어가기에 가장 적절한 곳은 ④이다.

구문풀이
3행 **It** is logical [**to postulate** {that organisms, such as human beings, (who grew up under different conditions) have developed different survival strategies, and different optimal levels of risk taking}].

: It은 형식상의 주어이고, [ ]로 표시된 to부정사구가 내용상의 주어이다. { }는 postulate의 목적어로 쓰인 명사절이고, ( )는 organisms를 수식하는 주격 관계대명사절이다.

6행 Prehistoric humans [living in environments {rich in vegetation} and {with little dangers from predators}] **were** hardly **encouraged** or **forced** to expose themselves to any of the dangers around.

: 문장의 핵심 주어는 Prehistoric humans이고, 동사는 were encouraged와 (were) forced이다. [ ]는 Prehistoric humans를 수식하는 현재분사구이고, 그 안에 두 개의 { }는 environments를 수식하는 형용사구와 전치사구이다.

어휘풀이

- predator *n* 포식자, 포식 동물
- logical *a* 논리적인
- prehistoric *a* 선사 시대의
- patient *a* 참을성 있는
- scarce *a* 부족한
- fierce *a* 격렬한, 극심한
- considerably *ad* 상당히
- overcome *v* 압도하다
- conflict *n* 갈등
- optimal *a* 최적의
- vegetation *n* 식물
- temperament *n* 기질, 성질
- inhabitant *n* 거주자
- offspring *n* 자식, 새끼
- cautious *a* 조심하는, 주의 깊은
- gain access to ~에 접근하다

072 답 ③

📖 사이버 범죄 관련 법제화가 어려운 이유

전문해석

대부분의 경우 경찰은 범죄자가 누구인지 알고 있는데, 주된 문제는 어떻게 유죄를 입증할 정도로 충분한 증거를 수집하느냐는 것이다. 그러나 **인터넷에 기반을 둔 범죄는 다른데, 경찰은 결코 범죄자가 누구인지 모른다!** 온라인 범죄에서는 신분을 감출 수 있는 방법이 아주 많이 있다. 다양한 서버를 통해 통신의 경로를 잡음으로써 사용자의 IP 주소를 숨겨 줄 수많은 서비스들이 있는데, 이는 범죄자 추적을 어렵게 만든다. 2009년에 일부 전문가들은 인터넷 사용자들의 상대적 익명성을 사이버 범죄를 가능하게 하는 주요 문제로 확인하고 그 문제와 싸우는 데 도움이 될 인터넷 '여권'을 제안했다. 하지만 온라인 신분을 더 잘 추적하려는 시도는 사생활 옹호자들에게 심각한 문제를 불러일으키고 정치적 반발이라는 결과를 낳는다. 그리고 인터넷상 익명성의 종결은 정부가 반대자를 처벌하는 국가에서 심각한 결과를 낳을 수 있다. 그래서 모든 온라인 사용자의 신분을 파악하는 것의 기술적인 난제가 극복될 수 있음에도 불구하고 많은 입법자들은 그것을 법제화하기를 주저할 것이다.

정답풀이

온라인상의 신분 추적은 사이버 범죄를 막는 데 도움이 되지만 사생활 침해의 문제점이 있어서 온라인상에서의 신분 확인을 법제화하기는 어렵다는 내용의 글이다. 주어진 문장은 온라인상의 익명성 문제를 제기하고 온라인 신분 확인의 필요성을 언급하며, However로 시작하는 ③ 다음 문장의 attempts to better track online identity는 주어진 문장의 Internet 'passports'와 논리적으로 연결된다. 따라서 주어진 문장이 ③에 들어가서 온라인 신분 확인이 필요하나 그것은 사생활 침해 문제를 불러일으킬 수 있다는 흐름으로 이어지는 것이 적절하다.

구문풀이

10행 There are numerous services [that will mask a user's IP address by routing traffic through various servers], [making **it** difficult {**to track** down the criminal}].

: 첫 번째 [ ]는 문장의 주어인 numerous services를 수식하는 주격 관계대명사절이다. 두 번째 [ ]는 분사구문으로, it은 making의 형식상의 목적어이고 { }로 표시된 to부정사구가 내용상의 목적어이다.

어휘풀이

- identify *v* 확인[인정]하다, ~의 신원을 파악하다 (*n* identity 신원, 신분)
- relative *a* 상대적인
- combat *v* ~와 싸우다, ~을 막다
- route *v* ~의 경로를 설정하다
- traffic *n* 소통(량)(정보 교환의 흐름 또는 그 양)
- anonymity *n* 익명성
- criminal *n* 범죄자

- track down ~을 찾아내다, ~을 밝혀내다
- advocate *n* 옹호, 옹호자
- consequence *n* 결과
- lawmaker *n* 입법자
- mandate *v* 명령하다, 법제화하다
- backlash *n* 반동, 반발
- dissenter *n* 반대자
- be hesitant to *do* ~하기를 주저하다

073 ①	**074** ①	**075** ①	**076** ③	**077** ②
078 ①	**079** ③	**080** ⑤	**081** ②	

073 답 ①

📖 주목할 만한 연구를 위한 분야별 순차적 연구

전문해석

평균적인 재능을 가진 사람들조차도 다양한 과학 분야에서 주목할 만한 성과를 낼 수 있는데, 한 번에 그것들 모두를 포괄하려 하지 않는 한 그렇다. 대신에 그들은 한 주제 다음에 다른 주제로 (즉, 다른 기간에) 주의를 집중해야 하는데, 나중의 연구가 다른 영역에서의 이전의 성취를 약화할 것임에도 그렇다. 이것은 뇌가 보편적인 과학에 '시간'상 적응하는 것이지 '공간'상 적응하는 것이 아니라고 말하는 것과 다름없다. 사실, 뛰어난 능력이 있는 사람들도 이런 식으로 나아간다. 따라서, 우리가 여러 다른 과학 분야에 출판물을 가진 사람에게 놀랄 때, 각 주제가 특정 기간에 탐구되었다는 것을 인식하라. 이전에 얻은 지식은 확실히 저자의 마음에서 사라지지 않았을 것이지만, 그것은 공식이나 크게 축약된 기호로 응축되어 단순화되었을 것이다. 따라서 대뇌 칠판에 새로운 이미지를 인식하고 학습할 수 있는 충분한 공간이 남아 있다.
→ 하나의 과학 주제를 탐구한 다음 다른 주제를 탐구하는 것은 과학 전반에 걸친 주목할 만한 연구를 가능하게 하는데, 이전에 습득된 지식이 뇌 안에서 단순화된 형태로 유지되어, 이것이 새로운 학습을 위한 공간을 남겨두기 때문이다.

정답풀이

과학 주제를 기간별로 하나씩 차례로 탐구하게 되면 이전에 습득한 지식이 뇌 안에서 공식이나 축약된 기호 등의 단순화된 형태로 간직되어 뇌에 새로운 학습을 위한 공간이 충분히 남아 있어 다양한 과학 분야에서 주목할 만한 성과를 낼 수 있다는 내용의 글이다. 따라서 요약문의 빈칸 (A)에는 enables(가능하게 하다)가, (B)에는 leaves(남겨두다)가 들어가는 것이 가장 적절하다.

구문풀이

6행 Thus, [when we are astonished by someone {with publications in different scientific fields}], **realize** [that each topic was explored during a specific period of time].

: 첫 번째 [ ]는 때를 나타내는 부사절이고, 그 안의 { }는 someone을 수식하는 전치사구이다. 주절은 동사원형 realize로 시작하는 명령문이고, 두 번째 [ ]는 realize의 목적어 역할을 하는 명사절이다.

어휘풀이

- notable *a* 주목할 만한
- concentrate *A* on *B* B에 A를 집중하다
- subject *n* 주제
- attainment *n* 성취, 성과
- amount to ~와 마찬가지이다
- astonish *v* 깜짝 놀라게 하다
- explore *v* 탐구하다
- abbreviate *v* 축약하다
- perception *n* 인식
- embrace *v* 포괄하다, 수용하다
- weaken *v* 약화하다
- sphere *n* 영역
- proceed *v* 나아가다, 진행하다
- publication *n* 출판(물)
- formula *n* 공식
- sufficient *a* 충분한

074 답 ①

📖 장인정신의 온전한 발전을 제약하는 요인

전문해석

'장인정신'은 산업 사회의 도래와 더불어 쇠락한 삶의 방식을 나타낼 수도 있겠지만, 이것은 오해의 소지가 있다. 장인정신은 지속적이고 기본적인 인간의 충동, 즉 일을 그 자체를 위해 잘하고 싶은 소망을 말한다. 장인정신은 숙련된 육체노동보다 훨씬 더 넓은 구획을 가르는데, 그것은 컴퓨터 프로그래머, 의사, 예술가에게 도움이 되고, 양육은 시민정신과 마찬가지로 그것이 숙련된 기술로서 실행될 때 향상된다. 이 모든 영역에서 장인정신은 객관적인 기준, 즉 그 자체의 것에 초점을 맞춘다. 그러나 사회적, 경제적 상황은 흔히 장인의 수련과 전념을 방해하는데, 즉 학교는 일을 잘하기 위한 도구를 제공하지 못할 수 있고, 직장은 품질에 대한 열망을 진정으로 가치 있게 여기지 않을 수 있다. 그리고 장인정신이 일에 대한 자부심으로 개인에게 보상을 줄 수 있겠지만, 이 보상은 간단하지 않다. 장인은 흔히 탁월함의 상충하는 객관적 기준에 직면하며, 어떤 일을 그 자체를 위해 잘하려는 소망은 경쟁적 압력에 의해, 좌절에 의해 또는 집착에 의해 약화할 수 있다.
→ 장인정신은 다양한 상황에서 오랜 시간에 걸쳐 존속해왔는데, 흔히 그것의 온전한 발전을 제한하는 요소들과 마주친다.

정답풀이

장인정신은 산업 사회가 도래한 이후에도 사라지지 않고 여러 분야에 계속 존재해왔지만, 장인의 수련과 전념을 방해하는 사회적 경제적 조건과 뛰어남에 상충되는 객관적 여건 등으로 인해 장인들이 장인정신을 발휘하는 데 지장을 받고 있다는 내용의 글이다. 따라서 요약문의 빈칸 (A)에는 장인정신이 사라지지 않고 지속되었다는 점을 나타내는 persisted(존속했다)가, (B)에는 장인정신 발휘에 지장을 받는다는 점을 나타내는 limit(제한하다)가 들어가는 것이 가장 적절하다.

오답풀이

②, ③, ④ 사회적 경제적 조건 및 여타 요인으로 인해 장인의 수련이 방해를 받거나 장인정신이 약화된다고 했으므로 (B)에 cultivate(양성하다), accelerate(가속화하다), shape(형성하다)가 들어가는 것은 적절하지 않다.

구문풀이

1행 "Craftsmanship" may suggest a way of life [that declined with the arrival of industrial society] — but **this** is misleading.

: [ ]는 a way of life를 수식하는 주격 관계대명사절이고, this는 but 앞 절의 내용을 가리킨다.

어휘풀이

- craftsmanship *n* 장인정신
- misleading *a* 오해의 소지가 있는
- impulse *n* 충동, 욕구
- manual *a* 육체노동의, 손으로 하는
- domain *n* 영역
- discipline *n* 수련, 수양
- aspiration *n* 열망
- frustration *n* 좌절
- decline *v* 쇠락하다, 쇠퇴하다
- enduring *a* 지속적인
- for one's own sake ~ 그 자체를 위해
- parenting *n* 양육, 육아
- stand in the way of ~을 방해하다
- commitment *n* 전념, 매진
- conflicting *a* 상충하는
- obsession *n* 집착

075 답 ①

📖 과학적 설명에 관한 두 가지 철학적 관점

전문해석

Philip Kitcher와 Wesley Salmon은 설명에 관한 철학 이론 중 두 가지 가능한 대안이 있다고 말했다. 하나는 과학적 설명이 최소한 수의 일반화 아래 광범위하게 많은 현상을 '통합'하는 데 있다는 관점이다. 이 관점에 따르면, 과학의 목표(혹은 어쩌면 한 가지 목표)는 모든 관찰 가능한 현상을 포섭할 수 있는 법칙이나 일반화의 경제적인 틀을 구축하는 것이다. 과학적 설명은 경험적 세계에 관한 우리의 지식을

조직하고 체계화하는데, 체계화가 더 경제적일수록, 설명되는 것에 대한 우리의 이해는 더 깊어진다. **또 하나의 관점은 '인과적/기계론적' 접근이다.** 그것에 따르면, 어떤 현상에 대한 과학적인 설명은 관심의 대상인 그 현상을 만들어 낸 메커니즘을 밝혀내는 것으로 이루어져 있다. **이 관점은 개별 사건들에 대한 설명을 일차적으로 보는데,** 일반화에 대한 설명이 그것들로부터 흘러나온다. 즉, 과학적 일반화에 대한 설명은 규칙성을 만들어 내는 인과적 메커니즘에서 나온다.

→ 과학적 설명은 모든 관찰을 아우르는 <u>최소한의</u> 원리를 찾거나 개별 현상으로부터 도출된 일반적인 <u>패턴</u>을 발견함으로써 이루어질 수 있다.

정답풀이

설명에 대한 철학적 이론 중 두 가지 가능한 대안이 있는데, 하나는 과학적 설명이 최소한으로 적은 수의 일반화 아래 광범위하게 많은 현상을 통합하는 데 있다는 관점이고, 다른 하나는 개별 사건에 대한 설명을 일차적으로 보고, 그로부터 일반화에 대한 설명이 나온다고 보는 인과적/기계론적 접근이라는 내용의 글이다. 따라서 요약문의 빈칸 (A)에는 최소한으로 적은 수와 관련된 least(가장 적은)가, (B)에는 일반화를 통해 만들어 내는 규칙성과 관련된 patterns(패턴)가 들어가는 것이 가장 적절하다.

구문풀이

14행 According to this view, the (or perhaps, a) goal of science is [to construct an economical framework of <u>laws or generalizations</u> {that are capable of subsuming all observable phenomena}].

: [ ]는 문장의 주격보어 역할을 하는 to부정사구이고, 그 안의 { }는 laws or generalizations를 수식하는 주격 관계대명사절이다.

16행 This view **sees** the explanation of individual events **as** primary, [**with** the explanation of generalizations **flowing** from them].

: 「see *A* as *B*」는 'A를 B로 여기다'라는 의미이다. [ ]는 「with+명사구+분사구」로 이루어진 분사구문으로 앞에 언급된 내용과 관련된 부수적 정보를 제공한다. 명사구가 의미상 분사와 능동적 관계이므로 현재분사 flowing이 사용되었다.

어휘풀이

- alternative *n* 대안
- unification *n* 통합,결합
- phenomenon *n* 현상 (*pl.* phenomena)
- minimal *a* 최소의, 아주 적은
- construct *v* 구성하다
- be capable of -ing ~할 수 있다
- systematize *v* 체계화하다
- mechanical *a* 기계론적인
- uncover *v* 밝혀내다, 알아내다
- primary *a* 일차적인, 주요한
- consist in ~에 있다
- generalization *n* 일반화
- framework *n* 틀
- observable *a* 관찰할 수 있는
- causal *a* 인과 관계의
- consist of ~로 구성되다
- mechanism *n* 메커니즘, 구조
- regularity *n* 규칙성, 규칙적임

076 답 ③

📖 **실행하기 어려운 계획이나 목표에 선뜻 동의하는 경향**

전문해석

여러분은 여러분이 왜 그렇게 자주 그 당시는 좋은 생각처럼 보이지만 그날이 다가올수록 점점 더 끔찍해지는 그런 미래의 어떤 것을 하기로 약속하는지 궁금해한 적이 있는가? "내가 도대체 왜 이것에 동의했지?"라고 우리는 탄식한다. "생물학에서 C를 받고 어떻게 내가 의대에 입학할 수 있다고 생각했을까?" "내가 왜 우리 집에 십여 명 이상이 들어갈 공간이 있다고 생각했을까?" 그리고 이제 공황 상태가 시작되는데, 왜냐하면 여러분의 목표가 의사가 되는 것이라고 결정할 때, 여러분이 남편의 가족으로 집을 채우기로 결정할 때, 그것이 잘 되어 가게 할 수 있을지 없을지에

대해 생각하는 데 실제로 그렇게 많은 시간을 보내지 않았기 때문이다. 여러분은 '무엇'이 아니라 '왜'를 생각하고 있었고, 그리고 위안이 될지 모르겠지만, 그것은 우리들 대부분이 계속해서 처하는 상황이라는 것이다. 우리는 미래의 일에 대해, 우리가 그것들을 '왜' 하고 싶어 하는지의 관점에서 더 많이 생각하고 우리가 실제로 어떻게 해낼지의 관점에서는 덜 생각하도록 편향되어 있기 때문에, 우리는 잠재적으로 풍부한 보상을 가졌지만 실제 실행상의 어려움이 있기도 한 목표와 계획을 채택한다.

→ 우리는 우리의 능력을 벗어난 목표나 계획에 쉽게 동의하는데, 우리가 그것들이 잘 될지의 여부보다는 그것들의 <u>이유</u>에 더 많이 주목하기 때문이다.

정답풀이

자신의 능력으로는 실행하기 어려운 미래의 목표나 계획을 쉽게 결정하고 그것에 동의하는 이유는, 우리가 실행보다는 그 일을 왜 하고 싶어 하는지의 관점에서 미래의 일을 생각하는 경향이 있기 때문이라는 내용의 글이다. 따라서 요약문의 빈칸 (A)에는 capacity(능력)가, (B)에는 causes(이유, 근거)가 들어가는 것이 가장 적절하다.

오답풀이

①, ②, ⑤ 우리의 능력으로는 실행할 수 없는 미래의 목표나 계획에 관한 내용이지, 우리의 초점을 벗어나거나 우리가 이해할 수 없는 것에 관한 내용은 아니므로 (A)에 focus(초점)나 comprehension(이해)이 들어가는 것은 부적절하다.

구문풀이

1행 Have you ever wondered [why you commit yourself so often to <u>something in the future</u> {that **seems** like a good idea at the time but **becomes** more and more awful / **as** the day approaches}]?

: [ ]는 wondered의 목적어 역할을 하는 명사절(의문사절)이고, 그 안의 { }는 something in the future를 수식하는 주격 관계대명사절이며, 관계절의 동사 seems와 becomes가 병렬구조를 이루고 있다. as는 '~하면서'라는 의미의 접속사로 쓰였다.

어휘풀이

- commit oneself to ~을 확실히 약속하다, ~에 전념하다
- awful *a* 끔찍한
- med school 의과대학
- set in *v* 시작하다
- biased *a* 편향된, ~에 더 관심을 두는
- potentially *ad* 잠재적으로
- application *n* 적용, 응용
- lament *v* 탄식하다, 후회하다
- panic *n* 공황 상태
- consolation *n* 위로, 위안
- in terms of ~의 관점에서
- work out 잘 풀리다, 잘 진행되다

077 답 ②

📖 **사건의 희귀성에 따른 예측 정확성의 가치**

전문해석

여러분이 막 사막에 있는 도시로 이주했고 고장의 일기 예보자가 화창할지 비가 올지를 정확히 예측할 수 있는지를 결정하려고 한다고 상상해보라. 그 예보자는 자주 햇빛을 예측하고 비는 좀처럼 예측하지 않는다. 어느 날, 여러분은 그 예보자가 햇빛을 예측하고 정확하다는 것을 목격한다. 또 다른 어느 날, 그녀가 비를 예측하고 정확하다. 이 정확한 예측 중 어떤 것이 그 예보자가 날씨를 정확하게 예측할 수 있다고 여러분을 더 확신하도록 하겠는가? 정보 이론적 설명에 의하면, 두 관찰 중 더 정보를 주는 것은 비에 대한 정확한 예측이다. 이는 햇빛에 대한 정확한 예측은 사막에서는 놀랍지 않기 때문인데, 그곳은 거의 매일 화창하다. 즉, 그 예보자가 사막이 화창하다는 것만 알고 있다고 하더라도, 여러분은 그녀가 단지 우연히 햇빛에 대해 많은 정확한 예측을 할 것으로 예상할 것이다. **비 오는 날은 사막에서 드물어서 비의 정확한 예측은 우연히 일어날 가능성이 더 적으며, 따라서 그 예보자가 미래의 화창한 날과 비 오는 날을 구분할 수 있다는 더 강한 증거를 제공한다.**

→ 어떤 한 사건에 대한 예측의 <u>정확성</u>이 유의미하게 여겨지는가 그렇지 않은가는 그 사건의 <u>희귀성</u>에 달려 있다.

정답풀이

사막 지역 도시에서 일기 예보자가 화창한 날씨를 정확히 예측했을 때와 비가 오는 날씨를 정확히 예측했을 때, 전자의 경우는 그 예보자의 예측 능력을 판단하는 증거로 유의미하지 않고, 후자의 경우는 유의미한데, 이는 사막의 경우 비가 오는 날씨가 매우 드물기 때문이라는 내용이다. 따라서 요약문의 빈칸 (A)에는 precision(정확성)이, (B)에는 rarity(희귀성)가 들어가는 것이 가장 적절하다.

구문풀이

1행 Imagine [that you **have** just **moved** to a desert town and **are trying** to determine {if the local weather forecaster can accurately predict (**whether** it will be sunny **or** rainy)}].

: [ ]는 Imagine의 목적어 역할을 하는 명사절이고, 명사절의 주어 you에 이어지는 두 개의 동사 have moved와 are trying이 and로 연결되었다. { }는 determine의 목적어 역할을 하는 명사절로 여기서 if는 '~인지 아닌지'라는 의미로 쓰였고, ( )는 predict의 목적어 역할을 하는 명사절로 「whether A or B」는 'A인지 아니면 B인지'라는 의미를 나타낸다.

17행 [Because rainy days are rare in the desert], a correct prediction of rain **is** less likely to occur by chance and therefore **provides** <u>stronger evidence</u> [that the forecaster can distinguish between future sunny and rainy days].

: 첫 번째 [ ]는 이유를 나타내는 부사절이고, 주절의 주어 a correct prediction of rain에 이어지는 동사 is와 provides가 and로 연결되었다. 두 번째 [ ]는 stronger evidence를 구체적으로 설명하는 동격절이다.

어휘풀이

- weather forecaster 일기 예보자
- predict *v* 예측하다
- theoretic *a* 이론적인
- informative *a* 정보를 주는, 유익한
- distinguish *v* 구별하다
- accurately *ad* 정확하게
- convinced *a* 확신하는
- account *n* 설명
- by chance 우연히, 뜻밖에
- significant *a* 유의미한, 중요한

078 답 ①

📖 인공지능이 특정한 기능이나 과업 수행에만 한정되는 이유

전문해석

'제한된' 그리고 '약한' 인공지능이라는 용어는 '강한', '인간 수준의', '범용' 또는 '완전한' 인공지능(때때로 AGI, 즉 범용 인공지능이라 불리는 것), 즉 우리가 영화에서 보는, 우리 인간이 할 수 있는 거의 모든 것을 할 수 있고, 어쩌면 훨씬 더 많은 것을 할 수 있는 인공지능과 대조하기 위해 사용된다. **범용 인공지능은 그 분야의 원래 목표였을 테지만, 그것을 성취하는 것은 예상보다 훨씬 더 어려운 것으로 드러났다.** 시간이 흐르면서 AI에서의 노력은 잘 정의된 특정 과제, 예컨대 발화 인식, 체스 두기, 자율 주행 등에 초점이 맞춰져 왔다. 그런 기능을 수행하는 기계를 창안하는 것은 유용하고 흔히 수익성이 있으며, 이 과제 각각이 개별적으로 '지능'을 필요로 한다고 주장될 수 있을 것이다. 하지만 어떠한 일반적인 의미에서든 지능적이라고 불릴 수 있을 어떤 인공지능 프로그램도 아직 창안되지 않았다. 그 분야에 대한 최근의 한 평가는 이 점을 잘 진술했다. '**한 무더기의 제한된 지능들이 결코 하나의 범용 지능이 되지 않을 것이다. 범용 지능은 능력들의 수에 관한 것이 아니라, 그 능력들 간의 통합에 관한 것이다.**'

→ 현재는 인공지능에 <u>특정한</u> 기능이나 과제를 수행할 수 있는 능력은 있지만, 그것의 능력들이 <u>결합되어</u> 범용 지능의 수준에 도달할 수는 없다.

정답풀이

인공지능의 원래 목표는 범용 지능 수준에 도달하는 것이었지만 그러한 목표를 성취하는 것은 예상보다 훨씬 어려웠고, 그래서 현재의 인공지능은 특정한 기능이나 과제를 개별적으로 수행하는 데 초점이 맞춰져 있으며 그 능력들을 통합해서 범용 지능에 도달하지는 못하고 있다는 내용의 글이다. 따라서 (A)에는 현재 인공지능이 수행하고 있는 기능이나 과제의 특성을 나타내는 specific(특정한)이, (B)에는 현재의 인공지능이 범용 지능 수준에 도달하지 못하는 이유를 나타내도록 combined(결합된)가 들어가는 것이 가장 적절하다.

구문풀이

11행 [Creating <u>machines</u> {that perform such functions}] is useful and often lucrative, / and **it** could be argued [**that** each of these tasks individually requires "intelligence."]

: 첫 번째 [ ]는 주어 역할을 하는 동명사구이고, 그 안의 { }는 machines를 수식하는 주격 관계대명사절이다. and 다음에서 it은 형식상의 주어이고, 두 번째 [ ]로 표시된 명사절이 내용상의 주어에 해당한다.

어휘풀이

- weak AI 약한 인공지능(한 임무에만 집중하는 인공지능)
- contrast *v* 대조하다
- general AI 범용 인공지능(인간처럼 자유로운 사고가 가능한 자아를 지닌 인공지능)
- full-blown *a* 완전히 발달한, 절정에 이른
- artificial *a* 인공의
- recognition *n* 인식
- appraisal *n* 평가
- add up to 결국 ~이라는 것이 되다
- subdivide *v* 세분하다
- original *a* 본래의, 원래의
- autonomous *a* 자율의, 자치의
- a pile of 한 더미의
- integration *n* 통합, 집성
- extend *v* 확대[확장]하다

079 답 ③

📖 옵션 제거와 선택에 따른 소비자의 상이한 태도

전문해석

한 연구는 사람들이 두 가지 조건 하에서 어떻게 자동차 구매 결정을 하는지를 비교했다. 한 조건에서 그들은 옵션이 장착된 자동차를 제안받았으며, 그들의 임무는 원하지 않는 옵션들을 제거하는 것이었다. 두 번째 조건에서 그들은 옵션이 없는 자동차를 제안받았으며, 그들의 임무는 그들이 원하는 옵션들을 추가하는 것이었다. **첫 번째 조건의 사람들은 두 번째 조건의 사람들보다 결국 더 많은 옵션을 갖게 되었다. 이것은 옵션들이 (구매를) 고려 중인 자동차에 이미 장착되어 있을 때, 그것들은 (차에) 부여된 일부가 되고 그것들을 포기하는 것은 상실감을 유발시키기 때문이다.** 옵션이 이미 장착되어 있지 않을 때 그것들은 (차에) 부여된 일부가 아니며 그것들을 선택하는 것은 이득으로 인식된다. 하지만 상실은 이득이 만족시키는 것보다 더 마음을 아프게 하기 때문에, 가령 이미 차량의 일부인 400달러짜리 스테레오 업그레이드를 (사기로) 결정하는 사람들은 그것을 포기하는 것이 그 가격인 400달러보다 더 마음을 아프게 할 것이라고 판단할 수 있다. 대조적으로, 업그레이드가 자동차에 부여된 일부가 아닐 때에 그들은 그것을 선택하는 것이 400달러만큼의 기분 좋은 감정을 만들어 내지는 않을 것이라고 생각할 것이다. 그러므로 사람들이 새 차에 대한 거래를 실제로 성사시키기도 전에 소유 효과가 나타나고 있는 것이다.

→ 연구는 손실이 상응하는 이득보다 더 많은 <u>심리적</u> 영향을 미친다는 것을 시사하는데, 왜냐하면 일단 어떤 것이 겉보기에 누군가에 의해 <u>소유되는</u> 것 같으면, 그것은 단순한 현금 가치보다 그 사람에게 더 가치가 있기 때문이다.

정답풀이

연구를 통해 사람들은 차에 옵션들을 추가할 때보다 이미 포함되어 있어서 차

의 일부라고 생각하는 옵션들을 포기해야 할 때 정신적으로 더 힘들어 한다는 것을 알 수 있다. 따라서 사람들은 자신이 '소유'한 것으로 보이는 것에 더 많은 가치를 부여하고 그것을 잃을 때 더 큰 '심리적' 상실감을 경험하게 된다는 것을 추론할 수 있으므로, (A)에는 psychological(심리적인)이, (B)에는 possessed(소유되는)가 들어가는 것이 가장 적절하다.

오답풀이
④ 이미 포함된 옵션에 대해 금전적인 가치가 아니라 심리적인 가치를 더 높이 두는 것이므로 (A)에 monetary(금전적인)는 적절하지 않고, abandoned(포기되는)는 possessed(소유되는)의 반대 의미로 볼 수 있기 때문에 (B)에 적절하지 않다.

구문풀이
8행 This is [**because** {**when** options are already attached to the car being considered}, {they become part of the endowment} and {passing them up triggers a feeling of loss}].

: because가 이끄는 절에서 첫 번째 { }는 시간 부사절이며, 두 번째와 세 번째 { }는 and로 연결되어 병렬구조를 이루는 절이다.

어휘풀이
- loaded *a* (짐을) 실은, 장전된
- end up with 결국 ~을 얻다
- endowment *n* 기본 재산, 주어진 것 (*cf.* endowment effect 소유 효과(자기가 갖게 된 대상의 가치를 갖기 전보다 높게 인식하는 것))
- pass up ~을 포기하다
- equivalent *a* 동등한, 상당하는
- abandon *v* 버리다, 포기하다
- eliminate *v* 제거하다
- attach *v* 붙이다, 첨부하다
- trigger *v* 유발하다
- monetary *a* 금전적인, 통화의

080 답 ⑤

📖 사회 불평등을 합리화하려는 사회 다윈주의의 의도

전문해석
사회 다윈주의는 찰스 다윈의 진화론 발표에 이어 19세기 후반과 20세기 초반에 생겨난 (결속이) 느슨한 일단의 이론을 나타낸다. 이때는 유럽 제국주의, 미국으로의 열띤 이주 그리고 산업 혁명으로 인한 도시화된 빈민 집단 증가의 시대였다. 따라서 **사회적 편견이 정복당한 자들과 빈곤한 자들은 어떤 식으로든 그런 지위에 있는 것이 마땅하다고 확신하는 유럽과 미국의 엘리트 계층 사이에서 퍼져나갔다. 마찬가지로, 적자생존 개념은 이 견해를 정당화하는 데 이용되었다.** 다윈은 진화가 인종 차별적이거나 사회적 불평등의 정당한 이유가 되는 것을 의도하지 않았다. 그의 이론은 동물들이 어떻게 그것들의 환경에 적응하는지에 대한 설명이었다. 그것은 사회를 위한 도덕적 규정이 아니었다. 하지만 그의 연구는 오직 최강자와 가장 가치 있는 자만이 생존하며 사회적 불리함은 유전적 열등함의 반영이라는 것을 의미하는 것으로 잘못 해석되었다.

→ 사회 다윈주의는 지배 집단을 위해 사회적 불평등을 합리화하고자 했기 때문에 다윈주의의 부당한 이용으로 여겨진다.

정답풀이
사회 다윈주의는 유럽과 미국의 엘리트 계층이 다윈의 진화론을 자신들에게 유리한 방향으로 악용하여 낮은 사회적 지위에 처한 사람들이 겪는 사회적 불평등을 정당화하려는 의도에서 생겨났다는 내용이다. 따라서 (A)에는 exploitation(부당한 이용)이, (B)에는 rationalize(합리화하다)가 들어가는 것이 가장 적절하다.

구문풀이
16행 But his work was misinterpreted to mean [that only **the strongest** and **most worthy** survive] and [that social

disadvantage is a reflection of genetic inferiority].

: 두 개의 [ ]로 표시된 명사절이 and로 연결되어 mean의 목적어 역할을 한다. the strongest와 (the) most worthy는 「the+형용사」의 구조로 복수 보통명사(~인 사람들)의 뜻을 나타낸다.

어휘풀이
- imperialism *n* 제국주의
- immigration *n* 이주
- prejudice *n* 편견
- conquer *v* 정복하다
- somehow *ad* 어떤 식으로든, 아무튼
- racist *a* 인종 차별적인
- inequity *n* 불공평, 불공정
- misinterpret *v* 잘못 해석하다
- inferiority *n* 열등(함)
- contradict *v* 부정하다, 반박하다
- intense *a* 열띤
- urbanized *a* 도시화된
- convince oneself 확신하다
- impoverished *a* 빈곤한
- be deserving of ~을 받아 마땅하다
- justification *n* 정당화
- prescription *n* 규정
- disadvantage *n* 불리, 불리한 점
- intensify *v* 강화하다

081 답 ②

📖 문화의 영향을 받는 성 역할

전문해석
문화 간 비교의 가장 큰 가치들 중 하나는 발달상의 현상이 보편적인지 그렇지 않은지를 우리들에게 말해 줄 수 있다는 것이다. 예를 들어, 남성과 여성의 역할은 보편적인가? 성(性)의 생물학적 차이가 필연적으로 행동의 성별 차이를 초래할 수 있는가? 여러 해 전에 인류학자 Margaret Mead는 뉴기니섬의 세 부족사회의 사람들에 의해서 채택된 성 역할을 비교했고, 그녀의 관찰은 확실히 많은 것을 생각하게 해 준다. Arapesh 부족에서는 남녀 모두 우리가 여성의 역할이라고 여기는 것을 하도록 교육받았다. 즉, 그들은 협력적이고 비공격적이고 타인의 필요에 민감했다. Mundugumor 부족의 남녀 모두는 서양의 기준에 의하면 남성의 행동 유형인 공격적이고 타인에게 정서적으로 둔감하도록 양육되었다. 마지막으로, Tchambuli 부족은 서양의 (행동) 유형과 정반대인 성 역할 발달 유형을 보여주었다. 즉, 남성들은 수동적이고 정서적으로 의존적이었으며 사회적으로 민감했던 반면에 여성들은 지배적이고 독립적이고 당당했다. Mead의 연구는 우리 사회에서 진실인 모든 것이 모든 곳에서 진실인 것은 아니라는 것을 보여준다.

→ Mead의 문화 간 비교는 문화적 학습이 생물학적인 차이보다 남녀의 특징적인 행동 유형과 훨씬 더 많은 관련이 있을 수 있다는 것을 시사한다.

정답풀이
서양의 전형적인 성 역할과는 다른 뉴기니섬 부족들의 성 역할을 통해서 성 역할이라는 것이 생물학적인 차이에서 기인하는 것이 아니라 문화의 소산이라는 것을 알 수 있다. 따라서 (A)에는 cultural(문화적인)이, (B)에는 biological(생물학적인)이 들어가는 것이 가장 적절하다.

구문풀이
1행 [One of the greatest values of cross-cultural comparisons] **is** [that they can tell us {**whether** a developmental phenomenon is or is not universal}].

: 첫 번째 [ ]가 문장의 주어부이고 주어의 핵은 one이므로 단수형 동사 is가 쓰였다. 두 번째 [ ]는 주격보어 역할을 하는 명사절이며, 그 안의 { }는 tell의 직접목적어 역할을 하는 명사절(~인지 아닌지)이다.

어휘풀이
- comparison *n* 비교
- masculine *a* 남성의
- inevitably *ad* 필연적으로
- thought-provoking *a* 깊이 생각하게 하는, 시사하는 바가 큰
- phenomenon *n* 현상
- feminine *a* 여성의
- anthropologist *n* 인류학자

- aggressive *a* 공격적인
- unresponsive *a* 둔감한
- dominant *a* 지배적인
- have more to do with ~와 더 관련 있다
- collective *a* 집단의, 공동의
- sensitive *a* 민감한, 예민한
- passive *a* 수동적인
- assertive *a* 당당한, 명확히 표현하는
- comparative *a* 상대적인, 비교적인

082 ②	083 ⑤	084 ①	085 ④	086 ②
087 ③	088 ⑤	089 ⑤	090 ②	091 ③
092 ⑤	093 ④	094 ④	095 ⑤	

082~083 답 ② / ⑤

📖 언론과의 접촉 여부에 대한 과학자의 개인적 선택

전문해석

이야기를 과대광고하는 것의 원인이 되는 것을 피하는 한 가지 방법은 아무 말도 하지 않는 것일 수 있다. 그러나 그것은 대중과 정책 입안자에게 정보를 전하고/전하거나 제안을 제공해야 한다는 강한 책임감을 느끼는 과학자들에게는 현실적인 선택안이 아니다. **언론 구성원들과의 대화는 메시지를 알려지게 하고 아마 호의적인 인정을 받을 수 있다는 장점이 있지만, 오해를 일으키고 반복적인 해명이 필요하며 끝없는 논란에 얽힐 위험을 감수한다. 따라서 언론과 대화할지 여부는 아주 개인적으로 결정되는 경향이 있다.** 수십 년 전에 지구과학자들이 언론의 흥미를 끄는 연구 결과를 가지는 것은 드문 일이었고, 따라서 언론과의 접촉이 예상되거나 권장되는 일은 거의 없었다. 1970년대에는, 언론과 자주 대화하는 소수의 과학자들은 흔히 그렇게 한 것에 대해 동료 과학자들로부터 비난을 받았다. 지금은 상황이 아주 다른데, 많은 과학자가 지구 온난화와 관련 문제의 중요성 때문에 공개적으로 말해야 한다는 책임감을 느끼고 있으며 많은 기자도 이런 감정들을 공유하고 있기 때문이다. 게다가, 많은 과학자는 자신이 언론의 주목과 그에 따른 대중의 인정을 즐기고 있다는 사실을 알아 가고 있다. 동시에, 다른 과학자들은 기자들과의 대화를 계속 물리치며, 그렇게 함으로써 자신의 과학을 위해 더 많은 시간을 지켜 내고, 잘못 인용되는 위험과 언론 보도와 관련된 다른 불쾌한 상황을 감수한다(→ 피한다).

정답풀이

082 과학자가 언론과 대화를 하면 메시지를 알리고 호의적인 인정을 받을 수 있다는 장점이 있지만 오해를 일으키고 해명할 필요와 논란의 위험이 있어서 언론과 대화할지의 여부는 개인적으로 결정되는 경향이 있는데, 최근 일부 지구과학자들은 지구 온난화와 관련 문제에 대해 언론을 통해 공개적으로 말하기도 하지만 다른 과학자들은 여전히 언론과의 대화를 물리치고 있다는 내용의 글이다. 따라서 글의 제목으로 가장 적절한 것은 ② '과학자의 선택: 언론과 접할 것인가, 말 것인가?'이다.

083 최근 많은 과학자들이 언론과 접하고 있지만, 일부 다른 과학자들은 언론과의 대화를 계속 물리치며 과학을 위한 더 많은 시간을 지켜 내고 잘못 인용되는 위험이나 언론 보도와 관련된 불쾌한 상황을 피하려 한다는 맥락이 적절하므로, (e) running(감수하다)을 avoiding(피하다)과 같은 낱말로 바꿔야 한다.

오답풀이

082 ① 과학자와 언론 간의 골치 아픈 관계

③ 과학자여! 언론에 말할 때 조심하시오
> 과학자의 메시지가 언론을 통해 공개될 때 오해나 논란을 불러일으킬 위험이 있으므로 언론과의 대화 여부는 과학자가 개인적으로 결정할 문제라는 내용이다.

일부 과학자가 언론과 접해서 생기는 오해나 곤란한 상황을 피한다는 것

④ 과학적 진실과 언론의 주목에 대한 딜레마

⑤ 누가 기후 문제에 책임이 있나, 과학자인가, 언론인가?

083 ① 언론과의 대화를 통해 메시지를 알리고 호의적인 인정을 받을 수 있다는 것은 언론과의 접촉이 가진 장점이라고 할 수 있으므로 advantages(장점들)는 문맥상 적절하다.

② 수십 년 전에 지구과학자가 언론과 접촉하는 것이 예상되거나 권장되는 일이 거의 없었던 것은 그들이 언론의 흥미를 끄는 연구 결과를 가지는 일이 드물었기 때문이라고 볼 수 있으므로 unusual(드문)은 문맥상 적절하다.

③ 지금은 과학자나 기후 문제에 대해 공개적으로 의견을 발표하는 것이 필요하다고 생각하지만, 과거에는 언론과 대화하는 과학자들이 동료들로부터 비판받았을 것이므로 criticized(비판받은)는 문맥상 적절하다.

④ 과학자가 언론과 접촉해도 된다고 생각하는 현재의 상황과 관련된 추가 진술이므로, 과학자들이 언론의 주목과 대중의 인정을 '즐기고(enjoy)' 있다는 문맥은 적절하다.

구문풀이

1행 However, that is not a realistic option for scientists [who feel a strong sense of responsibility] {to **inform** the public and policymakers} and/or {to **offer** suggestions}].

: [ ]는 scientists를 수식하는 주격 관계대명사절이고, 그 안에 두 개의 { }는 a strong sense of responsibility를 수식하는 형용사적 용법의 to부정사구로 병렬구조를 이루고 있다.

3행 [Speaking with members of the media] **has** advantages in [**getting** a message out] and [perhaps **receiving** favorable recognition], / but it runs [the risk of misinterpretations, the need for repeated clarifications, and entanglement in never-ending controversy].

: 두 개의 등위절이 but으로 연결된 문장이다. but 앞에서 첫 번째 [ ]는 주어 역할을 하는 동명사구이고, 동사는 has이다. 두 번째와 세 번째 [ ]는 전치사 in의 목적어 역할을 하는 동명사구로 병렬구조를 이룬다. 네 번째 [ ]는 runs의 목적어인 명사구로 「A, B, and C」의 형태로 되어 있다.

7행 Decades ago, **it** was unusual [for Earth scientists **to have** results {that were of interest to the media}], / and consequently few media contacts were expected or encouraged.

: it은 형식상의 주어이고 [ ]의 to부정사구가 내용상의 주어이며, for Earth scientists는 to have ~의 의미상 주어를 나타낸다. { }는 results를 수식하는 주격 관계대명사절이다.

13행 At the same time, other scientists continue to resist speaking with reporters, [thereby **preserving** more time for their science and **avoiding** the risk of being misquoted and the other unpleasantries {associated with media coverage}].

: [ ]는 결과를 나타내는 분사구문으로 preserving ~과 avoiding ~이 병렬로 연결되어 있고, { }는 the other unpleasantries를 수식하는 과거분사구이다.

어휘풀이

- contribute to ~의 원인이 되다, ~에 기여하다
- recognition *n* 인정
- run the risk of ~의 위험을 무릅쓰다[감수하다]
- misinterpretation *n* 오해
- clarification *n* 해명
- controversy *n* 논란, 논쟁
- fellow *n* 동료
- resist *v* 저항하다
- thereby *ad* 그렇게 함으로써
- preserve *v* 지키다, 보존하다
- misquote *v* (말이나 글을) 잘못 인용하다
- unpleasantry *n* 불쾌한 상황, 불쾌한 사건
- associated with ~와 관련된
- coverage *n* (언론의) 보도

084~085 답 ① / ④

📖 예측이나 의사 결정을 할 때 도움이 되는 간단한 공식

전문해석

매우 간단한 알고리즘조차도 간단한 예측 문제에 대한 전문가의 판단을 능가할 수 있다는 증거가 있다. 예를 들어, 가석방으로 풀려날 죄수가 계속해서 다른 범죄를 저지를 것인지 예측하거나, 잠재적인 후보자가 장차 직장에서 일을 잘할 것인지를 예측하는 데 알고리즘이 인간보다 더 정확하다는 것이 입증되었다. 많은 다른 영역에 걸친 100개가 넘는 연구에서, 모든 사례의 절반은 **간단한 공식이 인간 전문가보다 중요한 예측을 더 잘하고**, 그 나머지(아주 적은 소수를 제외하고)는 둘 사이의 무승부를 보여준다. 관련된 많은 다른 요인이 있고 상황이 매우 불확실할 때, 가장 중요한 요소에 초점을 맞추고 일관성을 유지함으로써 간단한 공식이 승리할 수 있는 반면, 인간의 판단은 특히 두드러지고 아마도 관련이 없는 고려 사항에 의해 너무 쉽게 영향을 받는다. 사람들이 편안하다고(→ 일이 너무 많다고) 느낄 때 중요한 조치나 고려 사항을 놓치지 않도록 함으로써 '체크리스트'가 다양한 영역에서 전문가의 결정의 질을 향상할 수 있다는 추가적인 증거가 유사한 아이디어를 뒷받침한다. 예를 들어, 집중 치료 중인 환자를 치료하려면 하루에 수백 가지의 작은 조치가 필요할 수 있으며, 작은 실수 하나로 목숨을 잃게 할 수 있다. 어떠한 중요한 조치라도 놓치지 않기 위해 체크리스트를 사용하는 것은 당면한 감염을 예방하는 것에서부터 폐렴을 줄이는 것에 이르기까지 다양한 의학적 상황에서 현저하게 효과적이라는 것이 입증되었다.

정답풀이

084 간단한 예측 문제에서 알고리즘이 인간 전문가보다 더 뛰어나며, 알고리즘처럼 인간도 체크리스트와 같은 간단한 공식을 마련해서 이용하면 다양한 영역에서 결정의 질을 향상할 수 있다는 내용의 글이다. 따라서 글의 제목으로 가장 적절한 것은 ① '의사 결정을 할 때의 간단한 공식의 힘'이다.

085 집중 치료 중인 환자에게 하루에 수백 가지의 작은 조치가 필요한 상황처럼 해야 할 일에 과부하가 걸릴 때, 중요한 사항을 놓치지 않도록 체크리스트를 만들어 활용하면 실수를 줄여 의사 결정의 질을 높이게 될 것이라는 맥락이므로, (d) relaxed(편안한)를 overloaded(일이 너무 많은) 정도의 단어로 바꿔야 한다.

오답풀이

084 ② 항상 우선순위를 결정하라: 빅 데이터 관리 요령
③ 알고리즘의 실수: 단순함의 신화
④ 준비하라! 만일의 경우를 대비해 체크리스트를 만들어라
└ 간단한 공식을 활용하면 의사 결정의 질을 향상시킬 수 있다는 주제를 설명하기 위해 간단한 공식의 예시로 든 체크리스트를 이용한 함정 오답! 너무 지엽적인 제목을 고르지 않도록 주의해야 한다.
⑤ 인간의 판단이 알고리즘을 이기는 방법

085 ① 알고리즘의 예측 능력은 인간을 능가한다는 증거에 대한 사례이므로 알고리즘의 예측이 인간보다 더 '정확하다(accurate)'는 문맥은 적절하다.
② 알고리즘과 같은 간단한 공식이 인간 전문가보다 예측을 '더 잘한다(better)'는 흐름은 문맥상 적절하다.
③ 중요한 요소에 초점을 맞추고 일관성을 유지하는 간단한 공식과는 달리, 인간은 '관련 없는(irrelevant)' 사항에도 영향을 받는다는 문맥은 적절하다.
└ 간단한 공식의 일관성 유지와 대조되고 있다는 점을 놓치고 관련이 있는 것의 영향을 받는다는 일반적인 생각으로 고를 수 있는 오답!
⑤ 의사 결정의 질을 향상시키는 간단한 공식의 예시로 체크리스를 들고 있으므로 체크리스트의 이용은 '효과적(effective)'이라는 문맥은 적절하다.

구문풀이

12행 [When {there are a lot of different factors involved} and {a situation is very uncertain}], simple formulas can win out **by** [**focusing** on the most important factors] and [**being** consistent], [while human judgement is too easily influenced by particularly salient and perhaps irrelevant considerations].

: 첫 번째 [ ]는 때를 나타내는 부사절로, 그 안에 { }로 표시된 두 개의 절이 and로 연결되어 있다. 두 번째와 세 번째 [ ]는 전치사 by에 이어지는 동명사구로 and에 의해 병렬구조로 연결되어 있으며, 「by+-ing」는 '~함으로써'라는 의미를 나타낸다. 네 번째 [ ]는 대조를 나타내는 부사절이다.

17행 A similar idea is supported by **further evidence** [that 'checklists' can improve the quality of expert decisions in a range of domains **by** {ensuring <that important steps or considerations aren't missed (when people are feeling overloaded)>}].

: [ ]는 further evidence와 동격 관계를 이루는 명사절이고, 그 안의 { }는 by의 목적어 역할을 하는 동명사구이다. < >는 ensuring의 목적어 역할을 하는 명사절이고, 그 안의 ( )는 때를 나타내는 부사절이다.

24행 [Using checklists {to ensure (that no crucial steps are missed)}] **has proved** to be remarkably effective in a range of medical contexts, **from** preventing live infections **to** reducing pneumonia.

: [ ]는 문장의 주어로 쓰인 동명사구이고, 문장의 동사는 has proved이다. [ ] 안의 { }는 목적을 나타내는 부사적 용법의 to부정사구이고, ( )는 ensure의 목적어 역할을 하는 명사절이다. 「from A to B: A에서 B까지」의 구문이 사용되고 있다.

어휘풀이
- outperform *v* ~을 능가하다
- accurate *a* 정확한
- commit *v* (범죄를) 저지르다
- candidate *n* 후보
- formula *n* 공식
- remainder *n* 나머지
- consistent *a* 일관성이 있는
- ensure *v* 확실하게 하다, 보장하다
- intensive care 집중 치료
- crucial *a* 중요한
- context *n* 상황, 맥락
- infection *n* 감염
- expert *a* 전문가의 *n* 전문가
- release *v* 풀어주다
- potential *a* 잠재적인
- domain *n* 영역
- significant *a* 중대한, 유의미한
- handful *n* 소수, 한줌
- irrelevant *a* 관련이 없는
- step *n* 조치
- cost *v* (목숨, 일 등을) 잃게 하다
- remarkably *ad* 현저하게
- live *a* 당면한, 생생한

086~087 답 ② / ③

언어의 본질적 특성으로 내재된 분류

전문해석
사물들을 묶어서 그룹으로 분류하는 것은 우리가 항상 하는 일이며, 그 이유를 이해하는 것은 어렵지 않다. 음식이 진열대에 마구잡이로 배열된 슈퍼마켓에서 쇼핑하려고 한다고 상상해 보라. 한 통로에서는 흰빵 옆에 토마토 수프가 있고, 치킨 수프는 뒤쪽에 있는 60와트 백열 전구 옆에 있고, 한 크림치즈 브랜드는 앞쪽에, 또 다른 하나는 쿠키 근처의 8번 통로에 있다. 여러분이 원하는 것을 찾는 일은, 불가능하지는 않더라도, 시간이 많이 걸리고 매우 어려울 것이다.
슈퍼마켓의 경우, 누군가는 분류 체계를 설계해야 했다. 하지만 우리 언어에 포함되어 있는 이미 만들어진 분류 체계도 있다. 예를 들어, '개'라는 단어는 특정 부류의 동물들을 함께 분류하여 다른 동물들과 구별한다. 분류라고 하기에는 그러한 분류가 너무 추상적으로(→ 분명해) 보일 수 있지만, 이것은 단지 여러분이 이미 그 단어를 숙달했기 때문이다. 말하기를 배우는 아이로서, 여러분은 부모님이 가르쳐주려 애썼던 분류 체계를 익히기 위해 열심히 노력해야 했다. 여러분이 그것을 이해하기 전에, 아마 고양이를 개라고 부르는 것과 같은 실수를 했을 것이다. 만약 여러분이 말하기를 배우지 않았다면, 온 세상이 정돈되지 않은 슈퍼마켓처럼 보일 것이다. 여러분은 모든 물건이 새롭고 낯선 유아의 처지에 있을 것이다. 그러므로 분류의 원리를 배우는 때, 우리는 언어의 핵심에 있는 구조에 대해 배우고 있는 것이다.

정답풀이
086 슈퍼마켓에서의 물건 분류 방식을 예로 들어 인간 언어에 내재된 분류적 특성에 대해 설명하는 글이다. 우리는 아이일 때 부모가 가르쳐주는 언어 분류 체계를 배우고, 우리가 말을 배우지 않았다면 세상은 정돈되지 않은 슈퍼마켓처럼 보일 것이며, 분류의 원리를 배울 때 우리는 언어의 핵심에 있는 구조에 대해 배우고 있다고 했으므로, 글의 제목으로 가장 적절한 것은 ② '분류: 언어의 본질적 특성'이다.
087 '개'라는 단어는 특정 부류의 동물들을 함께 분류하여 다른 동물들과 구별하는데, 우리가 '개'라는 단어를 이미 숙달하여 알고 있기 때문에 너무나 '추상적'으로 보일 수 있다는 문맥은 어색하다. 따라서 (c) abstract(추상적인)를 obvious(분명한) 정도의 단어로 바꿔야 한다.

오답풀이
086 ① 영업과 언어학습 전략의 유사점
③ 범주화를 통한 언어학적 문제 탐색
④ 기성의 분류 시스템이 정말 더 나은가?
⑤ 언어 교육에서 분류 활용의 딜레마
↳ 언어를 배우면서 분류 체계를 학습하고 이해하게 된다는 내용으로, 분류 활용의 딜레마에 대한 언급이 없다.
087 ① 물건들이 아무렇게나 배치된 슈퍼마켓에서 원하는 것을 찾으려면 '시간이 많이 소요될' 것이므로 time-consuming은 문맥상 적절하다.
② 슈퍼마켓에서는 소비자가 물건을 쉽게 찾을 수 있도록 분류 체계를 '설계해야' 한다는 것을 추론할 수 있으므로 design은 문맥상 적절하다.
④ 분류 체계를 이해하기 전에는 고양이를 개로 부르는 것 같은 실수를 했을 것이라는 내용이 이어지므로 말을 배울 때 분류 체계를 '배우기(learn)' 위해 열심히 노력해야 했다는 흐름은 적절하다.
⑤ 말하기를 배우지 않았다면 언어의 분류 체계를 배우지 못했을 것이고, 그러면 세상은 마치 물건들이 아무렇게나 배치된 슈퍼마켓처럼 보일 것이라 문맥이므로 unorganized(정돈되지 않은)의 쓰임은 적절하다.

구문풀이
1행 [Classifying things together into groups] **is** something [we do all the time], / and it isn't hard to see why.

: 첫 번째 [ ]는 주어로 쓰인 동명사구이며 하나의 개념으로 보아 단수 취급하기 때문에 단수형 동사 is가 쓰였다. 두 번째 [ ]는 something을 수식하는 관계절로 앞에 목적격 관계대명사 that이 생략되었다.

22행 If you **hadn't learned** to speak, / the whole world **would seem** like the unorganized supermarket; you **would be** in the position of an infant, [for whom every object is new and unfamiliar].

: 조건절에 가정법 과거완료 시제인 「had+과거분사」가, 주절에 가정법 과거 시제인 「조동사의 과거형(would)+동사원형」이 쓰인 혼합가정법 문장으로, 과거의 일이 현재에 영향을 미칠 때 그것을 반대로 가정하여 표현한다. [ ]는 an infant를 부연 설명하는 계속적 용법의 관계대명사절이다.

어휘풀이
- classify *v* 분류하다
- random *a* 마구잡이로 하는
- light bulb 백열 전구
- time-consuming *a* 시간이 많이 걸리는
- ready-made *a* 기성의, 이미 만들어진
- embody *v* 포함하다
- abstract *a* 추상적인
- get the hang of ~을 이해하다
- infant *n* 유아
- arrange *v* 배열[배치]하다
- aisle *n* 통로
- distinguish *v* 구별하다
- master *v* 숙달하다
- unorganized *a* 정돈되지 않은
- unfamiliar *a* 낯선

- core *n* 핵심
- inherent *a* 본질적인, 본래의

088~089 답 ⑤ / ⑤

📖 자신의 내면에 대한 이해를 늘릴 필요성

전문해석

우리 인생에 겉으로 보이는 것보다 훨씬 더 많은 생각, 감정, 기억, 환상, 그리고 욕망이 있다는 것을 깨닫는 것은 도움이 될 수 있다. 우리는 우리 내면세계의 한 부분에만 익숙한 한편 다른 부분에 대해서는 모르는 상태이다. 우리가 이해하지 못하는 경험들에 시달릴 때 결정적인 조치는 우리의 감정적인 삶의 덜 의식적인 영역에서 그것들의 기원을 찾아보는 것일지도 모른다. 우리가 모르는 채 우리의 삶을 결정하는 감정과 욕망, 상상력의 하위 흐름을 발견하는 것은 중요하다. 우리가 성공하면 무의식적인 감정적인 사건은 의식적인 경험으로 바뀐다. 이런 과정의 일부는 내면세계에 대한 점점 커지는 각성, 그것에 대해 말로 표현하는 것, 그리고 억압되고 가려진 동기의 숨겨진 논리와 원동력이 드러날 수 있게 하는 전기적 이해이다. 이런 과정의 끝에 나는 나의 내면세계에 대해 더 잘 알 수 있게 된다. 그리고 그것은 그저 아는 데서 멈추지 않는다. 자신을 더 잘 알게 되는 것은 해방적 변화와 더 큰 내면의 자율성으로 이어질 수 있다. 강박적 욕망과 불가해한 통제 불능의 감정들이 내가 그것들을 나 자신에게 설명한 다음에는 제어하기가 더 쉽고 어쩌면 심지어 온전히 사라질지도 모른다. 그것들은 불필요한 것이 된다. 이전에 이물질처럼 보였던 많은 경험이 점점 더 커지는 이해를 통해 그것의 낯섦을 잃게 되고 그 사람의 일부로 인식될 수 있고, 그것들이 '자신의 것이 될 수 있고' 자신의 감정적인 정체성의 명시적 일부로 만들어질 수 있다. 이렇게 자기 것으로 만든다는 것은 그것들이 더 이상 내면의 자율성을 고양하지(→ 위협하지) 않는다는 것을 의미한다.

정답풀이

088 자신의 무의식적인 내면을 탐구하여 이해하게 되면 통제하기 어려웠던 무의식적 감정 상태를 의식적으로 제어할 수 있는 자신의 것으로 바꿀 수 있고 내면의 자율성을 높일 수 있다는 내용이므로, 글의 제목으로는 ⑤ '내면적으로 자기이해를 확장할 필요성'이 가장 적절하다.

089 자기 이해가 커지면 이질적인 것으로 여겨지던 통제 불능의 감정들이 제어되고 그것들이 내면의 자율성을 더 이상 위협하지 않는다는 맥락이 자연스러우므로, (e) enhance(고양하다)를 threaten(위협하다) 정도의 낱말로 바꿔야 한다.

오답풀이

088 ① 내면의 자율성은 중요하지만 이루기 어렵다
② 내면의 갈등을 해결하려면 상담을 구해야 한다
③ 감정적인 반응이 여러분의 태도를 지시하도록 하지 말라
④ 무의식적 욕망: 일상생활의 숨은 장애물
089 ① 우리가 이해하지 못하는 경험들에 시달릴 때는 우리의 감정적인 삶의 '덜' 의식적인 영역에서 그것의 기원을 찾아야 할 것이라는 맥락이므로 less는 문맥상 적절하다.
② 무의식적인 감정적인 사건을 의식적인 경험으로 바꾸는 것은 내면세계에 대한 '각성'이 점점 커졌기 때문이므로 alertness는 문맥상 적절하다.
③ 억압되고 가려진 내면의 동기를 파악하는 것은 자신의 내면세계를 더 잘 알게 되는 것이므로 gain(얻다)은 문맥상 적절하다.
④ 자신의 감정의 원인을 자신에게 설명할 수 있게 됨으로써 그것을 '제어하기'가 더 쉬워진다는 맥락이므로 control은 문맥상 적절하다.

구문풀이

8행 **It** is important [**to uncover** the sub-streams of emotion, desire and imagination {that determine our life without us knowing

it}].

: It은 형식상의 주어이고 [ ]의 to부정사구가 내용상의 주어이다. { }는 the sub-streams of emotion, desire and imagination을 수식하는 주격 관계대명사절이다.

12행 Part of this process is [a growing alertness towards the inner world, / a verbal articulation of **it** / and a biographical understanding {that **allows** the hidden logic and dynamic of repressed and covered-up motives **to come** to light}].

: [ ]는 문장의 주격보어로 쓰인 명사구로 「*A*, *B* and *C*」의 구조로 되어 있고, 대명사 it은 the inner world를 가리킨다. { }는 a biographical understanding을 수식하는 주격 관계대명사절이고, 「allow+목적어+to부정사(목적격보어)」는 '~가 …하게 하다'라는 의미이다.

어휘풀이

- plague *v* 시달리게[성가시게] 하다
- uncover *v* 발견하다
- alertness *n* 각성
- articulation *n* 말로 표현함
- repressed *a* 억압된
- autonomy *n* 자율성
- dissolve *v* 사라지다
- identity *n* 정체성
- decisive *a* 결정적인
- sub-stream *n* 하위 흐름
- verbal *a* 말의, 언어적인
- biographical *a* 전기적인
- liberating *a* 해방적인
- compulsive *a* 강박적인
- explicit *a* 명시적인

090~091 답 ② / ③

📖 영리한 기계와 알고리즘으로 인해 사라질 인간의 직업들

전문해석

만약 인간이 택시뿐만 아니라 차량을 운전하는 것을 완전히 금지하고 컴퓨터 알고리즘에 교통에 대한 독점권을 준다면, 그러면 우리는 모든 차량을 하나의 네트워크에 연결할 수 있고, 그리하여 자동차 사고를 훨씬 덜 일어나게 만들 수 있다. 2015년 8월에 구글의 실험용 자율주행차들 중 한 대가 사고를 당했다. 그 차는 건널목에 접근해 보행자가 건너기를 원한다는 것을 감지했을 때, 그것의 브레이크를 밟았다. 잠시 후 그것은 부주의한 인간 운전자가 아마도 길을 보는 대신 우주의 신비에 대해 생각하고 있던 한 세단형 자동차에 의해 뒤를 받혔다. '두' 차량 모두 서로 연결된 컴퓨터에 의해 안내되었다면 이런 일은 일어날 수 없었을 것이다. 제어 알고리즘은 도로 위의 모든 차량의 위치와 의도를 알고 있었을 것이고, 그것의 꼭두각시들 중 둘이 충돌하는 것을 허용하지 않았을 것이다. 그러한 시스템은 많은 시간, 돈 그리고 인간의 생명을 구할[절약할] 것이지만, 또한 차를 운전하는 인간의 경험과 수천만 개의 인간의 일자리를 만들어 낼(→ 없앨) 것이다.
일부 경제학자들은 조만간 개선되지 않은 인간들은 완전히 쓸모없게 될 것이라고 예측한다. 로봇과 3D 프린터는 이미 셔츠 제작과 같은 육체노동에서 노동자들을 대체하고 있으며, 고도로 영리한 알고리즘은 사무직에도 동일한 것을 할 것이다. 얼마 전에는 자동화로부터 완전히 안전해 보였던 은행 직원과 여행사 직원들이 멸종위기에 처한 종이 되었다. 스마트폰을 사용해 알고리즘으로부터 비행기 표를 살 수 있을 때, 얼마나 많은 여행사 직원이 필요할까? 증권거래소 거래자들도 위기에 처해 있다. 오늘날 대부분의 금융 거래는 이미 1년에 사람이 할 수 있는 것보다 더 많은 데이터를 1초 안에 처리할 수 있고 사람이 눈을 깜빡일 수 있는 것보다 훨씬 더 빨리 데이터에 반응할 수 있는 컴퓨터 알고리즘에 의해 처리되고 있다.

정답풀이

090 지능을 갖춘 기계가 점차 인간이 해야 할 일을 빼앗아가고 있다는 것이 글의 핵심이므로, 글의 제목으로 가장 적절한 것은 ② '컴퓨터가 인류를 대체하는 길을 가고 있다'이다.

091 컴퓨터 알고리즘을 이용한 자율 운행 시스템이 우리의 시간과 돈을 절약해 주고 우리의 생명을 구해 줄 수 있지만, 자동차를 운전하는 인간의 경험

및 일자리를 빼앗아갈 것이라는 문맥이다. 따라서 (c) generate(만들어 내다)를 eliminate(없애다, 제거하다) 정도의 단어로 바꿔야 한다.

오답풀이

090 ① 인공지능은 그것이 없애는 것보다 더 많은 일자리를 창출할 것이다
③ 인공지능은 인간의 지능을 대체하는 것이 아니라 확장시킬 것이다
④ 컴퓨터 알고리즘의 장단점
⑤ 우리는 초지능 기계를 제어할 수 없을 것이다
  └→ 인공지능이 점점 인간의 일자리를 빼앗는다는 글의 핵심을 확대 해석한 함정 오답! 이처럼 글의 주제와 같은 방향이지만 너무 포괄적인 선택지를 고르지 않도록 주의해야 한다.

091 ① 자율 운행 시스템은 컴퓨터 알고리즘이 모든 것을 통제하는 시스템이므로 '독점권'이라는 의미의 monopoly는 문맥상 적절하다.
② 자율주행차량은 보행자를 감지하고 멈췄지만, 인간이 운전하는 그 뒤의 차량은 그러지 못해서 자율주행차량을 받았다고 했으므로 두 차량이 '서로 연결된(interlinked)' 하나의 컴퓨터에 의해 안내되었다면 그런 사고는 일어나지 않았을 것이라는 흐름은 자연스럽다.
④ 이미 여러 육체노동에서 로봇이 인간을 대체하고 있고, 앞으로는 사무직에서도 그럴 것이라는 내용이 이어지므로 일부 경제학자들이 개선되지 않은 인간들은 '쓸모없게(useless)' 될 것이라고 예측한다는 문맥은 자연스럽다.
⑤ 컴퓨터 알고리즘이 인간의 일을 하며 점차 인간을 대체하고 있는 상황이라고 했으므로 이전에는 컴퓨터 알고리즘, 즉 '자동화(automation)'로부터 안전해 보였던 사람들도 위협받는다는 흐름은 자연스럽다.

구문풀이

13행 The controlling algorithm **would have known** the position and intentions of every vehicle on the road, and **would** not **have allowed** two of its marionettes to collide.

: 「조동사의 과거형+have+과거분사」의 형태를 사용해 과거에 대한 추측을 나타내고 있는데, 가정법 과거완료의 주절 형태로 볼 수도 있다.

31행 Most financial trading today **is** already **being managed** by computer algorithms [that **can process** in a second more data than a human can in a year, and **can react** to the data much faster than a human can blink].

: 현재진행형 수동태가 쓰인 문장이다. [ ]는 computer algorithms를 수식하는 주격 관계대명사절이고, 이 절의 동사인 can process와 can react는 병렬구조를 이룬다.

어휘풀이

- forbid ⓥ 금지하다
- algorithm ⓝ 알고리즘(문제 해결 절차 및 방법)
- monopoly ⓝ 독점(권)
- crossing ⓝ 건널목
- pedestrian ⓝ 보행자
- marionette ⓝ 꼭두각시
- unenhanced ⓐ 향상되지 않은
- manual ⓐ 손으로 하는, 육체노동의
- automation ⓝ 자동화
- blink ⓥ 눈을 깜빡이다
- render ⓥ ~을 …하게 만들다
- detect ⓥ 감지[탐지]하다
- contemplate ⓥ 생각하다
- collide ⓥ 충돌하다
- replace ⓥ 대체하다
- occupation ⓝ 직업
- endangered species 멸종위기 종
- amplify ⓥ 확장하다, 증폭시키다

092~093 답 ⑤ / ④

📖📖 성인기의 성격 패턴을 형성하는 어린 시절의 경험

전문해석

불안한 성격을 가지고 있고, 마음이 계속 의심과 의혹으로 가득 차고, 사회로부터 자신을 고립시키는 방향으로 모든 노력을 기울이는 성인 환자는, 자신의 서너 살 때와 동일한 성격 특성과 심리적인 활동을 갖고 있다. 유일한 차이점은 그러한 특성이 어린 아이들에게서 더 투명하고 보기가 더 쉽다는 것인데, 어린 아이들은 자신의 실제 감정을 숨기는 법을 아직 배우지 못했다. 따라서 우리는 우리 연구의 보다 더 많은 부분을 우리 환자의 어린 시절에 집중시키는 것을 규칙으로 삼았다. 이런 식으로 우리는 종종 우리가 그들의 어린 시절에 대해 익숙해 있던 어떤 성인의 특성을 우리가 그것들에 대해 듣기 전에 추론할 수 있었다. 우리가 그 성인에게서 관찰하는 특성은 사실 어린 시절의 경험에 대한 직접적인 투영이다. 환자의 어린 시절에 대한 가장 생생한 기억을 듣고 이러한 기억을 올바르게 해석하는 방법을 안다면, 우리는 환자의 현재 성격 패턴을 정확하게 구성할 수 있다. 이렇게 할 때 우리는 개인이 어린 시절에 발달시킨 행동의 패턴을 벗어나는 것이 매우 어렵다는 사실을 명심한다. 성인의 삶에서 완전히 다른 상황에 처했을 수도 있지만, 자신의 어린 시절의 행동 패턴을 유지할(→ 바꿀) 수 있었던 사람은 거의 없다. 성년의 태도 변화가 반드시 행동 패턴의 변화로 이어지는 것은 아니다. 정신은 그 기초를 바꾸지 않으며, 사람들은 아동기와 성인기에 같은 성향을 가지고 있어서, 우리로 하여금 그들 성격의 많은 부분 또한 바뀌지 않는다고 추론하도록 이끈다.

정답풀이

092 성인기에 나타나는 성격 특성이나 행동 패턴은 어린 시절의 경험으로 인해 형성된 것이 그대로 투영된 것이라는 내용이 글의 핵심이다. 따라서 글의 제목으로 가장 적절한 것은 ⑤ '어린 시절의 경험, 인간 정신의 토대'이다.

093 어린 시절의 경험으로 인해 형성된 행동 패턴은 성인기에 그대로 나타나고 여기에서 벗어날 수 없다는 문맥이므로 (d) maintain(유지하다)을 change(바꾸다) 정도의 어휘로 바꿔야 한다.

오답풀이

092 ① 본성 대 양육, 어떤 것이 더 영향력이 있는가?
② 성격의 발달에 영향을 미치는 요인들
③ 왜 어떤 행동 패턴은 매우 변하기 쉬운가?
④ 어린 시절의 심리적인 문제를 극복하는 법

093 ① 정신적인 문제를 겪는 성인 환자의 치료를 위해 환자의 어린 시절에 집중하는 것을 규칙으로 삼았으며, 그러한 성인들에게서 관찰되는 특성은 어린 시절의 경험에 대한 직접적인 투영이라는 내용이 뒤에 나오므로, 환자가 어린 시절과 '동일한(identical)' 성격 특성과 심리적인 활동을 갖고 있다는 문맥은 자연스럽다.
② 정신적인 문제를 겪는 성인 환자와 어린 아이들의 유일한 차이점은 어린 아이들의 특성이 더 투명하고 쉽게 보인다는 것이라고 했으므로 어린 아이들이 자신의 감정을 잘 '숨기지(hide)' 못한다는 흐름은 자연스럽다.
③ 정신적인 문제를 겪는 성인 환자에게서 관찰되는 특성은 그들의 어린 시절의 경험에 대한 직접적인 투영이라고 했으므로, 환자의 어린 시절 기억을 올바르게 해석할 수 있다면 그들의 현재 성격 패턴을 정확하게 '구성할(construct)' 수 있다는 흐름은 자연스럽다.
⑤ 정신적인 문제를 겪는 성인 환자의 예시에서 볼 수 있듯이, 사람들은 대부분 어린 시절의 성향을 성인기까지 이어간다고 할 수 있으므로 우리 성격의 많은 부분이 '바뀌지 않는다(unaltered)'는 흐름은 자연스럽다.

구문풀이

1행 A mature patient [**who** has an anxious personality], [**whose** mind is constantly filled with doubts and suspicions], [**whose** every effort is directed towards isolating himself from society], **had** identical character traits and psychological activity in his third and fourth year of life.

: A mature patient가 문장의 핵심 주어이고 had가 동사이다. [ ]로 표시된 세 개의 관계절은 모두 A mature patient를 수식한다.

11행 In this way we were often able to infer the characteristics of a mature person [**whose** childhood we were familiar with] before we were told about **them**.

: [ ]는 a mature person을 수식하는 소유격 관계대명사절이며, them은 the characteristics of ~ familiar with를 가리킨다.

어휘풀이

- suspicion *n* 의심, 의혹
- trait *n* 특성
- investigation *n* 연구
- projection *n* 투사, 투영
- recollection *n* 기억, 회상
- extremely *ad* 아주, 극도로
- foundation *n* 기초, 토대
- tendency *n* 성향, 경향
- deduce *v* 추론하다
- changeable *a* 변하기 쉬운
- isolate *v* 고립시키다
- transparent *a* 투명한
- characteristic *n* 특성
- vivid *a* 생생한
- bear ~ in mind ~을 명심하다
- psyche *n* 정신, 마음
- retain *v* 보유하다, 간직하다
- maturity *n* 성숙, 완성
- unaltered *a* 바뀌지 않은, 변하지 않은

094~095 답 ④ / ⑤

📖 **인터넷 투표의 문제점**

전문해석

해가 지날수록 인터넷은 우리 생활에 더욱 통합되고 있다. 인터넷에 대한 신뢰는 점점 더 중요해진다. 이는 인터넷 투표의 경우에 특히 그러한데, 그것은 민주주의의 미래에 매우 중요한 역할을 할 수도 있다. 인터넷 투표는 주주 투표를 목적으로 기업들에 의해 이미 널리 사용되어 왔다. 하지만 민주적 선거를 위해 인터넷 투표를 사용하는 것은 특정한 문제들을 동시에 가져올 것이라는 점을 인식해야 한다. **인터넷은 부정, (신원) 확인 문제 및 배타성이라는 완전히 새로운 가능성을 열고, 이는 선거에 잠재적으로 파괴적인 영향을 미칠 수 있다.** 인터넷 투표가 극복해야 할 한 가지 장애물은 현재의 '디지털 양극화'이다. 즉, 이론상으로 인터넷 투표는 일반 대중을 위해 투표를 더 접근 가능하게 만들지만, 실제로는 부자들이 인터넷 접속을 할 가능성이 훨씬 더 크기 때문에 부유한 유권자와 가난한 유권자들 사이의 격차를 더 넓히는 데 기여할 뿐이다. 이 문제 외에도 발생할 다양한 새로운 보안 문제가 있다. 인터넷 신뢰성에 관한 논의에서 반복되는 주제는 (신원) 확인의 문제이고, 이는 특히 인터넷 투표의 상황에서 문제가 될 것이다. 투표가 투표소에서 멀리 떨어진 곳에서 일어나고 있을 것이기 때문에 유권자가 투표하는 동안 제3자가 그 자리에 있을 수 있어서 유권자 매수나 강압의 기회가 또한 더 클 것이다. 마지막으로, 해커가 유권자 데이터를 조작하거나 다른 어떤 식으로든 시스템을 교란시킬 위험이 항상 존재한다. 이러한 문제들을 처리할 수 있다고 하더라도 인터넷 투표가 현행 투표 방식보다 덜 믿을 만하다는 대중의 인식이 있는 한 인터넷 투표는 대중의 의심을 부추기도록(→ 잠재우도록) 개선되어야 한다. 현재의 투표 절차에서 이미 확립되어 있는 정도로 인터넷 투표에 대한 신뢰가 확립될 수 없다면 그것은 채택되어서는 안 된다.

정답풀이

094 인터넷 투표는 선거에 잠재적으로 파괴적인 영향을 미칠 수 있는 부정, 신원 확인 문제, 배타성의 가능성을 열어 주고, 대중은 인터넷 투표가 현행 투표 방식보다 신뢰할 만하지 못하다고 여기므로 현재의 투표 절차만큼 신뢰를 얻으려면 개선되어야 할 점이 있다는 내용의 글이다. 따라서 글의 제목으로 가장 적절한 것은 ④ '새로운 투표 시스템을 채택하는 데 있어서의 신뢰성 문제'이다.

095 인터넷 투표가 현재의 투표 방식보다 신뢰할 만하지 못하다는 대중의 인식이 있는데, 이러한 대중의 의심을 '부추기기' 위해 인터넷 투표가 개선되어야 한다는 흐름은 어색하다. (e) fuel(부추기다)을 put to rest(~을 잠재우다[가라앉히다]) 정도의 표현으로 바꿔야 한다.

오답풀이

094 ① 투표하기, 국민의 권리인가 아니면 의무인가?
② 투표권을 보호하기 위한 다양한 방법
③ 인터넷 투표, 민주주의를 위한 기회
 └ 인터넷 투표가 민주주의의 미래에 매우 중요한 역할을 할 수도 있지만, 여러 가지 극복해야 할 문제가 있고 인터넷 투표에 대한 대중의 신뢰가 확립되지 않으면 채택되어서는 안 된다는 것이 글의 핵심이므로 오답!
⑤ 투표율 높이기, 생각보다 더 어렵다

095 ① 이어지는 내용에서 인터넷이 부정, 신원 확인 문제, 배타성의 가능성을 열어 준 것의 부정적인 결과를 설명하고 있으므로, 이것이 선거에 잠재적으로 '파괴적인(devastating)' 영향을 미칠 수 있다는 문맥은 적절하다.
② 부유한 사람들이 인터넷에 접속할 가능성이 훨씬 더 높으므로, 인터넷 투표가 부유한 유권자들과 가난한 유권자들 사이의 격차를 더 '넓히는(widen)' 데 기여할 것이라는 문맥은 적절하다.
③ 이어지는 내용에서 설명하는 인터넷 투표 시 신원 확인 문제 및 인터넷 해킹 문제는 '보안(security)'과 관련된 문제라고 할 수 있다.
④ 해커들이 유권자 데이터를 '조작할(manipulating)' 위험성이 상존한다는 문맥은 적절하다.

구문풀이

[14행] That is, [**while** in theory Internet balloting would make voting more accessible for the masses], **it** would really only serve to further widen the gap between the rich and the poor voters, [**as** the rich are far more likely to have Internet access].

: 첫 번째 [ ]는 while이 이끄는 양보 부사절이고, 두 번째 [ ]는 as가 이끄는 이유 부사절이다. 주절의 주어인 it은 internet balloting을 가리킨다.

어휘풀이

- integrate *v* 통합하다
- share-holder *n* 주주
- fraud *n* 부정, 사기
- exclusivity *n* 배타성
- hurdle *n* 장애물
- digital divide 디지털 양극화
- the masses 일반 대중
- recurring *a* 반복되는
- polling station 투표소
- trustworthy *a* 신뢰할 수 있는
- turnout *n* 투표율, 투표자 수
- corporation *n* 기업
- bring ~ with it ~을 동시에 가져오다
- verification *n* (신원) 확인, 조회, 검증
- potentially *ad* 잠재적으로
- overcome *v* 극복하다
- balloting *n* 투표
- crop up 발생하다
- problematic *a* 문제가 있는
- disrupt *v* 교란시키다
- refine *v* 개선하다

PART I 어휘 REVIEW

01 글의 주제

01 왜곡하다 02 공개, 폭로, 드러냄 03 약화시키다 04 침식, 침해 05 특성, 속성 06 skeptical 07 ~을 주지 않다, 보류하다 08 제거하다 09 flexibility 10 증폭시키다 11 먹을 수 있는, 식용의 12 정당성, 합법성 13 무시하다, 소홀히 하다 14 regulation 15 영역 16 증식하다, 갑자기 증가하다 17 정권 18 특권을 주다 19 억제하다 20 ~을 방해하다

02 함축 의미 추론

01 적대적인 02 수용하다, 받아들이다 03 엄격한 04 자극하다, 촉진시키다 05 반박하다 06 가설 07 discipline 08 사라지게 하다 09 기준 10 paralyze 11 기업의 12 priority 13 붕괴, 와해 14 구성하다 15 열정, 열의 16 입자 17 대체의, 대안의 18 반증하다 19 유효하지 않은, 근거 없는 20 ~을 되돌아보다[반성하다]

03 어법

01 모호함 02 구별하다 03 자발적으로 04 탐험, 원정 05 조각하다 06 부차적인, 우연의 07 offspring 08 진행되다 09 absorb 10 숨을 헐떡이다 11 분리된, 고립된 12 reproduction 13 뒤의, 차후의 14 지름, 직경 15 뚜렷이 구별되는[다른] 16 신화 17 방법, 절차 18 그리다, 묘사하다 19 기관, 제도 20 ~을 보상하다

04 어휘

01 열망하다 02 양립할 수 없는 03 필연적인, 불가피한 04 의식, 의례 05 위계의, 서열의 06 artificial 07 변수 08 개별적인 09 이용하다 10 abstract 11 강요하다 12 minority 13 해결하다 14 통합 15 지배적인, 우세한 16 논쟁 17 분명히 밝히다 18 단체, 연합 19 결속, 단결 20 포괄적인

05 빈칸 추론(1)

01 전달하다 02 꺼림, 주저함 03 불러일으키다 04 일관성이 있는 05 필수의 06 영역 07 착각, 망상 08 exaggerate 09 비유, 유추 10 주장하다 11 biased 12 정교한 13 intuition 14 검증하다, 확인하다 15 경영진 16 공감하는 17 명제 18 역설적인 19 굴복, 항복, 복종 20 ~에 상응하다

06 빈칸 추론(2)

01 통합하다 02 은유 03 결함 04 탐지하다 05 엄청난, 거대한 06 고집하다, 끈질기게 계속하다 07 mutually 08 제한, 제약 09 수반하다 10 sustainability 11 단절시키다, 분리하다 12 colony 13 달아나다 14 부여하다 15 원초적인 16 희생자 17 공존 18 타협(안) 19 감소시키다 20 대립

07 글의 순서 파악

01 보존하다 02 이론적 근거 03 타고난, 선천적인 04 목록, 일람표 05 생생한 06 집념, 강박 관념 07 hatch 08 의도적인, 고의적인 09 겉으로 보기에, 외관상 10 감정을 상하게 하다 11 neutral 12 수정하다 13 predator 14 집단적인 15 소중히 여기다 16 변화, 차이 17 관용구, 숙어 18 착수하다 19 미신 20 ~이 없는

08 문장 삽입

01 비활성의 02 이행하다 03 일란성의, 동일한 04 성분, 재료 05 전술, 전략 06 구현하다 07 선례, 전례 08 advocate 09 부족한 10 optimal 11 조정하다 12 부분, 조각 13 합의, 해결 14 exceed 15 금지하다 16 거주자 17 명령하다, 법제화하다 18 보상 19 기질, 성질 20 익명성

09 요약문 완성

01 충동, 욕구 02 유의미한, 중요한 03 위로, 위안 04 전념, 매진 05 유발하다 06 자율의, 자치의 07 immigration 08 규정 09 monetary 10 잘못 해석하다 11 평가 12 abandon 13 대안 14 인과 관계의 15 지속적인 16 좌절 17 탄식하다, 후회하다 18 동등한, 상당하는 19 육체노동의, 손으로 하는 20 강화하다

10 장문(1지문 2문항)

01 독점(권) 02 충돌하다 03 나머지 04 본질적인, 본래의 05 추론하다 06 suspicion 07 성숙, 완성 08 생각하다, 심사숙고하다 09 infection 10 결정적인 11 explicit 12 투사, 투영 13 직업 14 기억, 회상 15 투명한 16 금지하다 17 특성 18 관련이 없는 19 부정, 사기 20 강박적인

II 3점 공략 모의고사

096 답 ⑤

📖 실용적 지혜의 일종인 도덕적 재즈

전문해석
재즈 색소폰 연주자인 Stan Getz는, 재즈는 '언어와 같다. 알파벳을 배우는데, 그것은 음계이다. 문장을 배우는데, 그것은 코드이다. 그리고 나서 리허설 없이 호른으로 이야기한다.'라고 말했다. 훌륭한 즉흥 연주는 무에서 유를 창조하는 것이 아니라 이전의 경험, 연습, 지식을 통해 유를 창조하는 것이다. 마찬가지로, 우리는 재즈 음악가들처럼 연습으로 우리 자신을 현명하게 만든다. 상황에 대한 관련 세부 사항을 인식하는 방법을 더 많이 배우고 즉흥으로 하는 것에 대한 기술을 더 많이 쌓을수록, 즉흥적으로 하는 것, 즉 예전의 기술과 지식을 새로운 방식으로 결합하여 예상치 못한 상황에 대처하는 것이 더욱 쉬워진다. 따라서 실용적 지혜는 일종의 '도덕적 재즈'이다. 그것은 때때로 페이지에 적힌 음표와 재즈의 기본 멜로디와 같이 규칙과 원칙에 의존한다. 하지만 규칙만으로는 그 일을 해낼 수 없다. 도덕적 즉흥 연주는 우리가 옳은 일을 하기 위해 이러한 음표와 멜로디를 중심으로 연주하는 해석적인 곡조이다.

정답풀이
재즈 음악가들이 기본적인 음계와 코드를 배우고 나서 리허설 없이 즉흥 연주를 하는 것처럼 우리가 상황의 세부 사항을 인식하는 방법을 배우고 즉흥으로 하는 것에 대한 기술을 쌓을수록 이전의 기술과 지식을 새로운 방식으로 결합하여 예상치 못한 상황에 대처하는 것이 더 쉬워진다는 내용이다. 규칙과 원칙을 상황에 맞게 실행하는 실용적 지혜의 비유적인 표현인 '도덕적 재즈'란 ⑤ '예측할 수 없고 변하기 쉬운 상황에서 올바른 행동을 적용하는 것'이다.

오답풀이
① 참가자들의 합의에 의해 이루어진 올바른 결정
② 사회의 진보를 위한 집단 구성원들의 화합
③ 우리가 좋은 음악을 들을 때 저절로 나타나는 감정의 표현
④ 기본적인 원칙을 따름으로써 이루어지는 효율성 향상

구문풀이
8행 **The more** we learn how to perceive the relevant details of our situations and **the more** we build our skills at improvisation, / **the easier it** becomes **to improvise**—[**to combine** old skills and knowledge in new ways {to deal with the unexpected}].

: '~하면 할수록, 더욱 …하다'를 뜻하는 「the+비교급 ~, the+비교급 …」 구문이 쓰였다. it은 형식상의 주어이고, to improvise가 내용상의 주어이다. [ ]는 to improvise를 구체적으로 설명하는 동격 어구이고, { }는 부사적 용법(결과)의 to부정사구이다.

어휘풀이
- saxophonist *n* 색소폰 연주자　　• scale *n* 음계
- improvisation *n* 즉흥 연주, 즉흥적으로 하기
- perceive *v* 인식하다　　• relevant *a* 관련된
- the unexpected 예상치 못한 일　　• note *n* 음, 음표

- interpretative *a* 해석의
- spontaneous *a* 자발적인, 자연스러운
- enhance *v* 향상시키다
- tune *n* 곡조
- unforeseen *a* 예측할 수 없는

- instantly *ad* 즉시
- set down ~을 기록하다, ~을 적어 두다
- act *n* 문서, 증서, 기록
- influential *a* 영향력 있는
- systematic *a* 체계적인
- arbitrary *a* 독단적인, 임의의
- transcription *n* 글로 옮긴 기록
- tremendously *ad* 굉장히, 엄청나게
- conceptualize *v* 개념화하다
- repeatable *a* 반복할 수 있는
- mount *v* 시작하다

097 답 ②

📖 세상을 개념화하는 방식과 사회의 조직화에 영향을 미치는 글쓰기

전문해석

글쓰기는 사회에 근본적인 변화를 가져온다. 그것은 언젠가 곧바로 사라졌을 것을 영구적이고 접근하기 쉽게 만든다. 예를 들어, 플라톤이 소크라테스의 말을 영속적인 방식으로 적어 두지 않았더라면 그것(소크라테스의 말)은 우리에게 알려져 있지 않을 것이지만, 우리는 거의 2500년이 지난 지금도 그 글로 옮긴 기록들을 읽을 수 있다. 이러한 먼 과거의 특정한 글로 된 기록은 우리가 세상을 개념화하는 바로 그 방식에 굉장히 영향을 미쳤다. 글쓰기는 또한 체계적이고 반복 가능한 방법으로 사회를 조직하는 것을 가능하게 하는데, 규정집들은 관료들이 각각의 특정한 사례의 세부 사항으로부터 모든 것을 해결해야 하기보다는 일반적인 원칙을 특정한 경우에 적용할 수 있게 해 준다. 문자화된 법률은 즉각적인 순간을 넘어 사용하기 위한 지침을 만듦으로써 독단적인 결정의 가능성을 줄이고, 결정에 대한 논쟁을 시작할 근거를 제공한다. 글쓰기는 글을 쓰는 사람들, 글을 읽는 사람들, 둘 다 하는 사람들과 둘 다 하지 않는 사람들로 사회를 나누게 될 수 있다. 만약 글쓰기가 특정 집단에만 국한된다면 촉진될 것은 바로 이러한 집단의 이익이 될 가능성이 있다.

정답풀이

② 가정법 도치: '플라톤이 소크라테스의 말을 영속적인 방식으로 적어 두지 않았다면 소크라테스의 말은 우리에게 알려져 있지 않을 것'이라는 의미로 가정법이 쓰인 문장이다. 플라톤이 소크라테스의 말을 영속적인 방식으로 적어 둔 것은 과거의 일이므로 조건절에는 가정법 과거완료 시제(had+과거분사)가 되어야 하는데, 조건절에서 if가 생략되면 주어와 조동사 had가 도치된다. 따라서 원래 if Plato had not set them down ~이었던 조건절에서 if가 생략되면 had Plato not set them down ~의 도치구문이 되므로 were를 had로 고쳐야 어법상 적절하다.

오답풀이

① 관계대명사 what: 문장의 동사인 makes의 목적어 역할을 하는 절을 이끌면서 뒤에 주어가 없는 불완전한 구조의 절이 이어지므로 선행사를 포함한 관계대명사 what은 어법상 적절하다.
  ↳ makes의 목적어인 what절과 목적격보어인 형용사구 permanent and accessible이 도치된 문장이다.
③ to부정사: 「make+형식상의 목적어 it+목적격보어+내용상의 목적어(to부정사)」 구문으로 내용상의 목적어 역할을 하는 to organize는 어법상 적절하다.
④ 병렬구조: provide는 문장의 주어인 Written laws에 연결되는 동사로 and 앞의 동사 reduce와 병렬구조를 이룬다.
⑤ it is ~ that... 강조구문: the interests of these groups를 강조하는 「it is+강조어구+that ~」의 강조구문을 이루는 that은 어법상 적절하다.

구문풀이

6행 [This particular act of writing from the distant past] **has been** tremendously influential on the very ways [in which we conceptualize the world].

: 첫 번째 [ ]가 주어이고, has been이 동사이며, 두 번째 [ ]는 the very ways를 수식하는 관계절이다.

어휘풀이

- bring about ~을 유발하다[초래하다]
- permanent *a* 영속적인, 오래가는
- fundamental *a* 근본적인
- accessible *a* 접근하기 쉬운

098 답 ⑤

📖 지불의 고통과 기억을 잊게 만드는 신용카드

전문해석

신용카드는 지불의 고통을 피하고자 하는 우리의 욕구를 활용한다. 그리고 그것(지불 고통의 회피)은 그것(신용카드)에게 우리가 가치를 인식하는 방식을 바꿀 수 있는 힘을 주었다. 더 쉽고 덜 눈에 띄는 지불 그리고 지불과 소비 사이의 시간 이동으로, 신용카드는 우리가 무언가를 구입하는 순간에 느끼는 지불의 고통을 최소화한다. 그것은 우리가 좀 더 기꺼이 소비하게 만드는 분리를 만들어 낸다. Elizabeth Dunn 과 Mike Norton이 언급한 바와 같이, 이러한 분리는 단지 우리가 그 순간에 어떻게 느끼는지에 관한 것만은 아니며, 그것은 또한 우리가 '얼마나 많은 돈을 소비했는지 기억하는 것을 더 어렵게 만드는' 방식으로 구매 경험을 기억하는 방식을 바꾼다. 예를 들어, 우리가 가게에 가서 양말, 파자마 그리고 볼품없는 스웨터를 산다면, 집에 도착하는 바로 그 순간 우리는 현금을 사용한 경우보다 신용카드를 사용한 경우에 지출한 돈의 액수를 기억할 가능성이 더 적다. 신용카드는 공상과학 영화에 나오는 기억 지우개와 비슷하지만, 그것들은 우리의 지갑 속에 산다. **연구는 사람들이 신용카드를 사용할 때 지불하고 싶은 기분이 더 들 뿐만 아니라, 더 많이 구매하고, 더 많은 팁을 남기고, 그들이 얼마나 썼는지를 과대평가할(→ 과소평가할) 가능성이 더 높고, 더 빠른 지출 결정을 내린다는 것을 밝혔다.**

정답풀이

⑤ 신용카드는 지불과 소비의 분리를 통해 지불액을 기억하기 어렵게 만듦으로써 소비를 더 쉽게 만든다는 문맥이므로, 신용카드를 쓰게 되면 실제 지불한 액수보다 더 적은 돈을 지불한 것처럼 느끼게 된다는 내용이 되어야 글의 흐름이 자연스럽다. 따라서 overestimate(과대평가하다)를 underestimate(과소평가하다)와 같은 낱말로 바꿔야 문맥상 적절하다.

오답풀이

① 신용카드는 지불을 더 쉽고 덜 눈에 띄게 만들고 소비와 지불 사이의 시간을 이동시키기 때문에 우리가 물건을 구입할 때 느끼는 지불의 고통을 줄여 준다는 흐름이 되어야 하므로 minimize(최소화하다)의 쓰임은 문맥상 적절하다.
② 신용카드는 소비 시점과 지불 시점을 분리시켜 지불을 더 쉽게 덜 눈에 띄게 하고, 이는 우리에게 더 '기꺼이' 소비하게 만든다는 것이므로 willing의 쓰임은 문맥상 적절하다.
③ 이어지는 예시에서 신용카드로 물건을 구입할 때 현금으로 구입할 때보다 지출한 돈의 액수를 잘 기억하지 못한다고 했으므로 신용카드는 우리가 돈을 얼마나 썼는지 기억하기 '더 어렵게(harder)' 만든다는 흐름은 적절하다.
  ↳ 어휘 자체는 어렵지 않지만 판단의 단서가 되는 어휘인 detachment(분리, 무관심)의 의미를 모르면 해당 문장의 의미를 제대로 파악하지 못할 수 있는 함정 오답이다.
④ 신용카드는 소비 시점과 지불 시점의 분리를 통해 지출 금액에 대한 기억을 어렵게 만든다고 했으므로 기억의 '지우개(erasers)'라는 표현은 문맥상 적절하다.

구문풀이

3행 With easier, less salient payment and the shifting of time between payment and consumption, / credit cards minimize the pain of paying [we feel at the moment {we buy something}].

: 「부사구+절」로 이루어진 문장이다. [ ]는 앞에 목적격 관계대명사가 생략된 관계절로 the pain of paying을 수식하며, 그 안의 { }는 the moment를 수식하는 관계절로 앞에 관계부사 when이 생략되었다.

어휘풀이
- capitalize on ~을 활용하다
- consumption *n* 소비
- pyjamas *n* 잠옷
- inclined *a* 마음이 내키는, ~하고 싶은
- shift *v* 바꾸다
- detachment *n* 분리
- moment *n* 순간, 때

099 답 ③

📖 개념적인 작업에서 분명한 경계선을 가지는 것의 이점

전문해석
개념적인 작업을 하는 것은 조각 그림 맞추기를 해결하는 것과 아주 비슷하다. 내가 생각하기에 많은 사람들이 자신의 작업에서 따분해지고 그리하여 온전한 호기심을 가지고 참여하지 못하는 이유 중 한 가지는 그들이 불확실성과 선택사항들에 의해 압도된다는 것이다. 그들은 문제의 한도를 엄밀하게 정의하지 못해왔다. 그 결과, 그들의 작업에 대한 접근은 조각 그림 전체를 탁자 위에 쏟고는 그들이 조립하려고 하는 것에 대한 이해가 거의 없거나 전혀 없이 일에 착수하는 것과 약간 비슷하다. 압도당한 그들은 포기한 채 적응을 하고, 한두 개가 우연히 일치하는 것을 발견하면 행복해한다. 하지만 과정의 초기에 여러분이 풀고 있는 문제의 '가장자리'를 정의하려는 약간의 의도적인 노력을 가지면, 보다 빨리 속도를 내고, 잠재적으로 더 적절한 해결책을 탐구하고, 여러분의 온전한 문제 해결 기술을 끌어내는 것이 가능하다. 여러분이 그 안에서 일할 분명한 경계선을 가질 때, 여러분은 매우 다양한 질문을 던지고 처음에 관련 없는 것처럼 보이는 가능성들을 탐구하면서 더 편안함을 느낄 수 있다.

정답풀이
개념적인 작업을 할 때 지루해서 전념하지 못하는 것은 문제의 한도를 엄밀하게 정의하지 못해서인데, 이것은 조각 맞추기 퍼즐의 모든 그림 조각들을 탁자에 쏟아 놓고 무엇을 맞춰야 하는지도 모르면서 작업을 시작하는 것과 같다고 설명하고 있다. 그래서 문제 해결 과정의 초기에 문제의 가장자리(한계)를 정의하려는 노력을 하면 더 빨리 문제를 해결할 수 있다고 했으므로, 빈칸에 들어갈 말로는 ③ '분명한 경계선'이 가장 적절하다.

오답풀이
① 다양한 선택사항
  └ 선택사항이 너무 많으면, 무엇부터 해야 할지 몰라 압도된다고 했으므로 적절하지 않다.
② 논리적 체계
④ 정의되지 않은 공간
⑤ 온전한 책임

구문풀이
2행 [**One** of the reasons {that (I believe) many people get bored in their work, and fail to engage with their full curiosity}], **is** [that they are overwhelmed by the uncertainty and options].

: 첫 번째 [ ]가 문장의 주어부이고 주어의 핵은 One이므로 단수 동사 is가 쓰였다. { }는 the reasons를 수식하는 관계부사절이고, 그 안의 ( )는 삽입절이다. 두 번째 [ ]는 주격보어로 쓰인 명사절이다.

10행 **Overwhelmed**, they may give up and settle in, [happy {to find (that a piece or two fall together by chance)}].

: Overwhelmed는 이유를 나타내는 분사구문으로 앞에 being이 생략되었다. [ ]는 부

대상황을 나타내는 분사구문으로 앞에 being이 생략되었고, 그 안의 { }는 감정(happy)의 원인을 나타내는 부사적 용법의 to부정사구이며, ( )는 find의 목적어로 쓰인 명사절이다.

12행 However, with a little intentional effort at the beginning of the process [to define the "edges" of the problem {you're solving}], / it's possible [**to get** up to speed more quickly, **explore** more potentially relevant solutions, and **leverage** your full creative problem-solving skill].

: 첫 번째 [ ]는 a little intentional effort를 수식하는 형용사적 용법의 to부정사구이고, 그 안의 { }는 the problem을 수식하는 목적격 관계대명사절이다. it은 형식상의 주어이고, 두 번째 [ ]의 to부정사구가 내용상의 주어이며, to에 이어지는 get, explore, leverage가 and에 의해 병렬구조로 연결되어 있다.

어휘풀이
- conceptual *a* 개념의, 개념적인
- overwhelm *v* 압도하다
- define *v* 정의하다
- set to ~에 착수하다
- settle in 적응하다
- intentional *a* 의도적인
- get up to ~에 이르다
- relevant *a* 적절한
- irrelevant-seeming *a* 관련 없어 보이는
- boundary *n* 경계선
- engage *v* 참여[관여]하다, 종사하다
- option *n* 선택사항
- dump *v* 쏟아 버리다
- assemble *v* 조립하다
- by chance 우연히
- edge *n* 가장자리, 테두리
- potentially *ad* 잠재적으로
- initially *ad* 처음에

100 답 ②

📖 문제 해결을 위한 통찰력에 다다르는 방식

전문해석
Wolfgang Köhler(1887~1967)는 게슈탈트[형태] 심리학의 창안에 기여한 독일의 심리학자였다. 그는 침팬지의 문제 해결 방법에 관한 일련의 유명한 연구를 수행했다. 그는 그 동물들이 닿을 수 있는 거리를 바로 벗어난 곳에 한 송이의 바나나를 놓은 다음 그것들이 어떻게 그 바나나에 닿는 방법을 생각해 내는지를 지켜보았다. 처음에는 좌절하다가, 침팬지들은 결국 이용 가능한 물체들을 도구로 사용하는 법에 대한 통찰력에 다다랐다. 이 통찰력은 흔히 일종의 아하! 하는 깨달음의 순간에 갑작스럽게 떠올랐다. 한 경우에, 한 침팬지는 바나나에 닿을 만큼 충분히 긴 도구를 만들어 내기 위해 두 개의 막대기를 이었다. 또 다른 한 침팬지는 천장으로부터 매달려 있는 과일에 닿기 위해 세 개의 상자를 각각의 위에 쌓았다. 이 연구는 우리에게 이 동물들의 놀라운 창의력을 보여줄 뿐만 아니라, 정신이 능동적으로 문제에 대한 완전한 해결책을 만들어 내며, 흔히 갑자기 그것에 도달한다는 게슈탈트 개념을 뒷받침했다. 이것은, 문제 해결은 오직 시행착오에 의해 서서히 진행될 수 있다는 행동주의적 가정과 대조된다.

정답풀이
문제 해결에 관한 침팬지 실험 결과는 침팬지들이 아하! 하는 깨달음의 순간에 갑작스럽게 문제 해결을 위한 통찰력을 얻는다는 것을 보여주었는데, 빈칸에는 이와 대조적인 의미를 가진 어구가 들어가야 한다. 따라서 빈칸에 들어갈 말로 가장 적절한 것은 ② '오직 시행착오에 의해 서서히 진행될 수 있다'이다.

오답풀이
① 오직 인간만이 가지는 능력이다
③ 보상과 처벌을 사용함으로써 강화된다
  └ 글의 내용과 관계없이 행동주의 심리학에 대한 상식을 토대로 한 함정 오답!
④ 갑작스런 통찰력의 결과로만 이루어질 수 있다
  └ 빈칸 앞에 나온 in contrast to의 표현을 간과하면 고를 수 있는 함정 오답!
⑤ 학습된 후에만 새로운 상황에서 사용된다

12행 Another chimp stacked three boxes on top of each other [to reach the fruit {hanging from the ceiling}].

: [ ]는 목적을 나타내는 부사적 용법의 to부정사구이고, 그 안의 { }는 the fruit을 수식하는 현재분사구이다.

어휘풀이
- a bunch of 한 송이의, 한 다발의
- frustrated *a* 좌절한, 낙심한
- A-Ha! moment 아하! 하는 깨달음의 순간
- stack *v* 쌓다
- remarkable *a* 놀라운, 훌륭한
- all at once 갑자기
- behaviorist *a* 행동주의적인
- proceed *v* 진행되다
- reinforce *v* 강화하다
- figure out ~을 생각해 내다
- insight *n* 통찰력
- ceiling *n* 천장
- ingenuity *n* 창의력, 독창성
- in contrast to ~와 대조되는
- assumption *n* 가정
- trial and error 시행착오

101 답 ⑤

📖 유사점을 가진 사람들이 서로 끌리는 경향

전문해석
우리가 친구나 연인으로 선택하는 경향이 있는 사람들에 관한 두 개의 금언이 있다. 하나는 '같은 깃털의 새들이 함께 모인다(유유상종)'이고, 나머지 하나는 '정반대의 사람에게 끌린다'이다. 그렇다면 우리는 우리와 비슷한 사람을 원하는가, 아니면 우리의 성격을 보완하기 위해서 다른 누군가를 찾는가? (C) 이러한 문제에 관한 연구는 실제로 '같은 깃털의 새들이 함께 모인다'는 것을 보여준다. 연인을 선택할 때, 우리는 우리와 비슷한 나이, 사회경제적 지위, 교육, 지능, 인종, 종교, 태도, 권력 그리고 신체적 매력을 가진 사람들에게 끌리는 경향이 있다. (B) 게다가, 유사점은 멕시코, 인도 그리고 일본을 포함해서 다양한 문화에 걸쳐 매력을 예측하는 것으로 보인다. 유사점은 또한 우리가 선택하는 친구들에 있는 한 요소처럼 보인다. (A) 유사점이 매력에 미치는 영향에 대한 한 가지 가능한 설명은 균형 이론인데, 이는 인지부조화(모순 또는 상반되는 신념·태도 등을 동시에 갖는 데서 오는 심리적 불안) 이론과 관련이 있다. 그것(균형 이론)은 우리가 좋아하는 것들을 좋아하지 않는 사람을 우리가 좋아할 때, 우리는 부조화를 야기하는 불균형을 경험한다고 설명한다. 이러한 부조화는 조화를 복원하는 변화를 자극한다.

정답풀이
'우리는 우리와 비슷한 사람을 원하는가, 아니면 우리의 성격을 보완하기 위해서 우리와 다른 누군가를 찾는가?'라는 의문을 제기한 주어진 글 다음에는, 제시된 질문에 대한 답을 보여주는 연구에 대해 언급하는 (C)가 오고, 유사점이 연인들을 서로 끌어당긴다는 (C)의 내용에 이어서, 이것이 다양한 문화에 적용되고 친구를 선택할 때도 해당된다는 내용인 (B)가 와야 한다. 그리고 이러한 유사점이 왜 매력에 영향을 미치는지를 설명하는 (A)가 마지막에 오는 흐름이 가장 자연스럽다. 따라서 적절한 글의 순서는 ⑤ (C)-(B)-(A)이다.

구문풀이
19행 [When choosing a romantic partner], we tend to gravitate to people [who are of similar age, socioeconomic status, education, intelligence, race, religion, attitudes, power, and physical attractiveness to ourselves].

: 첫 번째 [ ]는 의미를 분명히 하기 위해 접속사 When을 명시한 분사구문이고, 두 번째 [ ]는 주격 관계대명사절로 people을 수식한다.

어휘풀이
- adage *n* 격언, 금언
- complement *v* 보완하다

- personality *n* 성격
- similarity *n* 유사점
- imbalance *n* 불균형
- consonance *n* 조화
- gravitate *v* ~에 끌리다
- explanation *n* 설명
- attraction *n* 매력, 끌림
- restore *v* 회복하다
- indicate *v* 나타내다, 보여주다
- attractiveness *n* 매력, 끌림

102 답 ②

📖 현대 물질 사회의 추악한 이면

전문해석
값싼 아동용 무선 조종 탱크에는 여러분이 3분의 2가 넘는 주기율표의 원소를 그 안에서 발견하게 될 엄지손톱 크기의 마이크로칩이 들어있다. 이 원소들이 분류되어 사용될 준비가 되어 있는 깨끗한 유리 시험관에 담겨 땅속에서 나오지 않는다는 것을 잊지 말자. 반대로, 이 희귀 화합물은 수천 톤의 암석과 진흙 속에 담겨 있는데, 지구로부터 채굴되어 헤집어진다. 위험하고, 오염을 일으키며, 에너지 집약적인 추출과 정화 과정이 뒤따르는데, 우리 물질세계의 생태학적, 사회적 파괴의 대다수가 그 속에 숨어 있다. 하나의 산업 자체가 이 수준의 자원 전환을 차지하고서, 막후에서 지구의 희귀 자원을 신기한 현대적 물질로 탈바꿈시킨다. 우리를 에워싸는 차고 넘치는 전자 제품은 복합 광물, 귀금속, 그리고 유독성 화합물이 듬뿍 혼합되어 주입되어 있다. 우리 대부분에게, 이것들은 전혀 보이지 않으며, 우리의 물질적 경험 표면의 바로 아래 숨어 있다. 이 산업적 연금술의 경이로운 산물들은, 그것들의 천재성에도 불구하고, 놀랍도록 빠르게 폐기물이 되며, 확실히 그것들은 지속되도록 고안되지 않는다.

정답풀이
주어진 문장은 위험하고 오염을 일으키는 추출 및 정화 과정이 뒤따른다는 내용을 담고 있다. ② 앞 문장에는 자원 채굴에 관한 내용만 있는데, ② 다음 문장에서 this level of resource conversion(이 수준의 자원 전환)이라고 하여 가리킬 만한 내용이 없으므로 논리적 공백이 있다. this level of resource conversion은 문맥상 주어진 문장에서 말하는 자원의 추출 및 정화 과정을 가리키는 것이므로 주어진 문장은 ②에 들어가는 것이 가장 적절하다.

구문풀이
1행 [A hazardous, polluting, and energy-intensive process of extraction and purification] **follows**, [within which lurks the majority of our material world's ecological and social destruction].

: 첫 번째 [ ]는 문장의 주어 역할을 하는 명사구이고, follows가 술어 동사이다. 두 번째 [ ]는 첫 번째 [ ], 즉 주어에 대한 부가적 설명을 제공하는 계속적 용법의 관계절이다.

8행 **Let** us **not forget**, [these elements do not come out of the ground in clear glass test tubes, {labeled and ready for use}].

: 사역동사 Let의 목적격보어로 원형부사로 forget이 쓰였고, 원형부정사의 부정은 앞에 not을 붙여 나타낸다. [ ]는 forget의 목적어 역할을 하는 명사절이고, 그 안의 { }는 clear glass test tubes를 부가적으로 수식하는 분사구이다.

어휘풀이
- hazardous *a* 위험한
- energy-intensive *a* 에너지 집약적인
- extraction *n* 추출
- ecological *a* 생태학적인
- thumbnail-sized *a* 엄지손톱 크기의
- element *n* 원소
- test tube 시험관
- compound *n* 화합물
- claw *v* 헤집다
- occupy *v* 차지하다
- pollute *v* 오염시키다
- purification *n* 정화, 세정
- radio-controlled *a* 무선 조종의
- periodic table 주기율표
- label *v* 분류하다, 라벨을 붙이다
- mine *v* 채굴하다
- encase *v* 넣다
- conversion *v* 전환, 변환

- behind the scenes 막후에서, 무대 뒤에서
- transform ⓥ 바꾸다, 변형하다 • infuse A with B A에 B를 주입하다
- noxious ⓐ 유독성의

103 답 ⑤

📖 양자 역학의 무작위적 원자 운동 이론에 대한 아인슈타인의 반대론

전문해석

대부분의 과학자들은 코펜하겐 해석이라고 알려진 양자 역학에 대한 기술에 동의하는데, 그것은 아주 근본적인 수준에서 원자는 무작위로 운동한다고 말한다. 양자 역학은 하나의 원자가 이곳 또는 저곳에 존재할 가능성, 이런 속도 또는 저런 속도일 가능성, 이만큼의 에너지 수준 또는 저만큼의 에너지 수준일 가능성을 예측하는 데 사용될 수 있지만, 이러한 특성의 어느 것도 정확하게 예측할 수 없다. 아인슈타인은 양자 역학의 발달에서 중요한 선구자이며, 그는 그것이 믿을 수 없을 만큼 정확하게 이러한 가능성을 예측한다는 것을 알았지만, 다른 과학자들은 양자 역학의 정확성은 현실 그 자체가 무작위라는 것을 의미한다고 믿었다. 반면에, **아인슈타인은 현실이 명확한 인과의 법칙으로 작동한다고 믿었는데, 그것은 가능한 모든 정보를 갖고 있다면 정확하고 완벽하게 예측될 수 있는 운동이라는 것이다.** 생을 마감할 때까지 아인슈타인은 우리가 단지 자연을 제대로 이해하지 못하는 것이며, 우리가 아직 이해하지 못한 추가적인 요소, 즉 어떤 숨겨진 변수들이 틀림없이 작용한다고 주장했다.
→ 아인슈타인은 양자 역학의 근본적으로 확률론적인 성질에 반대하면서, 현실은 실제로 우리가 아직 확인하지 못한 어떤 결정론적인 숨겨진 변수들에 의해 지배된다고 제안했다.

정답풀이

원자가 무작위로 운동하므로 정확한 예측이 불가능하다는 것이 양자 역학이 취하는 입장인 반면에, 아인슈타인은 우리가 아직 모르고 있는 변수들이 있으며 그것들을 알게 된다면 완벽하게 원자의 운동을 예측할 수 있다고 주장했다는 내용이다. 따라서 (A)에는 양자 역학의 근본적인 성격을 나타내는 probabilistic(확률론적인), (B)에는 아인슈타인이 제안한 숨겨진 변수들의 성격을 나타내는 deterministic(결정론적인)이 들어가는 것이 가장 적절하다.

구문풀이

16행 To his death, Einstein insisted [that we simply didn't understand nature well enough], [there must be additional factors, some hidden variables at work {that we didn't yet understand}].

: 첫 번째 [ ]는 insisted의 목적어 역할을 하는 명사절이다. 두 번째 [ ]는 이 절의 내용(자연을 제대로 이해하지 못하는 것)을 구체적으로 기술하는 동격절이고, 그 안의 { }는 additional factors, some hidden variables를 수식하는 목적격 관계대명사절이다.

어휘풀이

- description ⓝ 기술, 묘사
- randomly ⓐd 무작위로
- incredible ⓐ 믿을 수 없는
- definite ⓐ 명확한
- additional ⓐ 추가적인
- identify ⓥ 확인하다
- interpretation ⓝ 해석
- pioneer ⓝ 개척자, 선구자
- accuracy ⓝ 정확성
- precisely ⓐd 정확하게
- variable ⓝ 변수

104 답 ②

📖 조직의 성공에 기여하는 이의 제기

전문해석

조직에서의 이의 제기는 좀처럼 아주 극적이지는 않다. 그것은 조직의 행동과 결정에 대한 직원들의 불만에 대한 피드백 형태로 맥락적 현상에 관한 의견 불일치 또는 상반된 의견의 표명으로 정의된다. 피드백 고리는 개인, 그룹 및 조직이 학습하고 그들의 실천을 개선하는 방법에 중요하다. 따라서 학습과 개선이 사람들이 주어진 목적, 임무 및 과업을 수행하는 데 중요하기 때문에 이의 제기는 환영받아야 한다. 이론가와 연구자들은 개인들이 그룹 내에서 공개적으로 이의 표명자 역할을 떠맡을 때, 사고와 행동에서의 순응을 막는 데 도움이 된다는 것을 보여주었다. **건설적인 사회적 갈등은, 기업을 더 효과적으로 만들기 위해 제안되고 전개되는데, 사회 시스템의 전 범위에서 반기능적이라기보다는 기능적이다.** 이의 제기가 없으면, 사람들은 반성적이라기보다는 반사적으로 행동하는 위험을 무릅쓰게 되며, 그들이 가지 말아야 할 곳으로 이끄는 길을 따라 무조건적으로 가게 된다. 동의라는 쉬운 흐름을 끊고, 다른 사람들에게 그들 자신의 가능한 편견을 숙고하도록 재촉하는 멈춤의 순간을 만드는 것은 그러므로 어떤 조직의 성공에도 필수적이다.

정답풀이

조직의 행동과 결정에 반대를 표명하는 이의 제기는 궁극적으로 조직의 발전에 기여하므로 환영받아야 한다는 내용의 글이다. 따라서 글의 주제로 가장 적절한 것은 ② '다수에 이의를 제기하는 것의 이로운 영향[효과]'이다.

오답풀이

① 조직에서 이의 제기를 하는 방법들
└ 이의 제기의 필요성을 언급하는 내용으로 이의 제기를 하는 방법에 대한 언급은 없다.
③ 기업에서 건설적인 피드백의 중요성
└ 건설적인 피드백은 이의 제기의 한 형태이므로 글의 주제로 부적절하다.
④ 사회적 갈등을 피하기 위해 반대자들의 목소리를 인정하기
⑤ 조직 내에서 불만족을 전달하는 구조적 수단들

구문풀이

13행 Social conflicts [that are constructive]—[offered and waged in the spirit of {**making** enterprises **more effective**}]—are functional rather than dysfunctional across the spectrum of social systems.

: 첫 번째 [ ]는 문장의 주어인 Social conflicts를 수식하는 주격 관계대명사절이다. 두 번째 [ ]는 주어를 부연 설명하는 어구이고, 그 안의 { }는 of의 목적어 역할을 하는 동명사구이며 making의 목적격보어로 형용사 more effective가 쓰였다.

17행 Without dissent, people risk acting reflexively rather than reflectively, [unquestioningly moving along paths {that lead to places (they ought not to go)}].

: [ ]는 부대상황을 나타내는 분사구문이고, 그 안의 { }는 paths를 수식하는 주격 관계대명사절이며, ( )는 places를 수식하는 관계부사절로 앞에 관계부사 where가 생략되었다.

20행 [**To interrupt** the easy flow of agreement and **create** moments of pause {that **press** others **to reflect** on their own possible biases}] **is** therefore essential to any organization's success.

: [ ]는 문장의 주어로 쓰인 to부정사구로 interrupt와 create가 병렬구조를 이루며, 문장의 동사는 is이다. { }는 moments of pause를 수식하는 주격 관계대명사절이며, 「press+목적어+to부정사(목적격보어)」는 '~가 …하도록 재촉하다'라는 의미를 나타낸다.

어휘풀이

- dissent *n* 반대, 이의 (제기)
- contradictory *a* 상반되는, 모순되는
- contextual *a* 맥락적인
- phenomenon *n* 현상 (*pl.* phenomena)
- discontent *n* 불만
- given that ~ ~을 고려[감안]하면
- fulfill *v* 수행하다
- assume *v* (역할 등을) 떠맡다
- constructive *a* 건설적인
- dysfunctional *a* 정상적으로 기능하지 않는
- reflexively *ad* 반사적으로
- interrupt *v* 방해하다, 중단시키다
- reflect on ~을 곰곰이 생각하다
- define *v* 정의하다
- regarding *prep* ~에 관한
- loop *n* 고리
- crucial *a* 중대한, 결정적인
- explicitly *ad* 명백히, 숨김없이
- conformity *n* 순응
- enterprise *n* 기업, 사업 (활동)
- reflectively *ad* 반성적으로
- press *v* 재촉하다, 다그치다
- bias *n* 편견, 편향

105 답 ③

📖 정당화와 설명 그리고 합리화의 차이

전문해석

정당화는 설명의 한 유형이지만, 정당화는 취해진 행동이 옳거나 적어도 이해할 만한 것이라고 듣는 사람을 설득하려는 시도를 포함한다. 설명은 듣는 사람이 언급되고 있는 것을 믿도록 납득시키는 어떠한 공공연한 시도도 포함하고 있지 않지만, 정당화는 그렇다(포함하고 있다). 물론, 좋은 정당화와 나쁜 정당화가 있다. 나쁜 정당화는 합리적이고 설득력 있는 설명을 제공하기보다는 그것을 제공하는 사람이 단지 자신이나 다른 사람을 위해 변명을 하고 있는 그런 것이다. 자기 잇속만 차리는 그리고 부적절한 정당화 시도에 대한 또 다른 단어는 합리화이다. 합리화는, 그 단어가 이성의 개념을 포함하고 있기 때문에 그것(합리화)이 논리적임에 틀림없는 것처럼 들린다는 사실에도 불구하고, 합리화를 제공하는 사람이 틀렸다고 알고 있는 행동을 변명하려고 시도하는 설득력 없는 설명이다. 연구의 자료를 조작하고서 연구 비용을 대는 제약회사로부터 많은 압박이 있었다고 말함으로써 그것을 정당화하려고 하는 교수는 합리화를 제시하고 있는 것이다.

정답풀이

③ 관계대명사 **which**: 이어지는 절이 주어(the person offering it), 동사 (is making), 목적어(excuses 이하)를 갖춘 완전한 구조를 이루므로 관계대명사 which는 쓸 수 없다. one(= a justification)을 선행사로 하며 관계사절에서 in the justification의 부사구 역할을 하도록 「전치사+관계대명사」 형태의 in which로 고쳐야 한다.

오답풀이

① 문장의 구조 파악: that절의 주어 the actions에 이어지는 복수형 동사 were는 어법상 적절하다. taken은 the actions를 수식하는 과거분사이다.
② 대동사: 반복되는 일반동사구 include any overt attempt to convince the listener to believe what is being said를 대신하는 대동사 do는 어법상 적절하다.
④ 문장의 구조 파악: that the person 이하는 behaviour를 수식하는 주격 관계대명사절로, the person offering the rationalization knows는 삽입절이고 was가 관계사절의 동사이므로 어법상 적절하다.
⑤ 분사의 태: 수식을 받는 the pharmaceutical company가 연구 비용을 지불하는 주체이므로 현재분사 paying은 어법상 적절하다.

구문풀이

13행 **Rationalizations**, [despite **the fact** {that they sound like they must be logical, because the word contains the idea of reason}], **are** weak explanations [which attempt to excuse behaviour {that <the person (offering the rationalization) knows> was wrong}].

: 문장의 주어는 Rationalizations이고 동사는 are이다. 첫 번째 [ ]로 표시된 부사구에서 { }는 the fact의 구체적인 내용을 설명하는 동격절이다. 두 번째 [ ]는 weak explanations를, 그 안의 { }는 behaviour를 수식하는 주격 관계대명사절이다. < >는 삽입절이고, 그 안의 ( )는 the person을 수식하는 현재분사구이다.

17행 The professor [who **falsifies** data in a study and then **tries** to justify it by saying {that there was a lot of pressure from the pharmaceutical company (paying for the research)}] **is offering** a rationalization.

: [ ]는 문장의 핵심 주어인 The professor를 수식하는 주격 관계대명사절이고, 문장의 동사는 is offering이다. 관계절의 동사는 falsifies와 tries이며, { }는 saying의 목적어 역할을 하는 명사절이다. ( )는 the pharmaceutical company를 수식하는 현재분사구이다.

어휘풀이

- justification *n* 정당화
- overt *a* 공공연한, 명백한
- rational *a* 합리적인
- excuse *n* 변명 *v* 변명하다
- inappropriate *a* 부적절한
- falsify *v* 조작하다
- persuade *v* 설득하다
- convince *v* 납득시키다
- compelling *a* 설득력 있는
- self-serving *a* 자기 잇속을 차리는
- rationalization *n* 합리화
- pharmaceutical *a* 제약의, 약의

106 답 ①

📖 진리 추구에서 도전에 대한 과학의 개방성

전문해석

세상과 그 안의 모든 것들은 과학자들의 관심 영역일 뿐만 아니라 신학자들, 철학자들, 시인들, 정치가들의 관심 영역이기도 하다. 그들의 관심사와 과학자들의 관심사를 어떻게 구분할 수 있는가? 과학자들은 이 세계가 무질서한 것이 아니라 어떤 방식으로 구조화되어 있으며, 전부는 아닐지라도 이 구조의 대부분의 측면은 과학적 조사의 도구를 따를 것이라고 가정한다. 모든 과학적 활동에서 사용되는 하나의 주요한 도구는 시험이다. 모든 새로운 사실과 모든 새로운 설명은 가급적이면 다른 방법을 사용하여 다른 조사자들에 의해 되풀이하여 시험되어야 한다. 모든 확증은 사실이나 설명이 '진리'일 가능성을 강화하며, 모든 반증과 반박은 상반된 이론이 옳을 가능성을 강화한다. 과학의 가장 특색을 이루는 특징 중 하나는 이 도전에 대한 개방성이다. 새롭고 더 좋은 것이 제안될 때 현재 받아들여지는 믿음을 기꺼이 버리는 마음은 과학과 종교적 교의 사이의 중요한 구분 요소이다.

정답풀이

과학에서는 서로 다른 조사자들이 서로 다른 방법으로 끊임없이 시험을 되풀이하여 사실이나 설명을 확인해 나가면서 진리에 접근하며, 그 과정에서 더 좋은 것이 제안되면 기꺼이 받아들이고 기존의 것을 버린다는 내용이다. 빈칸에는 이러한 과학의 특징을 설명하는 말이 들어가야 하므로 ① '도전에 대한 개방성'이 가장 적절하다.

오답풀이

② 사회에 대한 공헌
③ 권위에 대한 순응
④ 혁신에 대한 항거
⑤ 수정에 대한 반대

구문풀이

1행 [The world and <u>all</u> {that is in it}] are the sphere of interest **not only** of scientists **but also** of theologians, philosophers, poets, and politicians.

: 문장의 주어는 [ ]이고, 그 안의 { }는 all을 수식하는 주격 관계대명사절이다. 「not only A but also B」의 상관접속사가 of scientists와 of theologians 이하의 전치사구를 연결하고 있다.

어휘풀이

- sphere *n* 영역, 범위
- chaotic *a* 무질서한
- investigation *n* 조사, 연구
- confirmation *n* 확증
- opposing *a* 상반된
- abandon *v* 버리다
- contribution *n* 기여
- modification *n* 수정
- theologian *n* 신학자
- yield to ~을 따르다
- preferably *ad* 가급적이면
- refutation *n* 반박
- willingness *n* 기꺼이 ~하는 마음
- dogma *n* 교의
- conformity *n* 순응

107 답 ③

📖 집단 소속을 위한 비판적 사고에 대한 타고난 억제력

전문해석

수렵 채집인 사회에서, 자신의 집단에 의해 진정으로 속한 사람으로 여겨지는 것은 적응에 크게 도움이 되었다. 사람들은 어떻게 자신이 집단에 속한다는 것을 다른 이들에게 확신시키는 능력을 가장 잘 기를 수 있을까? 자기기만과 비판적 사고의 굽힘을 포함하여, 의식적이 아닌 정신 과정을 진화시킴에 의해서이다. 그러한 지식 저항 기반은 집단의 주요 지식 신념 및 가치관과의 긴장을 줄일 것이다. 우리가 한 집단의, 예컨대 종교, 정치, 또는 심지어 과학 단체의 구성원이기를 원할 때, 우리가 흔히 근본적인 지식 신념에 도전하지 않는 것은 단지 의식적, 책략적 이유에서만은 아니다. 우리는 문제가 되는 집단의 지배적인 지식 주장을 믿는 재능을 갖추고 있다. 왜 그런가? 우리의 신체 언어와 의식적이지 않은 신호가 우리의 영리하고 정제된 말이 하는 것보다 훨씬 더 많은 것을 다른 이들에게 전달하기 때문이다. 따라서, 수렵 채집인 사회에서 인간 적응의 중대한 부분은 <u>우리 자신이 어떤 문제에서는 다른 이들에게 속아 넘어가도록 허용하는</u> 능력을 포함한 것이 틀림없다.

정답풀이

수렵 채집인 사회에서 한 개인이 집단의 일원이라는 것을 다른 구성원들에게 확신시키는 것이 적응에 도움이 되었기 때문에, 이를 위해 자기기만과 비판적 사고를 굽히는 정신의 진화를 이루었다는 내용이다. 즉, 집단의 일원이 되고자 할 때, 그 집단의 지배적 지식 주장에 도전하지 않고 그것을 그대로 믿는다는 것은 집단의 주장에 자신의 의식을 속여서라도 맞춘다는 것이므로, 빈칸에 들어갈 말로 가장 적절한 것은 ③ '우리 자신이 어떤 문제에서는 다른 이들에게 속아 넘어가도록 허용하는'이다.

오답풀이

① 우리의 감정을 명확하면서도 정중하게 표현하는
└ 집단 소속을 위해 자신의 생각을 굽힌다는 지문의 내용과 반대되는 내용으로 오답!
② 우리의 오랜 믿음에 도전하고 새로운 신념을 받아들이는
└ 자기기만과 비판적 사고를 굽힌다는 것이 자신의 오랜 믿음에 도전한다는 것은 아니다.
④ 다른 이들의 안녕과 행복에 이바지하는
⑤ 한 집단의 사람들을 그 집단의 공동 목표를 향해 이끄는

구문풀이

1행 In a hunter-gatherer society, **it** was highly adaptive [to be seen by one's group as <u>someone</u> {who really belonged}].

: it은 형식상의 주어이고, [ ]의 to부정사구가 내용상의 주어이다. { }는 someone을 수식하는 주격 관계대명사절이다.

9행 [When we wish to be a member of a group—such as a religious, political, or even a scientific community —] **it** isn't just for conscious, tactical reasons [that we often don't challenge their fundamental knowledge beliefs].

: 첫 번째 [ ]는 때를 나타내는 부사절이며, 주절의 it은 형식상의 주어이고 두 번째 [ ]의 명사절이 내용상의 주어이다.

어휘풀이

- hunter-gatherer *n* 수렵 채집인
- equip A to *do* A에게 ~할 능력을 키워주다
- convince *v* 확신시키다
- self-deception *n* 자기기만
- resistance *n* 저항, 내성
- fundamental *a* 기본적인
- claim *n* 주장
- well-measured *a* 정제된, 잘 다듬어진
- crucial *a* 중대한
- devote oneself to ~에 헌신하다
- adaptive *a* 적응을 돕는
- nonconscious *a* 의식적이 아닌
- critical *a* 비판적인
- tactical *a* 책략적, 전술의
- dominant *a* 지배적인, 우세한
- fool *v* 속이다

108 답 ②

📖 이슬람 세계의 관습에 대한 서양인들의 가정과 해석

전문해석

서양인들이 이슬람 세계에서 베일을 쓰는 것과 같은 관습을 해석하기 위해 그들 자신의 문화적인 지식에 의존할 때, 그들은 베일을 쓰는 여성들에게 있어서의 그 베일의 의미를 잘못 해석할 수도 있다. (B) 예를 들어, 서양인들은 베일을 쓰는 것이 내켜 하지 않는 여성들에게 남성들이 강요하는 관습이라고 가정하거나 베일을 쓰는 이슬람 여성들이 그들의 아름다움을 감추기 위해 그렇게 한다고 가정할 수 있다. (A) 실제로, 이러한 결론 중 어느 것도 반드시 정확하지는 않은데, 예를 들어 일부 이슬람 여성들은, 때때로 남성 가족 구성원들의 소망에 반해서, 현대의 종교적이고 정치적인 정체성의 성명으로 자발적으로 얼굴을 가리는 것을 선택한다. (C) 마찬가지로, 일부 여성들은 베일을 아름다움을 가리는 것이 아니라 강조하는 하나의 방법으로 여긴다. 하지만 만약에 서양인들이 이러한 관행을 그들 자신이 이전에 가지고 있던 문화적인 지식과 가정의 렌즈를 통해서 해석한다면, 그들은 더 이상의 학습을 방해할 수 있는 왜곡된 이해를 가지고 나올 수도 있다.

정답풀이

서양인들이 자신의 문화적 지식에 의존하여 이슬람 여성들이 사용하는 베일의 의미를 잘못 이해할 수도 있다는 내용의 주어진 글 다음에는, 서양인들의 가정에 대한 예시가 시작되는 (B)가 와야 한다. 그리고 이슬람 여성의 베일에 대한 서양인들의 해석들 중 어떤 것도 정확하지 않을 수 있다고 하면서 이슬람 여성들은 베일을 자신들의 의견 표현으로 사용할 수 있다는 사실을 제시하는 (A)가 오고, By the same token(마찬가지로)으로 시작하며 이슬람 여성들의 베일에 대한 또 다른 사실을 계속해서 이어가는 (C)가 마지막에 오는 순서가 가장 적절하다. 따라서 적절한 글의 순서는 ② (B)-(A)-(C)이다.

구문풀이

1행 When Westerners draw on their own cultural knowledge **to interpret** <u>practices</u> [such as veiling in the Muslim world], / they may misinterpret the meaning of the veil to <u>the women</u> [who wear it].

: 부사절과 주절로 이루어진 문장이다. to interpret는 목적을 나타내는 부사적 용법의

to부정사이고, 첫 번째 [ ]는 practices를 수식한다. 두 번째 [ ]는 the women을 수식하는 주격 관계대명사절이다.

어휘풀이
- draw on ~에 의존하다
- voluntarily ad 자발적으로
- religious a 종교적인
- impose v 강요하다
- by the same token 마찬가지로
- assumption n 가정
- distorted a 왜곡된
- misinterpret v 잘못 해석하다
- statement n 성명(서), 진술(서)
- identity n 정체성
- unwilling a 내키지 않는
- conceal v 감추다, 숨기다
- emerge v 나오다, 나타나다
- impede v 방해하다, 지체시키다

109 답 ②

📖 유전자 변형이 야기하는 두 가지 문제

전문해석
유전자 변형(GM) 식물 기술의 발전은 두 가지 문제를 야기하는데, 과학적 그리고 윤리적인 문제이다. 과학은 우리가 살고 있는 세상을 이해하고, 특히 그 세상을 형성하는 인과관계를 이해하는 것과 관련이 있는데, 예를 들어 분자 배열로서의 유전자와 그 유전자가 표현하는 서리에 대한 내성과 같은 특징 사이의 연관성이 그것이다. 우리가 정보에 근거한 방법으로 식물의 특성을 바꾸거나 변화시키고자 한다면 그러한 패턴을 이해하는 것이 필요하다. 반면에, 윤리는 우리가 해야 하거나 하지 말아야 할 일과 관련이 있다. 윤리적 원칙은, 예를 들어 어떤 유전자 조작이 인간의 건강을 위협하거나 환경에 해를 줄 수 있기 때문에 그렇게 하는 것은 잘못일 수 있다는 것을 나타내는, 정책이나 관행의 평가에 대한 표준을 제공한다. 비록 어떤 실험을 하거나 상업적인 재배를 위한 새로운 종류의 농작물을 도입하는 것이 과학적으로 가능할 수 있을지라도, 결과적으로 그렇게 하는 것이 윤리적으로 옳은 것이라고 할 수 없다. 따라서 어떤 일을 행하는 것이 옳거나 허용될 수 있는지 파악하는 것은 개발되어 온 유전자 변형 능력을 고려하여 우리가 무엇을 해야 할지를 결정하기 위하여 우리의 과학적 이해와 우리의 윤리적 원칙을 결합하는 것을 포함한다.

정답풀이
주어진 문장의 Understanding such patterns는 ② 앞에 나온 분자 배열로서의 유전자와 그 유전자가 표현하는 특성의 연관성처럼 세상을 형성하는 인과관계를 가리킨다. 또한, 주어진 문장에서 언급하는 정보에 근거한 방법으로 식물의 특성을 바꾸는 것은 과학적인 문제와 관련이 있는 것이다. 따라서 주어진 문장은 유전자 조작의 윤리적인 측면을 언급하기 전인 ②에 들어가는 것이 가장 적절하다.

구문풀이
21행 [Working out {what **it** is right or permissible **to do**}] **involves**, therefore, [**bringing together** our scientific understanding **with** our ethical principles / **to decide** {what we should do} {**given** the capacities for genetic modification (that have been developed)}].

: 첫 번째 [ ]로 표시된 동명사구가 문장의 주어이고, 동사는 involves이다. 첫 번째 { }는 Working out의 목적어로 쓰인 명사절(의문사절)이며, to do는 형식상의 주어 it에 대한 내용상의 주어이다. 두 번째 [ ]는 involves의 목적어로 쓰인 동명사구이고, 「bring together A with B」는 'A와 B를 결합하다'의 의미를 나타낸다. to decide 이하는 목적을 나타내는 to부정사구이고, 두 번째 { }는 dicide의 목적어로 쓰인 명사절(의문사절)이며, 세 번째 { }는 전치사구(~을 고려하면)이고, ( )는 the capacities for genetic modification을 수식하는 주격 관계대명사절이다.

어휘풀이
- alter v 변경하다, 바꾸다
- genetically modified 유전자 조작의
- informed a 정보에 근거한
- ethical a 윤리적인

- causal relationship 인과관계
- sequence n 배열, 순서
- frost n 서리, 결빙
- practice n 관행, 실천
- undertake v ~에 착수하다
- it follows (that) ~ 결과적으로 ~라고 할 수 있다
- permissible a 허용할 수 있는
- molecular a 분자의
- resistance n 내성, 저항
- principle n 원리, 원칙
- modification n 조작, 변형

110~111 답 ③ / ③

📖 코끼리 보호 수단으로써의 사유재산화

전문해석
소는 귀중한 식량원이지만 누구도 소가 곧 멸종할까 봐 걱정하지 않는다. 사실, 많은 쇠고기 수요는 그 종이 계속 번성할 것임을 보장하는 것으로 보인다. 왜 쇠고기의 상업적 가치는 소를 보호하는 반면에 상아의 상업적 가치는 코끼리를 위협하는가? 그 이유는 코끼리는 공유 자원인 반면에 소는 사유재라는 것이다. 코끼리는 어떤 소유주 없이 자유롭게 돌아다닌다. 각 밀렵꾼은 자신이 발견할 수 있는 가능한 한 많은 코끼리를 죽일 강한 유인을 갖는다. 밀렵꾼들이 많기 때문에 각 밀렵꾼은 코끼리 개체 수를 보호할 유인이 거의 없다. 대조적으로, 소는 사적으로 소유되는 목장에서 산다. 각 목장주는 이익을 얻기 때문에 자기 목장의 소 개체 수를 유지하기 위해서 많은 노력을 한다.
정부들은 두 가지 방법으로 코끼리 문제를 해결하려고 노력해 왔다. 예를 들어, 케냐와 탄자니아는 코끼리를 죽이고 상아를 판매하는 것을 불법으로 만들었다. 하지만 이러한 법을 집행하기가 어려웠으며, 당국과 밀렵꾼들 사이의 싸움은 점점 더 격렬해져 왔다. 그 동안 코끼리의 개체 수는 계속 늘어(→ 줄어들어) 왔다. 대조적으로, 나미비아와 짐바브웨와 같은 다른 나라들은 사람들이 그들 자신이 소유한 코끼리에 대해서만 죽이는 것을 허용함으로써 코끼리를 사유재로 만들었다. 땅 주인들은 이제 그들 자신의 땅에서 그 종을 보존할 유인을 가지며, 그 결과 코끼리의 개체 수가 늘어나기 시작했다. 사적 소유와 이제 그에 따르는 이윤 동기로 인해, 아프리카 코끼리는 언젠가는 소처럼 멸종으로부터 안전해질 것이다.

정답풀이
110 소는 멸종 위기에 놓이지 않은 반면에 코끼리는 멸종 위기에 놓였는데, 이는 소가 코끼리와 달리 사유재산이기 때문이라고 하며 코끼리를 보호하기 위한 해법으로 소처럼 코끼리를 사유재산화하고 개체 수를 유지하는 가운데 거래를 하도록 한 일부 나라들의 사례를 소개하는 글이다. 따라서 글의 제목으로는 ③ '멸종 위기 종을 보호하기 위해 그것들을 소유되게 하라'가 가장 적절하다.
111 코끼리 사냥을 금지하는 법을 집행하기가 어려웠다는 현실에 대한 결과에 해당하므로 코끼리 개체 수가 계속 '줄어들었다'고 해야 자연스럽다. 따라서 (c) increase(증가하다)를 dwindle(줄어들다) 정도의 어휘로 바꿔야 한다.

오답풀이
110 ① 재산으로서의 동물의 개념 변화
② 멸종 위기에 놓인 몇몇 동물들의 경제적 가치
④ 공유 재산 자원의 지속 가능성에 대하여
⑤ 천연자원 정책의 개념으로서의 공유 재산
111 ① 밀렵꾼들은 코끼리를 죽이려는 강한 유인을 가진다고 했으므로 그들에게 코끼리 개체 수를 보호할 유인이 거의 '없다(little)'는 문맥은 적절하다.
② 목장주가 소의 개체 수를 유지하기 위해서 노력하는 이유는 목장주 자신이 '이익'을 얻기 때문이라는 문맥이므로 benefit은 적절하다.
④ 코끼리를 사유재산화해서 그 코끼리들만 죽일 수 있도록 '허용하는' 것이 오히려 코끼리 개체 수를 유지하고 멸종을 막을 수 있다는 문맥이므로 allowing은 적절하다.

⑤ 코끼리를 사유재로 만들면 자신의 이익을 위해 그 개체 수를 보존하게 되므로 결국 소처럼 멸종으로부터 '안전해질(safe)' 것이라는 문맥은 적절하다.

구문풀이

17행 For example, Kenya and Tanzania have made **it** illegal [**to kill** elephants and **sell** their ivory].

: it은 형식상의 목적어이고 [ ]로 표시된 to부정사구가 내용상의 목적어이다. to kill과 (to) sell이 등위접속사 and에 의해서 병렬구조로 연결되어 있다.

어휘풀이

- extinct *a* 멸종한 (*n* extinction)
- thrive *v* 번성하다, 번영하다
- ivory *n* 상아
- poacher *n* 밀렵꾼
- population *n* 개체 수
- ranch *n* 목장
- enforce *v* 집행하다
- property *n* 재산, 소유물
- ensure *v* 보장하다
- commercial *a* 상업의
- roam *v* 돌아다니다, 배회하다
- preserve *v* 보존[보호]하다
- cattle *n* 소
- reap *v* (이익 등을) 얻다[거두다]
- meanwhile *ad* 그 동안에, 한편
- endangered *a* 멸종 위기에 처한

112 답 ④

📄 메조아메리카 원주민들의 우수한 농법

전문해석

약 5,000년 전에, 메조아메리카 원주민들이 옥수수를 처음 길렀을 때, 그들은 그것 하나만을 재배할 정도로 어리석지 않았다. 그 자체로, 매우 생산성 있는 이 곡물은 토양에 있는 영양분들, 특히 질소를 빠르게 소모하고, 대규모 작물은 해충에 매력적일 것이며, 이는 그 작물을 대량으로 죽일 수도 있었다. 그래서 사람들은 옥수수와 함께 콩을 심었는데, 이것은 대기로부터 질소를 모으고 그것들 자신의 비옥함을 제공했다. 그들은 스쿼시도 심었는데, 이것은 넓은 잎으로 땅을 덮었고, 침식과 성장을 저지하는 잡초로부터 보호했다. 스쿼시는 심지어 잡초를 억제하는 특별한 화학물질을 잎에 포함했는데, 이것은 폭풍우 동안 침출되어 새어 나왔다. **옥수수, 콩 및 스쿼시는 함께 햇빛을 최대한 활용했고, 각각 다른 각도에서 태양 광선을 받았다. 간작물의 복잡한 3차원 구조는 해충을 혼란스럽게 만드는 반면, 유익한 곤충들에게 서식지를 제공했다. 농부들이 오랫동안 알고 연구자들이 최근 수십 년 동안 확인했듯이, 전체는 정말로 합쳐져서 그것의 부분들의 합계 이상이 된다.**

정답풀이

메조아메리카 원주민들이 처음 옥수수 재배를 시작했을 때 토양의 영양분을 빠르게 소모시키는 옥수수 한 작물만 심지 않고 콩을 함께 심음으로써 토양에 비옥함을 제공했고, 스쿼시를 심음으로써 침식과 성장을 저지하는 잡초로부터 보호하는 효과까지 얻었다는 내용으로, 밑줄 친 부분은 다양한 작물을 심음으로써 작물의 수확 이외에 토양의 비옥함과 해충 방지까지 추가적 이득을 얻게 되었음을 비유적으로 표현한 것이다. 따라서 밑줄 친 부분의 함축 의미로는 ④ '다양한 작물 재배로 엄청난 이익이 생긴다'가 가장 적절하다.

오답풀이

① 역동적인 생태적 균형은 다양한 작물의 성장을 지원한다
 └ 다양한 작물을 재배함으로써 생태적 균형과 이익을 이룬다는 내용이다.
② 생태계의 각 구성요소는 그 안에서 해야 할 역할을 가지고 있다
③ 인간과 자연의 조화는 더 큰 수확을 가져온다
⑤ 다양한 농법을 통합하는 것은 농업 성과를 향상시킨다
 └ 여러 작물을 함께 재배할 때의 이익이 단일 작물을 재배했을 때보다 크다는 내용으로, 농법의 통합을 말하고 있는 것이 아니다.

구문풀이

9행 They also planted squash, [which covered the ground with its broad leaves], [protecting against erosion and smothering weeds].

: 첫 번째 [ ]는 squash를 부가적으로 설명하는 계속적 용법의 주격 관계대명사절이고, 두 번째 [ ]는 결과적인 의미를 추가적으로 제시하는 분사구문이다.

어휘풀이

- indigenous *a* 원주민의, 토착의
- Mesoamerican *a* 메조아메리카의(현재의 멕시코 중부에서 코스타리카 북서부에 걸쳐 마야 문명이 번창했던 문화 영역)
- domesticate *v* 기르다, 길들이다
- know better than to *do* ~할 정도로 어리석지 않다
- use up ~을 소모하다[다 써버리다]
- nitrogen *n* 질소
- pest *n* 해충
- nutrient *n* 양분, 영양분
- stand *n* 작물, 입목(立木)
- atmosphere *n* 대기

- fertility *n* 비옥함
- squash *n* 스쿼시, 호박류
- erosion *n* 침식
- weed-suppressing *a* 잡초를 억제하는
- chemical *n* 화학물질
- leach out 새어 나오다
- make the most of ~을 최대한 활용하다
- three-dimensional *a* 3차원의
- intercrop *n* 간작물
- habitat *n* 서식지
- integrate *v* 통합하다

- substantial *a* 상당한, 실질적인
- pursue *v* 추구하다
- relevant *a* 타당한, 관련된
- pressure *v* ~에게 압박감을 주다
- intuitive *a* 직관적인, 직감에 의한
- literally *ad* 그야말로, 말 그대로
- incapacitate *v* (질병 등이) ~을 정상적으로 생활하지 못하게 하다
- bedridden *a* 아파서 누워 있는
- shatter *v* 망가뜨리다, 부수다
- circuit *n* 회로
- profound *a* 깊은, 심오한

113 답 ⑤

📖 조사와 질문을 통해 자신의 치료 시스템에 대해 이해해야 할 필요성

전문해석

나는 항상 나의 의뢰인들, 가족 그리고 친구들에게 누군가가 그들에게 주는 조언을 신뢰할 뿐만 아니라 어떤 행동을 추구해야 할지에 대해 정보에 근거한 결정을 하기 위해 그들이 어려움을 겪고 있는 상황들에 대한 상당히 많은 양의 연구도 해야 한다고 충고한다. 이 말은 그들이 의사 또는 기 치료사에 의해 이해하지 못하거나 편안함을 느끼지 못하는 어떤 것을 하도록 압박감을 받고 있을 때 특히 더 타당하다. 예를 들어, 나는 특정한 숨쉬기 기법들을 제대로 이해하지 못하고 상당히 많은 시간을 그것들을 하는 데 보내고, 자신들의 몸속에 있는 다른 회로와 신경 체계를 망가뜨려서 그야말로 정상적으로 생활하지 못하고 아파서 누워 있는 사람들을 만나 봤다. 나는 또한 치료에 수만 달러를 쓰고, 항상 다음번의 기적을 찾지만, 결국에는 이전보다 더 아프게 된 사람들도 알고 있다. **여러분이 실행에 옮기고 있는 어떤 치료 시스템이든지 조사해 보고, 많은 질문을 하며, 여러분이 하고 있는 것에 대해 깊이 이해하고 있는지 확인하라.**

정답풀이

⑤ **복합관계사**: that절에서 동사 research 다음에 목적어로 명사절이 와야 하므로 부사절을 이끄는 복합관계부사 whenever는 쓸 수 없다. 이어지는 명사 system을 수식하여 '어떤 치료 시스템이든지'라는 의미를 나타내는 복합관계형용사 whatever로 고쳐야 한다.

오답풀이

① **관계대명사 that**: any conditions를 선행사로 취하며 뒤에 나오는 전치사 by의 목적어 역할을 하는 목적격 관계대명사 that은 어법상 적절하다.
② **분사의 태**: when절의 주어 they는 앞에 나온 my clients, family, and friends를 가리키며, 이는 압박감을 받는 대상이므로 수동태 술어를 이루는 과거분사 pressured는 적절하다.
③ **대명사**: 앞에 나온 certain breathing techniques를 대신하는 목적격 대명사 them은 어법상 적절하다.
④ **to부정사**: 문맥상 완전한 구조의 절 다음에 와서 「only to *do*」의 형태로 '단지 ~하게 되다, 그 결과는 ~일 뿐이다'의 의미를 나타내는 to end up은 적절하다.

구문풀이

1행 I always **advise** my clients, family, and friends [**to not only trust** the advice {that someone gives them}] [**but to also do** a substantial amount of research on any conditions {that they are challenged by}] [to make informed decisions about what actions to pursue].

: 문장의 동사인 advise의 목적격보어로 두 개의 [ ]로 표시된 to부정사구가 「to not only trust ~ but to also do ....」의 형태로 연결되어 있다. 두 개의 { }는 각각 the advice와 any conditions를 수식하는 목적격 관계대명사절이고, 세 번째 [ ]는 목적을 나타내는 부사적 용법의 to부정사구이다.

114 답 ③

📖 세상에 대한 정보와 자극을 능동적으로 조직하는 우리의 감각

전문해석

우리는 보통 세상은 우리가 보는 그대로이며 다른 사람들도 세상을 똑같이 바라본다고, 즉 우리의 감각은 객관적이고 공유된 실제를 반영한다고 가정한다. 우리는 우리의 감각이 거울이 그것을 들여다보는 얼굴을 비추는 것처럼 정확하게 우리가 살고 있는 세상을 나타낸다고 가정한다. 물론 우리의 감각이 우리에게 어느 정도 정확한 정보를 제공하지 않는다면, 우리는 우리가 그러는 것처럼 그것들에 의존할 수 없을 것이나 그럼에도 불구하고 심리학자들은 인식에 대한 이러한 가정들이 완벽하다(→ 오해의 소지가 있다)는 것을 발견했다. 우리의 세계에 대한 정보를 얻는 것은 수동적이고 반사적인 과정이 아니라, 마음과 감각이 함께 어우러져서 우리가 실제에 대한 '인식'을 형성하도록 도와주는 복잡하고 능동적인 과정이다. 우리는 빛, 어둠, 색깔의 형태를 단지 보기만 하는 것이 아니라, 우리에게 의미 있는 사물을 보기 위하여 이러한 자극의 형태를 조직한다. 우리는 그것들에 이름을 붙이거나 알아보고, 다른 사물에 대해서 완전히 새롭거나 비슷한 것으로 그것들을 확인한다.

정답풀이

③ 우리는 우리의 감각이 객관적이고 정확하게 우리가 살고 있는 세상을 반영한다고 생각하지만, 사실 우리는 우리에게 의미 있는 것들을 보고 실제에 대한 인식을 형성하기 위해 능동적으로 정보와 자극의 형태를 조직한다는 내용이다. 즉, 세상의 정보와 자극을 받아들이는 우리의 감각은 우리가 가정하는 것처럼 객관적이거나 정확하지만은 않다는 것이므로, 심리학자들이 이러한 가정에 '오해의 소지가 있음'을 발견했다고 해야 문맥상 적절하다. 따라서 flawless(흠이 없는, 완벽한)를 misleading(오해의 소지가 있는) 정도의 어휘로 바꿔야 한다.

오답풀이

① 우리가 세상을 있는 그대로, 다른 사람들과 똑같이 바라본다고 가정한다는 것은, 곧 우리의 감각이 '객관적'이고 공유된 실제를 반영한다고 가정한다는 의미이므로 objective는 문맥상 적절하다.
② ①과 같은 맥락으로, 우리의 감각이 '정확하게' 세상을 반영한다고 생각한다는 문맥이므로 accurately는 적절하다.
④ 우리는 세상에 대한 정보를 수동적으로 받아들이는 것이 아니라, 능동적으로 받아들이면서 실제에 대한 인식을 스스로 '형성한다'는 문맥이므로 construct는 적절하다.
⑤ 우리가 세상으로부터 오는 자극의 형태를 스스로 조직하는 것은 우리 자신에게 '의미 있는' 것들을 보기 위해서라는 문맥이므로 meaningful은 적절하다.

구문풀이

3행 We assume [that our senses represent the world {**in which** we live} **as accurately as** a mirror reflects the face {that looks into it}].

: 첫 번째 [ ]는 assume의 목적절이고, 그 안의 첫 번째 { }는 the world를 수식하는 관계절로 in which는 관계부사 where로 바꿔 쓸 수 있다. 두 번째 { }는 the face를 수식하는 주격 관계대명사절이다. as ~ as 동등 비교 구문이 사용되었으며 accurately는 바로 앞의 live가 아니라 목적절의 동사인 represent를 수식한다.

어휘풀이
- reflect *v* 나타내다, 비추다 (*a* reflective)
- assumption *n* 가정, 추정 (*v* assume)
- perception *n* 지각, 인식
- flawless *a* 흠 없는, 완벽한
- passive *a* 수동적인
- stimulation *n* 자극
- entirely *ad* 완전히, 전부

- stimulus *n* 자극 (*pl.* stimuli)
- manner *n* 방식
- subject *n* 실험 대상자
- bias *n* 편향
- novelty *n* 새로움
- inconsistent *a* 일관되지 않은
- comparable *a* 비슷한, 비교할만한
- preference *n* 선호
- cognitive *a* 인지의
- invariably *ad* 항상, 변함없이
- peer *n* 동료, 또래

115 답 ①

📖 인간과 원숭이의 새로운 것에 대한 선호

전문해석
원숭이가 인간이 그런 것보다 훨씬 더 새로움에 이끌리는 경향이 있다고 주장될 수 있다. 1950년의 한 실험에서, 원숭이 한 마리는 이전에 보여준 것과 동일한 물건과 다른 물건 간에 선택을 해야 했다. 그 실험에서, 그 원숭이는 하나의 물건을 보았다. 그런 다음 그 원숭이는 그 미끼로 던진 물건과 동일한 또는 그것과 다른 한 물건을 보았다. 두 가지 조건이 비교되었는데, 동일한(친숙한) 물건을 선택하는 것이 강화되었을 때와 다른(새로운) 물건을 선택하는 것이 강화되었을 때였다. 대체로 원숭이들은 친숙한 자극보다는 새로운 자극에 더 빨리 반응했다. 비교 실험에서, 인간은 매우 다른 방식으로 행동한다. 인지 편향 과제에서(인간이 표적을 보고 나서 두 가지 선택 사항을 보고 그 후 자신이 '가장 좋아하는' 것을 선택하라고 요청받을 때) 인간 실험 대상자들이 보인 선호는 원숭이들의 그것(선호)과 매우 다르다. 인간은 거의 항상 표적과 더 큰 차이를 보이는 것들보다는 그것과 가장 비슷한 항목을 선택한다.

정답풀이
한 실험에서 원숭이가 친숙한 물건과 새로운 물건 각각에 반응하는 속도를 비교했을 때 새로운 물건에 반응하는 속도가 더 빨랐는데, 이는 비슷한 실험에서 친숙한 물건을 선택하는 인간의 선호와 매우 다르다는 내용이다. 빈칸이 있는 문장은 주제문에 해당하고 빈칸에는 원숭이의 성향을 나타내는 말이 들어가야 하므로 ① '새로움에 이끌리는'이 가장 적절하다.

오답풀이
② 차이를 알지 못하는
③ 자신의 동료들에 의해 영향을 받는
④ 자신의 선호에 있어서 일관되지 않은
⑤ 친숙하지 않은 것을 선택하기를 두려워하는
┗ 친숙하지 않은 것을 선택하기를 두려워하는 것은 원숭이의 성향과 반대되므로 오답!

구문풀이
2행 In a 1950 experiment, a monkey had to choose **between** an object [identical to one {previously shown}] **and** a different object.

: 「between *A* and *B*」 구문이 쓰였으며, [ ]는 an object를 수식하는 형용사구이고, 그 안의 { }는 one(= an object)을 수식하는 과거분사구이다.

5행 Then the monkey saw another object [which was **either** {identical to the baited object} **or** {different from it}].

: [ ]는 another object를 수식하는 주격 관계대명사절로, 이 절에는 「either *A* or *B*」의 상관접속사가 { }로 표시된 두 개의 보어를 연결하면서 '*A*이거나 *B*이거나 (둘 중 하나)'의 의미를 나타내고 있다.

어휘풀이
- experiment *n* 실험
- identical *a* 동일한, 똑같은
- previously *ad* 이전에
- bait *v* ~에 미끼를 달다
- familiar *a* 익숙한, 친숙한 (↔ unfamiliar)
- reinforce *v* 강화하다
- on the whole 대체로, 전반적으로

116 답 ③

📖 자신과 관련된 부정적인 증거를 쉽게 받아들이지 못하는 인간의 성향

전문해석
한 연구에서 동기가 부여된 인지에 평생을 바친 심리학자인 Ziva Kunda는 카페인 섭취가 유발하는 여성들의 섬유낭종성 질병 발병의 위험성에 관한 신문기사를 학생들에게 보여주었다. Kunda는 그들에게 그것이 〈뉴욕 타임스〉의 과학 섹션에 실린 것이라고 말했지만 실제로는 의학 저널에서 가져온 것이었다. 그녀는 이어서 그들에게 15년 이내에 그 질병에 걸릴 자신의 위험성을 평가하고 그 기사 자체가 얼마나 설득력이 있는지를 평가해 달라고 요청했다. 곧 호기심을 끄는 패턴이 나타났다. 카페인을 과하게 마시거나 제법 마시는 여학생들은 그들이 (병에 걸릴) 위험성이 높을 것이라는 것을 인정했지만 또한 그 기사에 대해서는 훨씬 더 회의적이기도 했다. 그들은 추가적인 증거를 보기를 원한다고 말했다. 그들에게 그 연구는 기껏해야 불확실한 것으로 보일 뿐이었다. 그러나 카페인을 거의 또는 전혀 마시지 않는 다른 모든 사람은 그 연구가 설득력이 있다고 생각했다. 그렇다면 이것은 무엇을 시사하는가? 단순히 말하자면, 우리 자신(우리의 특성, 우리의 삶, 우리의 결정)에 관한 한 우리의 개인적인 애착이 우리의 객관적인 지식을 압도한다.

정답풀이
사람들에게 자신의 건강 상태에 대해서 경고해 주는 부정적인 연구 결과를 받아들이지 않으려는 성향이 있다는 연구 결과를 통해서 우리 자신에 관한 한 자신을 보호하려는 성향(자신에 대한 애착)이 객관적인 지식을 넘어선다는 것을 추론할 수 있다. 따라서 빈칸에는 ③ '우리의 개인적인 애착이 우리의 객관적인 지식을 압도한다'가 들어가는 것이 가장 적절하다.

오답풀이
① 우리의 성향은 나쁜 것들을 외부의 사건에서 기인한 것으로 여기는 것이다
② 우리는 오직 듣도록 훈련받은 것만 듣기를 원한다
④ 우리는 건강과 관련된 뉴스 기사가 흔히 편향되어 있다고 의심한다
⑤ 우리는 일반적인 평판에 근거하여 증거를 체계적으로 잘못 판단한다

구문풀이
7행 She then **asked** them **to rate** their own risk for developing the disease within fifteen years and **to evaluate** [how convincing they found the article itself].

: asked의 목적격보어로 to rate와 to evaluate가 병렬구조로 연결되어 있으며, [ ]는 evaluate의 목적어로 간접의문문의 어순(의문사+주어+동사)을 취하고 있다.

어휘풀이
- devote *v* 헌신하다, 바치다
- consumption *n* 섭취, 소비
- rate *v* 평가하다
- emerge *v* 나타나다
- acknowledge *v* 인정하다
- shaky *a* 불확실한, 불안정한
- attribute *v* ~의 탓으로 돌리다
- overpower *v* 압도하다, 사로잡다
- cognition *n* 인식, 인지
- pose *v* 제기하다, 야기하다
- convincing *a* 설득력이 있는
- moderate *a* 중간의
- skeptical *a* 회의적인
- at best 기껏해야
- attachment *n* 애착, 집착
- reputation *n* 평판, 명성

117 답 ④

📖 무임승차자들이 사회적 유대에 미치는 영향

전문해석

무임승차자들이 착취하는 사회의 구성원들은 이타적으로 행동하는 수밖에 없는데, 그들은 자기 자신의 건강함을 잃어가며 무임승차자의 건강함에 기여한다. (C) 이러한 대가는 단기적으로는 작을지도 모르는데, 특히 그 대가가 그 사회의 모든 다른 구성원들 사이에 공유될 경우에 그러하다. 그러나 그 대가는 장기적으로 반드시 늘어난다. 그리고 그 압력이 충분히 크면, 무임승차자로 행동하는 많은 개인들의 영향이 그 공동체의 나머지 사람들에게 매우 큰 부담을 지우는 정도가 될 것이다. (A) 이 지점에서 사회를 하나로 묶는 암묵적 합의는 깨질 것이다. 의심과 상호 호혜적인 거래를 하는 것을 꺼리는 것이 증가하여 상호작용과 관계의 자연스러운 흐름을 덜 유동적으로 만들 것이다. 신뢰를 바탕으로 기꺼이 협력하려는 것은 줄어들고 사회 제도를 하나로 묶는 실제적인 유대는 점차 없어질 것이다. (B) 무임승차는 개별 무임승차자의 행동에 대한 우리의 개인적인 경험에 의해 결국 억제될 것인데, 한 번 물리고 나면 우리는 그 특정한 사람을 다시 신뢰하기를 꺼리게 될 것이다. 하지만 우리가 그 지점에 도달하게 되면, 사회를 하나로 묶는 데 도움이 되는 신뢰의 요소는 사라졌다.

정답풀이

무임승차자의 착취는 사회의 다른 구성원들의 건강함을 희생시키면서 얻어지는 것이라는 주어진 글 다음에는, 이런 대가(These costs)가 장기적으로 쌓여서 나머지 사람에게 큰 부담이 된다는 (C)가 와야 한다. 그리고 그렇게 부담이 커진 지점에서는(At that point) 사회적 유대가 점차 없어질 것이라고 말하는 (A)가 온 후, 결국 무임승차는 억제될 것인데 그 지점에 도달하면 이미 신뢰는 사라졌다는 (B)로 마무리되는 순서가 가장 자연스럽다. 따라서 적절한 글의 순서는 ④ (C)-(A)-(B)이다.

구문풀이

16행 But **once** we reach that point, / the element of trust [that helps to hold society together] has been lost.

: '일단 ~하면'이라는 의미의 접속사 once가 이끄는 부사절과 주절로 이루어진 문장이다. [ ]는 주절의 핵심 주어인 the element of trust를 수식하는 주격 관계대명사절이다.

어휘풀이

- exploit v 착취하다
- contribute to ~에 기여하다
- at the expense of ~을 잃어가며, ~을 희생하면서
- implicit a 암묵적인
- suspicion n 의심
- engage in ~을 하다
- fluid a 유동적인
- dissolve v 없어지다
- add up (조금씩) 늘어나다
- burden n 부담, 짐
- altruistically ad 이타적으로
- fitness n 건강함
- fall apart 무너지다
- reluctance n 내키지 않음, 꺼림
- reciprocal a 상호 호혜적인
- hold ~ together ~을 결속시키다
- hold ~ in check ~을 저지[억제]하다
- impose v 부과하다

118 답 ④

📖 생물분해성 제품에 대한 소비자 인식의 확산

전문해석

생물분해성 제품은 일반적으로 자연적 과정과 곰팡이 및 박테리아를 포함한 생물학적 유기체에 의해 분해될 수 있는 제품을 가리킨다. 최근까지 생물분해성 이면에 있는 문제들에 대한 소비자의 이해는 여러 가지 이유로 제한되었다. 용어의 급증과, 관련된 다양한 과정들의 복잡성은 일반 대중이 지속 가능한 관행의 이 특징적인 일에 참여하는 것을 막았다. 이러한 이해 부족의 결과로, 제품이나 포장의 수명에 대한 고려사항과 재사용 또는 재활용 가능성은 구매 의사 결정 과정에 충분히 영향을 끼치지 못했다. 그러나 분해 가능, 생분해 가능, 퇴비 가능이라는 관련 용어가 보다 일반적인 사용에 들어옴에 따라, 소비자들이 여전히 완전한 이해가 부족함에도 불구하고 그 용어들에 대한 소비자의 인식이 증가했다. 이것은 지방 정부의 재활용 계획 그리고 가두(街頭) 수집(재활용품 수거)과 결부되어, 더 많은 가정 재활용을 장려하는 정부의 캠페인에 의해 촉진되어 왔다. 증가하는 언론의 관심과 더불어 소매상 및 소비자 로비 활동, 특히 포장 및 일회용 비닐봉투의 감소에 관한 로비 활동 또한 소비자 참여 증대에 기여했다.

정답풀이

주어진 문장은 역접의 연결어 However로 시작하면서 생물분해성과 관련된 용어들에 대한 소비자의 인식이 증가했다는 내용을 담고 있다. ④ 다음의 문장에서 This가 가리키는 내용이 앞에 나와 있지 않고, 앞 내용과는 달리 긍정적인 내용이 전개되고 있어서 글의 흐름이 단절된다. This는 소비자의 인식이 증가한 것을 가리키며, 따라서 주어진 문장이 ④에 들어가 생물분해성 용어에 대한 소비자의 인식이 증가한 이유를 설명하는 흐름이 되어야 하므로 주어진 문장은 ④에 들어가는 것이 가장 적절하다.

구문풀이

11행 [The proliferation of terminology] and [the complexity of the different processes involved] **prevented** the general public **from engaging** with this feature of sustainable practice.

: 「A and B」의 구조로 연결된 두 개의 [ ]가 주어이며, 술부에는 '(목적어)가 ~하지 못하게 하다[막다]'라는 의미의 「prevent+목적어+from doing」 구문이 쓰였다.

어휘풀이

- terminology n 전문용어
- biodegradable a 생물분해성의 n 생물분해성 제품
- compostable a 퇴비로 만들 수 있는
- refer to ~을 가리키다, ~을 언급하다
- organism n 유기체
- appreciation n 이해, 올바른 인식
- proliferation n 급격한 증가, 확산
- sustainable a 지속 가능한
- consideration n 고려사항
- coupled with ~와 함께
- retailer n 소매상
- degradable a 분해할 수 있는
- awareness n 인식, 자각
- break down ~을 분해하다
- fungus n 곰팡이 (pl. fungi)
- biodegradability n 생물분해성
- feature n 특징적인 일[모습]
- duly ad 충분히, 정당하게, 당연히
- stimulate v 자극하다
- curbside n 가두, 보도 가장자리
- engagement n 참여, 개입

119 답 ②

📖 기술의 불확실성과 발달

전문해석

기술적 불확실성의 첫 번째 근원은 특정 과업을 수행하기 위한 다양한 해결책이 항상 존재한다는 운 좋은 사실에서 유래한다. 기술적 기준, 경제적 기준 및 사회적 기준을 고려할 때, 어느 것이 '최상'일지는 항상 불확실하다. 불확실성은 초기 설계 선택부터 시장에서의 성공 또는 실패, 궁극적인 환경적 영향 및 파급 효과에 이르기까지 기술 발달의 모든 단계에서 지배적이다. 기술과 경영에 관련된 문헌은 그러한 불확실성을 '뱀의 굴' 문제라고 규정하고 있다. 이것은 마치 모두 비슷하게 생긴 수백 개의 구덩이에서 특정 뱀을 고르려고 하는 것과 같다. 다른 이들은 '많은 사람들이 거명되지만, 선택되는 사람은 거의 없다'라는 성경에 나오는 인용문을 이용한다. 기술적 불확실성은 기술적 변화를 '예측하려는' 노력에서 지속적으로 악명 높은 당혹감이다. 그러나 '하늘이 맑아질 때까지 기다리자'는 전략으로 얻을 수 있는 것은 또한 아무것도 없다. 그것은 맑아지지 않을 것이고, 불확실성은 계속될 것이며, 올바른 전략은 기술적 다양성을 가진 실험이다.

→ 기술적 불확실성은 기술 발전의 모든 단계에서 <u>지속적</u>이므로, 결과의 불확실성에 대한 우려 때문에 실험을 <u>중단하는</u> 것은 타당하지 않을 것이다.

정답풀이

기술의 속성은 항상 불확실하기 때문에 불확실성을 인정하면서 현재 주어진 기술을 이용하여 여러 실험을 계속하는 것이 현명하다는 것이 이 글의 요지이다. 따라서 (A)에는 persistent(지속적인)가, (B)에는 suspend(보류하다, 일시 중단하다)가 들어가는 것이 가장 적절하다.

구문풀이

3행 **It** is always uncertain [which might be the "best]," [taking into account technical criteria, economic criteria, and social criteria].

: It은 형식상의 주어이고, 첫 번째 [ ]의 명사절(의문사절)이 내용상의 주어이다. 두 번째 [ ]는 분사구문이다.

어휘풀이

- derive from ~에서 유래하다
- criterion *n* 기준 (*pl.* criteria)
- initial *a* 초기의
- label *v* 규정하다
- quote *n* 인용문
- forecast *v* 예측하다
- unreasonable *a* 불합리한, 비이성적인, 터무니없는
- undertake *v* ~에 착수하다
- take into account ~을 고려하다
- prevail *v* 지배적이다, 우세하다
- eventual *a* 궁극적인
- pit *n* 구덩이
- notorious *a* 악명 높은
- postpone *v* 미루다[연기하다]

3점 공략 모의고사 4회				본문 p.088
120 ④	**121** ④	**122** ③	**123** ④	**124** ⑤
125 ②	**126** ③	**127** ④		

120 답 ④

📖 '역사의 아버지'로 인정받고 있는 Herodotus

전문해석

Herodotus는 로마의 작가 Cicero에 의해서 '역사의 아버지'라고 불렸지만, 고대와 현대의 비평가들에 의해서 '거짓말의 아버지'로 배척되기도 했는데, 이들은 그의 저술이 믿기 힘든 이야기일 뿐이라고 주장한다. Herodotus가 때때로 부정확한 정보를 전하거나 주의를 끌기 위해서 과장을 한 것은 사실이지만, 그의 진술은 다소 신뢰할 만한 것이 일관되게 밝혀져 왔다. **그의 저술에 대한 일부 초기의 비판은 그의 종종 비판받는 주장이 사실은 정확했으며, 그 시대의 받아들여지는 정보에 근거한 것임을 입증하는 후기의 고고학적 증거에 의해서 반박되었다.** 그가 현재는 틀린 것으로 인정되는 여러 주장을 한 것은 분명하지만, 여전히 그의 저술에는 옳은 것도 많이 있다. 그의 '역사서'는 그가 제공하는 세부 사항이 틀리거나 과장될 때조차도 종종 특정한 사건이나 문화적 패러다임을 이해하는 방법을 가리킨다. **현재 Herodotus는 대다수의 역사가들에 의해서 '역사의 아버지', 그리고 고대 세상에 대한 신뢰할 만한 정보원으로 계속 인정받고 있다.**

정답풀이

④ **분사의 태**: 앞의 claims를 수식하는 어구를 이끄는데, claims가 '인정하는' 것이 아니라 '인정받는' 수동적인 것이므로 recognizing을 recognized로 고쳐야 한다.

오답풀이

① **관계대명사 who**: 선행사 critics(비평가들)를 부연 설명하는 절을 이끌면서 claim의 주어 역할을 하는 주격 관계대명사 who의 쓰임은 어법상 적절하다.
  └→ 선행사가 멀리 떨어져 있는 경우로, 선행사를 *The Father of Lies*로 착각하면 which가 와야 한다고 생각할 수 있는 오답!

② **병렬구조**: 주어 Herodotus에 이어지는 동사 relays와 or에 의해 병렬구조를 이루고 있는 동사 exaggerates의 쓰임은 어법상 적절하다.

③ **접속사 that**: proves의 목적절을 이끄는데 뒤에 '주어+동사+보어'로 이루어진 완전한 절이 이어지고 있으므로 명사절을 이끄는 접속사 that의 쓰임은 어법상 적절하다.

⑤ **동명사**: 앞에 쓰인 to는 전치사이므로 동명사 understanding의 쓰임은 어법상 적절하다.
  └→ the way to는 '~하는 방법' 또는 '~로 가는 길'이라는 의미의 표현으로 이때 to는 전치사임에 유의한다.

구문풀이

8행 Some early criticism of his work has been refuted by <u>later archaeological evidence</u> [which proves {that his most-often criticized claims were, in fact, accurate, were based on accepted information of the time}].

: [ ]는 later archaeological evidence를 수식하는 주격 관계대명사절이며, 그 안의 { }는 proves의 목적어로 쓰인 명사절이다.

12행 [While **it** is clear {that he makes <u>a number of claims</u> (now recognized as wrong)}], there is still <u>much</u> in his work [that he has gotten right].

: 첫 번째 [ ]는 While이 이끄는 양보를 나타내는 부사절이며, 그 안의 it은 형식상의 주

어, { }의 명사절이 내용상의 주어이고, ( )는 a number of claims를 수식하는 과거분사구이다. 두 번째 [ ]는 much를 수식하는 목적격 관계대명사절이다.

어휘풀이
- reject *v* 거부[거절]하다
- critic *n* 비평가
- tall tale 믿기 힘든 이야기, 터무니없는 말
- relay *v* (말을) 전하다
- inaccurate *a* 부정확한
- exaggerate *v* 과장하다
- for effect 효과를 주기 위해, 주의를 끌기 위해
- account *n* 진술, 설명
- consistently *ad* 일관되게
- reliable *a* 신뢰성 있는
- refute *v* 반박하다
- archaeological *a* 고고학적인
- criticize *v* 비판하다, 비난하다
- recognize *v* 인정하다
- majority *n* 대다수, 대부분

121 답 ④

📖 위계적으로 조직되는 정보

전문해석
어떤 정보는 우리가 좀 더 하위의 개념을 이해하도록 돕는 일반적인 개념을 중심으로 저장되는 것으로 보인다. 그래서 예를 들면, 만일 누군가가 가자미에게 아가미가 있는지를 묻는다면, 당신은 전에 그 질문을 생각해 본 적 없이도 그리고 더 중요하게는 당신의 기억 속에 그 정보를 실제로 전혀 갖고 있지 않아도 쉽게 답할 수 있다. 당신이 알아야 할 전부는 가자미가 물고기이고 물고기는 아가미가 있다는 것뿐이다. 마찬가지로, 당신은 Buick(미국 GM사의 자동차)이 자동차이기 때문에 바퀴가 있다는 것을 알며, 암말이 포유동물이기 때문에 젖꼭지가 있다는 것을 안다. 의미 기억(경험에 의한 기억이 아닌 일반적인 개념에 관한 기억) 이면의 생각은 그저 이러한 종류의 정보가 위계적으로 공유된다는 것이다. 우리는 암컷 포유동물에게 젖꼭지가 있다는 정보를 저장하며 그러므로 말은 포유동물이기 때문에 젖꼭지를 가지고 있다고 추론한다. 명백히, 사람들은 그들이 실제로 경험해 온 것보다 훨씬 더 많이 알기 때문에 적어도 어느 정도는 이런 식으로 조직된 정보를 가지고 있음에 틀림없다.

정답풀이
가자미가 아가미를 가지고 있는지를 직접 경험하지 않더라도 알 수 있는데, 이는 가자미가 물고기라는 것과 물고기는 아가미가 있다는 보다 상위 개념의 지식을 가지고 있기 때문이라고 했다. 따라서 지식이나 정보가 위계적으로 조직되어 있기 때문에 사람들은 모든 것을 경험하지 않고도 훨씬 더 많은 지식이나 정보를 알 수 있음을 추론할 수 있으므로 빈칸에는 ④ '위계적으로'가 들어가는 것이 가장 적절하다.

오답풀이
① 다르게
② 집합적으로
③ 수평적으로
  └ 정보의 구성에 있어서 상위 개념과 하위 개념이 있다는 글의 내용과는 반대되는 오답!
⑤ 잠재의식적으로

구문풀이
7행 All [you need to know] is [**that** a flounder is a fish] and [**that** fish have gills].

: 첫 번째 [ ]는 All을 수식하는 목적격 관계대명사절이며, 두 번째와 세 번째 [ ]는 is의 보어 역할을 하는 명사절이다.

어휘풀이
- subordinate *a* 하위의, 부차적인
- gill *n* 아가미
- female *a* 암컷의, 여성의
- mammal *n* 포유동물
- semantic *a* 의미론적, 의미상의
- infer *v* 추론하다
- to some extent 어느 정도
- a great deal 훨씬 더

122 답 ③

📖 문화인류학에서 인지적 복잡성을 습득하는 과정

전문해석
새 천년 시대의 시민들은 인지적 복잡성이라고 불리는 것을 필요로 하는데, 그것은 구별과 통합이라는 두 가지 능력으로 구성되어 있다. 구별은 하나의 실체가 어떻게 많은 다른 부분들로 구성되어 있는지를 볼 수 있는 것을 수반하며, 반대로 통합은 다양한 부분들이 어떻게 상호 결합되어 있는지를 확인할 수 있는 능력을 수반한다. **인지적으로 복잡한 사람은 두 유형의 사고를 다 할 수 있으며 둘 사이에서 편안하게 이동할 수 있다.** 지역적인 상황의 독특한 필요에 집중할 수 있어야 하는 한편 동시에 그것이 어떻게 전체 조직의 작동 속에 맞춰 들어가는지를 이해할 수 있어야 한다. 문화인류학의 연구는 사람들에게 자신의 문화뿐만 아니라 다른 문화도 점검하고, 그 둘을 비교하며, 문화의 일반화된 개념에 대한 두 문화의 관계를 이해하도록 권장한다. 그리하여 인류학도는 특정한 부분들로부터 전체로 움직였다가 다시 돌아옴으로써 인지적으로 복잡해지는 연습을 하게 된다.

정답풀이
인지적 복잡성은 구별과 통합의 사고를 모두 할 수 있는 능력으로, 인지적 복잡성을 가진 사람은 지역적인 상황의 독특한 필요에 집중할 수 있는 동시에 그것이 전체에 어떻게 맞춰지는지도 이해할 수 있다고 했다. 또한, 문화인류학의 연구는 자신의 문화와 다른 문화를 점검해 문화의 일반화된 개념에 대한 두 문화의 관계를 이해하도록 권장한다고 하므로, 인류학을 공부하는 학생은 ③ '특정한 부분들로부터 전체로 움직였다가 다시 돌아옴'으로써 인지적인 복잡성을 얻게 될 것임을 추론할 수 있다.

오답풀이
① 실생활의 경험으로부터 많은 지식을 얻음
② 다양한 유형의 문화 상호 간의 의사소통을 분석함
④ 외부적인 사건의 영향에 대한 구체적인 사례를 조사함
⑤ 경쟁 우위를 주는 어떤 측면에 집중함

구문풀이
10행 One must be able to focus on the unique needs of the local situation [**while** at the same time **understanding** {how it fits into the operations of the total organization}].

: [ ]는 접속사를 생략하지 않은 분사구문이고, { }는 understanding의 목적어 역할을 하는 명사절(의문사절)이다.

어휘풀이
- millennium *n* 천년
- be referred to as ~라고 불리다[언급되다]
- complexity *n* 복잡성
- be made up of ~로 구성되다
- twin *a* 쌍을 이루는
- differentiate *v* 구별하다
- integrate *v* 통합하다
- involve *v* 수반하다
- entity *n* 실체
- integration *n* 통합
- engage in ~에 참여하다, ~을 하다
- cultural anthropology 문화인류학
- concrete *a* 구체적인
- competitive advantage 경쟁 우위

123 답 ④

📖 서로 다른 재료와 도구로 성취할 수 있는 예술적 목표

전문해석
어떤 종류의 재료와 도구가 서로 다른 예술적 매체에 관련되는가? 일부 재료와 도구들, 예를 들어 물감과 캔버스 또는 영화용 필름과 필름 카메라는 본질적으로 물리적이다. (C) 서로 다른 물리적인 재료와 도구들은 서로 다른 창작 목표의 실현을 허용

한다. 그림으로는 할 수 있지만 돌로는 할 수 없는 것들(예를 들어 2차원적이고 추상적인 표현주의적 구성을 만드는 것)이 있고, 그리고 연속적으로 움직이는 이미지(영상)가 특히 그리고 탁월하게 성취하기에 적합한, 이야기하기와 같은 예술적으로 중요한 기능들이 있다. (A) 물론 이야기하기는 그림으로도 가능하지만 이 기능은 영화 만들기에서와 뚜렷이 다른 방식으로 성취되며, 예를 들어 관례에 따라 일련의 사건을 나타내는 것으로 이해되는, 일련의 정지된 이미지나 이미지 부분으로 성취된다. 영화에는 때때로 연속된 이미지가 일련의 정지된 작품이라는 인상을 줄 때 회화 특유의 특성이 부여된다. (B) 역으로, 회화에는 때때로 사건을 전개하는 의식을 생생하게 전할 때 영화적 특성이 부여된다. 게다가 디지털 필름은 대부분 또는 전체적으로 구성될 때 회화적이 될 수 있다.

정답풀이
물감과 캔버스 또는 영화용 필름과 필름 카메라와 같은 물리적 재료와 도구가 서로 다른 예술 매체에 사용된다는 내용의 주어진 글 다음에, 서로 다른 물리적 재료와 도구는 서로 다른 창작 목표의 실현을 허용한다고 구체적 설명을 시작하는 (C)가 와야 한다. 연속적으로 움직이는 이미지, 즉 영상이 성취하기에 적합한 이야기하기 기능을 언급한 (C)의 후반부 다음에는, 물론 그런 이야기하기 기능이 회화에서도 성취될 수 있지만, 영화 만들기와는 아주 다른 방식으로 성취될 수 있음을 설명하는 (A)가 오고, 영화에 회화적 특성이 부여될 수도 있다는 (A)의 마지막 문장 다음에는, 역으로 회화에 영화적 특성이 부여되기도 한다고 하는 (B)가 오는 순서가 가장 적절하다.

구문풀이
10행 It is interesting [**to note** {that films are sometimes ascribed a painterly quality (when the image sequence gives the impression of a series of still compositions)}].

: It은 형식상의 주어이고, [ ]의 to부정사구가 내용상의 주어이다. { }는 note의 목적어 역할을 하는 명사절이고, 그 안의 ( )는 때를 나타내는 부사절이다.

20행 There are things [that you can do with paint] [that you can't do with stone]—for example, create a two-dimensional, abstract expressionist composition— / and there are artistically significant functions such as storytelling [that moving image sequences are particularly and distinctively well suited to accomplish].

: and로 두 개의 대등한 절이 연결된 구조의 문장이다. 첫 번째 [ ]는 things를 수식하는 관계절이고, 두 번째 [ ]는 things (that you can do with paint)를 수식하는 관계절이다. 세 번째 [ ]는 artistically significant functions를 수식하는 관계절이다.

어휘풀이
- film stock 영화용 (아날로그) 필름
- a sequence of 일련의, 연속의
- convention n 관례
- painterly a 회화 특유의, 그림 같은
- conversely ad 역으로
- convey v 전하다
- two-dimensional a 2차원적인
- expressionist a 표현주의적인
- distinctively ad 탁월하게, 뚜렷이
- markedly ad 뚜렷이
- still a 정지된
- represent v 나타내다
- composition n 작품
- vividly ad 생생하게
- unfold v 전개하다
- abstract a 추상적인
- significant a 중대한

124 답 ⑤

소매업자들의 격자망 구성 방식의 장단점

전문해석
소매업자들은 그들 가게 내부의 기초가 되는 많은 총괄적인 배치 방법들을 가지고 있다. 가장 흔한 접근법은 격자망인데, 그 안에서 선반을 양쪽에 둔 채로 통로가 서로 나란하게 조직된다. 이러한 배치는 그것이 효율적이기 때문에 인기가 있다. 고객들은 이런 유형의 가게에 익숙하며, 그 안에서 돌아다니기 편하고, 그들이 사고 싶은 상품을 빨리 찾을 수 있다. 그것은 또한 소매업자에게 비용 효과적인데, 왜냐하면 내부 붙박이들을 표준화할 수 있고 평방피트 당 많은 양의 상품을 전시할 수 있기 때문이다. 수만 개의 상품을 가진 보다 큰 식료품점과 할인 매장들은 효율성을 강조하고, 그 결과 격자망 배치를 선호한다. 하지만 효율성에 대한 대가로, 격자망 구성 방식은 소매업자가 구매자 통행의 흐름에 영향을 미치는 것을 더 어렵게 한다. 이러한 한계를 처리하기 위해, 가게는 그 표지와 상품 전시에 있어서 매우 창의적이 되어 왔다.

정답풀이
역접의 연결어 however가 있는 주어진 문장은 효율성에 대한 대가로 가게의 내부를 격자망으로 구성하는 것이 가지는 단점을 설명하고 있으므로 그것의 장점인 효율성에 대한 설명이 끝나는 부분인 ⑤에 들어가야 한다. ⑤ 다음 문장의 this limitation은 주어진 문장에 언급된 내용(고객의 통행에 영향을 미치는 것이 어려움)을 가리킨다.

구문풀이
1행 In exchange for efficiency, however, the grid format makes **it** more difficult [for the retailer **to influence** the flow of shopper traffic].

: it은 형식상의 목적어로 내용상의 목적어인 [ ]로 표시된 to부정사구를 대신한다. for the retailer는 to부정사구의 의미상의 주어를 나타낸다.

어휘풀이
- in exchange for ~에 대한 대가로
- grid n 격자(망)
- retailer n 소매업자
- layout n 배치
- parallel a 평행의
- fixture n 붙박이, 고정 장치
- merchandise n 상품
- warehouse store 할인 매장
- address v (문제 등을) 처리하다, 다루다
- limitation n 한계
- efficiency n 효율성 (a efficient)
- format n 구성 방식
- traffic n 왕래, 통행
- interior n 내부
- cost-efficient a 비용 효과적인
- standardize v 표준화하다
- square foot 평방피트
- emphasize v 강조하다
- signage n 신호, 표지판

125 답 ②

농업 보조금의 불균등한 배분이 미국의 농장에 미친 영향

전문해석
20세기 전반에 미국에는 600만 개 이상의 농장이 있었다. 현재는 그것의 겨우 3분의 1, 즉 200만 개의 농장이 남아 있다. 남아 있는 농장의 절반은 연 매출 5,000달러가 안 되는 소규모 시간제 운영을 한다. 지속적으로 성장해 온 유일한 농장들은 2,000에이커가 넘는 농장들이다. 세계화된 식료품 시스템은 규모의 경제(생산량이 증가함에 따라 평균 비용이 줄어드는 현상)에 보상을 하고, 미국의 농업 보조금 제도는 대규모의 기업형 생산에 기업 지원 정책인 현금 인센티브(장려책)를 제공함으로써 이것을 강화한다. 가장 큰 농장들은 전보다 더 많은 보조금을 받고 있다. 가장 큰 2퍼센트의 농장들이 미국 농업 보조금의 거의 30퍼센트를 받고 있는 한편, 가장 큰 30퍼센트의 농장들이 전체 보조금의 80퍼센트 이상을 받고 있다. 〈Des Moines Register〉지(아이오아주 신문)에 따르면 '시골은 연방 정부의 농장 지불금으로부터 가장 큰 혜택을 받는 월마트와 같은 초대형 농장과, 파산하지 않기 위해 거의 항상 농장 외적인 수입을 필요로 하는 틈새, 시간제 또는 취미로 하는 농부들로 구성된 수천 개의 작은 농장으로 나뉘고 있다.'

→ 세계화된 식료품 시스템에서 연방 보조금의 불공평한 분배 때문에 미국에서 대규모 농장들은 점점 더 번창해 왔다.

20세기 전반에는 600만 개에 달하던 미국 농장의 수가 많이 줄었으며, 남아 있는 농장 중에서도 지속적으로 번창하는 것은 기업형의 초대형 농장으로, 그 이유는 2퍼센트의 가장 큰 농장들이 농업 보조금의 30퍼센트를 받고, 상위 30퍼센트의 대규모 농장들이 농업 보조금의 80퍼센트를 가져가기 때문이라는 내용이다. 따라서 이러한 정부 보조금의 불공평한 분배로 인해 대규모 농장들이 더 번창해 왔다고 요약할 수 있으므로, (A)에는 thriving(번창하는)이, (B)에는 inequitable(불공평한)이 들어가는 것이 가장 적절하다.

오답풀이

①, ③ 앞부분에서 농장의 수가 3분의 1로 줄어들었다는 것만 보고 대규모 농장이 줄었다고 생각하여 (A)에 dwindling(점점 작아지는)이 들어가야 한다고 생각할 수 있는데, 대규모 농장은 농업 보조금으로 꾸준하게 성장해 왔으므로 dwindling은 적절하지 않다.

구문풀이

16행 The countryside **is being divvied** up into Wal-Mart-like mega-farms, [which profit most from federal farm payments], and thousands of small farms, [comprising niche, part-time or hobby farmers {who almost always require off-farm income to stay afloat}]

: 현재진행형 수동태가 사용되었으며, 첫 번째 [ ]는 Wal-Mart-like mega-farms에 대해 부연 설명하는 주격 관계대명사절이다. 두 번째 [ ]는 분사구문이며, 그 안의 { }는 niche ~ farmers를 수식하는 주격 관계대명사절이다.

어휘풀이

- consistently *ad* 지속적으로
- subsidy *n* 보조금
- incentive *n* 장려[우대]책
- mega-farm *n* 초대형 농장
- comprise *v* ~로 구성되다
- stay afloat 빚지지[파산하지] 않다
- equivalent *a* 동등한
- food commodity 식료품
- reinforce *v* 강화하다
- corporate welfare 기업 지원 정책
- federal *a* 연방(정부)의
- niche *a* (시장의) 틈새의
- dwindle *v* (점점) 줄어들다, 감소하다
- integrate *v* 통합시키다

126~127 답 ③ / ④

📖 의사 결정 상황에서 본능의 역할

전문해석

우리의 본능 혹은 우리가 때로로 직관이라고 부르는 것은 뭔가 마술적이라거나 신비한 것이 아니다. 그것은 타고난 보편적인 동물적 행동이다. 우리의 본능은 우리가 세상을 헤쳐 나가는 데 도움이 된다. 소크라테스는 '나는 시인들에게 그들의 시를 쓸 수 있게 해주는 것은 바로 지혜가 아니라 일종의 '본능'이라고 결정했다.'라고 썼다. 예술가들에게 본능은 자산이라고 여겨진다. 하지만 사람들 또는 상황에 관한 중요한 결정을 내리는 것에 관한 한, 우리가 항상 본능에 의존할 수 있는 것은 아니다. 다윈은 본능을 경험과 무관한 것으로 정의했지만, 더 최근의 심리학과 신경과학 연구는 그것이 끊임없이 연마되고 있다는, 즉 그것이 유동적이라는 것을 보여주었다. 새로운 기억이 우리의 뇌 안에 형성될 때, 우리 대뇌 피질에 있는 수많은 뉴런이 융합된다. 하지만 이 융합은 영구적이지 않으며 후속적인 사용과 강화에 상당한 정도로 좌우된다. 따라서 우리의 본능은 어떤 종류의 타고난 행동 패턴이 아니라 우리의 과거 경험, 상호작용, 우리의 상황과 맥락에 토대를 둔다. 우리의 본능은 축적된 지식의 결과이므로 그것의 가치는 폄하될 수 없는데, 신속한 결정을 내릴 때 특히 그렇다. 하지만 그것은 또한 우리의 편향과 편견에 의해 형성되므로, 증거에 따라 온전한 합리성을 가지고 행동하는 것보다 열등할(→ 것에 필적할) 리 없다. 핵심은 의사 결정을 위해 그것에 의존하는 것이 아니라 오히려 그것을 분석적 그리고 논리적 사고를

유발하기 위한 계기로 사용하는 것이다. 잠재의식 수준에서 재빨리 가능성을 걸러내고 우리의 의사 결정을 우리의 이성적, 의식적 정신이 떠맡는 지점, 즉 우리가 우리의 편향을 열린 마음으로 인정하고 평가할 수 있는 지점으로 향하게 하는 것이 중요하다.

정답풀이

126 본능은 우리의 축적된 지식의 결과로서 신속한 결정을 내릴 때는 중요한 가치를 지니지만, 우리가 중요한 결정을 내릴 때 전적으로 의존할 수 있지는 않고, 본능을 의사 결정을 내리기 위한 분석적, 논리적 사고를 불러일으키기 위한 계기로 삼아야 한다는 내용이다. 축적된 지식의 결과인 본능을 분석적, 논리적 사고로 나아가기 위한 출발점으로 삼으라는 것이 글의 핵심이므로, 글의 제목으로 가장 적절한 것은 ③ '본능의 역할: 이성적 추론을 위한 실마리를 제공하는 것'이다.

127 본능은 신속한 결정에서는 중요한 역할을 할 수 있으나 편향과 편견에 의해 형성된다는 단점이 있으므로 의사 결정을 내릴 때는 본능보다는 분석적, 논리적 사고에 의존해야 한다고 했다. 따라서 의사 결정 상황에서 본능은 분석적, 논리적 사고에는 미치지 못한다고 할 수 있으므로, 부정어 cannot을 고려할 때 (d) inferior(열등한)의 쓰임은 적절하지 않으며 comparable(필적하는) 정도의 낱말로 바꿔야 한다.

오답풀이

126 ① 예술적 창작에서 추정되는 본능의 기능
② 본능적 직관: 편향을 극복하는 것에 대한 장벽
④ 본능적인 동물적 행동이 변화하기가 얼마나 어려운가
⑤ 합리성은 오직 본능이 억제될 때만 활성화된다
127 ① 시인들은 본능으로 시를 쓴다고 한 소크라테스의 말에서 그것이 예술가들의 '자산(asset)'이라고 표현한 것은 문맥상 적절하다.
② 새로운 기억에 따른 대뇌피질의 수많은 뉴런 융합이 영구적이지 않으며 후속적인 사용과 강화에 크게 좌우된다는 내용이 이어지므로, 이러한 본능의 특성을 정의하는 표현인 fluid(유동적인)는 문맥상 적절하다.
③ 앞에서 본능을 구성하는 요소로 과거 경험, 상호작용, 상황, 맥락을 언급했으므로, 본능을 이러한 요소들이 '축적된(accumulated)' 지식의 결과라고 표현한 것은 문맥상 적절하다.
⑤ 의사 결정을 위해 우리의 편향과 편견에 의해 형성되는 본능에 의존하지 말라고 했으므로, 우리의 의사 결정을 이성적, 의식적 정신이 떠맡는 지점으로 '향하게 하라(direct)'는 문맥은 적절하다.

구문풀이

16행 So our instinct is **not** based [on some sort of innate behavioural patterns], **but** [on our past experiences, interactions, our situations and our contexts].

: 상관접속사 「not ~ but ....」이 based에 이어지는 두 개의 [ ]를 연결하면서 '~가 아니라 …에'라는 뜻을 나타내고 있다.

27행 **It** is vital [**to filter** possibilities quickly at a subconscious level and **direct** our decision-making to a point {where our rational, conscious mind can take over}, one {where we can acknowledge and evaluate our biases openly}].

: It은 형식상의 주어이고, [ ]로 표시된 to부정사구가 내용상의 주어이며, to filter와 (to) direct가 병렬로 연결되었다. 두 개의 { }는 각각 a point와 one을 수식하는 관계부사절이며, one은 a point를 대신하는 부정대명사이다.

어휘풀이

- intuition *n* 직관
- animalistic *a* 동물적인
- independent of ~와 무관한, ~와 별개인
- innate *a* 타고난, 선천적인
- navigate *v* ~을 헤쳐 나가다

- neuroscience *n* 신경과학
- permanent *a* 영구적인
- reinforcement *n* 강화, 보강
- bias *n* 편향, 편견
- rationality *n* 합리성
- in accordance with ~에 따라, ~에 부합하도록
- fall back on ~에 의지하다, ~에 기대다
- trigger *n* (유발하는) 계기
- analytical *a* 분석적인
- subconscious *a* 잠재의식의
- acknowledge *v* 인정하다
- barrier *n* 장벽
- suppress *v* 억제하다
- fuse *v* 융합되다, 하나로 합쳐지다
- subsequent *a* 후속의
- discount *v* 폄하하다
- prejudice *n* 편견
- spark *v* 유발하다
- filter *v* 걸러내다
- take over ~을 인수하다, ~을 넘겨받다
- evaluate *v* 평가하다
- activate *v* 활성화하다

128　답 ②

📖 탁월한 음악가가 훌륭한 스승인 것만은 아닌 이유

전문해석

유능한 교사가 된다는 것은 분명히 전문가 수준의 음악적 지식과 연주 실력보다 훨씬 더 많은 것을 필요로 한다. 이런 사실은 가르치는 일이 연주 경력을 떠나는 사람들을 위해 좋은 '대비용 직업'이 된다는 (일부 사람들 사이의) 전통적인 생각에 이의를 제기한다. 사실상 특출한 연주를 하는 음악가는 교사로서 음악을 배우는 학생에게 다가가는 데 있어서 분명 불리한 입장일 수 있다. 엘리트 음악가는 자신의 고급 실력 성장의 경험을 통해 확실히 많은 것을 배우지만 그들이 자신과의 다른, 다른 음악가의 음악적인 성장을 효과적으로 이끌 수 있을지는 보통 의심할 만한 이유가 있다. 기술 습득의 폭넓은 단계와 관련하여, 탁월한 음악가 중에, 그들의 많은 연주 실력이 매우 자동화되어서 그들은 그런 실력이 더 의식적인 주목이나 노력이 필요한 학습 전략을 필요로 했던 때를 기억하지 못할지도 모르는 정도다. 그들은 기술 발달의 초기 단계에 있는 다른 사람들을 이끄는 데 그들 자신의 경험을 이용할 수 없을지도 모른다.

정답풀이

뛰어난 연주를 하는 음악가라고 해서 음악을 잘 가르치는 유능한 교사가 되는 것은 아니라는 내용이다. 뛰어난 음악가는 연주 실력이 매우 자동화되어 있어서 그런 실력을 얻기 위해서 어떤 학습 전략이 필요했는지 기억하지 못할 정도이고 그래서 초기 단계의 학생들을 이끄는 데 자신의 경험을 이용하지 못할 수도 있다고 했으므로, 글의 주제로는 ② '음악을 가르칠 때 숙달된 연주자가 겪는 어려움'이 가장 적절하다.

오답풀이

① 학생이 전문가로부터 배우는 것의 중요성
 └ 전문가가 학생의 음악적인 성장에 자신의 경험을 효과적으로 이용하지 못할 수도 있다고 했다.
③ 음악을 연주하는 것과 음악을 가르치는 것의 유사성
④ 기술 발전을 위해 시합에 참가할 필요성
⑤ 가르치는 경험이 음악적 기술 개발에 미치는 영향

구문풀이

3행 This fact challenges **the traditional idea** (among some) [that teaching makes a good "fallback job" for <u>people</u> {who leave a performance career}].

: [ ]는 the traditional idea의 구체적 내용을 제시하는 동격절이고, 그 안의 { }는 people을 수식하는 주격 관계대명사절이다.

8행 [Although elite musicians surely learn a lot through the experience of their own advanced skill development], there is usually <u>reason</u> [to doubt {whether they can effectively guide the musical growth of <u>other musicians</u> (who are different from them)}].

: 첫 번째 [ ]는 양보를 나타내는 부사절이다. 두 번째 [ ]는 reason을 수식하는 형용사적 용법의 to부정사구이고, 그 안의 { }는 doubt의 목적어 역할을 하는 명사절이며, ( )는 other musicians를 수식하는 주격 관계대명사절이다.

13행 [With reference to the broad stages of skill acquisition], [among exceptional musicians], many of their performance skills have become highly automatized, [**such that** they may not remember {when those skills required more conscious attention or effortful learning strategies}].

: 첫 번째와 두 번째 [ ]는 부사구이다. 세 번째 [ ]는 such that(~할 정도로)이 이끄는 부사절이고, 그 안의 { }는 remember의 목적어 역할을 하는 명사절이다.

어휘풀이
- expert-level *a* 전문가 수준의
- fallback job 대비용 직업
- distinct *a* 분명한
- with reference to ~와 관련하여
- automatized *a* 자동화된
- effortful *a* 노력이 드는
- readily *ad* 쉽게
- challenge *v* 이의를 제기하다
- exceptional *a* 특출한
- advanced *a* 고급의
- acquisition *n* 습득
- conscious *a* 의식적인
- strategy *n* 전략
- draw upon ~을 이용하다

129 답 ③

📖 집중해서 효율적으로 공부하는 것의 중요성

전문해석
공부는 삶의 대부분의 것과 비슷한데, 그것은 어떤 일을 하는 데 얼마나 오래 걸리느냐가 아니라 그 시간 동안 무엇을 성취하느냐이다. 그래서 중요한 것은 얼마나 오래 책상에 앉아 있느냐가 아니라 그곳에 앉아 있는 동안 무엇을 배우느냐이다. 집중적으로 공부하는 15분이 부주의하게 공부하는 한 시간 전체보다 더 낫다. 지금 나는 15분 동안만 공부하라고 주장하고 있는 것이 아니라, 효과적으로 공부함으로써 책상에 앉아 있는 시간으로부터 더 많은 것을 얻을 수 있다고 말하고 있다. 나는 학생들이 시험에 떨어진 후에 그들에게서 자신들이 '이번 시험을 위해 정말 열심히 공부했다'고 하는 말을 자주 듣는다. 그러나 그들이 정말 열심히 공부했다고 말할 때 그들은 무슨 말을 하려는 것일까? 그들은 자신의 강의 노트를 데우기 위해 자신의 체온을 이용하면서 많은 시간을 보낸 것일까, 아니면 진정으로 공부를 했을까? 둘 다 가능하기는 하지만, 그들은 아마 오랫동안 자기 노트를 앞에 펼쳐진 상태로 두었지만 공부를 하고 있지는 않았을 것이다.

정답풀이
③ 관계대명사 which: 뒤에 완전한 구조의 절이 이어지므로 관계대명사 which는 쓸 수 없다. which를 문장의 동사인 hear의 목적어 역할을 하는 명사절을 이끄는 접속사 that으로 고쳐야 한다.

오답풀이
① 분사구문의 태: while you sit there를 분사구문으로 고치면서 접속사 while을 생략하지 않은 형태로, 현재분사 sitting은 어법상 적절하다.
② 부사: 바로 앞의 동명사 studying을 수식하는 부사인 effectively는 어법상 적절하다.
④ to부정사: 문맥상 '~하기 위해서'라는 목적의 의미를 나타내는 부사적 용법의 to부정사인 to warm은 적절하게 쓰였다.
⑤ 형용사: 앞의 동사 had의 목적격보어로 '펼쳐진'이라는 의미의 형용사 open을 쓴 것은 어법상 적절하다. 「have+목적어+형용사(목적격보어)」는 '~을 …한 상태로 두다[유지하다]'라는 의미를 나타낸다.

구문풀이
12행 [Did they **spend** a lot of hours **using** their body heat to warm their lecture notes] or [did they truly study]?

: 의문문인 두 개의 [ ]가 or로 연결된 구조이고, '~하면서 (시간)을 보내다'라는 의미의 「spend+시간+*doing*」 구문이 쓰였다.

어휘풀이
- accomplish *v* 성취하다
- intensive *a* 집중적인

- careless *a* 부주의한, 신중하지 않은
- lecture *n* 강의
- advocate *v* 주장[옹호]하다
- the probability is that ~ 아마 ~일 것이다

130 답 ②

📖 감정이 신체에 미치는 영향에 대한 연구의 활성화

전문해석
수 세기 동안 미국의 의학은 우리의 감정이 우리의 건강에 영향을 미치는가의 문제를 중요하지 않은 것으로 간주해 왔다. 200년의 기간에 걸친 우리의 의학적 기적은 감정이 우리의 건강에 미칠 수 있는 영향에 대해서는 거의 고려하지 않으며 우리가 기술적이고 과학적인 접근을 경시하도록(→ 중시하도록) 이끌었다. 대부분 그것은 매우 최근까지도 우리에게 우리의 감정이 우리의 신체적인 건강에 영향을 미칠 수 있다는 과학적인 증거가 부족했기 때문이다. 하지만 지난 20년 동안 연구원들은 우리의 감정이 우리의 두뇌에서 화학적이고 전기적인 활동을 변화시킴으로써 우리의 신체 세포에 어떻게 영향을 미치는지를 실시간으로 보는 기술을 개발했다. (정신과 육체를 다루는) 두 분야의 연구가 점점 겹치면서 정신과 육체를 오랫동안 분리시켜 왔던 경계선이 서서히 사라지기 시작하고 있고, 연구원들은 우리의 감정, 스트레스 수준 그리고 사고의 유형이 어떻게 우리의 기본적인 면역 세포에 영향을 미칠 수 있는지에 초점을 맞추고 있다.

정답풀이
② 우리가 감정이 신체에 미치는 영향을 중요하게 여기지 않았던 것은 과학적인 증거가 부족했기 때문인데, 최근에 기술의 발달로 상황이 바뀌고 있다는 내용이다. 따라서 지난 200년간의 의학적 발전은 감정이 건강에 미칠 수 있는 영향에 대해서는 거의 고려하지 않고, 우리로 하여금 기술적이고 과학적인 접근을 '중시하도록' 했다는 문맥이 적절하다. 따라서 disrespect(경시하다)를 반대 개념인 respect(중시하다)로 바꿔야 한다.

오답풀이
① 감정이 신체에 미치는 영향은 최근에 중시된 것이며 오랫동안 '중요하지 않은' 것으로 여겨져 왔다는 문맥이므로 unimportant는 적절하다.
③ 감정이 신체에 미치는 영향에 대한 과학적인 증거가 '부족해서' 최근까지 관심을 끌지 못했던 것이므로 lacked는 적절하다.
④ 감정이 두뇌에서 화학적이고 전기적인 활동을 변화시키는 것을 볼 수 있는 것은 '기술'과 관계된 영역이므로 technology는 적절하다.
⑤ 정신과 육체를 분리시켜 온 경계선이 사라지기 시작한 것은 두 분야의 연구가 서로 '겹치면서' 일어난 현상이므로 overlap은 적절하다.

구문풀이
3행 Our two-hundred-year span of medical miracles has **led** us **to respect** the technological and scientific approach [**while giving** little thought to the impact {that emotions might have on our health}].

: 「lead+목적어+목적격보어(to부정사): (목적어)가 ~하도록 이끌다」 구문이 쓰였다. [ ]는 접속사를 생략하지 않은 분사구문이고, { }는 the impact를 수식하는 목적격 관계대명사절이다.

13행 Slowly, the divide [that has long separated mind and body] is beginning to disappear [**as** the two spheres of study increasingly overlap], / and researchers are focusing on [how {our emotions, stress levels, and thought patterns} might influence our basic immune cells].

: 첫 번째 [ ]는 the divide를 수식하는 주격 관계대명사절이며, 두 번째 [ ]는 접속사

as(~하면서)가 이끄는 부사절이다. 세 번째 [ ]는 의문사절로 전치사 on의 목적어이며, { }는 의문사절의 주어이다.

어휘풀이
- regard A as B A를 B로 여기다
- divide n 경계선
- sphere n 분야, 영역
- immune a 면역의
- span n 시간, 기간
- separate v 분리시키다
- focus on ~에 초점을 맞추다

131 답 ②

📖 잘못된 것을 바로잡아주는 역할을 하는 미덕

전문해석
Philippa Foot에 따르면, 미덕의 한 가지 특징은 그것이 (잘못된 것을) 바로잡아준다는 것이다. 아리스토텔레스는 사람들에게 쾌락을 향한 타고난 성향이 있다는 것을 인식하고 그것이 우리의 삶에서 너무 지배적인 것이 되는 것을 막기 위해 우리에게 주의를 준다. 그리고 Foot은 '예를 들어, 단지 게으름이 유혹이기 때문에 근면함이라는 미덕이 있고, 단지 사람들이 자신을 너무 높게 평가하는 경향이 있기 때문에 겸손함이라는 미덕이 있다. 절망 역시 유혹이기 때문에 희망이 미덕이 되는데, 정말로 모든 것을 다 잃었다고 여기는 경우를 제외하고는 그러한 지경이라고 외치는 사람이 아무도 없을 것이고, 이 경우에 희망이라는 미덕이 없었을 것이라고' 덧붙여 말한다. 그러면 미덕은 우리가 일관되게 좋은 삶을 살아가는 데 장애물을 극복하도록 도와주고 자기중심적인 세계관에 수반되는 동기 및 성향과 함께 그것에 지나치게 사로잡히는 경향을 막아 준다. 즉, 미덕은 우리가 부족한 경우에 우리에게 동기를 부여하거나 우리가 선에 못 미치는 경향이 있는 경우에 우리를 북돋운다.

정답풀이
미덕은 쾌락에 빠져드는 성향이 지배적이게 되는 것을 막아 주고 게으름에 대해 근면함을, 자만에 대해 겸손함을, 절망에 대해 희망을 제시하여 잘못되거나 부족한 것을 바로잡아준다는 내용이다. 빈칸에는 이러한 미덕의 특징을 나타내는 말이 들어가야 하므로 ② '(잘못된 것을) 바로잡는'이 가장 적절하다.

오답풀이
① 주관적인
└ 게으름과 근면함, 자만과 겸손함, 절망과 희망 등의 개념이 상대적이라고 생각해서 미덕이 주관적인 것이라고 잘못 파악했을 때 고를 수 있는 함정 오답이다.

③ 자기 확증적인
④ 애매모호한
⑤ 자기 모순적인

구문풀이
[2행] Aristotle **recognizes** [that people have natural tendencies toward pleasure] and **cautions** us to ward against [them **becoming** too dominant in our lives].

: 동사 recognizes와 cautions가 and에 의해 병렬로 연결되었다. 첫 번째 [ ]는 recognizes의 목적어 역할을 하는 명사절이고, 두 번째 [ ]는 전치사 against의 목적어인 동명사구로 them(= natural tendencies toward pleasure)이 becoming ~의 의미상 주어이다.

[12행] Virtues, then, **help** us overcome obstacles to [living a consistently good life] and **guard against** the tendency [to get too caught up in a self-centered world-view with its attendant motives and inclinations].

: 주어 Virtues에 이어지는 술어 동사 help와 guard against가 and에 의해 병렬로 연결되었다. 첫 번째 [ ]는 전치사 to의 목적어 역할을 하는 동명사구이고, 두 번째 [ ]는 the tendency를 수식하는 형용사적 용법의 to부정사구이다.

어휘풀이
- virtue n 미덕
- ward against ~을 막다
- industriousness n 근면함
- temptation n 유혹
- think well of ~을 좋게 생각하다
- overcome v 극복하다
- consistently ad 일관되게
- caught up in ~에 사로잡히는
- attendant a 수반되는
- deficient a 부족한, 결핍된
- fall short of ~에 못 미치다, ~이 부족하다
- caution v ~에게 주의를 주다
- dominant a 지배적인
- idleness n 게으름, 나태
- humility n 겸손함
- despair n 절망
- obstacle n 장애물
- guard against ~을 막다
- world-view n 세계관
- inclination n 성향
- inclined a ~하는 경향이 있는

132 답 ③

📖 하나의 사례가 광범위한 일반화를 뒷받침할 수 없다는 일화적 증거의 오류

전문해석
여러분은 "나는 흡연이 사람들에게 안 좋다는 이 모든 주장들이 부풀려진 것이라고 생각합니다. 저희 할아버지는 평생 담배를 피우셨지만 90대에 돌아가셨습니다."라는 주장을 들어보았을 것이다. 이것은 비판적인 사고를 거의 필요로 하지 않는 주장이다. 그 추론에 무엇이 틀렸는지를 보여주기 위해 흡연과 관련된 사망자 수에 관한 끔찍한 통계 수치를 알 필요는 없다. '흡연이 안 좋은 생각이라는 것은 부풀려진 것이다'라는 주장은 모호하기도 하고 흡연의 위험에 관한 잘 확립된 증거에 반하는 것이기도 하다. 그 주장은 기존의 과학적인 증거와 상충되기 때문에 우리는 설득을 당하기 전에 어떤 정말로 타당한 증거를 원할 것이다. 할아버지의 인상적인 수명은 전혀 충분하지 않다. 이 인용문은 일화적 증거의 오류에 관한 전형적인 사례인데, 하나의 훌륭한 사례나 이야기가 광범위한 일반화를 뒷받침할 수 없다는 것이다. 그것이 우리가 연구와 통계 수치를 가지고 있는 이유이다. 그것은 또한 우리가 비판적인 사고를 필요로 하는 이유이다.

정답풀이
빈칸이 있는 문장은 글의 요지를 담고 있다. 할아버지가 흡연을 했는데도 오래 살았다는 하나의 일화적인 사례는 흡연의 폐해에 관한 주장이 부풀려진 것이라는 주장을 충분히 뒷받침할 수 없으며, 그래서 연구와 통계 수치가 필요하다는 내용이다. 즉, 일화적 증거의 오류란 ③ '하나의 훌륭한 사례나 이야기가 광범위한 일반화를 뒷받침할 수 없다'는 것임을 알 수 있다.

오답풀이
① 숫자나 통계 수치가 필요 이상으로 강조된다
② 분석될 필요가 있는 여러분의 주장을 뒷받침하는 결정적인 증거가 있다
④ 강한 주장은 진실된 전제와 잘못된 결론을 가질 수 있다
⑤ 기존의 증거가 잠재적인 증거보다 더 중요하다

구문풀이
[7행] The claim [that "smoking being a bad idea is overblown"] is **both** vague **and** contrary to well-established evidence of the dangers of smoking.

: [ ]는 문장의 핵심 주어인 The claim의 구체적인 내용을 설명하는 동격절이며, 술부에는 'A와 B 둘 다'를 의미하는 「both A and B」 구문이 쓰였다.

어휘풀이
- argument n 주장
- critical a 비판적인, 결정적인
- statistics n 통계 수치, 통계학
- vague a 모호한
- overblown a 잔뜩 부풀려진, 과장된
- horrifying a 끔찍한
- mortality n 사망자 수, 사망률
- contrary to ~에 반하여, ~와는 반대로

- well-established *a* 잘 확립된
- fallacy *n* 오류
- premise *n* 전제
- quote *n* 인용문, 인용구
- anecdotal *a* 일화의
- case *n* 주장, 논거

133 답 ②

📖 측정 방식에 따라 달라지는 농업의 생산성

전문해석

Kalahari의 !Kung 부시맨은 보통 식량을 채집하면서 일주일에 12시간에서 19시간을 보내고, 탄자니아의 Hazda 유목민들은 14시간 미만을 보낸다. 이는 여가 활동, 친교 등을 위한 많은 자유 시간을 제공한다. (B) 왜 자신의 부족민이 농업을 채택하지 않았는지 인류학자에게 질문을 받았을 때, 한 부시맨은 "세상에 과일과 견과류가 널려 있는데 왜 (농작물을) 심어야 하나요?"라고 대답했다. 사실상, 수렵 채집인들은 일주일에 2일을 일하고 5일간의 주말을 보낸다. 농경 이전 시대의 수렵 채집인들의 생활양식은 아마도 훨씬 더 즐거웠을 것이다. (A) 농업으로의 전환은 사람들에게 예술 활동, 새로운 기교와 기술의 개발 등에 할애할 더 많은 시간을 주었다고 생각되었다. 이러한 견해에서 농업은 수렵 채집인의 불안한 하루 벌어 하루 먹고 사는 생활로부터의 해방이었다. 하지만 사실상 그 반대가 사실임이 판명되고 있다. (C) 농업은 토지 단위당 더 많은 식량을 생산한다는 의미에서 더 생산적인데, 25명의 사람들로 이루어진 집단은 수렵과 채집으로 생계를 유지하기 위해 필요로 할 수만 에이커의 땅보다 훨씬 더 작은 면적인 단지 25에이커의 땅에서 농사를 지음으로써 생계를 유지할 수 있다. 하지만 농업은 노동 시간당 생산된 식량의 양으로 측정될 때는 덜 생산적이다.

정답풀이

식량을 채집하는 부시맨의 생활을 소개하는 주어진 글 다음에는, 인류학자로부터 왜 농업을 채택하지 않았는지 질문을 받은 부시맨의 답변이 제시되는 (B)가 오는 것이 적절하다. 농업을 채택하지 않은 수렵 채집인들의 여가 시간에 대해 언급하는 (B) 다음에는, 농업으로 전환한 이후에 여가 시간이 더 많아졌다는 통념과 그것이 틀렸음을 지적하는 내용의 (A)가 와야 한다. 그리고 기존의 통념이 틀린 이유를 구체적으로 설명하는 (C)가 마지막에 오는 순서가 가장 적절하다. 따라서 적절한 글의 순서는 ② (B)−(A)−(C)이다.

구문풀이

[6행] It **used to be thought** [that the switch to farming gave people more time {to devote to artistic pursuits, the development of new crafts and technologies, and so on}].

: It은 형식상의 주어이고 [ ]로 표시된 명사절이 내용상의 주어이다. 「used to+동사원형: ~하곤 했다, ~이었다」 구문은 현재와 대조되는, 오랫동안 지속되었던 과거의 상태나 동작[습관]을 나타낸다. { }는 more time을 수식하는 형용사적 용법의 to부정사구이다.

어휘풀이

- typically *ad* 보통, 전형적으로
- switch *n* 전환
- pursuit *n* 활동, 취미
- liberation *n* 해방
- hand-to-mouth *a* 하루 벌어 하루 먹고 사는
- existence *n* (불행한) 삶, 생활
- turn out (사실 등이) 밝혀지다, 판명되다
- hunter-gatherer *n* 수렵 채집인
- preagricultural *a* 농경 이전의
- nomad *n* 유목민
- devote *v* (시간·자금 등을) 할애하다
- craft *n* 기교
- anthropologist *n* 인류학자

134 답 ⑤

📖 광고에서 소비자의 관심을 끄는 한 가지 장점에 집중해야 할 필요성

전문해석

하나의 브랜드를 파는 것을 돕는 데 이용될 수 있는 많은 특징과 장점들이 있을 수 있지만, 판매대행사는 그러한 장점들 중에서 어떤 것이 가장 중요한 하나인지, 즉 광고 대상자에게 가장 흥미로울 것 같은 하나를 결정할 필요가 있다. 한 고위직 광고기획자는 그의 연설과 강연에 참석한 사람들 속으로 테니스 공 하나를 던짐으로써 광고학과 학생들에게 이것을 예증하곤 했다. 청중 속의 한 학생이 예외 없이 그 공을 잡아서 다시 던지곤 했다. 그런 다음 그 광고기획자는 그 학생에게 공을 다시 한 번 잡아보라고 지시했다. 그러나 이번에 그 광고기획자는 그 학생에게 여러 개의 공을 던졌고, 그(그 학생)는 예상대로 하나도 잡지 못했다. 이러한 비유적인 연습의 의미는 분명한데, '너무 많은 정보를 전달하려고 하면, 여러분은 아무것도 전달하지 못할 위험을 각오해야 한다'. 이 문제의 진실은 보통의 사람들이 하루에 무수한 광고에 노출되는 사회에서 광고 메시지는 아주 많은 가상의 '소음'을 뚫고 나가야 한다는 것이다.

정답풀이

주어진 문장의 this metaphorical exercise(이러한 비유적인 연습)는 광고기획자가 학생에게 공을 던진 사례를 가리키므로 이 사례가 언급된 후에 들어가야 한다. 따라서 주어진 문장이 들어갈 가장 적절한 곳은 ⑤이다. ⑤ 다음 문장의 the matter가 주어진 문장에서 언급한 너무 많은 정보를 전달하려고 하면 아무것도 전달하지 못할 수 있다는 문제를 가리키는 것도 단서가 된다.

구문풀이

[8행] One senior creative **used to demonstrate** this to advertising students **by throwing** a tennis ball into groups [**that** would attend his talks and lectures].

: 「used to+동사원형: ~하곤 했다」 구문은 과거의 습관을 나타내며, 「by+-ing」는 '~함으로써'라는 의미이다. [ ]는 groups를 수식하는 주격 관계대명사절이다.

[16행] The truth of the matter is [that {in a society (where the average person is exposed to thousands of advertisements a day)}, the advertising message has to cut through a great deal of virtual 'noise.']

: [ ]는 문장의 주격보어로 쓰인 명사절이고, 그 안의 { }는 부사구이며, ( )는 a society를 수식하는 관계부사절이다.

어휘풀이

- metaphorical *a* 비유적인, 은유적인
- risk *v* ~할 위험을 무릅쓰다, ~을 각오해야 하다
- agency *n* 판매대행사, 대리점
- demonstrate *v* 예증하다
- invariably *ad* 변함없이, 예외 없이
- cut through ~을 뚫고 나가다
- senior creative 고위직 광고기획자
- lecture *n* 강의
- predictably *ad* 예상한 바와 같이
- virtual *a* 가상의

135 답 ②

📖 지식과 노하우의 다른 점

전문해석

지식과 노하우는 정보의 축적에 매우 중요하다. 간단히 말해서, **지식은 독립체들 간의 관계를 수반한다. 이러한 관계는 종종 사건을 실행시킬 필요 없이 사건의 결과를 예측하는 데 사용된다.** 예를 들어, 우리는 담배 사용이 폐암의 가능성을 증가시킨다는 것을 알고 있으며, 그래서 우리는 그 관련성을 이용해서 담배를 직접 사용할 필요 없이 담배 사용의 결과를 예측할 수 있다. **노하우는 그것이 행동을 수행하는 능력을 수반하기 때문에 지식과 다른데, 그 능력은 암묵적이다.** 예를 들어, 비록 우리는 우

리가 어떻게 걷는지 모르지만 우리들 대부분은 걷는 법을 안다. 우리들 대부분은 어떤 이미지 속의 물체를 식별하고 명칭을 붙이는 법을 알고 있는데, 비록 우리가 어떻게 그러한 지각적이고 언어적인 과업을 완수하는지 알지 못하더라도 그러하다. 우리들 대부분은, 비록 우리가 어떻게 그것을 하는지 설명할 수 없지만, 다른 각도에서 사물을 인식하고, 얼굴을 식별하고, 감정을 인식하는 방법을 알고 있다. 하지만 우리는 노하우를 가지고 있기 때문에 이러한 과업들을 할 수 있다. 노하우는 우리가 행동을 할 수 있도록 하는 전술적인 계산 능력이며, 그것은 개별 및 집단 수준 둘 다에서 축적된다.
→ 지식은 우리에게 실제로 수행하지 않고도 행동들 사이의 관련성을 <u>추론함</u>으로써 행동의 결과를 예측할 수 있게 하는 반면, 노하우는 우리에게 우리가 무엇을 하고 있는지 <u>깨닫지 못한</u> 채 특정한 행동을 하도록 한다는 점에서 지식과 노하우는 다르다.

정답풀이
지식이 있으면 어떤 일들을 실제로 해보지 않고도 추론을 통해 그것들의 관련성을 알아내서 결과를 예측할 수 있는 데 반해, 노하우는 특정한 일을 구체적으로 어떤 절차를 거쳐서 하는지 알지 못한 채 그것들을 수행할 수 있도록 한다는 내용이다. 따라서 (A)에는 inferring(추론하다)이, (B)에는 unaware(깨닫지 못하는)가 들어가는 것이 가장 적절하다.

구문풀이
15행 Most of us know **how to** [**recognize** objects from different angles], [**identify** faces], and [**recognize** emotions], even though we cannot explain how we do it.

: 세 개의 [ ]는 and로 연결되어 how to에 이어져 '~하는 방법'을 나타낸다.

어휘풀이
- crucial *a* 매우 중요한
- simply put 간단히 말해서
- outcome *n* 결과
- tobacco *n* 담배
- anticipate *v* 예상[예측]하다
- perceptual *a* 지각의
- tactic *n* 전술의, 전략의
- linkage *n* 관련(성)
- mindful *a* 염두에 두는, 유념하는
- accumulation *n* 축적
- entity *n* 독립체
- act ~ out ~을 행하다[실연하다]
- likelihood *n* 가능성
- consequence *n* 결과
- verbal *a* 언어적인
- computational *a* 계산에 관한
- convinced *a* 확신하는

본문 p.096

3점 공략 모의고사 6회

136 ③	**137** ④	**138** ②	**139** ⑤	**140** ④
141 ④	**142** ①	**143** ③		

136 답 ③

📖 민들레의 '되로 주고 말로 받는' 생존 전략

전문해석
뜨락에서 민들레를 뽑아 본 적이 있는가? 행운을 빈다. 여러분은 바구니에 (뽑은 민들레) 20개를 가지고 시작할 것이고, 60개로 늘어날 것이며, '그것들을 몽땅 뽑아 버리는' 데 전념하지만, 결국 여러 시간 후에 80개를 뽑았다는 것과 (전에 보지 못한) 85개가 더 지금 여러분의 옆 뜰 등에 있다는 것을 발견하게 된다. 현대 뜨락의 진화 이야기에서, **민들레는 보기 드문 실패율을 보여주지만(그것은 많이 뽑히고 깎인다), 결국 훨씬 더 보기 드문 성공률이 그것(실패율)을 능가한다(그것은 좋은 환경을 발견하여 많이 자란다).** 민들레 그리고 참으로 많은 다른 자연의 생명체가 우리에게 가능한 한 가장 위대한 교훈을 주는데, '되로 주고 말로 받는' 것이다. 그리고 교훈은 이렇다. 민들레는 때때로 실패하지 않을 수 없다. 그것은 실패를 줄이도록 설계된 기제를 전혀 진화시키지 못한 듯하다! 그것은 물지 않고, (독소가 있다고 하더라도 극소수만이 있어) 실제로 먹기 좋으며, 무력하다! **오히려, 증식을 향한 그것의 전략은 다음과 같기가 더 쉬운데, 많이 자라고, 빨리 자라고, 어디에서나 자라고, 가능한 한 빨리 씨앗으로 변하는 것이다.** 민들레로 가득한 들판을 본 적이 있는가? 틀림없이 보았으리라. 그리고 그것은 이 특별한 진화된 전략, 즉 회복력이 작동하기 때문이다.

정답풀이
뜨락의 민들레는 사람들에게 뽑히거나 깎이는 실패를 겪지만, 많이 자라고, 빨리 자라고, 어디에서나 자라고, 가능한 한 빨리 씨앗으로 변하는 전략을 통해 성공적으로 증식한다는 내용이다. 밑줄 친 부분은 조금 주고 그 대가로 많이 받는 경우를 비유하는 말로, 이 글에서는 민들레의 증식 전략인 ③ '실패를 뚫고 더 큰 성공으로 나아가는 것'을 의미한다.

오답풀이
① 다른 이들의 실패와 성공으로부터 배우는 것
② 실패한 시도를 성공적인 시도로 대체하는 것
④ 같은 실패를 반복하지 않기 위한 전략을 개발하는 것
⑤ 성공적인 생존을 위해 다른 식물들과 협력하는 것

구문풀이
6행 In the evolutionary story of a modern yard, dandelions show an extraordinary failure rate (they get picked and mowed a lot), [**only to be outdone** by an even more extraordinary success rate (they find good environments and grow a lot)].

: [ ]는 「only+to부정사구」 구문으로 '결국 ~하게 되다'라는 결과를 나타낸다.

14행 They don't seem to have evolved <u>mechanisms</u> [designed to reduce failure at all]!

: [ ]는 mechanisms를 수식하는 과거분사구이다.

어휘풀이
- dandelion *n* 민들레
- extraordinary *a* 보기 드문, 엄청난
- outdo *v* 능가하다
- bushel *n* 부셸(약 35리터)
- toxin *n* 독소
- resilience *n* 회복력
- commit to *do* ~하는 데 전념하다
- mow *v* 깎다, 베다
- peck *n* 펙(약 881리터)
- mechanism *n* 기제, 구조
- helpless *a* 무력한, 무능력한

137 답 ④

📖 충실한 고객이 자신과 회사에 주는 이점

전문해석

여러분이 한 사업체와 충실한 고객의 관계를 확립할 때, 여러분은 본질적으로 그 사업체와 상호 이로운 동반자 관계를 형성하고 있는 것이다. 동반자 관계를 형성하는 것은 소비자인 여러분에게 여러분의 충실함을 값진 투자로 사용할 수 있게 해주는 것이다. 이러한 투자는 엄청난 보상으로 돌아오고, 이러한 회사들이 여러분을 대접하는 방식을 대단히 향상시킨다. 여러분이 얼마나 많이 (혹은 적게) 지출하든지 간에, 여러분의 반복된 거래는 가장 큰 기업에게조차도 가치를 갖는다는 것을 기억하라. 결국, 여러분의 거래가 한 회사에 가져다주는 적은 액수의 수입이라도 그것에 대한 장기적인 약속은, 특히 여러분과 똑같은 수십만 명의 다른 충실한 고객들에 의해 크게 증가될 때 대단히 큰 가치가 있다. 이것을 생각해 보자. 만약 여러분이 일류 항공사의 최고경영자라면, 수십만 명의 사람들이 매년 여러분의 항공사로 비행을 하면서 몇 백 달러라도 계속해서 지출할 것을 알면 안심하지 않겠는가?

정답풀이

④ **문장의 구조 파악**: 주어부는 the long-term promise ~ a company이고, 동사는 is이다. your business bringing to a company는 the modest amount of income을 수식하는 어구가 되어야 하는데, 동명사구의 형태여서 어법상 적절하지 않다. 앞에 있는 명사구를 수식하는 형용사절, 즉 앞에 목적격 관계대명사가 생략된 관계사절의 형태가 되도록 준동사 bringing을 your business를 주어로 하는 동사 brings로 고쳐야 한다.

오답풀이

① **관계대명사 what**: 앞에 나온 동사 is의 보어절을 이끌면서 이어지는 절의 동사 allows의 주어 역할을 하는 관계대명사 what은 어법상 적절하다.
② **병렬구조**: 주어 This investment에 대한 동사로 앞에 나온 pays와 병렬구조를 이루는 enhances는 어법상 적절하다.
③ **의문사 how**: 문맥상 '얼마나 ~하든지 간에, 아무리 ~해도'의 의미로 양보의 부사절을 이끄는 no matter how는 적절하게 쓰였다.
⑤ **분사구문의 태**: when[if] you know ~를 분사구문으로 쓴 knowing ~은 어법상 적절하다.

구문풀이

9행 After all, the long-term promise [of even the modest amount of income {your business brings to a company}] **is** worth a great deal, / especially **when multiplied** by the hundreds of thousands of other loyal customers [who are just like you].

: [ ]는 문장의 핵심 주어인 the long-term promise를 수식하는 전치사구이며, 그 안의 { }는 목적격 관계대명사가 생략된 관계절로 the modest amount of income을 수식하고, 문장의 동사는 is이다. when multiplied는 when it is multiplied에서 it is가 생략된 형태이고, 두 번째 [ ]는 the hundreds ~ customers를 수식하는 주격 관계대명사절이다.

어휘풀이

- establish *v* 확립하다
- mutually *ad* 서로, 상호 간에
- enhance *v* 향상하다, 높이다
- modest *a* (크기·중요성 등이) 대단하지 않은
- multiply *v* 크게 증가시키다
- loyal *a* 충실한, 충성스런 (*n* loyalty)
- beneficial *a* 유익한, 이로운
- secure *a* 안심하는, 안전한

138 답 ②

📖 느긋하고 깊이 있는 여행을 추구하는 추세

전문해석

느긋하고 깊이 있는 휴가의 추세는 다른 많은 것들처럼 베이비붐 세대의 사람들에게 기인한다. 그들은 열심히 일해 왔고 (그들의 사무직의 힘든 노동은 주로 지난 수년간의 세계적인 생산성 성장을 추진시켜 왔다) 이제 그들은 즐길 돈도 있고 시간도 있다. 십 대 때부터 여행자였던 그들은 유럽의 대형 박물관과, 아마도 아시아의 주요 기념물과 아프리카의 초원을 이미 보았다. 20일에 20개국을 재빨리 훑어보는 것보다 그들은 지역 주민들과 교류하고 새로운 풍습들을 맛보면서 한 나라의 외딴 구석에 오래 머무는 것에 더 관심이 있다. 인기 지역을 체크리스트에서 지워나가는 것보다(방문한 인기 지역을 여행 목록에서 삭제하는 것보다) 경험의 질과 깊이가 훨씬 더 중요하다. 이런 점이 여행 산업의 새로운 마케팅 캠페인에 반영되어 있다고 Deloitte의 세계 관광 실무의 관리 이사인 Alex Kyriakidis는 언급한다. "그리스는 '여러분의 감각을 탐험하도록' 초대합니다. Intercontinental 호텔은 '여러분은 대륙 간의 삶을 살고 계신가요?'라고 질문합니다."라고 그는 말한다. 휴가객들은 수박 겉핥기식으로가 아니라 자신의 삶을 맞추고 주제를 깊이 파고들 수 있는 충분한 시간과 공간을 얻고 있다.

정답풀이

빈칸이 있는 문장은 느긋하고 깊이 있는 휴가(leisurely, in-depth holidays)를 원하는 사람들에게 있어 여행의 진정한 의미에 해당한다. 그들은 한 곳에 느긋하게 머물면서 그곳의 사람들과 교류하고 문화를 경험하는 여행에 관심 있어 하므로, 빈칸에는 ② '경험의 질과 깊이가 훨씬 더 중요하다'가 가장 적절하다.

오답풀이

① 호화로운 고급 여행을 더 많이 찾는다
③ 자유분방한 즉흥 여행이 더 보람 있다
④ 아이들을 위한 교육적인 활동을 더하는 것이 우선순위가 더 높다
⑤ 가능한 한 많은 곳을 방문하는 것이 더 비용 효과가 있다

구문풀이

9행 **Rather than** zip through 20 countries in 20 days, they are more interested in [hanging out in a remote corner of one], [interacting with locals and sampling new customs].

: Rather than은 대조나 비교를 할 때 쓰는 표현이며, '~하기보다는'으로 해석한다. 첫 번째 [ ]는 전치사 in의 목적어에 해당하는 동명사구이며, 두 번째 [ ]는 동시상황을 나타내는 분사구문이다.

어휘풀이

- leisurely *a* 느긋한, 여유 있는
- stem from ~에 기인하다, ~에서 유래하다
- baby boomer 베이비붐 세대의 사람
- monument *n* 기념물, 기념비
- zip through ~을 빠르게 통과하다
- remote *a* 외딴, 외진
- sample *v* 맛보다, (잠깐) 시도해 보다
- cross ~ off ~을 지우다
- intercontinental *a* 대륙 간의
- high-end *a* 고급의
- improvisational *a* 즉흥적인
- in-depth *a* 깊이 있는, 면밀한
- toil *n* 노역, 수고
- plain *n* 초원, 평원
- hang out ~에서 많은 시간을 보내다
- local *n* 현지인
- hot spot 인기 지역, 방문자가 많은 곳
- holidaymaker *n* 휴가객
- free-wheeling *a* 자유분방한
- rewarding *a* 보람이 있는, 가치가 있는

139 답 ⑤

📖 호랑이나 대백상어가 현재의 최상위 포식자인 이유

전문해석

우리는 지구에 사나운 슈퍼드래곤이 진화하는 것이 왜 불가능한지 이해할 수 있다. 이것은 에너지 공급이 슈퍼드래곤의 부양까지 확대되지 않을 것이기 때문이다. 바다

의 대백상어 또는 범고래와 육지의 사자와 호랑이는 현재의 세계에서 생존할 수 있는 가장 가공할 동물인 듯하다. 그나마 이것들은 매우 드문드문 흩어져 있다. 한 사람은 생애 동안 아주 여러 번 세계의 해양에서 수영하면서도 대백상어와 마주치지는 않을 것이다. 옛 중국 속담은 하나의 산은 오직 한 마리의 호랑이에게만 살 곳을 제공한다고 단언한다. **진화의 원리는 우리에게 이 동물들의 존재가 다른 동물들이 그것들을 잡아먹도록 진화할 이론적 가능성을 만들어낸다고 말하지만, 대백상어와 호랑이를 사냥하는 이력과 활동 범위로부터 얻어지는 먹이 열량은 이것들만큼 크고 끔찍하게 사나운 동물의 최소 개체군을 부양하기에 너무 적다.** 따라서 그런 동물들은 결코 진화하지 않았다. 대백상어와 호랑이는 물리학의 법칙에 따라 현대의 지구가 부양할 수 있는 가장 큰 포식자를 대표한다.

정답풀이
현재의 최상위 포식자가 육지의 사자나 호랑이, 바다의 대백상어인 이유를 설명하는 내용이다. 이론적으로는 현재의 최상위 포식자인 사자나 호랑이, 대백상어나 범고래를 사냥해서 잡아먹는 더 상위 포식자의 진화가 가능하지만, 실제적으로 이 희소하게 분포하는 포식자를 사냥해서는 그 상위 포식자의 최소 개체군을 유지할 만큼의 열량을 확보하는 것이 불가능하므로 그러한 진화는 일어날 수 없다는 내용이다. 결국, 현재의 최상위 포식자가 대백상어와 호랑이인 것을 에너지 공급이라는 먹이 부양의 측면에서 설명하고 있으므로, 빈칸에 들어갈 말로는 ⑤ '물리학의 법칙에 따라 현대의 지구가 부양할 수 있는'이 가장 적절하다.

오답풀이
① 생태계가 균형을 유지하기 위해 의존하는
└ 생태계의 균형 유지에 대해서는 전혀 언급한 것이 없다.
② 진화 이론이 기원에 관해 설명을 하지 못하는
③ 지리적 한계가 특정 서식지에 남아있도록 강제하는
④ 파괴적인 인간 활동이 상대적으로 작은 영향을 주는

구문풀이
4행 [Great white sharks or killer whales in the sea], and [lions and tigers on the land], are apparently the most formidable animals [that can survive in the current world].

: 첫 번째와 두 번째의 [ ]는 and로 연결되어 문장의 주어 역할을 하는 명사구이다. 세 번째 [ ]는 the most formidable animals를 수식하는 주격 관계대명사절이다.

11행 Evolutionary principle tells us [that {the existence of these animals creates a theoretical possibility (for other animals to evolve to eat them)}, but {the food calories (to be won from a career or niches of hunting great white sharks and tigers) are **too few to support** a minimum population of animals (**as** large and horribly ferocious **as** these would have to be)}].

: [ ]는 tells의 직접목적어 역할을 하는 명사절로, { }로 표시된 두 개이 절이 but으로 연결되어 있는 구조이다. 첫 번째 { } 안의 ( )는 a theoretical possibility를 수식하는 형용사적 용법의 to부정사구로, for other animals는 to evolve ~의 의미상 주어를 나타낸다. 두 번째 { } 안의 첫 번째 ( )는 the food calories를 수식하는 형용사적 용법의 to부정사구이고, 두 번째 ( )는 animals를 수식하는 형용사구로 「as ~ as」 원급 비교 구문이 쓰였다. 「too+형용사[부사]+to부정사」는 '너무 ~해서 …할 수 없다, …하기에는 너무 ~한[하게]'이라는 의미를 나타낸다.

어휘풀이
- fierce *a* 흉포한, 사나운
- formidable *a* 가공할, 무시무시한
- spread *v* 퍼지다
- proverb *n* 속담
- shelter *v* 살 곳을 제공하다
- contemporary *a* 현대의, 동시대의
- apparently *ad* 외관상으로
- thinly *ad* 드문드문
- encounter *v* 마주치다
- assert *v* 단언하다
- predator *n* 포식자

140 답 ④

📖 우리에게 남아 있는 유목민의 정신

전문해석
수천 년 전에, 우리 인간들은 사냥하고 채집하면서 사막과 평야를 가로질러 방랑하는 유목생활을 했다. 그러다가 우리는 정착해서 살며 식량을 재배하는 것으로 바꾸었다. (C) 그 변화는 우리에게 편안함과 통제력을 가져다주었지만, 우리 정신의 어떤 부분에서 우리는 유목민으로 남아 있다. **우리는 배회하고 방랑하는 공간을 자유의 느낌과 연결시키지 않을 수 없다.** 고양이에게는 빈틈없고 둘러싸인 공간이 안락함을 의미할 수 있지만, 우리에게 그것은 질식을 떠오르게 한다. (A) 수세기에 걸쳐 이러한 반응은 보다 더 심리적인 문제가 되어, 우리가 어떤 상황에서 선택 사항을 가지고 있다는 느낌은 탁 트인 공간의 느낌과 같은 것으로 해석된다. **우리의 정신은 탈출할 가능성이 있다는 의식에서 발전한다.** (B) 역으로, 심리적인 울타리의 느낌은 우리에게 깊은 불안감을 주며, 종종 우리가 과잉 반응하도록 만든다. 누군가 혹은 무언가가 우리를 에워쌀 때, 우리는 우리의 감정에 대한 통제력을 잃어버리고 그 상황을 더 절망적이게 만드는 그러한 실수를 저지른다.

정답풀이
유목생활에서 정착생활로의 변화를 언급한 주어진 글 다음에는, 이 변화를 The change로 지칭하며, 자유롭게 배회할 수 있는 공간은 자유의 느낌으로 다가오고 둘러싸인 공간은 질식의 이미지를 떠오르게 한다는 내용의 (C)가 와야 한다. 그리고 인간의 이러한 반응을 this reaction으로 받아 부연 설명하는 (A)가 오고, (A)의 열린 공간에 대한 느낌과 반대로(Conversely) 둘러싸인 것에 대한 느낌을 설명하는 (B)가 마지막에 오는 순서가 가장 적절하다. 따라서 적절한 글의 순서는 ④ (C)-(A)-(B)이다.

구문풀이
5행 Over the centuries this reaction has become more psychological: **the feeling** [that we have options in a situation] **translates** into something like the feeling of open space.

: 콜론(:) 다음의 문장에서 핵심 주어는 the feeling이며 동사는 translates이다. [ ]는 the feeling의 구체적인 내용을 설명하는 동격절이다.

어휘풀이
- nomadic *a* 유목의, 방랑의
- settlement *n* 정착(지)
- translate into ~로 번역되다[해석되다]
- thrive *v* 번성하다, 번창하다
- enclosure *n* 울타리, 둘러쌈, 포위
- encircle *v* 둘러싸다
- render *v* ~을 (어떤 상태가 되게) 만들다
- nomad *n* 유목민
- wander *v* 돌아다니다, 헤매다
- cultivate *v* 재배하다
- break free 도망치다
- overreact *v* 과잉 반응하다
- suffocation *n* 질식

141 답 ④

📖 경제 규모의 확대에 따른 마케팅 전문가의 등장

전문해석
기업들이 발달하기 시작했을 때, 그것들은 처음에 규모가 작았고 공동체 내에 위치했다. 고객들이 구입하기를 원하는 상품들을 생산함으로써 그들을 만족시키는 것은 쉬웠다. 기업들이 공동체 내에 위치했기 때문에, 마케팅 업무는 고객의 필요와 욕구에 대한 그 소유주들의 개인적인 지식에 기반을 둘 수 있었다. **그러나 상품의 대량 생산으로 더 큰 지리적 범위에 걸쳐서 고객들에게 판매할 필요가 있는 더 큰 기업들이 나타났다.** 기업 소유주들은 더 이상 고객들과 개인적으로 소통할 수 없었기 때문에, 그들은 자신들의 상품을 판매할 방법을 진지하게 숙고해야 했다. 그들은 또한 이

제 선택할 상품이 많은 잠재적 고객들에게 상품의 장점들을 알려야만 했다. **이러한 복잡한 업무를 위해 기업은 마케팅 지식을 갖춘 사람들을 고용할 필요가 있었다.** 결과적으로, 20세기 초반에 훈련받은 마케팅 전문가들에 대한 기업들의 수요가 증가하기 시작했다. 이러한 전문가들을 공급하기 위해서 마케팅은 대학교에서 학문 연구 분야가 되었다.

정답풀이

주어진 문장의 these complicated tasks는 상품을 판매할 방법을 숙고하고 상품의 장점을 알리는 일을 지칭한다. 또한, 마케팅 지식을 갖춘 사람들을 고용할 필요가 있었기 때문에 마케팅 전문가들에 대한 기업의 수요가 증가했다는 흐름이 자연스러우므로 주어진 문장은 ④에 들어가는 것이 가장 적절하다.

구문풀이

4행 It was easy [to keep customers **satisfied** by producing goods {they wanted to buy}].

: It은 형식상의 주어이고 [ ]로 표시된 to부정사구가 내용상의 주어이다. satisfied는 keep의 목적격보어이고, { }는 goods를 수식하는 목적격 관계대명사절이다.

어휘풀이

- complicated *a* 복잡한
- geographic *a* 지리적인
- professional *n* 전문가
- practice *n* 업무, 영업
- potential *a* 잠재적인

142~143 답 ① / ③

📖 단순히 같다는 것이 유발하는 성취동기 증가

전문해석

한 연구에서 학부생들이 자신들이 다니는 대학의 수학과 대학원생이 수박 겉핥기식으로 쓴 보고서를 읽었다. 그 보고서는 그 학과에서의 긍정적인 경험을 기술했고 그 보고서 저자를 학업적으로 성공한 것으로 제시했다. 모든 참가자가 이렇게 수학의 긍정적 역할 모델을 접했다. 연구자들은 보고서에서 단 하나의 자료를 조작했는데, 바로 저자의 생일로, 그 저자의 이름, 고향과 더불어 작은 네모 칸에 넣어져 있었다. 같은 생일 조건에서는, 저자의 생일이 참가자의 생일과 일치했다. 다른 생일 조건에서는 두 생일이 여러 달 차이가 나게 달랐다. 과거의 연구가 보여주듯이, 같은 생일은 개인들 사이에 '단위(동질성) 관계'를 만들어내고, 더 큰 협력과 호감을 유발한다. 사람들이 사회적으로 동떨어졌다고(→ 연결되었다고) 느끼는 다른 사람들의 목표와 관심을 채택하면, 그들은 아마도 틀림없이 다른 생일 조건에서보다 같은 생일 조건에서 수학에서 성공하는 데 더 동기가 부여될 것이다.

그들은 그랬다. 동기의 주요한 평가 기준은 참가자들이 해결할 수 없는 수학 수수께끼 과제를 얼마나 오래 지속하는가였다. 그 과제는 다른 사람이 없는 데서 완료되어 사회적 바람직성이라는 압력을 최소화했고, 그렇게 함으로써 수학에 대한 내적 동기의 상대적으로 명확한 지표를 제공한다. 같은 생일 조건의 참가자들은 다른 생일 조건의 참가자들이 했던 것보다 그 수수께끼를 65% 더 길게 지속했다. 그들은 또한 (예컨대 수학을 잘하는 것이 자신들에게 '더 중요하다'라고 보고하는 등) 여러 가지 자기 보고 도구와 함께 수학에 대한 더 많은 동기를 보였다.

정답풀이

142 연구 참가자들은 두 집단으로 나뉘어 학업적으로 성공했다고 들은 수학과 대학원생의 보고서를 읽게 되었는데, 한 집단에는 보고서 저자의 생일이 자신과 생일이 같다는 조건이 설정되었고, 다른 집단에는 생일이 다르다는 조건이 설정되었다. 그리고 후에 해결할 수 없는 수학 과제를 얼마나 지속하는가를 통해 수학 성취의 동기를 측정해 보니 생일이 같은 조건이 설정된 집단이 65%나 더 길게 과제를 해결하려고 노력했으며, 여러 자기 보고 도구에서도 수학 공부에 동기가 높다는 것이 드러났다는 내용이다. 따라서 이 글의 제

목으로 가장 적절한 것은 ① '같다는 것이 성취에 대한 동기를 증가시킨다'이다.

143 앞에서는 과거의 연구가 생일이 같은 개인들 사이에 '단위(동질성) 관계'가 형성되고 호감이 유발된다는 것을 보여준다고 하였고, 뒤에서는 생일이 같은 사람의 목표와 관심을 채택할 가능성이 크다고 하였으므로, 결국 생일이 같다는 이유로 개인들 사이에 사회적 연결성이 생겼다고 할 수 있다. 따라서 (e) disconnected(동떨어진)를 connected(연결된) 정도의 낱말로 바꿔야 한다.

오답풀이

142 ② 끈기: 학업적 성공의 필수 불가결한 부분
└ 주어진 연구에서 수학 수수께끼 과제를 얼마나 끈기 있게 지속하느냐를 동기의 평가 기준으로 삼았을 뿐 끈기가 학업적 성공에 꼭 필요하다고는 하지 않았다.

③ 대학에서 훌륭한 역할 모델을 갖는 것의 중요성
④ 사회적 바람직함은 사람들이 협력하지 않도록 동기를 부여한다
⑤ 다름: 때로는 비슷함보다 더 매력적이다

143 ① 다음 문장에서 긍정적인 역할 모델이라고 규정하고 있으므로 보고서 저자를 학업적으로 '성공한(successful)' 것으로 제시했다는 문맥은 적절하다.
② 같은 생일 조건에 관한 설명이므로 보고서 저자와 참가자의 생일이 같다는 점을 나타내는 'matched(일치했다)'는 문맥상 적절하다.
④ 앞에서 사회적 바람직성 압력을 최소화했다고 했는데, 이것은 오로지 수학을 잘하려는 순수한 동기를 측정하기 위한 장치로 볼 수 있으므로 '내적(intrinsic)' 동기라고 표현한 것은 문맥상 적절하다.
⑤ 앞에서 수학 수수께끼 과제를 더 끈기 있게 지속했다고 했으므로 이와 논리적으로 부합하는 수학에 '더 많은(greater)' 동기를 보였다는 문맥은 적절하다.

구문풀이

13행 [As past research indicates], a shared birthday creates a "unit relationship" between individuals, [inducing greater cooperation and liking].

: 첫 번째 [ ]는 as(~하듯이)가 이끄는 부사절이다. 두 번째 [ ]는 부대상황을 나타내는 분사구문이다.

22행 The task **was completed** in private, [minimizing social desirability pressure], and thus **provides** a relatively clear index of intrinsic motivation for math.

: 주어 The task에 이어지는 동사 was completed와 provides가 and로 연결되었다. [ ]는 부대상황을 나타내는 분사구문이다.

어휘풀이

- undergraduate *n* 학부생, 대학생
- department *n* 학과
- academically *ad* 학업[학문]적으로
- embed *v* (끼워) 넣다
- cooperation *n* 협력
- insoluble *a* 풀 수 없는, 해결할 수 없는
- minimize *v* 최소화하다
- index *n* 지표
- instrument *n* 도구
- graduate *n* 대학원생
- describe *v* 기술하다, 묘사하다
- manipulate *v* 조작하다
- induce *v* 유발하다
- persist *v* 지속하다
- relatively *ad* 상대적으로
- intrinsic *a* 내적인
- integral *a* 필수 불가결한

144 답 ④

📖 기후 변화가 건강에 미치는 영향 분석을 위한 데이터 수집 및 이용의 어려움

전문해석

기후 변동성과 변화가 건강에 미치는 영향을 이해하는 데 있어 가장 큰 어려움 중 하나는 과학적으로 견실한 지식과 행동에 기반하여 증거를 뒷받침할 시간 및 공간적으로 호환되는 데이터가 부족하다는 것이다. 확고한 결과를 얻기 위해서는 건강, 의료, 사회 및 행동 과학에서부터 환경, 해양 및 기후 과학까지 다양한 분야의 데이터가 필요하다. 그리고 그것(데이터) 안에는, 데이터 모두를 사용할 수 없게 만들거나 사용 가능하지만 확고한 분석에 필요한 세분화 없는 일부 건강 데이터를 둘러싼 개인 정보 보호 문제와 민간 부문 소유권에서부터 대규모 기후 데이터 세트에 사용 가능한 방식으로 접근하는 것에 이르는 접근 가능성과 가용성에 대한 추가적인 어려움이 있다. 모순처럼 들릴 수도 있지만, 주어진 문제에 대해 시간 및 공간적으로 일치하는 확고한 데이터 세트가 없는 한편, 점점 더 많은 데이터가 여러 분야에 걸쳐 수집됨에 따라 어려움은 이 모든 빅데이터를 어떻게 통합하고 사용하느냐가 된다.

정답풀이

기후 변화가 건강에 미치는 영향을 이해하는 데 있어 과학적으로 견실한 지식과 행동에 기반하여 증거를 뒷받침할 시간 및 공간적으로 호환되는 데이터가 부족하고, 여러 분야에 걸쳐 수집된 데이터에 대한 접근성과 가용성 측면에서도 어려움이 있으며, 마지막으로 수집된 빅데이터를 어떻게 통합하고 사용하느냐의 문제가 있다는 내용이다. 따라서 글의 주제로 가장 적절한 것은 ④ '기후-건강 분석을 위한 데이터 확보와 활용에서의 걸림돌'이다.

오답풀이

① 세계적인 기후 변화와 그것이 공중 보건에 미치는 영향
 ↳ 기후 변화가 건강에 미치는 영향을 연구하는 데 있어 어려움이 있다는 내용이다.

② 기후 변화 적응을 위한 혁신적인 의료 시스템

③ 기후 데이터 인식에서 지역 사회 참여에 대한 필요성 증가

⑤ 기후 관련 건강 문제에 관한 연구에서의 사생활 보호
 ↳ 기후 변화가 건강에 미치는 영향을 연구하는 데 있어 하나의 어려움으로 언급되었을 뿐이다.

구문풀이

1행 [One of the great challenges in {understanding the health consequences of climate variability and change}] **is** the lack of temporally and spatially compatible data [to underpin evidence **based on** scientifically sound knowledge and action}].

: 첫 번째 [ ]가 주어부이고 주어의 핵은 One이므로 단수 동사 is가 쓰였고, { }는 전치사 in의 목적어 역할을 하는 동명사구이다. 두 번째 [ ]는 temporally and spatially compatible data를 수식하는 형용사적 용법의 to부정사구이고, based on은 '~에 기반하여[근거하여]'라는 의미를 나타낸다.

9행 And **within that** are further challenges to accessibility and availability — [**ranging from** privacy concerns and private sector ownership {surrounding some health data}, {making it altogether unavailable, or available but without the granularity (needed for robust analysis)}, **to** accessing massive climate data sets in a usable way].

: 장소를 나타내는 부사구 within that이 문두에 나오면서 주어(further challenges

to accessibility and availability)와 be동사(are)가 도치되었다. [ ]는 further challenges to accessibility and availability를 부가적으로 설명하는 분사구로, 「range from A to B: (범위가) A에서부터 B에 이르다」 구문이 쓰였다. 첫 번째 { }는 privacy concerns and private sector ownership을 수식하는 분사구이고, 두 번째 { }는 privacy concerns ~ some health data를 부가적으로 수식하는 어구이며, ( )는 the granularity를 수식하는 분사구이다.

어휘풀이

- challenge *n* 어려움, 과제
- climate *n* 기후
- temporally *ad* 시간적으로
- compatible *a* 호환되는
- sound *a* 견실한, 타당한
- discipline *n* (학문) 분야
- range from *A* to *B* (범위가) A에서부터 B에 이르다
- analysis *n* 분석
- integrate *v* 통합하다
- consequence *n* 영향, 결과
- variability *n* 가변성
- spatially *ad* 공간적으로
- underpin *v* 뒷받침하다, 보강하다
- robust *a* 확고한, 튼튼한
- oceanographic *a* 해양학의
- massive *a* 대규모의

145 답 ④

📖 질병 등과 같은 자연 속의 부정적인 가치

전문해석

질병은 유기체의 모든 집단을 완전히 없애거나 그것들에게 많은 고통과 통증을 유발할 수 있는 부정적인 가치이다. 질병은 대개 세상에서 자신의 목숨을 유지하려는 미생물에 기인할 수 있어서 질병은 적어도 단기적으로는 어떤 생명체의 번성함이 다른 생명체의 그것과 엇갈리게 되는 또 다른 방식이라는 것은 주목할 만하다. 다른 종을 희생시키고 얻은 하나 또는 더 많은 생물 종의 개체 수 과잉이 그러하듯이, 짝과 자손을 잃는 것과 서식지가 악화되는 것 역시 다른 종류의 부정적인 가치이다. 자연은 우리가 보아 왔듯이 역동적이고 급변할 수 있는 시스템이다. 그것의 다양한 측면은 근본적으로 서로에게 의존하고 있고, 그래서 모든 것은 변화에 매우 취약해진다. 자연의 생명체들에게 미래는 항상 믿을 수 있는 것이 아니며 그들에게 심각한 좌절, 실패 그리고 손실을 가져올 수 있다. 생명체의 '목적' 또는 발달과 번성의 특징적인 양상을 방해하는 것은 무엇이든지 자연에서 부정적인 가치이고, 인간이 자연 세계에서 할 수 있는 어떠한 역할과도 아주 별개로 그곳에는 많은 그러한 방해가 있다.

정답풀이

④ 재귀대명사: 재귀대명사를 목적어로 쓰는 경우는 주어와 목적어가 동일한 대상을 가리킬 때인데, and 다음에 이어지는 동사 can bring의 주어는 The future이고 목적어는 nature's creatures이다. 따라서 themselves를, nature's creatures를 가리키는 목적격 대명사 them으로 고쳐야 한다.

오답풀이

① 지시대명사: 앞에 나온 단수 명사 the flourishing을 대신하는 지시대명사 that은 어법상 적절하다.

② 주어와 동사의 수 일치: 접속사 as(~처럼)가 이끄는 절에서 주어 the overpopulation of one or more species at the expense of others와 도치된 be동사로 단수형 is는 어법상 적절하다. 이때 is는 대동사로 is a kind of a disvalue를 대신한다.

③ 형용사: '(목적어)를 ~하게 만들다'의 의미인 「make+목적어+목적격보어」 구문을 수동태로 바꾼 문장으로 원래 목적격보어에 해당하는 형용사 vulnerable은 어법상 적절하다.

⑤ 복합관계대명사: Whatever는 Anything that의 의미로서 선행사를 포함한 복합관계대명사로 여기서는 주어 역할을 하는 명사절을 이끌므로 어법상 적절하다.

구문풀이

1행 Disease is a disvalue, one [that may {wipe out whole groups of organisms} or {cause them much suffering and pain}].

: [ ]는 one(= a disvalue)을 수식하는 주격 관계대명사절이고, 이 절 안에서 두 개의 { }가 or로 연결되어 may에 이어진다.

3행 It is notable [that disease usually can be attributed to microorganisms {seeking to maintain their lives in the world}, so disease is yet another way {in which the flourishing of some creatures is at cross-purposes with that of others, at least in the short run}].

: It은 형식상의 주어이고, [ ]로 표시된 명사절이 내용상의 주어이다. 첫 번째 { }는 microorganisms를 수식하는 현재분사구이며, 두 번째 { }는 another way를 수식하는 관계절이다.

어휘풀이
- disvalue *n* 부정적인 가치
- organism *n* 유기체, 생명체
- be attributed to ~에 기인하다
- flourishing *n* 번성함
- at cross-purposes with ~와 엇갈리는
- in the short run 단기적으로
- overpopulation *n* 개체 수 과잉
- dynamic *a* 역동적인
- radically *ad* 근본적으로
- severe *a* 심각한
- setback *n* 실패
- apart from ~와 별개로
- wipe out ~을 완전히 없애다
- notable *a* 주목할 만한
- microorganism *n* 미생물
- deterioration *n* 악화
- at the expense of ~을 희생시키면서
- volatile *a* 급변할 수 있는
- vulnerable *a* 취약한
- frustration *n* 좌절
- interfere with ~을 방해하다

146 답 ③

📖 인간이 가지고 있는 다급해하는 본능

전문해석
다급함이라는 본능은 우리로 하여금 인지된 임박한 위험에 직면해서 즉각적인 행동을 취하고 싶어하게 만든다. 그것은 먼 과거에 우리 인간에게 이롭게 작용했을 것이 틀림없다. 만일 우리가 풀숲에 사자가 있을 것이라고 생각했다면 너무 많이 분석하는 것은 합리적이지 않았을 것이다. 멈춰서 가능성을 신중하게 분석했던 사람은 우리의 조상이 아니다. 우리는 **충분한(→ 불충분한)** 정보를 가지고 빠르게 결정하고 행동했던 사람들의 후손이다. 오늘날 우리는 여전히 예를 들어, 어디선가 자동차가 느닷없이 나타나서 우리가 피하는 행동을 취할 필요가 있을 때 다급함이라는 본능이 필요하다. 하지만 우리는 대부분의 즉각적인 위험을 제거했고 좀 더 복잡하고 종종 더 추상적인 문제를 가지고 있으므로, 다급함이라는 본능은 우리의 주변 세계를 이해하는 것에 관한 한 우리를 잘못된 길로 안내할 수 있다. 그것은 우리에게 스트레스를 주고, 우리의 다른 본능을 확대해서 통제하기 힘들게 만들고, 분석적으로 사고하는 것을 막고, 너무 빨리 결심하도록 유혹하고, 충분히 생각하지 않은 극적인 행동을 취하도록 부추긴다.

정답풀이
③ 임박한 위험에 직면했을 때 즉각적으로 행동하지 않고 여러 가지 가능성을 신중하게 분석했던 사람들은 멸종했을 것이기에 우리의 조상이 아니라고 했으므로, 신중하게 분석해서 얻은 충분한 정보가 없어도 본능에 의해 빠르게 행동했던 사람들이 우리의 조상이라는 흐름이 논리적으로 자연스럽다. 따라서 sufficient(충분한)를 반대 개념의 insufficient(불충분한)로 바꿔야 한다.

오답풀이
① 급하게 서두르는 본능을 가지고 있으면 임박한 위험에 직면했을 때 '즉각적으로' 행동할 것이므로 immediate는 적절하다.

② 임박한 위험에 처했을 때 빠르게 행동하지 않고 깊게 생각하는 것은 죽음을 초래할 수도 있으므로 합리적이라고 할 수 없다. 따라서 wasn't와 함께 쓰인 sensible(합리적인)은 적절하다.
④ 오늘날 여전히 다급함이라는 본능이 필요한 경우와 역접으로(But) 연결되어 있고, 다급함이라는 본능이 이제는 바람직하지 않게 된 하나의 배경에 해당하므로 오늘날에는 원시 시대에나 존재했을 즉각적인 위험이 대부분 '제거되었다(eliminated)'는 문맥은 적절하다.
⑤ 다급해하는 본능이 우리로 하여금 충분히 생각하지 않고 극적인 행동을 취하도록 하는 것이므로 encourages(부추긴다)는 문맥상 적절하다.

구문풀이
11행 But [now that we have eliminated most immediate dangers and are left with more complex and often more abstract problems], the urgency instinct can also lead us astray **when it comes to** [our **understanding** the world around us].

: 첫 번째 [ ]는 now that(~이므로)이 이끄는 이유를 나타내는 부사절이고, 두 번째 [ ]는 전치사 to의 목적어 역할을 하는 동명사구이며 our는 understanding ~의 의미상 주어이다. when it comes to는 '~에 관한 한'이라는 의미이다.

15행 It **makes** us stressed, **amplifies** our other instincts and **makes** them harder to control, **blocks** us from thinking analytically, **tempts** us to make up our minds too fast, and **encourages** us to take drastic actions [that we haven't thought through].

: 문장의 주어 It(= the urgency instinct)에 이어지는 동사 makes, amplifies, makes, blocks, tempts, encourages가 병렬구조로 연결되어 있다. [ ]는 drastic actions를 수식하는 목적격 관계대명사절이다.

어휘풀이
- urgency *n* 다급함, 긴급
- immediate *a* 즉각적인
- imminent *a* 임박한
- analysis *n* 분석
- ancestor *n* 조상
- sufficient *a* 충분한
- out of nowhere 갑자기, 예상치 못하게
- evasive *a* 회피하는
- abstract *a* 추상적인
- amplify *v* 증폭하다, 확대하다
- tempt *v* 유혹하다
- think through 충분히 생각하다
- instinct *n* 본능
- perceive *v* 인식하다
- sensible *a* 합리적인
- probability *n* 확률
- offspring *n* 후손, 자식
- eliminate *v* 제거하다
- lead ~ astray ~을 잘못된 길로 이끌다
- analytically *ad* 분석적으로
- drastic *a* 급격한, 과감한

147 답 ④

📖 자신이 만든 틀 안에서 이해하려는 방식의 문제점

전문해석
일상생활에서 우리의 개인적 선택과 해석에서 초래되는 한 가지 문제는 우리가 자기 충족적인 임무를 위한 만반의 준비가 되어 있다는 것이다. 다시 말해서, 우리는 세상을 다루기 위한 우리의 모형을 만들어 내고, 그런 다음 바로 그러한 모형의 틀에 의해서만 우리는 세상을 경험한다. **우리는 우리의 모형을 확인해 주거나 강화해 주는 정보를 수용하거나 받는 반면에 역으로 그것에 도전하거나 그것을 변화시키는 데 도움을 줄 수 있는 어떤 것이라도 거부한다.** 우리는 어떤 면에서 우리 자신의 해석 속에 '감금되어' 있다. 따라서 예를 들자면, 개인적인 관계에서 우리는 우리가 사람들에 대해 한 이전의 평가를 확인하는 데 도움이 되는 증거를 알아보고 기록하는 경향이 있다. 즉, 우리는 대체로 사람들의 행위를 '특징적으로' 그것들이 작용하고 있다고

계속해서 말할 수 있는 그런 방식으로 (다시 말해, 과거의 경험에 근거하여 우리가 그들에게 기대할 방식으로) 해석하며, 장기화된 '특징적이지 않은' 행동을 아주 방해가 되는 것으로 생각하여 우리는 아마도 그것을 우리 자신의 이전의 근본적인 잘못된 판단이라기보다 또 다른 사람의 일시적인 술 취한 상태 또는 정서 장애 탓으로 돌릴 것이다.

정답풀이
빈칸 앞에서는 우리가 세상을 다루는 한 가지 모형의 틀을 만들고 그 모형을 확인하거나 강화해 주는 정보는 받아들이고 그렇지 않은 것은 거부한다고 했으며, 빈칸 다음에서는 우리의 기대에 어긋나는 장기화된 특징적이지 않은 행동은 방해가 된다고 생각하고 그것을 우리 자신의 틀에 의한 잘못된 판단이라기보다 다른 외부적인 요인의 탓으로 돌린다고 했다. 따라서 대인 관계에서도 우리가 이전에 어떤 사람에 대해 내린 평가를 확인해 주는 증거만을 보고 기록하는 경향이 있다는 것을 추론할 수 있으므로, 빈칸에는 ④ '이전의 평가를 확인하는 데 도움이 되는'이 들어가는 것이 가장 적절하다.

오답풀이
① 우리가 고정관념에서 벗어나는 데 도움을 줄
② 호의적인 인상과 모순되는
③ 오로지 정서적인 유대를 강화하는
⑤ 우리가 오해를 인식하는 것을 가능하게 해주는

구문풀이
17행 ~ we find prolonged 'uncharacteristic' behavior **so** disturbing, **that** we would probably **attribute** it **to** another person's temporary drunkenness or emotional disorder, **rather than to** our own previous fundamental misjudgment.

: '매우 ~하여 …하다'라는 의미를 나타내는 「so ~ that ....」 구문이 쓰였으며, that절은 'A를 C의 탓이라기보다 B의 탓으로 돌리다'라는 의미의 「attribute A to B rather than to C」의 구조로 되어 있다.

어휘풀이
- be all set 만반의 준비가 되어 있다
- formulate v 만들다, 형성하다
- framework n 틀, 구조
- consolidate v 강화하다, 공고히 하다
- imprison v 가두다, 구속하다
- prolonged a 장기화된, 연장된
- attribute A to B A를 B의 탓으로 돌리다
- emotional disorder 정서 장애
- stereotype n 고정관념
- misconception n 오해, 잘못된 생각
- self-fulfilling a 자기 충족적인
- cope with ~에 대처하다, ~을 다루다
- confirm v 확인하다
- conversely ad 역으로
- on the basis of ~에 근거하여
- let go of ~을 놓아주다
- contradict v 모순되다

---

148 답 ③

📖 커피 거래 및 소비를 통해 본 세계화의 의미

전문해석
커피는 세계화, 국제무역, 인권과 환경 파괴에 대한 현시대 논쟁의 중심에 서 있는 제품이다. 커피가 인기를 끌게 됨에 따라 그것은 '상표가 붙게' 되고 정치적 논쟁거리가 되었다. 즉, 어떤 커피를 마실 것인지와 그것을 어디에서 구매할 것인지에 대해 소비자들이 하는 결정은 생활방식에 대한 선택이 되었다. 사람들은 오직 유기농 커피, 카페인을 뺀 커피 또는 (개발도상국의 소규모 커피 생산자들에게 온전한 시장 가격을 지불하는 제도를 통하여) '공정하게 거래된' 커피를 마실 것을 선택할 수 있다. 그들은 '기업의' 커피 체인점 대신 '독립적인' 커피 전문점을 애용하는 것을 선택할 수 있다. 커피를 마시는 사람들은 열악한 인권과 환경 기록을 가진 특정한 국가들에

서 온 커피에 대한 불매운동을 벌이기로 결정할 수도 있다. **커피의 거래와 소비에서 보이는 바와 같이, 세계화는 지구의 먼 구석에서 벌어지는 문제들에 대한 사람들의 인식을 높이고 그들이 그들 자신의 삶에서 새로운 지식에 따라 행동할 것을 촉구한다.**

정답풀이
이 글은 커피 거래와 소비를 통하여 세계화를 설명하고 있으며, 커피의 인기가 증가하면서 소비자들이 유기농 커피, 공정무역 커피, 인권이나 환경을 소홀히 하는 나라의 커피 등에 대해 선택을 할 수 있다는 내용이다. 즉, 세계화는 사람들이 세상에서 벌어지는 일들에 대해 관심을 갖고 그것에 따라 자기 삶의 방식을 결정하게 한다는 것이 글의 요지이므로, 빈칸에는 ③ '그들이 그들 자신의 삶에서 새로운 지식에 따라 행동할 것을 촉구한다'가 들어가는 것이 가장 적절하다.

오답풀이
① 개발도상국들이 그것의 이점을 공유할 수 있게 한다
② 회사들이 가져다줄 것에 대한 기대를 높인다
④ 회사들에게 더 엄격한 환경 지침을 따를 것을 촉구한다
⑤ 빈곤층이 그렇지 않으면 사용이 금지된 자원을 이용하도록 돕는다

구문풀이
4행 **As** coffee has grown in popularity, / it has become 'branded' and politicized: // the decisions [that consumers make / about what kind of coffee to drink and where to purchase it] **have become** lifestyle choices.

: As는 '~함에 따라'의 의미를 갖는 접속사이다. 콜론(:) 다음 문장에서 [ ]는 핵심 주어인 the decisions를 수식하는 목적격 관계대명사절이며, 동사는 have become이다.

어휘풀이
- stand at the heart of ~의 중심에 서다
- contemporary a 당대의, 현대의
- globalization n 세계화
- decaffeinated a 카페인을 뺀
- boycott v 거부하다, 대해 불매운동을 벌이다
- heighten v 높이다, 고양시키다
- urge v 촉구하다
- the have-nots 빈곤층
- debate n 논쟁, 토론
- politicize v 정치적 논쟁거리로 삼다
- scheme n 제도, 시책
- prompt v 촉발하다, 촉구하다
- comply to ~에 따르다, ~을 준수하다
- off-limits a 사용이 금지된

---

149 답 ⑤

📖 호환되는 소프트웨어를 사용하는 것의 장점

전문해석
파일을 공유하고 그것을 공동으로 사용하기를 원하는 컴퓨터 사용자들은 호환이 되는 소프트웨어 프로그램을 이용하고 있음에 틀림없다. **호환이 되는 소프트웨어 사용자들의 수가 증가함에 따라 파일을 공유하는 능력의 장점은 확대된다.** (C) 만일 MS Word가 다른 워드 프로세싱 프로그램보다 더 많은 컴퓨터 사용자들에 의해서 사용되면, 다른 사람들과 파일을 교환하기를 원하는 사람은 WordPerfect와 같은 (MS Word의) 경쟁 프로그램 대신에 MS Word를 구입하는 것이 이롭다. (B) MS Word의 모든 사용자들이 하나의 네트워크를 구성하고, 그 네트워크가 크면 클수록 MS Word를 사용하는 장점이 더 커진다. **가장 많은 사용자들을 끌어들일 수 있는 컴퓨터 프로그램은 시장에서의 분명한 우위를 행사할 것이다.** (A) 이것은 사용자들 간의 파일 호환성 때문일 뿐만 아니라 더 많은 사용자들이 특정한 프로그램에 익숙하게 되어 기업을 위한 훈련 비용을 줄이고 기업용과 가정용 사용자들 모두를 위해서 프로그램을 사용하는 법을 배우기 위한 지원의 비공식적인 원천의 이용 가능성을 증가시킬 것이기 때문에 참일 것이다.

정답풀이

호환이 되는 소프트웨어를 언급한 주어진 글 다음에는, 그 구체적인 사례로 MS Word를 소개하는 (C)가 먼저 와야 한다. 그리고 더 많은 사람들이 MS Word를 사용할 때의 장점을 소개한 (B)에 이어서 그러한 장점의 이유를 밝히는 (A)가 마지막에 이어지는 순서가 가장 적절하다. (A)의 This가 지칭하는 것이 (B)의 마지막 문장의 내용이라는 것도 단서가 된다.

구문풀이

13행 All the users of MS Word constitute a network, / and **the bigger** the network **the greater** the advantage of using MS Word.

: '~하면 할수록 점점 더 …하다'라는 의미의 「the+비교급 ~, the+비교급 …」 구문이 쓰였다.

어휘풀이

- utilize *v* 이용하다
- compatible *a* 호환되는 (*n* compatibility)
- familiar with ~에 익숙한
- constitute *v* 구성하다
- availability *n* 이용 가능성
- pay *v* (~에게) 이득이 되다
- as opposed to ~이 아니라, ~와는 반대로

150 답 ③

📖 신경계적으로 구별되는 '원하는 것'과 '좋아하는 것'

전문해석

우리가 가장 많이 먹는 음식이 항상 우리가 가장 좋아하는 것은 아니다. 1996년에 심리학자 Kent Berridge가 '원하는 것(어떤 것을 먹고자 하는 동기)'과 '좋아하는 것(음식이 실제로 주는 즐거움)'의 구별을 소개했을 때, 그는 많은 신경과학자들이 먹는 것에 대해 생각하는 방식을 변화시켰다. Berridge는 '원하는 것' 또는 갈망은 심리적으로뿐만 아니라 신경계적으로 '좋아하는 것'과 다르다는 것을 발견했다. 구체적으로 말하자면, 먹고자 하는 우리의 동기를 조절하는 뇌의 영역은 '측좌핵' 전체에 걸쳐 퍼져 있는 반면, 우리가 먹을 때 우리에게 즐거움을 주는 뇌의 부분은 이 동일 영역 내에서 더 작은 '민감점'을 차지하고 있다. Berridge에게 이 발견은 인간을 괴롭히는 일부 '욕구 장애'에 대해 생각해 보는 유익한 방법을 제공한다. 예를 들어, 폭식은 "상응하는 '좋아함'이 없는 과도한 원함"과 관련이 있을 수 있다. 치즈 맛 나초를 실제로 먹을 때 그것이 전달하는 즐거움이 기대한 것보다 훨씬 덜 강력함에도 불구하고, 여러분은 초대형 포장의 치즈 맛 나초를 구입하려는 강력한 욕구를 느낄 수 있다. 사실, 폭식가들은 종종 그들이 갈망하는 음식들을 먹고 있으면서도 맛이 없다고 보고하는데, 욕망이 즐거움보다 더 큰 것이다.

정답풀이

주어진 문장의 this discovery는 음식에 있어 원하는 것과 좋아하는 것이 다르다는 발견을 가리키고, 따라서 주어진 문장은 ②나 ③에 위치할 수 있다. 그런데 Specifically로 시작하는 ② 다음 문장은 바로 앞 문장의 내용을 구체적으로 설명하고 있고, ③ 다음 문장은 주어진 문장에서 언급한 욕구 장애의 예에 해당하는 폭식에 대해서 이야기하고 있으므로, 주어진 문장은 ③에 들어가야 한다.

구문풀이

12행 Specifically, **whereas** the zone of the brain [that controls our motivation to eat] stretches across the entire *nucleus accumbens*, / the sections of the brain [that give us pleasure when we eat] occupy smaller "hotspots" within this same area.

: whereas(~인 반면에)가 이끄는 부사절과 주절로 이루어진 문장이다. 첫 번째 [ ]는 the zone of the brain을, 두 번째 [ ]는 the sections of the brain을 수식하는 주격 관계대명사절이다.

어휘풀이

- fruitful *a* 유익한
- bedevil *v* 괴롭히다
- distinction *n* 구별
- neurally *ad* 신경계적으로
- stretch *v* 펼쳐 있다, 미치다
- hotspot *n* 민감점, 핫 스팟
- potent *a* 강력한
- disorder *n* 장애, 질환
- neuroscientist *n* 신경과학자
- craving *n* 갈망
- specifically *ad* 구체적으로 말하자면
- occupy *v* 차지하다
- corresponding *a* 상응하는
- consume *v* 먹다, 소비하다

151 답 ②

📖 미학적 디자인으로 인한 가시성 원칙의 위배와 사용의 불편함

전문해석

수많은 디자인들에서 매우 중요한 부분들이 꼼꼼히 숨겨져 있다. 캐비닛의 손잡이는 디자인의 미학으로부터 벗어나 있으므로, 그것들은 고의적으로 보이지 않게 만들어지거나 배제된다. 문의 존재를 나타내는 틈새 또한 디자인의 순수한 선에서 벗어나므로, 이 중요한 단서들 또한 최소화되거나 제거된다. 그 결과는 반짝거리는 재료가 매끄럽게 펼쳐진 것일 수 있는데, 문이나 서랍이 어떻게 열리는지는 고사하고 그것들의 흔적조차 없다. 이런 똑같은 미학적 원칙은 보통 전기 장치들에 적용이 되어서 많은 전기 장치들은 전원 스위치가 어딘가에 숨겨져 있다. 예를 들면, 많은 프린터와 복사기들은 전원 스위치가 뒤쪽이나 옆면에 있는데, 이는 그것을 찾기 힘들고 사용하기 불편하게 만든다. 게다가, 주방의 음식물 찌꺼기 처리기를 제어하는 스위치는 종종 숨겨져 있는데, 때로는 찾기가 거의 불가능하다. 많은 시스템들은 이제 눈에 보이지 않는 것을 보이게 만드는 행위에 의해 크게 개선될 수 있다.

→ 가시성의 원칙은 장치를 사용하는 것을 훨씬 더 수월하게 하는 것인데, 많은 일상적인 품목들의 디자인에서 위배되고 있다.

정답풀이

일상적인 시설이나 전자 기기의 디자인에서 작동 장치나 전원 장치가 미학적인 목적으로 인해 눈에 보이지 않게 처리되어 불편을 초래한다는 내용의 글이다. 일상생활에서 사용하는 시설이나 기기의 디자인에서 사용을 수월하게 하려면 문을 여는 손잡이나 전원 스위치 등이 잘 보이게 해야 한다는 점을 나타내도록 (A)에는 visibility(가시성)가 들어가야 하고, 그럼에도 불구하고 미학적인 목적으로 인해 이러한 가시성의 원칙이 지켜지지 않는다는 점을 나타내도록 (B)에는 violated(위배되는)가 들어가야 한다.

구문풀이

18행 Many systems can be vastly improved by the act of **making visible [what** is invisible] now.

: 「make+목적어+목적격보어」 구조에서 목적어에 해당하는 [ ]가 목적격보어인 visible 뒤에 위치한 형태로, 목적어가 긴 경우에 이러한 도치가 흔히 발생한다. [ ]는 선행사를 포함하는 관계대명사 what이 이끄는 명사절이다.

어휘풀이

- crucial *a* 매우 중요한
- aesthetics *n* 미학
- leave out ~을 제외하다[빼다]
- signify *v* 나타내다
- expanse *n* 널찍한 공간
- let alone ~은 고사하고, ~은커녕
- awkward *a* 불편한
- garbage disposal 음식물 찌꺼기 처리기
- unit *n* (한 벌의) 기구, 기계
- simplicity *n* 단일성, 단순성
- distract from ~로부터 벗어나 있다
- deliberately *ad* 고의적으로, 일부러
- crack *n* 틈, 균열
- minimize *v* 최소화하다
- gleaming *a* 반짝거리는, 빛나는
- photocopier *n* 복사기
- visibility *n* 가시성, 눈에 보임
- multi-function *n* 다기능

| 152 ② | 153 ② | 154 ① | 155 ② | 156 ② |
| 157 ③ | 158 ① | 159 ⑤ | | |

152　답 ②

📖 이슬람교도나 흑인에 대해서만 나타나는 외집단 동질성

전문해석
두 개의 범주가 주어지면 우리는 그 둘 간의 차이를 과대평가한다. 우리는 각 집단의 구성원 사이의 차이는 과소평가한다. 우리는 또한 우리 자신의 집단을 아름답게 다양하다고 여기고 그것 외부의 사람들은 동질적이라고 여기는 경향이 있다. 이것을 가리키는 전문 용어는 '외집단(外集團) 동질성'이며, 그것은 예를 들어 미국 언론 매체가 폭력을 보도하는 서로 다른 방법을 설명하는 데 도움이 된다. 백인의 그리스도교 사람들이 증오 범죄를 저지르면 그들은 주류 언론 매체에서 주로 정신적 장애가 있는 개인이나 그들의 행동은 그들 자신의 특정한 심리 상태에서 나오는 것으로 묘사된다. 이슬람교도가 저지른 범죄는 개인의 병리가 아니라 집단 정체성의 탓으로 돌릴 가능성이 큰데, 주변화된 집단 출신의 사람이 저지른 폭력 행위는 그들이 속한 그 집단의 반영으로 여겨진다. '흑인에 대한 흑인의 범죄'라는 용어는 존재하는 반면, '백인에 대한 백인의 범죄'라는 용어는 존재하지 않는데, 미국에서 백인 살인 피해자의 80퍼센트 이상이 다른 백인에게 살해되어도 그러하다. 문화적인 상상력에서 백인 가해자와 백인 피해자는 의미 있는 집단의 일부로 여겨지지 않는다. 철학자인 George Yancy가 말하듯이, 백인은 '그저 사람'이다.

정답풀이
미국 사회에서 주류 집단인 백인의 그리스도교 사람들은 범죄를 저지르면 해당 개인의 병리적 현상으로 해석되는 반면, 주변화된 다른 인종, 다른 종교에 속하는 이슬람교도나 흑인의 폭력에 대해서는 그들 집단 정체성이 반영된 행동으로 해석한다는 내용이므로, 백인에 대한 밑줄 친 부분이 의미하는 바로는 ② '집단 고정관념으로부터 자유로운 개인으로 인지된다'가 가장 적절하다.

오답풀이
① 어려운 처지에 있는 사람들에게 항상 너그럽다고 여겨진다
③ 그들의 사회에서 별개의 사회적 집단으로 흔히 인식된다
　└ 백인은 집단의 정체성을 반영하는 존재가 아니라 다양성을 가진 개인으로 여겨진다는 내용이다.
④ 종교적 차이와 상관없이 모든 인간을 존중하고 있다
⑤ 증오 범죄와 인종 관련 폭력에 반대하는 입장을 취하고 있다

구문풀이
[11행] Crime [committed by a Muslim person] is likely to **be ascribed not to** individual pathology **but to** group identity: violent acts by people from marginalized groups are seen as a reflection of that group [to which they belong].

: 첫 번째 [ ]는 문장의 핵심 주어인 Crime을 수식하는 과거분사구이다. 「A is ascribed not to B but to C」는 'A는 B의 탓이 아니라 C의 탓으로 여겨지다'라는 의미이다. 두 번째 [ ]는 that group을 수식하는 관계절이다.

어휘풀이
- overestimate *v* 과대평가하다
- variation *n* 차이
- commit *v* (죄 등을) 저지르다, 범하다
- portray *v* 묘사하다
- disturbed *a* 정신[정서]적 장애가 있는
- ascribe A to B A를 B의 탓으로 돌리다
- underestimate *v* 과소평가하다
- cover *v* 보도하다
- hate crime 증오 범죄
- mainstream *a* 주류의
- identity *n* 정체성
- marginalized *a* 주변화된
- victim *n* 희생자
- reflection *n* 반영
- put *v* 말하다, 언급하다

153　답 ②

📖 베이비부머와 X세대의 노동에 대한 견해 차이

전문해석
1946년과 1964년 사이에 태어난 베이비부머는 경제 침체기 동안 성년에 이른 그들의 부모와 대조적으로, 경제적 번영 가운데 성장했다. 그럼에도 불구하고, 부모와 마찬가지로 그들은 열심히 일하고 장시간 노동하는 것을 옳다고 생각하지만, 그들 이전 세대의 구성원들과 달리 자신의 노고에 대해 공적으로 인정받고 노력에 대해 보상받기를 기대한다. 베이비부머들은 그들 자신을 직업과 긴밀하게 연관 지으며, 많은 이들이 상당히 긴 시간을 일한다. 반면에, 1965년과 1980년 사이에 태어난 X세대는 노동에 대해 그들의 이전 세대들과 다른 관점을 가지고 있다. 수년간의 헌신과 충실한 근무에도 불구하고 그들의 부모가 해고되는 것을 목격했기 때문에, 그들은 자신들의 행복에 관심이 없는 것으로 보이는 고용주들에게 깊은 인상을 주기 위해 과도하게 오랜 시간 일하거나 특별히 열심히 일할 필요성을 알지 못한다. 대신, 그들은 '더 현명하게 일하는 것'이 옳다고 믿는데, 이는 보통 이전 가능한 기술을 개발하고 일에 더 적은 시간을 할애하는 것으로 해석된다. 그들은 업무보다 결과에 더 초점을 맞추면서 독립적으로 일할 수 있는 것을 더 중시한다.

정답풀이
② 대명사: 베이비부머들이 상당히 긴 시간을 일하는 것은 자신의 직업과 자신을 연관시키기 때문이라고 할 수 있다. 즉, 문맥상 associate의 목적어가 주어와 동일한 대상인 Baby Boomers를 가리키므로 them을 재귀대명사 themselves로 고쳐야 한다.

오답풀이
① 병렬구조: 문맥상 자신의 노고에 대해 공적으로 인정받고 노력에 대해 보상받기를 기대한다는 것이므로 and 앞의 to be acknowledged와 병렬구조를 이루는 (to be) rewarded는 어법상 적절하다.
③ 과거분사: 지각동사 witnessed의 목적어인 their parents가 해고를 당하는 대상이므로 목적격보어로 수동의 의미를 나타내는 과거분사 laid off를 쓴 것은 어법상 적절하다.
④ 관계대명사 which: 앞 절의 "working smarter"를 부연 설명하는 관계사절을 이끌며, 관계사절에서 주어 역할을 하는 관계대명사로 which를 쓴 것은 어법상 적절하다.
⑤ 분사구문: '~하면서'라는 의미로 부가적인 상황을 나타내는 분사구문을 이끄는 현재분사 focusing은 어법상 적절하게 쓰였다.

구문풀이
[13행] [**Having witnessed** their parents laid off despite years of dedication and loyal service], they don't see the necessity of [putting in excessively long hours] or [working extra hard to impress employers {they perceive as not likely to be concerned with their well-being}].

: 첫 번째 [ ]는 완료형 분사구문으로 문장의 시제보다 앞서 일어난 일을 나타낸다. or로 연결된 두 번째와 세 번째 [ ]는 전치사 of의 목적어로 쓰인 동명사구이다. { }는 employers를 수식하는 목적격 관계대명사절이다.

어휘풀이
- midst *n* 한가운데
- in contrast with ~와는 대조적으로
- depression *n* 침체
- associate A with B A를 B와 연관 짓다[결부시키다]
- prosperity *n* 번영
- come of age 성년에 이르다
- put in (~ 시간분의) 일을 하다

- considerably *ad* 상당히, 꽤
- lay off ~을 정리해고하다
- be concerned with ~에 관심이 있다
- predecessor *n* 전임자, 선배
- dedication *n* 헌신, 전념
- transferable *a* 이동[전이] 가능한

154 답 ①

📖 다원적 민주주의의 고질적인 문제점

전문해석

다원적 민주주의는 대립하고 있는 이해관계 사이에서 벌어지는 싸움을 이롭게 활용한다. 그것은 그 싸움을 조정하고 그 결과를 정부의 활동에 반영하는 정부를 찬성하는 입장이다. 다원적 민주주의에 따르면, 대중은 정부 구조가, 서로 다른 집단이 서로와의 경쟁 속에서 자신의 요구를 관철시키기 위한 통로를 제공하는 경우에 가장 잘 봉사받는다. 다원적 민주주의는 모든 집단이 정부의 결정에 대해 동일한 영향력을 가져야 한다고 주장하지 않는다는 것에 주목하라. 정치적인 분쟁에서 부유하고 잘 조직된 집단이 더 빈곤하고 제대로 조직되지 않은 집단보다 본질적 이점을 갖고 있다. 사실, 인구의 조직화되지 않은 부분은 심지어 그들의 관심사를 정부가 고려할 안건에 올리지도 못할 수 있다. 진정, 의회 안건에 대한 연구는 그것이 빈곤하거나 수입이 낮은 미국인들과 관계된 입법이라고 할 만한 것이 거의 없는 것으로 특징지어지며, 반면에 기업 관련 법안은 풍부하다는 것을 보여준다. 다원적 민주주의는 사회의 여러 다른 부분 사이에서의 정치적 조직과 자원의 수준에 존재하는 커다란 불균형을 정당화하는 듯하다.

정답풀이

다원적 민주주의에서는 사회의 모든 부분이 경쟁을 통해 각각의 이익을 도모하는 것을 추구하지만, 빈곤한 사람들과 관계된 입법은 거의 없는 반면에 기업 관련 법안은 풍부하다는 사실에서 볼 수 있듯이 각 부분의 조직화 정도와 보유 자원의 차이로 인해 생겨나는 불평등한 영향력이 발생한다는 내용이다. 따라서 빈칸에 들어갈 말로 가장 적절한 것은 이러한 다원적 민주주의의 특징을 나타내는 ① '커다란 불균형을 정당화하는'이다.

오답풀이

② 사회적 불평등을 해소하는
③ 의견의 다양성을 중시하는
└ 다원적 민주주의의 기본 취지이긴 하지만, 글의 핵심은 이러한 기본 취지가 균등하게 반영되지 않는다는 것이므로 오답!
④ 정치적 투쟁을 강화하는
⑤ 입법 활동을 지원하는

구문풀이

4행 According to pluralist democracy, the public is best served [**if** the government structure provides access {for different groups **to press** their claims in competition with one another}].

: [ ]는 접속사 if가 이끄는 부사절로 '~인 경우에'라는 의미를 나타낸다. { }는 access를 수식하는 형용사적 용법의 to부정사구로 for different groups가 to press ~의 의미상 주어를 나타낸다.

어휘풀이

- pluralist *a* 다원적인
- make a virtue of ~을 이롭게 활용하다
- argue for ~에 찬성 의견을 말하다
- channel *A* into *B* A를 B에 반영하다[넣다]
- press *v* 강조하다, 주장하다
- inadequately *ad* 불충분하게
- congressional *a* 의회의
- little in the way of ~라고 할 만한 것이 거의 없음
- legislation *n* 입법
- resolve *v* 해소하다, 해결하다
- accommodate *v* 수용하다
- inherent *a* 내재적인
- segment *n* 부분, 조각
- agenda *n* 안건
- disparity *n* 불균형

155 답 ②

📖 인류학 연구에 영향을 미치는 인류학자의 자기 민족 중심주의

전문해석

외국에서 연구를 수행할 때 인류학자들이 직면하는 장애물을 더하는 것은 그들 자신의 문화적 신념이다. 아마도 인류학자들에게 대부분의 사람들보다 자신들의 문화적 배경이 접근하는 것을 막는 더 큰 능력이 있다고 주장될 수 있을 텐데, 그것은 그들이 받는 훈련의 가장 중요한 부분이다. 하지만 그들이 태어날 때 특정 문화로 (혹은 더 엄밀하게 한 문화 내의 한 지역으로) 사회화되었다는 바로 그 사실은 특정한 가치와 관습을 포함하고 그들의 세계 질서에서 특유의 도덕적, 정치적 영역을 차지한다. 이것은 필연적으로, 개별적인 인류학자의 됨됨이를 고려하지 않아도, 어느 정도의 자기 민족 중심주의가 늘 생기기 마련이라는 것을 시사한다. 때때로 인류학자들은 최소한 사적으로는 우리의 민족지(民族誌: 현지조사에 바탕을 둔 여러 민족의 사회조직이나 생활양식 전반에 관한 내용을 체계적으로 기술한 자료)가 부분적으로는 연구 대상이 되는 사람들의 시각이 아니라 우리 자신의 세계관을 반영하는 문화적 투영과 개인적 고백으로 구성된다고 농담 삼아 말한다. 그러나 그 일을 더 잘 해낸 비교 문화 연구에 참여하는 다른 어떤 학문 분야도 언급하기 어려울 것이다.

정답풀이

인류학자들이 외국에 나가 연구할 때 자신들의 문화적 배경이 연구에 영향을 미치는 것을 막으려고 노력하지만 그들 또한 특정 문화 속에서 사회화된 존재이므로 어느 정도의 영향은 필연적이라는 내용이다. 따라서 빈칸에는 ② '어느 정도의 자기 민족 중심주의가 늘 생기기 마련이다'가 들어가는 것이 가장 적절하다.

오답풀이

① 많은 다른 학문 분야들이 인류학과 관련이 있다
③ 서로 다른 문화들 사이에 공통의 기반이 있다
④ 서로 다른 민족 집단들이 더 잘 통합되고 있다
⑤ 문화적 배경은 비교 문화 연구에 영향을 미치지 않는다

구문풀이

6행 Yet **the very fact** [that they have been socialized at birth into a particular culture (or more precisely a location within a culture)] **encompasses** specific values and institutions and **occupies** a particular moral and political niche in their world order.

: 문장의 핵심 주어는 the very fact이며, encompasses와 occupies의 두 동사가 병렬구조로 연결되어 있다. [ ]는 the very fact를 구체적으로 설명하는 동격절이다.

18행 However, **it** would be difficult [**to point** to any other discipline {engaged in cross-cultural studies} {that has done the job better}].

: it은 형식상의 주어이고, [ ]로 표시된 to부정사구가 내용상의 주어이다. 첫 번째 { }는 any other discipline을 수식하는 과거분사구이고, 두 번째 { }는 any other discipline ~ studies를 수식하는 주격 관계대명사절이다.

어휘풀이

- obstacle *n* 장애(물)
- anthropologist *n* 인류학자
- capacity *n* 능력, 수용력
- precisely *ad* 엄밀하게, 정확하게
- niche *n* 영역, 범위
- projection *n* 투영, 투사
- discipline *n* 학문 분야
- ethnocentrism *a* 자기 민족 중심주의
- integrate *v* 통합하다
- confront *v* 가로막다, ~에 직면하다
- baggage *n* 신념, 특정한 사고방식
- hold ~ at bay ~이 접근하는 것을 막다
- institution *n* 관습, 관례
- inevitably *ad* 필연적으로
- confession *n* 고백, 자백
- cross-cultural study 비교 문화 연구
- creep in ~이 생기기 마련이다
- ethnic *a* 민족의

156 답 ②

📖 **시간이 흐르면서 일어나는 생태계의 엄청난 변화**

전문해석

현대의 생태계와 그 안에 있는 식물과 동물의 발달을 연구하는 것은 우리가 어느 한 주어진 지역의 과거 생태계가 현재 그 지역을 특징짓는 동일한 기후, 토양 그리고 지형을 가졌다고 가정할 수 있다면 더 단순할 것이다. (B) 하지만 빈번히 화석 기록은 동일한 지역에서 오늘날의 그것과는 너무나도 다른 생태계를 드러내어 우리는 기후 그리고/또는 자연 환경에 상당한 변화가 있었음을 알게 된다. (A) 예를 들면, 중신세 동안에, 현재 동부 중앙 아이다호에 있는 새먼강이 된 곳 근방의 평원은 메타세쿼이아가 지배적이었지만 또한 많은 다른 수목 종들도 포함하고 있던 우거진 숲으로 덮여 있었다. (C) 오늘날 그 숲은 1,500만 년간 쌓인 화산재로 뒤덮여 있다. 재의 최상층에는 반사막 방목지가 있는데, 거기에는 산쑥과 풀이 자라고 있다. 약 100만 년 전 Cascade 산맥의 융기는 아이다호의 상당 부분을 비 그늘(산으로 막혀 강수량이 적은 지역) 사막으로 바꿔 놓았다.

정답풀이

현대와 과거 생태계의 동식물 발달 연구는 단순하지 않다는 내용의 주어진 글 다음에는, 그러나(however) 화석 증거를 통해 생태계의 변화를 확인할 수 있다는 내용의 (B)가 오고, 이어서 그 사례에 해당하는 (A)가 와야 한다. 그리고 과거 생태계에 대한 (A)의 언급에 이어 a dense forest를 that forest로 칭하며 과거(중신세)와 달라진 오늘날의 생태계에 대해 설명하는 내용의 (C)가 마지막에 오는 것이 가장 적절하다.

구문풀이

6행 For example, during the Miocene epoch, the plains near [**what** is now the Salmon River in east central Idaho] were covered with a dense forest [**dominated** by dawn redwood but also **containing** many other species of trees].

: 첫 번째 [ ]는 '현재 ~이 된 곳'의 의미를 나타내는 명사절이다. 두 번째 [ ]는 a dense forest를 수식하는 두 개의 분사구가 but으로 연결된 형태이다.

어휘풀이
- ecosystem *n* 생태계
- characterize *v* 특징짓다
- fossil *n* 화석
- accumulation *n* 쌓임, 축적
- rangeland *n* 방목지
- rain shadow 비 그늘(산으로 막혀 강수량이 적은 지역)
- assume *v* 가정하다, 추측하다
- dominate *v* 지배하다
- considerable *a* 상당한
- volcanic ash 화산재

157 답 ③

📖 **수치로 제시되는 데이터의 결과가 완벽하지 않을 가능성**

전문해석

데이터는 보통 숫자인데, 측정이나 셈, 또는 다른 과정의 결과이다. 우리는 그러한 데이터를 우리가 연구하고 있는 어떤 것이든 그것에 대한 단순화된 표현을 제공하는 것으로 생각할 수 있다. 만약 우리가 학교 아이들, 그리고 특히 그들의 학업 능력과 다양한 종류의 직업에 대한 적합성에 대해 관심이 있다면, 우리는 다양한 시험과 검사에서 그들의 결과를 제공하는 숫자를 연구하기로 선택할 수 있다. **이 숫자들은 그들의 능력과 성향의 표시를 제공할 것이지만, 그 표시는 완벽하지 않을 것이다.** 낮은 점수는 단순히 누군가가 시험 중에 아팠다는 것을 나타낼 수 있다. 같은 맥락에서 결측값은 그들의 능력에 대해 많이 말해주는 것이 아니라 단지 그들이 시험을 치르지 않았다는 것을 말해준다. 데이터의 질이 중요한데, 만약 우리가 가지고 작업하는 자료가 좋지 않으면 그 결과도 좋지 않을 것이라는 일반적인 원칙(그것은 단지 통계학

에서만이 아니라 평생에 걸쳐서 적용된다) 때문이다. 통계학자들은 숫자에서 이해를 추출하는 데 있어서 놀라운 업적을 수행할 수 있지만, 기적을 이룰 수는 없다.

정답풀이

③ 앞에서 학생들을 대상으로 실시한 시험과 검사의 숫자가 제공하는 표시가 있지만, 그것이 완벽하지 않을 수 있다고 지적했는데, ③ 뒤에는 같은 맥락에서 자료의 결측값은 아이들의 능력을 말해주는 것이 아니라 시험을 치르지 않았음을 말해준다고 해서 논리적으로 자연스럽게 연결되지 않는다. ③에 주어진 문장이 들어가면 아이들의 낮은 점수가 단지 아파서 생긴 결과일 수 있고, 같은 맥락에서 결측값이 시험에 결시했다는 사실만 나타낼 뿐이라는 문맥으로 자연스럽게 연결되므로 주어진 문장은 ③에 들어가는 것이 가장 적절하다.

구문풀이

6행 [If we are concerned with {school children}, and in particular {their academic ability and suitability for different kinds of careers}], we might choose to study the numbers [giving their results in various tests and examinations].

: 첫 번째 [ ]는 조건을 나타내는 부사절이고, 그 안에 and로 연결된 두 개의 { }는 전치사 with의 목적어이다. 두 번째 [ ]는 the numbers를 수식하는 현재분사구이다.

13행 A missing value, in the same vein, does **not** tell us [much about their ability], **but** merely [that they did not sit the examination].

: tell의 직접목적어에 해당하는 두 개의 [ ]가 「not A but B: A가 아니라 B」 구문에 의해 연결되어 있다.

16행 Data quality matters because of the general principle (which applies throughout life, not merely in statistics) [that {if we have poor material <to work with>} then the results will be poor].

: [ ]는 the general principle을 구체적으로 설명하는 동격절이고, 그 안의 { }는 조건을 나타내는 부사절이며, 〈 〉는 poor material을 수식하는 형용사적 용법의 to부정사구이다. ( ) 안에 주어진 which applies ~ in statistics는 the general principle을 부연 설명하는 주격 관계대명사절이다.

어휘풀이
- indicate *v* 나타내다
- simplified *a* 단순화된
- suitability *n* 적합성
- inclination *n* 성향
- matter *v* 중요하다
- statistics *n* 통계학, 통계 수치
- extract *v* 추출하다
- measurement *n* 측정
- representation *n* 표현
- indication *n* 표시
- in the same vein 같은 맥락에서
- apply *v* 적용되다
- feat *n* 업적

158~159 답 ① / ⑤

📖 **예술과 연예의 창작 과정이 비공개로 이루어지는 이유**

전문해석

제작자와 관객의 관계가 어떻게 변화하고 있는지 이해하기 위해서, 우리는 먼저 예술과 연예 산업이 전통적으로 어떻게 운영되는지를 상기해 보아야 한다. 그 공동 목표가 부분적으로 창작 과정을 드러내는 것인, 최근의 예술 교육 그리고 청중 개발 의제를 포함한 예술의 사회적 통합에도 불구하고 그리고 예술과 연예 매니지먼트라는 학문 분야의 증가하는 인기에도 불구하고, **창작 과정 자체는 종종 미스터리로 남아 있다.** 여기에는 다양한 이유가 있다. 첫째, 많은 예술가, 제작자 그리고 관객들은 그 과정 뒤에 숨겨진 비밀이 정확히 예술과 연예 경험에 그것의 가장 중요한 매력을 부여하는 것이라고 주장할 것이다. 무대를 천천히 드러내는 커튼의 강력한 이미지와 상징성은 폐쇄적이고 신비롭고 현실 도피적인 세계를 암시하는데, 이는 관객들을 커

튼의 한쪽에서 다른 쪽으로 잠시 이동시킬 수 있다. **둘째, 창작 과정 자체는 본질적으로 복잡하여** 새로운 경험을 계획하기 위해서 다양한 창의적인 에이전트들이 모여야 한다. 이것은 인간과 예술의 화학작용과 같은 많은 무형의 것들을 포함하는데, 그것들은 관객에게 알려지지 않은 새로운 요소를 만들어 내기 위해서 도가니 속에 넣어진다. **마지막으로, 다른 많은 전문적 활동들처럼** 쓰기, 작곡, 안무, 촬영, 리허설 그리고 다른 관련된 창작 활동들은 작가, 감독, 예술가들이 예술적 자유와 **투명성(→ 기밀 유지)**의 정신으로 실험하고, 집중하고, 작업할 수 있도록 일반적으로 **비공개**로 진행된다.

정답풀이

158 예술과 연예의 창작 과정이 미스터리로 남아 있는 이유로 그러한 비밀이 예술과 연예의 경험에 가장 중요한 매력을 제공하고, 창작 과정 자체가 본질적으로 복잡하며, 예술가들이 예술적으로 자유롭게 작업할 수 있다는 점을 들어 설명하는 글이다. 따라서 글의 제목으로 가장 적절한 것은 ① '예술적 과정을 숨기는 것은 자연스럽다'이다.

159 쓰기, 작곡, 안무 등과 같은 창작 활동이 비공개로 진행되는 것은 작가, 감독, 예술가가 자유롭게 그리고 비밀을 유지하며 실험하고 집중하고 작업할 수 있게 해줄 것이다. 따라서 (e) transparency(투명성)를 confidentiality (비밀성, 기밀 유지) 정도의 어휘로 바꿔야 한다.

오답풀이

158 ② 미술은 미술가의 비밀 유지에 대한 욕구를 반영한다
③ 예술은 사회적 그리고 문화적 경향을 반영한다
④ 예술품 감상의 큰 어려움
⑤ 예술 학문 분야들의 상호의존성

159 ① 예술의 사회적 통합의 공동 목표가 창작 과정을 '드러내는' 것임에도 불구하고 창작 과정은 여전히 미스터리로 남아 있다는 흐름이 자연스러우므로 reveal의 쓰임은 문맥상 적절하다.
② 창작 과정이 미스터리로 남아 있는 첫 번째 이유를 설명하는 문장이므로, 창작 과정 이면에 숨겨진 비밀이 예술과 연예 경험에 '매력(appeal)'을 제공한다는 문맥은 적절하다.
③ 창작 과정이 새로운 경험을 만들어 내려면 다양한 창의적인 에이전트들이 모여야 하므로 이는 '복잡한(complex)' 과정이라고 할 수 있다.
④ 인간과 예술의 화학작용은 눈으로 볼 수 있는 것이 아닌 '무형의 것'이므로 intangibles는 문맥에 맞는 표현이다.

구문풀이

15행 [The powerful image and symbolism of a curtain slowly revealing a stage] **hints** at [a closed, mysterious and escapist world], [which can briefly transport its audience from one side of the curtain to the other].

: 첫 번째 [ ]가 주어이고, 동사는 hints이다. 두 번째 [ ]는 전치사 at의 목적어인 명사구이다. 세 번째 [ ]는 앞 절의 내용을 부가적으로 설명하는 주격 관계대명사절이다.

어휘풀이

- social inclusion 사회적 통합
- communal *a* 공동의, 공동체의
- academic discipline 학문적 분야, 학과목
- contend *v* 주장하다
- stage *n* 무대 *v* 전개하다, 조직하다
- escapist *a* 현실 도피의
- inherently *ad* 본질적으로
- agenda *n* 의제, 안건
- overriding *a* 가장 중요한, 최우선적인
- hint at ~을 넌지시 비치다
- transport *v* 이동시키다
- chemistry *n* 화학작용, 화학
- behind the closed doors 비공개로, 비밀리에

3점 공략 모의고사 1회

01 분리 02 독단적인, 임의의 03 처음에 04 보완하다 05 유독성의 06 pioneer 07 위험한 08 마음이 내키는, ~하고 싶은 09 compound 10 회복하다 11 명확한 12 전환, 변환 13 insight 14 강화하다 15 격언, 금언 16 진행되다 17 영향력 있는 18 창의력, 독창성 19 오염시키다 20 추출

3점 공략 모의고사 2회

01 상반되는, 모순되는 02 돌아다니다, 배회하다 03 공공연한, 명백한 04 변경하다, 바꾸다 05 반대, 이의 (제기) 06 배열, 순서 07 강요하다 08 정보에 근거한 09 resistance 10 수행하다 11 설득력 있는 12 extinct 13 방해하다, 지체시키다 14 번성하다, 번영하다 15 순응 16 지배적인, 우세한 17 identity 18 수정, 조작, 변형 19 (이익 등을) 얻다[거두다] 20 반박

3점 공략 모의고사 3회

01 악명 높은 02 ~의 탓으로 돌리다 03 상당한, 실질적인 04 인식, 인지 05 중간의 06 reputation 07 회의적인 08 소매상 09 암묵적인 10 기르다, 길들이다 11 literally 12 비옥함 13 habitat 14 곰팡이 15 이타적으로 16 전문용어 17 원주민의, 토착의 18 동일한, 똑같은 19 새로움 20 상호 호혜적인

3점 공략 모의고사 4회

01 평가하다 02 동등한 03 억제하다 04 통합 05 역으로 06 장벽 07 subconscious 08 하위의, 부차적인 09 mammal 10 일관되게, 지속적으로 11 구별하다 12 상품 13 parallel 14 과장하다 15 추상적인 16 보조금 17 ~로 구성되다 18 편견 19 추론하다 20 (점점) 줄어들다, 감소하다

3점 공략 모의고사 5회

01 유목민 02 전술의, 전략의 03 장애물 04 예상[예측]하다 05 변함없이, 예외 없이 06 virtue 07 부족한, 결핍한 08 humility 09 지배적인 10 주장하다, 옹호하다 11 immune 12 특출한 13 시간, 기간 14 해방 15 오류 16 비유적인, 은유적인 17 축적 18 지각의 19 성향 20 수반되는

3점 공략 모의고사 6회

01 돌아다니다, 헤매다 02 회복력 03 충실한, 충성스런 04 조작하다 05 remote 06 monument 07 외관상으로 08 필수 불가결한 09 유발하다 10 단언하다 11 재배하다 12 contemporary 13 향상하다, 높이다 14 (끼워) 넣다 15 풀 수 없는, 해결할 수 없는 16 지속하다 17 안심하는, 안전한 18 정착(지) 19 크게 증가시키다 20 가공할, 무시무시한

3점 공략 모의고사 7회

01 취약한 02 강화하다 03 강력한 04 실패 05 다급함, 긴급 06 호화되는 07 stereotype 08 임박한 09 공간적인 10 만들다, 형성하다 11 immediate 12 모순되다 13 aesthetics 14 급격한, 과감한 15 가두다, 감금하다 16 오해, 잘못된 생각 17 후손, 자식 18 촉발하다, 촉구하다 19 회피하는 20 ~에 따르다, ~을 준수하다

3점 공략 모의고사 8회

01 번역 02 수용하다 03 내재적인 04 confession 05 의제, 안건 06 주장하다 07 statistics 08 헌신, 전념 09 ethnic 10 공동의, 공동체의 11 추출하다 12 업적 13 부분, 조각 14 통합하다 15 가로막다, ~에 직면하다 16 입법 17 이동시키다 18 필연적으로 19 전임자, 선배 20 묘사하다

3점 공략 모의고사 9회

3점 공략 모의고사 9회

본문 p.112

160 ⑤	161 ⑤	162 ⑤	163 ②	164 ②
165 ⑤	166 ④	167 ④		

160 답 ⑤

📖 사회학자들이 내리는 정의의 속성

전문해석

사회학자는 사회적 사실을 관찰할 뿐만 아니라 정의해야 하며, 각각의 정의에 도달하기 위한 규칙들이 있다. 주어진 정의에 포함시킬 수 있는 모든 사실들을 관찰하는 것은 불필요한데, 그것은 과학의 목적 중 하나인 노력의 경제성을 좌절시킬 것이기 때문이다. 살인에 대해 정의를 내리기 위해 모든 살인 사건을 일일이 관찰할 필요는 없다. 하나의 정의에 부합하는 현상의 모든 측면을 일일이 관찰할 필요도 없는데, 속성의 무한함이 이를 불가능하게 만들기 때문이다. 대신에, 사회학자는 자신의 목적에 필수적인 특징들에 도달하고, 이것들을 자신의 정의로 사용하고, 관찰에 의해 어떤 특정한 사례들이 정의를 내리는 특징들을 공유하는지 결정해야 한다. 이것들, 그리고 단지 이것들만 그렇게 정의된 세부 사항들의 부류에 속한다. Durkheim은 범죄를 예시로 들었다. 사회에 의한 처벌을 유발하는 모든 행동은 이러한 부류의 행동에 속한다. 따라서 처벌은 범죄의 정의이며, 모든 범죄는 이 속성을 공유한다. 이러한 집단적 반응을 이끌어 내지 못하는 모든 행동은 이 부류에 속하지 않으며, 따라서 그 정의에 맞지 않는다.

정답풀이

사회학자들이 사회적 사실에 대한 정의를 내릴 때, 모든 사실들을 관찰할 수 없기 때문에 자신들의 목적에 맞는 필수적인 특징들을 도출하고, 어떤 특정한 사례들이 그러한 특징을 공유하는지 결정을 내려야 한다고 말하고 있다. 따라서 '그렇게 정의된 세부 사항의 부류'가 의미하는 바로는 ⑤ '정의를 내리는 속성들을 공통으로 갖는 범주화된 사회적 사실'이 가장 적절하다.

오답풀이

① 노력을 아끼는 데 기반을 둔 전략
② 도덕적인 기준에 의해 판단되지 않는 행동의 종류
③ 모든 사회적 현상에 적용될 수 있는 보편적인 규칙
④ 모든 행동은 그 나름의 결과를 갖는다는 특정한 현상

구문풀이

`3행` It is unnecessary [**to observe** all the facts {that one can include under a given definition}], / **for** that would defeat the economy of effort, [which is one of science's purposes].

: It은 형식상의 주어이고, 첫 번째 [ ]로 표시된 to부정사구가 내용상의 주어이다. { }는 all the facts를 수식하는 목적격 관계대명사절이다. for는 부가적 이유를 나타내는 접속사이며, 두 번째 [ ]는 the economy of effort를 부가적으로 설명하는 주격 관계대명사절이다.

`10행` Instead, the sociologist **should arrive** at those characteristics [essential to his purpose], **use** these as his definition, and by observation **determine** [which particular instances share the defining characteristics].

: 조동사 should 다음에 동사원형 arrive, use, determine이 병렬로 이어진다. 첫 번째 [ ]는 those characteristics를 수식하는 형용사구이고, 두 번째 [ ]는 determine의 목적어로 쓰인 명사절로 which는 '어느, 어떤'을 의미하는 의문형용사로 쓰였다.

어휘풀이

- define *v* 정의하다 (*n* definition)
- given *a* 특정한, 정해진
- defeat *v* 좌절시키다, 패배시키다
- phenomenon *n* 현상 (*pl.* phenomena)
- fit *v* 잘 맞다, 부합하다
- attribute *n* 속성
- particulars *n* 상세한 내용, 세부 사항
- evoke *v* 유발하다, 불러일으키다
- fall under ~의 부류에 들어가다, ~에 해당되다
- elicit *v* 이끌어 내다, 유도하다
- murder *n* 살인
- infinity *n* 무한함, 무한대
- fall into ~에 속하다
- illustration *n* 예시
- in common 공통적으로, 공동으로

161 답 ⑤

📖 사회적 제도로서의 스포츠의 힘과 그것의 실현

전문해석

스포츠의 힘은 무수히 많은 사회적 목표를 다루는 데 사용될 수 있다. 강력하고 감정적인 사회경제적인 제도로서 스포츠는 개인, 단체 및 문화가 서로 관계를 형성하고 어울릴 수 있는 방법을 제공한다. 지역 차원에서 스포츠는 개인의 참여와 교류를 위한 장을 제공하고, 동시에 사회 제도로서의 그것의 구조적 힘과 기능은 그것이 또한 대규모로 사회에 영향을 주기 위해 사용될 수 있다는 것을 의미한다. 스포츠가 엄청나게 인기가 있고 실제로 많은 나라의 사회 구조에 퍼져 있기 때문에 사회적, 정치적, 경제적 분야에 미칠 수 있는 그것의 능력은 스포츠를 변화의 촉매제 역할을 할 수 있는 몇 안 되는 제도 중 하나가 되게 한다. 사회적인 제도인 스포츠의 힘은 엄청난 경제적 투자를 창출하며, 이것은 광범위한 사회적 영향을 미칠 기회를 만들어 낸다. 그 기회가 실현되는지의 여부는 스포츠의 수행에 달려 있으며, 그 수행은 현업 종사자와 업계에서 경력을 쌓기 시작한 야심찬 스포츠 매니저에 의해 궁극적으로 결정된다.

정답풀이

⑤ **문장의 구조 파악**: 두 개의 등위절이 and로 연결되어 있는 구조의 문장으로, and 앞 절의 주어인 Whether가 이끄는 명사절에 대한 동사가 없는 상태이다. 따라서 준동사 depending을 본동사 depends로 고쳐야 어법상 적절하다.

오답풀이

① **to부정사**: a way를 수식하는 표현으로 앞에 「for+의미상의 주어」 형태인 for individuals, groups, and cultures가 나왔으므로 to부정사인 to build는 어법상 적절하다.
② **접속사 that**: 뒤에 완전한 구조의 절이 이어지므로 문장의 동사 mean의 목적어 역할을 하는 명사절을 이끄는 접속사 that은 어법상 적절하다.
③ **주어와 동사의 수 일치**: 문장의 주어가 its ability ~ areas로 그 핵이 단수 명사인 ability이므로 단수형 동사 makes는 어법상 적절하다.
④ **관계대명사 which**: 앞에 나온 huge economic investment를 부가적으로 설명하는 절을 이끄는 주격 관계대명사 which는 어법상 적절하다.

구문풀이

`17행` [Whether or not that opportunity is realized] **depends** on the conduct of sport, / and that conduct **is** ultimately **determined** [by current practitioners and by aspiring sport managers embarking on careers in the industry].

: 두 개의 등위절이 and로 연결되었다. 첫 번째 절에서는 [ ]로 표시된 명사절이 주어이며, 동사는 depends이다. 두 번째 절에는 수동태가 쓰였으며, [ ]는 행위자를 나타낸다.

어휘풀이

- emotive *a* 감정적인
- engage with ~와 어울리다
- on a large scale 대규모로
- pervade *v* 만연하다, 널리 퍼지다
- institution *n* 제도, 기관
- arena *n* 장, 경기장
- enormously *ad* 엄청나게
- fabric *n* 구조, 조직, 직물

- generate *v* 발생시키다
- ultimately *ad* 궁극적으로
- aspiring *a* 야심찬, 열망 있는
- extensive *a* 광범위한
- practitioner *n* 종사자, 실무자
- embark on ~을 시작하다

162 답 ⑤

📖 불확실성의 기피 경향이 초래하는 결정 미루기

전문해석

불확실성은 우리 삶의 경험의 중요한 한 부분이다. 결정을 내리는 것은 이러한 불확실성의 느낌과 관련된 많은 것들 중 하나이다. 하지만 그것이 우리 모두가 친숙한 느낌임에도 불구하고 **그것은 여전히 우리가 회피하고자 열망하는 것이다.** 불확실성은 사람들이 혐오스럽게 경험하는 상태이다. 다시 말해서, **사람들은 이 상태를 자신의 삶에서 없애려는, 적어도 가능한 한 멀리 하려는 의욕이 매우 높다.** 우리가 하는 것과 우리가 성취하는 결과에 대해 우리가 통제력을 행사할 수 있다는 느낌은 더 위안을 주는 느낌이다. 이는 우리가 통제할 수 없는 것을 통제하려고 노력해야 한다는 생각에 대한 강한 믿음을 갖고 있다는 것을 의미한다. 이것은 분명히 가능하지 않지만, 우리가 노력하는 것을 멈추게 하지 못한다. **우리는 통제력의 환상을 경험하기를 간절히 바란다.** 통제력의 '거짓된' 느낌을 성취하려는 이 시도는 따라서 사실상 비이성적인 행동이다. 그리고 이 행동의 한 측면은, 우리가 흔히 이러한 방식으로 우리 자신을 속이려는 시도에서 사용하는데, 결정을 실행하는(→ 미루는) 것이다.

정답풀이

⑤ 결정을 내리는 것은 불확실성과 관련되는 반면, 우리 자신이 통제력을 가지고 있다는 느낌은 위안을 준다고 했다. 따라서 그러한 느낌을 유지하기 위한 시도로 결정을 내리지 않고 미룰 것임을 추측할 수 있으므로 implementing(실행하는 것)을 postponing(미루는 것)과 같은 낱말로 바꿔야 한다.

오답풀이

① 불확실성은 익숙한 느낌이지만 동시에 혐오스러운 경험이라고 했으므로, 사람들이 '회피하고자(avoid)' 열망하는 것이라는 흐름은 자연스럽다.
② 앞에 삶에서 불확실성을 겪는 것은 혐오스러운 경험이라는 내용이 있으므로 이러한 경험을 하지 않으려고 한다는 흐름이 되도록 eliminate(없애다)를 쓴 것은 문맥상 적절하다.
③ 뒤에 우리가 통제할 수 없는 것을 통제하려고 노력해야 한다는 강력한 믿음을 갖고 있다는 내용이 이어지므로, 통제력이 우리에게 긍정적인 느낌을 준다는 흐름이 되도록 comforting(위안이 되는)을 쓴 것은 문맥상 적절하다.
④ 우리가 통제할 수 없는 것을 통제하려고 노력하는 것을 통제력의 '거짓된' 느낌을 성취하려는 시도라고 했으므로, 이와 같은 맥락에서 false(거짓된)와 논리적으로 연결되는 illusion(환상)은 문맥상 적절하다.

구문풀이

3행 Yet although **it** is a feeling [that we are all familiar with], / it is still <u>something</u> [that we are anxious to avoid].

: 첫 번째 [ ]는 a feeling을, 두 번째 [ ]는 something을 수식하는 목적격 관계대명사절이다. 두 개의 it은 모두 uncertainty를 가리킨다.

어휘풀이

- associated with ~와 관련된
- aversively *ad* 혐오스럽게, 싫게
- be eager to *do* ~하기를 간절히 바라다
- illusion *n* 환상
- irrational *a* 비이성적인
- implement *v* 실행하다
- be anxious to *do* ~하고자 열망하다
- attempt *n* 시도
- trick *v* 속이다

163 답 ②

📖 과학 지식 생산에서 주관성의 역할

전문해석

과학자들의 이론적 방침, 신념, 이전의 지식, 훈련, 경험 그리고 기대가 실제로 그들의 연구에 영향을 미친다. 이 모든 배경 요인들이, 과학자들이 연구하는 문제와 그들이 그들의 연구를 수행하는 방식, 그들이 관찰하는 것 (그리고 관찰하지 않는 것) 그리고 그들이 그들의 관찰 결과를 이해하거나 해석하는 방식에 영향을 미치는 사고방식을 형성한다. 과학 지식 생산에서의 <u>주관성의 역할</u>을 설명하는 것은 바로 이 (때때로 집단적인) 사고방식이다. 세간의 믿음과는 반대로 과학은 중립적인 관찰로 시작되는 일이 거의 없다는 것은 주목할 만하다. 관찰은 (그리고 연구는) 질문 또는 문제에 의해 동기가 부여되고, 인도되며, 그(질문 또는 문제)와 관련하여 의미를 얻는데, 그것들은 결국 특정한 이론적 시각 안에서부터 생겨난다. 흔히 가설이나 모형 검증은 과학 연구에 대한 지침의 역할을 한다. 예를 들어, 진화론의 체제에서 연구하는 연구자는 자신의 노력을 전이 종(진화상 나타나야 하는 중간 종)의 위치 추적에 집중할지도 모른다. 대조적으로, 단속평형설을 믿는 사람의 관점에서 전이 종은 예상되지 않을 것이고, 진화론자가 전이 종으로 간주한 것도 그러한 것으로 여겨지지 않을 것이다.

정답풀이

과학 연구는 과학자들 각각이 지닌 특유의 배경 요인들에 의해 형성된 고유한 사고방식에 영향을 받고, 질문과 문제는 특정한 이론적 관점 안에서 생겨나므로 과학 연구는 중립적인 관찰로 시작되는 경우가 거의 없다는 내용이다. 따라서 빈칸에 들어갈 말로 가장 적절한 것은 ② '주관성의 역할'이다.

오답풀이

① 증거의 가치
③ 협력의 힘
④ 불확실성의 존재
⑤ 객관성의 중요성
└▸ 이 글은 과학 지식 생산에서 주관성이 어떤 역할을 하는지에 관한 내용이지, 주관성이 잘못되었다거나 객관성이 중요하다는 내용이 아니므로 오답!

구문풀이

8행 **It is** <u>this (sometimes collective) mind-set</u> **that** accounts for the role of subjectivity in the production of scientific knowledge.

: 「It is ~ that ...」 강조구문으로 주어인 This (sometimes collective) mind-set을 강조하고 있다.

12행 Observations (and investigations) [are motivated and guided by], and [acquire meaning in reference to], **questions or problems**, [which, in turn, are derived from within certain theoretical perspectives].

: questions or problems는 두 개의 [ ]로 표시된 동사구의 공통 어구이며, 세 번째 [ ]로 표시된 주격 관계대명사절은 questions or problems를 부연 설명한다.

어휘풀이

- commitment *n* 약속, 의무
- investigate *v* 연구하다, 조사하다
- interpret *v* 해석하다
- account for ~을 설명하다
- contrary to ~와 반대로
- in reference to ~와 관련하여
- theoretical *a* 이론의, 이론적인
- transitional *a* 과도기의, 전환기의
- mind-set *n* 사고방식
- make sense of ~을 이해하다
- collective *a* 집단적인
- noteworthy *a* 주목할 만한, 눈에 띄는
- neutral *a* 중립적인
- be derived 생겨나다
- hypothesis *n* 가설
- collaboration *n* 협력

164 답 ②

📖 1800년대 미국 서부에서 백인들의 인디언 토지 강탈

전문해석
유럽 출신의 미국인들은 1800년대에 더 서쪽으로 이동하여 아메리카 원주민들의 땅으로 들어갔다. 그 시기의 글 대다수는 아메리카 인디언의 몰살을 진보라는 이름으로 정당한 것 또는 필요한 것으로 나타냈다. '고결한 야만인(문명에 오염되지 않은 무구한 인간상)' 이미지가 강조되던 때조차도, 근원적인 이기적 목적들이 흔히 존재했다. 예를 들어, 1887년에 개별적인 인디언들이 자기 소유의 땅을 경작하거나 그곳에서 동물을 키우도록 하기 위해 부족의 땅을 구획으로 분리하는 것을 지지하도록 고안된 법안인 Dawes Act(단독 토지 소유 법령)가 통과되었다. 인디언들이 유럽에서 온 미국의 문화로 동화되도록 장려하기 위해 만들어진 '고결한 야만인' 이미지는 그 법령에 대한 지지를 구하기 위해 사용되었다. Dawes Act는 실제로 오랫동안 지속되는 부정적인 영향을 미쳤다. 그것은 악의적인 유럽 출신의 미국인들이 인디언 부족들의 소유였던 소중한 땅을 빼앗는 길을 닦아 주었고, 흔히 많은 아메리카 인디언들을 땅을 잃고 가난에 허덕이는 처지가 되게 만들었다. 1800년대 미국 서부에서 연민이라는 정서는 희귀한 것이 되었다.

정답풀이
1800년대에 유럽 출신의 미국인들, 즉 백인들이 서쪽으로 이동하여 그곳에서 아무 죄의식 없이 Dawes Act와 같은 수단을 동원하여 원주민들의 땅을 무자비하게 빼앗아서 원주민들이 땅을 잃고 가난에 허덕이게 만들었다는 것이 주요 내용이다. 따라서 1800년대 미국 서부의 상황을 나타내는 빈칸에 들어갈 말로는 ② '연민이라는 정서는 희귀한 것이 되었다'가 가장 적절하다.

오답풀이
① 갈등과 협력이 공존했다
③ 새로운 경제 활동들은 찾아볼 수 없었다
④ '고결한 야만인' 이미지가 법에 의해 훼손되었다
ᒐ 지문에 나온 어휘들이 포함되어 있어서 정확한 해석을 하지 못할 경우 고를 수 있는 함정 오답!
⑤ 식민지 개척자의 문화가 부족 문화에 투영되었다

구문풀이
7행 For example, in 1887, a bill, the Dawes Act, [designed to support the breakup of tribal lands into parcels {to allow individual Indians to farm or ranch their own land}] was passed.

: 문장의 주어 a bill과 바로 뒤의 the Dawes Act는 동격이며, 문장의 동사는 was passed이다. [ ]는 주어를 수식하는 과거분사구이고, 그 안의 { }는 목적을 나타내는 부사적 용법의 to부정사구이다.

어휘풀이
- savage *n* 야만인
- self-serving *a* 이기적인
- breakup *n* 분리, 해체
- parcel *n* (토지의) 한 구획
- ranch *v* (소·말 등을) 목장에서 사육하다
- assimilate *v* 동화되다
- ill-intentioned *a* 악의가 있는
- poverty *n* 가난
- sympathy *n* 연민, 동정
- undermine *v* 해치다, 훼손하다
- underlying *a* 근본적인, 근원적인
- bill *n* 법안
- tribal *a* 부족의
- summon *v* 구하다, 요청하다
- precious *a* 소중한
- sentiment *n* 정서
- rarity *n* 희귀(한 것)
- project *v* 투영하다

165 답 ⑤

📖 광범위한 상하 변동 속의 느린 추세를 파악하는 것의 어려움

전문해석
아마도 사회가 그 속에서 어떤 문제를 인식하지 못하는 가장 일반적인 상황은 그것이 광범위한 상하 변동으로 인해 감춰진 느린 추세의 형태를 취할 때이다. 현대의 주요한 사례는 지구온난화이다. (C) 우리는 주로 인간에 의해 야기된 대기의 변화 때문에 최근 수십 년 동안 지구상의 기온이 서서히 상승해 오고 있다는 것을 이제 깨닫고 있다. 하지만 매년 기후가 전년보다 정확히 0.01도 더 따뜻해졌다는 것은 사실이 아니다. (B) 그 대신, 우리 모두가 알고 있듯이, 기후는 매년 불규칙하게 위아래로 변동한다. 어떤 여름에 이전 여름보다 3도 더 따뜻해지고, 그러고 나서 다음 여름에는 2도 더 따뜻해지고, 그 다음 여름에는 4도가 내려가고, 다음 여름에 다시 1도가 내려가고, 그러고 나서는 5도가 올라가는 등등이다. (A) 그렇게 크고 예측 불가능하게 변동을 하기에, 그런 시끄러운 신호 안에서 평균적으로 연간 0.01도의 상승 추세를 식별하는 데는 오랜 시간이 걸렸다. 이것이 바로 지구온난화의 현실에 대해 이전에 회의적이었던 대부분의 전문 기후학자들이 확신을 하게 된 것이 불과 몇 년 전이었던 이유이다.

정답풀이
주어진 글에서 언급한 지구온난화에 대해 (C)에서 매년 기후가 정확히 0.01도씩 상승하고 있다는 것은 사실이 아니라고 말한 다음, (C)의 마지막 문장 다음에 Instead로 시작하는 (B)가 이어져서 실제로는 기후가 매년 불규칙하게 상하로 변동하고 있다는 점을 언급하는 것이 적절하다. 그리고 이러한 예측 불가능한 변동 속에서 연간 0.01도의 상승 추세를 식별하는 데는 오랜 시간이 걸렸다는 점을 말하는 (A)가 마지막에 오는 것이 자연스럽다. (A)의 such large and unpredictable fluctuations가 (B)의 내용을 지칭한다는 것도 단서가 된다.

구문풀이
9행 That's why **it was** only a few years ago **that** most professional climatologists previously skeptical of the reality of global warming became convinced.

: 「it was ~ that ....」의 강조구문에 의해 부사구인 only a few years ago가 강조되고 있다.

어휘풀이
- trend *n* 추세
- fluctuation *n* 변동, 오르내림
- discern *v* 식별하다
- skeptical *a* 회의적인
- atmospheric *a* 대기의
- conceal *v* 감추다
- unpredictable *a* 예측할 수 없는
- climatologist *n* 기후학자
- convinced *a* 확신한

166 답 ④

📖 글로 된 것 혹은 쓰기가 중요한 분야

전문해석
대부분의 학자들은 이제 '구술된 것과 글로 작성된 것 사이에는 어떤 확고한 선이 그어질 수 없다'는 인류학자 Ruth Finnegan의 의견에 동의할 것이다. 언어학적 구조나 사회적 기능 어느 것도 구술된 것과 글로 작성된 것 사이의 선을 깔끔하게 분리시키지 못한다. 글로 작성될 수 있거나 작성될 수 있었던 거의 모든 것은 말로 행해질 수 있고 그 반대도 가능하며, 하나에는 고유하지만 다른 하나에는 이용 가능하지 않은 어떤 문법이나 어휘도 없다. 심지어 단언하기와 약속하기 같은 발화 행위조차, 비록 사회마다 다소 다를지라도, 어떤 발화 행위도 글로 작성되는 전통에 고유하게 관련되지 않고, 거의 보편적이다(말과 글 둘 다 가능하다). 하지만 말하기와 상반된 것으로서 쓰기에 크게 의존하는 경향이 있는 학술 담론과 같은 몇몇 전문화된 분야가 있다. 우리 모두가 알고 있듯이 여러분이 심리학과 같이 어떤 전문화된 학문 분야에 참여하고 싶다면, 여러분은 심리학 논문과 교재를 읽고 쓰는 법을 배워야 한

다. 모든 학문 분야는 우리가 말하듯이 '저술 방식'을 갖고 있고, 참여를 위해서는 그 저술 방식을 알아야만 한다.

정답풀이

Yet으로 시작하는 주어진 문장은 쓰기가 중요한 분야가 있음을 언급하고 있으므로 말과 글의 구분이 명백하지 않다는 내용이 끝난 다음에 그리고 말과 상반된 것으로서의 글의 중요성에 관한 언급이 시작되는 문장 앞인 ④에 들어가는 것이 가장 적절하다.

구문풀이

12행 Even **speech acts** [**such as** asserting and promising], [although varying somewhat from one society to another], **are** more or less universal [**with** no speech act uniquely **associated** with the written tradition].

: 문장의 주어는 speech acts이고 동사는 are이다. such as는 '~와 같은'의 의미를 나타내며 앞에 쓰인 speech acts의 사례를 열거한다. 두 번째 [ ]는 삽입구로 접속사가 명시된 분사구문이고, 세 번째 [ ]는 「with+명사구+과거분사」의 구조이며 '~가 …하고서, ~가 …한 가운데'의 의미로 부대상황을 나타낸다.

어휘풀이

- genre *n* 분야, 장르
- discourse *n* 담론, 담화
- anthropologist *n* 인류학자
- linguistic *a* 언어학적인
- vice versa 역 또한 같음
- more or less 거의
- article *n* 논문, 논설
- literature *n* 저술 방식; 문학
- academic *a* 학술적인
- as opposed to ~와 상반된 것으로서
- observation *n* 말, 의견
- split *v* 나누다, 찢다
- assert *v* 단언하다
- discipline *n* 학문 분야
- possess *v* 소유하다

구문풀이

1행 Recent empirical work has examined **the interesting fact** [that our sense of {how long ago events occurred} does **not always** map onto their actual distance in time].

: [ ]는 the interesting fact를 구체적으로 설명하는 동격절이며, 그 안의 { }는 of의 목적어 역할을 하는 명사절이고, not always는 부분 부정으로 '항상 ~은 아닌'의 의미이다.

13행 **An interesting fact** about these images **is** [that they are not always pictured from the "first-person" visual perspective {that was experienced as the event unfolded}].

: 문장의 핵심 주어는 An interesting fact이므로 단수 동사 is가 쓰였다. [ ]는 주격보어로 쓰인 명사절이고, 그 안의 { }는 the "first-person" visual perspective를 수식하는 주격 관계대명사절이다.

어휘풀이

- empirical *a* 경험적인
- reunion *n* 동창회
- undergraduate *a* 대학(생)의
- awkward *a* 어색한
- contribute to ~에 기여하다
- involve *v* 관련시키다
- perspective *n* 관점
- observer *n* 관찰자
- map onto ~와 일치하다
- relive *v* 되새기다, 회상하다
- senior *n* 대학 4학년생
- freshman *n* 신입생, 대학 1학년생
- temporal *a* 시간의
- picture *v* 묘사하다
- unfold *v* 전개되다
- impartial *a* 공평한, 편견 없는

167 답 ④

📖 실제와는 다르게 인식되는 과거의 사건에 대한 시간적 거리와 관점

전문해석

최근의 경험적 연구는 사건이 얼마나 오래전에 일어났는지에 대한 우리의 감각이 항상 그것의 시간상의 실제 거리와 연결되지는 않는다는 흥미로운 사실을 조사했다. 대학 동창회 친구들은 '어제 일 같다'고 언급하면서 자신들의 대학생 때의 익살스러운 짓들을 되새길 것인 반면에, 대학 1학년 때의 어색한 순간들을 되돌아보는 대학 4학년생들은 그 일들이 마치 수년 전에 일어났던 것처럼 느낀다. **자아에 대한 믿음이 시간적 거리에 대한 느낌에 기여하고 시간적 거리에 대한 느낌이 자아에 대한 믿음에 영향을 미칠 수 있다는 것이 밝혀지고 있다.** 또 다른 최근의 관심 분야는 사람들이 과거의 사건들을 떠올릴 때 경험하는 정신적 이미지들을 관련시킨다. 이러한 이미지들에 대한 흥미로운 사실은 그것들이 사건이 전개될 때 경험되었던 '1인칭'의 시각적인 관점에서 항상 묘사되는 것은 아니라는 것이다. **때때로 사람들은 과거의 사건을 외부 관찰자의 '3인칭' 관점에서 묘사하며, 그리하여 그들은 그 이미지에서 과거의 자아를 본다.**

→ 우리가 과거를 돌아볼 때 시간적 거리는 <u>주관적으로</u> 측정되며, 때때로 우리는 우리에게 일어난 과거의 일을 <u>중립적인</u> 관점에서 본다.

정답풀이

과거의 일에 대한 시간적 느낌은 실제 시간의 거리가 아니라 자신에 대한 믿음의 영향을 받아 주관적으로 경험되며, 과거에 경험한 사건을 돌아볼 때 중립적인 제3자의 관점에서 묘사되기도 한다는 내용이므로, 요약문의 빈칸 (A)에는 subejctively(주관적으로)가, (B)에는 neutral(중립적인)이 들어가는 것이 가장 적절하다.

168 답 ①

📖 **토착민과 토착 문화에 대한 고정된 이미지**

전문해석

흔히 토착민들은 더 이국적이고 관광객들의 기대에 부응하기 위해 전통 의상을 입는다. 이 모든 것은 전통적인 문화의 모습을 살아 있게 하는 것을 증대시킨다. 1990년대 후반에 일부 학자들은 문화적 표지가 관광업의 맥락에서 변하지 않는 경향이 있다고 주장했고, 그들은 그것들을 '고정된 이미지'라고 불렀다. 그것은 많은 장소에서 달라졌을 수도 있지만 여전히 그러한 기대가 있는데, 그것은 충족되면 고정관념화, 타자화 그리고 관련된 현상과 같은 경향을 증대시킨다. 그럼에도 불구하고, 일부 학자들이 주목한 바와 같이 토착민들이 그러한 과정의 자동적으로 수동적인 희생자들인 것은 아니다. 그보다는, 그들은 때때로 경제적 이익을 얻기 위해 이 과정에 적극적으로 참여한다. 토착 관광에서 허용되는 것과 금지되는 것은 토착민과 비토착민 이해관계자들 사이에서 다양한 방식으로 검토되고 협상되며, 더 나아가 현재의 민족정치학적 담론에 따라 결정된다.

정답풀이

토착 문화를 관광 상품으로 만드는 관광업의 맥락에서 토착민과 토착 문화에 대한 변하지 않는 고정된 이미지가 있어 토착민들은 그것을 볼거리로 해서 이익을 얻기도 한다는 내용이다. 따라서 밑줄 친 부분이 의미하는 바로는 ① '토착민에 대한 변하지 않는 굳어진 표현'이 가장 적절하다.

오답풀이

② 토착민을 관광업의 수동적인 희생자로 보는 개념
③ 토착 관광을 필요악으로 부정적으로 묘사한 것
④ 토착 관광에서 무시된 전통적 가치 대 경제적 이득
⑤ 토착 관광을 위한 상품과 서비스에 옮겨진 문화적 표현

구문풀이

1행 Often, indigenous people wear traditional costumes [to be more exotic] and [to live up to the expectations of the tourists].

: and로 연결된 두 개의 [ ]는 목적의 의미를 나타내는 부사적 용법의 to부정사구이다.

7행 It might have changed in many places, but there are still such expectations [which, **when fulfilled**, add to tendencies {such as stereotyping, othering and related phenomena}].

: [ ]는 such expectations를 수식하는 주격 관계대명사절이다. when fulfilled는 when they(= such expectations) are fulfilled에서 주어와 be동사가 생략된 것이다. { }는 tendencies를 수식한다.

어휘풀이

- indigenous *a* 토착의
- exotic *a* 이국적인
- add to ~을 증가시키다
- fulfill *v* (기대 등을) 충족시키다
- othering *n* 타자화(他者化)
- victim *n* 희생자
- forbid *v* 금지하다
- stakeholder *n* 이해관계자
- discourse *n* 담론
- rigid *a* 굳어진, 엄격한
- costume *n* 의상
- live up to ~에 부응하다
- marker *n* 표지
- stereotyping *n* 고정관념화
- passive *a* 수동적인
- permit *v* 허용하다
- negotiate *v* 협상하다
- ethnopolitical *a* 민족정치학적인
- static *a* 고정된
- neglect *v* 무시하다

169 답 ⑤

📖 **문학이나 신화 같은 허구적 이야기의 기능[역할]**

전문해석

우리는 부분적으로 재미있거나 즐겁기 때문에 소설을 읽지만, 어떤 소설은 대인관계의 사례를 제공하기 때문에 읽기도 한다. 독서는 우리가 실수를 저지르는 것의 부정적인 영향을 겪어야만 하는 것 없이 대인 생활에서의 실험에 노출되게 한다. 우리 자신의 삶을 망치는 대신에 우리는 Tolstoy의 (소설 속 주인공) Anna Karenina가 자신의 삶을 망치는 것을 볼 수 있다. 우리의 특정한 상황에 맞춰진 것은 아니지만, 훌륭한 문학은 많은 독자에게 적용될 수 있다. 이러한 점에서, 문학은 일부 문화에서 신화가 하는 기능을 한다. 예를 들어, 일부 Apache 부족은 인생의 얽힌 것을 사람들이 헤쳐나가는 길을 안내하기 위해서 주변 풍경에서 특정한 장소와 관련된 이야기를 사용한다. 종교적, 문화적 신화는 사회의 젊은 구성원들의 (인생 항해의) 안내서로서 노인들에 의해서 종종 인용된다. Freud는 대부분 소년들의 심리에 대한 안내서로서 Oedipus 신화라는 특정한 신화를 사용했으며, Gilligan은 로맨틱한 사랑의 안내서로서 Cupid와 Psyche의 신화를 이용했다. 이러한 신화는 아마도 문학처럼 문화의 구성원들이 때때로 직면할 수 있는 상황에 맞도록 유지되고 수정되었을 것이다.

정답풀이

⑤ **관계부사 where**: 뒤에 face의 목적어가 없는 불완전한 절이 이어지므로 관계부사 where는 쓸 수 없다. 선행사 situations를 수식하는 절을 이끌면서 face의 목적어 역할을 할 수 있는 목적격 관계대명사 which[that]로 고쳐야 한다.

오답풀이

① **to부정사의 태**: expose는 '노출시키다'라는 의미의 타동사이고, 우리는 대인 생활에서의 실험에 '노출되는' 대상이므로 수동태 be exposed는 적절하게 쓰였다.

③ **지각동사의 목적격보어**: 지각동사 watch의 목적격보어 자리로, 목적어인 Tolstoy's Anna Karenina가 자신의 삶을 '망치는' 주체이므로 목적격보어로 동사원형 ruin은 적절하게 쓰였다.

② **대동사**: 앞에 언급된 일반동사 functions를 대신하는 대동사 do는 적절하게 쓰였다.

④ **to부정사**: 문맥상 길을 '안내하기 위해서' 특정한 장소와 관련된 이야기를 사용한다는 내용이 자연스러우므로 목적을 나타내는 부사적 용법의 to부정사인 to guide는 적절하다.

구문풀이

11행 Some Apaches, for example, use stories [associated with specific places in the surrounding landscape] [to guide people through life's tangles].

: 첫 번째 [ ]는 stories를 수식하는 과거분사구이고, 두 번째 [ ]는 '~하기 위해서'라는 목적의 의미를 나타내는 부사적 용법의 to부정사구이다.

어휘풀이

- suffer *v* 겪다, 경험하다
- ruin *v* 망치다
- specific *a* 특정한
- applicable *a* 적용할 수 있는
- landscape *n* 경치, 풍경
- religious *a* 종교적인
- cite *v* 인용하다
- presumably *ad* 아마도
- fit *v* ~에 들어맞다
- consequence *n* 영향, 결과
- tailor *v* (요구, 목적 등에) 맞추다
- literature *n* 문학
- associated with ~와 관련된
- tangle *n* 얽힌 상태, 엉킨 것
- myth *n* 신화
- navigational *a* 항해의
- retain *v* 유지하다

170 답 ②

📖 사물을 바라보는 카메라 각도가 영화 장면에 미치는 영향

전문해석

영화 카메라가 특정한 위치에 놓이게 되면, 카메라는 (관찰자가 정지하고 있을 때의) 인간의 눈과 마찬가지로 나란히 있는 대상들을 보는데, 하나가 다른 하나의 시야를 가린다. 그리고 이러한 제한은 꽤 특별한 효과를 얻는 데 도움을 준다. 에이젠슈타인의 영화 〈전선〉에서 한 가난한 여자 농부가 말 한 마리를 빌리기 위해 한 부유하고 뚱뚱한 남자의 농장에 찾아온다. 그 남자는 소파에 누워 있다. 그녀는 그 앞에 서서 겸손하게 사정한다. 그는 바로 앉지 않는다. 카메라는 이제 그의 뒤에 놓인다. 그의 넓은 등이 거대하고 뚱뚱한 모습으로 화면의 전경에 나타나며, 마침내 배경에 서 있는 여자를 완전히 덮어 가린다. 전체 화면은 갑자기 그의 거대한 등에 의해서 채워지면서 압도된다. 여기에서 그녀에 대한 그의 권력이 (카메라의) 교묘한 위치 선정의 방식으로 표현된다. 카메라 가까이에 있음으로써 그의 등은 유난히 비대하고 공간을 삼키는 것처럼 보인다. 배경에 있는 여자 농부는 대조적으로 매우 작다. 그 모습은 그녀가 할 수 있는 것이 거의 없다는 사실을 강조한다. 이렇게 해서, 권력이 무력함을 짓누른다는 아이디어가 암시되며 그 여자는 화면에서 완전히 사라진다.

정답풀이

카메라의 위치에 따른 효과를 설명하는 내용이다. 예시로 든 영화에서 카메라와 등장인물들의 교묘한 위치 선정을 통해 부자는 크게 부각되고 가난한 농부는 그 모습에 가려지는 장면이 연출되었는데, 이는 권력이 무력함을 압도한다는 것을 표현한다고 볼 수 있다. 따라서 빈칸에 들어갈 말로 가장 적절한 것은 ② '권력이 무력함을 짓누른다'이다.

오답풀이

① 영화는 그저 환상일 뿐이다
③ 성 고정관념이 영화에 만연해 있다
④ 클로즈업이 장면에 감동을 더한다
⑤ 카메라 각도가 모든 차이를 만든다

> ↳ 빈칸에는 글의 주제가 아니라 주어진 예시에서 카메라 각도가 주는 구체적인 효과에 해당하는 말이 들어가야 하므로 오답!

구문풀이

1행 If a film camera is placed in a particular spot, / it **sees** the objects one behind the other exactly / **as does** the human eye (when the observer is standing still), [one object **obstructing** the view of another]

: does는 앞에 나온 sees ~ the other를 대신하는 대동사이며, as가 이끄는 양태 부사절에 대동사가 쓰이면 주어(the human eye)와 대동사가 도치될 수 있다. [ ]는 분사구문으로 one object는 의미상의 주어이다.

어휘풀이

- one behind the other 나란히
- peasant *n* 소작농, 농부
- humbly *ad* 겸손하게
- loom *v* (무시무시하게) 어렴풋이 나타나다
- foreground *n* 전경
- dominate *v* 압도하다, 장악하다
- clever *a* 교묘한
- by contrast 대조적으로
- highlight *v* 강조하다, 두드러지게 하다
- illusion *n* 환상
- overshadow *v* 가리다, 그늘지게 하다
- helplessness *n* 무력함
- stereotype *v* ~에 대한 고정관념을 형성하다
- pervade *v* 만연하다, 널리 퍼지다
- obstruct *v* 방해하다
- address *v* ~에게 말을 건네다
- blot out ~을 완전히 덮어 가리다
- authority *n* 권력, 권위
- devour *v* 사로잡다, 엄습하다

171 답 ③

📖 과학 지식과 기적에 대한 믿음의 반비례 관계

전문해석

다양한 문화권을 여행하고 만나면서 나는 기적에 대한 중요한 것을 배웠다. 나는 사람들이 기초 과학에 대해 덜 알수록 그들이 기적에 대해 더 많이 이야기한다는 것을 알게 되었다. 예를 들어, 천문학과 의학에 대한 인식이 거의 없는 곳에서는 사람들이 기적의 식(蝕)과 치료에 대한 이야기를 많이 듣는다. 더 높은 수준의 과학 이해 능력을 가지고 있는 사회에서도 기적에 대한 주장을 듣지만, 그것들은 빈도가 덜 하고 사람들이 비행기 추락 사고에서 살아남은 것이나 일부 실종된 등산객의 구조와 같은 특이한 일들에 거의 항상 한정되어 있다. 그 상관관계는 분명한데, 자연 세계를 더 잘 이해하는 것은 사건을 설명하기 위해 기적에 덜 의존한다는 것을 의미한다는 것이다. 이것은 역사에서도 역시 볼 수 있다. 수세기 전에는 우리가 지금은 이해하는 일들이 설명할 수 없고 따라서 초자연적인 것으로 생각되었다. 이런 경향은 미래에도 사실일 것 같다. 우주가 작용하는 방식에 대한 미래 세대의 더 큰 이해 덕분에 오늘날의 기적적인 일은 아마도 내일의 일상적인 일이 될 것이다.

정답풀이

과학 지식이 많을수록 사람들은 기적과 같은 현상에 대해 덜 이야기하고, 수세기 전에는 설명할 수 없는 초자연적이라고 여겼던 일들이 현재에는 이해할 수 있는 일이 되었으며 이는 앞으로도 계속될 것이라는 내용이다. 따라서 사건을 설명하기 위해 기적에 덜 의존하게 되는 경우는 ③ '자연 세계를 더 잘 이해하게' 될 때라고 할 수 있다.

오답풀이

① 과학 문학에서의 더 큰 다양성
② 사회적 위계에서의 더 높은 지위
④ 종교적 믿음과의 덜 밀접한 관계
⑤ 초자연적인 사건의 덜 빈번한 발생

구문풀이

2행 I have learned [that **the less** people know about basic science, **the more** they talk about miracles].

: [ ]는 learned의 목적어 역할을 하는 명사절이며, 이 절에는 「the+비교급 ~, the+비교급 …」 구문이 사용되어 '~하면 할수록 더욱 더 …하다'의 의미를 나타내고 있다.

어휘풀이

- diverse *a* 다양한
- literacy *n* 이해력, 해독력
- correlation *n* 상관관계
- supernatural *a* 초자연적인
- occurrence *n* 일, 사건
- hierarchy *n* 위계
- awareness *n* 인식
- crash *n* 추락, 충돌
- reliance *n* 의존
- hold true 들어맞다, 계속 사실이다
- routine *a* 일상적인
- religious *a* 종교적인

172 답 ④

📖 증거를 얻기 위한 과학자들의 조건 조절과 관찰

전문해석

어떤 상황에서 과학자들은 그들의 증거를 얻기 위해 고의로 그리고 정확하게 조건들을 조절할 수 있다. (C) 예를 들어, 그들은 온도를 조절하거나 화학물질의 농도를 바꾸거나 어떤 유기체가 다른 것들과 짝을 이룰지를 선택할 수 있다. 한 번에 단 하나의 조건을 바꿈으로써, 그들은 다른 조건에서의 변화에 의해 복잡해지지 않고서, 발생하는 것에 대한 그것만의 효과를 확인하기를 희망할 수 있다. (A) 그러나 종종 조건의 조절은 (별을 연구할 때처럼) 비실용적이거나 (사람을 연구할 때처럼) 비윤리적

이거나 (갇혀 있는 야생동물을 연구할 때처럼) 자연 현상을 왜곡할 가능성이 있을 수 있다. (B) 그러한 경우에는, 다양한 요인들의 영향이 어떠할지 추론하기 위해 충분히 넓은 범위의 자연적으로 발생하는 조건에 대한 관찰이 이루어져야만 한다. 증거에 대한 이러한 의존 때문에 더 나은 관찰 도구나 기법의 발달에 큰 가치가 부여되고, 한 연구자나 집단에 의한 발견은 보통 다른 이들(연구자나 집단)에 의해 확인된다.

정답풀이

증거를 얻기 위해서 과학자들이 조건을 고의로 조절할 수 있다는 내용의 주어진 글 다음에는, 이러한 조건 조절에 대한 예를 들고 있는 (C)가 오고, 이어서 역접의 연결어 however로 시작하며 조건 조절의 문제점에 대해 언급하는 (A)가 와야 한다. 그리고 (B)의 such cases는 (A)에서 언급한 조건 조절이 문제가 되는 상황을 가리키므로 (B)가 마지막에 오는 순서가 자연스럽다. 따라서 적절한 글의 순서는 ④ (C)-(A)-(B)이다.

구문풀이

9행 In such cases, observations have to **be made** [over a sufficiently wide range of naturally occurring conditions] [to infer {what the influence of various factors might be}].

: observations는 '이루어지는 대상이므로 have to 다음에 수동형 be made가 쓰였다. 첫 번째 [ ]는 부사구이고, 두 번째 [ ]는 목적을 나타내는 to부정사구이며, { }는 infer의 목적어 역할을 하는 명사절(의문사절)이다.

어휘풀이

- deliberately *ad* 고의로, 일부러
- impractical *a* 비실용적인, 비현실적인
- unethical *a* 비윤리적인
- captivity *n* 감금 상태
- reliance *n* 의존, 의지
- concentration *n* 농도; 집중
- exclusive *a* 유일한, 배타적인
- distort *v* 왜곡하다
- sufficiently *ad* 충분히
- investigator *n* 연구원, 조사자
- organism *n* 유기체
- uncomplicated *a* 복잡하지 않은

173 답 ④

📖 생산성 증가율과 생산성 수준의 관계

전문해석

모든 사회의 개인은 자신의 삶에서 특정한 의미나 가치를 도출한다. 그 의미는 개별화되어 사람마다 다양하며, 그것은 특정 개인의 삶의 질을 구성한다. 사회가 발전하고 더 정교해짐에 따라, 창의적인 정신은 소비자의 삶을 더 좋게, 더 쉽게, 그리고 희망컨대, 더 즐겁게 만들기 위해 우리가 혁신이라고 부르는 새로운 것을 상상하고 창조한다. 바퀴에서 페니실린, 그리고 컴퓨터와 다른 많은 것에 이르기까지 각각의 모든 주요한 발전은 변화해 왔고 사람들이 사회에서 어떻게 살고 일하는지를 계속 변화시키고 있다. 그러나, 이런 혁신품들에 의해 만들어지는 변화와 진보의 속도는 모든 나라에서 같지 않다. '생산성 증가율은 생산성 수준에 따라 반대로 변하는 경향이 있다'는 가설이 있는데, 이것은 경제적으로 덜 발달된 나라들이 선진화된 나라들보다, 따라잡고 빠른 진전을 보일 수 있는 더 큰 기회를 가지고 있다는 것을 의미한다. 지난 수십 년 동안, 아시아의 네 마리 호랑이(홍콩, 싱가포르, 대만 그리고 한국) 같은 산업화된 신흥 국가들은 이런 가정이 옳다는 것을 보여주었다.

정답풀이

역접의 연결어(However)로 시작하여, 이런 혁신품들에 의해 만들어지는 변화와 진보의 속도가 모든 나라에서 같은 것은 아니라고 하는 내용의 주어진 문장 앞에는, 이런 혁신품들(these innovations)이 가리킬 수 있는 발명품들이 나와야 하므로, 주어진 문장은 바퀴에서 페니실린, 컴퓨터까지의 발명품에 대해 언급한 문장 뒤인 ④에 들어가야 한다. 그리고 주어진 문장에서 나라마다 다른 변화와 진보 속도를 보인다고 했으므로, 경제적으로 덜 발달된 나라

들이 선진국들보다 빠른 진전을 보일 수 있다는 내용이 주어진 문장 뒤에 오는 것이 문맥상 자연스럽다. 따라서 주어진 문장이 들어가기에 가장 적절한 곳은 ④이다.

구문풀이

15행 **It** is hypothesized [that "productivity growth rates tend to vary inversely with productivity levels"], [implying {that economically less developed countries have a **greater** opportunity (to catch up and forge ahead) **than do** industrialized countries}].

: It은 형식상의 주어이고, 첫 번째 [ ]의 명사절이 내용상의 주어이다. 두 번째 [ ]는 첫 번째 [ ]의 내용을 부가적으로 설명하는 분사구문이고, 그 안의 { }는 implying의 목적어 역할을 하는 명사절이다. 명사절에 greater ~ than ...의 비교급 구문이 사용되었고, ( )는 a greater opportunity를 수식하는 to부정사구이다. than 다음에는 주어(industrialized countries)와 동사(do)가 도치되었는데, do는 앞에 나온 동사구의 반복을 피하기 위해 쓰인 대동사로 have an opportunity to catch up and forge ahead를 나타낸다.

어휘풀이

- progress *n* 진보
- derive *v* 도출하다, 끌어내다
- vary *v* 다양하다, 변화하다
- sophisticated *a* 정교한, 세련된
- hypothesize *v* 가정하다, 가설로 세우다
- productivity *n* 생산성
- imply *v* 의미하다
- supposition *n* 가정
- innovation *n* 혁신(품)
- industrialized *a* 산업화된
- constitute *v* 구성하다
- inventive *a* 창의적인
- inversely *ad* 반대로, 역으로
- catch up 따라잡다

174~175 답 ① / ③

📖 21세기의 생물학에서는 무의미한 피부색에 의한 인종 구분

전문해석

인간을 집단으로 범주화하는 생각은 오래된 것인데, 우리 가족, 대가족, 마을, 종족, 종교, 지역, 국가 그리고 많은 다른 사회적인 범주의 구성원은 누구인가? 인식된 차이점들에 근거하여 집단을 만드는 것은 자연스러우며 우리는 엄청나게 많은 사회적인 범주에 근거하여 그렇게 한다. 그러나 인종은 특정한 생물학적인 의미를 가지고 있는데, 그 안에서 그것은 유전적으로 서로 구별되는 종 내의 유기체 집단을 위한 '아종(亞種)'이라는 용어와 일치한다. 사실, 우리는 침팬지나 고릴라와 비교하여 비교적 낮은 수준의 유전적 다양성을 보여준다. 그러면 우리는 다른 '인종'에 대해 뭐라고 말할 수 있을까? 유전적인 수준에서는, 아프리카, 유럽 혹은 아시아 출신의 사람 사이에 거의 아무런 차이가 없다. 지구상의 어떤 곳에서 온 사람이든지 무작위로 두 사람을 골라 그들의 유전자를 살펴보면 그들은 아주 밀접하게 연관되어 있을 것인데, 너무나 광범위하게 분산되어 있는 동물 종에서 일반적인 것보다 훨씬 더 많이 그럴 것이다.

명백한 사실은 현대 생물학이 우리가 서구 문명을 전 세계의 '표준'으로 만든 것뿐만 아니라 피부색을 이용해 전통적으로 다른 인종을 만들어 온 방식을 확증하고(→ 부정하고) 있다는 것이다. 두 가지 생각은 모두 크게 결함이 있다. 피부 색깔은 피부에 색소를 제공하는 멜라닌을 만들어 내는 세포인 멜라닌 (형성) 세포의 생산을 조절하는 간단한 유전 스위치에 의해 통제가 되지만, 이 차이는 아주 미미하다. 또한 교양 있음의 절대적인 척도로 서양 문화를 사용하는 것도 인간 사회의 범위와 다양성을 전혀 반영하지 않은 것이다. 간단히 말해, 서로 다른 '인종들'이 있다는 생각은 21세기 생물학의 관점에서는 전혀 유지될 수 없다.

정답풀이

174 인간은 인식된 차이점에 근거하여 집단으로 범주화하려는 자연적인 속성을 가지고 있지만, 21세기 생물학의 관점에서 보았을 때 피부 색깔에 따라

인종을 구분하는 것은 유전적인 측면에서 전혀 의미가 없는 것임을 지적하는 글이다. 따라서 제목으로는 ① '인종은 생물학적 실제가 아니라 환상이다'가 가장 적절하다.

175 이어지는 내용에서 피부 색깔의 차이는 멜라닌 형성 세포의 생산을 조절하는 간단한 유전 스위치에 의해 통제되며 그것은 아주 미미한 결과를 가져온다고 했다. 따라서 현대 생물학이 피부 색깔로 인종을 구분하는 방식을 완전히 '부정한다'는 문맥이 되어야 하므로, (c) confirms(확증하다)를 contradicts (부정하다, 반박하다) 정도의 어휘로 바꿔야 한다.

오답풀이

174 ② 인종 차별: 그것의 뿌리와 원인

③ 인간 생물학과 동물 생물학 간의 차이점

④ 생물학이 피부 색깔에 주목하는 이유

⑤ 유전학은 인종이라는 생물학적 개념이 타당하다는 것을 밝혀준다

175 ① 오래 전부터 인간을 집단으로 범주화해 왔다고 하므로 인식된 차이점들에 근거하여 집단을 만드는 것은 '자연스러운(natural)' 일이라고 한 것은 문맥상 적절하다.

② 지구상의 어디 출신의 사람이든지 무작위로 두 명의 유전자를 살펴볼 때 아주 밀접하게 연관되어 있을 것이라는 설명이 이어지므로, 유전적인 수준에서는 아프리카, 유럽, 아시아 출신의 사람 사이에 '차이(variation)'가 거의 없다는 문맥은 적절하다.

④ 이어서 피부 색깔로 인종을 나누고 서양 문화를 세계의 표준으로 만든 생각이 틀렸음을 밝히고 있으므로 flawed(결함이 있는)는 문맥상 적절하다.

⑤ 글 전체적으로 피부 색깔로 인종을 구분하는 것은 유전적인 측면에서 전혀 의미가 없음을 설명하고 있으므로 '서로 다른(separate)' 인종들이라는 개념이 유지될 수 없다고 한 것은 적절하다.

구문풀이

6행 But race has <u>a specific biological meaning</u>, [where **it** is identical to the term 'sub-species' for <u>groups of organisms</u> within a species {that are genetically distinct from one another}].

: [ ]는 a specific biological meaning를 부연 설명하는 관계부사절이고, it은 race 를 가리킨다. { }는 groups of organisms를 수식하는 주격 관계대명사절이다.

29행 In short, **the idea** [that there are separate 'human races'] **simply** cannot be sustained in light of twenty-first century biology.

: [ ]는 the idea의 구체적인 내용을 설명하고 있는 동격절이며, simply는 부정어를 강조하는 역할을 하고 있다.

어휘풀이

- categorize *v* 범주화하다
- tribe *n* 종족, 부족
- perceived *a* 인식된
- sub-species *n* 아종(亞種)
- genetic *a* 유전적인
- variation *n* 차이, 변화
- dispersed *a* 분산되어 있는
- melanocyte *n* 멜라닌 (형성) 세포, 멜라노사이트
- absolute *a* 절대적인
- sophistication *n* 세련됨
- simply *ad* (부정어 앞에서) 전혀, 결코
- in light of ~의 관점에서
- extended family 대가족
- religion *n* 종교
- identical *a* 동일한
- distinct *a* 구별되는, 서로 다른
- next to 거의
- at random 무작위로
- flawed *a* 결함이 있는
- measure *n* 척도
- separate *a* 서로 다른, 별개의
- sustain *v* 유지하다
- discrimination *n* 차별

3점 공략 모의고사 11회   본문 p.120

| **176** ⑤ | **177** ① | **178** ⑤ | **179** ② | **180** ② |
| **181** ⑤ | **182** ⑤ | **183** ④ | | |

176 답 ⑤

📖 서비스에 기반을 둔 후기 산업 사회가 경제 활동과 사회생활에 미치는 영향

전문해석

후기 산업 사회에는 사회적으로 해방시키는 효과가 있다. 서비스에 기반을 둔 경제는 산업 사회가 사람들의 일상적인 활동을 조직하는 기강이 있고 표준화된 방식을 뒤집는 경향이 있다. 산업화 시대에는 대량 생산 시스템이 노동력을 엄격한 중앙 통제의 지배하에 두었고 노동자들은 순응하라는 강한 압박이 있는 긴밀하게 짜인 집단에 박혀 있었다. 이와 대조적으로 후기 산업화는 경제 활동과 사회생활을 표준화에서 벗어나게 만든다. 서비스에 기반을 둔 경제의 유연한 조직화와 그것이 노동자들에게 주는 자율성은 생활의 모든 영역으로 퍼져, 인간의 상호작용은 긴밀하게 짜인 집단의 결속력 있는 유대로부터 점점 더 자유로워지고 사람들이 사회적 유대를 쉽게 만들고 깰 수 있게 한다. 복지 국가는 이런 개별화 경향을 지원한다. 예전에는 아이들의 생존은 주로 그들의 부모가 그들을 부양하는지에 달려 있었고 아이들은 그들의 부모가 노년에 이르렀을 때 그들을 돌봤다. 가족의 역할은 여전히 중요하지만 이 관계의 지극히 중대한 본질은 복지 국가에 의해 약화되었다.

정답풀이

서비스에 기반을 둔 후기 산업 사회는 이전 산업 사회의 엄격한 표준화에서 벗어나 조직이 유연해지고 구성원이 자율성을 가짐에 따라 사람들이 집단의 결속력 있는 유대에서 벗어나 자유롭게 상호작용할 수 있게 되었으며 복지 국가의 지원 덕분에 개별화 경향이 심화되었다는 내용이다. 따라서 글의 주제로는 ⑤ '후기 산업 사회가 경제와 사회 구조에 미치는 영향'이 가장 적절하다.

오답풀이

① 사회 변화에도 불구하고 사회적 유대 관계를 유지할 필요성

② 개인을 위한 복지 국가의 혜택과 한계

> 후기 산업 사회의 개별화 경향이 복지 국가에 의해 강화되었다고 언급되었지만, 복지 국가의 혜택이나 한계에 대한 구체적 내용은 없다.

③ 후기 산업 사회에서 경제적 불안정의 이유

④ 대량 생산 시스템의 문제점에 대한 다양한 해결책

구문풀이

9행 [{The flexible organization of the service-based economy} and {the autonomy (**it** gives workers)}] **radiate** into all domains of life: human interaction is increasingly freed from the bonding ties of closely knit groups, [**enabling** people **to make and break** social ties readily].

: 첫 번째 [ ]가 문장의 주어로 그 안에 두 개의 { }로 표시된 명사구가 and로 연결된 구조이며, 문장의 동사는 radiate이다. 두 번째 { } 안의 ( )는 the autonomy를 수식하는 목적격 관계대명사절이며, it은 the service-based economy를 가리킨다. 두 번째 [ ]는 결과를 나타내는 분사구문이고, 「enable+목적어+to부정사(목적격보어)」는 '~가 …할 수 있게 하다'라는 의미이다.

어휘풀이

- postindustrial society 후기 산업 사회
- liberate *v* 해방시키다
- disciplined *a* 기강이 있는
- mass-production system 대량 생산 시스템
- subject *A* to *B* A를 B의 지배하에 두다
- reverse *v* 뒤집다
- standardized *a* 표준화된

- rigid *a* 엄격한
- closely knit 긴밀하게 짜인
- destandardize *v* 표준화에서 벗어나게 하다
- flexible *a* 유연한
- radiate into ~로 퍼지다
- bond *v* 결합시키다
- individualization *n* 개별화
- erode *v* 약화시키다
- embed *v* 박아[끼워] 넣다
- conformity *n* 순응
- autonomy *n* 자율성
- domain *n* 영역
- tie *n* 유대(관계)
- provide for ~을 부양하다

- effectively *ad* 실제로, 사실상
- be grounded 땅에 내려앉다, 이륙하지 못하다
- pollen *n* 꽃가루
- be on the way 곧 일어날 것이다, 가까워지다
- precautionary measure 예방책
- decorative *a* 장식적인, 화려한
- striking *a* 놀라운, 인상적인
- fertilization *n* 수정
- petal *n* 꽃잎
- no less 같은 정도로, 그야말로, 역시
- not for nothing 그만한 이유가 있는

177 답 ①

📖 식물의 번식에 해로운 영향을 미치는 비

전문해석

한동안의 고기압의 맑은 날씨가 끝나고 저기압계가 아주 가까이에 위협적으로 내려 앉으면, 대기 습도는 점차 높아진다. 그리고 많은 식물들은 다가올 비가 그것들의 자 손에게 큰 피해를 입히기 때문에 이것을 좋아하지 않는다. 많은 종들은 그것들의 씨 앗을 가야 할 곳으로 보내는데, 그것(씨앗)들은 작은 솜털에 실려가고 이것들(작은 솜털들)은 부드러운 산들바람에도 운반된다. 그러나 그것들이 젖으면 이 작은 털은 **사실상 땅에 내려앉게 된다.** 새로운 영토를 정복할 기회는 사라진다. 동일한 것이 새 로 핀 꽃에 있는 꽃가루에도 적용되는데, **만약 빗물에 의해 땅에 떨어지면 그것은 벌 에 의해 운반되어 수정에 사용될 수 없다.** 곧 비가 올 것이라고 암시하면서 대기가 더 습해질 때 어떤 꽃들은 예방책으로 반응하는데, 그것들의 내부를 보호하기 위해 꽃잎을 닫는다. 하나의 예는 엉겅퀴인데, 그것의 큰 꽃은 특히 화려하고 접히는 방식 도 놀랍다. 독일어로 그것의 일반적인 이름이 '날씨 엉겅퀴'인 것에는 이유가 있다.

정답풀이

① **분사구문의 태**: bearing의 의미상의 주어는 their seeds이고, 씨앗들은 작은 솜털에 '실려가는' 대상이다. 따라서 bearing을 수동의 의미를 나타내는 과거분사 borne으로 고쳐야 어법상 적절하다.

오답풀이

② **주어와 동사의 수 일치**: 핵심 주어는 to conquer ~ territories의 수식을 받는 The opportunity이므로 단수형 동사 is는 어법상 적절하다.
③ **분사의 태**: if 다음에 「주어+be동사」인 it(= the pollen) is가 생략된 형태 이다. the pollen은 땅에 '떨어지는' 대상이므로 수동의 의미를 나타내는 과 거분사 knocked는 어법상 적절하다.
④ **관계대명사 whose**: the silver thistle을 부연 설명하는 관계사절을 이 끌며, 이어지는 명사구 large flowers와 함께 관계사절의 주어 역할을 하는 소유격 관계대명사 whose는 어법상 적절하다.
⑤ **접속사 that**: 뒤에 완전한 구조의 절이 이어지므로 형식상의 주어 It에 대한 내용상의 주어 역할을 하는 명사절을 이끄는 접속사 that은 어법상 적절하다.

구문풀이

5행 Many species send their seeds off on their way, [borne on small fluffy hairs], [which are carried away by even the gentlest breeze].

: 첫 번째 [ ]는 분사구문으로 의미상의 주어는 their seeds이다. 두 번째 [ ]는 small fluffy hairs를 부연 설명하는 주격 관계대명사절이다.

어휘풀이

- high-pressure 고기압의
- fine weather spell 맑은 날씨가 지속되는 기간
- subside *v* 진정되다, 내려앉다
- on the doorstep 아주 가까이에
- offspring *n* 자손, 새끼
- threateningly *ad* 위협적으로
- humidity *n* 습도
- fluffy *a* 솜털의, 보송보송한

178 답 ⑤

📖 식물의 섭식 저해 물질 생산

전문해석

정원에서 개별 식물, 균류, 그리고 곤충의 화학 작용은 따로따로 고려될 수 없다. 식 물의 화학 작용은 고유 특성의 총합이며 그것이 환경과 상호 작용한 결과이다. 식물 은 환경적 도전에 대한 반응으로 많은 천연물을 생산할 것이다. 식물은 본질적으로 고정되어 있다. 그것은 공격을 받으면 도망칠 수 있는 것이 아니라 싸워야 한다. 일 부 천연물의 형성은 미생물 또는 초식동물의 공격에 대한 반응으로 유발된다. 이러 한 천연물은 방어적 역할을 할 수 있고 포식자에게 독성이 있을 수 있다. 잎에서의 곤충 섭식 저해 물질 생산은 계절에 따라 다를 수 있다. 개화 전 잎에 존재하는 그것 들의 존재는 계절 초기에 포식자로부터 식물을 보호할 수 있다. 개화 후 및 그 해 후 반에는 섭식 저해 물질이 존재하지 않을 수 있고, 낙엽이 되어 부패하기 전에 잎이 손상된다. 손상된 조직은 가을의 부패에 관련된 미생물의 진입 경로를 차단한다 (→ 제공한다).

정답풀이

⑤ 미생물이나 곤충이 식물의 잎을 먹는 것을 방해하는 섭식 저해 물질이 개 화 후 잎에 존재하지 않게 되어 잎이 손상될 것이고 손상된 잎의 조직은 미생 물에게 부패를 위한 진입 경로를 '제공할' 것이라는 문맥이 자연스럽다. 따라 서 blocks(막다)를 provides(제공하다) 정도의 어휘로 바꿔야 한다.

오답풀이

① 식물은 환경적 도전에 대한 반응으로 천연물을 생산할 것이라는 내용이 이 어지므로, 식물의 화학 작용은 환경과 '상호 작용(interaction)'한 결과라고 하는 것은 문맥상 적절하다.
② 식물이 공격받을 때 도망갈 수 없는 이유는 본질적으로 한 자리에 '고정되 어 있기(stationary)' 때문이라는 것을 추론할 수 있다.
③ 미생물이나 초식동물의 공격에 대한 반응으로 생산되는 천연물은 잎을 먹 지 못하게 하는 방어적 역할을 하므로 '독성이 있는(toxic)' 것임을 추론할 수 있다.
④ 개화 전 잎에 곤충 섭식 저해 물질이 존재하면 계절[개화기] 초기에 포식자가 식물을 먹지 못하도록 식물을 '보호한다(protect)'는 흐름은 문맥상 적절하다.

구문풀이

18행 The damaged tissue provides a route of entry for micro-organisms [involved in autumnal decay].

: [ ]는 micro-organisms를 수식하는 과거분사구이다.

어휘풀이

- chemistry *n* 화학 작용, 화학
- in isolation 따로따로, 떨어져서
- intrinsic *a* 고유한, 본질적인
- consequence *n* 결과
- stationary *a* 정지해 있는, 움직이지 않는
- flee *v* 도망치다
- microbial *a* 미생물의
- toxic *a* 독성이 있는
- fungus *n* 균류 (*pl.* fungi)
- summation *n* 총합
- property *n* 특성, 속성
- essentially *ad* 본질적으로
- elicit *v* 유발하다, 끌어내다
- herbivore *n* 초식 동물
- predator *n* 포식자

- seasonal *a* 계절에 따라 다른, 계절적인
- decay *n* 부패, 부식
- entry *n* 진입, 입장
- autumnal *a* 가을의
- block *v* 막다, 차단하다
- micro-organism *n* 미생물

- worthwhile *a* ~할 가치가 있는
- requirement *n* 필요(한 것)
- streamline *v* 간소화하다
- extent *n* 범위, 정도
- alternative *n* 대체품

179 답 ②

📖 선택품목들의 수를 줄이는 것이 회사와 고객들에게 미치는 효과

전문해석

여러분이 한 제품의 다양한 변형 품목들을 팔고 있는 회사에서 일하고 있다고 가정해 보라. 비록 처음에는 여러분의 직관에 반하는 것처럼 보일지라도, **여러분이 판매하는 물건에 대한 최대한의 관심을 불러모으기 위해 여러분의 사업체에서 제공하는 선택품목들의 범위를 간소화하는 것이** 바람직할 수 있다. 때로는 제공받는 과도한 선택품목들에 대한 고객들의 그리 크지 않은 반발에 대한 반응으로, 최근 몇 년 동안 제품군을 검토하여 불필요한 품목들을 빼 버리고 있는 다양한 소비재의 많은 주요 제조업체들이 있다. 자신들이 무엇을 원하는지 불확실한 고객들은 과도한 선택항목으로 인해 경쟁사로 몰리고 있다. 간단히 말해서, **선택품목이 줄어들면 매출이 증가할 수 있다.** 물론, 덜 제공하는 것의 추가적인 이점이 있을 수 있는데, 예를 들면 더 많은 저장 공간, 원재료에 대한 줄어든 지출, 보다 적은 상품 목록을 유지하는 데 필요한 마케팅과 매장 재료의 감소 등이다. 해볼 만한 가치가 있는 연습은 여러분의 제품군의 범위를 검토하고 다음의 질문을 스스로에게 하는 것이다. 필요로 하는 것들에 대해 분명하지 않을 수 있는 고객들이 우리에게 있는 경우에, 우리가 제공하는 선택품목들의 수가 그들로 하여금 다른 곳에서 대체품목들을 찾도록 하는 것은 아닐까?

정답풀이

빈칸에는, 한 제품의 여러 변형 품목들을 판매하고 있는 회사가 판매 제품에 대한 관심을 최대화하고 특히 자신이 필요로 하는 것에 대해 분명하지 않은 고객이 다른 곳에서 대체품을 사지 않도록 하기 위해서 취할 수 있는 조치가 들어가야 한다. 빈칸 이후에서 제품군을 검토하여 불필요한 품목들을 빼 버리는, 즉 더 적은 선택품목을 제공하는 것에 대한 이점을 제시하며 선택품목의 수에 대해 고려해 보라고 제안하고 있으므로, 빈칸에 들어갈 말로는 ② '선택품목들의 범위를 간소화하는 것'이 가장 적절하다.

오답풀이

① 상품군을 확대하는 것
③ 각 선택품목에 대한 정보를 구체화하는 것
④ 마케팅 경로의 수를 줄이는 것
⑤ 상품 체험 전략을 중지하는 것

구문풀이

21행 **Where** we have customers [who may not be clear about their requirements], / might the number of choices [we offer] be **causing** them **to seek** alternatives elsewhere?

: where는 접속사의 기능을 하며 '~한 경우에'의 의미를 가진다. 첫 번째 [ ]는 주격 관계대명사절로 customers를 수식하고, 두 번째 [ ]는 목적격 관계대명사절로 choices를 수식한다. 주절에는 「cause+목적어+목적격보어(to부정사): (목적어)에게 ~하도록 야기하다」 구문이 쓰였다.

어휘풀이

- organization *n* 회사, 조직체
- drum up ~을 불러모으다
- review *v* 검토하다
- modest *a* 그리 크지 않은
- additional *a* 추가적인
- raw material *n* 원료
- intuition *n* 직관
- maximum *a* 최대한의
- redundant *a* 불필요한, 남아도는
- rebellion *n* 저항, 반항
- storage *n* 저장
- portfolio *n* 상품 목록

180 답 ②

📖 사회로부터 남성성을 강요받는 남자 아이들

전문해석

1999년에 두 심리학자 Dan Kindlon과 Michael Thompson은 〈Raising Cain〉이라는 제목의 책을 공동 집필했다. **저자들은 한 사회로서 미국이 남아들의 정서적 삶을 너무나 잘못 다루어서 많은 냉담하고 문제를 지닌 남자들을 키워 냈다고 주장한다.** 부모, 남녀 교사도 마찬가지로, 모두가 무의식적으로 **공모하여 남아들의 정서 발달에 제약을 가한다**고 그들은 말한다. Kindlon과 Thompson이 주장하듯이, 우리는 우리의 문화로부터 받아들이는 남성다움의 이미지를 근거로 남아들이 '거칠고' '강하기'를 바란다. 그래서 아이가 상처받고 있을 때, 즉 그가 슬프거나, 화가 나 있거나, 좌절해 있거나, 실망해 있거나 혹은 겁에 질려 있을 때, 우리는 그가 자신이 느끼는 것에 대해서 배우도록 허락하지 않는다. 우리는 그를 "씩씩하게 참고 견뎌야지." 혹은 "너는 강해져야지."와 같은 말로 자신의 감정을 안으로 감추고 움츠러들게 한다. **저자들은 우리가 남아들에게 '정서적 해독 능력', 즉 정서적인 경험을 인정하고 해석하고 이해할 수 있는 능력을 가르치지 않는다고 주장한다. 그 결과 남아들은 자신의 감정을 표현하는 능력이 부족할 뿐만 아니라 타인의 감정을 읽어내지도 못한다.**

정답풀이

사회가 남아들의 정서적 삶을 잘못 다루고 남아들에게 정서적인 경험을 인정하고 해석하고 이해할 수 있는 능력을 가르치지 않아서 자신의 감정을 표현하거나 타인의 감정을 읽는 능력이 부족한 남자로 키웠다는 것이 글의 핵심이다. 빈칸에는 사회를 대표하는 부모나 교사들의 태도가 남아들의 정서적 발달에 해가 되었다는 내용이 들어가야 하므로 ② '공모하여 남아들의 정서 발달에 제약을 가한다'가 가장 적절하다.

오답풀이

① 남아들에게 성 고정관념과 성 역할에 도전하도록 촉구한다
③ 정서적 개입으로 남아들의 공격성을 조절하려고 노력한다
④ 정서 발달보다는 지적 발달을 더 강조한다
⑤ 남아들에게 말보다는 행동을 통해서 그들의 감정을 표현하도록 압박한다
 ↳ 사회가 남아들에게 정서적 해독 능력을 가르치지 않았다는 내용을 확대 해석한 함정 오답!
 정서적 해독 능력을 가르치지 않았다는 것이 감정을 행동으로 표현하도록 압박하는 것과 동일한 맥락이라고 판단해서는 안 된다.

구문풀이

8행 As Kindlon and Thompson put it, we want our boys to be "tough" and "strong" [based on images of manliness {we absorb from our culture}].

: [ ]는 분사구문이고, 그 안의 { }는 images of manliness를 수식하는 목적격 관계대명사절이다.

17행 As a result, boys **not only** [lack the ability to express their own feelings], they **also** [fail to recognize emotions in others].

: 'A뿐만 아니라 B도'라는 의미의 「not only *A* (but) also *B*」 구문으로 [ ]로 표시된 두 개의 동사구가 연결되었다.

어휘풀이

- coauthor *v* 공동 집필하다
- mishandle *v* 잘못 다루다
- entitle *v* ~에 제목을 붙이다
- manliness *n* 남자다움, 용감함

- absorb *v* 흡수하다
- contend *v* 주장하다
- interpret *v* 해석하다
- conspire *v* 공모하다
- intervention *n* 개입
- frightened *a* 겁먹은
- literacy *n* (특정 분야의) 지식, 능력
- stereotype *n* 고정관념
- aggression *n* 공격성

181 답 ⑤

📖 나중을 위해 먹이를 보관할줄 모르는 침팬지

전문해석

미래의 더 큰 기쁨을 위해 현재의 기쁨을 희생한다는 생각은 대부분의 동물에게 낯설고, 어려우며, 심지어 이해 불가능할 것이다. 이 점에 대한 극적인 입증이 침팬지 연구에서 나타났다. (C) 그것들은 오직 하루에 한 번 언제나 같은 시간에 먹이가 주어졌고 원하는 모든 먹이를 먹도록 허용되었다. 인간과 다른 많은 동물들처럼 침팬지는 하루 동안 여러 번 먹는 것을 선호하므로, 그것들은 다음번에 예정된 먹이 제공 전의 마지막 두어 시간 동안에는 항상 배가 몹시 고팠다. (B) 현명한 대응은 차후를 위해, 특히 다음 날 아침 배가 고픈 몇 시간 동안을 위해 이용 가능한 먹이 일부를 보관하는 것이었을 테지만, 그 동물은 결코 이렇게 하는 것을 배우지 못했다. 그것들은 먹이가 나올 때 그것을 누렸다. 그것들은 배불리 먹고, 그런 다음 남은 먹이를 무시했는데, 심지어는 때때로 원치 않는 남은 먹이를 서로에게 던지며 먹이 싸움을 벌이곤 했다. (A) 그렇지만 반복된 시도에도 불구하고 그것들은 차후를 위해 먹이를 저장하는 것을 배우지 못했다. 24시간이라는 짧은 기간도 분명 행동을 조정하기 위한 그것들의 인지 능력을 넘어섰다. 대조적으로, 인간은 일상적으로 음식을 획득하여 여러 날 또는 심지어 여러 주와 여러 달 동안 저장한다.

정답풀이

침팬지를 비롯한 대부분의 동물들은 차후를 위해 먹이를 보관할 수 있는 인지 역량이 없다는 내용의 글이다. 동물에게는 미래의 더 큰 기쁨을 위해 현재의 기쁨을 희생하는 능력이 없다는 것이 침팬지 연구에서 입증되었다는 내용의 주어진 글 다음에는, 침팬지 연구 과정을 구체적으로 소개하기 시작하는 내용의 (C)가 이어진다. 그리고 실험에서 먹이를 주는 방식에 대한 (C)의 설명 다음에는, 그 방식으로 볼 때 남은 먹이를 보관하는 것이 지극히 타당하지만 침팬지들은 그렇게 하지 않고 남은 먹이를 가지고 딴 짓만 했다는 내용의 (B)가 오고, 반복된 시도에도 불구하고 침팬지는 먹이를 저장하는 방법을 배우지 못했는데, 이는 침팬지의 인지 능력의 한계 때문이라는 내용의 (A)로 마무리되는 것이 자연스럽다. 따라서 가장 적절한 글의 순서는 ⑤ (C)-(B)-(A)이다.

구문풀이

16행 They would eat their fill, and then they would ignore the rest, [sometimes even **engaging** in food fights {in which they would throw the unwanted leftover food at each other}].

: [ ]는 They를 의미상의 주어로 하는 분사구문으로 부수적 동작을 나타내고, 그 안의 { }는 food fights를 수식하는 관계절이다.

어휘풀이

- sacrifice *v* 희생하다
- incomprehensible *a* 이해 불가능한
- trial *n* 시도
- apparently *ad* 분명히, 명백히
- adjust *v* 조정하다
- sensible *a* 현명한
- eat one's fill 배불리 먹다
- leftover *a* (먹고) 남은
- for the sake of ~을 위해
- demonstration *n* 입증, 증명
- span *n* 기간
- cognitive *a* 인지의
- routinely *ad* 일상적으로
- rejoice *v* 누리다, 즐기다
- engage in ~에 참여하다

182 답 ⑤

📖 인간의 에너지 자원

전문해석

인간은 장작, 기름 그리고 가스와 같은 생물학적 재료들로부터 얻는 보충 에너지를 이용한다. 대부분의 인류 역사에서, 식물과 동물에게서 얻는 에너지는 여러 가지 일들을 해내기 위해 사람들에 의해 이용되어 왔다. 1850년대에 미국에서는, 사용되는 에너지의 약 91퍼센트가 나무와 여타 생물학적 재료를 태우는 것에서 나왔다. 21세기 초반에는 미국인들이 필요로 하는 기계에 동력을 공급하는 데 사용되는 보충 에너지의 약 81퍼센트가 가스, 석탄, 석유와 같은 화석 연료에서 나왔다. 화석 연료 에너지에 대한 이러한 수요는 또한 연방정부가 농부들이 농장 시설에 필요로 하는 가솔린과 같은 품목에 연료 보조금을 지급함으로써 특정 부문에서 지원을 받아 왔다. 하지만 현재는 화석 연료를 대체할 대체 에너지원을 개발하려는 노력이 이루어지고 있는데, 그것(화석 연료)은 환경을 오염시키고 재생이 불가능하기 때문이다. 어떤 사람들은 적절한 대안을 찾는 우리의 능력에 관해 매우 비관적이고 결과적으로 산업화된 문화의 종말을 예견하지만, 다른 사람들은 태양 에너지와 풍력 에너지에서의 현재의 발전이 이 운명을 피할 수 있게 해줄 것이라고 생각한다.

정답풀이

역접의 연결어 however가 있는 주어진 문장은 화석 연료의 문제점을 지적하면서 대체 에너지원을 개발하려고 노력하고 있다는 내용으로, 정부가 화석 연료 에너지의 수요에 보조금을 지급했다는 내용과 화석 연료의 대안을 찾는 것에 대한 사람들의 생각이 담긴 마지막 문장 사이인 ⑤에 들어가는 것이 가장 적절하다.

구문풀이

6행 For most of human history, the energy [derived from plants and animals] **has been used** by people [to accomplish various tasks].

: 첫 번째 [ ]는 문장의 핵심 주어인 the energy를 수식하는 과거분사구이며, 동사로 has been used의 수동태가 쓰였다. 두 번째 [ ]는 목적을 나타내는 부사적 용법의 to부정사구이다.

어휘풀이

- fossil fuel 화석 연료
- nonrenewable *a* 재생이 불가능한
- supplemental *a* 보충의, 추가의
- accomplish *v* 완수하다
- subsidy *n* 보조금, 장려금
- appropriate *a* 적절한
- avoidable *a* 피할 수 있는
- pollute *v* 오염시키다
- utilize *v* 이용[활용]하다
- derive *v* 얻다
- aid *v* 도와주다
- pessimistic *a* 비관적인
- predict *v* 예견하다

183 답 ④

📖 질문이 던져지는 맥락이 조사 결과에 미치는 영향

전문해석

질문이 던져지는 맥락이 어떻게 설문조사 결과에 영향을 미칠 수 있는가에 관한 사례가 미국인들의 '공적인 일에 대한 관심'에 관한 연구에 의해 제공된다. 설문조사 응답자들이 '정부와 공적인 일에서 무슨 일이 진행되고 있는지'를 얼마나 많이 지켜보고 있는지'에 관해 질문을 받았을 때, 이 질문이 그 설문조사에서 첫 번째 질문으로 던져졌을 때 자신들의 하원의원이 자신들의 지역구를 위해 했던 특별한 어떤 일과 자신들의 남녀 국회의원들이 어떤 법안에 어떻게 투표했는지 본인이 기억하고 있는지에 관한 질문들 이후에 이 질문이 던져졌을 때보다, 18퍼센트 더 많은 사람들이 자신들은 '대부분의 경우' 그것을 지켜보고 있다고 말했다. 대부분의 사람들은 자신

들의 하원의원이 지역구를 위해 했던 일이나 그들이 어떻게 투표했는지 기억하지 못하기 때문에 그들은 이 항목들에 대해 '모른다'고 말했다. 그런 다음 정부와 공적인 일을 얼마나 자주 지켜보고 있는지 질문을 받았을 때 그들은 '대부분의 경우'라고 대답할 가능성이 더 적었다. '어려운 지식'을 묻는 질문은 질문자가 말하는 '정부와 공적인 일을 지켜보고 있음'이 어떤 의미인지에 대해 다른 맥락을 제공했다.

→ 설문조사에서 질문의 순서는 그 결과에 큰 영향을 미칠 수 있는데, 이는 선행하는 질문들이 조사 참가자가 다른 질문들에 대해 어떻게 응답하는지에 영향을 줄 수도 있기 때문이다.

정답풀이

일반적인 태도를 묻는 질문에 앞서 구체적인 사실들에 대해 확인하는 질문을 했을 때 반대의 경우보다 긍정적인 응답을 한 응답자가 더 적었다는 연구 결과를 통해 설문조사에서 먼저 하는 질문이 다른 질문에 대한 응답에 영향을 미칠 수 있다는 결론을 내릴 수 있다. 따라서 (A)에는 order(순서)가, (B)에는 preceding(선행하는)이 들어가는 것이 가장 적절하다.

구문풀이

1행 **An example** of [how the context {in which a question is asked} can affect survey results] **is provided** by research on Americans' "interest in public affairs."

: An example이 문장의 핵심 주어이고, 동사는 is provided이다. [ ]는 전치사 of의 목적어 역할을 하는 명사절(의문사절)이고, 그 안의 { }는 the context를 수식하는 관계절이다.

어휘풀이

- public affair 공적인 일
- respondent *n* 응답자
- follow *v* (지속적으로) ~에 관심을 가지다, (계속) ~을 지켜보다
- representative *n* (미국) 하원의원
- district *n* 지역구, 선거구
- congressman *n* 국회의원
- legislative bill 법안
- subsequent *a* 차후의
- open-ended *a* 정해진 답이 없는
- validity *n* 타당성
- pointed *a* 정곡을 찌르는
- preceding *a* 선행하는
- exploratory *a* 탐구의, 예비의

3점 공략 모의고사 12회 　　본문 p.124

| 184 ⑤ | 185 ④ | 186 ③ | 187 ③ | 188 ④ |
| 189 ① | 190 ③ | 191 ③ | | |

184　답 ⑤

📖 서구 아동의 발달 표본을 보편적으로 적용하는 것의 문제점

전문해석

인간 발달에 관한 전형적인 이론과 연구 대부분은 서구 표본에 기반하고 있으며, 발달 연구원들은 한때 인간 발달의 과정이 보편적이라고 믿었다. 더 최근의 관찰은 발달이 맥락에 따라 극적으로 다르다는 것을 보여준다. 예를 들어, 아기가 걸음마를 시작하는 평균 나이 같은 중대 시점을 생각해 보라. 우간다에서는 아기가 약 10개월의 나이에 걷기 시작하고, 프랑스에서는 약 15개월 그리고 미국에서는 약 12개월에 걷기 시작한다. 이러한 차이는 문화별로 다른 육아 관행에 의해 영향을 받는다. 아프리카 부모들은 아기가 점프하고 걷는 기술을 연습하게 하는 놀이를 함으로써 걷기를 자극하는 방식으로 아기를 다루는 경향이 있다. 개인이 사는 문화적 맥락이 발달의 많은 양상들의 시기와 발현에 영향을 미치는데, 오랫동안 오직 생물학적 성숙에 의해서만 영향을 받는다고 여겨진 신체적 발달조차도 그렇다. 일부 과학자들은 서구 표본에서 추출된 발달 원리를 다른 문화의 아동에 적용하는 것은 비과학적이며 그것이 아동의 능력에 관한 오해의 소지가 있는 결론을 낳을 수 있기 때문에 비윤리적이기조차 하다고 주장한다.

정답풀이

⑤ **문장의 구조 파악**: argue의 목적어로 쓰인 that절에서 주어는 applying ~ cultures의 동명사구이고 unscientific and even unethical은 보어에 해당하므로 술어 동사가 없는 상태이다. 따라서 준동사 to be를 본동사 is로 고쳐야 한다. derived from Western samples는 「apply A to B(A를 B에 적용하다)」 구문에서 A에 해당하는 principles of development를 수식하는 과거분사구임에 유의한다.

오답풀이

① **주어와 동사의 수 일치**: believed의 목적어인 that절의 주어부에서 핵이 되는 명사는 processes이므로 복수형 동사 were를 쓴 것은 어법상 적절하다.
② **문장의 구조 파악**: milestones가 목적어이고, such as 이하는 milestones를 수식하는 어구에 해당하므로 명령문을 이끄는 동사원형 consider는 어법상 적절하다.
③ **관계대명사 that**: ways를 수식하는 절을 이끌면서 이어지는 절에서 stimulate의 주어 역할을 하는 주격 관계대명사 that의 쓰임은 어법상 적절하다.
④ **분사의 태**: 수식을 받는 physical developments가 영향을 받는다고 여겨지는 대상이므로 과거분사 thought는 어법상 적절하다. long thought 이하는 which have been long thought to be influenced ~에서 which have been이 생략된 형태로 이해할 수 있다.

구문풀이

15행 The cultural context [in which individuals live] **influences** the timing and expression of many aspects of development, [even physical developments {long **thought** to be influenced only by biological maturation}].

: 첫 번째 [ ]는 문장의 핵심 주어인 The cultural context를 수식하는 관계절이고, 문장의 술어 동사는 influences이다. 두 번째 [ ]는 many aspects of development에 대한 추가적인 설명을 제시하는 어구이며, 그 안의 { }는 physical developments 수식하는 과거분사구이다.

185 답 ④

📖 거절당할 큰 부탁을 한 후 작은 부탁을 해서 양보를 얻어 내는 전략

전문해석

협상에 참여하는 사람들에게 양보는 종종 보은(보답)의 초점이다. 양보를 받은 후에 대부분의 사람들은 그에 대한 보답으로 양보를 해야 한다는 의무감을 느낀다. 이렇게 느낀 의무감을 활용하도록 고안된 수락 전략은 보은적 양보 혹은 면전에서 문 닫기 기법이라고 불린다. 작은 부탁으로부터 출발해서 바라는 부탁으로 나아가는 대신에, 면전에서 문 닫기 기법을 사용하는 사람은 반대 방향으로 간다. 여기에서 부탁하는 사람은 큰 부탁으로 시작하는데, 만일 거절당하면, 그 이후의 좀 더 작은 부탁을 하자마자 "그래"라는 대답을 들을 가능성이 훨씬 더 커지는 독특한 상황에 일시적으로 놓이게 된다. 이러한 보은적 양보 전술은 실제로 거절을 통해서 부탁하는 사람에게 힘을 갖게 하기 때문에 독특한 영향력 행사 전략이다. 처음의 큰 부탁으로부터 두 번째의 작은 부탁으로 물러섬으로써 부탁하는 사람은 상대에게 양보를 하게 되는데, 그 상대는 (보은의 규칙을 통해서) 보답을 해야 한다는 의무감을 느낀다.

정답풀이

일부러 거절당할 큰 부탁을 먼저 하여 상대방이 거절한 것에 대해서 심리적으로 부담을 느끼고 이후의 작은 부탁을 들어주도록 만드는 보은적 양보 전술은 한 번의 거절을 통해서 부탁하는 사람에게 일종의 힘을 부여한다고 할 수 있다. 따라서 빈칸에 들어갈 말로 가장 적절한 것은 ④ '거절을 통해서 부탁하는 사람에게 힘을 갖게 하기'이다.

오답풀이

① 협상에서 교착 상태를 초래하기
② 상대방의 판단을 흐리게 하기
③ 호혜의 개념을 넘어서기
⑤ 부탁하는 사람에게 자신의 목표에 대해 타협하도록 강요하기
  └ 보은적 양보 전술은 처음의 큰 부탁에서 거절당할 것을 스스로 예상하고 전략을 짜는 것이므로 오답이다.

구문풀이

4행 A compliance tactic [designed to engage this felt obligation] **is called** the reciprocal concessions or door-in-the-face technique].

: [ ]는 문장의 핵심 주어인 A compliance tactic을 수식하는 과거분사구이며, is called가 문장의 동사이다.

어휘풀이

- negotiation *n* 협상
- reciprocation *n* 보답, 답례
- feel obligated to *do* ~해야 한다는 의무감을 느끼다
- compliance *n* 준수, 따름, 수락
- reciprocal *a* 호혜적인, 상호의, 보답의
- significantly *ad* 상당히, 의미 있게
- retreat *v* 물러나다
- empower *v* ~에게 힘을 갖게 하다
- concession *n* 양보
- tactic *n* 전술
- temporarily *ad* 일시적으로, 잠시
- subsequent *a* 이후의, 뒤이은
- deadlock *n* (협상의) 교착 상태

- compromise on ~에 대해 타협하다

186 답 ③

📖 인간을 특징짓고 문명을 가능하게 한 지식에 대한 갈망

전문해석

동물들은 어디에서 먹이를 찾고, 어떻게 포식자를 피하며, 어디에서 짝을 찾을지와 같은 자신들에게 즉시 쓸모가 있는 것이 무엇이고, 자신들의 생존에 필요한 것이 무엇인지 알지 못하고는 살 수 없다. 그러나 **인류는 우리의 개인적 필요를 훨씬 더 넘어서는 지식에 대해 갈망하기 때문에** 다른 동물들과 다르다. 우리는 우리 주변을 돌아보고 궁금해한다. 우리는 목적 없이 그리고 수동적으로 우리 주변에 대해 그리고 가까이와 멀리에서 우리가 관찰하는 것에 대해 궁금해하지만, 우리는 이 모든 것을 이해하고 싶어 한다. 사실 우리는 미지의 것을 두려워한다. **이러한 궁금한 것에 대한 느낌과 이해를 위한 절박한 욕구가 우리를 인간으로 만들 뿐 아니라 또한 문명의 초석 중 하나이기도 하다.** 해답에 대한 탐색과 일반적으로 접근 가능한 기억 속에 그것들을 보유하는 것이 조직적으로 추구될 때, 우리의 호기심을 만족하게 하는 것이 더욱 쉬워지고 더 능숙해지며, 이는 원시적인 집단들을 중국, 바빌로니아, 이집트, 마야, 인도, 고대 그리스, 현대 서구 문명 그리고 아마도 기록을 남기지 않은 다른 문명들처럼 우리가 문명이라고 부르는 거대한 역사적 연합으로 탈바꿈시키는 데 도움을 준다.

구문풀이

빈칸 이후의 내용에서 인류는 주변을 돌아보고 궁금해하며 주변에서 관찰하는 모든 것을 이해하고 싶어 하고, 궁금한 것에 대한 느낌과 이해를 위한 절박한 욕구는 우리를 인간으로 만들 뿐 아니라 문명의 초석이기도 하다고 말하고 있다. 따라서 인간이 동물들과 다른 이유는 ③ '우리의 개인적 필요를 훨씬 더 넘어서는 지식에 대해 갈망하기' 때문이라고 할 수 있다.

오답풀이

① 진화에 이로운 집단적인 안전을 추구하기
② 우리의 기억 속에 쉽게 저장되는 거의 모든 것을 상징화하기
  └ 글의 핵심인 '궁금한 것에 대한 느낌과 이해를 위한 절박한 욕구'에서 벗어나는 함정 오답!
④ 전체 종을 위험에 빠뜨릴 수 있는 불필요한 모험을 피하기
⑤ 적자생존에 이르게 하는 경쟁에 지배를 받기

구문풀이

13행 The satisfaction of our curiosity becomes [easier and more proficient] [**when** {the search for answers and their retention in a generally accessible memory} **is pursued** in an organized fashion], [helping to transform primitive groups into the grand historical confederations ...].

: The satisfaction of our curiosity가 주어, becomes가 동사이다. 첫 번째 [ ]는 보어이며, 두 번째 [ ]는 when이 이끄는 부사절이다. 이 부사절에서는 { }가 주어인데 '해답을 탐색하여 보유한다'는 하나의 개념으로 취급하여 단수형 동사 is pursued가 쓰였다. 세 번째 [ ]는 앞 절의 내용을 의미상의 주어로 하는 분사구문이다.

어휘풀이

- predator *n* 포식자, 육식동물
- the unknown 미지의 것
- foundation stone 초석
- curiosity *n* 호기심
- retention *n* 보유, 유지
- in an organized fashion 조직적으로
- transform *v* ~을 탈바꿈시키다, 변형시키다
- primitive *a* 원시적인
- aimlessly *ad* 목표 없이
- urgent *a* 절박한, 긴급한
- civilization *n* 문명
- proficient *a* 능숙한, 숙달된

- be subject to ~의 대상이다, ~의 지배를 받다
- survival of the fittest 적자생존

- attribute A to B A의 원인을 B에 돌리다
- attend v 주목하다
- reluctance to do ~하는 것을 꺼려함
- attribution n (원인 등을 ~에) 돌림, 귀속
- contribute to ~에 기여하다, ~의 원인이 되다
- analytic a 분석적인
- attribute n 속성
- in terms of ~의 측면에서
- assume v 생각하다
- apply v 적용되다
- dominance n 지배

187 답 ③

📖 동양인과 서양인의 세상을 바라보는 관점의 차이

전문해석

동양인들은 세상에 대한 '전체적인' 관점을 가지는 성향이 있다. 그들은 (사람들을 포함해서) 대상을 그것의 맥락 안에서 바라보고, 행동의 원인을 상황 요인에 돌리는 경향이 있으며, 사람들 사이 또는 사물들 사이의 관계에 면밀히 주목한다. (B) 서양인들은 좀 더 분석적인 관점을 가지고 있다. 그들은 사물에 주목하고, 그 속성을 알아내고, 그 속성을 근거로 사물을 분류하며, 그 특정한 범주의 사물에 적용된다고 생각하는 규칙에 따라 그 사물에 대해 생각한다. (C) 두 관점 모두 장점이 있다. 나는 분석적인 관점이 서양의 과학계에서 지배적인 위치를 차지하는 데 역할을 해왔다고 생각한다. 그리고 사실, 그리스가 과학을 탄생시킨 시기에 중국 문명은 수학과 다른 여러 분야에서 큰 진척을 이루긴 했지만, 근대적 의미의 진정한 과학 전통을 만들어 내지는 못했다. (A) 하지만 전체적인 관점은 동양인들이 다른 사람들의 행동을 이해할 때 심각한 오류를 피하게 한다. 게다가, 기질을 탓하지 않는 것은 사람들의 변화 능력에 대한 동양(인)의 믿음의 원인이 된다.

정답풀이

동양인의 세상에 대한 전체적인 관점을 설명한 주어진 글 다음에는, 서양인들의 분석적인 관점에 대해 언급하는 (B)가 오는 것이 적절하다. 두 관점을 Both perspectives로 받아 모두 장점이 있다고 하면서 분석적인 관점 덕분에 서양이 과학계에서 지배적인 위치를 차지하게 되었다고 언급하는 (C)가 그 뒤에 이어지며, 서양의 분석적 관점에 대한 장점을 말한 (C)의 마지막 내용 다음에 역접의 But으로 시작하면서 동양의 전체적인 관점의 장점을 언급하는 (A)가 마지막에 오는 순서가 가장 적절하다.

구문풀이

7행 But the holistic perspective saves Easterners from some serious errors **in understanding** [why other people behave {as they **do**}].

: 「in+-ing」는 '~할 때, ~함에 있어'라는 의미이다. [ ]는 동명사 understanding의 목적어로 쓰인 명사절이고, 그 안의 { }는 as가 이끄는 부사절이며, do는 대동사로 behave를 대신해서 썼다.

12행 They **attend** to the object, **notice** its attributes, **categorize** the object on the basis of those attributes, and **think** about the object in terms of the rules [that {they assume} apply to objects of that particular category].

: 문장의 주어 They에 이어지는 동사 attend, notice, categorize, think가 and에 의해 병렬구조를 이룬다. [ ]는 the rules를 수식하는 주격 관계대명사절이고, 그 안의 { }는 삽입절이다.

20행 And in fact, the Greeks invented science at a time [when **Chinese civilization**, {**though making** great progress in mathematics and many other fields}, **had** no real tradition of science in the modern sense].

: [ ]는 a time을 수식하는 관계부사절이고, 그 안의 { }는 관계절의 주어 Chinese civilization과 동사 had 사이에 삽입된 분사구문으로 의미를 분명히 하기 위해 접속사 though를 명시하였다.

어휘풀이

- perspective n 관점

188 답 ④

📖 합성비료를 사용하지 않는 유기농업의 문제점

전문해석

당신이 유기농업을 좋아하든 그렇지 않든 그것은 생산성이 낮다. 그 이유는 단순한 화학에 있다. 유기농업은 모든 합성비료를 피하기 때문에, 그것은 특히 인과 칼륨 같은 토양에 있는 광물성 영양분을 고갈시키는데, 결국에는 황, 칼슘 그리고 망간을 고갈시킨다. 유기농업은 잘게 분쇄한 광석이나 으깬 생선을 토양에 섞음으로써 이러한 문제를 완화시키는데, 이러한 것들은 채굴되거나 그물로 잡아야 한다. 하지만 유기농업의 주된 문제는 질소 결핍인데, 이는 공기로부터 질소를 고정시키는 콩과 식물(클로버, 알팔파, 콩)을 재배하고 그것들을 토양에 갈아엎거나 소 먹이로 주고 거기서 나오는 거름을 토양에 갈아엎어서 해결할 수 있다. 그러한 도움으로 특정한 유기농 경작지는 비유기농 산출에 필적할 수 있지만, 그러한 식물을 기르고 소를 먹이기 위해서 어딘가에 여분의 땅을 사용함으로써만 가능한데, 이는 사실상 쟁기질을 해야 하는 경작지를 두 배로 만든다. 대조적으로, (유기농이 아닌) 종래의 농업은 질소를 공장에서 얻는데, 공장은 공기로부터 질소를 고정시킨다. 이를 고려하면, 세계가 유기농을 선택하고, 즉 농업이 공장과 화석연료를 이용하여 공기에서 직접 얻는 것이 아니라 식물과 생선으로부터 질소를 얻고, 90억의 많은 사람들이 굶주리고 모든 열대우림이 벌채되도록 두어야 할까?

정답풀이

주어진 문장의 such help가 문맥상 콩과 식물을 재배하여 소를 먹이고 거기서 나온 거름을 토양에 섞는 것을 의미하고, 또한 those plants가 가리키는 대상이 legumes (clover, alfalfa or beans)에 해당하므로 주어진 문장이 들어가기에 가장 적절한 곳은 ④이다.

구문풀이

13행 Its main problem, though, is <u>nitrogen deficiency</u>, [which it can reverse by **growing** <u>legumes (clover, alfalfa or beans)</u>, {which fix nitrogen from the air}, and **either ploughing** them into the soil **or feeding** them to <u>cattle</u> {whose manure is then ploughed into the soil}].

: [ ]는 nitrogen deficiency를 부연 설명하는 목적격 관계대명사절이고, 그 안의 첫 번째 { }는 legumes (clover, alfalfa or beans)를 부연 설명하는 주격 관계대명사절이다. growing, ploughing, feeding이 병렬구조로 연결되었으며, 여기에는 「either A or B」의 구문이 쓰여 'A 또는 B'의 의미를 나타낸다. 두 번째 { }는 cattle을 수식하는 소유격 관계대명사절이다.

어휘풀이

- plot n 작은 땅, 소구획지
- effectively ad 사실상
- plough n 쟁기 v 갈다, 경작하다 (= plow)
- synthetic fertilizer 합성 비료
- exhaust v 고갈시키다
- phosphorus n 인
- potassium n 칼륨
- sulphur n 황
- get round ~을 해결[처리]하다
- squash v 으깨다
- nitrogen n 질소
- deficiency n 결핍
- reverse v 뒤집다, 바꿔 놓다
- fix v (질소를) 고정시키다
- manure n 동물의 배설물, 거름
- given prep ~을 고려하면

189 답 ①

📖 감상자의 배경에 따라 다르게 해석되는 음악의 의미

전문해석

음악 작품에 의미가 부여된다면, 그 의미는 아마도 똑같은 음악이 들려오더라도 과거의 기억과 결부되면서 보통 대단히 개인적인 성격을 지니게 될 것인데, 이는 '여보, 저 사람들이 우리의 선율을 연주하고 있어요' 증후군이다. Ian Cross가 최근에 말했듯이, '하나의 같은 곡도 연주자와 감상자 또는 두 명의 다른 감상자에게 아주 다른 의미를 지닐 수 있다. 심지어 그것은 특정한 시간의 한 감상자나 참여자에게 여러 가지 상이한 의미를 지닐 수도 있다.' 이것은 종교 음악의 경우에 가장 두드러진다. 즉, 나는 무신론자라서 헨델의 〈Messiah〉나 바흐의 〈St Matthew Passion〉처럼 신을 찬양하기 위해 작곡된 18세기의 위대한 합창곡을 들을 때, 그 것들은 종교적인 믿음을 가진 사람에게 의미하는 것과 아주 다른 어떤 것을 나에게 '의미한다'. John Blacking이 설명했듯이, 힌두교 문화의 맥락 밖에서 북부 인도 음악이 충분히 이해될 수 없는 것처럼 헨델과 바흐의 음악은 18세기의 세계관을 참작하지 않고서는 충분히 이해될 수 없다.
→ 감상자의 배경이 그 음악을 감상하는 데 결정적인 역할을 하기 때문에 음악 작품의 의미는 감상자에게 특유할 수 있다.

정답풀이

이 글은 음악에 의미가 부여되면 대단히 개인적인 특성을 갖게 된다고 말하며, 같은 음악이라도 감상자에 따라 서로 다른 의미를 가질 수 있다고 설명하고 있다. 음악의 의미가 개인마다 다른 이유는 감상자나 연주자가 다른 배경에 속해 있기 때문이라고 했으므로, (A)에는 distinctive(독특한, 특유의)가, (B)에는 background(배경)가 들어가는 것이 가장 적절하다.

구문풀이

11행 I am an atheist, so **when** I listen to the great eighteenth-century choral works [that were written to glorify God, such as Handel's *Messiah* or Bach's *St Matthew Passion*], / they 'mean' something quite different to me than they **would** to someone of religious faith.

: when이 이끄는 부사절에서 [ ]는 the great ~ choral works를 수식하는 주격 관계대명사절이다. would는 반복되는 동사구 would mean을 대신한다.

어휘풀이

- attach v 부여하다, 붙이다
- disparate a 상이한, 아주 다른
- choral a 합창곡의
- without reference to ~을 참작하지 않고, ~와 상관없이
- intricate a 복잡한
- bear v (특성 등을) 띠다
- evidently ad 분명히, 눈에 띄게
- glorify v 찬양하다

190~191 답 ③ / ③

📖 오락을 통해 경험하는 능력의 느낌

전문해석

오락은 도전이 거의 없거나 매체 사용자가 여전히 성공적으로 대처할 수 있는 만큼의 도전만 있는 활동으로 거의 항상 묘사되어 왔다. 물론, 이것은 최적의 도전일 것인데, 사람들에게 가장 큰 유능감을 느끼게 해주는 수준이다. 따라서 유능감이 거의 보장되며, 그것은 별다른 노력이 없이도 생겨날 수 있다. 어느 누가 다른 그 어느 곳에서 그렇게 자주, 그렇게 쉽고 그리고 그렇게 지대하게 유능하다고 느낄 수 있겠는가? 특히 젊은 남성들 사이에서 요즘 가장 매력적인 오락 촉진 수단 중 하나인 비디오 게임은 이것에 대한 훌륭한 사례를 제공한다. 어느 특정한 게임의 복잡성, 난이도 그리고 도전의 수준은 다양하며 플레이어에 의해 선택되거나 그 게임에 의해 자동적으로 설정되는 설정에 좌우된다. 그 게임 자체가, 플레이어가 이전에 드러냈던 기술 또는 전문성의 양을 토대로 하여 최적의 난이도를 선택할 수도 있다. 다시 말해서, 비디오 게임은 플레이어가 지루해지거나 압도되지 않고 숙달할 수 있는 수준에서 도전받는 것을 금지한다(→ 보장한다). 비디오 게임 플레이어의 오락 경험을 위한 경쟁과 도전의 중요성이 흔히 거론되는데, 그것은 사람들이 흔히 오락에서 능력을 경험하기를 추구한다는 개념을 뒷받침하는 듯 보인다. 플레이어들의 오락 경험의 많은 사례들에서처럼 우리는 그들이 지루함을 피하고 얼마간의 도전을 발견할 수 있을 상황을, 그 상황이 자신들을 압도하거나 자신들에게 무능력하다는 기분이 들게 하지 않도록 확실히 하면서 얼마나 조심스럽게 준비하는지를 생각해 볼 수 있다.

정답풀이

190 오락은 비디오 게임의 사례에서 볼 수 있듯이 참가자가 지루해하거나 압도되지 않으면서 숙달할 수 있는 최적의 수준으로 설정되고 경쟁과 도전을 가미하여 참가자로 하여금 자신에게 능력이 있다는 것을 경험할 수 있도록 해준다는 내용이다. 따라서 글의 제목으로는 ③ '오락은 유능감을 끌어낸다'가 가장 적절하다.

191 앞에서 비디오 게임 자체가 플레이어에 맞는 최적의 난이도를 설정한다고 했는데, 이는 플레이어가 게임을 할 때 지루해지지도 압도되지도 않는 수준에서 도전받는 것을 확실히 하기 위함이므로, (c) forbids(금지하다)를 guarantees(보장하다) 정도의 어휘로 바꿔야 한다.

오답풀이

190 ① 자기 조절 자원으로서의 오락
② 오락의 가치: 스트레스 완화 장치
④ 게이머의 심리: 게임을 흥미롭게 만드는 것
⑤ 게임에서의 지나친 경쟁: 자신감에의 타격

191 ① 사람들이 오락에서 최적의 도전에 임하면서 가장 큰 유능감을 느낄 수 있다는 내용이 이어지므로 successfully(성공적으로)는 문맥상 적절하다.
② 플레이어가 이전에 드러냈던 기술 또는 전문성의 양을 토대로 하여 게임 자체가 최적의 난이도를 설정할 수도 있다는 내용이 이어지면서 게임의 수준이 플레이어에 따라 달라질 수 있음을 말하고 있으므로 dependent(좌우되는)는 문맥상 적절하다.
④ 경쟁과 도전은 자신의 능력을 구현하는 수단 또는 통로의 역할을 하는데, 이는 오락 경험에서 능력을 경험하기를 추구한다는 개념과 부합하므로 support(뒷받침하다)는 문맥상 적절하다.
⑤ 플레이어가 자신이 압도되지 않도록 오락의 수준을 조심스럽게 조정하는 것은 능력이 없다는 느낌을 피하기 위해서이므로 incompetent(무능력한)는 문맥상 적절하다.

구문풀이

13행 [The level of complexity, difficulty, and challenge of a given game] **varies** and **is** dependent on the settings [that are **either** {chosen by the player} **or** {automatically set by the game}].

: 첫 번째 [ ]가 주어이고, 동사는 varies와 is이다. 두 번째 [ ]는 the settings를 수식하는 주격 관계대명사절인데, 이 절에는 「either A or B」 구문이 쓰여 are에 이어지는 분사구인 두 개의 { }를 연결하면서 'A이거나 B이거나 (둘 중 하나)'라는 의미를 나타내고 있다.

21행 The importance of competition and challenge for a video game player's entertainment experience is often mentioned, [which seems to support **the notion** {that individuals often seek to experience competence in entertainment}].

: [ ]는 앞에 언급된 내용에 대한 추가 설명을 제시하는 역할을 하는 계속적 용법의 주격 관계대명사절이다. { }는 the notion의 구체적인 내용을 설명하는 동격의 명사절이다.

- optimal *a* 최적의, 최선의
- competent *a* 능력 있는
- appealing *a* 매력 있는
- complexity *n* 복잡성
- automatically *ad* 자동적으로
- demonstrate *v* 드러내다, 보여주다
- forbid *v* 금지하다
- overwhelm *v* 압도하다
- boredom *n* 지루함, 권태
- self-regulatory *a* 자기 조절의
- engaging *a* 매력적인

- competence *n* 능력, 역량
- profoundly *ad* 완전히, 깊게
- facilitator *n* 촉진 수단, 촉진제
- dependent on ~에 좌우되는
- expertise *n* 전문성, 전문 지식[기술]
- previously *ad* 이전에
- master *v* 숙달하다
- notion *n* 개념
- incompetent *a* 무능력한
- bring out ~을 끌어내다
- confidence *n* 믿음, 신뢰

3점 공략 모의고사 13회   본문 p.128

192 ①	193 ②	194 ⑤	195 ③	196 ①
197 ⑤	198 ③	199 ④		

192   답 ①

📖 현대적 기술로 뇌를 관찰함으로써 가능해진 무의식에 관한 연구

전문해석

우리는 모두 습관적인 사고와 행동을 만들어 내는, 운이 좋으면 덜 극단적인, 암묵적인 기준들을 가지고 있다. 우리의 경험과 행동은 항상 의식적인 사고에 뿌리를 두고 있는 것'처럼 보이며', 우리는 그 이면에 숨겨진 힘이 작용하고 있다는 것을 받아들이기 어렵다고 생각할 수 있다. 그러나 비록 그러한 힘들이 보이지 않을 수도 있지만, 그것들은 여전히 강력한 힘을 발휘한다. 과거에는 무의식에 대한 수많은 추측이 있었지만, 뇌는 블랙박스와 같아서, 그것의 작용은 우리가 이해할 수 없었다. **현재의 무의식에 대한 사고의 혁명은, 현대 도구들로, 우리가 뇌의 다양한 구조와 하부 구조들이 느낌과 감정을 생성하는 것을 지켜볼 수 있기 때문에 일어났다.** 우리는 개별 뉴런의 전기 출력을 측정할 수 있고, 한 사람의 생각을 형성하는 신경 활동을 지도로 만들 수 있다. 오늘날 과학자들은, 우리의 경험이 우리에게 어떻게 영향을 미쳤는지 우리에게 이야기하고 추측하는 것을 넘어설 수 있으며, 오늘날 그들은 정신적 외상을 주는 초기 경험으로부터 비롯되는 뇌의 변화를 정확히 집어내고, 그러한 경험들이 스트레스에 민감한 뇌 영역에 어떻게 물리적 변화를 일으키는지 이해할 수 있다.

정답풀이

과거에는 무의식에 대한 수많은 추측만 있었을 뿐 뇌를 볼 수 없기 때문에 그것의 작용을 이해할 수 없었지만, 현대 도구들에 의해 뇌 구조들의 활동이 관찰 가능해짐에 따라 무의식에 대한 사고의 혁명이 일어나 우리의 경험이 뇌의 변화에 어떻게 영향을 미치는지를 이해할 수 있게 되었다는 내용이다. 따라서 글의 주제로는 ① '현대의 기술에 의한 무의식에 대한 통찰'이 가장 적절하다.

오답풀이

① 충격적인 초기 경험이 뇌의 변화에 미치는 영향
  ↳ 현대 기술의 도움으로 이러한 영향을 이해할 수 있게 되었음을 설명하는 내용이다.

③ 느낌과 감정을 만들어 내는 두뇌의 복잡한 작용
  ↳ 두뇌의 복잡한 작용을 관찰할 수 있게 되어 무의식에 관한 연구가 가능해졌음을 설명하는 내용이다.

④ 우리의 사고와 행동에 영향을 미치는 기준틀

⑤ 의식과 무의식을 구별하는 어려움

구문풀이

3행 Our experiences and actions always *seem* to be rooted in conscious thought, and we can find **it** difficult [to accept {that there are hidden forces at work behind the scenes}].

: it은 형식상의 목적어이고 [ ]의 to부정사구가 find의 내용상의 목적이며, { }는 accept의 목적어 역할을 하는 명사절이다.

17행 Today scientists can go beyond [**talking** to us and **guessing** {how our experiences affected us}]; today they **can** actually **pinpoint** the brain alterations [that result from traumatic early experiences] and **understand** [how such experiences cause physical changes in stress-sensitive brain regions].

: 첫 번째 [ ]는 전치사 beyond의 목적어 역할을 하는 동명사구로 talking과 guessing이 병렬구조를 이루며, 그 안의 { }는 talking과 guessing의 공통 목적어로 쓰인 명사절이다. 세미콜론(;) 다음에서 can에 이어지는 동사원형 pinpoint와 understand가 병

렬구조를 이루며, 두 번째 [ ]는 the brain alterations를 수식하는 주격 관계대명사절이고, 세 번째 [ ]는 understand의 목적어로 쓰인 명사절이다.

어휘풀이
- implicit *a* 암묵적인, 내재하는
- frame of reference 기준틀, 준거 기준
- extreme *a* 극단적인, 극도의
- habitual *a* 습관적인
- be rooted in ~에 뿌리를 두다
- conscious *a* 의식적인
- at work 작용하는
- behind the scene 이면에
- invisible *a* 눈에 보이지 않는
- exert a pull 힘[견인력]을 발휘하다
- speculation *n* 추측
- unconscious mind 무의식
- inaccessible *a* 접근하기 어려운
- revolution *n* 혁명
- come about 생겨나다
- substructure *n* 하부 구조
- generate *v* 발생시키다
- output *n* 출력, 산출
- neuron *n* 뉴런, 신경 단위
- pinpoint *v* 정확하게 집어내다
- alteration *n* 변화, 변경
- traumatic *a* 정신적 외상을 주는
- stress-sensitive *a* 스트레스에 민감한
- region *n* 영역
- intricate *a* 복잡한, 뒤얽힌
- distinguish *A* from *B* A를 B와 구별하다

193 답 ②

📖 의료 분야에서 손 세척이 표준 관행이 된 유래

전문해석
의료 분야에서는 19세기가 되어서야 비로소 손 세척이 표준 관행이 되었다. 헝가리의 의사 Ignaz Semmelweis는 Vienna 병원의 산부인과 병동에서 근무하는 동안 아기가 의사들에 의해 분만되었던 여성들이 아기가 조산사들에 의해 분만되었던 여성들이 그런 것보다 '산욕열'로 사망할 가능성이 상당히 더 높다는 것을 깨달았다. Semmelweis는 의사들에 의해 돌보아진 여성들의 그 형편없는 결과가 어떤 식으로든 의사들이 분만을 돕는 일과 병행하는 검시 작업과 관련이 있다는 가설을 가지고 자신의 산부인과 병동에서 적극적인 손 세척 방침을 실시했다. 이것은 '산욕열'로 인한 산모 사망률을 크게 감소시켰다. 이것에도 불구하고, 다른 사람들을 자신의 새로운 방식으로 전환시키려는 그의 강력한 캠페인은 거의 결실을 맺지 못했다. 그가 수천 명의 여성의 불필요한 죽음으로 본 것으로 인해 고통받으며 그는 점점 더 불안해졌고 결국 정신병원에서 사망했다. Semmelweis의 이론은 그가 사망하고 나서야 비로소 널리 받아들여졌는데, Louis Pasteur의 미생물 연구가 Semmelweis의 방책이 효과를 나타낼 수 있었던 이해 가능한 구조를 제공했을 때였다.

정답풀이
② **관계대명사 which**: 뒤에 완전한 구조의 절이 이어지므로 관계대명사 which는 적절하지 않다. 문맥상 the hypothesis와 동격을 이루는 명사절을 이끄는 접속사 that으로 고쳐야 한다.

오답풀이
① **접속사 that**: Hungarian physician Ignaz Semmelweis가 주어, realized가 동사이다. while ~ Hospital은 부사구이며 that 이하가 realized의 목적어로 쓰인 명사절로 접속사 that은 어법상 적절하다.
③ **to부정사**: to convert는 앞의 명사구 his forceful campaign을 수식하는 형용사적 용법의 to부정사로 적절하게 쓰였다.
④ **분사구문의 태**: 의미상의 주어인 he가 고통을 받는 대상이므로 과거분사 Pained를 쓴 것은 어법상 적절하다.
⑤ **동사의 태**: when이 이끄는 부사절에서 주어 Louis Pasteur's work with microorganisms에 이어지는 동사인데 뒤에 목적어 an understandable mechanism이 있으므로 능동형 provided를 쓴 것은 어법상 적절하다.

구문풀이
8행 Semmelweis instituted an aggressive policy of hand washing

---

on his maternity ward with **the hypothesis** [that the poor outcomes of the women {attended by doctors} were somehow related to the autopsies {that doctors performed alongside their obstetric work}].

: [ ]는 the hypothesis의 내용을 설명하는 동격의 명사절이다. 첫 번째 { }는 the women을 수식하는 과거분사구이고, 두 번째 { }는 the autopsies를 수식하는 목적격 관계대명사절이다.

어휘풀이
- maternity ward 산부인과 병동
- deliver *v* 분만시키다
- significantly *ad* 상당히
- childbed fever 산욕열
- institute *v* 실시하다
- aggressive *a* 공격적인
- hypothesis *n* 가설
- attend *v* 돌보다
- convert *v* 전환시키다
- microorganism *n* 미생물
- mechanism *n* 구조, 기제
- tactics *n* 방책

194 답 ⑤

📖 민주주의적 과정에 대한 환멸의 증가

전문해석
Anthony Giddens는 민주주의의 역설을 언급하는데, 그것은 민주주의가 전 세계적으로 확산되고 있지만 동시에 성숙한 민주주의에서 사람들은 민주적인 과정에 점점 더 환멸을 느끼게 되고 있다는 것이다. 이것은 결국 더 적은 사람들이 투표하러 나오고 정치인에 대한 신뢰가 낮다는 것을 의미했다. Giddens는 민주주의에 대한 관심 부족은 부분적으로 세계화의 영향 때문임을 보여준다. 민족 국가 차원에서 민주주의는 증가한 생태적 위험, 경제의 세계화, 그리고 기술적 변화와 같은 세계적인 변화에 대해 제한된 영향을 미친다. 그래서 개인들은 국가적 정치에 참여해서 바꿀 수 있는 게 거의 없다고 느낀다. 이와 대조적으로 전통적인 민주적 과정에 대한 대중의 불신은 '단일 사안' 정치에 관여하는 집단의 증가로 이어졌다. 게다가 세계화 과정은 민족 국가들이 점점 더 일방적인 결정을 할 수 없게 하는 그러한 방식으로 민족 국가에 영향을 미치고 있고 그것은 결국 개인은 나라의 정부가 내리는 결정에 대한 통제력이 거의 없다는 견해에 이의를 제기한다(→ 견해를 강화한다).

정답풀이
⑤ 세계화는 민족 국가가 일방적인 결정을 내릴 수 없게 하는 방식으로 영향을 미친다고 했으므로, 같은 맥락으로 논리가 연결되려면 정부가 내리는 결정에 대해서 개인은 통제력이 거의 없다는 견해가 '강화된다'는 문맥이 자연스럽다. 따라서 challenges(이의를 제기하다)를 enhances(강화하다) 정도의 어휘로 바꿔야 한다.

오답풀이
① 민주주의에 대한 역설을 설명하고 있으므로, 민주주의에 대한 모순적 상황이 나와야 한다. 따라서 민주주의가 전 세계로 확산되면서 동시에 민주주의가 성숙한 나라에서 민주주의적 과정에 대해 '환멸을 느낀다(disillusioned)'는 문맥은 적절하다.
② 더 적은 사람들이 투표하러 나온다는 내용으로 보아 민주주의에 대한 관심이 '부족하다(lack)'는 문맥은 적절하다.
③ 사람들이 국가적 정치에 참여해서 바꿀 수 있는 게 거의 없다고 느끼는 이유에 해당하므로 세계적인 변화에 대해 민족 국가 차원의 민주주의의 영향력이 '제한되어 있다(limited)'는 문맥은 적절하다.
④ 개인들이 정치에 참여해도 바꿀 수 없다는 것을 느꼈다는 앞 내용과 In contrast로 연결되므로 이러한 불신이 단일 사안에 관련된 집단 정치의 '증가(increase)'로 이어졌다는 문맥은 적절하다.

1행 Anthony Giddens refers to the paradox of democracy [which is {that (democracy is spreading throughout the world), yet at the same time (people in mature democracies are becoming increasingly disillusioned with democratic processes)}].

: [ ]는 the paradox of democracy를 수식하는 주격 관계대명사절이고, 그 안의 { }는 주격보어로 쓰인 명사절로, ( )로 표시된 두 개의 절이 yet으로 연결되어 있다.

17행 Moreover, the globalization process is affecting nation-states in such a way [that **they** are increasingly unable to make unilateral decisions], [which in turn enhances **the view** {that individuals have little control over decisions (made by national governments)}].

: 첫 번째 [ ]는 a way를 수식하는 관계부사절이고, they는 nation-states를 가리킨다. 두 번째 [ ]는 앞 절의 내용을 부연 설명하는 계속적 용법의 주격 관계대명사절이고, 그 안의 { }는 the view와 동격 관계의 명사절이며, ( )는 decisions를 수식하는 과거분사구이다.

어휘풀이
- refer to ~을 언급하다
- mature *a* 성숙한
- in turn 결국
- globalization *n* 세계화
- affect *v* 영향을 미치다
- paradox *n* 역설
- disillusion *v* 환멸을 느끼게 하다
- politician *n* 정치인
- ecological *a* 생태의

195 답 ③

📖 기업의 성공을 이끄는 경영자와 직원 사이의 신뢰

전문해석
고객을 중심에 두는 것으로 유명한 회사인 사우스웨스트 항공사는 방침상 고객이 언제나 옳다고는 믿지 않는다. 사우스웨스트 항공사는 그들의 직원을 함부로 대하는 고객들을 용인하지 않을 것이다. 그들은 그런 고객들이 다른 항공사를 이용하기를 원할 것이다. 국내 최고의 고객 서비스를 제공하는 회사들 중 하나가 고객들보다 직원들에게 초점을 맞추는 것은 약간 아이러니하다. 신조가 아닌, 경영자와 직원들 사이의 신뢰는 최고의 고객 서비스를 만들어 내는 것이다. 그렇다면 그 문화의 가치와 신념을 공유하기 위해서 그들이 일하는 문화를 신뢰하는 것은 전제 조건이다. 그것이 없으면, 예를 들어 그 직원은 그저 (조직에) 잘 맞지 않게 되며 더 큰 이익에 대한 고려 없이 자기 이득을 위해서만 일하기가 쉽다. 하지만 조직 내부에 있는 사람들이 조직에 잘 맞으면, 탐구하고, 투자하고, 혁신하고, 발전하고, 더 중요하게는 계속해서 그렇게 하기 위해서 '한층 더 노력하는' 기회가 극적으로 증가한다. 상호 신뢰를 가지고서만이 위대한 조직이 될 수 있다.

정답풀이
고객이 항상 옳다고는 믿지 않으며 직원에게 함부로 대하는 고객을 용인하지 않는다는 내용을 통해서 고객 중심의 서비스를 지향하는 사우스웨스트 항공사가 아이러니하게도 직원을 고객보다 우선시한다는 것을 추론할 수 있다. 따라서 빈칸에 들어갈 말로 가장 적절한 것은 ③ '고객들보다 직원들에게 초점을 맞추는'이다.

오답풀이
① 고객들에게 신경을 쓰지 않는
 └ 직원과의 신뢰를 중시하여 직원에게 함부로 하는 고객들을 용인하지 않는다는 것이지 고객에게 신경을 쓰지 않는다는 것은 아니므로 오답!
② 회사 이익보다 고객 신뢰를 더 중시하는
④ 고객 서비스를 직원들에게만 의존하는
⑤ 개인의 가치보다 조직의 가치를 우선시하는

15행 But if those inside the organization are a good fit, / [the opportunity {to "go the extra mile}," {**to explore**, **to invest**, **to innovate**, **to advance** and, more importantly, **to do so** again and again and again}], **increases** dramatically.

: [ ]는 주절의 주어이고, 동사는 increases이다. 첫 번째 { }는 the opportunity를 수식하는 형용사적 용법의 to부정사구이고, 두 번째 { }는 부사적 용법(목적)의 to부정사구로 5개의 to부정사(구)가 and로 병렬 연결되어 있다.

어휘풀이
- renowned for ~으로 유명한
- abuse *v* 폭언을 하다, 학대하다
- irony *n* 아이러니, 역설적인 점
- fit *n* (서로) 잘 맞음
- go the extra mile 한층 더 노력하다, 특별히 애를 쓰다
- innovate *v* 혁신하다
- solely *ad* 오로지
- tolerate *v* 참다, 용인하다
- subtle *a* 미세한, 감지하기 힘든
- prerequisite *n* 전제[필수] 조건
- consideration *n* 고려
- mutual *a* 상호 간의, 서로의
- prioritize *v* 우선시하다

196 답 ①

📖 직원에게 회사의 상황을 알려야 하는 이유

전문해석
만약 내가 재고 담당 직원이고 여러분이 회사의 이익을 위해 내가 나의 지식을 이용하기를 원한다면, 여러분은 내가 그것이 무엇을 의미하는지 정확하게 이해하도록 도울 필요가 있다. 예를 들어, 우리가 재정적으로 어려움을 겪고 있다는 것을 내가 모른다면, 나는 재고 관리가 더 저렴하고 더 간단하도록 굳이 그것을 재설계하려고 애쓰지 않을지도 모른다. 물론, 나는 모든 윗사람들의 권고에 근거하여 항상 내 업무를 향상시켜야 한다는 것을 알지만, 솔직히 말해서 나는 재고 담당 업무 이외의 삶도 갖고 있다. 나는 관심을 기울여야 할 설득력 있는 이유가 있어야 그렇게 할 따름이다. 지식과 혁신은 명령될 수 없고 권유될 수 있을 뿐이다. 모든 관리자들의 어려운 과제는 그 권유를 매우 거부할 수 없게 만들어서 모두가 응하도록 하는 것이다. 관심을 기울이지 않을 수 없는 그러한 권유의 일부는 근로자가 회사에서 무슨 일이 일어나고 있는지 알도록 분명히 하는 것이다. 이것은 흔히 지금까지 주로 관리자의 분야였던 정보(예를 들면, 재정적인 그리고 여타의 비밀 정보)를 공개하는 것과 사람들이 그것이 어떻게 자신들의 업무에 관련되는지 이해하도록 돕는 것을 수반한다.

정답풀이
직원들이 자신들의 지식을 이용하고 혁신하기를 원한다면 일상적인 권고 정도로는 충분하지 않고, 회사의 실제적인 상황에 대한 정보를 공개하여 직원이 담당 업무 외에도 관심을 기울이고 그 상황과 자신의 업무와의 관련성을 이해하게 해야 한다는 것을 재고 담당 직원을 예로 들어서 설명하고 있다. 따라서 빈칸에 들어갈 말로 가장 적절한 것은 ① '회사에서 무슨 일이 일어나고 있는지'이다.

오답풀이
② 그들에게 어떤 전문 분야가 필요한지
 └ 글의 핵심은 직원에게 회사 상황에 대한 정보를 공개해서 그것에 대한 이해를 바탕으로 자신의 지식을 이용하도록 유도하라는 것이므로 오답!
③ 얻을 수 있는 재정적 보상이 무엇인지
④ 무엇이 프로젝트 관리에서 수용할만한 위험인지
⑤ 비판적인 사고가 회사의 미래에 얼마나 중요한지

16행 This often entails [**releasing** information {that has hitherto been largely management's province (e.g., financial and other confidential information)}] and [**helping** people to understand {how it relates to their jobs}].

: 두 개의 [ ]는 문장의 동사 entails의 목적어 역할을 하는 동명사구로 and로 병렬 연결되어 있다. 첫 번째 [ ] 안의 { }는 information을 수식하는 주격 관계대명사절이다. 두 번째 [ ] 안의 { }는 understand의 목적어 역할을 하는 명사절이다.

어휘풀이

- stock clerk 재고 담당 직원
- bother *v* 일부러 ~하다
- compelling *a* 관심을 기울이지 않을 수 없는, 설득력 있는
- invitation *n* 제안, 권유
- entail *v* 수반하다
- province *n* 분야
- expertise *n* 전문 지식
- financially *ad* 재정적으로
- inventory control 재고 관리
- irresistible *a* 거부[저항]할 수 없는
- hitherto *ad* 지금까지
- confidential *a* 비밀의
- critical *a* 비판적인

197 답 ⑤

📖 식사하는 속도를 늦추어 과식을 하지 않는 방법

전문해석

식사를 하는 속도를 천천히 느긋하게 유지하려고 애써라. 처리를 위해서 여러분의 위가 '배가 부르다'라는 메시지를 뇌에 전달하는 데는 약 20분이 걸린다. (C) 여러분이 충분히 먹었으며 포크를 내려놓을 시간이라는 메시지를 여러분의 뇌가 손으로 보내는 데에 또 약간의 시간이 걸린다. 여러분의 가족이 전체 식사를 딱 5분 만에 먹는 것을 좋아하는 빨리 먹는 사람들로 이루어져 있다면, 그들은 아마도 몸이 필요로 하는 것보다 결국 더 많은 양을 먹게 될 것이다. (B) 그들의 뇌가 배가 부르다는 신호를 받기 전에, 그들은 아마도 두 그릇째의 음식을 먹으려고 손을 뻗고 있을 것이다. 자녀들이 먹는 동안 속도를 늦추는 데 도움이 필요하다면, 섬유질이 풍부한 음식을 많이 제공하라. (A) 그런 음식들은 더 많이 씹어야 하기 때문에, 섬유질이 적은 음식보다 먹는 데 시간이 더 오래 걸린다. 자녀들이 먹는 속도를 늦추면, 그들은 자신이 먹고 있는 음식에 더 충분히 집중할 수 있을 것이다. 이러한 더 높은 수준의 자각은 끼니때마다 그들이 덜 먹도록 도움을 줄 것이다.

정답풀이

배가 부르다는 메시지를 위가 두뇌에 전달하는 데 20분이 걸린다는 주어진 글 다음에는, '충분히 먹었으니 포크를 내려놓아야 한다'는 메시지를 두뇌가 손에 전달하는 데 약간의 시간이 더 걸린다는 내용의 (C)가 이어져야 한다. 이어서 (C)의 fast eaters를 their로 지칭하며, 빨리 먹는 사람들의 먹는 속도를 늦추려면 섬유질이 풍부한 음식을 많이 제공해야 한다는 내용의 (B)가 오고, (B)의 fiber-rich foods를 they로 가리키며, 이러한 음식은 먹는 데 시간이 더 걸린다고 설명하는 (A)가 마지막에 오는 순서가 가장 적절하다. 따라서 적절한 글의 순서는 ⑤ (C)-(B)-(A)이다.

구문풀이

2행 **It takes** about twenty minutes **for** your stomach **to communicate** the "I'm full" message to your brain for processing.

: 「It takes+시간+for *A*+to부정사: *A*가 ~하는 데 …의 시간이 걸리다」 구문이 쓰였다.

17행 If you have a family of fast eaters [who like to eat the entire meal in five minutes flat], / they'll probably **end up eating** more than their bodies need.

: [ ]는 fast eaters를 수식하는 주격 관계대명사절이다. 주절에서 「end up *doing*」은 '결국 ~하게 되다'의 의미이다.

어휘풀이

- pace *n* 속도
- fiber *n* 섬유질
- chew *v* 씹다
- awareness *n* 인식, 자각

- seconds *n* 한 그릇 더, 두 그릇째
- flat *ad* (수와 함께) 꼭, 정확히
- entire *a* 전체의, 완전한

198 답 ③

📖 편견과 오류로 가득 찬 이야기들을 없애는 과학

전문해석

여러분 이전에 세상을 살았던 사람들은 여러분이 경험하는 것을 이해하고 설명하는 자연스러운 방식이 형편없기 때문에 과학을 발명했다. 증거가 없을 때, 모든 가정은 기본적으로 같다. 여러분은 결과보다는 원인, 소음 속의 신호, 무작위 속의 패턴을 보는 것을 선호한다. 여러분은 쉽게 이해할 수 있는 이야기를 선호하며, 그리하여 복잡한 문제들이 쉬워질 수 있도록 삶의 모든 것을 이야기로 바꾼다. 과학자들은 이야기를 없애려고, 즉 그것을 증발시켜버리고 가공하지 않은 사실만 남기려고 노력한다. 그러한 자료는 무방비로 노출된 상태로 있어서 매번 새로운 방문자에 의해 심사숙고되어 재조정될 수 있다. 과학자들과 일반인들은 그 자료를 이용하여 새로운 이야기들을 만들어 낼 것이고, 그들이 논쟁을 하겠지만 그 자료는 조금도 움직이지 않을 것이다. 그것들은 100년 이상이 지나도 타당하지 않을 수도 있지만, **과학적인 방법 덕분에 편견과 오류로 가득 찬 그 이야기들은 사실과 충돌해 역사 속으로 물러날 것이다.**

정답풀이

주어진 문장의 the narrative는 ③ 앞 문장의 a narrative를 지칭하며, ③ 다음에 오는 문장의 Those data는 주어진 문장의 the raw facts를 가리키므로 주어진 문장은 ③에 들어가는 것이 가장 적절하다.

구문풀이

3행 The people [who came before you] **invented** science / **because** your natural way of **understanding** and **explaining** [what you experience] is terrible.

: 「주절+이유의 부사절」로 이루어진 문장으로 주절에서 핵심 주어는 The people이고, 동사는 invented이다. 첫 번째 [ ]는 The people을 수식하는 주격 관계대명사절이고, 두 번째 [ ]는 병렬구조를 이루고 있는 understanding과 explaining의 공통 목적어이다.

어휘풀이

- narrative *n* 이야기, 서술
- randomness *n* 무작위성
- naked *a* 무방비 상태의, 벌거벗은
- reflect upon ~에 대해 숙고하다
- conjure up ~을 만들어 내다, ~을 꾸며 내다
- make sense 이해가 되다, 일리가 있다
- bias *n* 편견
- crash against ~와 충돌하다
- assumption *n* 가정
- complicated *a* 복잡한
- exposed *a* 노출된
- laypeople *n* 일반인
- fallacy *n* 오류
- recede *v* 물러나다, 멀어지다

199 답 ④

📖 지리적 고립으로 인한 섬 난쟁이 종의 진화

전문해석

2003년 동안 인도네시아 Flores Island의 Liang Bang 선사 시대 주거지에서의 발굴에서 완전히 다 자란 성인임에도 불구하고 신장이 단지 1미터에 지나지 않는 일곱 명의 유해가 나왔다. 이들은 새로운 종으로 명명되었는데, '호모 플로레시언시스'이다. 이 발견에 대한 한 가지 해석은 그 섬에서 발견된 석기 유물의 시대를 비춰보면 한 작은 집단의 '호모 에렉투스'가 약 80만 년 전에 가까운 거리의 물을 건너 Flores Island에 갔다는 것이다. 그 집단은 고립되었고 '호모'의 난쟁이 형태로 진

화했다. 이것은 대형 육상 포유류가 작은 섬에 고립될 때 일어나는 것으로 알려진 과정인데, 특히 포식자가 부재한 경우에 그렇다. 그리하여 난쟁이 코끼리, 하마, 사슴, 매머드의 유해가 전 세계의 섬에서 발견되어 왔다. 정확하다면, 이것은 난쟁이 인간의 유일한 발견이며, 우리의 속(호모)이 생리학적으로 얼마나 다양할 수 있는지를 보여준다. 아마도 몸의 크기만큼 주목할 만한 것은 그 유해의 얼마 안 된 지질 연대이다. 화석의 나이는 74,000년에서 18,000년 사이이며, 그중 후자는 구세계(유럽, 아시아, 아프리카)와 어쩌면 정말로 신세계(아메리카)의 다른 곳에 있는 현생인류의 범위 안에 잘 들어맞는다.

→ '호모' 속에서 생물학적 다양성의 새로운 범위를 보여주는 '호모 플로레시언시스'는 장기간의 지리적 고립의 결과로 작은 체격을 발달시켰을지도 모르며, 이 종은 현생인류와 공존했다고 추측된다.

정답풀이
호모 플로레시언시스는 지금까지 유일하게 발견된 난쟁이 종으로서 소규모의 호모 에렉투스 집단이 물을 건너 Flores Island로 이주하여 고립되면서 작은 체격을 발달시켰고 이 종은 현생인류와 동시대에 존재했다는 내용이다. 따라서 (A)에는 작은 체격을 발달시킨 원인을 나타내는 isolation(고립)이, (B)에는 현생인류와 같은 시기에 살았음을 나타내는 coexisted(공존하다)가 들어가는 것이 가장 적절하다.

구문풀이
[11행] This is a process [known to happen to any large terrestrial mammal {when isolated on small islands}, {especially if predators are absent}].

: [ ]는 a process를 수식하는 과거분사구이고, 그 안에 두 개의 { }는 각각 시간과 조건을 나타내는 부사절인데, 첫 번째 { }에서는 when 다음에 it is 정도가 생략된 것으로 이해할 수 있다.

어휘풀이
- excavation *n* 발굴
- designate *v* 명명하다
- in light of ~에 비추어, ~의 관점에서
- dwarf *n* 난쟁이
- predator *n* 포식자
- genus *n* (생물 분류상의) 속(屬)
- physique *n* 체격
- remains *n* 유해
- interpretation *n* 해석
- isolate *v* 고립시키다
- terrestrial *a* 육생의, 뭍의
- physiologically *ad* 생리학적으로
- speculate *v* 추측[짐작]하다

200 답 ③

📖 시합을 진행하면서 전략을 구체화하기

전문해석
축구에 혁명을 일으킨 전략인 '전원 공수형(攻守型) 축구'로 이끈 아이디어를 설명해 달라고 요청받았을 때, 네덜란드의 코치 Rinus Michels는 '시작할 때는 얻으려고 애쓸 목적에 관한 정확한 아이디어가 없다'고 주장했다. 그가 계속해서 설명하기를, 어떤 의미에서는 그저 몇 가지를 시도해 봄으로써 시작하고, 만약 관찰력이 뛰어나며 좋은 영향을 쉽게 받아들이고 상황이 전개됨에 따라 아이디어를 서로 연결시킬 수 있다면 좋은 전략은 분명해지기 시작한다. 유명한 오스트리아 축구 선수 Matthias Sindelar에 대한 Alfred Polgar의 설명보다 이 생각에 관한 더 나은 표현은 없었다. '어떤 면에서 그는 다리에 명석한 두뇌가 있었다 ... 그리고 그들이 달리고 있는 동안 많은 놀랍고 예상치 못한 일들이 그들에게 일어났다.' 우리에게 이런 수준의 예술성이 부족할 수도 있지만, 우리가 참여해 왔던 최선의 전략적 아이디어 중 많은 것들이 일단의 떠오르는 생각들을 화이트보드에 쓰고 있었을 때에만 생겨났다.

정답풀이
시합을 시작할 때는 목표 달성을 위한 정확한 아이디어가 없지만 몇 가지 시도를 해 보고 상황이 전개됨에 따라 아이디어들을 연결시키면서 좋은 전략을 찾게 된다는 내용의 글이다. 따라서 밑줄 친 부분이 의미하는 바로는 ③ '몇 가지 시도를 실행하면서 적절한 전략을 찾았다'가 가장 적절하다.

오답풀이
① 코치의 지시에 따라 경기를 했다
② 경기 내내 달릴 수 있는 신체 조건을 가졌다
④ 새로운 것을 배움으로써 자신의 신체뿐만 아니라 두뇌도 훈련시켰다
⑤ 경기의 맨 처음부터 자신의 몸과 마음을 조절했다

구문풀이
[14행] While we may lack this level of artistry, / [many of the best strategic ideas {we have been a part of}] have occurred only [as a group's emergent thoughts were whiteboarding].

: While은 '~이기는 하지만'이라는 뜻으로 양보 부사절을 이끈다. 첫 번째 [ ]가 주절의 주어이고, 그 안의 { }는 the best strategic ideas를 수식하는 관계절로 앞에 목적격 관계대명사가 생략되었으며, 주절의 동사는 have occurred이다. 두 번째 [ ]는 as가 이끄는 시간 부사절이다.

어휘풀이
- strategy *n* 전략
- strive after ~을 얻으려고 애쓰다
- observant *a* 관찰력이 뛰어난
- articulation *n* 표현
- remarkable *a* 놀랄 만한, 놀라운
- emergent *a* 떠오르는, 창발적인
- revolutionize *v* ~에 혁명을 일으키다
- go on to *do* 계속해서 ~하다
- unfold *v* 전개되다
- description *n* 설명, 묘사
- artistry *n* 예술가적 기교, 예술성
- whiteboard *v* 화이트보드에 쓰다

201 답 ②

📖 돈을 목표로 삼지 말고 일을 잘한 결과로 여기기

전문해석
슈퍼스타와 슈퍼맨은 돈을 좇지 않는다. **돈은 자본주의에서 득점이 기록되는 방법이고 그것은 돈을 추구되어야 할 목표가 아니라 일을 잘한 것의 결과로 만든다.** 돈을 벌기 위해 너무 열심히 애쓰는 것은 돈을 버는 데 역효과를 낳는다는 것을 입증할 것이다. 일어나는 일은 목표를 달성하는 데 매우 중요한 기본적인 것보다 목표에 초점을 두는 것이다. 두 영역 모두에서 추구하는 것이 획득한 것보다 훨씬 더 매력적이다. 이상하게 들리겠지만 사실이 그렇다! **목표에 초점을 두는 것은 모든 종류의 나쁜 결정과 이기적인 조치로 이어진다.** 사람들은 목표에 너무 매혹되어 즉각적인 만족과 빠른 획득을 추구하기 시작한다. 정말로 큰 획득은 그것이 영혼의 짝을 찾는 것이든 성공적인 직업을 찾는 것이든 시간과 돌봄이 필요하다. 빠른 성공과 즉각적인 성공에 빠진 사람들은 항상 최고의 성공을 운 덕분으로 돌리는 사람들이다. 명성과 부로 가는 여정은 길고 고된 것으로 대부분의 경우 20년 정도 걸린다. 빨리 부자가 되는 계획은 실패하게 되어 있으므로 그러한 함정에 걸리지 않도록 조심하라.

정답풀이
② **문장의 구조 파악**: 동명사구 주어 Focusing on the target에 이어지는 동사가 없는 상태이므로 준동사 leading을 본동사 leads로 고쳐야 한다.

오답풀이
① **지시대명사**: 여기서 that은 앞 절의 내용을 받는 지시대명사로 어법상 적절하게 쓰였다.
③ **접속사 whether**: 문맥상 '~이든지'라는 양보의 의미로 부사절을 이끄는 접속사 whether는 적절하게 쓰였다.
④ **분사의 태**: 수식을 받는 the ones가 최고의 성공을 운으로 돌리는 주체이므로 현재분사 attributing은 어법상 적절하다.
⑤ **주어와 동사의 수 일치**: 핵심 주어는 The trek이므로 단수형 동사 is는 어법상 적절하다.

구문풀이
[1행] Money is the way [score is kept in capitalism] / and **that** makes **it** a result of doing well, not a goal [that should be pursued].

: 두 개의 절이 and로 연결된 구조의 문장이며, 첫 번째 [ ]는 the way를 수식하는 관계부사절이다. and 다음의 that은 앞 절 Money ~ capitalism의 내용을 가리키고, it은 money를 대신하는 대명사이다. 두 번째 [ ]는 a goal을 수식하는 주격 관계대명사절이다.

어휘풀이
- capitalism *n* 자본주의
- counterproductive *a* 의도와는 반대되는, 역효과를 낳는
- fundamental *n* 기본, 근본
- arena *n* 활동 영역
- catch *n* 포획(물), 획득(물)
- self-serving *a* 이기적인, 자기 잇속만 차리는
- enamor *v* ~의 마음을 사로잡다
- attribute *A* to *B* A를 B의 덕분으로 돌리다
- trek *n* 여정
- beware *v* 조심하다
- pursue *v* 추구하다
- critical *a* 중요한
- tempting *a* 매력[유혹]적인
- weird *a* 이상한
- nurturing *n* 돌봄, 양육
- be destined for ~하게 되어 있다

202 답 ②

📖 **늘 보거나 들어 왔던 것을 선호하는 심리**

전문해석
진정, 사람들은 보통 그들이 더불어 성장한 종류의 그림을 좋아한다. 예를 들면, 코넬 대학교 학생들은 코넬 대학교 도서관에 소장된 책들에 가장 빈번히 묘사된 인상파 그림들을 선호했다. 그림의 묘사가 나타나는 빈도가 학생들이 평생 동안에 그 그림을 보았던 빈도의 대용물로 간주되었다. 더 빈번한 그림에 대한 동일한 선호가 더 나이가 많은 성인들에게서는 발견되었지만 아이들에게서는 발견되지 않았는데, 그들은 명백히 학생들이나 성인들만큼 많은 그림을 본 적이 없다. 비슷한 맥락에서, **사람들은 그들이 더불어 성장한 종류의 음악을 좋아한다.** 사회학자 Pierre Bourdieu는 서로 다른 사회 계층은 가정에서 서로 다른 종류의 음악을 접하며 성장하기 때문에 음악에 대한 기호가 다르다고 말했다. **사람들이 좋아하고 아름답다고 생각하는 것은 자신들이 전에 접해 보았던 것**에 달려 있다.

정답풀이
사람들은 성장하면서 많이 접해 보았던 종류의 그림이나 음악을 선호하는 경향이 있다는 내용을 두 가지 근거를 들어 설명하고 있는 글이며, 빈칸에는 글 전체의 내용을 요약하는 어구가 들어가면 된다. 따라서 빈칸에는 ② '그들이 전에 접해 보았던 것'이 들어가는 것이 가장 적절하다.

오답풀이
① 그들이 정신적으로 성장하도록 돕는 것
③ 그들이 교육받아 온 것
④ 그들에게 강한 인상을 남긴 것
⑤ 예술적으로 가치가 있다고 여겨지는 것

구문풀이
[5행] Frequency [with which depictions of paintings appeared] **was taken as** a substitute for the frequency [with which students had seen the painting in their lifetime].

: 두 개의 [ ]는 각각 Frequency와 the frequency를 수식하는 관계절이다. 「take *A* as *B*: A를 B로 여기다」 구문이 수동태로 전환되어 「*A* is taken as *B*」 형태가 되었다.

어휘풀이
- Impressionist *a* 인상파(화가)의
- depict *v* 묘사하다 (*n* depiction)
- substitute *n* 대용물
- observe *v* ~라고 말하다
- frequently *ad* 빈번히
- frequency *n* 빈도
- in a similar vein 비슷한 맥락에서

203 답 ①

📖 **외국어 학습에 대해 증가하는 관심**

전문해석
세계 공용어가 성인들이 다른 언어를 배울 동기를 없앨까? 공통된 관찰에 따르면, 모든 사람이 영어를 말하는 것으로 그리고 그렇지 않다면 그것은 어찌됐든 현지인들의 잘못이라고 간주하며 세계를 여행하는 전형적인 영국인 또는 미국인 관광객에게서 언어적 만족의 분명한 징후가 이미 나타나고 있다. **그러나 오늘날 영어를 사용하는 지역 사회 내에서 전통적인 단일 언어에 대한 편견으로부터 깨고 나올 필요성에 대한 인식이 커지고 있는 조짐들이 있다.** 경제적으로 어려운 시대에 수출을 늘리고 외국 투자를 유치하는 것에 있어서의 성공은 미묘한 요소들에 달려 있으며, 한 나라의 잠재적인 외국 파트너가 사용하는 언어에 대한 민감성은 특히 영향력이 있는 것으로 알려져 있다. 적어도 사업이나 산업의 수준에서 많은 회사들은 이러한 방향에서 새로운 노력을 하기 시작했다. 그러나 일반 여행자들의 수준에서도, **다른 문화에 대한 존중이 더해지고 언어 학습에 참여하고자 하는 보다 큰 자발성의 조짐들이 있다.** 언어에 대한 태도는 항상 변화하고 있으며, 점점 더 많은 사람들이 매우 기쁘게도 그들이 **외국어를 습득하는 것**에 있어 결코 서툴지 않다는 것을 알아가고 있다.

정답풀이
단일 언어를 고집하는 것에서 깨고 나올 필요성, 외국의 경제 파트너가 사용하는 언어에 대한 민감성, 언어 학습에 대한 더 커진 자발성 등의 단서를 통해 외국어 학습에 대한 관심이 더욱 커지고 있는 경향에 대해 이야기하는 글임을 알 수 있다. 따라서 빈칸에는 ① '외국어를 습득하는 것'이 들어가는 것이 가장

적절하다.

오답풀이
오답풀이
② 2개 국어를 사용하는 소수민족에 대한 편견을 없애는 것
③ 세계 공용어로서 영어의 존재감을 높이는 것
④ 통역 소프트웨어가 있는 기기의 도움을 받아 여행하는 것
⑤ 외국 투자자들을 유치하고 경제 성장을 발전시키는 것

구문풀이

10행 In economically hard times, success [in boosting exports and attracting foreign investment] can depend on subtle factors, / and sensitivity [to the language {spoken by a country's potential foreign partners}] is known to be particularly influential.

: 두 개의 [ ]는 각각 success와 sensitivity를 수식하는 전치사구이고, { }는 the language를 수식하는 과거분사구이다.

20행 Language attitudes are changing all the time, / and more and more are discovering, **to their great delight**, [that they are not at all bad at picking up a foreign language].

: and 다음의 절에서 [ ]는 discovering의 목적어로 쓰인 명사절이다. 「to one's+감정 명사」는 '~가 …하게도'라는 의미를 갖는다.

어휘풀이
- eliminate *v* 없애다, 제거하다
- awareness *n* 인식, 인지
- monolingual *a* 단일어를 사용하는
- boost *v* 신장시키다, 늘리다
- sensitivity *n* 민감성, 감성
- readiness *n* 준비가 됨, 자발성
- pick up ~을 익히다, ~을 귀동냥하다
- minority *n* 소수민족, 소수집단
- linguistic *a* 언어의, 언어적인
- break away from ~에서 탈피하다
- bias *n* 편향, 편견
- subtle *a* 미묘한
- influential *a* 영향력 있는, 유력한
- engage in ~에 참여하다
- bilingual *a* 2개 국어를 사용하는
- foster *v* 발전시키다, 육성하다

204 답 ④

📖 미디어에 의해 만들어지고 공유되는 감정적 반응

전문해석
우리가 좋아하든 그렇지 않든, 우리가 보는 모든 미디어 메시지는 우리의 현실을 구성한다. 그것들은 우리가 주변의 세계를 보고 느끼는 데 도움을 준다. 사회학자들은 오랫동안 뉴스 매체가 사회적 의견을 반영할 뿐만 아니라 그것을 또한 구성할 수 있음을 인정해 왔다. (C) 감정에 대해서도 마찬가지인데, 미디어는 관객에게 감정적인 공동체로서 그들에게 무엇이 중요할지를 알려 줄 수 있으며, 상황이나 자극에 어떻게 감정적으로 반응해야 하는지를 제안할 수도 있다. 공포를 심어 주는 것에서 희망을 불러일으키는 것까지 미디어는 감정적인 반응을 만들어 낸다. (A) 그러나 저자 또는 편집자의 의도와 받아들이는 것 사이에는 직접적인 상관관계가 있는 것은 결코 아니다. 감정적인 반응은 개인적이지만, 동시에 개별적인 반응은 공유된 문화적 그리고 사회적 맥락에 의해 형성된다. (B) 결과적으로, 메시지는 때때로 공유된 관심사를 이용하여 감정의 공유된 의식을 촉진하고, 소셜미디어 덕분에 그러한 메시지가 결국 '공유되어' 유포될 수 있다.

정답풀이
미디어가 사회적 의견을 반영할 뿐만 아니라 그것을 구성할 수 있다는 내용의 주어진 글 다음에는, 감정도 마찬가지라고 하며(The same goes for emotions) 미디어가 어떻게 감정적으로 반응해야 할지를 제안할 수 있다고 하는 (C)가 온다. 이어서 However로 시작하며 저자 또는 편집자의 의도와 그것을 받아들이는 것 사이에 직접적인 상관관계가 있는 것은 아니고, 감정적

반응이 개인적인 것을 넘어서 공유된 문화적, 사회적 맥락에 의해 형성된다고 하는 (A)가 오고, (A)에 대한 결과로 미디어의 메시지가 감정의 공유된 의식을 촉진하고 소셜 미디어를 통해 공유되어 유포된다는 내용의 (B)가 마지막에 오는 순서가 가장 적절하다. 따라서 적절한 글의 순서는 ④ (C)-(A)-(B)이다.

구문풀이

12행 As a result, messages can sometimes tap into a shared concern, [promoting a shared sense of feeling] / and, thanks to social media, such messages can be in turn 'shared,' [becoming viral].

: 두 개의 절이 and로 연결된 구조이며, 두 개의 [ ]는 분사구문이다.

어휘풀이
- constitutive *a* 구성하는
- authorial *a* 저자의
- reception *n* 받아들임, 수용, 이해
- tap into ~에 다가가다, ~을 이용하다
- viral *a* 유포되는, 퍼지는
- instill *v* 심어주다, 주입시키다
- inspire *v* (감정 등을) 고취시키다[불러일으키다]
- correlation *n* 상관관계
- editorial *a* 편집자의
- simultaneously *ad* 동시에
- in turn 차례로, 결국
- stimulus *n* 자극 (*pl.* stimuli)

205 답 ③

📖 브랜드의 성공을 위한 부가 가치 제공

전문해석
장기적으로 성공하기 위해서 브랜드는 기본 제품 특성 이상의 부가 가치를 제공해야 한다. 서비스 분야에서 다른 모든 요소가 동일할 때, 이것은 은행에서 환전할 때 이름을 불러주는 것처럼 간단하다. 기업 대 기업 시장에서 이것은 브랜드를 위험이 없는 구매로 제시하는 빈틈없는 영업 엔지니어에 의해 전달될 수 있다. 이것은 테스트의 철저함, 조직의 신뢰성, 업계 표준 준수, 그리고 다른 사용자의 사례 이력 등을 통해서 달성될 수 있다. 부가 가치는 제조사나 유통사뿐만 아니라 고객과 관련이 있어야 한다는 것을 깨닫는 것이 가장 중요하다. 안전벨트를 착용하지 않았을 때 '컴퓨터 언어'를 방출하는 전자 회로의 부가 가치가 자신의 브랜드에 있다고 발표한 자동차 제조사들은 이 소위 말하는 혜택을 고객들이 대단히 싫어한다는 것을 발견하는 데 오래 걸리지 않았다. 양질의 서비스를 홍보하는 호텔은 단순히 객실 주변에 홍보물을 배치하는 대신 특별한 심야 음식 메뉴를 제공함으로써 단골 고객을 확보할 것이다.

정답풀이
주어진 문장의 This는 철저한 테스트, 업계 표준 준수, 사용자 이력 등을 통해서 달성된다고 했으므로, 문맥상 ③ 앞 문장에서 언급한 기업 대 기업 거래에서 영업 엔지니어가 '브랜드를 위험이 없는 구매로 제시하는(presenting the brand as a no-risk purchase)' 것을 지칭하는 것이 적절하다. 따라서 주어진 문장이 들어갈 위치로 가장 적절한 곳은 ③이다. ③ 뒤에는 고객 차원의 부가 가치의 제공에 대한 설명이 논리적 공백 없이 이어지고 있다.

구문풀이

12행 It is most important [to realise {that the added values must be relevant (to the customer) and **not just** (to the manufacturer or distributor)}].

: It은 형식상의 주어이고, [ ]의 to부정사구가 내용상의 주어이다. { }는 realise의 목적어로 쓰인 명사절이고, 그 안에 and로 연결된 두 개의 ( )는 relevant에 이어지는 전치사구이며, not just는 '~뿐만 아니라'의 의미이다.

15행 Car manufacturers [who announced {that their brands had the added value of electronic circuits (emitting 'computer speak'

<when seat belts were not worn>)}] **didn't take** long to discover [that this so-called benefit was intensely disliked by customers].

: 문장의 핵심 주어는 Car manufactures이고 문장의 동사는 didn't take이다. 첫 번째 [ ]는 Car manufacturers를 수식하는 주격 관계대명사절이며, 그 안의 { }는 announced의 목적어로 쓰인 명사절이고, ( )는 electronic circuits를 수식하는 현재분사구이며, < >는 때를 나타내는 부사절이다. 두 번째 [ ]는 discover의 목적어로 쓰인 명사절이다.

어휘풀이

- accomplish *v* 달성하다, 성취하다
- credibility *n* 신뢰성
- industry standard 업계 표준
- added value 부가 가치
- sector *n* 분야
- address ~ by name ~을 이름으로 부르다
- foreign exchange 외국환 거래
- relevant *a* 관련 있는
- distributor *n* 유통 회사, 배급사
- electronic circuit 전자 회로
- intensely *ad* 대단히, 몹시
- loyal customer 단골 고객
- thoroughness *n* 철저함
- compliance *n* 준수, 따름, 순종
- case history 사례 이력
- characteristic *n* 특성
- convey *v* 전달하다
- manufacturer *n* 제조사
- announce *v* 발표하다, 공표하다
- emit *v* 방출하다
- promote *v* 홍보하다
- promotional literature 홍보물

206~207 답 ③ / ③

📖 유전적 요인과 환경적 요인에 의해 영향을 받는 동물과 인간

전문해석

새들에 관한 연구는 언어적 행동과 비언어적 행동에 관한 유전–환경 문제에 대한 분명한 답을 제공한다. 유럽의 수컷 울새는 번식기에 자신의 영역에 들어오는 낯선 울새들을 공격한다. 박제된 모델을 사용한 연구는 붉은색의 가슴만으로도 이러한 공격 기제를 유발한다는 것을 보여주었다. 그러나 둥지를 공유하고 있는 암컷 울새도 또한 붉은색의 가슴을 가지고 있지만 공격받지 않는다. 따라서 타고난 것으로 믿어지는 이러한 공격적 행동은 환경 내에서의 특정한 조건이나 상황에 의해 수정된다. 또 다른 예로, 어떤 새들은 본능적으로 다른 새가 노래하는 것을 들은 적이 없어도 자신들의 종에게 공통되는 노래를 부른다. 이러한 새들은 자신들의 특정한 집단의 노래를 듣고 나서 지역의 방언을 반영하는 멜로디의 변형을 만들어 낼 수 있다. 성숙한 노래에의 노출 없이는 어린 새들의 노래는 완전한(→ 불완전한) 상태로 남는다는 것 역시 주목되어 왔다. 그리고 어떤 새가 기본적인 노래를 갖고 태어났을 때조차도, 그것은 지저귐으로 누구를 불러야 하는지, 어떤 상황에서인지 그리고 다른 새들로부터 오는 신호를 어떻게 알아봐야 하는지를 배워야만 할 수도 있다. 인간 행동의 선천적인 요소들 중 많은 것이 유사하게 수정된다. 그것은 우리 인간들의, 음성 언어에 대한 성향 또는 음성 언어를 배우는 능력과 같다. 우리가 언어를 배우는 능력을 가지고 태어나긴 하지만 문화적인 훈련이 없이는 배울 수 없다. 인간의 접촉으로부터 고립된 아이들은 언어 능력을 발달시키지 못한다. 어떤 비언어적인 신호들은 아마도 주로 유전된 신경 프로그램에 달려 있고, 다른 것들은 아마도 주로 환경에 따른 학습에 달려 있으며, 물론 많은 행동들은 둘 다에 의해 영향을 받는다.

정답풀이

206 동물과 인간은 타고난 선천적 능력뿐만 아니라 환경에 따른 학습에 의해서도 많은 행동을 배운다는 것이 글의 요지이므로, 제목으로는 ③ '생명작용(생물학적인 측면)과 환경이 공동으로 행동을 형성한다'가 가장 적절하다.

207 바로 뒤에서 기본적인 노래를 타고 나도 지저귐의 대상이 누구인지 다른 새들의 신호를 어떻게 알아봐야 하는지 등에 대해서 배워야 한다고 했으므로, 성숙한 노래를 접해 보지 않은 어린 새들의 노래는 불완전한 상태로 남을 것임을 추론할 수 있다. 따라서 (c) perfect(완전한)를 반대 개념인 imperfect(불완전한)로 바꿔야 한다.

오답풀이

206 ① 새의 노랫소리에서 진화한 인간의 언어
② 행동의 생물학적 뿌리에 대한 이해
④ 의사소통은 인간만의 특징인가?
⑤ 새와 인간의 발성 학습의 차이

207 ① 수컷 울새는 본능적으로 번식기에 자기 영토에 침입하는 낯선 울새들을 붉은색 가슴만 보고도 공격하는데, 똑같이 붉은색 가슴을 가졌어도 같은 둥지에서 사는 암컷 울새들은 공격하지 않는다고 했다. 이는 타고난 행동이 환경에 의해 수정되는 것이라고 할 수 있으므로 modified(수정하다)는 문맥상 적절하다.

② 다른 새의 노랫소리를 들어 본 적 없어도 자신들의 종에게 공통되는 노래를 부를 수 있는 것은 본능 때문이라고 할 수 있으므로 instinctively(본능적으로)는 문맥상 적절하다.

④ 새들과 마찬가지로 인간 행동의 선천적인 요소들도 환경에 의해 영향을 받는다는 내용이 이어지므로 similarly(유사하게)의 쓰임은 문맥상 적절하다.

⑤ 인간의 접촉으로부터 고립된 아이들은 언어 능력을 발달시키지 못한다고 했으므로, 언어 학습 능력을 가지고 태어나지만 '문화적인(cultural)'인 훈련이 없으면 언어를 배울 수 없다는 문맥은 적절하다.

구문풀이

[8행] Thus, this aggressive behavior, [which is believed to be innate], **is modified** by certain conditions or situations in the environment.

: [ ]는 문장의 주어인 this aggressive behavior를 부연 설명하는 주격 관계대명사절이다. 주어가 수정되는 대상이므로 수동태 동사 is modified가 쓰였다.

어휘풀이

- nurture *n* 양육, 교육
- robin *n* 울새
- breed *v* 번식하다, 기르다, 양육하다
- trigger *v* 유발하다
- aggressive *a* 공격적인
- dialect *n* 방언, 통용어
- address *v* ~에게 말을 걸다, ~에게 전하다
- component *n* 요소, 성분
- isolated *a* 고립된
- neurological *a* 신경의
- concerning *prep* ~에 관한
- territory *n* 영역, 영토
- stuffed *a* 박제된
- mechanism *n* 기제, 메커니즘
- innate *a* 타고난, 선천적인
- exposure *n* 노출, 접함
- alter *v* 바꾸다, 수정하다
- inherited *v* 유전된
- biology *n* 생태, 생명작용

208 ⑤	209 ③	210 ③	211 ②	212 ⑤
213 ③	214 ③	215 ⑤		

208 답 ⑤

📖 대의 민주주의의 대표성 상실에 대한 비판

전문해석

어떤 나라들은 국가 헌법에 일단 의회에 선출되면 오직 구성원 자신의 양심이 그의 투표를 인도해야 한다는 구절을 담고 있다. 이는 아마도 공정하겠지만 대의 기능을 없앤다. 의회 구성원들은 더는 그들의 유권자가 그들을 선출한 목적이 되는 문제를 도모할 필요가 없다. 상황은 의회가 정당에 기반하고 있으면 더 나빠지는데, 이는 대부분의 당이 어떤 개인적 '양심'과 관계없이 당 지도자 혹은 수상이 지시한 대로 그들의 대리자들이 투표할 것을 요구하기 때문이다. 사실 이것은 내각 책임의 도입과 연결되는데, 정부가 항상 의회 다수에 의해 뒷받침되어야 한다는 것을 의미한다. 이러한 요구는 의회가 지지하지 않는 '임시법'으로 통치한 이른바 민주 정부에 관한 몇몇 사례 후에 여러 나라의 헌법에 추가되었다. 어떤 경우든, 이 모든 문제는 정부에 대한 국민의 영향력을 약화 또는 제거한 것에 대하여 대의 민주주의를 비판하는 방향으로 향한다.

정답풀이

의원들은 자신을 선출한 유권자들을 대표하여 유권자들의 문제를 다루는 것을 도모해야 하지만, 일단 선출되고 나면 자신의 양심에 따라, 또는 자신이 속한 정당의 명령에 따라, 또는 내각 책임에 의해 정부를 지지하는 방향으로 자신의 투표권을 행사해야 하므로 유권자들의 권익을 대표하는 역할을 제대로 할 수 없게 된다는 내용으로, 대표성을 상실하게 되는 대의 민주주의의 맹점을 지적하는 글이다. 결국, 의원들이 유권자의 대표자이면서도 이러저러한 이유로 대표자 역할을 하지 못하게 된다는 것이 핵심 내용이므로, 글의 주제로 가장 적절한 것은 ⑤ '대의 민주주의가 대표성을 상실하게 하는 요인들'이다.

오답풀이

① 대표자들이 자신의 양심에 따라 행동해야 할 필요성
   ↳ 대표자들이 자신을 선출한 유권자들의 문제를 도모하지 않고 자신의 양심에 따라 투표하는 것도 대의 민주주의 대표성 상실의 하나의 요인으로 제시하고 있다.

② 대의 민주주의에서 선거의 중차대한 역할

③ 정부가 의회의 지지를 받아야 하는 이유들

④ 구성원들이 양심에 따라 투표하지 못하게 함으로써 발생하는 문제점들

구문풀이

1행 Some countries have **the phrase** in their constitutions [that {**once** elected to the parliament} only the member's own conscience should guide his or her voting].

: [ ]는 the phrase의 구체적인 내용을 제시하는 동격절이고, 그 안의 { }는 once(일단 ~하면)가 이끄는 부사절로 once 다음에 '주어+be동사'인 he/she is가 생략된 것으로 볼 수 있다.

13행 This requirement was added to the constitution of several countries, after several cases of so-called democratic governments [ruling by 'provisional laws' {which were not supported by parliament}].

: [ ]는 democratic governments를 수식하는 현재분사구이고, 그 안의 { }는 'provisional laws'를 수식하는 주격 관계대명사절이다.

어휘풀이

- phrase *n* 구절, 글귀
- elect *v* 선출하다
- conscience *n* 양심
- dictate *v* 지시하다, 명령하다
- cabinet *a* 내각의
- requirement *n* 요구 (조건)
- representative democracy 대의 민주주의
- eliminate *v* 제거하다
- constitution *n* 헌법
- parliament *n* 의회
- prime minister 수상, 국무총리
- independent of ~와 관계없이
- majority *n* 다수
- criticize *v* 비판하다

209 답 ③

📖 생태계 기능 유지와 관련된 생물학적 원리를 이해할 필요성

전문해석

인간은 살아 있는 유기체의 세계 속에 존재하고 그것에 의존한다. 우리가 호흡하는 공기 중의 산소는 무수한 수십억의 개별적 유기체들에 의해 수행되는 광합성에 의해 생산된다. 우리 몸에 연료를 공급하는 먹거리는 다른 살아 있는 유기체의 조직으로부터 나온다. 우리의 차를 움직이게 하고 우리의 전력 시설에 동력을 공급하는 연료는 대부분 살아 있는 유기체들에 의해 대개 수백만 년 전에 생산된 다양한 형태의 탄소 분자들이다. 안팎으로 우리의 몸은 살아 있는 단세포 유기체들의 복잡한 군집으로 뒤덮여 있는데, 그것들의 대부분은 우리가 우리의 건강을 유지하는 데 도움을 준다. 또한 우리의 몸에 침입하여 가벼운 것에서부터 심각한 것에 이르는 질병 또는 심지어 죽음조차 초래할 수 있는 해로운 종들도 있다. 다른 종들과의 이러한 상호작용은 인간에게만 국한되지 않는다. 생태계 기능은 지구에 거주하는 수백만 종들 사이의 무수히 많은 복잡한 상호작용에 의존한다. 다시 말해서, 생물학적 원리를 이해하는 것은 우리가 알고 있고 의존하고 있는 바와 같이 우리의 삶과 지구의 기능을 유지하는 데 필수적이다.

정답풀이

③ 문장의 구조 파악: our bodies are covered ~ organisms가 첫 번째 절에 해당하고, 두 번째 절이 이어져야 하는 구조이다. 따라서 most 앞에 등위 접속사 and를 쓰거나 them을 관계대명사 which로 고쳐야 한다.

오답풀이

① 분사의 태: 수식을 받는 photosynthesis가 수행되는 대상이므로 수동의 의미를 가진 과거분사 conducted를 쓴 것은 적절하다.

② 관계대명사 that: 뒤에 drive와 power의 주어가 없는 불완전한 구조의 절이 이어지고, 이 절은 앞의 명사구 The fuels를 수식하므로, 주격 관계대명사에 해당하는 that은 어법상 적절하다.

④ 주어와 동사의 수 일치: These interactions가 핵심 주어이므로 복수형 동사 are는 어법상 적절하다.

⑤ 문장의 구조 파악: 문장의 동사는 is이므로 주어부를 이끄는 동명사 understanding은 어법상 적절하다.

구문풀이

2행 The oxygen in the air [we breathe] is produced by photosynthesis [conducted by countless billions of individual organisms].

: 첫 번째 [ ]는 The oxygen in the air를 수식하는 목적격 관계대명사절이고, 두 번째 [ ]는 photosynthesis를 수식하는 과거분사구이다.

어휘풀이

- organism *n* 유기체
- countless *a* 셀 수 없는, 무수한
- molecule *n* 분자
- photosynthesis *n* 광합성
- tissue *n* (신체) 조직
- inside and out 안팎으로

- unicellular _a_ 단세포의　　• invade _v_ 침입하다
- inhabit _v_ 거주하다, 서식하다

210 답 ③

📖 자본주의의 팽창과 부의 증가

전문해석
자본주의는 흔히 개인들이 자유롭게 다른 이들의 노동을 고용하여 수익을 최대화하기 위해 사유 재산과 생산 수단을 소유하는 시장 기반의 사회 및 경제 체제로 정의된다. 자원 할당은 가격 제도를 통하여 결정된다. 다시 말해서, 노동을 포함한 모든 상품이 시장에서의 공급과 수요의 상대적인 힘을 통해 자연가격이 정해진다. 부족한 자원은, 어떤 특정 시기에 기술을 갖춘 노동력, 금 또는 진정 어떤 상품도 될 수 있는데, 높은 가격을 점한다. 게다가, 그런 높은 가격은 이 부분에 대한 투자와, 수요를 충족시키기 위해 이 특별한 상품의 더 많은 공급을 초래하는 것을 억제한다(→ 부추긴다). 따라서 자본주의는 팽창하며 끊임없이 더 많은 양과 개선된 품질의 상품을 생산한다. 이러한 이유로 자본주의는 이전까지 자본주의 이전 사회에서 상상할 수 있었던 것보다 더 많은 부를 인간 사회에 가져왔다.

정답풀이
③ 부족한 자원은 높은 가격에 팔리고, 그러면 그러한 상품에 대한 수요를 충족시키기 위해 투자와 공급이 늘어나게 될 것이다. 따라서 discourage(막다, 억제하다)를 encourage(촉진[조장]하다) 정도의 단어로 바꿔야 한다.

오답풀이
① 자본주의에서 다른 이들의 노동을 고용하는 것은 수익을 최대한 많이 올리기 위해서이므로 maximize(최대화하다)는 적절하게 쓰였다.
② 가격은 공급과 수요 사이의 균형에 의해 정해지므로 relative(상대적인)는 문맥상 적절하다.
④ 자본주의는 수요에 대한 끊임없는 공급으로 인해 계속 규모가 커질 수밖에 없으므로 expansive(팽창하는)는 문맥상 적절하다.
⑤ 끊임없이 더 많은 양과 개선된 품질의 상품을 생산하여 더 많은 부를 창출했다는 문맥이므로 wealth(부)의 쓰임은 적절하다.

구문풀이
16행 For this reason, capitalism has brought greater wealth to human society [**than** was ever imaginable in precapitalist society].

: [ ]에서 than은 일종의 관계대명사(유사관계대명사)로, 관계절에서 주어의 역할을 하며 '자본주의 이전 사회에서 이전까지 상상할 수 있었던 것(부)보다' 정도의 뜻을 나타내는 절을 이끈다.

어휘풀이
- capitalism _n_ 자본주의　　• private property 사유 재산
- allocation _n_ 할당　　• commodity _n_ 상품
- natural price 자연가격(생산요소의 원가에 이윤을 더한 가격)
- relative _a_ 상대적인　　• scarce _a_ 부족한, 결핍된
- command _v_ ~의 값에 팔리다　　• expansive _a_ 팽창하는
- constantly _ad_ 끊임없이, 계속　　• imaginable _a_ 상상할 수 있는
- precapitalist _a_ 자본주의 이전의

211 답 ②

📖 안전이 동물의 집단생활에 미치는 영향

전문해석
우리는 높은 수준의 상호의존성을 가지고 집단으로 사는 긴 계보의 영장류 후손이

다. 안전에 대한 필요성이 어떻게 사회적인 삶을 형성하는가는 영장류 동물학자들이 인도네시아 군도의 여러 다른 섬에 있는 긴꼬리원숭이들을 세웠을 때 분명해졌다. 어떤 섬들에는 (호랑이와 구름표범과 같은) 고양잇과 동물들이 있는 반면에 다른 섬들은 그렇지 않았다. 같은 원숭이들은 고양잇과 동물들이 있는 섬에서는 큰 무리를 지어 이동하는 것이 발견되었지만, (고양잇과 동물들이) 없는 섬에서는 작은 무리를 지어 이동하는 것이 발견되었다. 따라서 포식(잡아먹히는 것)은 개별 동물들을 함께 뭉치게 한다. 일반적으로, 어떤 종이 더 취약할수록, 그것의 집합체는 더 커진다. 개코원숭이처럼 지상에 거주하는 원숭이들은 나무에 거주하는 것들보다 더 큰 집단을 이루어 이동하는데, 그것들(나무 거주 동물들)은 더 나은 탈출 기회를 누린다. 그리고 그것의 크기 때문에 낮 동안에 두려워할 것이 거의 없는 침팬지는 보통 혼자나 작은 무리를 지어 먹이를 찾는다.

정답풀이
포식, 즉 잡아먹히는 것에 대한 두려움에 따라 무리의 크기가 달라지고, 보통 취약한 종일수록 무리의 크기가 커진다는 내용이다. 따라서 안전에 대한 필요성이 무리의 크기에 영향을 주는 것으로 추론할 수 있으므로, 빈칸에 들어갈 말로 가장 적절한 것은 ② '안전에 대한 필요성이 어떻게 사회적인 삶을 형성하는가'이다.

오답풀이
① 무리의 크기가 어떻게 집단 행동에 영향을 미치는가
　└ 포식에 대한 두려움으로 동물들이 무리를 지어 생활하게 되었다는 내용의 글이지, 무리의 크기와 집단 행동에 관한 글이 아니므로 오답!
③ 왜 적자생존이 과학적인 진실인가
④ 복잡한 계층구조는 지능과 관계가 있다는 것
⑤ 사냥 방법이 어떻게 무리의 안전에 영향을 미치는지

구문풀이
13행 And chimpanzees, [which (because of their size) have little to fear in the daytime], typically **forage** alone or in small groups.

: 문장의 핵심 주어는 chimpanzees이고, 동사는 forage이다. [ ]는 chimpanzees를 부연 설명하는 주격 관계대명사절이다.

어휘풀이
- descend from ~의 후손이다　　• primate _n_ 영장류
- interdependence _n_ 상호의존(성)
- long-tailed macaque 긴꼬리원숭이
- Indonesian archipelagoe 인도네시아 군도
- clouded leopard 구름표범　　• predation _n_ 포식
- vulnerable _a_ 취약한, 연약한　　• aggregation _n_ 집합체
- dwell _v_ 살다, 거주하다　　• baboon _n_ 개코원숭이
- forage _v_ 먹이를 찾다　　• survival of the fittest 적자생존
- hierarchy _n_ 계층

212 답 ⑤

📖 생산량과 창의성과의 관계

전문해석
여러분이 창의적인 조직을 원한다면, 행동하지 않는 것은 최악의 형태의 실패인데, 즉 처벌을 받아야 할 유일한 실패이다. 많은 연구들로부터 연구원 Dean Keith Simonton은 무엇이 창의성을 이끌어 내는가에 대한 강력한 증거를 제공한다. Picasso, da Vinci 그리고 물리학자 Richard Feynman과 같은 유명한 천재들이 그들의 동료보다 더 높은 비율로 성공하지는 않았다. 그들은 단지 더 많이 생산했을 뿐이고, 이것은 그들의 알려지지 않은 동료들보다 그들이 훨씬 더 많은 성공과 실패를 경험했다는 것을 의미했다. 작곡가, 예술가, 시인에서부터 발명가와 과학자

에 이르기까지 Simonton이 연구한 모든 직업에서 상황은 같은데, 즉 창의성은 생산된 일의 양의 함수이다. **이러한 발견은 사람들이 뭔가를 하고 있는가 또는 아무것도 하고 있지 않는가를 측정하는 것이 창의적인 일을 하는 사람들의 업무 수행을 평가하는 방법들 중 하나임을 의미한다.** 회사는, 자신이 무엇을 할 것인가에 대해 말하거나 계획을 세우는 데 매일 매일을 보내지만 전혀 아무것도 하지 않는 사람들을 강등시키거나 전출을 보내고 심지어는 해고해야 한다.

정답풀이

창의성으로 유명한 사람들은 단지 남들보다 더 많은 일을 한 것이며, 일을 하는가 또는 하지 않는가가 창의적인 일에 종사하는 사람들의 업무 수행을 가늠하는 척도가 된다고 했으므로, 창의성은 생산량과 관련이 있음을 알 수 있다. 따라서 빈칸에 들어갈 말로 가장 적절한 것은 ⑤ '생산된 일의 양의 함수이다' 이다.

오답풀이

① 아무것도 하지 않는 기술에 영감을 받는다
② 측정하기 어려운 변수이다
③ 사회 문화적 기반에서 성장한다
④ 능동적인 무의식적 과정의 결과이다

구문풀이

16행 Companies should demote, transfer, and even fire <u>those</u> [who **spend** day after day **talking about** and **planning** {what they are going to do} but never do anything].

: [ ]는 those를 수식하는 주격 관계대명사절이다. 그 안에는 「spend+시간+*doing*」 구문이 쓰였는데, talking about과 planning이 병렬구조를 이룬다. { }는 talking about과 planning의 공통 목적어(의문사절)이다.

어휘풀이

- inaction *n* 활동하지 않음
- renowned *a* 유명한
- peer *n* 동료, 또래
- assess *v* 평가하다
- inspire *v* 영감을 주다, 고무하다
- matrix *n* 기반, 모체
- lead to ~을 초래하다
- physicist *n* 물리학자
- occupation *n* 직업
- transfer *v* 전출시키다
- variable *n* 변수

---

213 답 ③

📖 사고 피해자를 돕는 것과 관련된 법과 도덕의 문제

전문해석

어느 날 당신이 차로 출근하고 있는데, 충격 상태에 빠져 있고 의료적인 도움을 필요로 하는 것이 분명한 교통사고 피해자가 길 옆에 앉아 있는 것을 본다고 가정해 보자. 당신은 응급처치 방법을 알고 목적지에 도착하는 데 그다지 급하지 않기 때문에, 쉽게 멈춰서 그 사람을 도울 수도 있다. (B) 그러나 법적으로 말하면 당신이 멈춰서 도움을 줄 의무는 없다. 멈춤으로써 당신은 합리적인 조치를 하도록 당신 자신을 구속하는 것이고, 따라서 당신이 그렇게 하지 못하고 피해자가 그것으로 부상의 고통을 겪는다면 법적인 책임을 물게 되기 때문에, 관습법에 따르면 신중한 행동은 계속 운전하는 것일 수도 있다. (C) 많은 주에서 (중과실이나 심각한 불법 행위를 제외하고는) 도움을 주는 사람에게 피해로부터 면책권을 주는 소위 착한 사마리아인 법을 제정하였다. 그러나 대부분 주에서의 법은 사람들에게 그러한 도움을 주거나 구급차를 부르는 것조차 의무화하지 않는다. (A) 그러나 도덕론자들은 당신이 만약 도움을 주거나 도움 요청조차도 하지 않고 빨리 지나쳐 버리면, 당신의 행동은 지극히 합법적일지라도 도덕적으로는 의심스럽다는 것에 동의할 것이다. 법과 상관없이 그러한 행동은 거의 틀림없이 잘못된 것일 것이다.

정답풀이

출근길에 교통사고 피해자를 도와주는 것에 대해 가정하는 내용인 주어진 글 다음에는, 도와줄 수는 있지만(though) 피해자를 돕다가 잘못되면 법적인 문제가 생길 수 있다는 내용의 (B)가 와야 한다. 그 다음에 그러한 법적인 문제를 해결하기 위한 법안 제정을 언급하며 많은 주에서 응급처치나 구급차를 부르는 것을 법적으로 의무화하지 않는다는 내용의 (C)가 오고, (C)에 대한 반론으로(however) 도덕론자들의 생각을 언급하고 있는 (A)가 마지막에 오는 순서가 자연스럽다. 따라서 적절한 글의 순서는 ③ (B)-(C)-(A)이다.

구문풀이

7행 Moral theorists would agree, however, [that **if you sped** away without rendering aid or even calling for help, / your action **might be** perfectly legal but **would be** morally suspect].

: [ ]는 agree의 목적어에 해당하는 명사절이고, 이 절에는 가정법 과거(if+주어+동사의 과거형 ~, 주어+조동사의 과거형+동사원형 …) 구문이 쓰였다.

13행 Under common law, the prudent thing would be to drive on, // **because** by stopping you **would bind** yourself to use reasonable care and thus **incur** legal liability / **if** you fail to do so and the victim thereby suffers injury.

: because가 이끄는 부사절은 주절과 조건 부사절로 이루어져 있으며, 주절의 동사는 would bind와 (would) incur이다.

어휘풀이

- first aid 응급처치
- render *v* ~을 주다, ~을 해주다
- regardless of ~에 관계없이
- be obligated to *do* ~해야만 하다, ~할 의무가 있다
- common law 관습법
- incur *v* 초래하다, 물게 되다
- enact *v* (법 등을) 제정하다
- Good Samaritan law 착한 사마리아인 법
- immunity *n* 면책, 면역
- misconduct *n* 잘못된 행위, 위법[불법] 행위
- moral theorist 도덕론자
- suspect *a* 의심스러운, 수상한
- prudent *a* 신중한
- liability *n* (법적) 책임

---

214 답 ③

📖 교통사고와 부상을 줄일 수 있는 제품과 환경 설계의 필요성

전문해석

교통 상해를 줄이기 위한 대부분의 노력은 '사고 예방' 캠페인이라고 불린다. 우리는 '사고 예방'이 효과적인 도로 교통 상해 관리 프로그램에 사용되는 훨씬 더 광범위한 대응책의 한 가지 측면일 뿐이며 항상 가장 가치 있는 측면은 아님을 분명히 해야 한다. **모든 프로그램에 충돌이 실제로 발생하는 경우에 부상의 심각성을 줄이는 조치와 충돌 후 응급 처치, 치료 및 재활을 위한 잘 설계된 시스템 또한 포함시키는 것이 중요하다.** 왜냐하면 실수를 하는 것은 특정 집단의 대다수 사람들과 관련된 활동에서 매우 '정상적인' 것이지 '비정상적인' 것이 아니기 때문이다. 전문적인 운전자가 장시간 운전 중 어느 때 동안에 주의가 산만해지는 것은 정상이고, 운전하여 출근하는 (기업의) 임원이 이동 중 어느 시점에 공상에 잠기는 것은 정상이며, 십 대가 나이 지긋한 사람보다 오토바이를 운전하면서 더 많은 위험을 무릅쓰는 것은 정상적인 일이다. 간단히 말해, 우리는 일상적인 활동에서 부주의, 방심, 심지어 소홀을 결코 없애지 못할 것이다. 그러나 **인간의 수행에서 이러한 정상적인 변화에 더 잘 견뎌내는 제품과 환경을 설계함으로써 우리는 사고와 부상 발생 건수를 최소화할 수 있다.**

정답풀이

주어진 문장의 This는 모든 도로 교통 상해 관리 프로그램에 충돌 시 부상의

심각성을 줄이는 조치와 충돌 후 응급 치료, 치료 및 재활을 위한 잘 설계된 시스템을 포함시켜야 한다는 내용을 가리키고, 운전자가 운전 중에 잠깐 산만해지거나 십 대가 오토바이를 더 위험하게 타는 것은 정상적인 일이라는 내용의 ③ 다음 문장은 실수를 하는 것은 매우 정상적인 것이라는 주어진 문장의 내용을 부연한다. 따라서 주어진 문장은 ③에 들어가는 것이 가장 적절하다.

구문풀이

5행 We should be clear [that *accident prevention* is just one aspect—and not always the most rewarding one—of a much larger range of underlined{countermeasures} {used in effective road traffic injury control programmes}].

: [ ]는 be clear의 목적어에 해당하는 명사절이다. { }는 countermeasures를 수식하는 과거분사구이다.

어휘풀이

- abnormal *a* 비정상의
- term *v* (…을 ~이라고) 칭하다[일컫다]
- rewarding *a* 보람 있는, 가치 있는
- measures *n* 조치, 대책, 수단
- distracted *a* 주의가 흐트러진, 집중을 못하는
- executive *n* (기업의) 임원
- take a risk 모험을 하다
- neglect *n* 무시(하는 것), 소홀
- variation *n* 변화, 변형
- injury *n* 상해, 부상
- prevention *n* 예방
- countermeasure *n* 대응책, 대책
- severity *n* 심각성, 가혹함
- day-dreaming *n* 공상
- absentmindedness *n* 방심, 건성
- tolerant *a* 견디는, 아량 있는
- minimize *v* 최소화하다

215 답 ⑤

📖 **동료들의 행동에 대한 아이들의 순응 경향**

전문해석

한 흥미로운 연구는 '문제를 해결하는 것에 동료들이 얼마나 영향을 미치는가에서 침팬지, 오랑우탄 그리고 두 살배기 아이가 다른가?'라는 질문을 던졌다. 이것을 확인하기 위해서 연구원들은 처음에 세 집단 모두에게 해결해야 할 과제를 주었다. 그 과제는 공을 세 개의 상이한 구멍을 가진 일련의 상자에 떨어뜨려 넣는 것이었다. 그 구멍들 중 오직 하나에 공을 떨어뜨려 넣어야만 보상이 배출되었는데, 유인원에게는 땅콩이, 인간 아이에게는 초콜릿칩이 보상이었다. 일단 세 집단이 스스로 공을 떨어뜨림으로써 어떤 구멍이 먹을 것을 배출하는지를 찾아내면, 그런 다음 그들은 비슷한 동료들이 역시 먹을 것을 배출하는 다른 구멍에 공을 떨어뜨려 넣는 것을 지켜보았다. 그다음에 그 세 집단에게 그 일련의 상자로 되돌아가 공을 다시 떨어뜨려 넣을 기회가 주어졌다. 그 결과는 오직 인간 아이들만 그들의 동료가 넣었던 구멍에 공을 떨어뜨려 넣음으로써 바꿀 가능성이 있었다는 것을 분명히 보여주었다. 유인원들은 자신의 원래 해결책을 계속했다. 게다가, 인간 아이들은 또래가 같은 방에 있을 경우에 타인의 행동을 모방할 가능성이 훨씬 더 높았다. 유인원들에게 동료의 존재는 그들의 행동에 영향을 미치지 않았다.

→ 연구는 유인원에 비해 인간 아이들이 동료의 행동에 underlined{순응할} 가능성이 더 크며, 이는 그 방에 있는 동료의 존재에 의해 underlined{강화되었다는} 것을 보여 주었다.

정답풀이

침팬지, 오랑우탄, 두 살배기 아이를 대상으로 하여 문제 해결 상황에서 동료들이 얼마나 영향을 미치는가를 실험했을 때, 유인원(침팬지와 오랑우탄)은 동료들의 해결책을 따르지 않았고 오직 인간 아이들만 해결책을 따랐는데, 특히 같은 방에 동료들이 함께 있을 때 그러한 행동을 할 가능성이 더 높았다고 한다. 따라서 요약문의 빈칸 (A)에는 conform(순응하다)이, (B)에는 reinforced(강화하다)가 들어가는 것이 가장 적절하다.

구문풀이

13행 The three groups **were** then **given the chance** [to go back to the set of boxes] and [to drop balls in again].

: 「give+간접목적어+직접목적어」의 5형식 문장을 간접목적어(the three groups)를 주어로 하여 수동태로 전환한 형태이며, the chance는 능동태의 직접목적어에 해당한다. 두 개의 [ ]는 the chance를 수식하는 to부정사구이다.

어휘풀이

- fascinating *a* 흥미진진한
- peer *n* 동료, 또래
- (great) ape 유인원
- switch *v* 바꾸다, 전환하다
- presence *v* 존재
- influential *a* 영향을 미치는
- release *v* 배출하다
- figure out ~을 찾아내다, ~을 파악하다
- stick with ~을 계속하다
- trigger *v* 촉발하다, 일으키다

216 답 ①

📖 살아 있는 것에만 초점을 맞춘 과학의 문제점

전문해석

우리 자신이 살아 있기 때문에 우리는 죽음과 부패에 포함된 과정을 알고 있는 것보다 성장의 과정에 대해 훨씬 더 많이 알고 있다. 이것은 지극히 자연스럽고 타당한 것이다. 사실, 그것은 우리 안의 매우 강력한 본능이며 건강한 본능이다. 그러나 우리가 완전히 성장한 인간이라면, 우리의 교육은 '인생의 수레바퀴'의 다른 한쪽 또는 더 숨겨져 있는 쪽을 구성하고 있는 과정들에 의해 우주에서 수행되는 광대한 역할을 우리가 지적으로 이해할 수 있을 정도로 많은 지식과 숙고를 우리 마음속에 발달시켰어야 했다. 그러나 이러한 면에서 과거 우리의 일반 교육은 부분적으로 과학 자체가 아주 슬프게도 우리를 잘못 이끌어 왔기 때문에 심각하게 결함이 있었다. 식물계와 동물계를 다루는 지식의 그러한 분야, 즉 식물학과 동물학은 스스로를 거의 전적으로 '살아 있는' 것에 대한 연구로 한정해 왔고, 우주의 이러한 구성요소들이 죽을 때 그것들에게 무슨 일이 일어나는지 그리고 그것들의 노폐물과 유해가 식물과 동물의 세계 모두가 의존하는 일반 환경에 영향을 주는 방식에 거의 또는 전혀 관심을 기울이지 않았다.

정답풀이

밑줄 친 부분 앞뒤의 내용에서 살아 있는 것에만 초점을 맞추고 죽음과 부패에 포함된 과정을 무시한 것이 과학의 문제점이라고 반복하여 말하고 있다. 그러므로 밑줄 친 '과학 자체가 아주 슬프게도 우리를 잘못 이끌어 왔다'가 의미하는 바로는 ① '과학적 연구는 단지 살아 있는 것에만 초점을 맞춰 왔다'가 가장 적절하다.

오답풀이

② 모든 학문은 상호의존적으로 발달해 왔다
③ 최근까지 생태계의 균형은 등한시되어 왔다
④ 과학은 보존이 아니라 발달을 위해 이용되어 왔다
⑤ 과학은 인간과 다른 생물체 간의 연관성을 찾지 못했다

구문풀이

13행 [Those branches of knowledge {dealing with the vegetable and animal kingdoms}—botany and zoology—] **have confined** themselves almost entirely to the study of *living* things and **have given** little or no attention [to what happens to these units of the universe when they die] and [**to** the way {in which their waste products and remains affect the general environment (on which both the plant and animal world depend)}].

: 첫 번째 [ ]가 주어이며, 동사는 and로 연결된 have confined와 have given이다. 첫 번째 { }는 Those ~ knowledge를 수식하는 현재분사구이다. 두 번째와 세 번째 [ ]는 attention에 연결되는 전치사구이며, 두 번째 { }는 the way를, ( )는 the general environment를 수식하는 관계절이다.

어휘풀이

- be conscious of ~을 알고 있다, ~을 의식하다
- decay *n* 부패
- instinct *n* 본능
- grasp *v* 이해하다
- defective *a* 결함이 있는
- confine *v* 한정하다
- justifiable *a* 타당한, 정당화할 수 있는
- reflection *n* 숙고
- gravely *ad* 심각하게, 예사롭지 않게
- botany *n* 식물학
- waste product 노폐물, 폐기물

- remains *n* 잔해, 유해
- conservation *n* 보호, 보존
- discipline *n* 학문 부문[분야]

217 답 ④

📖 마케팅을 하기 위해 여성을 이해할 필요성

전문해석

여성들은 오늘날 구매 결정에 있어 커다란 영향력을 가지고 있고, 거대한 기업의 지도적 위치에서 종종 볼 수 있으며, 그들의 빈틈없는 투자 덕분에 전 세계의 주요 사업에 지배지분(기업의 경영권을 행사할 수 있는 지분)을 가지고 있다. 이런 사실에도 불구하고, 대부분의 기업들은 아직도 광고 대상자들이 모두 남성인 것처럼 취급하는 경향을 띠고 있다. 모든 매체 광고의 5분의 1이 남성보다는 여성을 대상으로 하고 있다는 사실에도 불구하고, 몇 년 전에 실시된 영국의 한 설문조사에서 여성들 중에서 91퍼센트가 광고주들이 그들을 이해하지 못한다는 느낌을 받는다는 것이 밝혀졌다. 여성들에게 마케팅을 하는 것은 오늘날 관심이 많은 주제이고, 그들의 여성 대상자들에 이르기 위해 마케팅 자료나 로고에 핑크색을 약간 입히는 것으로 충분할 것이라고 생각하는 기업들은 결국 빠르게 패배자의 자리에 있게 된다. 브랜드 전략에 여성을 성공적으로 포함하기 위해서 우리는 여성들이 남성들과 다르게 생각하는 방식을 이해할 필요가 있다.

정답풀이

④ **문장의 구조 파악**: and 다음의 절에서 주어 businesses에 이어지는 동사가 없는 상태이다. 따라서 준동사 ending을 본동사 end로 고쳐야 한다. that assume ~ female targets는 businesses를 수식하는 주격 관계대명사절이다.

오답풀이

① **동사의 태**: 주어인 Women을 공통의 주어로 하여 동사 have, can be found, have가 병렬구조를 이루고 있다. 문맥상 여성들이 거대한 기업의 지도적 위치에서 발견된다는 의미이므로 수동형 be found는 어법상 적절하다.
② **가정법**: '마치 ~인 것처럼'이라는 의미의 as though가 이끄는 절에 가정법이 쓰인 문장이다. 현재 사실과 반대되는 일을 가정하므로 가정법 과거 동사 were를 쓴 것은 어법상 적절하다.
③ **대명사**: understand의 주어는 광고주들(advertisers)이고 목적어는 여성들(women)이므로 서로 다른 대상이다. 따라서 목적격 대명사 them을 쓴 것은 어법상 적절하다.
⑤ **전치사+관계대명사**: the ways를 선행사로 하며 뒤에 완전한 구조의 절이 이어지므로 관계사절에서 부사구의 역할을 하는 「전치사+관계대명사」 형태인 in which는 어법상 적절하다.

구문풀이

11행 Marketing to women is a hot topic today, / and businesses [that assume {that (adding a few pink shades to their marketing materials or logo) **will suffice** (to reach their female targets)}] **end up** in the loser's seat quickly.

: 두 개의 절로 이루어진 문장으로, 두 번째 절의 주어는 businesses이고, 동사는 end up이다. [ ]는 주격 관계대명사절로 businesses를 수식하며, { }는 assume의 목적절이다. 이 목적절의 주어는 첫 번째 ( )로 표시된 동명사구이고 동사는 will suffice이다. 두 번째 ( )는 부사적 용법(목적)의 to부정사구이다.

어휘풀이

- corporation *n* 회사, 기업
- operation *n* 사업, (대규모) 기업
- be aimed at ~을 대상으로 하다, ~을 겨냥하다
- assume *v* ~라고 생각하다[추측하다]
- suffice *v* 충분하다, 만족시키다
- controlling interest 지배지분
- target audience 광고 대상자
- shade *n* 색조, 그늘
- strategy *n* 전략, 계획

218 답 ③

전문해석

이유를 불문하고 많은 상이한 사회학적, 심리학적 그리고 생물학적 이론들은 사람들이 개인적 이득의 유무와 관계없이 그들의 집단을 다른 집단들과 구별하려고 시도하는 '차이를 최대화하기'라 불리는 과정을 인정한다. 사람들은 자기 자신의 집단과 강하게 일체감을 가지며, 긍정적인 특성들을 과장하는데, 특히 덜 존중되는 다른 집단들을 희생시키면서 그렇게 한다. 집단과 사회는 일부 집단이 다른 집단보다 우월함을 정당화하는 신화와 이론적 근거를 만들어 낸다. 그런 이야기와 신화는 차이가 근본적이고, 타고난 것이며, 인간의 고안 혹은 사회적 관습을 넘어선다는 믿음을 약화시킨다(→ 강화한다). 인종, 민족, 성은 특히 사회적으로 구성된 차이의 좋은 사례인데, 크게 확대되고 신화와 관습으로 덮여 있다. 하지만 이 집단들 사이에 존재하는 유전적이고 생물학적인 천부적 자질에서의 어떤 차이도 대단히 작으며, 결코 사회적 역할과 대우에서의 방대한 차이를 뒷받침해주지 않는다.

정답풀이

③ 신화와 이론적 근거는 집단의 우월성에 대한 믿음을 공고히 하려는 시도에서 생겨나는 것이므로 undermine(약화시키다)을 reinforce(강화하다)나 undergird(떠받치다) 정도의 단어로 바꿔야 한다.

오답풀이

① 차이를 최대화하기란 사람들이 자신의 집단을 다른 집단들과 '구별하려고' 하는 것이므로 distinguish의 쓰임은 적절하다.

② 사람들은 자신이 속한 집단의 차별성을 추구하므로 긍정적 특성들을 '과장한다(exaggerate)'는 문맥은 적절하다.

④ 앞에서 집단의 우월성을 정당화하기 위해 신화와 이론적 근거가 생겼다고 했으므로, 인종, 민족, 성과 같은 사회적으로 구성된 차이가 신화와 관습에 의해 '확대된다(magnified)'는 문맥은 적절하다.

⑤ 인종, 민족, 성과 같은 집단의 차이는 유전적이고 생물학적인 자질이라는 측면에서 보면 사회적으로 구축된 차이만큼 크지 않다는 문맥이므로 small(작은)은 적절하다.

구문풀이

1행 Regardless of the reason, [many different sociological, psychological, and biological theories] **acknowledge** a process [**called** *maximizing the difference*] [**through which** people attempt to **distinguish** their group **from** others, whether or not there is personal gain].

: 첫 번째 [ ]가 문장의 주어이고, acknowledge가 동사이다. 두 번째와 세 번째 [ ]는 각각 a process를 수식하는 과거분사구와 관계절이며, 관계절에는 「distinguish A from B: A와 B를 구별 짓다」 구문이 사용되었다.

16행 However, [whatever differences in genetic and biological endowments {that exist among these groups}] **are** exceedingly small and by no means **support** the vast differences in social roles and treatment.

: [ ]가 문장의 주어로 쓰인 명사절이고, are와 support가 병렬로 연결되어 문장의 동사 역할을 한다. { }는 genetic and biological endowments를 수식하는 주격 관계대명사절이다.

어휘풀이

- regardless of ~에 관계없이
- identify with ~와 일체감을 갖다
- lesser-regarded *a* 덜 존중되는
- justify *v* 정당화하다
- distinguish *v* 구별하다
- exaggerate *v* 과장하다
- rationale *n* 이론적 근거
- dominance *n* 우월, 지배
- undermine *v* 약화시키다
- convention *n* 관습
- magnify *v* 확대하다
- endowment *n* 천부적 자질
- by no means 결코 ~이 아닌
- fundamental *a* 근본적인
- ethnicity *n* 민족(성)
- mythology *n* 신화
- exceedingly *ad* 대단히, 매우

219 답 ②

전문해석

때때로 우리에게 시기심을 갖도록 하는 것은 바로 물질적인 소유물이 아니라 다른 사람들의 아이들이다. 이것은 우리가 아이들을 우리 자신의 연장으로 간주하고 그들이 성취한 것이 우리에게 반영된다고 믿을 경우에 일어날 가능성이 더욱 크다. 우리에게 질투할 기회를 무한히 주면서 우리 아이들보다 더 잘하거나, 더 빠르거나, 더 영리하거나, 더 매력적인 아이들이 항상 있게 마련이다. 그러나 여기에서 다시, 우리는 상황을 어떻게 바라볼 것인가를 결정할 수 있다. 우리 아이들의 무능력을 보는 대신, 그들의 장점에 초점을 맞추는 것이 훨씬 더 이롭다. 그러면 비교해야 할 상황이 불가피하게 생길 때 우리는 아이들 각자의 특별한 점을 인정할 수 있게 될 것이다. 게다가, 우리는 우리 아이들의 성공과 실패가 그들 자신의 것이지 우리의 것이 아니라는 것을 인식해야만 한다. 우리는 우리 아이들을 사랑하며, 우리가 그들이 성공했을 때 기뻐하고 그들이 그러지 못했을 때 고통을 느끼는 것은 그저 자연스러운 것이다. 그러나 우리는 우리 아이들에 대한 우리의 희망과 기대가 실현하지 못한 우리 자신의 소망이 아닌, 그들의 성격과 장점에 맞춰져야 한다는 것을 확실히 해야만 한다.

정답풀이

아이들을 우리 자신의 연장으로 보고 그들의 성취가 우리에게 반영된다고 믿을 때 끊임없이 다른 사람들의 아이들과 비교하게 되어 문제가 생기므로, 우리 아이들의 성격과 장점에 맞춰 희망과 기대를 가져야 한다는 것이 글의 요지이다. 아이들의 성공과 실패는 그들의 것이지 우리의 것이 아니라고 했으므로 그들에 대한 희망과 기대를 ② '실현하지 못한 우리 자신의 소망'에 맞추지 말아야 한다는 것을 추론할 수 있다.

오답풀이

① 그들의 성장을 지원할 수 있는 우리의 능력
③ 차근차근 발전하고자 하는 그들의 노력
④ 스스로 목표를 설정할 수 없는 그들의 무능력
⑤ 그들이 직면하게 될 지속적인 도전

구문풀이

1행 Sometimes **it's not** material possessions **that** make us envious, **but** other people's kids.

: 「it is ~ that ....」 강조구문과 'A가 아니라 B인'의 의미인 「not A but B」 구문이 쓰인 문장으로, Sometimes it's not material possessions but other people's kids that makes us envious.에서 but other people's kids를 문장의 끝으로 보낸 형태이다.

어휘풀이

- possession *n* 소유(물)
- extension *n* 연장, 확장
- inability *n* 무능함
- comparison *n* 비교
- appreciate *v* ~의 진가를 인정하다
- be tailored to ~에 맞춰지다
- unfulfilled *a* 실현[충족]하지 못한
- step by step 점차, 착실히
- envious *a* 시기하는, 질투심이 강한
- reflect *v* 반영하다, 반사하다
- strength *n* 장점, 강점
- inevitably *ad* 불가피하게
- rejoice *v* 기뻐하다, 좋아하다
- personality *n* 성격
- endeavor *n* 노력, 시도
- continuous *a* 끊임없는, 지속적인

220 답 ④

📖 생명의 미(美)와 조화를 가져오는 무작위적인 유전적 변화와 자연 선택

전문해석

생명은 아름답고 조화로우며, 대부분의 사람들이 이러한 인식을 공유한다. 그러한 아름다움과 질서의 원인은 무엇인가? 찰스 다윈이 이 어려우면서 아마도 가장 중심적인 과학적이고 철학적 질문들 중 하나에 답했다. (C) 그는 최고로 중요한 두 가지의 힘이 있다는 결론에 이르렀다. **그중 하나는 무작위적인 유전적 변이인데, 그것은 자연의 사납고 맹목적인 힘이다. 또 다른 하나의 힘은 자연 선택인데, 이러한 무작위성을 적응과 조화로 탈바꿈시킬 수 있다.** (A) 이 엄청난 시현과 다윈의 그 견해를 시험하고 심지어 논박하려는 무수한 시도가 이루어져 온 150년 후 지금, 이것은 가장 설득력 있고 사실적으로 뒷받침되는 진화론이다. (B) 확실히 그러한 노력들은 헛되지 않았다. 난해한 생명 과정의 이해에 있어서의 진보는 놀라웠으며, 이것은 무작위적인 유전적 변이와 자연 선택 둘 다에 매우 깊은 관련이 있다.

정답풀이

생명의 아름다움과 조화를 가져오는 힘이 무엇인가라는 질문에 대한 답을 찰스 다윈이 내놓았다는 내용의 주어진 글 다음에는, 그 답을 구체적으로 설명하는 내용의 (C)가 이어지고, 그러한 다윈의 견해가 150년의 검증을 거쳐 진화론으로 굳어졌다는 내용의 (A)가 온 후, 그러한 노력으로 생명 과정의 이해에 있어서의 놀라운 진보가 이루어졌다는 내용의 (B)로 마무리되는 순서가 가장 적절하다. 따라서 적절한 글의 순서는 ④ (C)-(A)-(B)이다.

구문풀이

15행 He came to **the conclusion** [that there are two forces of paramount importance].

: [ ]는 the conclusion의 내용을 구체적으로 설명하는 동격절이다.

18행 Another force is natural selection, [**capable** of transforming this randomness into adaptations and harmony].

: [ ]는 which is capable of ~에서 「주격 관계대명사+be동사」인 which is가 생략된 형태로 볼 수 있다.

어휘풀이

- perception *n* 인식
- disprove *v* 논박하다
- in vain 헛되이, 허사가 되어
- relevant *a* 관련된
- variation *n* 변화, 변이
- paramount *a* 최고의, 지상의
- incredible *a* 엄청난
- convincing *a* 설득력 있는
- intricate *a* 난해한
- random *a* 무작위의
- conclusion *n* 결론
- adaptation *n* 적응

221 답 ⑤

📖 이성적으로 해결할 수 없는 윤리적 신념 사이의 갈등

전문해석

특정한 윤리적 신념에 따르면 인간의 생명, 모든 인간의 생명은 최고의 가치이다. 결과적으로, 이러한 윤리적 신념에 따르면 심지어 전쟁에서나 사형으로도 인간을 죽이는 것은 절대적으로 금지된다. 이것은, 예를 들면, 군 복무 수행을 거부하는 소위 양심적 병역 거부자의 견해이며, 원칙적으로 그리고 어떠한 경우에도 사형을 거부하는 사람들의 견해이다. 그러나 또 다른 윤리적 신념이 있는데, 이것에 따르면 최고의 가치는 국가의 이익과 명예이다. 결과적으로, 모든 사람은, 이 견해에 따르면, 국가의 이익이나 명예가 그러한 행동을 요구한다면 자신의 생명을 희생하고 전쟁에서 국가의 적인 다른 인간들을 죽여야 하는 도덕적 의무를 가지게 되며, 사형을 집행해서 범죄자인 인간을 죽이는 것이 정당화된다. 이러한 두 개의 상반되는 가치 판단 사이에서 이성적이고 과학적인 방법으로 결정을 내리는 것은 불가능하다. 이러한 갈등을 판결하는 것은 최종적으로 우리의 감정, 우리의 의지인 것이지 우리의 이성이 아니다. 즉, 우리 양심의 감정적인 요소이지 이성적인 요소가 아니다.

정답풀이

주어진 문장에 these two conflicting judgments of value(이러한 두 개의 상반되는 가치 판단)라는 말이 있으므로, 앞에는 두 가지 가치 판단에 관한 진술이 나와야 한다. 따라서 주어진 문장은, 인간을 절대로 죽여서는 안 된다는 신념과 국가의 이익을 위해서라면 인간을 죽이는 것이 정당화된다는 신념인 두 가지 상반되는 가치 판단이 제시된 다음인 ⑤에 들어가는 것이 가장 적절하다.

구문풀이

8행 This is, for instance, the opinion of so-called conscientious objectors [who refuse to perform military service]; **and of** those [who repudiate in principle, and in any case, the death penalty].

: 두 개의 [ ]는 모두 주격 관계대명사절로 각각 conscientious objectors와 those를 수식하며, and of 사이에는 the opinion이 생략되었다.

어휘풀이

- conflict *n* 갈등, 충돌 *v* 대립하다, 모순되다
- rational *a* 이성적인, 합리적인
- conviction *n* 신념, 확신
- capital punishment 사형
- morally *ad* 도덕적으로
- sacrifice *v* 희생하다
- in the last instance 최후에, 중심에서
- ethical *a* 윤리적인
- forbid *v* 금지하다
- military service 군 복무
- be obliged to *do* ~할 수밖에 없다
- inflict *v* (벌 등을) 과하다

222~223 답 ④ / ③

📖 진정한 신뢰를 바탕으로 상호작용하는 인터넷 공간

전문해석

신뢰가 부족한 상황에 처해 있을 때, 우리는 상호작용에 제약을 강요하는 도구와 방법을 사용한다. 우리는 어두운 골목에서 낯선 사람을 만나지 않고, 제3자를 이용해 주요 금융거래를 보증하며, 친구와 함께 클럽에 가는 등등을 한다. 온라인도 마찬가지이다. 우리는 우리가 완전히 신뢰하지 않는 사람과 의사소통을 할 때, 의사소통을 제약하는 메커니즘을 발동한다. 우리는 확인, 검증, 증인(신뢰할 수 있는 제3자) 등등을 원한다. 우리는 도착하는 이메일에서 바이러스가 제거되기를 원하고, 스팸이 완전히 제거되는 등등을 원한다. **그러나 행동에 대한 그러한 제약들이 신뢰를 위한 기초가 아니다. 제약은 어떤 의미에서 신뢰의 정반대이다.** 왜냐하면 한 사람이 다른 사람을 신뢰하게 되면, 신뢰를 받는 사람은 비록 외부적으로 그렇게 하도록 제약을 받지 않더라도 '올바른 일을 할' 것으로 기대되기 때문이다. 경찰 국가는 시민들이 하는 일을 크게 제약할 수 있고, 이것이 특정한 종류의 예측 가능성과 행동에 대한 확신을 제공할 수는 있지만, 그것이 신뢰를 유발하지는 않는다. 진정한 신뢰가 생기려면, 그 신뢰가 검증될 수 있는 자유가 반드시 있어야 하는데, 그 신뢰가 유지될 (→ 위반될) 가능성이 반드시 있어야 한다. 인간 신뢰의 본질은 바로 이러한 위험과 그에 수반되는 자유이다. 사회는 우리에게 상호작용을 제약할 수 있는 도구에 덧붙여 그것을 피할 수 있는 도구도 제공한다. **'개방적' 또는 '투명한'이라고 불려온 최초 인터넷의 본질은 신뢰하는 당사자들이 상호작용하는 제약 없는 환경이다. 그리고 우리가 가장 쉽게 혁신, 새로움, 독창성을 찾을 수 있는 것은 바로 상호작용의 간접비가 가장 낮은 곳인 신뢰 당사자들 사이이다.**

정답풀이

222 신뢰가 부족할 때 상호작용에 제약을 강요하는 도구나 방법을 사용하지만 진정한 신뢰는 이러한 제약에 의해서가 아니라 신뢰가 검증될 수 있는 자유로운 환경에서 발생하는데, 인터넷의 본질이 바로 신뢰하는 당사자들이 상

호작용하는 환경이며, 이러한 제약 없는 환경에서 혁신이나 독창성을 찾을 수 있다는 내용이다. 따라서 글의 제목으로는 ④ '인터넷: 진정한 신뢰를 통한 상호작용 공간'이다.

223 앞에서는 진정한 신뢰가 생기려면 그 신뢰가 검증될 수 있는 자유가 있어야 한다고 했고 뒤에서는 신뢰의 본질은 이러한 위험과 그에 수반되는 자유라고 했다. 즉, 신뢰를 '위반할' 가능성이 있어야 하고, 신뢰를 테스트할 자유가 있어야만 진정한 신뢰가 있는지가 검증된다는 문맥이 자연스럽다. 따라서 (c) maintained(유지되는)를 violated(위반되는) 정도의 어휘로 바꿔야 한다.

오답풀이

222 ① 온라인상에서 진정한 신뢰를 확보하기 어려운 이유
  └ 온라인에서는 자유로운 검증을 통해 진정한 신뢰를 확보할 수 있다고 했다.

② 신뢰의 부족을 보충하는 다양한 방법

③ 자유: 신뢰 확인의 필수적인 요소
  └ 진정한 신뢰의 중요한 요소로 자유가 언급되었지만, 전체 글의 내용을 담고 있지 않은 제목이다.

⑤ 점차 정교해지고 복잡해지는 온라인 규제

223 ① 신뢰가 부족한 상황에서는 금융거래를 할 때 당사자 이외의 제3자를 통해서 보증을 한다는 문맥이므로 assure(보증하다)는 적절하다.

② 제약은 신뢰를 위한 기초가 아니며, 진정한 신뢰는 제약이 없는 자유로운 환경에서 생긴다고 했으므로 제약이 신뢰의 '정반대(opposite)'라고 한 것은 문맥상 적절하다.

④ 진정한 신뢰 형성을 위한 자유로운 환경의 필요성을 말하고 있으므로 제약을 '피할(bypass)' 수 있도록 한다는 문맥은 적절하다.

⑤ 상호작용 당사자들이 서로 신뢰하면 상호작용에 제약을 가하기 위한 노력이 필요 없을 것이므로 상호작용의 간접비가 '가장 낮을(lowest)' 것이라는 문맥은 적절하다.

구문풀이

21행 **It is** [this risk, and the freedom {that accompanies it}], **that** is the essence of human trust.

: 「It is ~ that ...」 강조구문을 사용하여 문장의 주어인 [ ]를 강조하고 있고, { }는 the freedom을 수식하는 주격 관계대명사절이다.

25행 The nature of the original Internet, [which has been called "open" or "transparent,"] is the constraint-free context [in which trusting parties interact].

: 첫 번째 [ ]는 문장의 주어인 The nature of the original Internet을 부연 설명하는 계속적 용법의 관계대명사절이고, 두 번째 [ ]는 the constraint-free context를 수식하는 관계절이다.

28행 And **it is** [among trusting parties, {where the overhead of interaction is lowest}], **that** we most easily find innovation, novelty, and originality.

: 「It is ~ that ...」 강조구문을 사용하여 [ ]의 부사구를 강조하고 있고, { }는 trusing parties를 부연 설명하는 계속적 용법의 관계부사절이다.

어휘풀이

- impose *v* 강요하다, 부과하다
- alley *n* 골목
- transaction *n* 거래
- validation *n* 검증
- strip out ~을 완전히 제거하다
- predictability *n* 예측 가능성
- accompany *v* 동반하다
- transparent *a* 투명한
- novelty *n* 새로움
- constraint *n* 제약, 구속
- assure *v* 보증하다
- constrain *v* 제약하다
- witness *n* 증인
- trustee *n* 신뢰를 받는 사람
- induce *v* 유발하다
- bypass *v* 피하다, 우회하다
- context *n* 상황, 맥락
- originality *n* 독창성

3점 공략 모의고사 9회

01 만연하다, 널리 퍼지다 **02** 실행하다 **03** 약속, 의무 **04** 야만인 **05** 경험적인 **06** 공평한, 편견 없는 **07** illusion **08** 사고방식 **09** temporal **10** 식별하다 **11** 연구하다, 조사하다 **12** tribal **13** 담론, 담화 **14** 중립적인 **15** 동화되다 **16** 변동, 오르내림 **17** 해치다, 훼손하다 **18** 어색한 **19** 궁극적으로 **20** ~을 시작하다

3점 공략 모의고사 10회

01 권력, 권위 **02** 방해하다 **03** 차별 **04** 정교한, 세련된 **05** 유지하다 **06** deliberately **07** 상관관계 **08** 유일한, 배타적인 **09** 고정된 **10** distort **11** 이국적인 **12** landscape **13** 망치다 **14** 소작농, 농부 **15** 도출하다, 끌어내다 **16** 위계 **17** 압도하다, 장악하다 **18** (요구, 목적 등에) 맞추다 **19** 굳어진, 엄격한 **20** 유지하다

3점 공략 모의고사 11회

01 뒤집다 **02** 약화시키다 **03** 습도 **04** 개입 **05** 고유한, 본질적인 **06** 꽃가루 **07** 저항, 반항 **08** decay **09** 보충의, 추가의 **10** sacrifice **11** 이용[활용]하다 **12** 타당성 **13** pessimistic **14** 선행하는 **15** 진정되다, 내려앉다 **16** 꽃잎 **17** 유연한 **18** 정지해 있는, 움직이지 않는 **19** 그리 크지 않은 **20** 이해 불가능한

3점 공략 모의고사 12회

01 능숙한, 숙달된 **02** 준수, 따름, 수락 **03** 고갈시키다 **04** 상이한, 아주 다른 **05** 물러나다 **06** 능력 있는 **07** 결핍 **08** 복잡한 **09** analytic **10** 압도하다 **11** yield **12** (협상의) 교착 상태 **13** misleading **14** 양보 **15** (원인 등에 ~에) 돌림, 귀속 **16** 지루함, 권태 **17** 으깨다 **18** 힘을 갖게 하다 **19** 이후의, 뒤이은 **20** ~에 대해 타협하다

3점 공략 모의고사 13회

01 환멸을 느끼다 **02** 미세한, 감지하기 힘든 **03** 발굴 **04** 추측[짐작]하다 **05** 비밀의 **06** 명명하다 **07** 폭언을 하다, 학대하다 **08** 변화, 변경 **09** mature **10** 수반하다 **11** tolerate **12** 육생의, 뭍의 **13** 하부 구조 **14** deliver **15** 고립시키다 **16** 물러나다, 멀어지다 **17** 지금까지 **18** 전제[필수] 조건 **19** 우선시하다 **20** ~을 만들어 내다, ~을 꾸며 내다

3점 공략 모의고사 14회

01 대용물 **02** 발전시키다, 육성하다 **03** 소수민족, 소수집단 **04** 떠오르는, 창발적인 **05** 신장시키다, 늘리다 **06** 2개 국어를 사용하는 **07** 양육, 교육 **08** dialect **09** 유전된 **10** 방출하다 **11** 동시에 **12** territory **13** 심어주다, 주입시키다 **14** 신뢰성 **15** 전개되다 **16** 자극 **17** 묘사하다 **18** 활동 영역 **19** counterproductive **20** 표현

3점 공략 모의고사 15회

01 살다, 거주하다 **02** 제거하다 **03** 영장류 **04** 양심 **05** 흥미진진한 **06** 신중한 **07** constitution **08** 유명한 **09** 주의가 흩어진, 집중을 못하는 **10** invade **11** (법 등을) 제정하다 **12** 먹이를 찾다 **13** 의회 **14** inspire **15** 지시하다, 명령하다 **16** 광합성 **17** 할당 **18** 부족한, 결핍된 **19** (기업의) 임원 **20** ~해야만 하다, ~할 의무가 있다

3점 공략 모의고사 16회

01 검증 **02** 한정하다 **03** 잔해, 유해 **04** 결함이 있는 **05** 확대하다 **06** 피하다, 우회하다 **07** 제약, 구속 **08** accompany **09** 금지하다 **10** 충분하다, 만족시키다 **11** 시기하는, 질투심이 강한 **12** 보호, 보존 **13** reflect **14** 천부적 자질 **15** (벌 등을) 과하다 **16** conviction **17** 이론적 근거 **18** 논박하다 **19** 최고의, 지상의 **20** 거래

224 답 ④

📖 이윤 지향적 박물관 운영의 부정적 측면

전문해석

박물관의 보이지 않는 구역에서 일어나는 활동보다 갤러리에서 발생하는 것을 강조하게 만드는 박물관 '내부의' 압력이 있다. 박물관의 수입을 늘리도록 박물관이 강요당하는 시대에, 박물관은 점점 더 많은 관객을 문으로 데려오기 위해 자기 갤러리를 현대화하거나 일시적인 전시회를 시작하는 데 흔히 자기 에너지를 집중시킨다. 다시 말해서, 박물관이 경쟁 경제에서 살아남기 위해 고군분투할 때, 그것의 예산은 흔히 갤러리의 인포테인먼트, 카페와 상점의 상품과 서비스와 같은 소비할 수 있는 박물관 자체의 부분을 우선시한다. 불이 켜져 있지 않은 매력 없는 저장실은, 그것들이 논의가 된다고 해도, 기껏해야 전시 홀에 둘 물건을 처리하는 서비스 공간으로 제시된다. 그리고 최악의 경우 박물관이 공개적으로 보이는 겉면에 점점 더 많은 자원을 쏟아붓기 때문에, 저장 공간의 현대화가 보류되거나 확장되는 소장품을 보관하고 그것의 복잡한 보존상의 요구를 충족시킬 공간이 점점 줄어들게 되어 저장 공간은 더 나빠질지도 모른다.

정답풀이

박물관이 수익 늘리는 것을 강요당하는 시대이기 때문에, 관객을 끌기 위해 눈에 보이는 갤러리의 현대화나 일시적 전시회 같은 것에만 에너지를 집중시킴으로써, 정작 눈에 보이지 않는 소장품을 보관하는 공간은 더 나빠질지도 모른다는 내용의 글이다. 따라서 글의 주제로 가장 적절한 것은 ④ '이윤 지향적 박물관 운영의 결과'이다.

오답풀이

① 박물관 전시 공간을 우선시하는 것의 중요성
② 관객을 위한 박물관에서의 다양한 활동의 이점
③ 물건 전시를 위해 저장실을 확장할 필요성
⑤ 공공의 이익에 대한 박물관의 헌신을 늘리는 방법

구문풀이

1행 There are pressures *within* the museum [that cause it to emphasise {what happens in the galleries} over the activities {that take place in its unseen zones}].

: [ ]는 pressures를 수식하는 주격 관계대명사절이고, 그 안의 첫 번째 { }는 emphasise의 목적어 역할을 하고, 두 번째 { }는 the activities를 수식하는 주격 관계대명사절이다.

14행 And at worst, [**as** museums pour more and more resources into their publicly visible faces], the spaces of storage may even suffer, [their modernisation **being kept** on hold or **being given** less and less space {**to house** the expanding collections and **serve** their complex conservation needs}].

: 첫 번째 [ ]는 접속사 as(~함에 따라)가 이끄는 부사절이다. 두 번째 [ ]는 부대상황을 나타내는 독립분사구문으로 their modernisation이 병렬구조로 연결된 being kept ~와 being given ~의 의미상 주어이고, { }는 목적을 나타내는 부사적 용법의 to부정사구로 house와 serve가 병렬구조를 이룬다.

어휘풀이

- mount *v* (~을 조직하여) 시작하다
- budget *n* 예산
- prioritise *v* 우선시하다
- consumable *a* 소비할 수 있는
- infotainment *n* 인포테인먼트(정보(information)와 오락(entertainment)의 합성어)
- unlit *a* 불이 켜져 있지 않은
- unglamorous *a* 매력 없는, 따분한
- storeroom *n* 저장실
- house *v* 보관하다
- suffer *v* 더 나빠지다
- conservation *n* 보전

225 답 ②

📖 과학 발전과 대비되는 역사적 통찰의 발전

전문해석

정확성과 확정성은 모든 의미 있는 과학 토론을 위해 없어서는 안 될 필요조건이고, 과학에서의 발전은 상당 부분 점점 더 높은 정확성을 달성하는 진행 중인 과정이다. 그러나 역사적 진술은 진술의 증식을 더 중요시하는데, 이는 한 가지 진술의 정제가 아니라 더 다양한 일련의 진술의 생성을 중요시하는 것이다. 역사적 통찰은 이전에 선택한 것들을 지속적으로 '좁혀 가는' 것의 문제, 즉 진리에 대한 근접함의 문제가 아니라, 반대로 가능한 관점들의 '폭발적 증가'이다. 따라서 그것은 이전의 진술들에서 무엇이 옳고 그른지에 대한 주의 깊은 분석에 의해 진리를 획득하는 것이 아니라, 새롭고 대안적인 진술의 생성에 의해 확정성과 정확성에 대한 이전의 환상의 정체를 밝혀내는 것을 목표로 한다. 그리고 이러한 관점에서 볼 때, 역사적 통찰의 발전은 과학에서처럼 진리에 점점 더 많이 근접함보다는, 점점 더 큰 혼란을 만들어 내는 과정, 즉 이미 획득된 것으로 보이는 확실성과 정확성에 대한 지속적인 의문 제기로 외부인에게 정말로 여겨질 수도 있다.

정답풀이

정확성과 확정성이 중요한 과학과 달리 역사적 진술에서는 한 가지 진술을 정제하는 것이 아니라 더 다양한 일련의 진술을 생성하는 것이 중요하다는 내용의 글이다. 역사적 통찰은 진리에의 근접함이 아니라 가능한 관점들의 폭발적 증가로, 이전에 확실하다고 여겨졌던 것의 정체를 드러내는 것을 목표로 한다고 했다. 따라서 외부인에게 역사적 통찰의 발전은 ② '이미 획득된 것으로 보이는 확실성과 정확성'에 지속적으로 의문을 제기하는 것으로 보일 수 있다고 할 수 있다.

오답풀이

① 역사적 진술을 평가하는 기준
③ 어떤 사건에 대한 대안적 해석의 가능성
└ 역사적 통찰은 대안적 해석의 가능성을 지향하므로 오답!
④ 역사 저술에서 다수의 관점의 공존
⑤ 수집된 역사적 증거의 정확성과 신뢰성

구문풀이

17행 And from this perspective, the development of historical insight may indeed be regarded by the outsider [as {a process of creating ever more confusion}, {a continuous questioning of certainty and precision (seemingly achieved already)}], **rather than**, [as in the sciences, an ever greater approximation to the truth].

: 두 개의 [ ]는 각각 「A rather than B(B라기보다는 A)」 구문의 A와 B에 해당한다. 첫 번째 [ ] 안에서 두 개의 { }는 동격 관계를 이루며, ( )는 certainty and precision을 수식하는 과거분사구이다.

226 답 ④

📖 **결과 기반 가격 책정인 승소 시 보수 약정 제도**

전문해석

결과 기반 가격 책정 중 가장 일반적으로 알려진 형태는 변호사들이 사용하는 '승소 시 보수 약정'이라고 불리는 관행이다. (C) 승소 시 보수 약정은 개인 상해 및 특정 소비자 소송에 대해 비용이 청구되는 주요 방식이다. **이 방식에서 변호사는 소송이 해결될 때까지 수수료나 지불금을 받지 않는데, 해결되었을 때 그들은 의뢰인이 받는 금액의 일정 비율을 받는다.** (A) 따라서 의뢰인에게 유리한 결과만 보수가 지불된다. 의뢰인의 관점에서 보면, 이러한 소송의 의뢰인 대부분이 법률 사무소에 익숙하지 않고 아마도 겁을 먹을 수 있다는 부분적인 이유로 그 가격 책정은 타당하다. 그들의 가장 큰 두려움은 해결하는 데 몇 년이 걸릴 수 있는 소송에 대한 높은 수수료이다. (B) 승소 시 보수 약정을 사용함으로써 의뢰인은 합의금을 받을 때까지 수수료를 지불하지 않도록 보장받는다. 승소 시 보수 약정의 이런 경우와 여타 경우에서 서비스의 경제적 가치는 서비스 전에 결정하기 어렵고, 공급자는 구매자에게 가치를 전달하는 위험과 보상을 그들이 나눌 수 있게 하는 가격을 전달한다.

정답풀이

결과 기반 가격 책정의 한 형태로 승소 시 보수 약정이 있다고 언급한 주어진 글 다음에는, 승소 시 보수 약정의 방식에 대해 설명하는 (C)가 오는 것이 적절하다. 변호사가 승소한 경우에 의뢰인이 지불받는 금액의 일정 비율을 받는 방식의 가격 정책이라고 설명하는 내용의 (C) 다음에는, 그 방식이 결과적으로 의뢰인에게 유리하다고 의뢰인의 입장에서 설명하는 (A)가 이어지고, 마지막으로 공급자의 입장에서 승소 시 보수 약정에 대해 설명하는 (B)가 와야 한다.

구문풀이

12행 In these and other instances of contingency pricing, / the economic value of the service is hard to determine before the service, and providers develop a price [that allows them to share the risks and rewards of delivering value to the buyer].

: the economic ~ service가 주어1, is가 동사1이며, providers가 주어2, develop가 동사2이다. [ ]는 a price를 수식하는 주격 관계대명사절이다.

19행 In this approach, lawyers do not receive fees or payment / until the case is settled, [when they are paid a percentage of the money {that the client receives}].

: [ ]는 '소송이 해결된 때'를 부연 설명하는 관계부사절이고, 그 안의 { }는 the money를 수식하는 목적격 관계대명사절이다.

어휘풀이

- practice *n* 관행

227 답 ⑤

📖 **아날로그에서 디지털 기술로의 변화가 음악 제작 방식에 미친 영향**

전문해석

아날로그 기술에서 디지털 기술로의 전환은 음악이 제작되는 방식에 크게 영향을 미쳤다. 무엇보다도, 소리의 디지털화, 즉 그것의 숫자로의 변환은 음악 제작자들이 기존의 작업을 되돌릴 수 있게 해주었다. 다시 말해, 원본을 희생하지 않으면서 소리를 비틀고 구부려서 어떤 새로운 것으로 만들 수 있었다. 이러한 '되돌리기' 기능은 실수를 훨씬 덜 중대하게 만들어, 창작 과정을 촉발하고 일반적으로 더 실험적인 사고 방식을 장려했다. 또한, 디지털로 변환된 소리는 물리적인 도구를 사용하기보다는 단순히 디지털 메시지를 프로그래밍함으로써 조작될 수 있어서, 편집 과정을 크게 간소화했다. 예를 들어, 예전에 편집 과정은 음성 녹음테이프를 물리적으로 자르고 합쳐 잇기 위해 면도기 칼날의 사용을 수반했지만, 이제 그것은 컴퓨터에 기반한 순서기 프로그램의 커서와 마우스 클릭을 수반했고, 그것은 분명 시간을 덜 소모했다. 디지털로 변환된 소리의 조작은 2진법의 정보를 재프로그래밍하는 것을 의미했으므로, 편집작업은 1,000분의 1초의 정밀도로 수행될 수 있었다. 이런 미시적 수준의 접근은 (무음 지점에서 트랙을 결합하는 것과 같은) 조작의 흔적을 숨기는 것을 더 쉽게 만든 동시에, 들릴 수 있고 실험적인 방식으로 소리를 조작할 새로운 가능성을 내놓았다.

정답풀이

디지털로 변환된 소리의 조작으로 인해 편집 작업이 1,000분의 1초의 정밀도로 수행될 수 있었다는 내용의 주어진 문장은, ⑤ 뒤의 This microlevel access(이런 미시적 수준의 접근)와 연결되므로 주어진 문장이 들어가기에 가장 적절한 곳은 ⑤이다. 앞에 This microlevel access라고 가리킬 만한 내용이 없는 논리적 공백이 주어진 문장을 ⑤에 넣으면 채워진다.

구문풀이

18행 For example, while editing once involved razor blades to physically cut and splice audiotapes, / **it** now involved the cursor and mouse-click of the computer-based sequencer program, [which was obviously less time consuming].

: 주절의 주어 it은 부사절의 주어 editing을 가리키는 대명사이다. [ ]는 앞절(it ~ program)의 내용을 부연 설명하는 주격 관계대명사절이다.

22행 This microlevel access at once <u>made</u> **it** easier [**to conceal** any traces of manipulations (such as joining tracks in silent spots)] and <u>introduced</u> new possibilities for manipulating sounds in audible and experimental ways.

: it은 made의 형식상의 목적어이고, [ ]의 to부정사구가 내용상의 목적어이며, made와 introduced는 문장의 동사로 병렬구조를 이룬다.

어휘풀이

- manipulation *n* 조작
- edit *v* 편집하다
- millisecond *n* 1,000분의 1초, 밀리초
- precision *n* 정밀도
- significantly *ad* 크게
- convert *v* 변환하다
- analog *a* 아날로그 방식의

- first and foremost 무엇보다도, 가장 중요하게
- digitization *n* 디지털화
- conversion *n* 변환
- bend *v* 구부리다
- undo *v* 되돌리다
- sacrifice *v* 희생하다
- momentous *a* 중대한
- experimental *a* 실험적인
- mindset *n* 사고방식
- razor blade 면도날 칼날
- audiotape *n* 음성 녹음테이프
- sequencer *n* 순서기(전자 녹음 장비의 하나)
- microlevel *a* 매우 작은 수준의, 미시적 수준의
- access *n* 접근
- conceal *v* 숨기다
- trace *n* 흔적
- track *n* 트랙(테이프나 디스크의 데이터 구획 단위)
- audible *a* 들릴 수 있는

228~229 답 ③ / ②

📖 협상은 고정된 파이라는 잘못된 통념에서 벗어나야 할 필요성

전문해석

많은 협상가는 모든 협상이 고정된 파이를 수반한다고 가정한다. 협상가들은 종종 통합적인 협상 기회를 제로섬 상황이나 승패 교환으로 접근한다. 허구의 고정된 파이를 믿는 사람들은 당사자들의 이해관계가 통합적인 합의와 상호 이익이 되는 절충안의 가능성이 없는 반대 입장에 있다고 가정하기 때문에 그것을 찾으려는 노력을 억누른다. 고용 협상에서 급여가 유일한 문제라고 생각하는 구직자는 고용주가 7만 달러를 제시할 때 7만 5천 달러를 요구할 수 있다. 두 당사자가 가능성에 대해 더 자세히 논의할 때만 이사 비용과 시작 날짜 또한 협상할 수 있다는 사실을 발견하게 되는데, 이는 급여 문제의 해결을 방해할(→ 촉진할) 수 있을 것이다. 협상을 고정된 파이 관점에서 보는 경향은 사람들이 주어진 갈등 상황의 본질을 어떻게 보느냐에 따라 달라진다. 이는 Harinck, de Dreu와 Van Vianen의, 징역형에 대한 검사와 피고측 변호인 간의 모의 협상을 포함하는 기발한 실험에서 밝혀졌다. 어떤 참가자들은 개인적 이득의 관점에서 그들의 목표를 보라는 말을 들었고(예를 들어, 특정 징역형을 정하는 것이 당신의 경력에 도움이 될 것이다). 다른 참가자들은 그들의 목표를 효과성의 관점에서 보라는 말을 들었으며(특정 형은 상습적 범행을 방지할 가능성이 가장 크다). 그리고 또 다른 참가자들은 가치에 초점을 맞추라는 말을 들었다(특정 징역형은 공정하고 정당하다). 개인적 이득에 초점을 맞춘 협상가들은 고정된 파이에 대한 믿음의 영향을 받아 상황에 경쟁적으로 접근할 가능성이 가장 컸다. 가치에 초점을 맞춘 협상가들은 문제를 고정된 파이 관점에서 볼 가능성이 가장 낮았고 상황에 협력적으로 접근하려는 경향이 더 컸다. 시간 제약과 같은 스트레스가 많은 조건은 이러한 흔한 잘못된 생각의 원인이 되며, 이는 결국 더 적게 통합적인 합의로 이어질 수 있다.

정답풀이

228 협상을 고정된 파이의 관점에서 접근하기 때문에 통합적인 합의에 이르지 못하는 상황을 고용 협상과 징역형에 대한 모의 협상의 사례를 통해 설명함으로써, 고정된 파이의 관점에서 벗어나야 함을 강조하는 내용이다. 따라서 글의 제목으로 가장 적절한 것은 ③ '협상가들이여, 고정된 파이라는 미몽에서 깨어나라!'이다.

229 고용 협상에서 두 당사자가 급여 문제뿐만 아니라 협상의 다른 가능성인 이사 비용과 시작 날짜를 논의하게 되면, 막혔던 협상이 새로운 국면으로 진척될 수 있다는 맥락이므로, (b) block(방해하다)을 facilitate(촉진하다)와 같은 낱말로 바꿔야 한다.

오답풀이

228 ① 고정된 파이: 제로섬 게임에서 성공의 열쇠
 ↳ 협상을 고정된 파이의 관점에서 접근함으로써 합의에 이르지 못함을 설명하고 있으므로 제목으로 부적절하다.

② 고정된 파이는 여러분에게 가장 큰 급여를 받는 방법을 알려 준다
④ 더 공정한 징역형을 원하는가? 고정된 파이를 고수하라
⑤ 어떤 대안이 고정된 파이 효과를 극대화하는가?

229 ① 협상을 고정된 파이의 관점에서 접근하면, 합의 도출을 위한 다른 절충안을 찾으려는 노력을 '억누른다(suppress)'는 것은 문맥상 적절하다.

③ 징역형에 대한 모의 협상의 목표(본질)를 어떻게 보게 하느냐에 따라 고정된 파이의 관점에도 차이가 있다는 내용이 이어지므로 varies(달라진다)는 문맥상 적절하다.

④ 개인적 이득의 관점에서 협상을 하게 되면 고정된 파이의 관점에 가장 영향을 받았다고 했으므로, 그로 인해 상황을 '경쟁적으로(competitively)' 접근한다는 흐름은 문맥상 적절하다.
 ↳ 고정된 파이라는 믿음에 영향을 받게 되면 협상을 제로섬 상황의 경쟁적인 것으로 볼 것이므로 competitively는 적절하다.

⑤ 스트레스가 많으면, 협상으로 고정된 파이로만 접근하는 잘못된 생각을 하게 됨으로써, '더 적게(less)' 통합적인 합의로 이어진다는 흐름은 문맥상 적절하다.

구문풀이

4행 Those [who believe in the mythical fixed pie] assume [that parties' interests stand in opposition, with no possibility for integrative settlements and mutually beneficial trade-offs], / so they suppress efforts to search for **them**.

: 첫 번째 [ ]는 문장의 핵심 주어진 Those를 수식하는 주격관계대명사절이고, 두 번째 [ ]는 동사 assume의 목적어 역할을 하는 명사절이다. 마지막의 them은 integrative settlements and mutually beneficial trade-offs를 가리킨다.

11행 **Only** when the two parties discuss the possibilities further / **do they discover** [that moving expenses and starting date can also be negotiated], [which may facilitate resolution of the salary issue].

: Only가 이끄는 부사절이 문두에 와서 주절의 주어와 동사가 도치되었다. 첫 번째 [ ]는 discover의 목적어 역할을 하는 명사절이고, 두 번째 [ ]는 앞 절을 부연 설명하는 관계대명사절이다.

어휘풀이

- negotiator *n* 협상가
- assume *v* 가정[추정]하다
- integrative *a* 통합의
- mythical *a* 허구의, 신화적인
- party *n* 당사자
- interest *n* 이익, 이해관계
- opposition *n* 반대
- settlement *n* 합의
- mutually *ad* 상호 간에
- trade-off *n* 절충, 타협
- suppress *v* 억누르다
- resolution *n* 해결
- simulated *a* 모의의
- defense lawyer 피고측 변호인
- jail sentence 징역형
- arrange *v* 정하다
- competitively *ad* 경쟁적으로
- constraint *n* 제약
- contribute to ~의 원인이 되다
- misperception *n* 오해, 잘못된 생각

230 답 ②

📖 고객이 아닌 전문가를 만족시키려고 시도하는 프로젝트의 문제점

전문해석
프로젝트에서 금도금은 예상되는 결과를 불필요하게 향상하는 것, 즉 비용이 많이 들고 필요하지 않으며 목표와 관련하여 부가 가치가 낮은 특성을 추가하는 것으로, 다시 말해 자신의 재능을 입증하는 것 외에는 실질적인 명분이 없는 더 많은 것을 제공하는 것을 의미한다. 금도금은 특히 프로젝트팀원들에 대해서 흥미로운데, 이는 전문적인 요소가 뚜렷한 프로젝트, 다시 말해 검증된 경험과 폭넓은 전문적 자율성을 갖춘 전문가가 참여하는 프로젝트에서 일반적이기 때문이다. 이러한 환경에서 전문가들은 종종 프로젝트를 자신의 다양한 능력을 테스트하고 강화할 기회로 여긴다. 따라서 선의로 금도금에 참여하려는 유혹, 즉 전문가를 만족시키지만, 고객의 요청에 가치를 더하지 않는 동시에 프로젝트에서 귀중한 자원을 없애는 더 많은 또는 더 높은 품질의 성과를 달성하려는 유혹이 있다. 속담에 있듯이, '최고는 좋음의 적'이다.

정답풀이
프로젝트에서 금도금을 한다는 것은 필요 이상으로 결과를 향상하는 것, 즉 자신의 재능을 입증하기 위해 명분도 없이 더 많은 것을 제공하는 것을 의미하며, 이런 일은 특히 검증된 전문가가 참여하는 프로젝트에서 일반적이라고 한다. 따라서 밑줄 친 '최고는 좋음의 적'이 의미하는 바로 가장 적절한 것은 ② '오로지 자신을 증명하기 위해 성과의 질을 올리는 것은 바람직하지 않다.'이다.

오답풀이
① 일에서 완벽을 추구하면 팀원 간 갈등이 일어난다.
③ 프로젝트에 필요 이상의 자격을 갖춘 전문가를 끌어들이는 것은 나쁜 결과를 가져온다.
└ 프로젝트에 참여한 전문가들이 필요 이상으로 결과를 높이려고 한다는 내용이지, 필요 이상의 자격을 갖춘 전문가를 참여시키는 것 자체가 나쁜 결과를 가져온다는 것이 아니다.
④ 고객의 변화하는 요구에 대응하는 것은 불필요하다.
⑤ 프로젝트에 필요한 다양한 기술을 습득한다고 해서 성공이 보장되는 것은 아니다.

구문풀이
1행 Gold plating in the project means needlessly **enhancing** the expected results, namely, **adding** characteristics [that are costly, not required], and [that have low added value with respect to the targets] — in other words, **giving** more with no real justification other than to demonstrate one's own talent.

: enhancing ~ results, adding ~ targets, giving ~ talent는 모두 동사 means 의 목적어 역할을 하는 동명사구이다. 두 개의 [ ]는 모두 characteristics를 수식하는 주격 관계대명사절이다.

13행 There is therefore a strong temptation, in all good faith, [to engage in gold plating], namely, [to achieve more or higher-quality work {that **gratifies** the professional but **does not add** value to the client's requests, and at the same time **removes** valuable resources from the project}].

: 두 개의 [ ]는 모두 a strong temptation을 수식하는 to부정사구이다. { }는 more

or higher-quality work를 수식하는 주격 관계대명사절이며, 그 안에 gratifies, does not add, removes는 병렬구조로 연결된 that절의 동사들이다.

어휘풀이
- gold plating 금도금
- added value 부가 가치
- justification *n* 명분, 정당화
- component *n* 요소
- autonomy *n* 자율성
- temptation *n* 유혹
- gratify *v* 만족[충족]시키다
- overqualified *a* 필요 이상의 자격[경력]을 갖춘
- namely *ad* 즉, 다시 말해
- with respect to ~에 관하여
- demonstrate *v* 보여주다
- extensive *a* 광범위한
- enrich *v* 강화하다, 향상시키다
- in all good faith 선의로

231 답 ③

📖 유기농 경작 방식의 제약과 이점

전문해석
천연 제품만 투입물로 사용될 수 있는 방식으로 정의되는 '유기농' 방식이 생물권에 피해를 덜 줄 것이라고 시사되어 왔다. 그러나 **대규모로 '유기농' 경작 방식을 채택하면 여러 주요 작물의 수확량이 감소하고 생산비가 증가할 것이다.** 무기 질소 공급은 많은 비(非)콩과 작물 종의 생산성을 중상 수준으로 유지하는 데 필수적인데, 질소성 물질의 유기적 공급이 흔히 무기 질소 비료보다 제한적이거나 더 비싸기 때문이다. 또한, '친환경적인 거름' 작물로 거름이나 콩과 식물을 광범위하게 사용하는 것에는 **이점(→ 제약)**이 있다. 많은 경우에 화학 물질이 사용될 수 없다면 잡초 방제는 매우 어렵거나 많은 수작업이 필요할 수 있는데, 사회가 더 부유해짐에 따라 이러한 일을 기꺼이 하려는 사람은 더 적다. **그러나 윤작의 현명한 사용 및 경작과 축산업의 특정한 조합과 같은 '유기농' 경작에서 사용되는 일부 방식은 농촌 생태계의 지속 가능성에 중요한 기여를 할 수 있다.**

정답풀이
③ 유기농 경작 방식을 대규모로 채택하면 주요 작물의 수확량이 감소하고 생산비가 증가한다는 내용 다음에 또 다른 단점을 덧붙이는 흐름이다. 따라서 거름이나 콩과 식물을 광범위하게 사용하는 것에는 잡초 방제의 어려움이 따른다는 문맥이 되도록 benefits(이점)를 constraints(제약)와 같은 낱말로 바꾸어야 한다.

오답풀이
① 유기농 방식을 대규모로 채택하는 것의 단점에 대해 언급하는 문장으로 주요 작물의 수확량이 '줄고(reduce)' 생산비가 증가한다는 문맥은 적절하다.
② 유기농 방식을 대규모로 채택할 경우 생산비가 증가하는 이유를 밝히는 문장이다. 따라서 무기 질소 공급은 많은 비콩과 작물 종의 생산성을 유지하는 데 '필수적(essential)'인데, 질소성 물질의 유기적 공급이 제한적이고 비싸기 때문이라는 문맥은 적절하다.
④ 화학 물질을 쓰지 않으면 잡초 방제를 수작업으로 해야 하는데, 사회가 부유해짐에 따라 그런 일을 할 사람들이 '더 적을(fewer)' 것이라는 문맥은 적절하다.
⑤ 유기농 경작 방식의 단점을 극복할 수 있는 방법을 소개하는 문장으로 윤작 등의 방식을 통해 농촌 생태계의 지속 가능성에 '기여(contributions)'할 수 있다는 문맥은 적절하다.

구문풀이
17행 Some methods [used in "organic" farming], however, **such as** [the sensible use of crop rotations] and [specific combinations of cropping and livestock enterprises], **can make** important contributions to the sustainability of rural ecosystems.

: 첫 번째 [ ]는 문장의 핵심 주어인 Some methods를 수식하는 과거분사구이고 문장의 동사는 can make이다. and로 연결된 두 번째와 세 번째 [ ]는 such as에 이어져서 Some methods ~ farming의 구체적인 예를 제시한다.

어휘풀이

- organic *a* 유기농의
- input *n* 투입물
- adoption *n* 채택
- inorganic nitrogen 무기 질소
- productivity *n* 생산성
- weed control 잡초 방제
- sensible *a* 현명한
- combination *n* 조합
- contribution *n* 기여, 공헌
- rural *a* 농촌의
- define *v* 정의하다
- biosphere *n* 생물권
- yield *n* 수확량, 산출량
- moderate *a* 보통의, 중간의
- extensive *a* 광범위한
- chemical *n* 화학 물질
- crop rotation 윤작, 돌려짓기
- livestock enterprise 축산업
- sustainability *n* 지속 가능성
- ecosystem *n* 생태계

232 답 ④

📖 받아들여지기 위해 한 걸음만 앞서야 하는 혁신

전문해석

시대를 너무 앞서간 발명이나 발견은 가치가 없는데, 누구도 따라갈 수 없기 때문이다. 이상적으로, 혁신은 알려진 것으로부터 단지 다음 단계만을 가능하게 하고, 그 문화가 한 걸음 앞으로 나아가도록 요청한다. 지나치게 미래지향적이거나 관행을 벗어나는 혹은 비현실적인 발명은 처음에는 실패할 수도 있지만(아직 발명되지 않은 필수적인 재료나 중요한 시장 또는 적절한 이해가 부족할 수 있다) 아이디어를 뒷받침하는 생태 환경이 따라잡을 때 나중에 성공할 수도 있다. Gregor Mendel의 1865년 유전 이론은 옳았지만 35년 동안 무시되었다. 그의 날카로운 통찰력은 생물학자들이 그 당시에 가졌던 문제들을 설명하지 않았기 때문에 받아들여지지 않았고, 그의 설명 역시 알려진 메커니즘에 의해 작동하지 않았기 때문에 그의 발견은 얼리 어댑터들에게도 이해하기 어려웠다. 수십 년 후 과학은 Mendel의 발견이 답할 수 있는 긴급한 질문에 직면했다. 이제 그의 통찰력은 단 한 걸음만 떨어져 있었다. 서로 몇 년 간격으로, 세 명의 다른 과학자들이 각각 독립적으로 Mendel의 잊혀진 연구를 재발견했는데, 물론 그 연구는 줄곧 그곳에 있었다.

정답풀이

동시대 사람들이 혁신으로 받아들이려면 한 걸음 정도만 앞서야 하는데, 너무 앞서간 발명이나 발견은 시간이 한참 흐른 후에야 받아들여질 수 있다고 설명하고, 그 사례로 Mendel의 유전 이론이 제시되었다. 따라서 시대를 너무 앞서 나갔기 때문에 받아들여지지 않던, Mendel의 유전 이론은 시간이 지난 후에는 받아들여질 수 있을 정도의 앞선 이론이 되었다고 해야 하므로, 빈칸에 들어갈 말로 가장 적절한 것은 ④ '단 한 걸음만 떨어져 있었다'이다.

오답풀이

① 현대의 문제를 따라잡았다
  ↳ 현대의 문제를 따라잡았는지에 대해 언급된 것이 없다.

② 훨씬 더 많은 의문을 제기했다

③ 과거와 현재의 주제를 동일하게 다루었다

⑤ 대중에게 다시 수용되었다
  ↳ 대중에게 수용된 적이 없었기에 다시 수용되었다고 할 수 없다.

구문풀이

2행 Ideally, an innovation **opens** up only the next step from [what is known] and **invites** the culture to move forward one hop.

: opens와 invites는 문장의 주어 an innovation에 대한 동사로 병렬구조를 이룬다. [ ]는 from의 목적어 역할을 하는 명사절(관계절)이다.

11행 His sharp insights were not accepted because they did not explain the problems [biologists had at the time], / **nor** did his explanation operate by known mechanisms, so his discoveries were out of reach even for the early adopters.

: [ ]는 the problem을 수식하는 관계절로 목적격 관계대명사 that[which]이 생략되었다. 부정어 nor가 문두에 쓰이면서 뒤에는 '조동사(did)+주어+동사원형'의 어순으로 도치가 일어났다.

어휘풀이

- invention *n* 발명
- innovation *n* 혁신
- overly *ad* 지나치게
- unconventional *a* 관습에 얽매이지 않는
- visionary *a* 비현실적인
- catch up 따라잡다
- insight *n* 통찰력
- early adopter 얼리 어답터(남들보다 먼저 신제품을 사서 써 보는 사람)
- urgent *a* 긴급한
- discovery *n* 발견
- open up ~을 가능하게 하다
- initially *ad* 처음에는
- genetic *a* 유전의
- biologist *n* 생물학자
- all along 줄곧

233 답 ②

📖 단순한 요소를 다양하게 발전시켜 만드는 멋진 작품

전문해석

전개부는 매우 복잡하면서 환상적일 수 있다. Johann Sebastian Bach의 푸가는 하나의 멜로디 라인, 때로는 단지 소수의 음표가 그 작곡가가 일관된 구조 내에서 많은 복잡한 전개부를 포함하는 훌륭한 작품을 만들기 위해 필요한 전부였을 때, 이 과정이 얼마나 효과를 보일 수 있을지를 보여준다. Ludwig van Beethoven의 유명한 5번 교향곡은 클래식 작곡가가 몇 개의 음표와 단순하며 리듬감 있는 두드림으로 얼마나 많은 이익을 얻어낼 수 있는지에 대한 이례적일 정도로 우수한 예를 제공한다. 모든 사람들이 어디선가 들어본 시작 부분의 다-다-다-덤은 일종의 반복 악구나 연결 끈처럼, 시작 악장뿐만 아니라 나머지 3악장 내내 엄청나게 다양한 방식으로 나타난다. 우리가 그림 작품 하나를 완성하는 데 들인 복잡한 붓놀림을 항상 볼 수 있는 것이 아니듯이, Beethoven이 자신의 반복 악구를 어떻게 계속 새롭게 사용하는 것을 찾는지 또는 그의 제재를 거대하고 응집력 있는 진술로 어떻게 전개하는지를 항상 알아보지는 못할 수도 있다. 그러나 그 강력한 교향곡에서 우리가 얻는 즐거움의 많은 부분은 그 이면의 독창성, 즉 음악적 아이디어의 인상적인 전개에서 비롯된다.

정답풀이

전개부는 복잡하면서도 환상적일 수 있다고 하면서 Bach의 푸가와 Beethoven의 5번 교향곡을 그 예로 설명하고 있다. 하나의 멜로디 라인, 혹은 소수의 음표를 다양하게 발전시켜서 훌륭한 작품이 된 것이 Bach의 푸가이고, Beethoven의 5번 교향곡 또한 몇 개의 음표와 리듬감 있는 단순한 두드림을 다양하게 전개하여 멋진 작품을 탄생시킨 사례라고 했으므로, 들어본 듯한 도입부의 단순한 음이 다양하게 발전되어 나가면서 시작 악장뿐만 아니라 나머지 3악장 내내 멋진 음악으로 등장할 것임을 추론할 수 있다. 따라서 빈칸에 가장 적절한 것은 ② '엄청나게 다양한 방식으로 나타난다'이다.

오답풀이

① 작곡가의 음악적 아이디어를 모순되게 만든다
  ↳ 단순한 음이 작곡가의 음악적 아이디어를 모순되게 만든다는 내용은 전혀 등장하지 않았다.

③ 광범위한 음악적 지식을 창의적으로 제공한다

④ 구조 내에서 상당히 조용하게 남아 있다

⑤ 자기 자신의 즐거움과 깊이 관련된다
  ↳ 마지막 문장의 즐거움이란 단어를 이용했지만 글의 내용과는 전혀 관련 없는 내용이다.

2행 A fugue by Johann Sebastian Bach illustrates [how far this process could go], / when [a single melodic line, sometimes just a handful of notes], was all [that the composer needed {to create a brilliant work (containing lots of intricate development within a coherent structure)}].

: 첫 번째 [ ]는 문장의 동사 illustrates의 목적어 역할을 하는 명사절이고, 두 번째 [ ]는 when이 이끄는 시간 부사절의 주어이며, 세 번째 [ ]는 when절의 보어인 all을 수식하는 목적격 관계대명사절이다. 세 번째 [ ] 안의 { }는 목적을 나타내는 부사적 용법의 to부정사구이고, ( )는 a brilliant work를 수식하는 현재분사구이다.

15행 **Just as** we don't always see the intricate brushwork [that goes into the creation of a painting], / we may not always notice [how Beethoven keeps finding fresh uses for his motto] or [how he develops his material into a large, cohesive statement].

: Just as ~는 '~와 마찬가지로'라는 의미를 나타내는 부사절을 이끌고, 첫 번째 [ ]는 the intricate brushwork를 수식하는 주격 관계대명사절이다. 두 번째와 세 번째 [ ]는 notice의 목적어 역할을 하는, 의문사 how가 이끄는 명사절이다.

어휘풀이
- development *n* 전개부
- fanciful *a* 별난, 공상적인, 멋진
- illustrate *v* 보여주다
- note *n* 음표
- exceptional *a* 이례적일 정도로 우수한, 예외적인
- mileage *n* 이익
- connective *a* 연결[결합]하는
- motto *n* 반복 악구
- cohesive *a* 응집력 있는
- inventiveness *n* 독창적임
- complicated *a* 복잡한
- fugue *n* 푸가[둔주곡]
- a handful of 소수의
- brilliant *a* 훌륭한
- movement *n* 악장
- thread *n* 끈
- material *n* 제재
- mighty *a* 강력한, 장대한
- contradictory *a* 모순적인

는 내용과 연결되므로 (C) 다음에 (B)가 와야 하고, 마지막에 대조적으로 영양이 풍부한 경우일 때 식물의 반응에 대해 말하는 (A)가 오면 된다.

6행 At all developmental stages, plants respond to environmental changes or unevenness **so as to** be able to use their energy for growth, survival, and reproduction, **while limiting** damage and nonproductive uses of their valuable energy.

: so as to *do*는 '~하도록'의 의미를 나타내고, while ~ing는 '~하는 동안'의 의미를 나타낸다.

19행 But if a plant does not have a caretaker [to provide supplemental minerals], / it can **proliferate** or **lengthen** its roots and **develop** root hairs [to allow foraging in more distant soil patches].

: if ~ minerals는 조건의 부사절이고, 첫 번째 [ ]는 a caretaker를 수식하는 to부정사구이다. it 이하 주절에서 proliferate, lengthen, develop은 can에 연결되는 동사로 병렬구조를 이루고, 두 번째 [ ]는 목적의 의미를 나타내는 to부정사구이다.

어휘풀이
- finely *ad* 미세하게
- adaptive response 적응 반응
- abundance *n* 풍부
- unevenness *n* 불균형
- availability *n* 가용성
- lengthening *n* 연장
- proliferate *v* 증식시키다
- temporal *a* 시간의
- variation *n* 변화
- tune *v* 조정하다
- gardener *n* 정원사
- risk averse *a* 위험을 회피하는
- reproduction *n* 번식, 복제
- rist-taking *a* 위험을 감수하는
- supplemental *a* 보충의
- patch *n* 작은 땅, 지대
- spatial *a* 공간의

---

234 답 ⑤

📖 영양분이 제한적일 때와 풍부할 때 식물의 적응 반응

전문해석
식물은 영양분이 제한적일 때 미세하게 조정된 적응 반응을 보인다. 정원사는 노란 잎을 영양 부족과 비료가 필요하다는 신호로 인식할 수도 있다. (C) 그러나 식물에 보충하는 미네랄을 공급해 줄 관리자가 없다면, 그것은 더 먼 토양에서 구하러 다닐 수 있도록 뿌리를 증식하거나 길게 늘리고 뿌리털을 발달시킬 수 있다. 식물은 또한 영양 혹은 자원 가용성의 시간적 또는 공간적 변화의 역사에 대응하기 위해 자신의 기억을 사용할 수 있다. (B) 이 분야의 연구는 식물은 공간과 시간 모두의 측면에서 환경에서 자신의 위치를 지속적으로 인식한다는 것을 보여주었다. 과거에 다양한 영양소 가용성을 경험한 식물은 잎 생산 대신 뿌리 길이를 연장하는 데 에너지를 소비하는 것과 같은 위험을 감수하는 행동을 보이는 경향이 있다. (A) 반대로, 영양분이 풍부했던 이력을 가진 식물은 위험을 회피하고 에너지를 절약한다. 모든 발달 단계에서 식물은 성장, 생존, 번식에 에너지를 사용할 수 있도록 환경 변화나 불균형에 반응하는 동시에, 귀중한 에너지의 손상과 비생산적인 사용을 제한한다.

정답풀이
영양분이 제한적일 때 식물이 보이는 적응 반응을 정원사는 영양 부족이나 비료의 필요로 인식할 수도 있다는 내용의 주어진 글 다음에는, (정원사 같은) 관리자가 없으면 식물은 영양분을 위해 뿌리를 증식시키거나 시간과 공간에 대한 자신의 기억을 활용한다는 내용의 (C)가 올 수 있다. 식물이 시간과 공간의 측면에서 자신의 위치를 인식한다는 것을 연구로 보여주었다는 내용의 (B)는 (C) 마지막 부분의 식물이 시간과 공간에 대한 기억을 이용할 수 있다

---

235 답 ②

📖 둘러싸고 있는 주변 환경만큼 강한 나무

전문해석
나무가 함께 자랄 때는 각 나무가 가능한 최고의 나무로 성장할 수 있도록 영양분과 물이 그것들 모두 사이에서 최적으로 분배된다. 만약 여러분이 경쟁자로 여겨지는 나무를 제거하여 개별 나무를 '도와주면' 나머지 나무를 잃게 된다. 그것들은 그루터기 외에는 무엇도 남아있지 않기 때문에 이웃 나무들에 메시지를 보내지만, 소용이 없다. 이제 모든 나무가 그것 나름대로 자라 생산성에 큰 차이가 생긴다. 어떤 개체들은 당분이 줄기를 따라 확연히 흘러넘칠 때까지 미친 듯이 광합성을 한다. 그 결과, 그것들은 건강하고 더 잘 자라지만 특별히 오래 살지는 못한다. 그것은 나무가 자신을 둘러싸고 있는 숲만큼 강할 수 있기 때문이다. 그리고 지금 숲에는 많은 패자가 있다. 한때는 강한 구성원들의 지원을 받았을 약한 구성원들이 갑자기 뒤처진다. 그것들의 쇠락 원인이 위치와 영양분 부족이든, 일시적인 질병이든, 혹은 유전적 구성이든, 이제 그것들은 곤충과 균류의 먹이가 된다.

정답풀이
주어진 문장은 그것들이 건강하고 더 잘 자라지만 특별히 오래 살지는 못한다고 했으므로 건강하고 잘 자랄 수 있는 상황이 주어진 문장 앞에, 그리고 특별히 오래 살지는 못하는 이유를 설명하는 내용이 주어진 문장의 뒤에 나와야 한다. ② 앞에서 어떤 나무는 미친듯이 광합성을 하여 당분이 줄기를 따라 흘러넘친다고 했고, ② 뒤에서는 나무가 자신의 둘러싼 숲만큼 강할 수 있기에 아무런 이웃 없이 혼자 잘 자란 나무는 오래 살지 못한다고 이유를 설명하고 있으므로, 주어진 문장이 들어가기에 가장 적절한 곳은 ②이다.

3행 When trees grow together, / nutrients and water can be optimally divided among them all **so that** each tree can grow into the best tree [it can be].

: When ~ together는 시간 부사절이고, nutrient ~ 이하가 주절이다. so that은 '~하도록'의 의미를 나타내는 부사절을 이끌고, [ ]는 the best tree를 수식하는 관계대명사절이다.

17행 [**Whether** the reason for their decline is their location and lack of nutrients, a passing sickness, **or** genetic makeup], / they now fall prey to insects and fungi.

: [ ]에는 「Whether *A*, *B*, or *C*」 구조가 쓰여 'A이든지, B이든지, 아니면 C이든지'라는 의미를 나타내고, they ~ 이하가 주절이다.

어휘풀이
- nutrient *n* 영양분
- competition *n* 경쟁자, 경쟁
- trunk *n* 줄기
- fungus *n* 균류, 곰팡이류 (*pl.* fungi)
- optimally *ad* 최적으로
- bubble *v* 흘러넘치다
- fall behind 뒤처지다

| 236 ② | 237 ③ | 238 ② | 239 ⑤ | 240 ① |
| 241 ⑤ |

236 답 ②

📖 집단 구성원이 혼자 개인적인 아이디어를 창안할 시간을 갖도록 해야 할 지도자의 임무

전문해석
협업의 전등 스위치를 탁 하고 누르는 것은 지도자가 할 수 있는 유일한 위치에 있는 것인데, 사람들이 자발적으로 혼자 일하는 것을 여러 장애물이 방해하기 때문이다. 우선, 상황을 잘 모르고 혼자 남겨진다는 두려움은 그들이 계속 자신의 기업 소셜미디어에 붙어 있도록 할 수 있다. 사람들은 고립되거나 고립된 듯 보이는 것을 원하지 않는다. 또 다른 이유로는, 자신의 팀 동료들이 무엇을 하고 있는지를 아는 것이 편안하고 안전하다는 느낌을 제공하는데, 사람들은 집단과 조화를 이루도록 그들 자신의 행동을 조정할 수 있기 때문이다. 아마도 바로 처음부터 성공적이지 않을 뭔가 새로운 것을 시도하기 위해 홀로 벗어나는 것은 위험하다. 하지만 사람들이 과잉 연결되어 있다는 것이 안도감을 준다고 느껴질지라도, 그들이 주기적으로 (조직을) 벗어나 스스로 생각하여 그다지 성숙하지는 않더라도 다양한 아이디어를 창안하는 것이 조직을 위해 더 좋다. 따라서 사람들이 그것을 스스로 선택하지 않는 때에도, 처벌처럼 보이게 하지 않으면서 간헐적인 상호작용을 시행함으로써 전체에게 유익한 여건을 조성하는 것이 지도자의 임무가 된다.

정답풀이
집단 구성원들은 보통 고립되는 것에 거부감을 느끼고 동료들과 함께할 때 편안함과 안전함을 느끼지만, 그들이 조직을 벗어나 스스로 생각하여 다양한 아이디어를 창안하는 것이 조직에 유익하므로 지도자는 이런 일이 가능하게 하는 여건을 조성해야 한다는 내용이다. 따라서 밑줄 친 부분이 의미하는 바로 가장 적절한 것은 혼자만의 시간을 가지면서 개인의 창의력을 발휘하는 것과 관련된 ② '사람들이 함께 일하는 것을 멈추고 개인적으로 일하기 시작하도록 하는 것'이다.

오답풀이
① 협력을 막는 물리적 장벽과 집단 규범을 깨는 것
③ 사람들이 온라인 협업에 더 많은 시간을 할애하도록 격려하는 것
④ 더 높은 생산성이 요구되는 환경을 조성하는 것
⑤ 직원들이 집단 프로젝트에 관심을 집중하도록 요구하는 것

구문풀이

12행 But even though **it** feels reassuring [for individuals **to be hyperconnected**], / **it**'s better for the organization [**if** they periodically go off and think for themselves and generate diverse — {**if** not quite mature} — ideas].

: 양보 부사절과 주절로 이루어진 문장이다. 두 개의 it은 모두 형식상의 주어이고, 두 개의 [ ]가 각각의 내용상의 주어에 해당한다. 첫 번째 [ ] 안에서 for individuals는 to부정사의 의미상 주어에 해당한다. 두 번째 [ ] 안의 { }는 '~일지라도'의 뜻을 나타내는 부사절로 if they(= ideas) are not quite mature에서 they are가 생략된 형태로 이해할 수 있다.

16행 Thus, **it** becomes the leader's job [**to create** conditions {that are good for the whole by enforcing intermittent interaction even when people wouldn't choose **it** for themselves, without making **it** seem like a punishment}].

: 첫 번째 it은 형식상의 주어이고, [ ]로 표시된 to부정사구가 내용상의 주어에 해당하며, { }는 conditions를 수식하는 주격 관계대명사절이다. 두 번째와 세 번째 it은 intermittent interaction을 대신하는 대명사이다.

어휘풀이
- flick *v* (스위치 등)을 탁 하고 누르다
- obstacle *n* 장애물
- out of the loop 상황을 잘 모르는
- isolated *a* 고립된
- go off 자리를 벗어나다
- periodically *ad* 주기적으로
- enforce *v* 시행하다
- collaboration *n* 협업
- stand in the way of ~을 방해하다
- enterprise *n* 기업
- adjust *v* 조정하다
- hyperconnected *a* 과잉 연결된
- mature *a* 성숙한, 무르익은

237 답 ③

📖 자신이 원하는 것은 이미 가지고 있었음을 깨닫게 되는 오즈로 가는 여행

전문해석
〈오즈의 마법사〉를 동기 부여에 관한 심리학적 연구로 생각해 보라. Dorothy와 그녀의 세 친구는 에메랄드 시로 가기 위해 열심히 노력하면서, 장벽을 극복하고, 모든 적에게 끈질기게 맞선다. 그들은 마법사가 그들에게 없는 것을 줄 거라고 기대하기 때문에 그렇게 한다. 대신에, 그 멋진 (그리고 현명한) 마법사는 자신이 아니라 그들이 항상 자신들의 소원을 실현할 힘을 가지고 있었음을 그들이 깨닫게 한다. Dorothy에게, '집'은 장소가 아니라 그녀가 사랑하는 사람들과 함께하는 편안한 느낌, 안전하다는 느낌이며, 그녀의 마음이 있는 곳이면 어디든 집이다. 사자가 원하는 용기, 허수아비가 바라는 지성, 양철 인간이 꿈꾸는 감정은 그들이 이미 가지고 있는 속성이다. 그들은 이러한 속성을 내적인 조건이 아니라 이미 자신들이 다른 이들과 관계를 맺는 긍정적인 방식으로 생각할 필요가 있다. 결국, 그들은 자신들이 원하는 뭔가를 얻을 수 있을 거라는 미래의 가능성에 관한 생각, 즉 어떤 '기대'에 지나지 않는 것에 의해 동기가 부여된 여행, 오즈로 가는 여정에서 그러한 자질들을 보여주지 않았는가?

정답풀이
③ **문장의 구조 파악**: 문장의 주어는 The courage ~, the intelligence ~ and the emotions ~이고, 밑줄 친 부분은 문장의 술어 동사가 와야 할 자리이므로, 준동사 being을 주어의 수와 문장의 시제에 맞게 동사 are로 고쳐야 한다.

오답풀이
① **대명사**: to give의 의미상 주어는 the Wizard고, give의 목적어는 Dorothy and her three friends이므로 목적어로 대명사 them은 어법상 적절하다.
② **to부정사**: 앞의 the power를 수식하는 to부정사 to fulfill은 어법상 적절하다.
④ **전치사+관계대명사**: positive ways를 수식하는 관계절을 이끄는데, 뒤에 완전한 구조의 절(they are ~ to others)이 이어지고 있으므로, 「전치사+관계사」의 구조인 in which는 어법상 적절하다.
⑤ **분사의 태**: 분사의 수식을 받는 a journey와 수동 관계에 있으므로 과거분사 motivated는 어법상 적절하다.

구문풀이
10행 [The courage {the Lion wants}, the intelligence {the Scarecrow longs for}, and the emotions {the Tin Man dreams of}] **are** attributes they already possess.

: [ ]가 문장의 주어이고, 동사는 are이다. 세 개의 { }는 각각 The courage, the intelligence, the emotions를 수식하는 목적격 관계대명사절이다.

16행 After all, didn't they demonstrate those qualities on the journey to Oz, a journey [motivated by little more than an *expectation*, an idea about the future likelihood of getting something {they wanted}]?

: a journey ~는 the journey to Oz와 동격으로 쓰여 여행에 대해 부연 설명하고, [ ]는 a journey를 수식하는 과거분사구이다. an idea ~도 an *expectation*과 동격으로 쓰여 부연 설명하고 있고, { }는 something을 수식하는 목적격 관계대명사절이다.

어휘풀이
- motivation *n* 동기 부여
- barrier *n* 장벽
- fulfill *v* 실현하다, 성취하다
- scarecrow *n* 허수아비
- possess *v* 가지고 있다, 소유하다
- demonstrate *v* 보여주다
- likelihood *n* 가능성
- overcome *v* 극복하다
- persist *v* 끈질기게 계속하다
- security *n* 안전, 안정
- attribute *n* 속성
- relate *v* 관계를 맺다
- little more than ~에 지나지 않는

238 답 ②

📖 제조업자들에게 받아들여지기 어려운 리드유저가 개발한 혁신

전문해석
제조업자들은 자신들이 생각하기에 그 과정이 작동되는 방식에 맞춰 자신들의 혁신 과정을 설계한다. 제조업자의 대다수는 제품 개발과 서비스 개발은 항상 제조업자들에 의해 이루어지며, 자신들의 일은 가끔 리드유저(시장 경향을 선도하는 사용자)가 이미 개발한 혁신을 발견하고 상업화하기보다는 항상 필요를 발견하고 그것을 채우는 것이라고 여전히 생각한다. 그래서, 제조업자들은 표적 시장 사용자들의 필요를 탐구하기 위한 시장 연구 부서, 그러한 필요에 대처하기에 적절한 제품을 고안하기 위한 제품 개발 집단 및 기타 등등을 설치해 왔다. 리드유저의 필요와 시제품 해결책은, 만일 정말 마주치기라도 한다면, 대체로 전혀 흥미롭지 않은 아웃라이어(해당 범위에서 많이 벗어나는 것)로 거부된다. 정말로, 리드유저의 혁신이 그 회사의 제품 라인에 정말로 들어가게 될 때—그리고 그것은 많은 회사의 여러 주요 혁신의 실질적인 원천이 되는 것으로 알려졌는데—그것은 대체로 지연 후에 이례적이고 비체계적인 경로를 통해 도착한다.

정답풀이
제조업자들은 이미 개발된 혁신적인 것을 발견해서 상업화하는 것은 제조업자의 일이 아니고, 직접 제품과 서비스를 개발해서 상품화하는 것이 제조업자의 일이라고 생각한다는 내용이다. 빈칸에는 제조업자들이 발견해서 상품화하지 않고 오히려 제조업자들에게 거부당하기도 하는, 혁신을 수식하는 내용이 들어가야 하므로 제조업자가 아닌 ② '리드유저(시장 경향을 선도하는 사용자)가 이미 개발한'이 빈칸에 들어갈 말로 가장 적절하다.

오답풀이
① 리드유저가 간과하는 경향이 있던
③ 리드유저가 시장에서 마주친
  └ 리드유저가 시장에서 마주친 혁신은 리드유저가 아닌 다른 사람들이 개발한 혁신이므로 적절하지 않다.
④ 다른 회사들이 자주 실행한
⑤ 사용자와 회사 둘 다 소중하게 여긴

구문풀이
2행 The vast majority of manufacturers still think [that product development and service development are always done by manufacturers, / and that their job is always {to find a need and fill it **rather than** to sometimes find and commercialize an innovation

(that lead users have already developed)}].

: [ ]는 문장의 동사 think의 목적어 역할을 하는 명사절이다. 명사절 안에서 { }는 동사 is의 보어 역할을 하는 to부정사구로, 'B라기보다는 A'라는 의미를 나타내는 「A rather than B」로 to find ~ fill it과 to sometimes find ~ developed가 연결되었다. ( )는 an innovation을 수식하는 목적격 관계대명사절이다.

8행 Accordingly, manufacturers have set up market-research departments [to explore the needs of users in the target market], product-development groups [to think up suitable products to address those needs], and so forth.

: 첫 번째 [ ]는 market-research departments를 수식하는 to부정사구이고, 두 번째 [ ]는 product-development groups를 수식하는 to부정사구이다.

어휘풀이

- manufacturer *n* 제조업자
- commercialize *v* 상업화하다
- target market 표적 시장
- prototype *n* 시제품
- outlier *n* 관련 없는 것, 범위를 벗어난 것
- unsystematic *a* 비체계적인
- the vast majority of ~의 대다수
- accordingly *ad* 그래서
- address *v* 대처하다

239 답 ⑤

📖 사진과 달리 시공간적 제약이 많았던 그림

전문해석

사진이 나오기 전에는 장소들이 잘 이동하지 않았다. 화가들이 항상 특정한 장소를 그것의 '거주지'에서 벗어나게 해 다른 곳으로 이동시켜 왔지만, 그림은 제작에 시간이 많이 걸렸고, 상대적으로 운반이 어려웠고, 단품 수주 생산이었다. 사진의 증가는 특히, 신문, 정기간행물, 책 그리고 광고에서 사진의 기계적인 복제를 가능하게 한 1880년대 하프톤 판의 도입으로 이루어졌다. 사진은 소비자 자본주의와 결합하게 되었고 이제 세계는 '이전에는 전혀 사용되지 않았거나 단 한 명의 고객을 위한 그림으로만 사용되었던 인물, 풍경, 사건들을 무제한의 양으로 제공받았다'. 자본주의가 세계를 '백화점'으로 정리함에 따라, '표현물의 확산과 유통은… 극적이고 사실상 피할 수 있는 세계적 규모를 달성했다'. 점차 사진은 세계를 가시적이고, 미적이며, 탐나게 만드는 값싼 대량생산품이 되었다. 경험들은 그것을 저렴한 이미지로 바꿈으로써 '대중화'되었다. 가볍고 작고 대량으로 제작된 사진은 장소의 시공간적 순환을 위한 역동적인 수단이 되었다.

정답풀이

빈칸에는 사진이 나오기 전, 화가의 그림을 통해 세계를 경험하던 시대의 제약이 나와야 한다. 그림으로 특정한 장소를 경험하는 것은 제작 시간, 운반, 대량 생산의 측면에서 제약이 많았으나, 사진의 등장으로 인해 인물, 풍경, 사건의 경험이 신문, 잡지, 광고 등에 무제한의 양으로 소비자에게 제공되어 대중화되었다는 내용이다. 즉, 사진이 나오기 전 그림으로는 장소의 시공간적 순환, 즉 언제 어디서든 그 장소를 경험하는 것이 어려웠으므로, 빈칸에 들어갈 말로 가장 적절한 것은 ⑤ '장소들이 잘 이동하지 않았다'이다.

오답풀이

① 그림만이 자연과 연관되었다
② 그림은 예술의 주요한 형식이었다
  └ 그림의 시공간적 한계를 지적하는 내용이며, 그림이 예술의 주요한 형식이었던 점은 글에서 언급하지 않았다.
③ 예술은 세상을 비추는 거울을 떠받쳤다
  └ 세상을 비추는 거울로서 그림이 많은 한계를 가지고 있었던 점을 지적하는 내용이지, 세상을 비추는 거울로서의 예술을 설명한 내용이 아니다.

④ 여행을 위한 욕구가 강하지 않았다

구문풀이

5행 The multiplication of photographs especially took place with the introduction of the half-tone plate in the 1880s [that **made possible** {the mechanical reproduction of photographs in newspapers, periodicals, books and advertisements}].

: [ ]는 the half-tone plate를 수식하는 주격 관계대명사절이고, 그 안의 { }는 made의 목적어로 목적격보어인 possible 뒤에 위치해 있다.

10행 Photography became coupled to consumer capitalism / and the globe **was** now **offered** 'in limitless quantities, figures, landscapes, events [which had not previously been utilised **either** at all, **or** only as pictures for one customer]'.

: figures, landscapes, events는 동사 was offered의 목적어이며, [ ]로 표시된 주격 관계대명사절이 수식하는 선행사들이다. 「either A or B: A 또는 B」에 의해 두 개의 부사구가 연결되어 있다.

18행 Gradually photographs became cheap massproduced objects [that made the world visible, aesthetic and desirable].

: [ ]는 cheap massproduced objects를 수식하는 주격 관계대명사절이다.

어휘풀이

- prior to ~ 이전에
- lift ~ out of ~을 들어서 벗어나게 하다
- transport *v* 이동시키다, 수송하다
- multiplication *n* 증가, 증식
- reproduction *n* 복제
- couple *v* 결합하다
- figure *n* 인물
- circulation *n* 유통, 순환
- virtually *ad* 사실상
- democratise *v* 대중화하다, 민주화하다
- translate *v* 바꾸다
- spatiotemporal *a* 시공간적인
- photography *n* 사진(술)
- dwelling *n* 거주지
- one-of-a-kind *n* 단 하나뿐인 것
- mechanical *a* 기계적인
- periodical *n* 정기간행물
- capitalism *n* 자본주의
- landscape *n* 풍경
- spectacular *a* 극적인
- vehicle *n* 수단

240 답 ①

📖 공간 기준점이 거리 추정에 미치는 영향

전문해석

공간 기준점은 자기 자신보다 더 크다. 이것은 사실 역설적이지 않은데, 랜드마크(특정 지역을 대표하는 건축물이나 자연물)는 그 자체이기도 하지만, 또한 그 주변의 지역을 (자신의 범위로) 규정하기도 한다. (A) 많은 대학 캠퍼스에서 반복되어 온 한 전형적인 예에서, 연구원들은 먼저 학생들에게서 캠퍼스 랜드마크의 목록을 수집한다. 그런 다음, 그들은 또 다른 학생 집단에게 쌍으로 이루어진 장소 사이의 거리, 즉 캠퍼스에 있는 어떤 장소에서 랜드마크까지, 어떤 장소에서 평범한 건물까지의 거리를 추정해 달라고 요청한다. (C) 주목할 만한 결과는 평범한 장소에서 랜드마크까지의 거리가 랜드마크에서 평범한 장소까지의 거리보다 더 짧다고 추정된다는 것이다. 그래서 사람들은 Pierre의 집에서 에펠탑까지의 거리가 에펠탑에서 Pierre의 집까지의 거리보다 더 짧다고 추정할 것이다. 블랙홀처럼, 랜드마크는 평범한 장소를 자기 자신 쪽으로 끌어들이는 것처럼 보이지만, 평범한 장소들은 그렇지 않다. (B) 거리 추정에 관한 이러한 비대칭은, A에서 B까지의 거리는 B에서 A까지의 거리와 같아야 한다는 가장 기초적인 유클리드 거리 법칙에 위배된다. 그렇다면 거리에 대한 추정은 반드시 일관성이 있는 것은 아니다.

공간 기준점의 상대적 크기에 관해 언급하는 주어진 글 다음에는, 공간 기준점인 랜드마크에 관한 실험의 예를 제시하는 (A)가 와야 한다. (C)의 The remarkable finding은 (A)에서 제시한 실험의 결과를 나타내고, (B)의 This asymmetry of distance는 (C)에서 언급한 랜드마크에서 평범한 장소까지의 추정된 거리와 평범한 장소에서 랜드마크까지의 추정된 거리 사이의 불일치를 나타낸다. 따라서 적절한 글의 순서는 ① (A)-(C)-(B)이다.

구문풀이

11행 This asymmetry of distance estimates violates **the most elementary principles of Euclidean distance**, [**that** the distance from A to B must be the same as the distance from B to A].

: [ ]는 the most ~ distance와 동격을 이루는 명사절이며, that 앞의 콤마(,)는 긴 어구가 이어지므로 독자를 배려한 것이다.

어휘풀이

- spatial *a* 공간의
- landmark *n* 랜드마크, 주요 지형지물
- paradigm *n* 패러다임, 전형적인 예
- ordinary *a* 평범한, 보통의
- elementary *a* 기본적인, 기초적인
- coherent *a* 일관성이 있는
- reference point 기준점
- define *v* 규정하다
- estimate *v* 추정하다 *n* 추정
- violate *v* 위반하다
- judgment *n* 추정, 판단
- remarkable *a* 주목할 만한

241 답 ⑤

글 대량 생산에서 소비자 파편화, 소비자 공동체 형성으로의 변화

전문해석

식품 선택을 결정하는 사회적 역학이 복잡해지면서 마케팅 담당자와 광고주 업무가 점점 더 어려워지고 있다. 과거에 대량 생산은 제품의 광범위한 유통뿐만 아니라 제품의 입수 가능성과 구입 비용의 감당을 가능하게 했고 발달의 신호로 받아들여졌다. 요즘 그것은 개인의 선호를 반영해야 하는 점점 더 작은 부문 사이에서 소비자 파편화에 의해 점차 대체되고 있다. 모든 사람은 서로 다르고 특별하다고 느끼며, 자신의 기호를 만족시키는 제품을 기대한다. 실제로, 이러한 개인적 선호라고 여겨지는 것들은 결국 문화적 감수성, 사회적 정체성, 정치적 감수성 그리고 식생활과 건강에 관한 관심을 중심으로 공고해지는, 신생의, 일시적이며, 늘 바뀌고, 거의 부족적인 형성물과 겹치게 된다. 개인의 이야기는 새로운 정체성을 만들어 내며 더 큰 이야기와 연결된다. 이런 소비자 집단은 국경을 넘어 개념, 이미지 그리고 관습의 전 세계의 널리 공유된 저장소로 인해 더 강해진다.

정답풀이

개인의 이야기가 새로운 정체성을 생성하며 더 큰 이야기와 연결된다는 내용의 주어진 문장은, 개인적 선호가 문화, 사회, 정치, 식생활, 건강 등을 중심으로 하는 더 광범위한 형성물과 겹쳐진다는 ⑤ 앞 문장의 내용을 요약하고 있다. 따라서 주어진 문장이 들어가기에 가장 적절한 곳은 ⑤이다.

구문풀이

5행 In the past, mass production [**allowed** for accessibility and affordability of products, **as well as** their wide distribution], and [**was** accepted as a sign of progress].

: and로 연결된 두 개의 [ ]는 주어인 mass production에 이어지는 술부이다. 「A as well as B」는 'B뿐만 아니라 A'라는 뜻이다.

어휘풀이

- narrative *n* 서사, 이야기
- complexity *n* 복잡성
- identity *n* 정체성
- dynamics *n* 역학

- mass production 대량 생산
- accessibility *n* 입수 가능성
- affordability *n* 적당한 가격으로 구입할 수 있는 것, 감당할 수 있는 비용
- distribution *n* 유통
- inclination *n* 성향, 기호
- supposedly *ad* 추정상, 아마도
- emerging *a* 신생의, 최근에 생겨난
- tribal *a* 부족적인, 부족의
- solidify *v* ~을 공고히 하다
- social identification 사회적 정체성
- feed on ~ 때문에 더 강해지다
- allow for ~을 가능케 하다
- segment *n* 부문
- in reality 실제로
- overlap with ~와 겹치다
- temporary *a* 일시적인
- formation *n* 형성물, 구조(체)
- sensibility *n* 감수성
- national boundary 국경

PART Ⅲ 어휘 REVIEW

고난도 기출 모의고사 1회

01 대안적인 **02** 통합의 **03** 근접, 근사 **04** 변환 **05** 들릴 수 있는 **06** 제약 **07** 사고방식 **08** 모의의 **09** 변환하다 **10** 폭발적 증가 **11** manipulation **12** 억누르다 **13** 절충, 타협 **14** 오해, 잘못된 생각 **15** party **16** 정제, 개선 **17** 되돌리다 **18** (~을 조직하여) 시작하다 **19** 진술, 설명 **20** settlement

고난도 기출 모의고사 2회

01 응집력 있는 **02** 강력한, 장대한 **03** autonomy **04** 필요 이상의 자격[경력]을 갖춘 **05** 작은 땅, 지대 **06** 미세하게 **07** 만족[충족]시키다 **08** 독창적임 **09** 명분, 정당화 **10** 보충의 **11** 증식시키다 **12** 번식 **13** 공간의 **14** 모순적인 **15** 지속 가능성 **16** 시간의 **17** 관습에 얽매이지 않는 **18** yield **19** 불균형 **20** 비현실적인

고난도 기출 모의고사 3회

01 대처하다 **02** 증가, 증식 **03** periodical **04** 끈질기게 계속하다 **05** 유통 **06** 거주지 **07** 신생의, 최근에 생겨난 **08** 시행하다 **09** 성향, 기호 **10** 상업화하다 **11** 대중화하다, 민주화하다 **12** 기준점 **13** 장벽 **14** 안전, 안정 **15** 일관성이 있는 **16** 부문 **17** ~을 공고히 하다 **18** 수단 **19** violate **20** 속성

메가스터디 고등학습 시리즈

메가스터디 N제

영어영역 고난도·3점

정답 및 해설

메가스터디BOOKS

내용 문의 02-6984-6908 | 구입 문의 02-6984-6868,9 | www.megastudybooks.com

중고등부터
성인까지

태블릿으로
공부하는

meBOOK 스토어

보고, 듣고, 읽고, 풀고!
학습 기능을 접목한 디지털 수험서로 합격하세요.

모의고사
응시

동영상
강의

정답/해설
보기

음원
듣기

정답/해설
가리기

지문
보기

정오답
체크

앱스토어

 구글플레이

미북스토어

Notice

수험서별 적용된 미북Special(AI 학습기능)은 상이할 수 있으며,
미북스토어에서 구매한 전자책은 미북 APP에서만 열람하실 수 있습니다.